Instructor's Resource Manual

PUBLIC SPEAKING

Randall Parrish Osborn
Indiana University, Bloomington

Suzanne Osborn
University of Memphis

Instructor's Resource Manual

PUBLIC SPEAKING

FOURTH EDITION

Michael Osborn
University of Memphis

Suzanne Osborn
University of Memphis

HOUGHTON MIFFLIN COMPANY   BOSTON NEW YORK

Sponsoring Editor: George T. Hoffman
Senior Manufacturing Coordinator: Marie Barnes
Marketing Manager: Pamela J. Laskey

Text Credits

Chapter 1: "Time to Stop Shouting" adapted from Michael Kramer, *Time,* May 1, 1995, p. 66. Copyright © 1995 Times Inc. Reprinted with permission.

The following material appeared in *Speech Communication Teacher,* published by the Speech Communication Association. Used by permission of the Speech Communication Association.

Chapter 1: Terilyn Goins Phillips, "Name That Analogy: The Communication Game" *Chapter 2:* Lou Davidson Tillson, "Building Community and Reducing Communication Apprehension: A Case Study Approach" *Chapter 3:* Craig Newburger, "Testing Students' Ability to Distinguish Facts from Inferences" *Chapter 6:* James Kauffman, "Collecting and Evaluating Evidence" *Chapter 7:* Mary Mino, "Structuring: An Alternate Approach for Developing Clear Organization" *Chapter 9:* Mary Ann Danielson, "A Critical Thinking Approach to the Use of Visual Aids" *Chapter 10:* Edwin R. Rowley, "More Than Mere Words" *Chapter 11:* Pamela Hayward, "Delivery Cards" *Chapter 12:* Katherine Rowan, "The Speech to Explain Difficult Ideas" *Chapter 13:* Howard N. Schreier, "Analyzing Persuasive Tactics" *Chapter 14:* Joan A. Yamasaki, "Teaching the Recognition and Development of Appeals"

Printed in the U.S.A.

ISBN: 0-395-80884-7

23456789-HS-00 99 98 97

CONTENTS

INTRODUCTION

This *Instructor's Resource Manual* to accompany *Public Speaking*, Fourth Edition, is designed to assist both new and experienced instructors. New instructors should find a wealth of materials to draw upon for classroom activities and assignments, and experienced teachers should find that the materials add an element of freshness to their courses. The IRM complements the text with suggestions for teaching and additional teaching materials that can be adapted and incorporated into most course formats.

"Teaching Public Speaking," opens by discussing the purpose and philosophy of the basic course. It covers most of what you should need in order to format a class: the preparation of syllabi, planning class schedules, and formatting major assignments to meet the requirements of both regular and general education courses. In this edition, we have added a sample syllabus, and schedules to accommodate classes meeting once, twice, and three times weekly for a regular semester. There is also a section on options for grading individual assignments and for preparing final semester grades. We also include a troubleshooting guide for new instructors, giving advice for dealing with common problems that may at first be difficult. Finally, we include an extensive bibliography that may help to enrich your knowledge of teaching methods and techniques.

The "Chapter-by-Chapter Guide to Teaching Public Speaking" offers activities and assignments to engage your students for every chapter and major concept in the text. Beyond some minor editing work, we have deleted very little from the last edition, and added much in the way of critical applications and exercises. Each chapter includes a list of learning objectives, general suggestions for teaching, chapter outlines of major concepts, suggestions for using the Discussion and Application items at the end of each chapter, a variety of additional activities and exercises for putting ideas into practice, a list of supplementary materials, master copies of transparencies and handouts, and a bibliography of further readings.

Many of the activities in this IRM refer to the "Speech Designer" computer software program developed specifically for use with *Public Speaking.* The guidelines for each design, skeleton outline formats, and outlining check lists from the software have been reproduced for use as handouts in the appropriate chapters of this IRM.

Many people deserve credit and thanks for their help and advice with the preparation of this manual. Special thanks to Dr. Pat Andrews of Indiana University who provided extensive feedback on both the text and bibliography of this IRM, and allowed one of the authors to meet with her graduate class in communication education. A number of invaluable insights, many of which have found their way into this manual, came from graduate students at Indiana University, including Larry Lambert, Jim Cherney, Kara Maltzahn, Rustom Bhathena, Stephanie Grey, Jeneatte Heidewald, Amy Jester, Irwin Mallin, Jeff McKinney, Carolyn Novak, Teresa Palmitessa, Stephanie Reding, and Rebecca Townsend. The indirect influence of a number of outstanding professors is (hopefully) present in this manual, including Bob Brown of the University of Memphis; Thomas Frentz, Janice Rushing, Dennis Bailey and Stephen Smith of the University of Arkansas; and Jim Andrews, Mike Hogan, John Lucaites, and Bill Wiethoff of Indiana University.

R. P. O.
S. S. O.

Instructor's Resource Manual

PUBLIC SPEAKING

PART I
Teaching Public Speaking

THE PURPOSE AND PHILOSOPHY OF THE COURSE

The art of public speaking has a time-honored place in the history of Western education that dates to the early Greeks, when pioneer teachers such as Gorgias, Protagoras, and Isocrates helped shape the foundations of the rhetorical tradition. Taught effectively, it can be one of the most rewarding classes your students will ever take. In *Public Speaking* we teach the basic skills that are the mark of an educated and competent person, skills by which your students will be evaluated later in their lives. In addition to developing and polishing their presentation skills, we teach them how to compose meaningful and coherent messages and adapt them to particular situations and audiences, to conduct responsible research, to argue and engage opposing viewpoints constructively, and to develop critical and constructive listening skills. It is therefore not surprising that the teaching of public speaking has always been an important priority in societies that promote open, democratic deliberation of important issues. These skills also have personal benefits, promoting individual achievement in school, work, and life in general.

Teachers have long disagreed as to whether we should emphasize *theory* or practice in our courses. This assumes a false dichotomy, exemplifying the persuasive fallacy *either-or thinking*. We prefer to focus on offering practical advice to assist students in developing public communication skills that will outlast the classroom experience, but we believe that this advice must be grounded in an understanding of the basic principles that underlie it. In *Public Speaking* our primary focus is on building the skills students need to make effective public presentations. To this end, we tell them *what* to do, *how* to do it, and *why* it should be done in that particular way. We try to provide just enough understanding of the *why* to make the *what* and the *how* more meaningful and lasting.

We believe in learning through examples and critical application—the "show and tell" approach to education. We try to show students what to do and how to do it by providing them with many short examples throughout the text. In addition, we provide sample speeches by both students and public figures, and also sample outlines. When we teach the course ourselves, we use videotaped student speeches to prepare students for each major speaking assignment. We find that students who are shown examples of quality speeches tend to give better speeches.

We take a step-by-step approach to teaching public speaking, beginning with the most simple materials and assignments and working up to the more complex. We feel that it is important for students to have successful early experiences in order to build self-confidence and generate enthusiasm for the course, and to that end we provide an overview of vital skills in the first two chapters of the text. Subsequent chapters cover these important skills in more depth and detail so that they can be mastered incrementally. Throughout the text and this IRM, we include exercise materials to provide your students with opportunities to practice the skills they are acquiring in preparation for their major speaking assignments. Although you might grade these activities, their relative weight in the student's final grade should be small enough to minimize the perception of threat that is often associated with major graded assignments. Using such exercises prior to the informative and persuasive speaking assignments can help your students master the skills they will need for later work.

We emphasize the content and structuring of speeches and the ethical responsibilities of speakers. We want to avoid turning out students who sound good, but say nothing. Public speaking should be viewed as a participative sharing of information and ideas aimed at increasing understanding and shaping values, beliefs, and behavior. Its practice is vitally important to the fabric of a healthy community. We stress the importance of *responsible knowledge* as basic to all forms of public speaking, and we focus attention on the ethical and social responsibilities a speaker must assume. We impress upon students the possible abuses of stylistic techniques, supporting materials, proofs, and arguments so that they may avoid committing them in their own speeches and better detect their presence in the barrage of public messages to which they are exposed daily.

Because the classroom climate is crucial to the success of the course, we offer suggestions in this IRM for improving that climate. In Chapter 2 we suggest the formation of small support groups to encourage cooperative learning. We realize that there is no *one right way* to teach the course—that no single approach works for all teachers with all students all of the time. We have personally experienced situations where what works great in one section bombs dreadfully in another. Each class is different, and each student in each class is different. To help you meet this challenge, we provide a variety of materials covering a broad range of interests and difficulty levels. We have also included activities and readings to help the course meet the general education requirements that are now mandated for many college and university public speaking courses.

To make your job easier, we have tried to prepare an outstanding ancillary package of supplemental materials for the public speaking instructor. This edition of the text is available in an "Annotated Instructor's Edition" that includes teaching tips for both general and English as a Second Language classrooms. Also included in the package are a CD-ROM for those instructors with multimedia-equipped classrooms; transparencies for use on an overhead projector; student speeches videos and a guide for their use in class; "The Speech Designer" computer software, which students can use to help them better structure their presentations; the *Speech Outlining Workbook*, which steps students through the process of outlining their messages; an ESL guide for public speaking instructors to use in classrooms in which English is a second language; a test bank, available in both computer and hard-copy formats; a video on using presentation aids (to keep you from having to carry samples to class for your lecture); and a printed supplement *Origins of Classical Rhetoric*.

We hope this manual helps make your job as a teacher easier and more satisfying. We realize that many of you are teaching the course for the first time, and that others of you have been teaching the course for so long you have reached a state of "burnout" and could benefit from updating your knowledge of the subject area and teaching methods. We provide for each chapter a list of "Readings for Enrichment" to help you stay abreast of the latest ideas and experiment with diversifying your curriculum with alternative ideas and teaching methods. We appreciate the time pressures on full-time teachers and especially graduate assistants, and have provided materials that can be copied directly from this manual for use. We have also provided detailed guidelines for the use of activities and samples of appropriate responses.

Finally, we believe that a course in public speaking ought to be fun—both to take and to teach. We hope the exercises and materials in this manual will not only help to improve the quality of your course but also offer an occasional change of pace from the usual classroom experience. We hope they help facilitate more interest in and enthusiasm for the course among students and instructors alike.

PREPARING A SYLLABUS

An effective syllabus is an important component of any course. It should orient the students to the course and provide a written account of assignments and expectations. Experienced instructors generally have a backlog of old syllabi to work from. Unless there is a departmental syllabus, new instructors should prepare one for distribution at the first class meeting. A syllabus should contain the following information:

- The goals of the course in terms of what the students must accomplish

- The organization of the course, complete with a schedule

- Explanations of assignments, class policies, and grading standards

Most course descriptions cover objectives such as instilling in students a basic understanding of the general principles underlying effective and ethical public speaking, having them enact those principles by composing and presenting their own speeches in class, developing their critical and constructive listening skills, and instilling in them an appreciation for the broader significance of public communication in their lives and communities. We offer here a "Check List for a Course Syllabus," adapted from guidelines provided at the University of Nebraska—Lincoln, as well as a sample syllabus with a variety of class schedules that can be modeled for use in your courses.

After preparing a syllabus for class distribution, you should also prepare a "working syllabus" for your own use. If your class syllabus is on a computer disk, simply duplicate the application, and in distinguishable type, enter additional information to remind you of things like ancillary materials to use, classroom exercises, homework to assign and/or collect, etc.

Check List for Developing a Syllabus

- Instructor's title and name, office location, phone, and hours; E-mail address and/or fax number; and where to leave messages in case of an emergency

- Course title and number, with spaces for section number, meeting days, time, room, and building

- General description of the course, including goals and objectives

- Required purchases: text and readings packets or a reading list

- Topics to be covered, in sequence, with dates and assignments

- Specific explanations of oral and written assignments and examinations, with dates

- Place, date, and time of final examination

- Grading standards and criteria

- Policy regarding attendance

- Policy regarding late or missed assignments

- Policy regarding academic dishonesty and plagiarism

- Spaces for "Important Dates to Remember"

SAMPLE SYLLABUS: PUBLIC SPEAKING CLASS

Speech 101   **Sugartree State University**
Course section:
Instructor's name; office location, hours, and phone; and E-mail address and fax number
Time/room/building:

Required Text: Michael and Suzanne Osborn, *Public Speaking*, 4th Edition.

Course Description/Objectives: Speech 101 is an introductory course in public speaking that assumes no previous experience on your part. Its objectives are to familiarize you with some basic principles of effective and ethical public speaking, to give you experience in enacting those principles through practice, and to instill in you a sense of the importance of public communication in shaping our lives and your ethical obligations as a participant in that process.

Assignments and Student Evaluations: Students will complete four graded speech assignments and a written speech critique. In addition, you are expected to keep up with assigned readings and be familiar with material introduced in class lectures and discussions. Students are expected to attend and participate in class discussions and activities. Short quizzes will be administered on a regular basis, and there will be a comprehensive final at the end of the semester. Final grades will be determined on the basis of . . . [*see subsequent sections on specific assignments and working final grades*].

Attendance/Makeups/Tardiness: Public speaking is an audience-centered activity, and we need your active participation to make the class more rewarding. In this case, being fair means being firm. Students who miss too many classes typically perform poorly on their assignments. Therefore, your attendance at this class is mandatory. You are allowed four unexcused absences without penalty. After that, each recorded absence will cost a weighted percentage of your final grade. I reserve the right to make judgments regarding excused absences, but generally some sort of written documentation as to why you were absent is necessary. In the case of an unexcused absence, students will be allowed to make up *only one* major assignment and will incur a letter grade deduction on that assignment.

 Please try to come to class on time. If you are late, enter quietly to minimize the disruption. When you are late on speech presentation days, wait outside the door to avoid disrupting a speech in progress. Remember that it is your responsibility to remind me of your presence *on that day* to avoid being counted absent. I reserve the right to begin treating habitual and unexcused tardiness as absences.

Academic Honesty: You are expected to do original work on your speeches and written assignments. Your textbook and your student handbook both have thorough statements on plagiarism. As a student at Sugartree State, it is your responsibility to be familiar with them. Presenting somebody else's words and ideas as your own is a serious academic violation and will result in a 0 on the assignment and referral to appropriate university officials.

Consultation: If you want to do well in this class, I strongly encourage you to consult me in preparation for every major graded assignment. I respond to my E-mail daily, and I welcome your visits during office hours. If you want high-quality, sympathetic feedback, consult with me prior to the day before your assignment is due. After you've had some time to digest my comments, I am always happy to further explain a grade, and even change it in the rare case that I have made a mechanical error. Otherwise, grades are nonnegotiable. Postspeech consultations are especially encouraged as a means of improving your performance on future assignments.

Schedule of Classes and Important Dates: [*see subsequent sections on scheduling classes and assignments*]. Public speaking classes typically include three to five graded presentations, depending on class size and available time. In this section, we offer sample schedules for a class with four major speeches meeting once, twice, and three times weekly for a typical semester. A similar schedule should be included in your syllabus for distribution during the first class meeting.

Dates to Remember:

_____	Examination 1
_____	Final examination
_____	Self-introductory presentation
_____	Informative outline due
_____	Informative presentation
_____	Persuasive outline due
_____	Persuasive presentation
_____	Ceremonial presentation

Sample Schedule for a Class with Forty Sessions

Day	Topic	Assignment
1	Orientation and overview	
2	Public speaking as communication	Chapter 1
3	Your first speech assignment	Chapter 2
4	The importance of ethos and coping with communication apprehension	
5	Listening and critical thinking	Chapter 3
6–8	Self-introductory speech presentations	
9	Audience analysis	Chapter 4
10	Selecting and researching your topic	Chapter 5
11	Structuring and outlining your speech	Chapters 7 and 8
12	Informative speaking	Chapter 12
13	Supporting materials	Chapter 6
14	Supporting-a-point presentations	
15	Using presentation aids	Chapter 9
16	Examination 1 on Chapters 1–9 and 12	
17	The speaker's language	Chapter 10
18	Informative speech preparation outlines	
19	Presentation skills	Chapter 11
20–23	Informative speech presentations	
24–25	Persuasive speaking	Chapter 13
26–27	Evidence, proof, and argument	Chapter 14
28	Persuasive speech preparation outlines	
29	Evaluating persuasive messages	
30–34	Persuasive speech presentations	
35	Ceremonial speaking	Chapter 15
36–39	Ceremonial speech presentations	
40	Exercise in critical evaluation	
Final exam date and time	Examination 2 on Chapters 10, 11, 13, 14, and 15	

Sample Schedule for a Class with Twenty-eight Sessions

Day	Topic	Assignment
1	Orientation and overview	
2	Public speaking as communication; your first speech assignment	Chapter 1
3	The importance of ethos; coping with communication apprehension	Chapter 2
4	Listening and critical thinking	Chapter 3
5–6	Self-introductory speech presentations	
7	Audience analysis	Chapter 4
8	Informative speaking; selecting and researching your topic	Chapters 5 and 12
9	Supporting materials	Chapter 6
10	Supporting-a-point presentations	
11	Structuring and outlining your speech; using presentation aids	Chapters 7, 8, and 9
12	Examination 1 on Chapters 1–9 and 12	
13	The speaker's language	Chapter 10
14	Informative speech preparation outlines; presentation skills	Chapter 11
15–17	Informative speech presentations	
18	Persuasive speaking	Chapter 13
19	Evidence, proof, and argument; evaluating persuasive messages	Chapter 14
20	Persuasive speech preparation outlines	
21–23	Persuasive speech presentations	
24	Ceremonial speaking	Chapter 15
25–27	Ceremonial speech presentations	
28	Exercise in critical evaluation	
Final exam date and time	Examination 2 on Chapters 10, 11, 13, 14, and 15	

Sample Schedule for a Class with Fourteen Sessions

Day	Topic	Assignment
1	Orientation and overview; public speaking as communication; your first speech assignment	
2	The importance of ethos; coping with communication apprehension; listening and critical thinking	Chapters 1, 2, and 3
3	Self-introductory speech presentations; audience analysis	Chapter 4
4	Informative speaking; selecting and researching your topic; supporting materials	Chapters 5, 6, and 12
5	Structuring and outlining your speech; using presentation aids; supporting-a-point presentations	Chapters 7, 8, and 9
6	Examination 1 on Chapters 1–9 and 12; the speaker's language	Chapter 10
7	Informative speech preparation outlines; presentation skills	Chapter 11
8	Informative speech presentations; persuasive speaking	Chapter 13
9	Informative speech presentations; evidence, proof, and argument	Chapter 14
10	Evaluating persuasive messages; persuasive speech preparation outlines	
11	Persuasive speech presentations	
12	Ceremonial speaking	Chapter 15
13	Ceremonial speech presentations	
14	Exercise in critical evaluation	
Final exam date and time	Examination 2 on Chapters 10, 11, 13, 14, and 15	

After you determine the dates and order of assignments for your class, you can modify your own schedule to guide your presentation and remind you of materials you need for each session. The following is a sample working schedule.

Sample Working Schedule for a Class with Forty Sessions

Day	Topic	Assignment
1	Orientation and overview	

Distribute syllabus.

2	Public speaking as communication	Chapter 1

Have students complete audience analysis questionnaire.

3	Your first speech assignment	Chapter 2

Show tape of self-introductory speech.

4	The importance of ethos and coping with communication apprehension	

Use Discussion items 1 and 4 (text). Assign speaking dates.

5	Listening and critical thinking	Chapter 3

Use pop quiz to structure listening discussion. Bring evaluation forms and show video of student speech for students to critique.

6–8	Self-introductory speech presentations	
9	Audience analysis	Chapter 4

Share results of questionnaire with class. Distribute "Library Trivia Quiz" forms for homework and have students prepare a personal interest inventory for use during session 10.

10	Selecting and researching your topic	Chapter 5

Collect homework. Use Application item 1 to generate topic possibilities.

11	Structuring and outlining your speech	Chapters 7 and 8

Show videotape of poorly organized student speech: have students look for the problems in its organization and structure. Introduce computer outlining program. Return graded homework.

12	Informative speaking	Chapter 12

Show videotape of good student informative speech.

13	Supporting materials	Chapter 6

Distribute outline formats for supporting-a-point exercise.

14	Supporting-a-point presentations	
15	Using presentation aids	Chapter 9

Show presentation aids video.

| 16 | Examination 1 on Chapters 1–9 and 12. | |

| 17 | The speaker's language | Chapter 10 |

Return and review examinations. Assign speaking dates; instruct students to have preparation outlines for class work during session 18.

| 18 | Informative speech preparation outlines | |

Use Discussion item 1 format from Chapter 8 for group discussion for revision of preparation outlines.

| 19 | Presentation skills | Chapter 11 |

Show videotapes illustrating good and poor presentation skills.

| 20–23 | Informative speech presentations | |

| 24–25 | Persuasive speaking | Chapter 13 |

Show videotape of student persuasive speech. Assign homework. Distribute text of a different persuasive speech from video guide for written analysis, due class session 28.

| 26–27 | Evidence, proof, and argument | Chapter 14 |

Use "Find the Fallacy" exercise from IRM. Assign speaking dates for persuasive presentations.

| 28 | Persuasive speech preparation outlines | |

Use Discussion item 1 format from Chapter 8 for group discussion to revise preparation outlines.

| 29 | Evaluating persuasive messages | |

Return graded homework. Show videotape of speech assigned for critique. Discuss critiques of speech.

| 30–34 | Persuasive speech presentations | |

| 35 | Ceremonial speaking | Chapter 15 |

Show videotape of ceremonial speech. Assign speaking dates for ceremonial presentations.

| 36–39 | Ceremonial speech presentations | |

| 40 | Exercise in critical evaluation | |

Show videotape of short speech and have students write a critique of the speech.

| Final exam date and time | Examination 2 on Chapters 10, 11, 13, 14, and 15 | |

Public speaking courses have become an integral part of many collegiate general education curricula. Many programs attempt to integrate subjects such as group and mass communication, which can cause scheduling problems for instructors who are intent on maintaining four major speaking assignments. One way to deal with this is to assign Appendix A, on group communication processes, early in the term and then incorporate mass communication and group discussion applications through assigned readings and scheduled activities.

The following schedule offers various types of readings and activities that may help meet the special requirements of a general education course. To demonstrate the availability of such materials and activities, more are included than you would probably want to schedule or assign.

Sample Schedule for Class Meeting General Education Requirements

(See guide to journal abbreviations on p. 37)

1   Introduction and overview of course
         Activity: Administer "Audience Survey Form"

2   Public speaking as communication
         Readings:
             Text: Chapter 1
             Michael Osborn, "Our Communication Heritage: The Genetic Tie That Binds," *SSCJ*
                 (Winter 1979), 147–158.
             Franklyn S. Haiman, "Erosions of the First Amendment: A Challenge to Speech
                 Communication," *Free Speech Yearbook* (1986), 1–10.
         Activities:
             Mass communication application: Text Discussion item 3, on ethics and television
                 advertising.

3   Group communication processes
         Readings:
             Text: Appendix A.
             Ernest G. Bormann, "Ethics and Small Group Communication," *The Speech Association of
                 Minnesota Journal* (1985), 20–25.
         Activities:
             Have students complete "Group Communication Skills Analysis Form" on page 419 of the
                 text.
             Group communication exercise: "Panty Hose Problem" (from Chapter 5, IRM).
             Have Students complete "Group Discussion Participant Evaluation Form" (from Appendix
                 A, IRM).

4   Your first speech assignment
         Readings:
             Text: Chapter 2.
             Lawrence B. Rosenfield, "Self-Disclosure Avoidance: Why I Am Afraid to Tell You Who I
                 Am," *CM* (Mar. 1979), 63–66.
             Michael T. Motley, "Taking the Terror Out of Talk," *Psychology Today* (Jan. 1988), 46–49.
         Activities:
             Show videotape of self-introductory speech.
             Group discussion activity: Use "Creating a Supportive Classroom Climate," (from
                 Chapter 2, IRM).

5   The importance of ethos
         Readings:
             R. Larry Overstreet, "Understanding Charisma Through Its History," *CSSJ* (Winter 1978),
                 275–282.
             Carolyn Calloway-Thomas and Raymond G. Smith, "Images of Leadership: Black vs.
                 White," *SSCJ* (Spring 1981), 263–277.
         Activities:
             Mass communication application: Use Discussion item 3 (in text Chapter 2) for analysis of
                 ethos in videotaped political advertisements

6   Listening and critical thinking skills
         Readings:
             Text, Chapter 3.

Donald F. Roberts, Peter Christenson, Wendy A. Gibson, Linda Mooser, and Marvin J. Goldberg, "Developing Discriminating Consumers," *JC* (Summer 1980), 94–105.

S. I. Hayakawa and Alan R. Hayakawa, "Reporters, Inferences, Judgements," in *Language in Thought and Action,* 5th ed. (San Diego: Harcourt Brace Jovanovich, 1990), pp. 22–32.

Activities:

Use T-F quiz (in Chapter 3 IRM) to structure discussion of listening and critical thinking.

7–9   Self-introductory speech presentations

10   Audience analysis

Readings:

Text, Chapter 4.

Peter Menneer, "Audience Appreciation: A Different Story from Audience Members," *Journal of the Market Research Society* (July 1987), 241–263.

James Atlas, "Beyond Demographics," *Atlantic Monthly* (Oct. 1984), 49–58.

Jean Kilbourne, "Beauty and the Beast of Advertising," *Media & Values* (Winter 1989), 8–10.

Barbie White, "Sexist Advertisements: How to See Through the Soft Sell," *Media & Values* (Winter 1989), 10.

Activities:

Discuss results of class "Audience Survey Form" administered during session 1.

11   Selecting and researching your topic

Readings:

Text, Chapter 5.

John H. Boyer, "How Editors View Objectivity," *Journalism Quarterly* (Spring 1981), 24–28.

William S. Maddox and Robert Robins, "How People Magazine Covers Political Figures," *Journalism Quarterly* (Spring 1981), 113–115.

Norman R. Luttbeg, "News Consensus: Do U.S. Newspapers Mirror Society's Happenings?" *Journalism Quarterly* (Autumn 1983), 484–488.

Activities:

Group discussion exercise: Use Discussion item 1 to generate topic possibilities. Assign Application item 1 from Chapter 7 as written homework.

12   Organizing and outlining your presentations

Readings:

Text, Chapters 7 and 8.

John L. Vohs, "An Empirical Approach to the Concept of Attention," *CM* (Aug. 1964), 355–360.

Walter W. Stevens, "Attention Through Language," *CQ* (Nov. 1963), 23–25.

Activities:

Show videotape of poorly organized student speech. Have students look for and discuss problems in its organization and structure.

Introduce students to computerized outlining program.

13   Informative speaking

Readings:

Text, Chapter 12.

Walter B. Weimer, "Why All Knowing Is Rhetorical," *JAFA* (Fall 1983), 63–71.

Jay Davis, "Beyond the Myth of Objectivity," *Media & Values* (Summer 1990), 21.

"How to Analyze a News Story: Eight Guidelines for Reading Between the Lines," *Media & Values* (Summer 1990), 22.

Activities:

Show videotape of student informative speech.

Mass communication application: Use Discussion item 3 from Chapter 12 for viewing a short "pseudodocumentary" film and discussing the differences between informing and persuading.

14   Using and evaluating supporting materials
      Readings:
          Text, Chapter 6.
          J. Deighton, "The Interaction of Advertising and Evidence," *Journal of Consumer Research* (1984), 763–770.
          Hellmut Geissner, "Commercials as Narratives," in *On Narrative,* ed. Hellmut Geissner (Frankfurt: Scriptor, 1987), 297–303.
          Barry K. Spiker, Tom D. Daniels, and Lawrence M. Bernabo, "The Quantitative Quandary in Forensics: The Use and Abuse of Statistical Evidence," *JAFA* (Fall 1982), 87–96.
          Jerry Cederblom and David Paulsen, "Making Reasonable Decisions as an Amateur in a World of Experts," in *Selected Issues in Logic and Communication,* ed. Trudy Govier (Belmont, Calif.: Wadsworth, 1988), 138–149.
      Activities:
          Mass communication application: Use Application item 2 for the analysis of supporting materials in television advertisements

15   Supporting-a-point presentations

16   Using presentation aids
      Readings:
          Text, Chapter 9.
      Activities:
          Mass communication and group discussion application: Use Discussion item 4 from Chapter 9 for small-group analysis of the principles of design in magazine ads.

17   Examination 1: text Chapters 1–9 and 12 plus assigned readings.

18   The speaker's language
      Readings:
          Text, Chapter 10.
          Michael Osborn, "In Quest of Metaphor: The Story of an Odyssey," *The Florida Communication Journal* (1989), 1–9.
          Robert E. Denton, Jr., "The Rhetorical Effect of Slogans: Classification and Characteristics," *CQ* (Spring 1980), 10–18.
          Martin Peretz, "Symbolic Politics," *The New Republic,* 24 Oct. 1988, p. 50.
          Morris K. Udall, "Stalking the Elusive Malaprop," *Saturday Evening Post* (Oct. 1988), 38–41.
      Activities:
          Group communication application: Use "Exercise in Divergent Thinking" from Chapter 10, IRM.

19   Informative speech preparation outlines
      Activities:
          Group communication exercise: Use Discussion item 1 from Chapter 8 for group participation in revision of preparation outlines.

20   Presentation skills
      Readings:
          Text, Chapter 11.
          John Townsend, "Paralinguistics: It's Not What You Say, It's the Way That You Say It," *Management Decision* (May 1988), 36–40.

Bruce Bower, "Faces of Emotion: Social or Innate?" *Science News,* 5 Sept. 1987, p. 150.

Srully Blotnick, "So You're Going to Be on TV," *Forbes,* 17 Jan. 1986, pp. 118–119.

Activities:

Show videotapes illustrating good and poor presentation skills.

21-24   Informative speech presentations

25   Persuasive speaking

Readings:

Text, Chapter 13.

Wayne C. Minnick, "A New Look at the Ethics of Persuasion," *SSCJ* (Summer 1980), 352–362.

Ernest R. Alexander, "After Rationality: Planning, Politics, and Power," *Society* (Nov.–Dec. 1988), 15–19.

Jack D. Karetz, "Rational Arguments and Irrational Audiences: Psychology, Planning, and Public Judgment," *Journal of the American Planning Association* (Autumn 1989), 445–456.

Activities:

Mass communication application: Use Application item 1 for the analysis of videotaped television advertisements

26–27   Evidence, proof, and argument

Readings:

Text, Chapter 14.

Michael Osborn, "The Abuses of Argument," *SSCJ* (Fall 1983), 1–11.

Murray Edelman, "Language, Myths, and Rhetoric," *Transaction: Social Science and Modern Society* (July–Aug. 1975), 14–21.

Janice Hocker Rushing, "The Rhetoric of the American Western Myth,"*CM* (Mar. 1983), 14-32. (not sure about this one)

Donald Kipnis and Stuart Schmidt, "The Language of Persuasion," *Psychology Today* (Apr. 1985), 40–46.

Activities:

Mass communication application: Use Discussion item 1 for the analysis of magazine advertisements.

28   Persuasive speech preparation outlines

Activities:

Group communication application: Use Discussion item 1 from Chapter 8 for group participation in revision of preparation outlines.

29   Evaluating persuasive messages

Activities:

Show videotape of a short persuasive speech. Have students analyze the evidence, proofs, and arguments advanced by the speaker.

30–34   Persuasive speech presentations

35   Ceremonial speaking

Readings:

Text, Chapter 15.

J. Richard Chase, "The Classical Conception of Epideictic," *QJS* (Oct. 1961), 293–300.

Bernard K. Duffy, "The Platonic Functions of Epideictic Discourse," *Philosophy and Rhetoric* (1983), 79–93.

Joanne R. Cantor, "What is Funny to Whom? The Role of Gender," *JC* (Summer 1976), 164–172.

Activities:
Show videotape of ceremonial speech
Group communication application: Use Discussion item 3, having the students work in small groups to generate lists of heroes and share them with the class as a whole.

36–39   Ceremonial speech presentations

40   "Toasting Your Hero/Heroine" activity, Chapter 15 IRM

SPEAKING ASSIGNMENTS

As noted earlier, the class typically involves three to five major speaking assignments. Some instructors like to specify the requirements for each major assignment in the class syllabus. For example:

Self-introductory speech: A three- to five-minute extemporaneous presentation with an introduction, body, and conclusion. Choose something about yourself through which the audience can gain a better understanding of who you are as a unique individual. Try to think of something original that makes you different from other people. If you feel your topic may be too personal or too sensitive, discuss it with your instructor. Do not try to tell us everything about yourself or your entire life story in two to three minutes. Instead, focus on one experience, interest, etc., and use it to illustrate a specific point about who you are. As with all speeches, you may speak from note cards or a key-word outline.

Informative speech: A four- to six-minute extemporaneous presentation. Choose a topic that is important to you and either potentially important or interesting to your audience, and that can be adequately researched and covered in the four to six minutes allotted. Your speech should be timely and "news" to your audience. You should have a clear thesis statement that is developed in the body of your speech with two or three main points. Your main points should be arranged in one of the informative designs covered in Chapter 12 of your text. Each main point must be supported with a variety of supporting materials. Your speech should reflect responsible, balanced knowledge of your topic, and should be as objective as possible. You need to submit a formal outline and a bibliography with at least four reference sources.

Persuasive speech of contention: A six- to eight-minute extemporaneous presentation. This assignment stresses the development of a sound argument in support of a contested thesis on a timely topic. Try to pick timely issues with which your audience may not be familiar or on which they have not made up their minds yet. In this assignment you should address the major opposing viewpoints and offer reasoning and evidence in support of your position. Your thesis should be free of blatant fallacies. The main points of the body of your speech should be arranged in an appropriate design (see Chapter 13 of the text). You must submit a formal outline and a bibliography with at least six references.

Persuasive speech to move to action: A six- to eight-minute extemporaneous presentation. Choose a topic that is timely and important—something that you feel represents a problem that needs collective action. Craft a speech that (1) establishes the existence of a problem in the minds of your audience and (2) offers a clear and explicit set of actions that your audience can take to help resolve the matter. You need a well-organized message that reflects a clear sense of purpose. Your main points should be arranged in an appropriate design (see Chapter 13 of the text). Try to focus on something tangible that your audience can actually do something about. Speeches addressing local or campus-related issues can be very effective. You should incorporate strategies for involving your audience with your speech. You need to submit a formal outline and a bibliography with at least six references.

Ceremonial speech: A four- to six-minute extemporaneous presentation. You may select the type of ceremonial speech you wish to present from the following: (1) a speech of tribute, (2) a speech of inspiration, (3) an after-dinner speech. Turn in a cover sheet that explains which of the ceremonial functions discussed in Chapter 15 you hope to accomplish with your presentation and how you intend to work in the principles of magnification and identification.

Other speech options: These include impromptu speeches and contests, manuscript presentations, question-and-answer sessions, campus issues or local interest speeches, media presentations, revised presentations, problem-solving discussions, and panel discussions of important local issues. There are short speaking activities and exercises presented throughout the chapters of this IRM (see especially Chapters 2 and 11).

EVALUATING AND GRADING SPEECHES

Your evaluation of students' speeches should be part of your students' learning experience. The goal is to help them improve on later speeches, not to make them look or feel bad. Research on effective learning indicates that immediate feedback is important. We suggest that you provide short oral critiques to provide this immediate feedback, followed by written critiques after the completed round of speeches. To aid in the preparation of written critiques, we have developed "The Speech Evaluator" computer software, which contains a list of the common problems students have in presenting speeches and automatically refers them to appropriate text material that they should review.

When giving oral critiques, instructors should focus first on the positive aspects of the presentation, even though this is sometimes difficult. We have all heard speeches where the most positive comment we can come up with is, "What a wonderful learning opportunity you've given us!" An oral critique should never be embarrassing or humiliating to the student. Keep in mind the old management adage, "Praise in public, reprimand in private." Address areas for improvement in a constructive, supportive, and optimistic manner. It often helps to preface such comments with something like, "Did you give any thought to . . ." or "Do you think it would have been helpful to . . . "

The perception of fairness is of major importance in grading. Students need to know how they will be evaluated and what is expected for different grades. Let your students know the type of evaluation you will use and provide them with a statement of criteria for grading. Many instructors like to use explicitly defined criteria for each grade level. The "Criteria for Grading Speeches" on p. 21 has been adapted from Cassandra L. Book, et al., *Contract Grading in Speech Communication Courses*. The "Speech Evaluation Form" on p. 22 reflects the criteria for effective speaking discussed in the text. You might tailor it to a given assignment by starring items of particular importance or placing the letters *NA* ("not applicable") before items that you will not be considering.

Prescriptive grading criteria such as these offer several advantages. They force instructors to be more thorough and consistent in their grading practices, and they tend to reduce perceptions of subjective or arbitrary grading. However, such methods can confuse students and even intimidate them, so that they simply accept their grades without question. Furthermore, they can be cumbersome, and they constrain appreciation for the artistry of public speaking. The principles we teach, while usually pertinent, do not always hold true. Would you give a young Winston Churchill an A– because he spoke with a lisp? Would you admonish a future Martin Luther King, Jr. for over-relying on biblical metaphors and narratives? The point is, do not let prescriptive grading criteria blind your appreciation of your students' creative endeavors.

As a simplified alternative, you might customize a statement regarding what you want for an A on each particular assignment, then specify grade reductions for common problem areas (thesis clarity, citing sources, eye contact, etc.). The following statement is customized from the speech criteria offered in the text emphasizing substance, structure, and presentation:

> You will not be graded on whether your presentations "glow" or seem to "capture the moment." I focus on three major areas when assigning speech grades. First, an A speech is *substantive*. It develops an original topic and idea that is relevant to the interests and moral sensibilities of your audience. It should be supported by a variety of high-quality researched information and (if necessary) reasoning. Researched information should be cited orally at least twice during the presentation of your speech. Second, an A speech is well *structured*, so that it can be easily followed by your audience. Your entire speech should develop your thesis statement and reflect a clear sense of general and specific purpose. It should adhere to the principles of good form, and be developed with an introduction, a body, and a conclusion. The main ideas should be developed in accordance with a coherent speech design strategy. Your choice of language and sentence structure should be as simple and clear as possible. Third, an A speech is effectively *presented*, using an extemporaneous speaking style. Note that I do not expect you to look "slick" your first time in front of an audience, and a jittery presentation does not necessarily mean a bad grade so long as you keep forcing yourself to make contact with your audience. If you do this, your

presentation skills should improve with every speech. In addition, in an A speech, the details are well polished. All these variables should come together in your presentation.

Tell your students they need to excel in all three areas to make A range, emphasizing that this is difficult to achieve and rare on first presentations. A B range grade reflects a really good speech that falls short in one major area, or is plagued by a couple of minor problems that add up. A C range grade reflects a lot of time and effort, but there are numerous problems that need to be addressed next time. A D range grade is poor in all three areas and does not impress you as reflecting a lot of work. An F range speech is not delivered and never made up. Impress upon students that infractions in different areas are always a matter of degree, which is necessarily left to your discretion. Go out of your way to use the grading criteria you have established, and always explain how students can improve on future assignments.

Although it gets easier with experience, grading is hard work. It is absolutely crucial that you be as fair and consistent as possible when assigning grades. This is often easier said than done, for it can be hard to give students you really like grades you're sure will upset them. Unless you give excessively high grades, you will have disgruntled students after nearly every round of speeches. Remember that angry students will often compare their grades with those of classmates and will be quick to assume that you are being arbitrary or showing favoritism, especially if you are a young and inexperienced instructor. Impress upon them that this is not the case, and make sure that this is true.

To help you gain confidence in grading and critiquing speeches, we have developed a "Speech Assessment" package that contains a videotape of student speeches and a printed guide in which seven experienced professors share their observations on critiquing and grading speeches. The guide also includes material on the nature of the assignment for each speech, written transcripts of the speeches, a copy of the evaluation form each professor uses, and a completed written evaluation of each speech by each of the professors.

Some instructors supplement written evaluations with self- and/or peer evaluations of classroom presentations. Students can be objectively critical of themselves in self-evaluations and are often tougher in suggested grades than an instructor might be. Research suggests that students find peer evaluations useful, and that they are generally consistent with instructor evaluations. Forms for both types of evaluations may be found on pp. 23–24 . Another option for evaluating and grading student speeches is to establish specific objectives for an assignment and evaluate how well the student meets the stated objectives. A form for this procedure may be found on p. 25. If you have never done this or feel uncertain of your ability to evaluate speeches, we suggest that you practice with videotaped student speeches, comparing your evaluations with those of other, more experienced instructors.

Criteria for Grading Speeches

To receive a C on your speeches, you must meet the following standards:

Your speech must be original, appropriate to the assignment and audience, sufficiently focused and timed, and presented on the assigned day. Your speech should reflect a clear sense of purpose, and its main ideas should be supported with facts and figures, appropriate testimony, examples, and narratives. Your speech should be developed with an introduction, a body, and a conclusion, and its main ideas should be arranged using an appropriate design strategy. Your speech should be delivered extemporaneously with effective language use. Finally, your speech must satisfy the technical requirements of the specific assignment.

To receive a B on your speeches, you must meet the following standards:

You must meet and exceed the requirements of a C speech by choosing a challenging topic and adapting it appropriately to your audience, reflecting a greater depth of research, identifying the sources of your information and ideas, creating and sustaining your audience's attention throughout the speech, making effective use of transitions, making a poised presentation, and having a good oral style.

To receive an A on your speeches, you must meet the following standards:

You must meet and exceed the requirements for a B speech by demonstrating imaginative creativity in topic selection and development; developing and sustaining strong bonds of identification among the speaker, audience, and topic; consistently adapting information and supporting materials to the experiences of your audience; having an even greater depth of research; making creative use of language and stylistic techniques, and giving a polished presentation that artfully integrates verbal and nonverbal techniques.

A D speech does not meet one or more of the standards for a C speech or:

It is obviously unrehearsed, and/or it is based entirely on biased information or unsupported opinions.

An F speech does not meet three or more of the standards for a C speech, reflects either of the problems associated with a D speech, or:

It uses fabricated supporting material, deliberately distorts evidence, and/or is plagiarized.

Speech Evaluation Form

Speaker _____ Date _____ Topic _____

5 = excellent   4 = good   3 = average   2 = below average   1 = poor

Overall Considerations

_____ Did the speaker seem committed to the topic?
_____ Did the speech meet the requirements of the assignment?
_____ Was the speech adapted to fit the audience?
_____ Did the speech promote identification among topic, audience, and speaker?
_____ Was the purpose of the speech clear?
_____ Was the topic handled with imagination and freshness?
_____ Did the speech meet high ethical standards?

Substance

_____ Was the topic worthwhile?
_____ Had the speaker done sufficient research?
_____ Were the main ideas supported with reliable and relevant information?
_____ Was testimony used appropriately?
_____ Were the sources documented appropriately?
_____ Were examples or narratives used effectively?
_____ Was the reasoning clear and correct?

Structure

_____ Did the introduction spark your interest?
_____ Did the introduction adequately preview the message?
_____ Was the speech easy to follow?
_____ Could you identify the main points of the speech?
_____ Were transitions used to tie the speech together?
_____ Did the conclusion summarize the message?
_____ Did the conclusion help you remember the speech?

Presentation

_____ Was the language clear, simple, and direct?
_____ Was the language colorful?
_____ Were grammar and pronunciation correct?
_____ Was the speech presented extemporaneously?
_____ Were notes used unobtrusively?
_____ Was the speaker appropriately enthusiastic?
_____ Did the speaker maintain good eye contact?
_____ Did gestures and body language complement ideas?
_____ Was the speaker's voice expressive?
_____ Were the rate and loudness appropriate to the material?
_____ Did the speaker use pauses appropriately?
_____ Did visual aids make the message clearer or more memorable?
_____ Were visual aids skillfully integrated into the speech?
_____ Was the presentation free from distracting mannerisms?

Self-Evaluation Form

Name _____ Date _____

Topic _____

Strengths in this assignment: _____

_____

_____

_____

_____

Areas I need to work on: _____

_____

_____

_____

_____

Grade I deserve _____

_____

Instructor's evaluation:

Grade:

Student Feedback Form

Speaker _____ **Topic** _____ **Date** _____

Introduction:

1. Did the introduction grasp your attention? How? _____

    _____

2. Did the speaker establish credibility to speak on the topic? How? _____

    _____

3. Did the speaker adequately preview the main points? _____

Body:

1. Was the speech easy for you to follow? _____ Identify the main points:

    (1) _____

    (2) _____

    (3) _____

2. Were the main points arranged effectively? _____ What type of design was used? _____

    _____ Might a different design have been better? _____ What design

    would you suggest? _____

3. Was supporting material sufficient and appropriate? _____ Please comment: _____

    _____

4. Did you find the speech interesting? _____ Why or why not? _____

    _____

Conclusion:

1. Did the speaker summarize the message? _____

2. Did you feel the speech was complete? _____

3. Were you left with something to remember? _____ What? _____

    _____

Suggestions for Improvement (Please note two things the speaker could do to improve his or her next presentation):

1. _____

2. _____

Speaking by Objectives

Name _____

Assignment _____

Taking into consideration the evaluation of your previous speech(es) and the nature of the assignment, you are to establish specific objectives for your next speech. For example, if the evaluation of your last speech suggested that you were too dependent on your notes, one of your objectives might read: "To be more extemporaneous in my presentation." Your objectives should also contain a statement of the specific purpose and thematic statement of your speech.

Objectives

1. Specific purpose _____

   _____

2. Thematic statement _____

   _____

   _____

3. Objective related to previous evaluation _____

   _____

   _____

4. Objective related to previous evaluation _____

   _____

   _____

5. Objective specific to assignment _____

   _____

   _____

6. Objective specific to assignment _____

   _____

   _____

PREPARING FINAL GRADES

Your syllabus should explain how your students' final grades will be determined at the end of the semester. Many instructors like to give letter rather than numerical grades; these can then be converted to a twelve- or fifteen-point numerical scale to tabulate and compute final grades. Such a grading scheme can help reduce perceptions of subjectivity in your grading practices. Emphasize that your students' grades are a composite of their performances throughout the course of the semester, not a personal decision made by you at the last moment. In your syllabus, you should list the weighted percentage of each assignment or assigned grade in respect to the final grade. A sample list might read:

Introductory speech	5 percent	Essay or outside speech critique	10 percent
Informative speech	15 percent	Final exam	25 percent
Persuasive speech	20 percent	Miscellaneous	10 percent
Ceremonial speech	15 percent		

The letter grade of each evaluated assignment should be converted to a numerical scale, such as:

A+ = 15	B+ = 12	C+ = 9	D+ = 6	F = 0
A = 14	B = 11	C = 8	D = 5	
A− = 13	B− = 10	C− = 7	D− = 4	

To compute final grades, simply multiply each grade's numerical equivalent by its weighted percentage, sum the totals, and convert the result back to the numerical scale. Emphasize that this establishes clear numerical boundaries between grade ranges at the end of the semester, and that you will not "bump" grades in either direction at that time. Impress upon students that with numerical grading schemes, every grade is important, no matter how small the percentage—they all add up! In the sample grade that follows, the student barely made a B. A B+ instead of an A+ on the miscellaneous grade would have meant a C in the course. If students keep up with their scores, they should have no problem calculating their own grades.

Introductory speech (5 percent)	C+	$9 \times 0.05 = 0.45$
Informative speech (15 percent)	B	$11 \times 0.15 = 1.65$
Persuasive speech (20 percent)	B−	$10 \times 0.2 = 2$
Ceremonial speech (15 percent)	C	$8 \times 0.15 = 1.2$
Essay/speech critique (10 percent)	C+	$9 \times 0.1 = 0.9$
Miscellaneous grade (10 percent)	A+	$15 \times 0.1 = 1.5$
Final exam (25 percent)	B−	$10 \times 0.25 = 2.5$

Total = 10.2 (B or B−)

If you intend to give students an opportunity for extra credit, you need to let them know this from the beginning of the term. It's not fair to hint at such work and then never assign it. Keep in mind that you are not obliged to do this, and that it means extra work for you at the end of the semester, when you may well have other things to do with your time.

TROUBLESHOOTING GUIDE FOR BEGINNING INSTRUCTORS

Beginning instructors may encounter many problems that seem difficult to handle at first. This section explores common problem situations and offers suggestions for handling them.

Appreciating Cultural Diversity

Public speaking has often been criticized for promoting the values and ideals of the dominant culture. Speech instructors may reinforce this sort of cultural elitism by implicitly teaching their students that there is only one right way to communicate. Fortunately, people are now learning to recognize and appreciate the value of cultural differences in strengthening the fabric of a community, understanding that diversity is not a liability but an asset to be cherished and nurtured for the good of the whole. Tragic examples such as Bosnia continue to remind us of what can happen in multicultural societies when constructive communication breaks down.

As a public speaking instructor, you can help by emphasizing (as the text does) that effective and ethical public speaking begins with the development of a humane sensitivity and appreciation for cultural diversity. Your students will probably represent a broad spectrum of backgrounds. Emphasize the value of learning public speaking skills as a means of exposing us to diversity as well as discovering and affirming our own distinct identities. Remember that public speaking is a means of empowerment, and that some of your students will use the skills you teach them to influence the lives of other people. Therefore, the assumptions we pass to them regarding its effective and ethical practice are crucial.

Seek to exercise this humane sensitivity yourself in class and in your interactions with students. This is not easy, as all instructors must develop standards and use them to evaluate their students. But speech teachers should be flexible enough to recognize that there is no one right way to communicate that works in all contexts. For instance, an exchange student from Southeast Asia might have trouble with eye contact because in most Asian communities it is considered offensive to stare at people when you talk to them. In situations such as these, you have to rely on your best judgment, but if the speech shows that the student has put considerable effort into preparing and presenting it effectively, your own humane sensitivity should lead you to be flexible and tactful. You cannot simply ignore such problems, as students will not learn to speak effectively before Western audiences without learning to make better eye contact. But as instructors we should acknowledge and respect the value of the differing communication styles our students bring to the classroom.

Most people are very sensitive about the way they talk. Grammar and pronunciation are one thing, but speech teachers should avoid the temptation to "correct" what they deem to be deviant dialects or speech patterns. While most audiences are predisposed to people who talk their own language, a Latino, southern, or black vernacular pattern can be blended into an effective public speaking style. Our last three Democratic presidents have all been southerners with distinctively regional accents. A black vernacular is certainly not a hindrance to eloquence in the speeches of Barbara Jordan or Martin Luther King, Jr. The lesson here is to encourage your students to discover and affirm their own distinctiveness as they develop their unique communication styles.

Finally, developing a sense of humane sensitivity and respect for cultural differences may be enhanced by some healthy self-criticism on your part. Few of us like to think of ourselves as prejudiced, but many of us harbor tacit assumptions based on social and cultural stereotypes that lead us to say and do insensitive things without being aware of them or thinking about them. Be honest with yourself. Do you sometimes group people into categories rather than perceiving them as unique individuals? How much do you know about the various cultural backgrounds represented in your classes? All of us come from limited backgrounds that can blind us to the concerns and experiences of other people. We strongly recommend that you take every opportunity to educate yourself. Look for social activities and "mixers" sponsored by minority student associations, and consider taking the cultural diversity seminars offered at most universities at the beginning of the fall semester.

Detecting and Dealing with Plagiarism

Be certain your students understand clearly what plagiarism is and what the penalties are for this serious academic violation. Include a statement on plagiarism in your syllabus. There is probably one in your institution's student handbook, or you might use or adapt the statement from Chapter 1 of this IRM. Most policies stipulate an F on the assignment, an F in the course, or even expulsion from the university pending student judiciary action. Check with your course director or faculty handbook for specific policies and procedures regarding academic dishonesty.

Speech instructors may encounter a variety of forms of plagiarism. Be wary of speeches that are pulled from fraternity, dormitory, or computer network "files." Students may also parrot a recent article from a popular periodical or even fabricate sources of information. Make sure they understand that academic dishonesty includes adapting speeches from previous essays and class assignments or getting all their materials from a single source. Some students have even been known to memorize a speech from the appendix of your or another text and present it as their own.

Accusations of plagiarism are very serious and can have legal repercussions. You must have some sort of proof before bringing formal charges against a student. Look up the articles the student cites in his or her bibliography to see if they actually exist. If they are all dated but from the same time period (say, three or four years ago), you have good reason to be suspicious. If a speech sounds like something that was parroted right out of a magazine, check recent popular periodicals for articles on the subject. Some departments keep a file of speeches delivered on common topics (donating body parts, safe sex, avoiding tanning booths, drinking and driving, etc.) so that speeches that sound "strangely familiar" can be checked. Even if your department doesn't keep such a file, tell your students you do to inhibit their baser inclinations. Ask other instructors in your department if they have heard similar speeches.

Because plagiarism is difficult to prove, instructors often end up with good reasons to be suspicious, but no real proof. In such cases a direct confrontation may be in order. Call the student to your office for a meeting, or ask her or him to stay after class. Be polite, but firm and to the point. Tell the student that you are concerned about this work and uncertain whether in fact it is actually the student's. Keep your composure if the student becomes emotional. You might have another instructor present to act as a witness to your discussion. If the student insists that the work is his or hers, and you're convinced it's not, read through it with the student, asking how he or she came up with particular ideas or information. You might even photocopy the articles the student cited ahead of time and read through them as well. If the student is guilty, it will be difficult for him or her to make up one lie after another without collapsing into a remorseful confession. Remember that this is a very serious charge that could end up in litigation. Regardless of whatever actions you intend to take, *always consult your course director or department chair* before pursuing this very serious charge.

Students Not Prepared to Speak on the Assigned Day

Set a clear policy in your syllabus concerning speaking on assigned days. Most instructors lower the assignment grade by one letter for each class period a student is late in presenting an oral assignment. Many instructors also stipulate that they will allow a student only one chance to make up a speech without a formal, written excuse. Some instructors pass around a list of days for a round of speeches and have students sign up for a particular date and time on a first-come, first-served basis. This should give students a chance to avoid being scheduled on days when they have legitimate conflicts. Other instructors draw names or arbitrarily appoint dates and times, asking students ahead of time for preferable dates.

When faced with requests for delays, keep in mind that you are dealing with adult students who may have legitimate adult problems. Documented illnesses, deaths in the family, car accidents, rapes, or other traumatic occurrences warrant flexibility and good judgment on your part. Still, college is an adult priority, and once you start allowing students to delay their presentations, you're in for many headaches before the end of the term. Make sure they understand that in most situations you will enforce the stated policy concerning grade deductions, and be firm and consistent about enforcing that policy. A legitimate excuse must have some form of reasonable documentation (letters from Mom will not do). Be wary of last-minute telephoned excuses the night before students are scheduled to speak.

Absenteeism

Public speaking is a participative course, and students will not learn anything if they are not in class. Also, students make better presentations when they have a full audience to simulate a realistic speaking environment. Your course director, department, or college may have an absenteeism policy that prescribes how you should handle this problem. If so, this should be clearly stated in your syllabus. If no statement is available, you may wish to adapt the following to meet your particular needs.

> Public speaking requires an audience; therefore, attendance is especially important in this course. Students also are expected to participate in class activities and contribute to class discussions of topics. Five or more absences will result in a lowering of your final grade by one letter. Additional absences will result in further lowering of your grade.

Habitual absenteeism may be a sign of more serious problems. When students have used up their last unexcused absence before suffering a grade reduction, make it a point to pull them aside, let them know you are concerned, and remind them of your policy.

Tardiness

Students who wander in late disrupt class just as it is getting started. This can be frustrating when you are lecturing or conducting a class discussion or activity—and even more problematic if a student is presenting a speech. Set a clear policy regarding tardiness and stick to it. Often students will "feel you out" on this one; if you let them get away with it, they will start walking into class five minutes late every day. You are only reinforcing this tendency by stopping class politely and starting over again. Students may have legitimate excuses or reasons for being a few minutes late on a regular basis, and there are situations calling for tolerance on this policy. Otherwise, instructors generally allow only a limited number of unexcused tardys before counting them as unexcused absences. When students do come late, they should enter as quietly as possible to minimize the disruption. When they arrive late on speech days, they should be especially careful not to disrupt a speech in progress. Obviously, instructors should set an example by always being on time themselves. Finally, make sure your students understand that quizzes missed because of unexcused tardiness will not be made up and that if they miss roll call, it is their responsibility to let you know they are present *on that day* to avoid being counted absent.

Emotional Outbursts

Most students take grades very seriously and are especially sensitive to criticism they perceive as biased or personally motivated. Most veteran instructors have experienced upset students crumpling evaluation forms, cursing the instructor, and storming out of the room. Should this happen, *keep your cool*. Don't respond in kind. Document what happened by writing an account of the encounter and reporting the incident to your course director or chairperson. Wait to see what the student will do next. Young students often feel chagrined after such incidents and frequently apologize. Accept their apologies, but let them know that you will not tolerate further outbursts.

Grade Complaints

Every instructor deals with students who are upset over their grades almost every semester. It's part of the job. Remember that grading is serious business, and that students have a right to understand the marks they receive. Be certain that they know your grading criteria and that you explain the reasons for their grade on your evaluation form. Keep in mind the pressures that students are under to make good grades and be as tactful as possible when they are obviously upset.

Establish a policy of being willing to explain and discuss but never to negotiate grades unless it is obvious that you have made an error. Tell students to see you as soon as possible after receiving grades that they are unhappy with, and impress upon them that such postspeech consultations are encouraged as a means of improving on future presentations. Emphasize that you will not hear grade complaints concerning early assignments at the end of the semester. Having said this, you might also establish a twenty-four-hour cooling-off period after returning graded evaluation forms in which you will not discuss anyone's grade in order to prevent hostile or unproductive encounters. Students should use this time to read your comments, and consider whether and why they feel their grade is unreasonable. As always, keep your composure should your students lose theirs. If a student is unsatisfied with your explanation, inform her or him of the appeal process or refer the student to your course director or department chair. On rare occasions you may find yourself having to politely ask students who will not take no for an answer to leave your office. Some instructors offer an "extra credit option" near the end of the semester to allow borderline students to improve their grades. If you decide to institute such a policy, it should be noted in your syllabus and worked into your formula for computing final grades.

Students Who Are Overly Critical of Classmates in Oral Critiques

Sometimes domineering students can make others feel inhibited by unsolicited negative criticism. Although this problem is really quite rare, you can help head it off by emphasizing the importance of constructive listening and feedback and requiring students who make negative comments to offer suggestions for improvement as well. Don't compound the problem by publicly attacking such students. If they are persistently obnoxious, you might approach them before or after class. Such students often fail to recognize that their remarks are upsetting others, or that their tone of voice may carry a message different from what they intend. Ask your students to be supportive of their classmates, suggesting the value of constructive criticism in learning public speaking skills.

Students Not Reading Assignments or Not Participating in Discussions

Let students know from the beginning that they are expected to read assigned materials and be prepared for class activities. Many instructors establish a participation grade that is contingent on being prepared for class activities and readings. If you habitually spoon-feed assigned readings through lectures, students will not bother to read the material until test time. When students are habitually unprepared for class, many instructors resort to pop quizzes. As an alternative, you might have your students keep a reading log in which they are asked to identify two to three points of interest from assigned readings for class discussion (see Chapter 1 of this IRM).

Work to involve students with the material from the first days of class. Use thought-provoking questions to stimulate discussion rather than questions that require only the recitation of memorized information. Ask direct questions: "Was there anything in the reading that you didn't understand? Anything you would like to take issue with? Anything you felt was especially valuable?" Be willing to wait for students to think about and formulate answers. Be patient. Groups are uncomfortable with silence, so if you pause long enough, someone will usually volunteer a response. It may seem like an eternity, but if you time it, you'll probably find that it's not more than ten or fifteen seconds. Don't inhibit class involvement by jumping in prematurely with answers. If no one volunteers, call on someone by name. Try to steer students toward the correct answers without "correcting" them. Offer hints as necessary and at all costs avoid humiliating them.

When students do participate, be receptive and tactful with your responses. Acknowledge correct answers without embarrassing praise, and don't humiliate students for asking what you think is a dumb question or comment. Remember, the only "dumb question" is one that is not asked. If an answer is partially correct, acknowledge the correct portion but probe for more detail. If a response is off the mark, you should acknowledge the student's effort—"That's an interesting perspective"—then tactfully explain why it might be off the mark. Be careful—if you ever start humiliating students, others will be reluctant to participate.

One Student Dominating a Discussion

Occasionally you will have a student in your classes who is always the first to respond and insists on being heard on everything. While it is nice to have one student in a section that you can always count on to get discussion going, sometimes such students can dominate class discussion and inhibit others from participating. If this is the case, politely intervene and solicit input from other students. As soon as you see the student pause for breath, say something like, "That's interesting, Bob. Jane, what do you think?" Be tactful, and (as always) avoid humiliating students. Let them know that you appreciate their enthusiastic participation, but that you want everyone to have a chance. If a student persists in dominating class discussions, call him or her to your office to discuss the problem in private. Solicit the student's support in helping you involve others in the discussion rather than criticizing him or her directly.

Students Talking During Lectures, Films, or Speeches

It's disconcerting to discover during a lecture that two students at the back of the room are carrying on an animated discussion about something that probably has no bearing on your class. This is rude, unacceptable behavior that infringes upon other students' right to learn, and instructors should not let it go for long. It is even more problematic when such a situation occurs during a student speech. You can forestall such problems by establishing a code of listening behavior early in the course, or giving your students critical and constructive listening activities to complete in conjunction with their classmates' presentations. Before each round of speeches, remind the class of their role and function as listeners in the communication process.

If students are talking while you are lecturing, a long pause accompanied by direct eye contact is often sufficient to restore quiet. If this doesn't work, you may have to ask them directly to be quiet and tell them that you find their behavior disconcerting and rude. You might revert to the old standbys: "I know what you're discussing is really relevant . . . so please share it with us" or "Do I have to separate you two?" If the problem persists, approach the students and tell them unambiguously that their behavior is rude and unacceptable. It's sad but true that you might actually find yourself having to separate college-age students who otherwise simply will not shut up.

Inattentive Students

Even the best students are occasionally inattentive. However, some students seem never to pay attention, and all experienced instructors have had students who use their class for nap time or a study hall for other classes. On the one hand, if the inattention is self-contained and causes no distraction, then it's their prerogative to fail. However, it is rude and distracting for students to sleep or do their homework for other classes in your class. It is also often an indirect challenge to your ethos as a teacher. If such behavior persists, suggest that such students leave and take an unexcused absence (unless, of course, the students are sick or medicated, in which case they really should not be there in the first place). Again, critical and constructive listening activities usually make for a more attentive classroom audience for student speeches.

If an inordinate number of your students prove chronically inattentive, some healthy self-evaluation of your teaching may well be in order. Holding a class's undivided attention for fifty or seventy-five minutes is no easy task, and instructors should constantly critique themselves to improve and personalize both their lesson plans and their manner of teaching. Simply put, this is hard work, and it doesn't come overnight. As you seek to improve your own skills in speech instruction, you might consider the following questions:

- Are you actively involving students with the subject matter?
- Are you using the attention-creating and -sustaining techniques we discuss in the text?
- Are you boring students with long lectures that simply repeat what they've heard or read elsewhere?
- Have you overestimated or underestimated the ability of your students?

- Are you conveying enthusiasm for teaching in general and your subject in particular?
- Do you speak in a monotone?
- Do you spend most of your time writing on the blackboard with your back to the class?
- Are you disorganized and hard to follow?
- Do you follow the same format for every class?

Students Coming to You with Personal Problems

Public speaking classes are small by most college and university standards, and the need to promote a warm classroom environment means that you may give your students more personal attention than most other instructors. This situation sets you up for the role of counselor par excellence. Don't let this go to your head. You are not a trained counselor or therapist, and you shouldn't try to act like one. If a student comes to you with a serious problem, listen empathetically, but do not try to solve the problem. If the student just wants to talk, fine—but learn to recognize when students may need professional services or advice that you are not trained to provide. Giving out faulty legal, psychological, or relational advice is unprofessional and can have serious consequences. On rare occasions, it could actually result in legal action being taken against you or your institution. Familiarize yourself with the services available on your campus or in your community so that you can direct troubled students to a place where they can get the help they need.

Students with Disabling Communication Apprehension

Most people experience some anxiety when asked to make presentations in front of more than five people at a time, especially when they have never done so before. Nervous students will often approach you early in the course to express their concern. Keep in mind that communication apprehension is a well-documented phobia that warrants sensitivity. However, few students are actually disabled by it. For most, the butterflies become progressively more manageable once they've had a little experience. Refer students to the material in the text concerning coping with speech anxiety. Impress upon them that it is perfectly natural and can be channeled into an effective presentation. Because all students are in the same situation, the classroom tends to make for a nonthreatening and supportive environment. Assure them that nervousness will not necessarily hurt their grades, especially on earlier presentations.

However, sooner or later you will encounter students with extreme communication anxiety who, despite being prepared (or even overprepared), cannot manage an effective presentation. Students may start out trying to present a speech extemporaneously, freeze, and proceed to read the rest of the speech from their notes. Sometimes they may simply freeze and sit down without explanation. Try to keep them going. Often nervous students will stop and ask to start over, which you should not let them do if they are already well into their speech. If students sit down, remember that they are probably very upset, so avoid saying anything that will further humiliate them. Tactfully try to get them to go again at the end of the class. If they refuse, have them talk to you after class. Get a copy of the outline to see if they prepared a speech, and, if they did, let them know that the world has not just ended—the sun will rise again tomorrow. Let them know that, although they may not believe it, many of their classmates will remember their discomfort and try to be especially supportive during their next presentation. Try to get these students to reschedule the speech at the beginning of the next class day. Impress upon them the benefits of getting over this "hump" and learning to address large groups of people effectively.

As a last option, you might consider allowing students with extreme communication apprehension to present their speeches in your office in front of a smaller audience of instructors and/or classmates. This is one of the most uncomfortable situations you will ever have to deal with as an instructor. On the one hand, students will not learn much without presenting their speeches before a real audience. On the other hand, if communication apprehension is a physically debilitating phobia, then it would hardly be fair to give students failing grades for it. Such situations are generally upsetting to students, and they rarely fake a "freeze" experience in order to get out of completing an assignment. You will know acute communication anxiety when you see it, and you'll know if it's the real thing. Getting such students to deal constructively with their fear and manage extemporaneous presentations can be a tremendous victory and valuable breakthrough experience for them. Some larger departments have developed special courses for high-communication-apprehension students.

Flirting with, Fraternizing with, or Dating Students

Getting to know your students can be nice, and many instructors develop long-term relationships with people who were once their students. However, becoming personally, and especially romantically, involved with students while they are taking your course is asking for trouble. Dating or even flirting with students can leave you, your department, and your university open to charges of conflict of interest and sexual harassment. Some friendly or flirtatious students may come on to you because they know you have the power to evaluate them. Using that power to make them flirt with or become personally involved with you is *absolutely unethical* and a disgrace to the teaching profession. Always maintain a polite but professional distance from your students until they have completed your course.

Also remember that students who are disgruntled with grades may be prone to assume favoritism and capriciousness on your part. You want to avoid the obvious impression that one or two of your students have developed a special status with you personally and are therefore sure to get an A on every assignment. This same advice holds true for "partying" with or meeting students you like at bars on weekends. Save yourself and your department the hassle by not acting on personal attraction until the class is over and they are no longer your students.

Students Not Respecting You as an Instructor

Gross insubordination is less common than most beginning instructors fear, but it does happen from time to time, especially with young teachers and graduate assistants. Make no mistake, when students refuse to shut up or to quit flirting with you or exhibit other distracting behaviors, they are challenging your authority. Often such students are upset over a grade or have suddenly realized that public speaking is not such an "easy" course after all. These students create an unpleasant classroom atmosphere, which is unfair and counterproductive. If this happens, avoid a heated confrontation in front of other students. If things get out of hand, pull the problem students aside and tell them in no uncertain terms that your find their behavior disconcerting and will not tolerate it in the future. If they keep pushing it, suggest a meeting with your course director or department chair.

However, if this happens to you often, some healthy self-evaluation may well be in order. Beginning instructors are most commonly bothered by such problems. They have legitimate power because of their position, but this doesn't mean automatic respect. Just as a speaker must establish ethos to be effective, so must a teacher. So let's look at the four dimensions of ethos and consider how they relate to teaching effectiveness and respect.

Do you come across as competent? Do you know the material you are teaching well enough to answer student questions? If you are not personally confident of your knowledge of the field, students will quickly pick up on this. The chapter-by-chapter guide in this IRM offers an extensive list of readings for enrichment on the topics covered in the corresponding sections of the text. Use readings from this list to increase your own knowledge of the field and your confidence in handling student questions.

Are you well prepared for class? Have you planned and organized each class session? Have you outlined a lecture or series of questions to stimulate discussion? Have you gone over your notes before class? Have you planned activities and made certain you have all the necessary materials? It is estimated that instructors spend at least three hours preparing for each hour in the classroom. Experienced teachers typically have more material than they can use in the time they have for class. Follow their lead and be overprepared. The chapter-by-chapter guide in this IRM contains an abundance of materials and activities to keep you supplied with different things to do.

Do you look competent? Are you neatly groomed and dressed appropriately for work? Older, more experienced teachers may be able to be casual and still command respect. However, younger beginning instructors can boost their self-confidence and ethos by dressing as if they've got a real job.

Do you act competent? Does your demeanor send cues that you are confident of yourself and in control of the classroom? If students sense that you lack confidence, respect will be hard to come by. The more confident you appear, the more positive feedback you will get and the more true confidence you will acquire. Keep in mind that the class is in your hands and that one of your primary responsibilities as a teacher is to maintain control. *Control does not imply heavy-handedness.* You need not be a tyrant to stay on top of things. Simply deal with problems as they arise and don't let the situation get out of hand.

Do you come across as trustworthy? Are you evaluating your students fairly? Have you established a clear set of grading criteria and communicated it effectively to your students? Are your criteria reasonable? Are you firm and consistent in your application of those criteria?

Are you careful to differentiate fact from opinion when presenting your ideas? It's not wrong to express opinions, as long as you let your class know that they are not required to agree with them. Opinions are necessarily biased, and we all have them. We get into trouble when, by denying their existence, we allow them to influence our objectivity. When covering argumentation and reasoning, you want your students to talk about and even argue positions on politically significant issues. It can be extremely detrimental to an atmosphere of free and open deliberation if a domineering instructor imposes her or his viewpoint on every issue that comes up and attacks any students who are bold enough to disagree.

When appropriate, are you willing to say, "I don't know"? You can come across as competent without having to know the answer to every question directed to you in class. Don't bluff answers. You'll end up talking in circles and look the worse for it. If the question is worth consideration, tell the students that you honestly don't know, but you will have an answer for them by the next class period. Then do it! Be willing to learn as you teach. The true test of education is not knowing all the answers, but knowing how and where to find them.

Can you admit mistakes? No matter how hard we try, all of us are going to make mistakes at one time or another in our teaching. We may misgrade an exam, write unclear or ambiguous test questions, allow personal bias to influence our grading, and so on. Be willing to accept that you can and will make mistakes. Also be willing to correct them.

Do you show respect for your students? Can they trust you not to belittle them when they make comments or express their opinions in class? Can you help them see their mistakes or problems as growth opportunities rather than something they should feel embarrassed about? One of the nicest compliments a teacher can receive is that he or she never made students feel bad about themselves. You need to be able to step on their toes without messing up their shoeshines.

Do you come across as likable? Are you a positive and optimistic person? Do you check your personal problems and concerns at the classroom door? Do you work to create identification among yourself, the class, and the material? Can you handle close identification and still maintain the role differences you must observe as an instructor? Are you a good role model for your students? You want your students to identify with you as a teacher, not as one of the gang.

The concepts of immediacy and affinity-seeking behaviors are closely related to likability. They are also related to learning motivation and to both cognitive and affective learning. Behaviors associated with immediacy include:

- Smiling at the class and at individual students
- Maintaining eye contact
- Using gestures and movement
- Demonstrating vocal variety
- Having a relaxed rather than tense body posture while teaching

Affinity-seeking behaviors include:

- Making the class enjoyable
- Not acting superior or snobbish
- Being cheerful and optimistic
- Not complaining or being highly critical of others
- Showing respect for students
- Helping students feel good about themselves and their abilities
- Being respectful of the opinions and ideas students express

Do you come across as forceful? Forcefulness relates to perceptions of power. *Power* is not a four-letter word! Depending on its type, it may be perceived positively or negatively. Power in the classroom is usually one of five different types:

1. *Coercive power* is based on the teacher's ability to inflict punishment. It is negatively associated with motivation and with cognitive and affective learning.

2. *Reward power* is the opposite of coercive power. Although it is not directly associated with motivation or with cognitive or affective learning, it may be used effectively to sustain desired behaviors while a teacher builds a base of referent or expert power.

3. *Legitimate power* is power vested in the position, not in the person holding the position. Reliance on legitimate power does not result in high levels of motivation and cognitive or affective learning.

4. *Referent power* is based on attractiveness and identification. It is highly related to motivation and to both cognitive and affective learning.

5. *Expert power* is based on the perceived competence of the teacher. It is positively related to motivation and to both cognitive and affective learning.

As an instructor you have immediate access to legitimate, coercive, and reward power, but those alone are not enough. To be an effective teacher, you must work on developing your referent and expert power base. The first issue of *Speech Communication Teacher* listed the following characteristics of effective teachers, most of which relate to referent or expert power.

1. They know their subject and its current relevance.
2. They make their classes interesting.
3. They try to be fair to everyone.
4. They are friendly and interested in their students.
5. They try to make learning easy.
6. They maintain control of their classes.
7. They organize their lessons and presentations well.
8. They display a controlled sense of humor.

Strive to attain these goals for yourself.

SPECIFIC TEACHING SUGGESTIONS FOR BEGINNING INSTRUCTORS

In putting together this instructional package for teaching public speaking, we have tried to provide you with a variety of materials that will make your job easier and more rewarding. This *Instructor's Resource Manual* is one part of that package. Part II, "Chapter-by-Chapter Guide to Teaching Public Speaking," contains learning objectives; suggestions for teaching the specific topics covered in each chapter; chapter outlines for quick access to textbook information; suggested ways to use the end-of-chapter Discussion and Application items; additional activities geared to experiential learning; a list of available supplementary materials, such as films and videos, transparencies, and handouts; and a bibliography of readings suitable for both instructor and student enrichment. Part III contains annotated versions of the speeches in Appendix B of *Public Speaking*. Both experienced and inexperienced instructors should find a wealth of information and materials to enrich their teaching effectiveness. Feel free to adapt these materials to fit the needs of your particular students and teaching approaches. The test bank has now become a separate ancillary item, and continues to be available on computer disk.

We have developed a well-received computerized speech-outlining program for students. It contains outline formats for preparation, formal, and key-word outlines. Each major speech design discussed in the text has a skeleton outline form, sample formal and key-word outlines that students may use for examples, and a check list of processes completed. The program is self-directed in that it walks students through the outlining process, and it should help improve the structure and comprehensibility of student speeches presented in your classes. A *Speech Outlining Workbook* for students is also available.

Our teaching package also contains an assortment of color transparencies that may be used to enhance your lectures. Additional transparency masters are available in Part II of this IRM. Adopters whose schools order a minimum number of books will receive a package of videotapes containing speeches presented by students. They may be used as models for students to critique and emulate—a basic part of learning public speaking skills.

Beyond what we personally offer as a teaching package, we encourage you to affiliate with your state, regional, and national speech communication associations. Their meetings and journals are valuable sources of information and ideas for teaching communication courses. Of particular interest to instructors of public speaking are *Speech Communication Teacher* and *Communication Education*, two publications of the Speech Communication Association (SCA), 5105 Backlick Road, Suite E, Annandale, VA 22003. SCA also makes available additional teaching resource materials, many of which are listed in the bibliographies throughout this IRM.

Videotapes of speeches and discussions by prominent contemporary figures are available from C-Span. Its bimonthly publication *C-Span in the Classroom* is available free of charge, and its copyright usage policy is quite liberal. It also conducts a seminar series for professors, maintains archives at Purdue University, and publishes a weekly newspaper, *C-Span Update*. For more information, contact C-Span in the Classroom, 400 North Capitol Street, NW, Washington, DC 20001 or call its educator's hotline at 1-800-523-7586.

GUIDE TO ABBREVIATIONS OF JOURNAL TITLES

ACAB	*Association for Communication Administration Bulletin*
CE	*Communication Education* (formerly *Speech Teacher*)
CM	*Communication Monographs* (formerly *Speech Monographs*)
CQ	*Communication Quarterly* (formerly *Today's Speech*)
CRR	*Communication Research Reports*
CR	*Communication Reports*
CSMC	*Critical Studies in Mass Communication*
CS	*Communication Studies* (formerly *CSSJ, Central States Speech Journal*)
HCR	*Human Communication Research*
JAFA	*Journal of the American Forensic Association*
JBEM	*Journal of Broadcasting and Electronic Media*
JC	*Journal of Communication*
JQ	*Journalism Quarterly*
P&R	*Philosophy and Rhetoric*
QJS	*Quarterly Journal of Speech*
SCJ	*The Southern Communication Journal* (formerly *SSCJ, Southern Speech Communication Journal*)
WJSC	*Western Journal of Speech Communication*

READINGS FOR ENRICHMENT

See guide to journal abbreviations on p. 37.

General Resources for Communication Instructors

Andersen, Kenneth E. "Ethical Issues in Teaching." In *Teaching Communication: Theory, Research, and Methods,* edited by John A. Daly, Gustav W. Friedrich, and Anita L Vangelisti, pp. 459–470. Hillsdale, N.J.: Lawrence Erlbaum, 1990.

Beall, Melissa. "The Affective Component in Communication Classrooms." *SCT* (Summer 1992), 12–13.

Book, Cassandra L. "Communication Education: Pedagogical Content Knowledge Needed." *CE* (Oct. 1989), 315–321.

Briggs, Nancy, and Mary Pinola. "A Consideration of Five Traditional Educational Philosophies for Speech Communication." *CSSJ* (Winter 1985), 305–314.

Christophel, Diane M., and Joan Gorham, "A Test-Retest Analysis of Student Motivation, Teacher Immediacy, and Perceived Sources of Motivation and Demotivation in College Classes." *CE* (Oct. 1995), 292–306.

Comstock, Jamie, Elisa Rowell, and John Waite Bowers. "Food for Thought: Teacher Nonverbal Immediacy, Student Learning and Curvilinearity." *CE* (July 1995), 251–266.

Conville, Richard L. "Cognitive Goals in Communication Learning." *CE* (Mar. 1977), 113–120.

———. "Change, Process, and the Future of Communication Education." *SSCJ* (Spring 1978), 265–282.

Dalle, Teresa, and Margaret Inglis, "'Teacher Talk'—Discourse Markers as Guideposts to Learning." Available through ERIC.

Deethardt, John F. "A Future for Speech Communication," *CQ* (Fall 1982), 274–281.

Dolin, Danielle J. "An Alternative Form of Teacher Affinity-Seeking Measurement." *CRR* (Fall 1995), 220–226.

Fackler, Mark. "My First Public Speaking Class: An Oral Culture Adventure." *SCT* (Spring 1991), 6–7.

Friedrich, Gustav W. "Speech Communication as a Required University Course." *ACAB* (Oct. 1982), 7–9.

Friedrich, Gustav W., and Don M. Boileau. "The Communication Discipline." In *Teaching Communication: Theory, Research, and Methods,* edited by John A. Daly, Gustav W. Friedrich, and Anita L Vangelisti, pp. 3–18. Hillsdale, N.J.: Lawrence Erlbaum, 1990.

Frymier, Ann Bainbridge. "The Impact of Teacher Immediacy on Student's Motivation: Is It the Same for All Students?" *CQ* (Fall 1993), 454–465.

———. "A Model of Immediacy in the Classroom." *CQ* (Spring 1994), 133–144.

———. "The Use of Affinity-Seeking in Producing Liking and Learning in the Classroom." *ACR* (May 1994), 87–105.

Fusani, David S. "'Extra Class' Communication: Frequency, Immediacy, Self-Disclosure, and Satisfaction in Student-Faculty Interaction Outside the Classroom." *ACR* (Aug. 1994), 232–255.

Gibson, James W., Charles R. Gruner, Michael S. Hanna, Mary-Jeanette Smythe, and Michael T. Hayes. "The Basic Course in Speech at U.S. Colleges and Universities: III." *CE* (Jan. 1980), 1–9.

Gibson, James W., Michael S. Hanna, and Bill M. Huddleston. "The Basic Course at U.S. Colleges and Universities, IV." *CE* (Oct. 1985), 281–291.

Giroux, H. *Schooling and the Struggle for Public Life: Critical Pedagogy in the Modern Age.* Minneapolis: University of Minnesota Press, 1988.

Goldsmith, Daena, and Terrance Albrecht, "The Impact of Supportive Communication Networks on Test Anxiety and Performance." *CE* (Apr. 1993), 142–158.

Gouran, Dennis S. "Speech Communication: Its Conceptual Foundation and Disciplinary Status." *CE* (Jan. 1979), 1–8.

Hart, Roderick P. "Why Communication? Why Education? Toward a Politics of Teaching." *CE* (Apr. 1993), 97–105.

Haynes, W. Lance. " Public Speaking Pedagogy in the Media Age." *CE* (Apr. 1990), 89–102.

Hertzog, Robert L. "Active Learning in the Basic Public Speaking Course." *SCT* (Winter 1992), 8.

Hiemstra, Glen E., and Ann Q. Staton-Spicer. "Communication Concerns of College Undergraduates in Basic Speech Communication Courses." *CE* (Jan. 1983), 29–37.

Katula, Richard A. "Excellence in the Speech Communication Classroom." *CQ* (Fall 1986), 341–343.

McCroskey, James C., Virginia P. Richmond, Aino Sallinen, Joan M. Fayer, and Robert A. Barraclough. "A Cross-Cultural and MultiBehavioral Analysis of the Relationship Between Nonverbal Immediacy and Teacher Evaluation." *CE* (Oct. 1995), 281–291.

Mongeua, Paul A., and Jennifer Blalock. "Student Evaluations of Instructor Immediacy and Sexually Harassing Behaviors: An Experimental Investigation." *ACR* (Aug. 1994), 256–272.

Moore, Michael R. "Toward Effective and Efficient Instruction in the Basic Speech Communication Course: A Position." *ACAB* (Aug. 1977), 39–45.

Myers, Scott A. "Student Perceptions of Teacher Affinity-Seeking and Classroom Climate." *CRR* (Fall 1995), 192–199.

Neuliep, James W. "A Comparison of Teacher Immediacy in African-American and Euro-American College Classrooms." *CE* (July 1995), 267–277.

Nevins, Randi J., and Cassandra L. Book. "The Gift of Oration for the Gifted and Talented." *SCT* (Spring 1991), 4–5.

Nussbaum, Jon F. "Effective Teacher Behaviors." *CE* (Apr. 1992), 167–180.

Osborn, Michael. "The Study of Communication Flourishes in a Democratic Environment." *The Chronicle of Higher Education*, 17 Jan. 1990, pp. B2–B3.

Phillips, Gerald M. "Treatment/Training of Speaking Problems: A Study in Reification." *CQ* (Fall 1986), 438–450.

Preiss, Ray. "Meta-Analysis and Curriculum Development." *SCT* (Winter 1991), 11–12.

Richmond, Virginia P., and K. David Roach. "Willingness to Communicate and Employee Success in U.S. Organizations." *ACR* (Feb. 1992), 95–115.

Roach, K. David. "Temporal Patterns and Effects of Perceived Instructor Compliance-Gaining Use." *CE* (July 1994), 236–251.

Schwartz, Omar. "Exercises in Critical Pedagogy for the Basic Communication Course," *SCT* (Winter 1996), 11–12.

Sensenbaugh, Roger. "How Effective Communication Can Enhance Teaching at the College Level." Available through ERIC Digest.

Sevitch, Benjamin. "Trends in General Education Speech Requirements: Can We Be Optimistic About the Future?" *ACAB* (Jan. 1980), 70–71.

Smagorinsky, Peter, and Pamela K. Fly. "The Social Environment of the Classroom: A Vygotskian Perspective on Small Group Process." *CE* (Apr. 1993), 159–171.

Special Issue of *CE*, October 1993, "When Teaching 'Works': Stories of Communication in Education."

Sprague, Jo. "The Goals of Communication Education." In *Teaching Communication: Theory, Research, and Methods*, edited by John A. Daly, Gustav W. Friedrich, and Anita L Vangelisti, pp. 19–38. Hillsdale, N.J.: Lawrence Erlbaum, 1990.

——. "Retrieving the Research Agenda for Communication Education: Asking the Pedagogical Questions that Are 'Embarrassments to Theory.'" *CE* (Apr. 1993), 106–122.

Thompson, Carol, and Christina Standerfer, "Interactive Public-Speaking Activities." *SCT* (Summer 1992), 2–3.

Trank, Douglas M. "An Overview of Present Approaches to the Basic Speech Communication Course." *ACAB* (Apr. 1985), 86–89.

Van Hoeven, Shirley A. "What We Know About the Development of Communication Competence." *CSSJ* (Spring/Summer 1985), 33–38.

Wartella, Ellen. "Challenge to the Profession." *CE* (Jan. 1994), 54–62.

Weaver, Richard L. "Effective Lecturing Techniques: Alternatives to Classroom Boredom." In *New Directions in Teaching*, edited by Wilbert J. McKeachie, pp. 25–35. San Francisco: Jossey-Bass, 1980.

Work, William. "Communication Education for the Twenty-First Century." *CQ* (Fall 1982), 265–269.

Communication Education: History and Teachers of Note

Arnold, Carroll C. "Herbert August Wichelns (1894–1973)." *SSCJ* (Winter 1982), 124–130.

Beider, P. G., ed. *Distinguished Teachers on Effective Teaching: Observations on Teaching by College Professors Recognized by the Council for Advancement and Support of Education.* San Francisco: Jossey-Bass, 1986.

Blankenship, Jane. "The Song of the Open Road: Marie Hochmuth Nichols as Teacher." *CQ* (Fall 1986), 419–428.

Braden, Waldo W. "A Symposium on Liberalizing Influences: Great Teachers." *SSCJ* (Winter 1982), 107–108

Brownell, Judi. "Elwood Murray: Innovator, Integrator, Educator." *CQ* (Fall 1986), 405–413.

Brownell, Winifred W. "Agnes G. Doody: An Inspiring Communicator at the University of Rhode Island." *CQ* (Fall 1986), 389–397.

Burns, David G. "William Norwood Brigance and Wabash College." *CQ* (Fall 1986), 349–356.

Cappella, Joseph N., Donald J. Cegala, Thomas B. Farrell, Robert D. McPhee, Peter R. Monge, Marshall Scott Poole, Ted J. Smith III, and Joseph N. Woelfel. "Donald Cushman: Larger than Life." *CQ* (Fall 1986), 379–388.

Clark, Jeanne E. "Masterman King: Rhetorical Raconteur." *CQ* (Fall 1986), 401–404.

Dresser, William R. "Lionel Crocker: Teacher, Scholar, and Good Man Skilled in Speaking." *CQ* (Fall 1986), 372–378.

Duffy, Bernard K. "Robert P. Newman: American Don." *CQ* (Fall 1986), 414–418.

Einhorn, Lois J. "Carroll C. Arnold: Another Roar for the Lion." *CQ* (Fall 1986), 344–348.

Hickson, Mark III. "Thomas Jennings Pace: Learning to Cope with Ambiguity." *CQ* (Fall 1986), 429–431.

Katula, Richard A. "Excellence in the Speech Communication Classroom." *CQ* (Fall 1986), 341–343.

McBath, James H. "James Milton O'Neill (1881–1970)." *SSCJ* (Winter 1982), 108–115.

Oliver, Robert T., and Eugene E. White. *History of Public Speaking in America,* 2nd ed. (Boston: Allyn & Bacon), 1975.

Peterson, Owen. "A. Craig Baird (1883–1979)." *SSCJ* (Winter 1982), 130–134.

"Preferred Profs: The Ten Best in California May Be the Ten Best Anywhere." *California* (Aug. 1986), 66.

Reid, Loren. "James A. Winans (1872–1956)." *SSCJ* (Winter 1982), 115–123.

———. "John P. Ryan: A Teacher with Several Imperative Pluses." *CQ* (Fall 1986), 432–437.

Schuetz, Janice. "Dimensions of Teaching: The Methods, Relationships, and Ideas of Wayne Brockriede." *CQ* (Fall 1986), 357–364.

Sevitch, Benjamin. "Gorden F. Hostettler." *CQ* (Fall 1986), 398–400.

Wallace, Karl R., ed., *History of Speech Education in America: Background Studies.* New York: Appleton-Century-Crofts, 1954.

Washington, Earl M. "Charles T. Brown, Trailblazer of Communication Education." *CQ* (Fall 1986), 365–371.

Teaching Techniques

General

Andersen, Janis F., Robert W. Norton, and Jon F. Nussbaum. "Three Investigations Exploring Relationships Between Perceived Teacher Communication Behaviors and Student Learning." *CE* (Oct. 1981), 377–393.

Angelo, T. A. *Fourteen General, Research-based Guidelines to Inform Assessment and Teaching and Improved Higher Education.* Academic Development Center, Boston College, Chestnut Hill, Mass., 1994.

Arnett, Ronald C. *Dialogic Education: Conversation About Ideas and Between People.* Carbondale, Ill.: Southern Illinois University Press, 1992.

Baker, Eva L. "Can Educational Research Inform Educational Practice? Yes!" *Phi Delta Kappan* (Mar. 1984), 453–455.

Baker, Moira P. "Mentoring as Teaching and Learning." Paper presented at the Conference on College Composition and Communication Convention, 1993; available through ERIC.

Booth-Butterfield, Melanie. *Interpersonal Communication in Instructional Settings.* Edina, Minn.: Burgess, 1992.

Booth-Butterfield, Steve. *Influence and Control in the Classroom.* Edina, Minn.: Burgess,1992.

Bruschke, Jon C., and Carrie N. Gartner. "Teaching as Communication: Advice for the Higher Education Classroom." *ACR* (Aug. 1992), 197–216.

Cooper, Pamela, and Kathleen Galvin, "What Do We Know About Research in Teacher Training in Instructional Strategies?" *CSSJ* (Fall 1985), 186–192.

Cruickshank, Donald R. "Profile of an Effective Teacher." *Educational Horizons* (Winter 1985), 90–92.

Dedrick, Charles, and Len Froyen, "Motivation Maxims: Why They Fail to Motivate." *The Education Forum* (Mar. 1980), 295–303.

Donald, Janet G. "The State of Research on University Teaching Effectiveness." In *Using Research to Improve Teaching,* 7–20. San Francisco: Jossey-Bass, 1985.

Eble, K. E., and R. E. Young, eds. *College Teaching and Learning: Preparing for New Commitments.* San Francisco: Jossey-Bass, 1988.

Eble, Kenneth. "The Mythology of Teaching." In *The Craft of Teaching,* 9–21. San Francisco: Jossey-Bass, 1981.

Eisner, Elliot W. "The Art and Craft of Teaching." *Educational Leadership* (Jan. 1983), 4–13.

Ferguson, Jeanne, and Maria Miller. "A Creative Approach to Improving Teaching Skills." *ACAB* (Oct. 1979), 57–58.

Frymier, Ann Bainbridge, and Gary M. Shullman, "'What's In It For Me?': Increasing Content Relevance to Enhance Student's Motivation." *CE* (Jan. 1995), 40–50.

Galvin, Kathleen M. "Classroom Roles of the Teacher." In *Teaching Communication: Theory, Research, and Methods,* edited by John A. Daly, Gustav W. Friedrich, and Anita L Vangelisti, pp. 95–206. Hillsdale, N.J.: Lawrence Erlbaum, 1990.

George, Don. "Peer Support in Speech Preparation." *SCT* (Spring 1993), 4–5.

Glasser, Robert. "Ten Untenable Assumptions of College Instruction." *Educational Record* (Spring 1968), 154–159.

Gorg, Robert. "The Use of Model Speeches on Videotape (or See, Your Friends Can Do This Too!)." *SCT* (Fall 1993), 11–12.

Gorham, Joan, and Diane M. Christophel. "The Relationship of Teachers' Use of Humor in the Classroom to Immediacy and Student Learning." *CE* (Jan. 1990), 46–62.

Hahn, Dan F. "Toward Excellence: Seven Rules for Teachers." *SCT* (Fall 1992), 8.

Hayward, Pamela A. "Getting It Right the First Time: An Exploration of Instructor Beliefs and Strategies for the First Day of Class." Paper presented at the National Conference on the Training and Employment of Graduate Teaching Assistants, 1993; available through ERIC.

Hill, Nancy K. "Scaling the Heights: The Teacher as Mountaineer." *Chronicle of Higher Education,* 16 June 1980, p. 48.

Jorgensen-Earp, Cheryl R., and Ann Q. Stanton. "Student Metaphors for the College Freshman Experience." *CE* (Apr. 1993), 123–141.

Kearney, Patricial, et al. "College Teacher Misbehaviors: What Students Don't Like About What Teachers Say and Do." *CQ* (1991), 309–324.

Klopf, Donald W., and Catherine A. Thompson. *Communication in the Multicultural Classroom.* Edina, Minn.: Burgess, 1992.

Knapp, Mark L. "Communicating with Students." *Improving College and University Teaching* (Summer 1976), 167–168.

Lederman, Linda C. *Communication Pedagogy: Approaches to Teaching Undergraduate Courses in Communication.* Norwood, N.J.: Ablex, 1992.

Martin, George I. "Using Student Response Journals to Assess Your Teaching." *SCT* (Summer 1993), 7.

McClish, Glen, and Susan Browne. "Planting the Seed: A Mentor Approach to Middle-School and College-Level Communication Instruction." *SCT* (Fall 1993), 6–8.

McCroskey, James C. *An Introduction to Communication in the Classroom.* Edina, Minn.: Burgess, 1992.

McCroskey, James C., and Virginia P. Richmond. *Communication in Educational Organizations.* Edina, Minn.: Burgess,1992.

McDaniel, Thomas R. "The Ten Commandments of Motivation." *The Clearing House* (Sept. 1985), 19–23.

McKeachie, Wilbert J., P. R. Pintrich, Y. G. Lin, and D. A. F. Smith. *Teaching and Learning in the College Classroom: A Review of the Research Literature.* Ann Arbor, Mich.: National Center for Research to Improve Postsecondary Teaching and Learning, 1986.

Mino, Mary. "Using Student Responses to Strengthen Course Objectives." *SCT* (Summer 1991), 14.

Morris, Tracy L., Joan Gorham, Stanley H. Cohen and Drew Huffman. "Fashion in the Classroom: Effects of Attire on Student Perceptions of Instructors in College Classes." *CE* (Apr. 1996), 135–148.

O'Donnell, Karen, "Computer Laboratory Assistant Interactions with Communication Students." Paper presented at the Speech Communication Association Convention, 1993; available through ERIC.

Powers, William G., Richard Nitcavic, and David Koerner, "Teacher Characteristics: A College Level Perspective." *CE* (July 1990), 227–233.

Richmond, Virginia. "Communication in the Classroom: Power and Motivation." *CE* (July 1990), 181–195.

———. *Nonverbal Communication in the Classroom.* Edina, Minn.: Burgess, 1992.

Richmond, Virginia P., and Joan Gorham. *Communication, Learning and Affect in Instruction.* Edina, Minn.: Burgess, 1992.

Richmond, Virginia, and James C. McCroskey, "Power in the Classroom II: Power and Learning." *CE* (Apr. 1984), 125–136.

Roach, K. David. "Teaching Assistant Argumentativeness: Effects on Affective Learning and Student Perceptions of Power Use." *CE* (Jan. 1995), 15–29.

Robbins, Bruce, ed. *The Phantom Public Sphere.* Minneapolis: University of Minneapolis Press, 1993.

Smith, Lindsley F., and Peter M. Kellett. "Self-Directed Teams in the Classroom." *SCT* (Fall 1995), 14–15.

West, Richard. "Teacher-Student Communication: A Descriptive Typology of Students' Interpersonal Experiences with Teachers." *CR* (Summer 1994), 109–118.

Will, Tony. "Empowering the Student." *SCT* (Summer 1994), 14–15.

Womack, Sid T. "Modes of Instruction: Expository, Demonstration, Inquiry, Individualized," *The Clearing House* (Jan. 1989), 205–209.

The Novice Instructor

Allen, R. R., and Theodore Rueter. *Teaching Assistant Strategies.* Dubuque, Iowa: Kendall/Hunt, 1990. A good basic introduction for the novice instructor covers teaching assistant roles, interpersonal relationships, planning for classes, creating a supportive classroom environment, methods of teaching and assessment.

Andrews, Patricia Hayes. "Creating a Supportive Climate for Teacher Growth: Developing Graduate Students as Teachers." *CQ* (Fall 1983), 259–265.

Brown, N. M., and S. M. Keeley. "Achieving Excellence: Advice to New Teachers." *College Teaching* (1985).

DeBoer, Kathryn D. "Teacher Preparation for Graduate Assistants." *CE* (Sept. 1979), 328–331.

Ferris, Jim. "A Review of Communication Research on Graduate Teaching Assistants." Paper presented at the Speech Communication Association Convention, 1992; available through ERIC.

Hendrix, Katherine Grace. "Preparing Graduate Teaching Assistants to Effectively Teach the Basic Course." Paper presented at the Southern States Communication Association Convention, April 1995; available through ERIC.

Lambert, Leo M., and Stacey Lane, eds. *Preparing Graduate Students to Teach: A Guide to Programs that Improve Undergraduate Education and Develop Tomorrow's Faculty.* Available from American Association for Higher Education, One Dupont Circle, Suite 360, Washington, DC 20036-1110.

Mandeville, Mary Y., and Scott A. Blakemore. "Using the Team Building Approach as a Management Tool for the Training of Graduate Teaching Assistants in the Basic Speech Communication Course." Paper presented at the Speech Communication Association Convention, 1994; available through ERIC.

McKeachie, Wilbert J. *Teaching Tips: A Guidebook for the Beginning College Teacher,* 8th ed. Lexington, Mass.: D. C. Heath, 1986.

Nyquist, J. D., and D. H. Wulff, eds. *Preparing Teaching Assistants for Instructional Roles: Supervising TAs in Communication.* Annandale, Va.: Speech Communication Association, 1992.
————. *Working Effectively with Graduate Assistants.* Thousand Oaks, Calif.: Sage, 1996.
Nyquist, Jody D., Robert D. Abbott, and Donald H. Wulff, eds. *Teaching Assistant Training in the 1990s: New Directions for Teaching and Learning.* San Francisco: Jossey-Bass, 1989.
Nyquist, Jody, Ann Stanton, and Brooke Quigley. *Encounters With Teaching.* Available from Speech Communication Association, 5105 Backlick Road, Suite E, Annandale, VA, 22003, undated. This program, which combines videotaped scenarios of problem situations and instruction manuals, is suitable for use in faculty development workshops or for training teaching assistants. Some of the problems covered include: handling grade complaints, plagiarism, requests for extra time, language problems, inappropriate subjects, complaints about racism/sexism, and social interactions with students.
Philllips, Gerald M., and Mary-Linda Merriam. "Growing as a Professional." In *Teaching Communication: Theory, Research, and Methods,* edited by John A. Daly, Gustav W. Friedrich, and Anita L Vangelisti, pp. 481–92. Hillsdale, N.J.: Lawrence Erlbaum, 1990.
Rowley, Edwin N. "Keeping the Faith: Teaching Assistants and the Pursuit of Teaching Excellence." Paper presented at the Joint Meeting of the Southern States Communication Association and the Central States Communication Association, 1993; available through ERIC.
Stanton, Ann Q., and Ann L. Darling, "Socialization of Teaching Assistants." Available through ERIC.
Staton-Spicer, Ann Q., and Jody L. Nyquist. "Improving the Teaching Effectiveness of Graduate Teaching Assistants." *CE* (July 1979), 199–205.
Woolever, Kristin R. "Issues in TA Training: Does Postmodernism Preclude Teaching Structure." Paper presented at the Conference on College Composition and Communication Convention, 1993; available through ERIC.
Worthen, Thomas K. "The Frustrated GTA: A Qualitative Investigation Identifying the Needs Within the Graduate Teaching Assistant Experience." Paper presented at the Speech Communication Association Convention, 1992; available through ERIC.

Scheduling and Preparing a Syllabus

Andrews, Patricia Hayes. "The Importance of a Good Syllabus." *Notes on Teaching and Learning,* Teaching Resources Center, University of Indiana, Feb. 1986.
"Preparing a Course Syllabus." Illinois Instructor Series, University of Illinois at Urbana-Champaign, #3.
Rubin, Sharon. "Professors, Students, and the Syllabus." *The Chronicle of Higher Education,* 7 Aug. 1985.
Wilson, Susan. "The Flexible Loop: A New Look at the Public Speaking Schedule." *SCT* (Summer 1995), 14–15.

Lecturing

Andrews, Patricia Hayes. "Improving Lecture Skills," *Notes on Teaching and Learning,* Teaching Resources Center, University of Indiana, Feb. 1989.
Broadwell, Martin M. "It's so Technical, I Have to Lecture." *Training: The Magazine of Human Resources Development* (Mar. 1989), 41–43.
Clarke, John M. "Building a Lecture that Really Works." *Education Digest* (Oct. 1987), 52–55.
Frederick, Peter. "The Lively Lecture: Eight Variations." *College Teaching* (1986), 43–50.
McKeachie, Wilbert J. "Improving Lectures by Understanding Students' Information Processing." In *New Directions for Teaching and Learning: Learning, Cognition, and College Teaching,* edited by Wilbert J. McKeachie, pp. 25–35. San Francisco: Jossey-Bass, 1980.
Thompson, C. Lamar. "Suggestions for Making Lectures More Effective." *The Clearing House* (Dec. 1987), 186–187.
Weaver, Richard L. "Effective Lecturing Techniques: Alternatives to Classroom Boredom." *Teacher-Educator* (Summer 1980), 2–8.

Other Teaching Techniques

Andersen, Janis, and Jon Nussbaum. "Interaction Skills in Instructional Settings." In *Teaching Communication: Theory, Research, and Methods*, edited by John A. Daly, Gustav W. Friedrich, and Anita L Vangelisti, pp. 301–316. Hillsdale, N.J.: Lawrence Erlbaum, 1990.

Blom, Patricia. "Using Group Activities in Basic Public Speaking." *SCT* (Fall 1989), 10–11.

Dwyer, Karen Kangas. "Group Mini-Speeches: Experiential and Cooperative Learning in the Public Speaking Course." *SCT* (Summer 1994), 15.

Frederic, Peter. "The Dreaded Discussion: Ten Ways to Start." *Improving College and University Teaching* (Summer 1981), 109–114.

Karp, David A., and William C. Yoels. "The College Classroom: Some Observations on the Meanings of Student Participation." *Sociology and Social Research* (1976), 421–439.

Nyquist, Jody D., and Donald H Wulff. "Selected Active Learning Strategies." In *Teaching Communication: Theory, Research, and Methods*, edited by John A. Daly, Gustav W. Friedrich, and Anita L Vangelisti, pp. 337–362. Hillsdale, N.J.: Lawrence Erlbaum, 1990.

West, Richard, and Judy C. Pearson. "Antecedent and Consequent Conditions of Student Questioning: An Analysis of Classroom Discourse Across the University." *CE* (Oct. 1994), 299–311.

Optional Approaches to Teaching Public Speaking

Auer, J. Jeffrey. "Creating an Extra and 'Real Life' Public Speaking Assignment." *SCT* (Spring 1991), 3.

Bate, Barbara. "Assertive Speaking: An Approach to Communication Education for the Future." *CE* (Jan. 1976), 53–59.

Blankenship, Jane, and Sara Latham Stelzner. *Speech Communication Activities in the Writing Classroom.* Urbana, Ill.: ERIC Clearinghouse on Reading and Communication Skills, 1979. (Available through the Speech Communication Association, 5105 Backlick Road, Suite E, Annandale, VA 22003.)

Bochin, Hall W., and John A. Cagie. "Instructional Practices: San Francisco Simulation." *CE* (Mar. 1977), 154–157.

Cheatham, T. Richard, and Keith V. Erickson. "Simulation Learning Experiences in Speech Communication." *CSSJ* (Summer 1976), 113–119.

Ellingsworth, Huber W., Sarah Sanderson King, and Richard D. Newman. *A Learning Center Approach to Basic Communication Courses.* Urbana, Ill.: ERIC Clearinghouse on Reading and Communication Skills, 1977. (Available through the Speech Communication Association, 5105 Backlick Road, Suite E, Annandale, VA 22003.)

Feltzer, Ronald C. "An Alternative Approach to Teaching Public Speaking." *CE* (Sept. 1977), 261–270.

Heun, Linda, Richard Heun and Linnea Ratcliff. "Individualizing Speech Communication Instruction." *CE* (Sept. 1976), 185–190.

Kane, Pat. *A TV News Approach to Oral Communication.* Urbana, Ill.: ERIC Clearinghouse on Reading and Communication Skills, undated. (Available through the Speech Communication Association, 5105 Backlick Road, Suite E, Annandale, VA 22003.)

Newman, Gemma. "Teaching the Basic Speech Course with Career Orientation: An Affirmative Case." *ACAB* (Aug. 1975), 45–46.

Ostrander, Tammy. "The Use of Role-Plays in Introductory Speech Courses." *The Florida Communication Journal* (1989), 31–32.

Scott, Michael D., and Thomas J. Young. "Personalizing Communication Instruction." *CE* (Sept. 1976), 211–221.

Staton-Spicer, Ann Q., and Ronald E. Bassett. "A Mastery Learning Approach to Competency Based Education for Public Speaking Instruction." *CE* (May 1980), 171–182.

Webb, Lynne. "A Program of Public Speaking Training: One Consultant's Approach." *SSCJ* (Fall 1989), 72–86.

Wolvin, Andrew D., and Darlyn R. Wolvin. "Developing the Speech Communication Course for the Technical/Career Student." *ACAB* (Jan. 1977), 37–42.

Evaluation and Grading

Anderson, Susan, and Jeff Butler, "An Assessment of Speech Students' Perceptions of the Use of Videotapes as a Supplement to Instructor Critiques." *The Florida Communication Journal* (1989), 33–35.

Backlund, Phillip M., Kenneth L. Brown, Joanne Gurry, and Fred Jandt. "Recommendations for Assessing Speaking and Listening Skills." *CE* (Jan. 1982), 9–17.

Bassett, R. E., N. Whittington, and A. Staton-Spicer. "The Basics in Speaking and Listening for High School Graduates: What Should Be Assessed?" *CE* (Nov. 1978), 293–303.

Behnke, Ralph R., and Michael R. Beatty. "Critiquing Speaker Behavior Through Immediate Video Display." *CE* (Nov. 1977), 345–348.

Benson, James A., and Sheryl A. Friedley. "An Emperical Analysis of Evaluation Criteria for Persuasive Speaking." *JAFA* (Summer 1982), 1–13.

Bock, Douglas, and Hope Bock. *Evaluating Classroom Speaking.* Urbana, Ill.: ERIC Clearinghouse on Reading and Communication Skills,1981. (Available through the Speech Communication Association, 5105 Backlick Road, Suite E, Annandale, VA 22003.)

Bollinger, Lee. "Tough Self-Evaluators." *SCT* (Summer 1995), 14.

Book, Cassandra L. "Providing Feedback: The Research on Effective Oral and Written Feedback Strategies." *CSSJ* (Spring/Summer 1985), 14–23.

Book, Cassandra, and Katrina Wynkoop Simmons. "Dimensions and Perceived Helpfulness of Student Speech Criticism." *CE* (May 1980), 135–145.

Book, Cassandra L., Shirley Van Hoeven, Marcia Kreger, and Jo Sprague. *Contract Grading in Speech Communication Courses.* Urbana, Ill.: ERIC Clearinghouse on Reading and Communication Skills, 1978. (Available through the Speech Communication Association, 5105 Backlick Road, Suite E, Annandale, VA 22003.)

Booth-Butterfield, Melanie. "The Interpretation of Classroom Performance Feedback: An Attributional Approach." *CE* (Apr. 1989), 119–131.

Boyd, Stephen D. "Insights on Speech Evaluation from Toastmaster's and Dale Carnegie." *CE* (Nov. 1975), 379–381.

Carlson, Robert E., and Deborah Smith-Howell."Classroom Public Speaking Assessment: Reliability and Validity of Selected Evaluation Instruments." *CE* (Apr. 1995), 87–97.

Cronen, Vernon E., and Robert Fuller. "Freshman Perceptions of Instructor Fairness and Expertise: A Problem in Course Evaluation." *CQ* (Winter 1976), 45–47.

Dedmon, Donald N. "Criticizing Student Speeches: Philosophy and Principles." In *Dimensions of Oral Communication Instruction,* edited by K. Erickson, pp. 271–281. Dubuque, Iowa: William C. Brown, 1970.

Erhart, Joseph F. "The Performance Appraisal Interview and Evaluation of Student Performances in Speech Communication Courses." *CE* (Sept. 1976), 237–246.

Goulden, Nancy Rost, and Charles J. G. Griffin. "The Meaning of Grades Based on Faculty and Student Metaphors." *CE* (Apr. 1995), 110–125.

Hallmark, James R. "Using Your Computer to Evaluate Speeches." *SCT* (Winter 1994), 3–4.

Haynes, W. Lance. "Grading Student Speeches: An Experiential Approach." *SCT* (Fall 1989), 1–2.

LaFleur, Gary B. "A Special Tool for Offering Criticism: The Post Speech Transcript." *ACAB* (Oct. 1985), 63–64.

Littlefield, Valgene. "Behavioral Criteria for Evaluating Performance in Public Speaking." *CE* (Mar. 1975), 143–145.

———. "Selected Approaches to Speech Communication Evaluation: A Symposium: Behavioral Criteria for Evaluating Performance in Public Speaking." *CE* (Mar. 1975), 143–145.

Miles, Paul L. "Student Video Self-Critiques." *CE* (July 1981), 280–283.

Mino, Mary, and Dale A. Bertelsen. "Critiquing Student Speeches: Two Approaches." *SCT* (Winter 1993), 15–16.

Mino, Mary, and Marilyn N. Butler. "Using Oral Self-Evaluations to Assess and Improve Public Speaking Skills." *SCT* (Spring 1995), 4.

Mulac, Anthony, and A. Robert Sherman. "Relationships Among Four Parameters of Speaker Evaluation: Speech Skills, Source Credibility, Subjective Speech Anxiety, and Behavioral Speech Anxiety." *CM* (Nov. 1975), 302–310.

Phillips, Gary. "Put Your Test on ICE." *SCT* (Summer 1991), 8–9.

Rollman, Steven A. "Leading Class Discussions Which Evaluate Student's Oral Performance." *SCT* (Spring 1992), 10–12.

Rubin, Rebecca B. "Assessing Speaking and Listening Competence at the College Level: The Communication Competency Assessment Instrument." *CE* (Jan. 1982), 19–32.

———. "Communication Assessment Instruments and Procedures in Higher Education." *CE* (Apr. 1984), 178–180.

———. "Evaluating the Product." In *Teaching Communication: Theory, Research, and Methods,* edited by John A. Daly, Gustav W. Friedrich, and Anita L Vangelisti, pp. 379–401. Hillsdale, N.J.: Lawrence Erlbaum, 1990.

Rubin, Rebecca B., John Sisco, Michael R. Moore, and Richard Quianthy. *Oral Communication Assessment Procedures and Instrument Development in Higher Education.* (Undated report available from the Speech Communication Association, 5105 Backlick Road, Suite E, Annandale, VA 22003. Commissioned by the Committee on Assessment and Testing, this recent report covers the procedures and/or instruments used to assess oral communication skills at 45 institutions of higher learning. The schools surveyed included junior and community colleges as well as major universities.)

Rubin, Rebecca B., and Jess Yoder. "Ethical Issues in the Evaluation of Communication Behavior." *CE* (Jan. 1985), 13–17.

Stahl, Michael G. "Critiques That Count." *SCT* (Summer 1994), 5–6.

Stiggins, Richard J., Philip M. Backlund, and Nancy J. Bridgeford. "Avoiding Bias in the Assessment of Communication Skills." *CE* (Apr. 1985), 135–141.

Stohl, Cynthia. "Developing a Communicative Competence Scale." In *Communication Yearbook 7,* edited by Robert N. Bostrom, pp. 685–716. Beverly Hills, Calif.: Sage, 1983.

Wolvin, Andrew D., and Darlyn R. Wolvin. "Contract Grading in Technical Speech Communication." *CE* (Mar. 1975), 139–142.

Additional readings on evaluation and grading may be found at the end of Chapter 3 in this IRM.

Problems in the Classroom

Handling Communication Apprehensive Students

Adams, Lori. "Speech Anxiety Simulation." *SCT* (Fall 1992), 13.

Adler, Ronald B. "Integrating Reticence Management into the Basic Communication Curriculum." *CE* (July 1980), 215–221.

Allen, Mike, and Steven B. Hunt. "Legal Issues in the Treatment of Communication Apprehension." *ACR* (Nov. 1993), 385–390.

Ayres, Joe. "Comparing Self-constructed Visualization Scripts with Guided Visualization" *CR* (Summer 1995), 193–199.

Ayres, Joe, Debbie M. Ayres, Gary Grudzinskas, Tim Hopf, Erin Kelly, and A. Kathleen Wilcox. "A Component Analysis of Performance Visualization." *CR* (Summer 1995), 185–192.

Ayres, Joe, and Theodore S. Hopf. "The Long-Term Effect of Visualization in the Classroom: A Brief Research Report." *CE* (Jan. 1990), 75–78.

———. "Visualization: A Means of Reducing Speech Anxiety." CE (Oct. 1985), 318–323.

Ayres, Joe, and Tim Hopf. "Visualization: Reducing Speech Anxiety and Enhancing Performance." *CR* (Winter 1992), 1–10.

———. *Coping with Speech Anxiety.* Norwood, N.J.: Ablex, 1993.

Ayres, Joe, Tim Hopf, and Debbie M. Ayres. "An Examination of Whether Imaging Ability Enhances the Effectiveness of an Intervention Designed to Reduce Speech Anxiety." *CE* (July 1994), 252–258.

Beatty, Michael J., and Matthew H. Friedland. "Public Speaking State Anxiety as a Function of Selected Situational and Predispositional Variables." *CE* (Apr. 1990), 142–147.

Behnke, Ralph R., Chris R. Sawyer, and Paul E. King. "Contagion Theory and the Communication of Public Speaking State Anxiety." *CE* (July 1994), 246–251.

Booth-Butterfield, Melanie, and Steve Booth Butterfield. *Communication Apprehension and Avoidance in the Classroom.* Edina, Minn.: Burgess, 1992.

———. "The Role of Cognitive 'Performance Orientation' in Communication Anxiety." *CQ* (Spring 1993), 198–209.

Booth-Butterfield, Steven. "Instructional Interventions for Reducing Situational Anxiety and Avoidance." *CE* (July 1988), 214–223.

Bowers, John Waite, and Members of 36C:009. "Classroom Communication Apprehension: A Survey." *CE* (Oct. 1986), 372–378.

Brownell, Winifred W., and Richard A. Katula. "The Communication Anxiety Graph: A Classroom Tool for Managing Speech Anxiety." *CQ* (Summer 1984), 243–249.

Cohen, Herman. "Teaching Reticent Students in a Required Course." *CE* (July 1980), 222–228.

Cronin, Michael W., George L. Grice, and Richard K. Olsen, Jr. "The Effects of Interactive Video Instruction in Coping with Speech Fright." *CE* (Jan. 1994), 42–53.

Daly, John A., Anita L. Vangelisti, and David J. Weber. "Speech Anxiety Affects How People Prepare Speeches: A Protocol Analysis of the Preparation Processes of Speakers." *CM* (Dec. 1995), 383–397.

Daly, John A., Anita L. Vangelisti, Heather L. Neel, and P. Daniel Cavanaugh. "Pre-Performance Concerns Associated with Public Speaking Anxiety." *CQ* (Winter 1989), 39–53.

Duran, Robert L., and Lynne Kelly. "The Cycle of Shyness: A Study of Self-Perceptions of Communication Performance." *CR* (Winter 1989), 30–38.

Foss, Karen A. "Communication Apprehension: Resources for the Instructor." *CE* (July 1982), 195–203.

Frymier, Ann Bainbridge. "The Relationships Among Communication Apprehension, Immediacy, and Motivation to Study." *CR* (Winter 1993), 8–17.

Glaser, Susan R. "Oral Communication Apprehension and Avoidance: The Current Status of Treatment Research." *CE* (Oct. 1981), 321–341.

Hamilton, James P. "The Development of a Communication Specific Locus of Control Instrument." *CR* (Summer 1991), 107–112.

Hawes, Ruhemah. "Using Group Speaking to Overcome Apprehension." *SCT* (Fall 1990), 10.

Hopf, Tim, and Joe Ayres. "Coping with Public Speaking Anxiety: An Examination of Various Combinations of Systematic Desensitization, Skills Training, and Visualization." *ACR* (May 1992), 184–198.

Isaacson, Zelda. "Paradoxical Intention: A Strategy to Alleviate the Anxiety Associated with Public Speaking." *SCT* (Summer 1993), 13–14.

Johnson, Craig. "Nothing to Fear But Fear . . . Or Is There." *SCT* (Winter 1990), 1.

Kelly, Lynne. "Implementing a Skills Training Program for Reticent Communicators." *CE* (Apr. 1989), 85–101.

King, Stephen W., Janis Andersen, and B. Robert Carlson. "The Dimensionality of the PRCA-24: An Explication of Content Dimensions." *CR* (Winter 1988), 1–8.

Kougl, Kathleen M. "Dealing with Quiet Students in the Basic College Speech Course." *CE* (July 1980), 234–238.

Langdon, Harry. "A Course on Stage Fright." *SCT* (Summer 1990), 15.

MacIntyre, Peter, and Kimly A. Thivierge, "The Effects of Audience Pleasantness, Audience Familiarity, and Speaking Contests on Public Speaking Anxiety and Willingness to Speak," *CQ* (Fall 1995), 456–466.

McCroskey, James C. "Classroom Consequences of Communication Apprehension." *CE* (Jan. 1977), 27–33.

McCroskey, James C., and Michael J. Beatty. "Communication Apprehension and Accumulated Communication State Anxiety Experiences: A Research Note." *CM* (Mar. 1984), 79–84.

McCroskey, James C., Steven Booth-Butterfield, and Steven K. Paynes. "The Impact of Communication Apprehension on College Student Retention and Success." *CQ* (Spring 1989), 100–107.

McGuire, John, Cherise Stauble, David Abbott, and Randy Fisher. "Ethical Issues in The Treatment of Communication Apprehension: A Survey of Communication Professionals." *CE* (Apr. 1995), 98–109.

Motley, Michael T., and Jennifer L. Molloy. "An Efficacy Test of a New Therapy ('Communication Orientation Motivation') for Public Speaking Anxiety." *ACR* (Feb. 1994), 48–58.

Parks, Malcolm R. "A Test of the Cross-Situational Consistency of Communication Apprehension." *CM* (Aug. 1980), 220–232.

Pederson, Douglas J. "Systematic Desensitization as a Model for Dealing with the Reticent Student." *CE* (July 1980), 229–233.

Phillips, Gerald M. "The Practical Teachers' Symposium on Shyness, Communication Apprehension, Reticence, and a Variety of Other Common Problems." *CE* (July 1980), 213–214.

Proctor, Russell F. II, Annamae T. Douglas, Teresa Garera-Izquierdo, and Stephanie L. Wartman. "Approach, Avoidance, and Apprehension: Talking with High-CA Students About Getting Help." *CE* (Oct. 1994), 312–321.

Rose, Heidi M., Andrew S. Rancer, and Kenneth C. Crannell. "The Impact of Basic Courses in Oral Interpretation and Public Speaking on Communication Apprehension." *CR* (Winter 1993), 54–60.

Rosenfield, Lawrence B., Charles H. Grant III, and James C. McCroskey. "Communication Apprehension and Self-perceived Communication Competence of Academically Gifted Students." *CE* (Jan. 1995), 79–86.

Rubin, Alan M. "The Effect of Locus of Control on Communication Motivation, Anxiety, and Satisfaction." *CQ* (Spring 1993), 161–171.

Tillson, Lou Davidson. "Building Community and Reducing Communication Apprehension: A Case Study Approach." *SCT* (Summer 1995), 4–5.

Watson, Arden K., and Carley H. Dodd. "Alleviating Communication Apprehension Through Rational Emotive Therapy: A Comparative Evaluation." *CE* (July 1984), 257–266.

Additional readings on communication apprehension may be found at the end of Chapter 2 in this IRM.

Technology in the Classroom

Aitken, Joan E. "A CD-ROM (Compact Disk-Read Only Memory) and World Wide Web Computerized-Assisted Approach to Teaching Basic Public Speaking." *SCT* (Spring 1996), 15–16.

Allen, Terre H., and Scott H. "New Media for the Communication Classroom." *SCT* (Winter 1996), 13–14.

Bailey, Elaine K., and Morton Cotlar. "Teaching Via the Internet." *CE* (Apr. 1994), 184–193.

Benson, Thomas W. "Electronic Network Resources for Communication Scholars." *CE* (Apr. 1994), 120–128.

Kuehn, Scott A. "Computer-Mediated Communication in Instructional Settings: A Research Agenda." *CE* (Apr. 1994), 171–183.

Madsen, Amie. "Computer-Assisted Comments for Research Papers and Speeches." *SCT* (Spring 1995), 15–16.

McComb, Mary. "Benefits of Computer-Mediated Communication in College Courses." *CE* (Apr. 1994), 159–170.

Diversity in the Classroom

Araujo, Alice R. "Multicultural Instruction: Strategies for Training Teaching Assistants to Incorporate Diverse Perspectives and Communication Styles into the Basic Communication Course." Paper presented at the Speech Communication Association Convention, 1991; available through ERIC.

Banks, Stephen P., and Anna Banks. "Translation as Problematic Discourse in Organizations." *ACR* (Nov. 1991), 223–241.

Bantz, Charles R. "Cultural Diversity and Group Cross-Cultural Team Research." *ACR* (Feb. 1993), 1–20.

Brown, William J. "Culture and AIDS Education: Reaching High-risk Heterosexuals in Asian-American Communities." *ACR* (August 1992), 275–291.

Carbaugh, Donal. "Comments on 'Culture' in Communication Inquiry." *CR* (Winter 1988), 38–41.

Delgado, Fernando Pedro. "Chicano Movement Rhetoric: An Ideographic Interpretation." *CQ* (Fall 1994), 446–455.

Donald, J., and A. Rattansi, eds. *'Race,' Culture and Difference*. Newbury Park, Calif.: Sage, 1992.

Fayer, Joan M., ed. *Puerto Rican Communication Studies*. San Juan: La Fundacion Arqueological, Antropologica e Historica de Puerto Rico, Inc., 1993.

Garbowitz, Fred. "Changing Classroom Populations Call for Increased Cultural Sensitivity." *SCT* (Summer 1990), 13–14.

Hammer, Mitchell R., and Judith N. Martin. "The Effects of Cross-Cultural Training on American Managers in a Japanese-American Joint Venture." *ACR* (May 1992), 162–183.

Hart, Russell D., and David E. Williams. "Able-Bodied Instructors and Students with Physical Disabilities: A Relationship Handicapped by Communication." *CE* (April 1995), 140–154.

Hawkinson, Ken. "Through the Eyes of Djeli Baba Sissoko: The Malian Oral Tradition." *SCT* (Winter 1991), 1–2.

Johnson, Scott D. "Exploring the Influences of Culture on Small Groups." *SCT* (Winter 1995), 6–7.

Klopf, Donald W., and Catherine A. Thompson. *Communication in the Multicultural Classroom.* Edina, Minn.: Burgess, 1992.

Kondo, David Shinji. "Strategies for Reducing Public Speaking Anxiety in Japan." *CR* (Winter 1994), 20–26.

Lee, Wen Shu. "On Not Missing the Boat: A Processual Method for Inter/cultural Understanding of Idioms and Lifeworld." *ACR* (May 1994), 141–161.

Lu, Xing, and David A. Frank, "On the Study of Ancient Chinese Rhetoric/Bian." *WJC* (Fall, 1993), 445–463.

Mandeville, Mary Y. "Are Our Basic Speech Communication Courses Targeting Today's Diverse Student Audience? Teacher Perceptions of Course Rigidity and Its Effect on Student Learning." Paper presented at the Speech Communication Association Convention, 1994; available through ERIC.

Martin, Judith N., Mitchell R. Hammer, and Lisa Bradford. "The Influence of Cultural and Situational Contexts on Hispanic and Non-Hispanic Communication Competence Behaviors." *CQ* (Spring 1994), 160–195.

McLaurin, Patrick. "An Examination of the Effect of Culture on Pro-Social Messages Directed at African-American At-Risk Youth." *CM* (Dec. 1995), 301–326.

Nieto, Sonia. *Affirming Diversity: The Sociopolitical Context of Multicultural Education.* New York: Longman, 1992.

Olaniran, Bolanie A., and K. David Roach. "Communication Apprehension and Classroom Apprehension in Nigerian Classrooms." *CQ* (Fall 1994), 379–389.

Orbe, Mark P. "African American Communication Research: Toward a Deeper Understanding of Interethnic Communication." *WJC* (Winter 1995), 61–78.

Ralston, Steven Michael, Robert Ambler, and Joseph N. Scudder. "Reconsidering the Impact of Racial Differences in the College Public Speaking Classroom on Minority Student Communication Anxiety." *CR* 43–50.

Robie, Harry. "A Native American Speech Text for Classroom Use." *SCT* (Summer 1991), 12.

Rosenfield, Lawrence B. "The Effects of Perceived Sexism in Female and Male College Professors on Students' Descriptions of Classroom Climate." *CE* (July 1985), 205–213.

Sanders, Judith, Robert Gass, Richard Wiseman, and Jon Bruschke. "Ethnic Comparison and Measurement of Argumentativeness, Verbal Aggressiveness, and Need for Cognition." *CR* (Winter 1992), 50–56.

Sprague, Joe. "The Reduction of Sexism in Speech Communication Education." *CE* (Jan. 1975), 37–45.

Sternglanz, Sarah, and Shirley Lyberger-Ficek. "Sex Differences in Student-Teacher Interactions in the College Classroom." *Sex Roles* (1977), 345–352.

Summerfield, E. *Crossing Cultures Through Film.* Yarmouth, Me.: Intercultural Press, 1993.

Suzuki, Shinobu, and Andrew S. Rancer. "Argumentativeness and Verbal Aggressiveness: Testing for Conceptual and Measurement Equivalence Across Cultures." *CM* (Sept. 1994), 256–279.

Thompson, Dawn, and Myra Cullen. *Collidascope: An Intercultural Learning Experience* [a learning game]. Available from Collidascope, 188 Blakeslee Hill Road, Newfield, NY 14867.

Tuana, Nancy. "Sexual Harrassment in Academe." *College Teaching* (1985), 53–63.

Walter, Suzanne. "Experiences in Intercultural Communication." *SCT* (Summer 1995), 1–3.

Wood, Julia. "Diversity and Commonality: Sustaining Their Tension in Communication Courses." *WJC* 367–380.

Zimmerman, Stephanie. "Perceptions of Intercultural Communication Competence and International Student Adaptation to an American Campus." *CE* (Oct. 1995), 321–335.

Adapting to Adult Learners

Query, Jim L. Jr., Doug Parry, and Lyle J. Flint. "The Relationship Among Social Support, Communication Competence, and Cognitive Depression for Nontraditional Students." *ACR* (Feb. 1992), 78–94.

Tifft, Susan. "The Over-25 Set Moves In: Adults Are Fast Becoming the Majority on College Campuses." *Time,* 24 Oct. 1988, 90–91.

Wolvin, Andrew D. "Meeting the Communication Needs of the Adult Learner." *CE* (July 1984), 267–271.

General Problems

"Dealing With Disruptive Behavior in the Classroom." *The Teaching Professor* (Feb. 1988), 4.

"Ideas for Managing Your Classroom Better," *The Teaching Professor* (Feb. 1988), 3.

Bardine, Rudy. "Why Some Students Fail to Participate in Class." *Marketing News* (18 July 1986), 23–24.

Chiodo, John J. "The Effects of Exam Anxiety on Grandma's Health." *Education Digest* (Jan. 1987), 45–47.

Infante, Dominic A. "The Argumentative Student in the Speech Communication Classroom: An Investigation and Implications." *CE* (Apr. 1982), 141–148.

Williams, Glen L. "Alleviating Attendance Woes for Instructors and Students." *SCT* (Winter 1995), 9.

Teaching in the Junior/Community College

Burchett, Brenda Harnage. "Speech Communication in the Community-Junior College: A Bibliography." *ACAB* (Aug. 1976), 31–39.

Corley, Diane. "Some Practical Criteria for Developing Courses for Community Colleges." *ACAB* (Apr. 1977), 36–37.

D'Aponte, Mimi, Susan Goldstein, and Andrew McKenzie. "Teaching Speech in an Open Admissions Program." *CE* (Nov. 1977), 327–332.

Miller, Maria B. "Developmental Education and Speech Communication in the Community College." *CE* (Jan. 1984), 5–11.

Miller, Maria, and Tyler Tindall. "Speech Communication in the Community-Junior College: The El Pomar Conference Report." *ACAB* (Apr. 1982), 32–38.

Muchmore, John. "National Implications of the Denver Conference on Speech Communication in the Community College." *ACAB* (Apr. 1977), 32–33.

Ratliffe, Sharon A. "Speech Communication in the Community College." *CE* (Jan. 1984), 1–4.

Reynolds, Beverly C. "Speech Communication in the Community-Junior College: An Annotated Bibliography of Non-Print Materials." *ACAB* (Jan. 1981), 83–89.

Ritter, Ellen M. "Training Speech Communication Teachers for the Community College: A Competency-Based Approach." *CQ* (Summer 1975), 3–10.

Spivey, Clayton, Shirley Mitchell, Ruth Louise Jones, and Roy Berko. "A Basic Communication Course for Community College Technical Career Students: A Structural Design." *CQ* (Summer 1975), 15–18.

Strain, Barbara, and Patrica Wysong. "Teaching the Community College Student: Methods and Procedures for a Developmental Course in Speech Communication." *ACAB* (Aug. 1976), 42–56.

———. "A Report of Developmental Speech Courses in Selected Community Colleges." *ACAB* (Jan. 1981), 76–77.

Wolvin, Darlyn R., and Isa N. Engleberg. "Community Colleges and Communication Education." *CE* (Oct. 1989), 322–326.

Wolvin, Darlyn R., and Andrew D. Wolvin. "Communication in the 2-Year College." In *Teaching Communication: Theory, Research, and Methods,* edited by John A. Daly, Gustav W. Friedrich, and Anita L Vangelisti, pp. 427–436. Hillsdale, N.J.: Lawrence Erlbaum, 1990.

PART II
Chapter-by-Chapter Guide to Teaching Public Speaking

CHAPTER 1
You as a Public Speaker

OBJECTIVES

- To introduce your students to the field of speech communication studies through public speaking.
- To impress upon your students the personal benefits of a course in public speaking.
- To help your students appreciate the social and cultural benefits of developing improved public communication skills.
- To impress upon students their ethical responsibilities as participants in the communication process.
- To help students understand the nature of public speaking as communication.

SUGGESTIONS FOR TEACHING

An effective introduction can be as important to the success of a course as it is to that of a speech. It should involve, interest, and orient your students to the class itself. Simply drawing a communication model on the board and spoon-feeding various components and principles of communication is rarely effective. We suggest that during the first class session you distribute your syllabus and orient your students to the general format, goals, and policies of the course (see Part I for more on syllabi and first-day preparations). You might follow that with some sort of short activity and give your students a homework assignment that sets up your second-day lesson plans. During your early class meetings, strive to develop a supportive and positive climate in the classroom that will help students feel more comfortable when making their presentations. Encourage their involvement and interaction.

Many instructors like to get their students in front of the class during its first meeting or as early as possible. There are a variety of short speaking activities to choose from in Chapter 2 of this IRM. You may want to skip forward to Chapter 4 and administer an audience analysis questionnaire early in the term. In this chapter, we offer activities to emphasize the personal, social, and cultural benefits of public speaking and free speech, to demonstrate the function and importance of feedback in the communication process, to highlight the ethical responsibilities of participants in the communication process, and to help promote the participative interaction that fosters a warm and familiar classroom environment.

CHAPTER OUTLINE

I. There are five essential ingredients to developing public speaking skills. *(text p. 4)*
   A. Student commitment to learning.
   B. Experience in giving speeches.

    C. A helpful instructor.

    D. A supportive audience of classmates.

    E. A text illustrating the "hows" and "whys" of public speaking.

II. Public speaking benefits the students and society. *(text pp. 4–12)*

    A. The *personal benefits* of developing improved communication skills include:

        1. promoting personal growth and self-knowledge.

        2. developing basic skills of preparing and presenting speeches.

        3. developing critical and constructive listening skills.

        4. promoting intercultural sensitivity through interacting with diverse audiences.

        5. exposure to creative learning through interactions.

        6. improved performance in school and career.

        7. developing the ability to publicly defend your values and interests.

    B. There are many *social benefits* of developing improved public speaking skills.

        1. Social beings develop identities through public interaction.

        2. Public speaking skills allow us to defend causes we find important.

        3. Societies that promote democratic deliberation of significant issues depend upon effective and responsible public advocates.

    C. There are many *cultural benefits* of developing improved public speaking skills.

        1. The United States is a multicultural nation, and increased public speaking skills can counter the impulse toward ethnocentrism by obliging participants to recognize and appreciate the diversity of their audiences.

            a. Metaphoric images such as Lozano's bouillabaisse or Lincoln's chorus may be more appropriate for characterizing our society than the stereotype implied by the traditional image of a melting pot.

III. As communication, public speaking represents an expansion of basic language and conversational skills that most of us develop early in life. *(text pp. 12–23)*

    A. Effective public speaking preserves at least three aspects of a conversation.

        1. It preserves natural directness and spontaneity.

        2. It is colorful and compelling.

        3. It is tuned to specific listeners.

            a. Speakers can make immediate and long-term adjustments in response to feedback.

            b. Speakers need to show audiences why they should be interested in what the speakers have to say, how they know it is true, and what they can do.

    B. Public speaking differs from conversation in that it is less spontaneous, has clearly defined roles for speakers and listeners, and is more carefully planned and structured.

        1. Speakers and listeners have complementary roles.

            a. Speakers' roles are defined in terms of the audience's impressions of ethos, which consists of:

                (1) credibility (competence and integrity).

                (2) charisma (likability and forcefulness).

            b. Listeners play an important role in public communication.

                (1) They should be supportive yet critical, seeking value in messages.

                (2) Their responses shape the meanings that emerge.

        2. Whereas conversations are fragmentary and unpredictable, public speaking consists of well-planned messages that are internally consistent and complete, carefully researched, rehearsed, and worded to have a desired effect on the audience.

            a. Speakers encode their messages through words, tones, and gestures, and invite an audience to decode their intention and determine the value of their messages.

            b. Shaping messages consists of choosing topics, organizing your ideas, and supporting them with substantive facts, examples, testimony, and narratives.

            c. Effective wording can make or break a message, as well as a speaker's ethos.

            d. The medium of transmission can greatly affect a speaker's message.

                (1) Speakers may need to adjust their volume to the acoustics of the speaking site.

        (2)   Electronic media present speakers with challenges.
            (a)   Radio emphasizes the value of an attractive and expressive voice.
            (b)   Television magnifies the significance of intimacy, personality, and personal appearance.
            (c)   The electronic media generally preclude the possibility of direct feedback, so speakers should be clear, concise, and colorful.

    e.   The communication environment consists of the physical setting in which communication takes place and the moods and interests of your audience.
        (1)   The physical environment of classroom speeches is predictable.
        (2)   Recent events and audience expectations can influence the meaning of messages.
        (3)   Interference can be physical or psychological and can create communication problems.
            (a)   An unfamiliar audience can make speakers appear nervous, distant, or even suspicious.
            (b)   Audience members may be distracted by personal concerns or beset by stereotypes, fears, and indifference.
        (4)   The art of public speaking is an effort to overcome interference so that listeners can accept the invitation to meaning offered by the message.
            (a)   "Interference Mountain" provides a useful metaphor for characterizing the barriers of fear, suspicion, indifference, distraction, and prejudice that speakers and audiences must overcome.

  C. Communication as transformation goes beyond the sharing of information, ideas, and advice to facilitating the moral exploration, unity, and growth of speakers and audiences.

IV. Because communication affects the lives of others, ethical considerations affect every aspect of successful public speaking. *(text pp. 23–28)*
  A. Ethics involve the moral dimensions of conduct: how we treat others and wish to be treated by them.
    1.   Ethical public speaking emphasizes respect for the integrity of ideas, responsible knowledge, considered use of techniques, and avoidance of plagiarism.
      a.   Responsible knowledge entails knowledge about the main points of concern, familiarity with expert opinions, knowledge of recent events, and concern for the effects of this information on your listeners.
      b.   Careful use of communication techniques can help avoid such common abuses as misrepresenting authorities by quoting them out of context.
      c.   Plagiarism, presenting the ideas and words of others as though they were your own, without acknowledging their source, can have serious academic and professional consequences.
        (1)   Speakers plagiarize when they summarize single articles from newspapers and magazines and do not credit their sources.
    2.   Ethical communication entails concern for how words affect listeners.
      a.   Effective speaking entails developing sensitivity to listeners that helps speakers transcend egocentrism.
      b.   Speakers can appeal to the audiences within an audience by invoking universal values such as love, truthfulness, fairness, freedom, unity, tolerance, responsibility, and respect for life.

USING END-OF-CHAPTER ITEMS

Discussion *(text p. 30)*

1. **Look for symptoms of ethnocentrism and egocentrism among newspapers of the day. What impact do these attitudes have on events and on the ethos of those who speak in connection with them? Share your ideas in class.**

   This makes a good homework assignment followed by in-class discussion. As an alternative, pull the clippings yourself and bring them to class for a small-group discussion. Look especially at front-page stories and editorial pages. You should review ethnocentrism, egocentrism, and ethos with your students in preparation for this exercise. Keep in mind that this activity invites students to discuss personal and political convictions, which may differ. Use this exercise as a good first opportunity to encourage a climate of critical tolerance and openness to consideration of opposing views.

2. **Identify some stereotypes at work in your own thinking and in your conversations with friends. Why do these stereotypes exist? What is the result of their existence?**

   This exercise makes a good homework writing assignment followed by in-class discussion. It emphasizes the type of self-evaluation that enhances sensitivity to audiences of different backgrounds and with different experiences. Push your students to be honest about the stereotypes they disclose before opening class discussion to the consequences of these stereotypes. Emphasize that all of us inevitably put one another into categories—it's unavoidable. The point is to constantly reflect on this impulse and its implications for communication transactions. As the text notes, we get into trouble when we allow stereotypes to guide our evaluations of other people instead of considering those people as unique individuals.

3. **Discuss how the ethics of communication might be applied to advertising. Bring to class an example of an advertisement that you think is unethical and explain why.**

   This makes an effective homework assignment and second-day discussion piece to emphasize the practical and ethical differences between advertising and public speaking. Have your students present their ads to the class and explain why they think these ads are unethical. As you probe them with questions and critique their ideas, focus discussion on the following standards for ethical persuasion:

   1. *Respect for the audience:* To what type of consumer is this advertisement directed? What assumptions have been made about consumers? Is the consumer treated as a rational adult capable of making informed decisions? How are women, men, and minorities portrayed in the ad? Does it perpetuate positive or negative stereotypes?

   2. *Responsible knowledge:* Does the product or service advertised require a reasoned decision for its selection? If so, does the ad contain the information consumers would need to make such a decision? What other types of appeal (emotional, mythic, celebrity endorsement, need-based) are used?

   3. *Accuracy and objectivity:* Does the ad present information accurately and objectively? Are claims about the product or service reasonable? Does the ad encourage a false expectation or ideal? What techniques are used to convey an image of objectivity?

   4. *Concern for consequences:* Beyond making a sale, do the advertisers seem concerned about the consequences of the ad? Does the ad try to create unnecessary needs for the product or service? Does it portray an unrealistic or unhealthy lifestyle?

To structure their messages, your students should make a statement, defend it using the above criteria, and then make the statement again. If this is your first speaking activity, many of your students will be nervous. Push them to speak up and maintain eye contact (see the comments on first speaking activities in the next chapter).

4. **What personal and social benefits are lost in societies that do not encourage the free and open exchange of ideas?**

This exercise can be used for small-group or general class discussion. Again, you might have your students prepare some ideas as homework in preparation for class discussion. Have them present their ideas to the class. Use this as an opportunity to introduce the personal, social, and cultural benefits of public speaking as discussed in the text. You might wish to write the student comments on the chalkboard.The list of lost personal benefits may include creative expression, personal development opportunities, improved decision making, and critical thinking ability. The list of lost social benefits might include participation in policy making, open deliberation, personal freedom, and living in an open society. Lost cultural benefits might include cultural diversity, minority empowerment, and creative input from differing cultures and experiences. You might mention that public speaking both as an art form and as an educational priority has always flourished in democratic societies encouraging free and open deliberation. Why is this so? Extend the discussion by having your student prioritize their list of social and personal benefits and consider the appropriate functions of a public speaking course with respect to promoting these benefits.

5. **Do you agree that it is better to think of American culture as a "chorus" rather than as a "melting pot"? What images of American identity do you prefer, and why?**

This makes an excellent outside writing assignment or small-group activity to introduce the intercultural significance of rhetoric. You might want to start by discussing some basic ideas about metaphor (see Chapter 10), emphasizing its potential for organizing thoughts and perceptions about abstract or complex ideas. Many of your students will be familiar with the "melting pot" theory of American history and culture—an image that is becoming progressively less fashionable. Some may express reservations about multiculturalism and defend the old image. As an instructor, you should avoid the impulse to take sides, and welcome the inclusion of opposing views. Try to steer the discussion toward the pros and cons of both images to characterize American culture, as well as their implications for minority cultures and identities. Your students should recognize that the melting pot image favors one predominant "alloy" culture and corresponding value/belief systems. The chorus image would obviously favor diverse input and harmonious interaction. Other multicultural images might include a quilt or a montage. Have your students present their ideas for class discussion. Remember that there may be benefits and drawbacks to both images and encourage your students to discuss these constructively.

Application *(text p. 30)*

1. **Develop your own personal statement of commitment. What do you hope to gain from your public speaking class? Plan time during the week that you can work to achieve these benefits.**

This makes a good homework writing assignment, which may be followed by in-class or small-group discussion. You might review the basic personal, social, and cultural benefits of public speaking in preparation for this exercise. Have your students think in terms of ends and means—what they want from the course (beyond a passing grade) and how they intend to get it. Push them to address the likely benefits of public speaking skills in fulfilling their basic educational, career, and life interests, and to be specific regarding times of the week they will work to achieve their stated aims.

2. The Speech Communication Association has adopted the following code of ethics concerning free expression [see text pp. 30–31]. Working in small groups, discuss how you would adapt this credo into a code of ethics for use in your public speaking class. Each group should present the code it proposes to the class, and the class should collectively determine a code of ethics to be used during the term.

You will accomplish three important goals if you allow students to have a voice in determining a code of ethical behavior for the class. First, students who have input into the code are less likely to feel that arbitrary rules are being forced upon them, and will have a vested interest in seeing therules followed. Second, the students will be engaging in the process of constructive deliberation, which is crucial to developing improved public speaking skills. Finally, this item gets students talking openly about course-related issues early in the term. Students also get a chance to become familiar with one another, which can help later with communication apprehension.

As the instructor, you may act as leader for this first exercise in group deliberation, establishing some ground rules for both the discussion and the code of ethics. For example, you might advise the students that the code should cover both speaking and listening behaviors, and also policies concerning plagiarism. Although students will have many suggestions, the discussion should focus on areas such as implications for topic selection, respect, responsibility, and concern for consequences. Try to steer the class toward concrete manifestations of these abstractions, such as, "If you are late for class, do not enter the room while another student is presenting a speech," and "Do not do your homework for another class while another student is speaking."

3. Begin keeping a speech evaluation notebook in which you record comments on effective and ineffective, and ethical and unethical speeches you hear both in and out of class. As you observe speeches, ask yourselves the following twelve questions:

    1. How did the speaker rate in terms of ethos?
    2. Was the speech well adapted to its listeners' needs and interests?
    3. Did the speech take into account the cultural complexity of its audience?
    4. Did the speech make an effective connection with universal values?
    5. Was the message clear and well structured?
    6. Did the medium pose any problems?
    7. Were the language and presentation of the speech effective?
    8. How did listeners respond, both during and after the speech?
    9. Did the communication environment have an impact?
    10. Did the speech overcome interference to achieve its goal?
    11. Did the speaker respect the integrity of ideas by developing an original speech that exhibited responsible knowledge and a careful use of communication techniques?
    12. Did the speaker exhibit proper concern for the impact of the message on listeners?

This exercise can be fruitfully developed throughout the course of the semester. It helps students discover the complexity of public communication. As with any continuing assignment, students will be more diligent if you collect and grade the notebooks on a regular basis (two or three times a semester). You might specify a minimum number of speech analysis entries per review. It is also helpful to solicit constructive classroom criticism as you offer oral critiques of classroom speeches (remind students to emphasize the positive and make suggestions for improvement). Use this activity as an opportunity to let your students know what you focus on when evaluating class speeches.

ADDITIONAL ACTIVITIES

Know-U Icebreaker

Purpose: To stimulate interaction among your students so that they can begin to get familiar with one another.

Directions: Most people feel more comfortable addressing people if they feel familiar with them. Therefore, it's a good idea to get your students talking to one another as soon as possible. Once you have distributed your syllabus and discussed your class priorities and policies, this makes a good conclusion to the first class. Make copies of the "Know-U" game card and give one to each student. Explain that the game is similar to Bingo, except that they should mingle until they find someone who fits the description in a square. Then they should write that person's name in the appropriate square and continue to mingle. The first student who fills in five squares in a row comes to you and is pronounced the winner. The student who wins reads out the names for each of the squares, and the students identified explain how and why they fit that description.

K	N	O	W	U
grew up in rural area	is an environmentalist	has no driver's license	works twenty or more hours per week	played high school basketball
has traveled in Europe	is of Native American lineage	is under eighteen years old	was born outside the United States	is a Republican
played high school soccer	writes poetry as a hobby	FREE	voted in last election	likes rock 'n' roll music
is a Democrat	has five or more brothers and sisters	is over thirty years old	is of Latino heritage	has been to Hawaii
likes classical music	has never had a job	has signed an organ donor card	paints or draws as a hobby	grew up in an urban area

The Importance of Feedback

Purpose: To impress upon students the importance of feedback in the communication process.

Directions: It is rarely effective (and usually boring) to simply lecture about the communication process. You can enliven this material by using the following exercise inspired by a classic experiment by Harold J. Leavitt and Ronald A. H. Mueller ["Some Effects of Feedback on Communication," *Human Relations*, 4 (1951), 401–410] that illustrated the effects of feedback on the communication process by asking students to reproduce drawings of geometrical forms as described by other subjects with varying degrees of allowed feedback. As expected, both the accuracy of the drawings and the speaker's sense of communicative competence increased dramatically in the higher-feedback situations, at considerable cost in time. Obviously, receivers preferred the free-feedback situation. Indeed, the zero-feedback situation aroused continued hostility toward the speaker in subsequent free-feedback situations.

Ask for two student volunteers to "describe an arrangement of tables" to the class. Give one of them a copy of Arrangement 1 and the other a copy of Arrangement 2 from p. 70. Have the first volunteer sit at the front of the room, facing away from the audience. Using only words (no gestures or drawing on the chalkboard allowed), have the volunteer describe Arrangement 1. The class should use the information to draw the arrangement as well as they can without asking any questions of the volunteer. Have the second volunteer sit at the front of the room facing the audience as he or she describes Arrangement 2. The speaker may supplement words with gestures but may not use the chalkboard. This time, students may interrupt and ask follow-up questions of the volunteer. Show enlarged originals of the arrangements. Ask how many students got Arrangement 1 correct (typically, few can even approximate it). Ask how many got Arrangement 2 correct (usually around 70 percent). Discuss the importance of feedback in completing the communication process. Be sure to thank both student volunteers, reassuring the first zero-feedback speaker as well as the class that it was not his or her speaking skill that was deficient, but a lack of adequate feedback.

What Constitutes Ethical Speaking?

Purpose: To provide students with an opportunity to discuss the concerns of ethical speaking with references to real-life examples.

Directions: Show videotapes of student speeches, and have your students critique them in accordance with the ethical criteria offered in the text, i.e., respect for the integrity of ideas, responsible knowledge use, and concern for audience implications. Have your students take notes and share their observations for general discussions after each viewing. Use this as an opportunity to discuss the tension that sometimes exists between effective and ethical speaking, the place of ethical considerations in your course, and your students' responsibilities as speakers and listeners in facilitating ethical public communication.

Public Speaking vs. War

Purpose: To emphasize for students the immense social and ethical significance of constructive public communication.

Directions: One of the noblest potentials of ethical and effective public communication is that it allows people to mediate differences and potential conflicts without resorting to violence. Indeed, during uprisings and armed conflicts, controlling the means of public communication generally becomes a central focus of dispute. The past decade has witnessed an unprecedented number of revolutions and armed conflicts throughout the world. Choose one, and have each student locate two relevant articles for class discussion, looking especially for statements on freedom of news coverage and reasons for its restriction during wartime. Focus the discussion on how different sides seek to manipulate the dominant means of communication. Governments under attack typically censor the mass media, forcing opposing groups to use such alternative forms as pamphlets and audiovisuals. During most conflicts, all sides eventually become hostile toward or skeptical about the idea of free and open press coverage. Push your students to consider whether armed conflicts would be more or less likely to occur if neither faction were allowed absolute control over the dominant means of public communication. Again, use this as an opportunity to underscore the ethical and political significance of free and open public speech.

Reading Logs

Purpose: To push students to engage their assigned readings with in-class experiences and personal applications.

Directions: Speech instructors complain that students do not read assigned materials. Many students assume that public speaking is strictly a performance course, and that outside readings are really not necessary. Rhetoricians have always known that their students must make applications in order to learn and integrate ideas with practice. Instead of resorting to "pop quizzes," which more often results in last-minute and short-term memorization, consider having your students keep a reading log in which they make a one-page entry after each major reading assignment. Emphasize that students should not spend too much time on their logs and should make their entries while they are reading. Use the format on p. 62.

The point is not to bog students down with busywork or force them to memorize text materials, but rather to get them to seek out creative applications of the ideas they read about to their own experiences as listeners and speakers in public communication both in and outside the classroom. Have your students turn in their logs periodically for a brief pass/fail-type evaluation. You might coordinate this with the suggested speech log activity in Chapter 3 of this IRM.

READING LOG

Name: _____ Date: _____

Title (or text chapter): _____

Author (if not from text): _____

Source (if not from text): _____

Applicability to current assignment:_____

_____

_____

_____

_____

_____

Applicability outside of class: _____

_____

_____

_____

_____

_____

Case Study: Freedom of Speech

Purpose: To provide students with an opportunity to relate the concept of freedom of speech to an actual situation involving a student speaker.

Directions: Read the following short article from *USA Today*, 5 June 1995, to your students, then have them discuss whether or not the situation depicted is an example of censorship. On what basis could it be justified? On what basis is it a violation of freedom of speech? How should the student involved have handled the situation?

Paul Leavitt, "Student Mum After Speech Altered."*

> An Oak Bluff, Mass., high school salutatorian sat silent at her graduation Sunday rather than deliver a speech in which her principal had deleted reference to her rape by a school football star three years ago. Megan Cryer, 17, said she wouldn't change her wording because "I would be letting myself down if I didn't deal with the experience head on." The offending remark: "Terrible things can happen, even something as terrible as rape. But you can overcome it, and I wanted people to know that," she said. Martha's Vineyard Regional High School Principal Gregory Scotten said he wanted to make the speech more appropriate as a welcoming address. "I think there was a misinterpretation of our intentions."

Responsible Communication

Purpose: To stimulate discussion of the importance of responsibility in public communication.

Directions: Distribute the following excerpt on responsibility in communication to your classes. After students have read the article, break them out into small groups and have them discuss the situation involved. Have the students relate their discussions to the ethics of communication and the idea of freedom of speech. Each group should report the results of their discussion to the class as a whole.

---

* "Student Mum After Speech Altered" by Paul Leavitt, *USA Today*, June 5, 1995. Copyright © 1995 *USA TODAY*. Reprinted with permission.

Adapted from Michael Kramer, "Time to Stop Shouting," *Time*, 1 May 1995, p. 66.

If they agree on nothing else, Big Government liberals and conservative devolutionists view national security and the preservation of domestic order as Washington's two primary roles. There is a third and equally important federal function on which any public figure can help instruct the nation: the role of civil discourse in a democracy.

But civil discourse is virtually an oxymoron today. Cannot the prevalence of ad hominem attacks and demonization in our politics be seen as having helped inspire last Wednesday's insanity [the Oklahoma City Federal Building bombing]? The dots need not be connected for some connections to be considered.

Last month the National Rifle Association ran full-page ads denouncing the federal Bureau of Alcohol, Tobacco and Firearms for a "tyrannical record of misconduct and abuse of power." Assuming those responsible for Oklahoma City have ties to the gun-toting "citizen militias" whose leaders advocate armed conflict against governmental "intrusion," shouldn't the NRA reconsider at least the tone of such heated calls to arms?

Newt Gingrich recently praised incendiary language as a key to winning elections. Use words like "liar" and "traitor" to attack Democrats, he said. Should anyone who values honest debate condone such advice? Is it much wonder that the unhinged can't make the distinction between mere name calling and damning opponents as the embodiment of evil?

There is of course no straight line between any of this and Oklahoma City—just as there was no straight line between the 1960s antiwar movement and the left-wing terrorists who robbed banks and killed cops in the name of patriotism. But didn't "Hey, hey, L.B.J., how many kids did you kill today?" encourage more extreme expressions of division?

If the perpetrators of the Oklahoma City bombing really view government as the people's enemy, the burden of fostering that delusion is borne not just by the nut cases who preach conspiracy but also to some extent by those who erode faith in our governance in the pursuit of their own ambitions. Inflamed passions produce unintended consequences. In the effort to get attention, to startle, to motivate, a crucial self-control is lost. The gulf between hyperbolic words and last week's despicable treachery is not all that great.

Everyone is obliged to demand a more honest and more civil discourse. But those who seek to lead bear the largest responsibility. Both the right and left need to lower their voices.

Terilyn Goins Phillips (Christopher Newport University, Va.), "Name That Analogy: The Communication Game," *SCT* (Winter 1996), 10–11.

Goal: To help students understand the nature of communication as a transactional rather than a linear or interactive process.

What is communication? I suppose it depends on whom you ask. "Definitions of communication reflect fields at almost every conceivable level ranging from all behavior to meaningful, purposive behavior of human beings in conscious interaction."* If communication scholars debate the nature of communication, surely students find it difficult to answer the seemingly simple question, "What is communication?" So, how do we as educators address this most fundamental question within a basic communication course?

Name that Analogy is an activity whereby students can discover for themselves what makes up the communication process. The *objectives* of this activity are for students to:

- Determine the components of communication.
- Analyze how these components interact.
- Gain a more thorough understanding of the transactional nature of communication.
- Receive the satisfaction of creating their own model of communication.
- Measure their intellectual discoveries with those of communication scholars.

* R. L. Applebaum, O. O. Jensen, and R. Carroll. *Speech Communication: A Basic Anthology*, New York: Macmillan, 1975.

Instructions

First, students get into small groups and are told to complete the statement,

"Communication is like a game of _____ because _____." The analogy can be made to a board game, a computer game, a card game, or a type of sports, so long as the group can justify their comparative choice.

Second, after completion of the exercise, I ask each group to explain and justify their communication game analogy.

Third, I conduct a brief lecture on the transactional nature of communication, to include discussion of various linear and interactive communication models.

Finally, I ask that students identify each analogy as an example of a linear, interactive, or transactional communication process. As the analogies are identified, we discuss the characteristics associated with each model, the limitations of linear and interactive communication, and the advantages of viewing communication as transactional.

Though simplistic, this exercise creates discussion regarding the nature of communication. Students come up with rather interesting analogies that lend themselves nicely to discussion about the communication process as a whole. For instance, students, when comparing communication to a volleyball game, explain it this way: One person serves (starts the interaction). Another hits the ball back (responds), passes it to someone else (includes more interactants), or fails to hit the ball at all (provides no feedback). During the game, a person may hit the ball out of bounds (miscommunicate), spike it (drive an idea home), or score a point (get an idea across). In this example, the players function as both senders and receivers... the ball represents the message...the net serves as noise ... the different plays demonstrate the interactive nature of communication, the involvement of a third person illustrates different types of communication. ... Other game comparisons include battleships, poker, golf, football, basketball, soccer, and the list goes on.

From these simple comparisons, we discuss the communication components and all that is involved in the communication process. We then contrast and compare the various analogies to help students understand the differences between linear, interactive, and transactional communication. For instance, one group compares communication to bowling, stating that communicators often fail to get their point across, like a gutter ball, or they miscommunicate, as with a spare ball (where they get a second chance), or all goes well in the communication encounter, such as when one bowls a strike. This analogy provides an example of linear communication. The communication encounter is unidirectional, and the burden of responsibility regarding communication efficiency rests entirely with the message source.

Another group compares communication to tennis, where communication involves a back and forth proposition, with a limited number of attempts to get it right. This analogy provides an example of interactive communication. The communicative encounter (tennis game) has a definite beginning and ending. The communicators bat ideas back and forth with little knowledge of the person(s) with whom they are communicating (volleying). The object is to get the idea (ball) across, wait for the feedback (return ball), and speak (hit) again. Cultural issues such as the communicators' identity, origin, or lifestyle are left unaddressed. The interactants simply take their turn when the time arrives and continue doing so until the end of the interaction.

Finally, communication is compared to a chess game, where the players must have an in-depth knowledge of the game to successfully achieve their goal. This provides an example of transactional communication. Each communicator (player) has the same objective, to get their idea accepted (to capture the king). The communicators (players), however, cannot communicate (move their piece) without considering the other's perspective. They must always anticipate the other person's move as they make their own move. This process may involve thinking well ahead with regard to strategic choices. Moreover, the encounter (chess game) may be ongoing and, though abandoned for a period, always remains to be returned to at a later time.

Needless to say, most of these analogies, if carried to their out limits, would probably break down. The use of this activity in my classes has provided fertile ground for discussions regarding definitional issues related to communication. Additionally, I have found that when students are given opportunity to ask themselves what communication is all about, they generally answer most, if not all, of the questions that arise relating to the communication process in its entirety.

SUPPLEMENTARY MATERIALS

Films and Videos

"Be Prepared to Speak," Kantola-Skeie Productions, color, 27 minutes.

"When You Have to Get Up and Talk," BBP, 24 minutes.

"Beyond Hate," Educational Video Group, 60 minutes.

"The Communication Process," RMI Media Productions, 28 minutes.

"How to Get Your Point Across in 30 Seconds or Less," Coronet/MTI Film and Video, 30 minutes.

"Crediting Your Sources," RMI Media Productions, 30 minutes.

"Ten Vital Rules for Giving Incredible Speeches and Why They're Irrelevant," Video Publishing House, 32 minutes.

"Diversity Series," Quality Media Resources, 4 segments, 20 minutes each.

"The Public Speaker and the Audience," RMI Productions, 28 minutes.

"Sending a Message," Films for the Humanities, color, 15 minutes.

"For Goodness Sake," CRM Films, 24 minutes.

"Speaking Effectively to One or One Thousand," CRM Films, 21 minutes.

"First Amendment Freedoms," Insight Media, 30 minutes.

Student Speeches Videos to accompany *Public Speaking* .

"The Communication Cycle," Insight Media, 28 minutes.

Transparencies and Handouts *(see following pages)*

How to Create a Good Public Speech

A Questionnaire on Freedom of Speech

Statement on Student Plagiarism

Arrangements 1 and 2

HOW TO CREATE
A GOOD PUBLIC SPEECH

1. Choose a subject that is important to you and your listeners.

2. Select a topic that interests you, that you know something about, and that you can bring to life for your audience.

3. Decide on a clear purpose. What would you like your audience to do as a result of your speech?

4. Involve your listeners by asking for their response and relating your topic directly to them.

5. Use testimony, facts, examples, and stories to add substance to your speech.

6. Organize your ideas into a logical design.

7. Use clear, colorful, concrete language.

8. Practice your speech until you can present it smoothly.

9. Be concerned about the ethical consequences of your speech.

"HOW FREE IS TOO FREE?"

Please respond using the following code:

> 7 = Strongly agree
> 6 = Agree
> 5 = Agree somewhat
> 4 = Neutral or not sure
> 3 = Disagree somewhat
> 2 = Disagree
> 1 = Strongly disagree

1 2 3 4 5 6 7   There is too much violence on TV.

1 2 3 4 5 6 7   There is too much sexually explicit content on TV.

1 2 3 4 5 6 7   There is too much intolerance (e.g., racist, sexist, anti-gay, or anti-Semitic material) on TV.

1 2 3 4 5 6 7   Viewing violent movies causes people to be violent.

1 2 3 4 5 6 7   Sexually explicit materials provide an outlet for bottled-up impulses.

1 2 3 4 5 6 7   Sexually explicit materials lead to rape.

1 2 3 4 5 6 7   Sexually explicit materials lead to the breakdown of morals.

1 2 3 4 5 6 7   The government should officially restrict blatantly violent, sexually explicit, or intolerant expression on television.

1 2 3 4 5 6 7   The media should restrict unusually violent, sexually explicit, or intolerant expression on television.

1 2 3 4 5 6 7   Unusually violent, sexually explicit, or intolerant expression should not be restricted.

1 2 3 4 5 6 7   Individuals should be free to voice their disapproval of unusually violent, sexually explicit, or intolerant material.

1 2 3 4 5 6 7   One problem with laws against offensive speech is that once certain messages are banned, any material could be banned.

1 2 3 4 5 6 7   Not censoring offensive messages puts at risk many of our cherished values.

1 2 3 4 5 6 7   Campus speech codes will not combat the problems of prejudice and insensitivity to others' beliefs.

1 2 3 4 5 6 7   Leaving censorship up to the media will guarantee that more offensive messages will be permitted.

1 2 3 4 5 6 7   Restrictions on free speech, whether by government or by media, threaten our obligation as a democratic society to protect minority views.

1 2 3 4 5 6 7   One good way to deal with racist attitudes on campuses is to encourage open discussions about racial differences.

1 2 3 4 5 6 7   Unlimited free speech carries individual rights to such an extreme that responsibilities to the community are neglected.

STATEMENT ON STUDENT PLAGIARISM*

Plagiarize: To use or pass off as one's own (the ideas or writings of another). To appropriate for use as one's own passages or ideas from (another). *(The American Heritage Dictionary)*

Derivation: Greek *plagios:* oblique, crooked, treacherous
Latin *plagium:* kidnapping

Honesty requires that any ideas or materials taken from another source for either written or oral use must be fully acknowledged. *Offering the work of another as one's own is plagiarism. Any student who fails to give credit for ideas or materials that he or she takes from another source is guilty of plagiarism.*

　　Penalties for plagiarism are often severe. Depending on the specific nature of the act, a student found guilty of plagiarism may receive an F in the course or even be dismissed from the university with a notation of the offense on his or her transcript. If you are in doubt about the legitimate use of sources for your speeches, *check with your instructor.* He or she will assist you in ensuring the originality of your ideas and avoiding subsequent confrontations and penalties.

---

* Adapted from *Handbook for Teaching Assistants*, Department of Speech Communication, Indiana University. Used by permission.

Arrangement 1

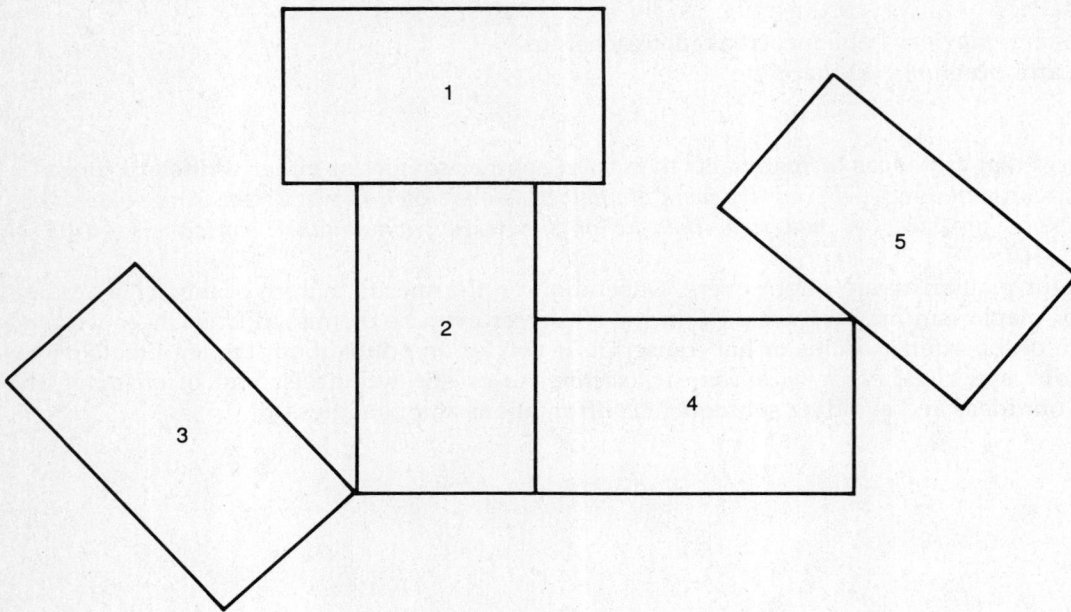

Arrangement 2

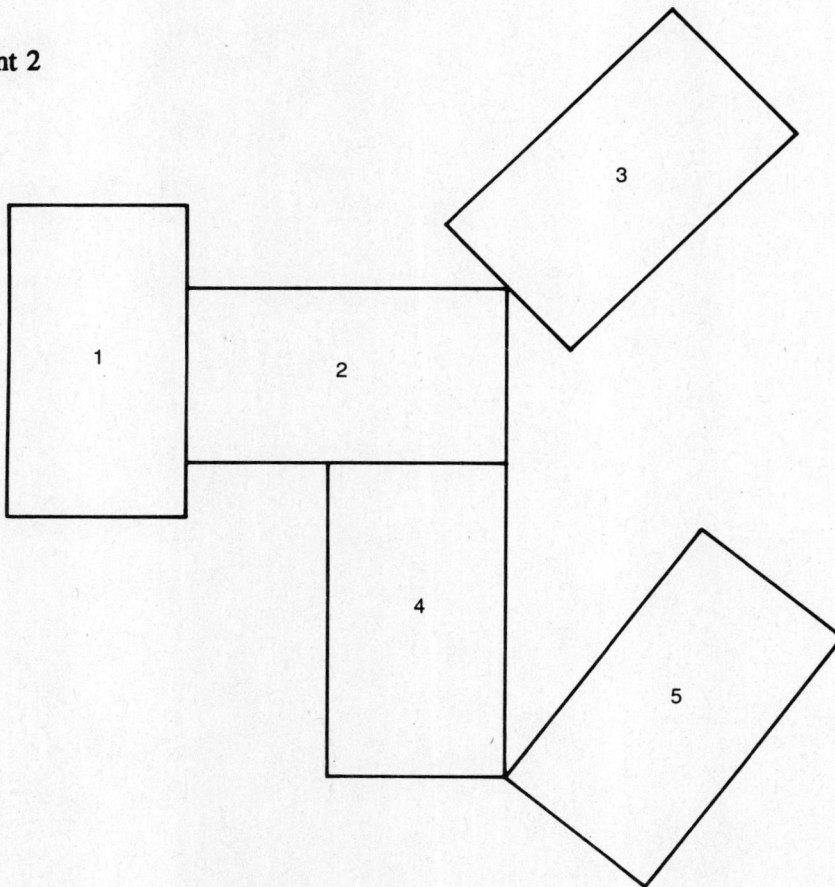

READINGS FOR ENRICHMENT

See guide to journal abbreviations on p. 37.

*Items marked with an asterisk are suitable for student enrichment.

General Background

Bitzer, Lloyd F. "Rhetoric and Public Knowledge," In *Rhetoric, Philosophy, and Literature: An Exploration,* edited by Don M. Burks, pp. 67–93. West Lafayette, Ind.: Purdue University Press, 1978.
———. "Rhetorical Public Communication." *CSMC* (Dec. 1987), 425–428.
Blumer, Jay G. "Communication and Democracy: The Crisis Beyond and the Ferment Within." *JC* (Summer 1983), 166–173.
Braden, Waldo W. "Public Address and the Humanities." *SSCJ* (Winter 1976), 151–157.
Cronkite, Gary. "On the Focus, Scope, and Coherence of the Study of Human Symbolic Activity." *QJS* (Aug. 1986), 231–246.
Curtis, Dan B., James Floyd, and Jerry L. Winsor. "A Case for Oral Communication Skills." *ACAB* (Jan. 1982), 42–44.
Dance, Frank E. X. "Speech Communication as a Liberal Arts Discipline." *CE* (Sept. 1980), 328–331.
Dannefer, Dale, and Nicholas Poushinsky. "Language and Community." *JC* (Summer 1977), 122–126.
* Dienstag, Eleanor Foa. "The Fine Art of Speaking in Public." *Working Woman* (Feb. 1986), 78–81.
Golden, James L. "Contemporary Trends and Historical Roots in Communication: A Personal View." *CCSJ* (Fall/Winter 1987), 262–270.
Goodnight, G. Thomas. "Public Discourse." *CSMC* (Dec. 1987), 428–432.
Hart, Roderick P. "Why Communication? Why Education? Toward a Politics of Teaching." *CE* (Apr. 1993), 97–105.
Hauser, Gerard A. "Features of the Public Sphere." *CSMC* (Dec. 1987), 437–441.
Havelock, Eric A. "The Coming of Literate Communication to Western Culture." *JC* (Winter 1980), 90–98.
Heath, Shirley Brice. "The Functions and Uses of Literacy." *JC* (Winter 1980), 123–133.
Hitchcock, Orville. "Public Address and Liberal Education." *CSSJ* (Fall 1976), 169–175.
Hostettler, Gordon F. "Speech as Liberal Study." *CE* (Sept. 1980), 332–347.
Jamieson, Kathleen Hall. "The Cunning Rhetori, the Complicitous Audience, The Conned Censor, and the Critic." *CM* (Mar. 1990), 73–78.
Kramer, Cheris. "Women's and Men's Ratings of Their Own and Ideal Speech." *CQ* (Spring 1978), 2–10.
Lustig, Myron W. "Theorizing About Human Communication." *CQ* (Fall 1986), 451–459.
Marlier, John T. "What Is Speech Communication Anyway?" *CE* (Sept. 1980), 324–327.
McBath, James H. "Speech Communication and Society." *WJSC* (Spring 1976), 76–82.
McBath, James H., and Robert C. Jeffrey. "Defining Speech Communication." *CE* (Sept. 1978), 181–188.
McFarland, J. L. "The Role of Speech in Self Development, Self-Concept, and Decentration." *CE* (July 1984), 231–236.
Modaff, John, and Robert Hopper. "Why Is Speech 'Basic'?" *CE* (Jan. 1984), 37–42.
* Ong, Walter. "Literacy and Orality in Our Times." *JC* (Winter 1980), 197–204.
* Osborn, Michael. "Our Communication Heritage: The Genetic Tie That Binds." *SSCJ* (Winter 1979), 147–158.
Phillips, Gerald M. "Rhetoric and the Proper Study of Man." *CE* (Sept. 1978), 189–201.
Powell, Jon T., and Donald Ary. "Communication Without Commitment." *JC* (Summer 1977), 118–121.
Robie, Harry. "Defining Communication: An Opening Experience for a Mixed Group." *SCT* (Fall 1990), 14.
Rowley, Edwin N. "More Than Mere Words." *SCT* (Fall 1992), 5.
Thompson, Wayne N. "The Implications of the Classical Concept of Rhetoric for Today's Programs in Speech Communication." *ACAB* (Oct. 1977), 11–14.

Vangelisti, Anita L., and John A. Daly. "Correlates of Speaking Skills in the United States: A National Assessment." *CE* (Apr. 1989), 132–143.

Wood, Roy V. "Keeping Communication Human." *ACAB* (Apr. 1985), 56–58.

Ethics and Responsibility

Arnett, Ronald C. "The Status of Communication Ethics Scholarship in Speech Communication Journals from 1915 to 1985." *CSSJ* (Spring 1987), 44–61. Contains an extensive bibliography on ethics.

———. "The Practical Philosophy of Communication Ethics and Free Speech as the Foundation for Speech Communication." *CQ* (Fall 1990), 208–217.

Bennett, W. Lance. "Communication and Social Responsibility." *QJS* (Aug. 1985), 259–288.

Bineham, Jeffery L. "Some Ethical Implications of Team Sports Metaphors in Politics." *CR* (Winter 1991), 35–42.

Borger, Gloria. "The Story the Pictures Didn't Tell." *U.S. News & World Report,* 22 Feb. 1993, 6–7.

Communication, 6, No. 2 (1981). Entire issue on ethical problems in various communication contexts such as small group, rhetoric, interpersonal, mass media, and intercultural.

Condit, Celeste Michelle. "Crafting Virtue: The Rhetorical Construction of Public Morality." *QJS* (Feb. 1987), 79–97.

Crossen, Cynthia. *Tainted Truth: The Manipulation of Fact in America.* New York: Simon & Schuster, 1994.

Cunningham, Stanley B. "Sorting Out the Ethics of Persuasion." *CS* (Winter 1992), 233–245.

Day, Louis A. *Ethics in Media Communication: Cases and Controversies.* Belmont, Calif.: Wadsworth, 1991.

Denton, Robert E., ed. *Ethical Dimensions of Political Communication.* New York: Praeger. 1991.

Eubanks, Ralph T. "Reflections on the Moral Dimension of Communication." *SSCJ* (Spring 1980), 297–312.

Herrick, James A. "Rhetoric, Ethics, and Virtue." *CS* (Fall 1992), 133–149.

Jaska, James A., and Michael S. Pritchard. *Communication Ethics: Methods of Analysis,* 2nd ed. Belmont, Calif.: Wadsworth, 1994.

Jensen, J. Vernon. "Ethics in Speech Communication: Focus on Minnesota." *The Speech Association of Minnesota Journal* (1985), 1–10.

———. "Teaching Ethics in Speech Communication." *CE* (Oct. 1985), 324–330.

———. *Ethics in Human Communication,* 3rd ed. Prospect Heights, Ill.: Waveland, 1990.

Johannesen, Richard L. "Teaching Ethical Standards for Discourse." *Journal of Education* (Spring 1980), 5–20.

* Katz, Stephen B. "The Ethics of Expediency: Classical Rhetoric, Technology, and the Holocaust." *College English* (1992), 255–275.

* Kramer, Michael. "Time to Stop Shouting." *Time,* 1 May 1995, p. 66.

* Mallon, Thomas. *Stolen Words: Forays into the Origins and Ravages of Plagiarism.* New York: Penguin, 1991.

McCaleb, Joseph L., and Kevin W. Dean. "Ethics and Communication Education: Empowering Teachers." *CE* (Oct. 1987), 410–416.

McGuire, Michael. "The Ethics of Rhetoric: The Morality of Knowledge." *SSCJ* (Winter 1980), 133–148.

* Nyberg, David. *The Varnished Truth: Truth Telling and Deceiving in Ordinary Life.* Chicago: University of Chicago Press, 1993.

* Posner, Ari. "The Culture of Plagiarism." *New Republic,* 18 Apr. 1988, pp. 19+.

Rice, George P. Jr. "Do We Need a Code of Ethics?" *ACAB* (Oct. 1976), 77–13.

* Shapiro, Walter. "Lies, Lies, Lies: How to Tell if a Politician Is Lying." *Time,* 5 Oct. 1992, p. 38.

Sproule, J. Michael. "Whose Ethics in the Classroom? An Historical Overview." *CE* (Oct. 1987), 317–326.

Freedom of Expression

Anderson, Rob. "Exploring Student Rights in Speech Communication Classes." *CE* (Jan. 1978), 47–52.

Beall, Melissa L. "Censorship and Self-Censorship: A Problem in the Schools." *CE* (Oct. 1987), 313–316.

Bosmajian, Haig A. "Freedom of Speech and the Language of Oppression." *WJSC* (Fall 1978), 209–221.

* Bozell, L. Brent, III. "Incisive 'Deep Truth'?" *Washington Times,* 18 July 1993, p. B4.

Eich, Ritch K., and Charles M. Feldman. "Suppression of Expression: Rights in Jeopardy." *CSSJ* (Fall 1976), 225–229.

* Haiman, Franklyn S. "Erosions of the First Amendment: A Challenge to Speech Communication." *Free Speech Yearbook* (1986), 1–10.

* McGaffey, Ruth. "Freedom of Speech for the Ideas We Hate: Nongovernmental Abridgment of Freedom of Expression." *Free Speech Yearbook* (1987), 90–103.

Medhurst, Martin J. "The First Amendment vs. Human Rights: A Case Study in Community Sentiment and Argument from Definition." *WJSC* (Winter 1982), 1–19.

* O'Neil, Robert M. "An Inquiry into the Legal and Ethical Problems of Campus Hate Speech." In *Free Speech Yearbook: 1991,* edited by Raymond S. Rogers, pp. 26–30. Carbondale, Ill.: Southern Illinois University Press, 1991.

*Sakharov, Andrei. "Censored: Excerpts from Memoirs." *Time,* 14 May 1990, pp. 47+.

Smolla, Rodney M. *Free Speech in an Open Society.* New York: Random House, 1992.

Sunstein, Cass R. *Democracy and the Problem of Free Speech.* New York: Free Press, 1993.

* "Targeting the Radios," *Washington Times,* 11 Mar. 1993, p. G2.

Tedford, Thomas L. *Freedom of Speech in the United States,* 2nd ed. New York: McGraw-Hill, 1993.

Walker, Samuel. *Hate Speech: The History of an American Controversy.* Lincoln, Neb.: University of Nebraska Press, 1994.

The Communication Process

Clement, Donald A., and Kenneth D. Frandsen. "On Conceptual and Empirical Treatments of Feedback in Human Communication." *CM* (Mar. 1976), 11–28.

Cusella, Louis P. "The Effects of Feedback Source, Message, and Receiver Characteristics on Intrinsic Motivation." *CQ* (Summer 1984), 211–221.

Fisher, B. Aubrey, Thomas W. Glover, and Donald G. Ellis. "The Nature of Complex Communication Systems." *CM* (Aug. 1977), 231–240.

Frandsen, Kenneth D., and Michael A. Millis. "On Conceptual, Theoretical and Empirical Treatments of Feedback in Human Communication." *CR* (Summer 1993), 79–91.

Practical Applications of Public Speaking Skills

Berko, Roy M. "Adult Literacy and Lifelong Learning: A Communicative Perspective." In *Rationale Kit: Information Supporting the Speech Communication Discipline and Its Programs.* Annandale, Va.: Speech Communication Association, 1994.

* Book, Cassandra L. "Student Leadership: Improvement Through Communication Skills." *CE* (Sept. 1977), 237–240.

Cohen, Jodi R. "The Relevance of a Course in Public Speaking." *SCT* (Winter 1988), 14–15.

Curtis, Dan B., Jerry L. Winsor, and Ronald D. Stephens. "National Preferences in Business and Communication Education. " *CE* (Jan. 1989), 6–14.

DiSalva, Vincent, David C. Larsen, and William J. Seiler. "Communication Skills Needed by Persons in Business Organizations." *CE* (Nov. 1976), 269–275.

Ford, Wendy, S. Zabava, and Andrew D. Wolvin. "The Differential Impact of a Basic Communication Course on Perceived Competencies in Class, Work, and Social Contexts." *CE* (July 1993), 215–223.

Hanna, Michael S. "Speech Communication Training Needs in the Business Community." *CSSJ* (Fall 1978), 163–172.

Johnson, John R., and Nancy Szczupakiewicz. "The Public Speaking Course: Is It Preparing Students with Work Related Public Speaking Skills?" *CE* (Apr. 1987), 131–137.

Rubin, Rebecca B., and Elizabeth E. Graham. "Communication Correlates of College Success: An Explanatory Investigation." *CE* (Jan. 1988), 14–27.

Trank, Douglas M., and Joe M. Steele, "Measurable Effects of a Communication Skills Course: An Initial Study." *CE* (Apr. 1983), 227–236.

Communicating in a Diverse Society

Axtell, Roger E. *Gestures: The Do's and Taboos of Body Language Around the World.* New York: Wiley, 1991.

Bowser, Benjamin P., Gale S. Auletta and Terry Jones. *Confronting Diversity Issues on Campus.* Newbury Park, Calif.: Sage, 1993.

Brunson, Deborah A. "A Perceptual Awareness Exercise in Interracial Communication." *SCT* (Fall 1994), 2–4.

Donald, J., and A. Rattansi, eds. *'Race,' Culture, and Difference.* Newbury Park, Calif.: Sage, 1992.

Ekachai, Daradirek "Gee." "Diversity Icebreaker." *SCT* (Spring 1996), 14–15.

Garbowitz, Fred. "Changing Classroom Populations Call for Increased Cultural Sensitivity." *SCT* (Summer 1990), 13–14.

Gleason, Philip. *Speaking of Diversity: Language and Ethnicity in Twentieth-Century America.* Baltimore: Johns Hopkins University Press, 1992.

Gonzalez, Alberto, Marsha Houston, and Victoria Glen, eds. *Our Voices: Essays in Culture, Ethnicity, and Communication.* Los Angeles: Roxbury, 1994.

Hankins, Gail Armstead. "Don't Judge a Book by Its Cover." *SCT* (Summer 1991), 8.

Hochel, Sandra. "An Exercise in Understanding Ethnocentrism," *SCT* (Summer 1994), 10–11.

Johnson, Scott D. "Exploring the Influences of Culture on Small Groups." *SCT* (Winter 1995), 6–7.

Kaye, Tom. "Respecting Others' Point of View." *SCT* (Spring 1990), 12.

Kidder, Rushworth M. *Shared Values for a Troubled World: Conversations with Men and Women of Conscience.* San Francisco: Jossey-Bass, 1994.

Klopf, Donald W. *Intercultural Encounters: The Fundamentals of Intercultural Communication,* 2nd ed. Englewood, Colo.: Morton, 1991.

Klopf, Donald W., and Catherine A. Thompson. *Communication in the Multicultural Classroom.* Edina, Minn.: Burgess, 1992.

* "The New Face of America." Special Issue of *Time,* Fall 1993.

Nieto, Sonia. *Affirming Diversity: The Sociopolitical Context of Multicultural Education.* New York: Longman, 1992.

Schlesinger, Arthur M. *The Disuniting of America: Reflections on a Multicultural Society.* New York: Norton, 1993.

Spicer, Karin-Leigh. "Stereotypes and Appearances." *SCT* (Winter 1995), 10.

Summerfield, E. *Crossing Cultures Through Film.* Yarmouth, Me.: Intercultural Press, 1993.

Walter, Suzanne. "Experiences in Intercultural Communication." *SCT* (Summer 1995), 1–3.

Wood, Julia. "Diversity and Commonality: Sustaining Their Tension in Communication Courses." *WJC* (Summer 1993), 367–380.

Yook, Eunkyong Lee. "Students Creating Intercultural Sensitizers: Storytelling and Attribution." *SCT* (Spring 1996), 11–12.

Pedagogy

Auer, J. Jeffrey. "Creating an Extra and 'Real Life' Public Speaking Assignment." *SCT* (Spring 1991), 3.

Boatman, Sara A. "Introducing Communication Resources." *SCT* (Summer 1995), 7–8.

Dwyer, Karen Kangas. "Group Mini-Speeches: Experiential and Cooperative Learning in the Public Speaking Course." *SCT* (Summer 1994), 15.

Fackler, Mark. "My First Public Speaking Class: An Oral Culture Adventure." *SCT* (Spring 1991), 6–7.

George, Don. "Peer Support in Speech Preparation." *SCT* (Spring 1993), 4–5.

Gorg, Robert. "The Use of Model Speeches on Videotapes (or See, Your Friends Can Do This Too!)." *SCT* (Fall 1993), 11–12.

Hayward, Pamela A. "Getting It Right the First Time: An Exploration of Instructor Beliefs and Strategies for the First Day of Class." Paper presented at the National Conference on the Training and Employment of Graduate Teaching Assistants, 1993; available through ERIC.

Hertzog, Robert L. "Active Learning in the Basic Public Speaking Course." *SCT* (Winter 1992), 8.

Menzel, Kent E., and Lori J. Carrell. "The Relationship Between Preparation and Performance in Public Speaking." *CE* (Jan. 1994), 16–17.

Mohsen, Raed A. "Out on Campus: A Challenging Public Speaking Experience." *SCT* (Summer 1993), 10–11.

Nevins, Randi J., and Cassandra L. Book. "The Gift of Oration for the Gifted and Talented." *SCT* (Spring 1991), 4, 5.

Schwartz, Omar. "Exercises in Critical Pedagogy for the Basic Communication Course." *SCT* (Winter 1996), 11–12.

Smagorinsky, Peter, and Pamela K. Fly. "The Social Environment of the Classroom: A Vygotskian Perspective on Small Group Process." *CE* (Apr. 1993), 159–171.

Smith, Lindsley F., and Peter M. Kellett, "Self-Directed Teams in the Classroom." *SCT* (Fall 1995), 14–15.

Stoebig, Joe. "Speech Logs with a Twist." *SCT* (Spring 1992), 13.

Will, Tony. "Empowering the Student." *SCT* (Summer 1994), 14–15.

CHAPTER 2
Your First Speech

OBJECTIVES

- To provide your students with a speaking opportunity early in the term.

- To teach students how to manage the impressions they make as speakers.

- To teach students how to develop and present an introductory speech.

- To teach students how to develop an effective introduction, body, and conclusion for a speech.

- To show students how to compose outlines for their first speeches.

- To teach basic presentation skills.

- To provide students with some guidelines for dealing with communication apprehension.

SUGGESTIONS FOR TEACHING

Instructors who schedule first speeches early in the term face the challenge of teaching their students enough about public speaking in a few class periods to get them through their first oral assignment. This chapter previews the basic areas of preparing and presenting effective speeches, and takes your students step by step through an introductory speaking assignment. We offer a variety of activities to teach the fundamentals of topic selection, structuring, outlining, presenting, and critiquing short speeches.

We suggest that you establish "peer-review" teams of students to work on one another's ideas for speaking assignments. We also suggest that you get your students in front of the class for ungraded speaking activities (for which there are plenty of suggestions in this chapter) as often as possible. You should try to critique their speaking skills early in the course so that they will know what they need to work on for their major assignments. You should also give them some understanding of how their speeches will be evaluated and graded. They deserve a written critique along with suggestions for improvement after their first major speeches. You might make the grades on these first speeches of minimal importance or give the students the option of dropping the grades afterwards so that you can critique them thoroughly without doing too much damage.

Having said this, do not go easy in terms of grades on the first round. You can always ease up as the semester wears on, but it is unfair to suddenly get more demanding. If you expect quality work, you need to make that clear from the start.

For most students, actual experience in speaking is the best cure for nervousness. Many of them (more than will admit it) will be experiencing feelings of anxiety, as they are not accustomed to addressing more than three to five people at a time. Let them know that this nervousness is normal and can be channeled into an effective presentation, and that a jittery first speech will not result in a failing grade. Students should focus their nervous energy into preparation and practice. Other activities included in the text can help them through the process of visualizing successful presentations and the cognitive restructuring of negative thoughts. As an instructor, you should remember that acute communication apprehension is a valid and well-documented phobia that warrants sensitivity on your part. You can help by getting your students to interact and become familiar with one another through various course-related activities early in the course.

CHAPTER OUTLINE

I. Speeches of self-introduction can help foster a supportive classroom environment, help students become familiar with one another, give them a first chance to establish their credibility as a source of ideas, and teach practical skills that may help them make favorable first impressions at job interviews and social gatherings. *(text p. 36)*

II. *Ethos* is based upon audience perceptions of a speaker's competence, integrity, likability, and forcefulness. *(text pp. 37–41)*
   A. Competence relates to perceptions of a speaker's relevant knowledge, intelligence, and preparation. Speakers can enhance this by:
      1. choosing topics they know and citing personal experience.
      2. doing sufficient research and citing authoritative sources.
      3. delivering well-organized, appropriately worded, and thoroughly practiced speeches.
   B. Speakers who convey integrity appear ethical, honest, and dependable. Enhanced integrity is related to audience perceptions that speakers are:
      1. straightforward, responsible, and concerned for the consequences of their words.
      2. addressing all sides of an issue before advancing their own positions.
      3. personally committed and willing to follow their own advice.
      4. competent in their knowledge of the issue at hand.
   C. Speakers who convey likability radiate a sense of warmth and good will that inspires audience affection.
      1. Smiles, eye contact, and self-directed humor can enhance perceptions of likability.
      2. True likability results only when a speaker truly cares for his or her audience and is willing to adapt to their needs and concerns.
      3. Perceived likability can help to establish identification, or feelings of closeness or sharing between speakers and their audiences that can transcend cultural barriers. Speakers can enhance identification by:
         a. cultivating a natural, conversational presentation style.
         b. speaking and dressing in a formal yet nonextravagant way.
         c. making references to shared stories, experiences, and values.
   D. The perception of forcefulness makes speakers appear confident, decisive, and enthusiastic.
      1. Speakers should seek to appear confident, even when they do not feel that way.
      2. While they should weigh all the options, speakers do not want to appear ambiguous as to where they stand and why.
      3. Speakers can enhance perceived enthusiasm by animating face, voice, and gestures.

III. The first assignment in a public speaking course may be a speech of introduction. *(text pp. 41–46)*
   A. Speeches of introduction should tell the audience something unique and interesting about the speaker or person being introduced, and avoid either simply relating a few superficial facts or trying to tell a complete life story.
   B. Students may discover ideas for self-introductory speeches by conducting a self-awareness inventory.
      1. Is your cultural background the most important thing about you?
      2. Is the most important thing about you the environment in which you grew up?

       3.   Was there some particular person who had a major impact on your life?

       4.   Have you been marked by some unusual experience?

       5.   Are you best characterized by an activity that brings meaning to your life?

       6.   Is the work you do a major factor in making you who you are?

       7.   Are you best characterized by your goals or purpose in life?

       8.   Are you best described by some value that you hold dear?

IV. First presentations (self-introductions, descriptions, supporting a point) should be carefully planned and structured for simplicity and brevity. *(text pp. 46–51)*

    A. The keys to success in your first speech are to select your topic, decide on your purpose, focus what you want to say, and determine the design that is best suited for developing the speech.

       1. A design for arranging the main points of a speech should be suggested by the speaker's topic, purpose, and main ideas.

          a. Categorical designs develop related points in a way that advances an overall purpose and idea.

          b. Sequential designs cover events in the actual time sequence in which they occur.

          c. Causation designs can help to explain the meaning and influence of something.

    B. A well-chosen topic should suggest strategies for introductions, bodies, and conclusions.

       1. Introductions should arouse interest, orient and preview audiences, and help establish rapport between speakers and listeners.

          a. Speakers should not prepare the introduction until they have completed the body of a speech.

       2. A speech's body is its most important part because it develops the speaker's main ideas.

          a. Short speeches should not develop more than two or three main points.

          b. Each main point should be developed with some form(s) of supporting material— facts and figures, testimony, examples, or narratives.

             (1) Examples and narratives are especially effective in introductory speeches because they promote feelings of closeness between speaker and audience.

       3. Conclusions usually offer a summary statement of the speaker's main ideas, and concluding remarks provide the message with a sense of closure.

V. Outlining can help speakers organize their ideas and information. *(text pp. 51–52)*

    A. Formal outlines should demonstrate how the major parts of a speech (introduction, thesis statement, main ideas, supporting materials, transitions, and conclusion) fit together.

       1. Main points and subpoints should be written as complete sentences to help organize thoughts.

       2. Thesis statements, introductions, and conclusions should be written out as they will be presented in order to facilitate a smooth presentation.

    B. Key-word outlines are good for practice and presentation.

       1. Ideas and cues should be written as key words or phrases to prompt the speaker's memory.

VI. Effective presentations spotlight ideas and come across as if the speaker is interacting with the audience, not reading or reciting from memory. *(text pp. 52–55)*

    A. Speakers should strive to spotlight ideas as they express them.

    B. Speakers should present their messages in a natural or extemporaneous fashion.

       1. *Extemporaneous speaking* emphasizes careful preparation and practice, but not memorizing or writing speeches word for word.

       2. Audience interaction is more desirable than exact wording.

    C. Speakers should make their actual presentations using key-word outlines or note cards, and never from formal outlines or written manuscripts.

    D. Speakers should practice thoroughly, first from full and then from key-word outlines.

       1. Speakers should practice their entire presentations, working in gestures, movements, vocal flexibility, pauses, eye contact, and other forms of anticipated interaction with an imaginary audience.

2. Students who use lecterns should place their notes high on its surface and be conscious of maintaining eye contact with their audiences.

VII. Almost all public speakers experience some degree of communication anxiety. *(text pp. 55–58)*
   A. Nervousness occurs because public speaking occasions are highly significant, and most people lack familiarity with the experience.
   B. Nervousness is desirable in that it conveys respect for the speaking situation, and students can learn to channel it into positive energy.
   C. The following suggestions, used in combination, can help students channel nervous energy into an effective presentation:
      1. Deep breathing and relaxation exercises.
      2. The identification and cognitive restructuring of negative thoughts.
      3. Visualizing themselves successfully presenting their speeches.
      4. Selecting topics they know and find interesting and/or important.
      5. Using presentation aids that prompt gestures that can help release nervous energy.
      6. Thorough practice.
      7. Developing a positive attitude toward listeners as positive and supportive.
      8. Acting confident, even when they do not feel that way.
         (1) Students should not open their speeches with pleas for audience sympathy.
      9. Maintaining eye contact throughout their presentations.
      10. Focusing on their messages, and not on themselves.
   D. Audience members can help create a positive environment by listening attentively and constructively.

USING END-OF-CHAPTER ITEMS

Discussion *(text pp. 59–60)*

1. **Although we have defined ethos in terms of public speakers, other communicators also seek to create favorable impressions of competence, integrity, likableness, and forcefulness. Advertisers always try to create favorable ethos for their products. Bring to class print advertisements to demonstrate each of the four dimensions of ethos we have discussed. Explain how each ad uses ethos.**

   You might have your students find appropriate ads for homework, or select them and bring them to class yourself. Break your students into small groups to critique and evaluate one another's ads in terms of the four dimensions of ethos. Ads presenting "experts" (actors playing doctor or financial wizard) seek to create favorable impressions of competence, whereas ads sporting celebrity endorsements rely more on likability and associated popularity. Which dimensions of ethos do your students' ads rely most heavily on, and how might similar appeals be used in public speaking? If you ask students to bring advertisements to class, remind them not to deface library materials.

2. **Select a prominent public speaker and analyze his or her ethos. On which dimensions is this speaker especially strong or weak? How does this affect the person's leadership ability? Present your analysis for class discussion.**

   This works well as a homework assignment or a small-group activity followed by general class discussion to get your students thinking about the ethos of contemporary public figures. Using the chalkboard, construct a chart with selected names across the top and the four dimensions of ethos down the left side. Break your students into small groups and have them rate each figure as very negative (1), negative (2), positive (3), very positive (4), or neutral (x) on each dimension. They should then present and justify their ratings. Try to move the class to a consensus for each rating.

Explore reasons (such as political and cultural differences) for differing ratings on each dimension. A sample ethos chart follows:

	Carol Moseley-Braun	Boris Yeltsin	Newt Gingrich	Bill Clinton
Competence	3	3	3	3
Integrity	4	3	4	2
Likability	4	2	4	3
Forcefulness	3	2	3	3

As an alternative, show a videotaped contemporary speech, and discuss the way speeches themselves can influence perceptions of ethos. Have students assess the speaker's ethos before and after the viewing and focus discussion on how viewing the speech changed their perceptions of the speaker's competence, integrity, likability, and forcefulness.

3. **Political ads often do the work of introducing candidates to the public and disparaging their opponents. Study the television ads in connection with a recent political campaign. Bring to class answers to the following questions:**

   a. **What kinds of positive and negative identities do the ads establish?**
   b. **Which of these ads are most and least effective in creating the desired ethos? Why?**
   c. **Which of the Self-awareness Inventory questions discussed in this chapter might explain how the candidates are introduced?**

Instructors should videotape political ads for use in this in-class exercise. Look especially for "attack" ads and mini-biographies of new candidates. There was a short film aired at the 1992 Democratic convention entitled "The Man From Hope" intended to improve Bill Clinton's ethos and increase the American people's familiarity with him that would be perfect for this exercise. As an alternative, bring political brochures that serve similar functions. Break your students into small groups and have them consider contrasting images of candidates and their opponents with regard to the four dimensions of ethos—competence, integrity, likability, and forcefulness. Which dimensions do candidates project when they cite qualifications such as personal experience and past accomplishments (military, business, academic, athletic); a modest background and values such as family, religion, and hard work; past political leaders and other personal heroes; identification with "common" people and culture; and, in general, an image of active and tireless leadership?

Consider which ads your students find most effective and why. Compare the techniques these ads use with those that were less effective, and speculate on how the latter ones might be improved. As an alternative, evaluate the ads or brochures using the Self-awareness Inventory questions from the text (see p. 46). Do any of them mention the candidate's cultural background, his or her childhood environment, a person that influenced his or her life, unusual life-shaping experiences, some activity that is especially meaningful to the candidate, work experience to establish competence, central goals and life purposes, or important values? How might these factors relate to the candidate's overall impression of ethos?

Application *(text pp. 60–63)*

1. **As the introductory speeches are presented in your class, build a collection of "word portraits" of your classmates as revealed by their speeches. At the end of the assignment, analyze these "bios" to see what you have learned about the class as a whole. What kind of topics do they prefer? Did you detect any strong political or social attitudes to which you might have to adjust?**

Submit one copy of your analysis to your instructor, and keep another for your own use in preparing later speeches.

Instruct your students to take notes on their classmates' introductory speeches and the discussions that follow. Have them review their notes after the opening round of speeches, listing the topics that they found the most interesting or that generated the most discussion, the types of supporting materials (examples, narratives, facts and figures, testimony) that seemed to work best, and the attitudes or values that emerged as important to the class as a whole. Compile and distribute this information for class discussion. Focus the discussion on common social or political attitudes, areas of common interest, and possible topic ideas for future speeches.

2. **Prepare a full outline of your speech of introduction. On an attached page, identity the design you are using and discuss why this design is most appropriate. Turn in a copy of your outline and this rationale to your instructor.**

This works well as homework in preparation for the first speaking assignment. Duplicate and distribute the "Outline Format for a Self-Introductory Speech" on p. 93 to help students structure their presentations, or have them use the computer software program, "Speech Designer." Evaluate these first outlines in terms of the body's structural clarity, the use of supporting materials (examples and narratives), introductions and conclusions, and appropriate format (symbols and indention, etc.).

3. **Identify any negative messages you might send yourself concerning public speaking. How might you change these messages, using the principles of cognitive restructuring?**

Use this for homework and class discussion, or on an individual basis with students who experience severe communication anxiety. Have your students volunteer their negative thoughts, and solicit positive reconstructions from the students who expressed the negative thoughts or from the class as a whole. If you are concerned that students may be inhibited in volunteering their concerns, have them submit these concerns anonymously in writing for class discussion. To break the ice, you might offer a sample concern, such as "Everyone will notice how nervous I am," or discuss your own experiences with communication anxiety (surely you have had some!).

You might note that effective cognitive restructuring also corresponds with the process of visualization described in this chapter. By using this application, you can help make your students aware that, in fact, most of them are at least a little nervous about giving their first presentations, and that they are not alone. Instructors can help facilitate constructive cognitive restructuring by emphasizing early in the term that they do not expect novice speakers to look "slick" in their early speaking experiences, that nervousness is both expected and natural, and that a jittery first presentation will not necessarily mean a low grade.

4. **To help you visualize yourself succeeding as a speaker, write a script in which you describe specific details of an ideal experience of speaking. Start with getting up in the morning on the day of your speech to the moments of satisfaction after you have concluded. Once you have completed your script, relax, concentrate on it, and bring it to life in your mind. As a model both for your own script and for your mental enactment of it, consider the following script and instructions for an informative speech developed by Professors Joe Ayers and Theodore S. Hopf.** *[see text pp. 60–61].*

This can be an effective homework activity in preparation for the first speech—especially for dealing with communication apprehension. The process of "going through the numbers" and visualizing a successful presentation is an inherent part of preparing an effective speech. You might review the concept of cognitive restructuring with your students in preparation for this exercise. To compel students to go through the process of visualization in preparation for their first speeches, take up their scripts and give them a quick pass or fail evaluation.

ADDITIONAL ACTIVITIES

Creating a Supportive Classroom Climate

Purpose: To create a supportive, cooperative climate in the classroom.

Directions: Divide the class into small groups or peer-review teams of four to five students who will work together throughout the semester in and/or out of class. Encourage them to exchange phone numbers and to help one another with their speeches by

- Generating topic ideas and checking them for audience adaptation
- Reviewing design plans and outlines
- Serving as practice audiences

We encourage you to break your students into such groups in preparation for every major assignment. This should also offer some help with restructuring negative messages for those who develop the last-minute jitters. Impress upon students that the feedback they get may help them fine-tune and improve their presentations even if they already feel relatively comfortable with them. Consider reserving the last class session before the first speech for team presentations, allowing students one last chance to practice before familiar faces and obtain critical feedback without having to worry about grades. Refer the groups to the "Practice Presentation Feedback Form" (p. 94) to guide their critiques and suggestions.

Exploring Ethos

Purpose: To offer students an opportunity to explore the concept of ethos as it applies to organizations, groups, and products as well as to individuals.

Directions: This works well as a homework assignment followed by group discussion. Select about four recent situations in which a group, product, or organization had its reputation tarnished by an unfortunate accident or occurrence. The Tylenol poisonings, the Exxon Valdez oil spill, the Tonya Harding incident, and the Valujet airplane crash are the types of situations you should look for. Assign the students to groups, and have each group work on a particular incident. Have each student find, copy, and summarize two newspaper or newsmagazine accounts of the incident and the way the organization attempted to cope with it. Students should make copies of their summaries for the other members of their group. When the class reconvenes, have the groups discuss the aspects of ethos that were damaged by the incident, what steps were taken to restore ethos, and whether or not these were successful. After the small-group discussion, the class should reconvene as a whole for the groups to report on their conclusions.

Outlining Practice

Purpose: To provide your students an opportunity to practice outlining before their first graded assignment.

Directions: This exercise can be a homework assignment or a group discussion activity. Distribute the "Outline Format for a Self-Introductory Speech," p. 93. Review some basic concepts of outlining, such as outlining the body of the speech first and ensuring that the introduction and conclusion fit with the rest of the speech. Have each student (or group) complete a preparation outline on one of the following topics: "Registering for Classes," "Finding a Parking Place on Campus," "Adjusting to Living with a Roommate," "My First Adventure on my Own," or "How I Plan to Deal with Communication Apprehension." Focus discussion on evaluating introductions and conclusions, thematic statements, the relation of main points to the central idea, and the use of supporting materials with each main point.

The Speech I Liked Best

Purpose: To get your students to begin systematically evaluating their classmates' presentations from the first round of graded speeches.

Directions: In preparation for the first round of speeches, inform your students that they will be expected to write a one- to two-page paper on the speech (not their own) that makes the biggest impression on them. Emphasize that these papers will not influence their classmates' grades in any way. Push your students to engage the ideas in Chapter 3 on what makes an effective speech. Why did they like this particular speech more than those presented by other classmates? Was it the presentation? Was it the speaker's main points or their effective organization? What, in general, do they feel they learned about this speaker? How did the speech work to develop ethos in terms of competence, integrity, likability, and forcefulness? For an alternative, assign each student a specific classmate to evaluate, and have them share their constructive comments with each other in addition to your own oral and written critiques.

Evaluating Ethos in Student Speeches

Purpose: To give your students an opportunity to evaluate student speeches in terms of the four major categories of ethos.

Directions: It can be difficult for students to grasp the significance of ethos without reflecting on the reasons for their own responses to actual speeches. You might use this as a follow-up to a short mini-lecture on the major components of ethos—competence, integrity, likability, and forcefulness. Show videotapes of introductory speeches and have your students evaluate them in terms of these categories. Ask them to first recognize their own intuitive responses, then consider the speeches in terms of the discussion of ethos in the text. As an alternative, show videotapes of speeches by contemporary popular and political figures and discuss them in terms of the same four categories.

Critiquing a Self-Introductory Speech

Purpose: To give your students an opportunity to apply basic concepts of organizational structure to the critique of an actual student's speech.

Directions: This works well for homework or as a small-group activity. Have your students prepare rough outlines of the main ideas of one of the self-introductory speeches provided in the text. They should consider whether the speech seems to flow smoothly, and why or why not. How might the structure have been improved? What type of supporting material does the speaker use? Is this supporting material used effectively? Have your students prepare a one-paragraph written statement in response to these questions as the basis for in-class discussion. Use that discussion to introduce such concepts as the basic design strategies; symmetry; the functions of introductions, transitions, and conclusions; an ideal model of supporting information; etc. The following material is based on the self-introductory speech by Sandra Baltz, which may be found at the end of Chapter 2 in the text. Additional texts of self-introductory speeches may be found in Appendix B of the text.

Sample Outline of "MY THREE CULTURES," by Sandra Baltz

Introduction

Attention-arousing and Orienting Material:
   A. Opens with a story from a local newspaper that illustrates a typical lack of understanding of Middle Eastern cultural traditions.
   B. Arabic proverb spoken in Spanish that explains the misunderstanding.

Thematic Statement: My life is unique because of my Middle Eastern–Central American–American family background.

Body

Main Point 1: There were many advantages to being raised in this tricultural background.
   A. Speaking both Spanish and English made getting A's in high school Spanish easy.
   B. Being bilingual made travel to Central America more rewarding.
   C. Being bilingual should help me in my career as a doctor.

Main Point 2: There were also some disadvantages to being raised in this tricultural environment.
   A. I picked up my mother's accent as well as her language.
   B. Family reunions were confusing.

Conclusion

Summary Statement: Being exposed to three different cultures has been rewarding.
   A. It has made a difference in the music I enjoy.
   B. It has influenced the food I eat.
   C. It has helped me understand and appreciate my own culture.

Concluding Remarks:
   A. *Adios* and *allak konn ma'eck*
   B. Good-bye and may God go with you.

Sandra's speech has a clear structure with two main points: the advantages and disadvantages of her multicultural background. One plausible criticism that many students may make is that she takes a long time getting to a preview statement, and hence the listener is forced to wait for a while before being able to assess her central point and purpose. But Sandra's speech is genuinely creative and interesting, and in the end she keeps our attention long enough to make her point clear. You might tell your class that this is a combination of a topical and a comparison-and-contrast design. That is, her speech implicitly contrasts her multicultural qualities with the monoculturalism typified by the reporter's ethnocentric comments. Sandra's main ideas are supported with short, personal narratives and examples, which constitutes an appropriate model of support for an introductory speech. Finally, her use of self-directed humor helps to make her more human and attractive.

Impromptu and Short Speaking Activities

Purpose: To provide your students with opportunities to make ungraded presentations before the same class audience they will address in their formal speeches. A round or two of ungraded speaking activities early in the semester can greatly improve the quality of a first round of speeches. Offer oral critiques of each presentation, focusing on the organization of messages and the speaker's presentation skills. Push your students to spotlight their ideas, improve their voice and gestures, and maintain eye contact with their audience. For more advanced speaking activities, see Chapter 11. Emphasize strengths as well as weaknesses, and always offer suggestions for improvement.

What is it?

Directions: Bring a grab bag containing pictures of common objects glued on index cards. Be sure to have about ten more pictures than you have students. Have each student draw three cards from the bag, select one, and return the remaining two to the bag. Give students about ten minutes to sort and organize their ideas before presenting a one- to two-minute description of their objects without using their common names. The audience should try to identify the object upon completion of each speech. Solicit comments from the audience on why the speech was or was not effective at describing the object, and how it might have been made more effective.

Brown Bag Introduction*

Directions: This works well as a first-day speaking activity. Visual aids can sometimes help students overcome initial communication apprehension. This exercise allows students to make their first presentations using a visual aid and offers them a way to structure their self-introductions. At the beginning of class, give each student a small brown lunch bag as he or she enters the room. Let them wonder about the purpose of the bag as you go over your syllabus and assignments. At the end of the class, tell your students that during the next two class meetings, they should be prepared to tell the class how they view themselves. To do this, they should place three or four items inside the paper bag (using a larger one if necessary). Suggest some typical items—a floppy disk for a computer whiz; an employee badge from work; a picture of a best friend, child, or spouse; a bag of M&Ms for a "chocaholic," etc. Beginning with the next class meeting, have students make two- to three-minute presentations at the front of the room, using the objects in the bag and explaining how they are descriptive of the way(s) they see themselves.

Anything But Human

Directions: This exercise can help with communication apprehension, especially the added trauma some students experience when asked to speak about themselves in front of a large group. Inform your students that they will be making a short (no more then two minutes) impromptu presentation using the following format:

  A. If I could be anything other than human, I would like to be a(n) _____.

  B. Explain why you would like to be a(n) _____.

  C. Tell us what this reveals about you as a person.

Discuss the similarities and differences among students, exploring what gets revealed about the attitudes and values of the class.

Sharing Feelings Speech**

Directions: This exercise was developed to help students use self-disclosure to reduce communication apprehension due to lack of familiarity or identification with an audience. For homework preceding this exercise, have your students prepare a one- to two-minute presentation on a poem, piece of literature, song, or some other form of expression that they find personally meaningful. They should begin by introducing the material and reading choice selections. They should then explain their personal reactions and solicit comments from the audience as to what similar or different feelings or impressions the material evokes in them. Impress upon your students the need for honesty and the value of sharing feelings for promoting identification with audiences and dealing with communication apprehension.

---

* Adapted with permission from an exercise developed by Trudy L. Hanson, West Texas State University.

** Adapted from Robert S. Littlefield and Timothy L. Sellnow, "The Use of Self-Disclosure as a Means for Reducing Stage Fright in Beginning Speakers," *CE* (Jan. 1987), 62, by permission of the Speech Communication Association.

Introducing a Classmate

Directions: This can be a fun icebreaker for the first class period. In addition to helping increase familiarity and curb communication apprehension, it can help instructors teach the basics of introductory speaking. Break your students into dyads and allow them ten to fifteen minutes to interview each other regarding how they would like to be introduced to their other classmates. They should prepare a one- to two-minute, one-point introduction of the other member of the pair, focusing on what their classmate's professional or educational goals are, and how improved public speaking skills might benefit that student in pursuit of those goals. They should include at least one illustrating example (real or hypothetical) of the benefits of improved speaking skills for that person.

Yesterday and Today

Directions: This exercise can be used as a short speaking activity or as an interesting alternative to the first graded speech assignment. Have your students go to the library to find out what happened in the world on the day or in the week they were born. They should look in the *New York Times,* a local newspaper, or one of the weekly national newsmagazines such as *Time, Newsweek,* or *U.S. News & World Report* for a short article that they think reveals something important about what we have become, or how things have changed and/or haven't changed over the years. They should then craft a one- to two-minute speech around their selected article (which should be summarized as the introduction to the speech). In the body of the speech, they should offer two or three reasons why or how the article is still relevant today. They should plan an effective conclusion that summarizes their ideas and leaves the audience with something to remember.

Lou Davidson Tillson (Murray State University, Murray, Ky.), "Building Community and Reducing Communication Apprehension: A Case Study Approach," *SCT* (Summer 1995), 4–5.

Goal: To build a sense of classroom community and reduce communication apprehension in the introductory public speaking class by using a case study approach.

Students report feeling very apprehensive about delivering speeches in most public speaking classes. One of the best ways I have found to reduce this anxiety is by building a supportive classroom climate. To build an empathetic environment, I provide students with several opportunities to develop their public speaking skills through oral presentations of ungraded speeches, jokes, and children's stories. Additionally, peer evaluators prepare positive and constructive comments following each speech. Students report that these experiences help to build feelings of competence, confidence, and camaraderie. Unfortunately, communication apprehension still exists.

Although it is impossible to completely eradicate communication apprehension, I have found that incorporating an original case study based on actual events that occurred in a public speaking class is helpful. This approach enables students to objectively discuss the behavior of Lisa, a student who "falls apart" during a presentation and flees the classroom before its conclusion. It also builds classroom community by allowing students to collectively experience (and survive) a public speaking worst case scenario. According to former students, "The case study makes for good classroom discussion and debate . . . it encourages cooperation and interaction . . . gives insight into others' reactions and enables you to widen your scope on possible situations."

Early in the semester, I distribute copies of the case study for students to read and ponder outside of class. In my class they are assigned to small groups of four to five students and asked to analyze the case. Discussion time is limited to 15–20 minutes. Sample questions may include:

- What might have caused Lisa to feel/react the way she did?

- Pretend you were one of her classmates. How would you have felt?

- What was the instructor's reaction? How could he/she have prevented Lisa from "falling apart"?

- What could Lisa have done to prevent reacting the way she did?

- What advice can you give Lisa to help her prepare for the next speech assignment?

- How can the instructor/students show support for Lisa when she returns to class?

Following the small group discussion, we reconvene as a whole class and conduct a pull-out session. Group responses are recorded on the blackboard. Some of the key learning points that invariably arise include:

- Apprehension is a normal reaction to a stressful situation like public speaking.

- Classmates (and the instructor) want you to succeed, not fail.

- In-depth preparation increases the likelihood for a successful presentation.

- Little mishaps may occur, but try not to sweat the small stuff!

The power of this strategy lies in the reflection and transference that occurs. I have found this approach enables students to almost anonymously share their own feelings and fears about public speaking by transferring them to the student in the case study. Students are able to visualize themselves in Lisa's shoes, without revealing that image to their classmates. Collectively, they are given the opportunity to vicariously experience the worst case scenario for PS 101. This surrogate experience serves as an inoculation against "bombing a speech" because it enables students to identify what went wrong, why it went wrong, and how to prevent it from going wrong in future presentations. They are able to reach conclusions on their own that are much more meaningful than a dry (or even an entertaining) lecture about speech preparation and communication apprehension. In the words of a former student: "The case study allows you to look at the situation from all sides more objectively than if you were in such a situation yourself . . . I believe that the case study is, in a sense, a 'hands-on' method of learning because it requires an application of the concepts discussed rather than rote memorization. It also allows the student to think of what he or she would do in such a 'real life' situation."

Public Speaking 101: A Case Study

It was the first day of graded speeches in Public Speaking 101. Scott, the football team captain and a 4.0 student, was near the end of his speech on the use of steroids in high school athletics. He efficiently reviewed his main points and concluded with a poignant story about a teenager who died because he wanted to play football as best he possibly could, even if that meant taking drugs to do so.

"... Jason Robinson died in pursuit of excellence. There is no need for other youngsters to follow in his footsteps to an early grave."

His words ended on a quiet note and his classmates tentatively began to applaud before breaking into a loud ovation. Breathing a sigh of relief, Scott gathered his notecards from the podium and began walking back to his desk in the third row of the classroom. His classmates were obviously impressed.

"Way to go, man! Where'd you learn to talk like that?" "Geez, I'm glad I don't have to go next." "Was that a true story or did you just make it all up?"

I asked the students to write down their comments on Scott's presentation while I finished writing my own evaluation. A couple of minutes passed and students began talking among themselves. I checked my sign-up sheet to see who would be delivering the next speech. It was Lisa. My heart went out to the timid girl sitting two seats away from me. Lisa had registered for my section of Public Speaking 101 last semester, but had dropped it before she had to make any oral presentations in class. I knew she was nervous—probably more so than any of the other students. As she dropped her stack of 4 x 6 notecards and busily tried to reorganize them, a niggling little voice spoke in my mind, "Maybe you should have touched base with her last week to see if she was ready for the assignment." And then the voice of reason and practicality spoke up, "You don't have time to spoon feed every scared student."

"OK, Lisa. You're up next," I said in what I hoped was an encouraging tone of voice.

A petite, blonde girl wearing wire-rimmed glasses and clasping notecards stood, took a few audible gulps of air, and walked toward the front of the classroom. Twenty-seven pairs of eyes looked in her direction. Lisa cleared her throat and placed the notecards on the podium as the class had been instructed to do. Her hands immediately grabbed onto the edge of the podium in a white-knuckled, death grip. A flush slowly inched its way from her chest to her throat. As her cheeks turned a blotchy, fire-engine red, she cleared her throat again and began to talk in a faltering, timid voice.

"My speech is on ... why children who commit violent crimes ... should be tried as adults in the court system," she stumbled. "There are three reasons why children who commit violent crimes should have to face adult penalties for their actions ..."

Lisa got off to a rough start. "How many times have I told the class not to introduce a speech with 'my speech is about' or 'today I want to talk about'?" I asked myself. "Where is the clever attention getter no speech should be without?"

She continued, "The first reason why children who commit violent crimes should be tried as adults is because ..." Lisa fumbled through her preview. As she arranged her notecards, one fell off the podium and slid under a nearby desk. No one else seemed to notice—except Lisa. She appeared to freeze in time as she apparently wondered whether to retrieve the card or try to continue without it. Her eyes looked scared and wild, like an animal caught by surprise in car headlights on a dark road.

Several seconds passed before Lisa decided what to do. As she stepped out from behind the podium she bumped into it and the rest of the cards fluttered to the floor. That mishap was the proverbial last straw. With a dumbstruck expression on her face, Lisa abandoned her search for the lost notecard, turned, and ran out of the room. Tears of frustration and embarrassment already stained her blotchy cheeks. The classroom was uncomfortably quiet except for the haunting sound of Lisa's footsteps running down the tile hallway. With a sinking feeling in my stomach, I looked away from the empty doorway and faced twenty-seven pairs of eyes looking at me.

SUPPLEMENTARY MATERIALS

Films, Videos, and Tapes

"Stage Fright," Coronet/MTI Film and Video, color 13 minutes.

Student Speeches Videos to accompany *Public Speaking*.

"Building Speech Confidence," an audiotape package that students may use to help reduce communication apprehension. Produced by James Lohr, published by the National Textbook Company, 1976.

"How to Make a More Effective Speech," Time-Life, 25 minutes.

"Learning to Live with Fear," ACI Media, 5 minutes.

"Stage Fright," Centron, 14 minutes.

"Conquering the Fear of Public Speaking," by Michael Motley, *Psychology Today* Tapes.

"Mental Imagery: Your Hidden Potential," by Arnold A. Lazarus, *Psychology Today* Tapes.

Computer Software

"Speech Outlining," Houghton Mifflin, 1991.

Transparencies and Handouts *(see following pages)*

Steps in the Preparation of a Self-Introductory Speech

Dealing with Speech Anxiety

Speaker Ethos

Outline Format for a Self-Introductory Speech

Practice Presentation Feedback Form

STEPS IN THE PREPARATION OF A SELF-INTRODUCTORY SPEECH

I.   Conduct the Self-awareness Inventory described on pp. 41–46.

II.   Decide on a thematic statement that spells out what you want to say in your speech.

III. Compose a preparation outline for your speech.

   A. Determine the main points of your speech. (Limit to two or three.)
      1. Decide how to arrange your main points.
      2. Develop examples or narratives to support each point.

   B. Prepare an introduction for your speech.
      1. Include material to gain attention.
      2. Include a preview of your message.

   C. Prepare a conclusion for your speech.
      1. Include a summary of your message.
      2. Develop concluding remarks that give the audience something to remember.

IV.   Condense your preparation outline into a key-word outline that will fit on a single sheet of paper or three index cards.

V.   Practice presenting your speech using your key-word outline at least three times.

VI.   Be ready the day you are assigned to speak.
   A. Try to get a good night's sleep before your speech.
   B. Do not eat or drink carbonated beverages immediately before your speech.

DEALING WITH SPEECH ANXIETY

I. Put nervousness into perspective.
   A. Nervousness is natural and desirable.
   B. Your classmates are likely to be supportive.
      1. Most of them are giving their first speeches too.
      2. They are less concerned with your nervousness than you are.
   C. You will not receive a low grade for simply appearing nervous your first time.

II. Be thoroughly prepared.
   A. Choose a topic and prepare a speech that reflects responsible knowledge and a clear sense of purpose.
   B. Practice until you feel comfortable.

III. Compose yourself before starting.
   A. Practice deep breathing and relaxation techniques.
   B. Practice cognitive restructuring of negative thoughts.
   C. Visualize yourself successfully making your presentation.
   D. Focus on your message, not yourself.
   E. Take a deep breath and establish eye contact.

IV. Act confident, even if you don't feel that way.
   A. Never start by apologizing for nervousness.
   B. Speak slowly and clearly, pausing to breathe when it feels natural.
   C. Keep going if you stumble over your own tongue.
      1. Repeat the idea if necessary, but never start over on the entire presentation.
   D. Establish and maintain eye contact with your audience.
   E. Work on movements and gestures to reinforce your message.

SPEAKER ETHOS

Ethos is the audience's perception of the speaker's competence, integrity, likability, and power.

A. Competence refers to education and knowledge, training, preparation, and personal experience. It can be enhanced by:
1. Choosing topics you know and citing personal experience.
2. Citing authoritative sources.
3. Confidently delivering well-organized messages.
4. Using appropriate language.

B. Integrity relates to perceptions of honesty and reliability. You can enhance this by:
1. Being straightforward in your presentation.
2. Addressing all sides of the issues.
3. Being personally committed and willing to follow your own advice.

C. Likability means radiating warmth and good will.
1. Smiles and eye contact increase likability.
2. Likability engenders audience identification, which can be enhanced by:
   a. Using a personable and conversational presentation style.
   b. Making references to shared stories and values.

D. Power makes people want to listen.
1. Perceptions of power are related to self-confidence, integrity, likability, competence, decisiveness, commitment, and enthusiasm.

OUTLINE FORMAT FOR A SELF-INTRODUCTORY SPEECH

Introduction

I.   Attention-arousing and orienting material: _____

_____

II.   Thematic statement: _____

_____

Body

I.   Main point 1: _____

      Supporting material: _____

_____

_____

II.   Main point 2: _____

      Supporting material: _____

_____

_____

III. Main point 3: _____

      Supporting material: _____

_____

_____

Conclusion

I.   Summary statement: _____

_____

II.   Concluding remarks: _____

_____

PRACTICE PRESENTATION FEEDBACK FORM

1. Did the introduction gain attention effectively? What other techniques might the speaker want to consider?

2. Did the introduction provide an adequate preview of the speech? Would such a preview be desirable or necessary?

3. Was the specific purpose of the speech clear? What was it?

4. Could you pick out the main points of the speech? What were they?

5. Was there sufficient supporting material? Were examples or narratives interesting?

6. Did the conclusion effectively summarize the message?

7. Did the concluding remarks leave you with something to remember?

8. Did the presentation sound natural and spontaneous?

READINGS FOR ENRICHMENT

See guide to journal abbreviations on p. 37.

* Items marked with an asterisk are suitable for student enrichment.

Chapter 2, General

Jorgensen-Earp, Cheryl R., and Ann Q. Stanton. "Student Metaphors for the College Freshman Experience." *CE* (Apr. 1993), 123–141.

Menzel, Kent E., and Lori J. Carrell. "The Relationship Between Preparation and Performance in Public Speaking." *CE* (Jan. 1994), 17–26.

Stearns, Susan A. "Small Group Activities and Student Empowerment." *SCT* (Summer 1995), 3–4.

Ethos

Adams, Julie K. "The Mask." *SCT* (Summer 1991), 11.

Ailes, Roger, and Jon Kraushar. *You Are the Message.* New York: Doubleday, 1988.

———. "How to Make an Audience Love You." *Working Woman* (Nov. 1990), 118+.

Benoit, William L., and Susan L. Brinson. "AT&T: 'Apologies Are Not Enough.'" *CQ* (Winter 1994), 75–88.

Benoit, William L., and Robert S. Hanczor. "The Tonya Harding Controversy: An Analysis of Image Restoration Strategies." *CQ* (Fall 1994), 416–433.

Berko, Roy. "Getting to Know You and Talking About It." *SCT* (Winter 1993), 5–6.

Bock, Douglas G., and Thomas J. Saine. "The Impact of Source Credibility, Attitude Valence, and Task Sensitization on Trait Errors in Speech Evaluation." *CM* (Aug. 1975), 229–236.

Boster, Franklin J., Dean Kazoleas, Timothy Levine, Randall G. Rogan, and Kil Ho Kang. "The Impact of Power on Communicative Persistence, Strategic Diversity, and Bargaining Outcomes." *CR* (Summer 1995), 136–144.

* Burgoon, Judee K. "The Ideal Source: A Reexamination of Source Credibility Measurement." *CSSJ* (Fall 1976), 200–206.

* Calloway-Thomas, Carolyn, and Raymond G. Smith. "Images of Leadership: Black vs. White." *SSCJ* (Spring 1981), 263–277.

Carbone, Tamara. "Stylistic Variables as Related to Source Credibility: A Content Analysis Approach." *CM* (June 1975), 99–106.

* Carrocci, Noreen M. "Trust and Gender Ten Years Later: The More Things Change. . . . " *Women's Studies in Communication* (Fall 1988), 63–89.

Cronkite, Gary, and Jo Liska. "A Critique of Factor Analytic Approaches to the Study of Credibility." *CM* (June 1976), 91–107.

Delia, Jesse G. "A Construct Analysis of the Concept of Credibility." *QJS* (Dec. 1976), 361–375.

Downey, Sharon D. "The Evolution of the Rhetorical Genre of Apologia." *WJC* (Winter 1993), 42–64.

Hosman, Lawrence A. "The Evaluative Consequences of Hedges, Hesitations, and Intensifiers: Powerful and Powerless Speech Styles." *HCR* (Spring 1989), 383–406.

Infante, Dominic A., Kenneth R. Parker, Christopher H. Clarke, Laverne Wilson, and Indrani A. Nathu. "A Comparison of Factor and Functional Approaches to Source Credibility." *CQ* (Winter 1983), 43–48.

Johnson, Craig, and Larry Vinson. "'Damned If You Do, Damned If You Don't?': Status, Powerful Speech, and Evaluations of Female Witnesses." *Women's Studies in Communication* (Spring 1987), 37–44.

* Kelly, Rex. "Speakers and the Bottom Line: The Character of the Speaker." *Vital Speeches of the Day*, 1 Nov. 1987, pp. 47–50.

* Kripalani, Manjeet. "The Image Merchants." *Forbes*, 25 Nov. 1991, 212–214.

Lashbrook, William R., William B. Snavely, and Daniel L. Sullivan. "The Effects of Source Credibility and Message Information Quality on The Attitude Change of Apathetics." *CM* (Aug. 1977), 252–262.

MacIntrye, Peter D., and Kimly A. Thivierge. "The Effects of Speaker Personality on Anticipated Reactions to Public Speaking." *CCR* (Fall 1995), 125–133.

McCroskey, James C., and Thomas J. Young. "Ethos and Credibility: The Construct and Its Measurement After Three Decades." *CSSJ* (Spring 1981), 24–34.

Mills, Cary G. "Relationships Among Three Sources of Credibility in the Communication Configuration: Speaker, Message, and Experimenter." *SSCJ* (Summer 1977), 334–351.

* Overstreet, R. Larry. "Understanding Charisma Through Its History." *CSSJ* (Winter 1978), 275–282.

Overton, Julia. "On the Line: A Self-Concept Discovery Activity." *SCT* (Spring 1995), 8.

Parker, Rhonda G., and Dale G. Leathers. "You Be the Judge: Impression Management in the Courtroom." *SCT* (Fall 1992), 4.

Portnoy, Enid J. "The Impact of Body Type on Perceptions of Attractiveness by Older Individuals." *CR* (Summer 1993), 101–108.

Richmond, Virginia P., and James C. McCroskey. "Whose Opinion Do You Trust?" *JC* (Spring 1975), 42–50.

Rosenfeld, Lawrence B., and Timothy G. Plax. "The Relationship of Listener Personality to Perceptions of Three Dimensions of Credibility." *CSSJ* (Winter 1975), 274–278.

Rowland, Robert C., and Thea Rademacher. "The Passive Style of Rhetorical Crisis Management: A Case Study of the Superfund Controversy." *CS* (Winter 1990), 326–341.

Schumer, Alice. "To Tell the Truth." *SCT* (Fall 1992), 4–5.

Wakshlag, Jacob J., and Nadyne G. Edison. "Attraction, Credibility, Perceived Similarity, and the Image of Public Figures." *CQ* (Fall 1979), 27–34.

West, Richard. "Can We Talk? Using the Personal Reference Inventory as an Icebreaker." *SCT* (Summer 1993), 12–13.

Williams, David E., and Glenda Treadaway. "Exxon and the Valdez Accident: A Failure in Crisis Communication." *CS* (Spring 1992), 56–64.

Wood, Julia T. "Alternate Portraits of Leaders: A Contingency Approach to Perceptions of Leadership." *WJSC* (Fall 1979), 260–270.

Communication Apprehension

Adams, Lori. "Speech Anxiety Simulation." *SCT* (Fall 1992), 13.

Allen, Mike, and Steven B. Hunt. "Legal Issues in the Treatment of Communication Apprehension." *ACR* (Nov. 1993), 385–390.

Ayres, Joe. " Perceptions of Speaking Ability: An Explanation for Stage Fright." *CE* (July 1986), 275–287.

———. "Coping with Speech Anxiety: The Power of Positive Thinking." *CE* (Oct. 1988), 289–296.

———. "Comparing Self-constructed Visualization Scripts with Guided Visualization." *CR* (Summer 1995), 193–199.

Ayres, Joe, Debbie M. Ayres, Gary Grudzinskas, Tim Hopf, Erin Kelly, and A. Kathleen Wilcox. "A Component Analysis of Performance Visualization." *CR* (Summer 1995), 185–192.

Ayres, Joe, and Theodore S. Hopf. "Visualization: A Means of Reducing Speech Anxiety." *CE* (Oct. 1985), 318–323.

———. "Visualization: Is It More than Extra-Attention?" *CE* (Jan. 1989), 1–5.

Ayres, Joe, Theodore S. Hopf, and Jeff Ady. "Coping with Speech Anxiety." *SCT* (Spring 1988), 11–13.

Ayres, Joe, and Tim Hopf. "Visualization: Reducing Speech Anxiety and Enhancing Performance." *CR* (Winter 1992), 1–10.

———. *Coping with Speech Anxiety*. Norwood, N.J.: Ablex, 1993.

Ayres, Joe, Tim Hopf, and Debbie M. Ayres. "An Examination of Whether Imaging Ability Enhances the Effectiveness of an Intervention Designed to Reduce Speech Anxiety." *CE* (July 1994), 252–258.

Beatty, Michael J., Ralph R. Behnke, and Karin McCallum, "Situational Determinants of Communication Apprehension." *CM* (Aug. 1978), 187–191.

Beatty, Michael J., and Matther H. Friedland. "Public Speaking State Anxiety as a Function of Selected Situational and Predispositional Variables." *CE* (Apr. 1990), 142–147.

Behnke, Ralph R., Chris R. Sawyer, and Paul E. King. "Contagion Theory and the Communication of Public Speaking State Anxiety." *CE* (July 1994), 246–251.

Booth-Butterfield, Melanie, and Steve Booth-Butterfield. "The Role of Cognitive 'Performance Orientation' in Communication Anxiety." *CQ* (Spring 1993), 198–209.

Carlile, Larry W., Ralph R. Behnke, and James T. Kitchens. "A Psychological Pattern of Anxiety in Public Speaking." *CQ* (Fall 1977), 44–46.

Cronin, Michael W., George L. Grice, and Richard K. Olsen, Jr.. "The Effects of Interactive Video Instruction in Coping with Speech Fright." *CE* (Jan. 1994), 42–53.

Daly, John A., and Gustav Friedrich. "The Development of Communication Apprehension: A Retrospective Analysis of Contributory Correlates." *CQ* (Fall 1981), 243–255.

Daly, John A., Anita L. Vangelisti, and David J. Weber. "Speech Anxiety Affects How People Prepare Speeches: A Protocol Analysis of the Preparation Processes of Speakers." *CM* (Dec. 1995), 383–397.

Duran, Robert L., and Lynne Kelly. "The Cycle of Shyness: A Study of Self-Perceptions of Communication Performance." *CR* (Winter 1989), 30–38.

Frymier, Ann Bainbridge. "The Relationships Among Communication Apprehension, Immediacy, and Motivation to Study." *CR* (Winter 1993), 8–17.

Hamilton, James P. "The Development of a Communication Specific Locus of Control Instrument." *CR* (Summer 1991), 107–112.

Hawes, Ruhemah. "Using Group Speaking to Overcome Apprehension." *SCT* (Fall 1990), 10.

Hopf, Tim, and Joe Ayres. "Coping with Public Speaking Anxiety: An Examination of Various Combinations of Systematic Desensitization, Skills Training, and Visualization." *ACR* (May 1992), 184–198.

Isaacson, Zelda. "Paradoxical Intention: A Strategy to Alleviate the Anxiety Associated with Public Speaking." *SCT* (Summer 1993), 13–14.

Johnson, Craig. "Nothing to Fear but Fear . . . Or Is There." *SCT* (Winter 1990), 1.

King, Stephen W., Janis Andersen, and B. Robert Carlson. "The Dimensionality of the PRCA-24: An Explication of Content Dimensions." *CR* (Winter 1988), 1–8.

Kondo, David Shinji. "Strategies for Reducing Public Speaking Anxiety in Japan." *CR* (Winter 1994), 20–26.

Langdon, Harry. "A Course on Stage Fright." *SCT* (Summer 1990), 15.

* Lederman, Linda C. "High Communication Apprehensives Talk About Communication Apprehension and Its Effects on Their Behavior." *CQ* (Summer 1983), 233–237.

MacIntyre, Peter, and Kimly A. Thivierge. "The Effects of Audience Pleasantness, Audience Familiarity, and Speaking Contests on Public Speaking Anxiety and Willingness to Speak." *CQ* (Fall 1995), 456–466.

McGuire, John, Cherise Stauble, David Abbott, and Randy Fisher. "Ethical Issues in the Treatment of Communication Apprehension: A Survey of Communication Professionals." *CE* (Apr. 1995), 98–109.

Mester, Cathy Sargent. "Peer Support Groups." *SCT* (Fall 1987), 2.

* Motley, Michael T. "Taking the Terror Out of Talk." *Psychology Today* (Jan. 1988), 46–49.

Motley, Michael T., and Jennifer L. Molloy. "An Efficacy Test of a New Therapy ('Communication Orientation Motivation') for Public Speaking Anxiety." *ACR* (Feb. 1994), 48–58.

Olaniran, Bolanie A., and K. David Roach. "Communication Apprehension and Classroom Apprehension in Nigerian Classrooms." *CQ* (Fall 1994), 379–389.

* "Picture Yourself Successful." *Prevention* (Mar. 1990), 15–18.

Proctor, Russell F., II, Annamae T. Douglas, Teresa Garera-Izquierdo, and Stephanie L. Wartman. "Approach, Avoidance, and Apprehension: Talking with High-CA Students About Getting Help." *CE* (Oct. 1994), 312–321.

Ralston, Steven Michael, Robert Ambler, and Joseph N. Scudder. "Reconsidering the Impact of Racial Differences in the College Public Speaking Classroom on Minority Student Communication Anxiety." *CR* 43–50.

Rose, Heidi M., Andrew S. Rancer, and Kenneth C. Crannell. "The Impact of Basic Courses in Oral Interpretation and Public Speaking on Communication Apprehension." *CR* (Winter 1993), 54–60.

Rosenfield, Lawrence B., Charles H. Grant III, and James C. McCroskey. "Communication Apprehension and Self-perceived Communication Competence of Academically Gifted Students." *CE* (Jan. 1995), 79–86.

Rubin, Alan M. "The Effect of Locus of Control on Communication Motivation, Anxiety, and Satisfaction." *CQ* (Spring 1993), 161–171.

Stowell, Jessica. "Free Writing to Deal with Speech Anxiety." *SCT* (Spring 1992), 15.

Tillson, Lou Davidson. "Building Community and Reducing Communication Apprehension: A Case Study Approach." *SCT* (Summer 1995), 4–5.

Self-Disclosure

Berg, John H., and R. L. Archer. "The Disclosure-Liking Relationship: Effects of Self-Perception, Order of Disclosure, and Topical Similarity." *HCR* (Winter 1983), 269–281.

Berko, Roy. "The Public 'I' And the Private 'I'." *SCT* (Fall 1986), 6.

Dichter, Ernest. *Total Self-Knowledge.* New York: Stein & Day, 1976. This book is a collection of self-knowledge quizzes and exercises some of which you might find useful in teaching communication courses.

* Fisher, B. Aubrey. *Pragmatics of Human Relationships.* New York: Random House, 1987, pp. 117–156.

Gill, Mary. "Successful Self-Disclosure." *SCT* (Spring 1988), 7, 16.

Keen, Sam, and Anne Valley Fox. *Telling Your Story: A Guide to Who You Are and Who You Can Be.* New York: New American Library, 1973.

Kennedy, Eugene. *If You Really Knew Me, Would You Still Like Me?* Niles, Ill.: Argus Communications, 1975.

Knapp, Mark. *Interpersonal Communication and Human Relationships.* Boston: Allyn & Bacon, 1984, pp. 208–214.

Lair, Jess. *I Ain't Much Baby—But I'm All I've Got.* New York: Doubleday, 1972.

Littlefield, Robert S., and Timothy L. Sellnow. "The Use of Self-Disclosure as a Means of Reducing Stage-Fright in Beginning Speakers." *CE* (Jan. 1987), 62–64.

* Rosenfield, Lawrence B. "Self-Disclosure Avoidance: Why I Am Afraid to Tell You Who I Am." *CM* (Mar. 1979), 63–66.

Schelle, Elizabeth B., and Susan H. Koester. "The Alter Ego: Self-Disclosure Without Anxiety." *SCT* (Spring 1990), 2–3.

Steele, Fritz. *The Open Organization: The Impact of Secrecy and Disclosure on People and Organizations.* Reading Mass.: Addison-Wesley, 1975.

Stull, James B. "Rewards for 'Openness.'" *JC* (Winter 1978), 124–129.

Tardy, Charles H., Lawrence A. Hosman, and James J. Bradac. "Disclosing Self to Friends and Family: A Reexamination of Initial Questions." *CQ* (Fall 1981), 263–268.

* Weaver, Richard L., II. *Understanding Interpersonal Communication,* 3rd ed. Glenview, Ill.: Scott, Foresman, 1984, pp. 40–73.

Wenburg, John R., and William W. Wilmot. *The Personal Communication Process.* New York: Wiley, 1973, pp. 217–230.

Optional First Speech Assignments

Auer, Jeffrey J. "Creating an Extra and 'Real Life' Public Speaking Assignment." *SCT* (Spring 1991), 3.

Bahti, Cynthia L. "What's Your Gripe?" *SCT* (Fall 1992), 12–13.

Bowers, A. Anne, Jr. "Happy Birthday to Me." *SCT* (Summer 1995), 11.

Corey, James. "The 'I Am' Speech." *SCT* (Summer 1988), 1.

Ehrler, Rhonda. "Extemporizing Through Humor and Repetition." *SCT* (Summer 1988), 2–3.

Garvin, Janet Allen. "Where Is It and How Do We Get There?" *SCT* (Spring 1990), 15.

Gschwend, Laura L. "Creating Confidence with the Popular Recording Speech." *SCT* (Summer 1995), 9–10.

Hankins, Gail A. "Hometown Analysis Project: A Cultural Awareness Exercise." *SCT* (Summer 1989), 5–6.

Hawkinson, Ken. "Performing Personal Narratives." *SCT* (Spring 1995), 3–4.

Hibben, Jane. "A Key Address." *SCT* (Spring 1996), 9–10.

McAvoy, Malcolm L. "Self-Concept Builder." *SCT* (Fall 1986), 7.

McClarty, Wilma. "Nomination Speech: The Ideal Date." *SCT* (Summer 1991), 9–10.

Mohsen, Raed A. "Out on Campus: A Challenging Public Speaking Experience." *SCT* (Summer 1993), 10–11.

Nagel, George, Jr. "'Peculiarity': An Exercise in Sharing, Caring, and Belonging." *SCT* (Fall 1989), 3–4.

Powell, Kimberly A. "Increasing Appreciation for Diversity Through the Group Culture Speech." *SCT* (Winter 1996), 3–4.

Raftis, Sean. "Brush With Greatness." *SCT* (Winter 1991), 5.

Reid, Louann. "Doing What Comes Naturally—Naturally!" *SCT* (Spring 1987), 1–2.

Ross, Roseanna. "What Is in the Shoe Box?" *SCT* (Spring 1991), 12.

Schelle, Elisabeth B., and Susan H. Koester. "The Alter Ego: Self Disclosure Without Anxiety." *SCT* (Spring 1990), 2–3.

Schneider, Valerie L. "The Personal Experience Speech in Public Speaking." *SCT* (Fall 1986), 15–16.

Schumer, Allison. "Structure and Substance in a One-Minute Speech." *SCT* (Spring 1987), 5.

———. "Custom Comparison Speeches." *SCT* (Fall 1989), 1.

Snyder, Lee. "Twenty-Five Speeches an Hour." *SCT* (Spring 1990), 1.

Sutton, David L. "Impromptu Speaking Exercise: Academy Award Acceptance Speeches." *SCT* (Fall 1994), 15.

Thompson, Carol, and Christina Standerfer. "Interactive Public Speaking Activities." *SCT* (Summer 1992), 2–3.

Walter, Suzanne. "Introduction of a Speaker: Multipurpose and Multicultural." *SCT* (Spring 1993), 3.

Webb, Lynn. "The Analogy Speech," *SCT* (Fall 1986), 2.

CHAPTER 3
Developing Your Listening Skills

OBJECTIVES

- To impress upon your students an appreciation for the significance of effective listening.

- To help your students overcome barriers to effective listening.

- To help your students improve their critical thinking skills.

- To help your students conduct constructive speech evaluations.

- To help your students appreciate their ethical responsibilities as listeners.

SUGGESTIONS FOR TEACHING

Most instructors and course syllabi stress the development of listening and critical thinking skills as a primary objective of an introductory public speaking course. However, it is all too easy to pay lip service to the importance of listening early in the term and then ignore it for the rest of the semester. Listening affects every other aspect of the communication process.

You should emphasize the ethical and practical significance of the listener's role and responsibility in public speaking. Besides providing immediate feedback and a warm atmosphere, effective listeners improve the overall quality of communication by demanding high standards of rationality and constructively engaging messages for their positive value. Question-and-answer sessions after speeches offer an excellent means of stimulating audience interaction. Here we've included activities to emphasize constructive as well as critical listening skills and the value of a balanced approach. In a practical sense, critical and constructive evaluation of one's own and other speeches and artifacts is a basic part of learning just about every skill involved with public speaking. Certainly it is an essential part of learning to argue, structure, and present messages more effectively. Consequently, there are exercises intended to engage your students' listening and thinking skills in almost every chapter of this IRM. Some of the activities in this chapter have your students critique other speeches, illustrate the differences between facts and inferences, flush out adjectives for describing good and poor speakers, observe audience listening behaviors, and even work on improving their class note-taking abilities. They also have you establish and communicate your own grading criteria.

CHAPTER OUTLINE

I. Effective listening entails actively seeking out intended meanings in messages, considering apparent and not-so-apparent motives, evaluating reasoning and supporting materials, calculating the value and risk of accepting recommendations, and creatively integrating the messages into the world of the listener. *(text pp. 68–73)*
   A. Effective listening is essential to quality communication.
      1. We spend more of our communication time listening than speaking.
      2. Listening is vital to effective citizenship skills.
      3. Many non-Western cultures place a higher emphasis on listening skills than we do.
   B. What constitutes effective listening?
      1. Hearing and listening are not the same thing.
         a. Hearing is an involuntary physical process.
         b. Listening is a voluntary effort to hear, attend, comprehend, and interpret the meaning of a message.
      2. Critical listening entails analyzing and evaluating messages for their potential value, and responding with appropriate and constructive feedback.
         a. Feedback consists of the visual and verbal cues listeners provide to let speakers know how they are responding.
      3. Constructive listening adds to the meaning of a message by seeking out valuable applications.
         a. Constructive listeners often engage speakers in subsequent dialogues of participative communication in which both share responsibility for creatively extending the meaning of a public transaction.
         b. Constructive listeners are typically able to empathize and identify with speakers even as they disagree with their positions.
      4. Critical and constructive listening skills complement each other in making possible the transformative effect of successful public speaking.
   C. Effective listening benefits both listeners and speakers.
      1. Effective listeners benefit from their skills in that they:
         a. are less likely to succumb to questionable persuasion.
         b. are more likely to succeed in the workplace and in school.
         c. become better public speakers themselves.
      2. Speakers also benefit from an audience of good listeners in that they provide:
         a. he feedback necessary for participative communication.
         b. a supportive environment that helps alleviate communication anxiety.
         c. for an experience that helps to elevate self-esteem.

II. The first step in developing effective listening skills is to become aware of the external and internal barriers that may prevent us from being good listeners. *(text pp. 73–81)*
   A. External sources of interference may arise from the environment, from the message, or from the presentation.
      1. Noise is the most common form of environmental interference.
         a. Listeners may close a window that is letting in noise, or sit closer to the speaker.
      2. Poorly organized speeches and the use of unfamiliar jargon are also sources of external interference.
         a. Listeners might read relevant literature in advance and/or take notes, listening for main ideas.
      3. Rate of speech, annoying habits, and even dress and hair styles can distract a listener's attention.
         a. Listeners should be wary of such responses and consciously focus on the speaker's message.
   B. Internal sources of interference cause the most important listening problems.
      1. Listeners may drift off because their minds can process information faster than people speak.

2. Internal sources of interference may include reactions to words, personal concerns, attitudes, cultural differences, or bad listening habits.
   a. Trigger words can evoke powerful positive or negative reactions that dominate the meaning of the discourses in which they occur.
      (1) Students should train themselves to look at the overall message and the particular case, rather then letting their reactions to trigger words or chance associations dictate their responses to messages.
      (2) Students can improve their concentration skills by keeping a listening log during their lecture classes.
   b. Personal concerns such as lack of sleep, hunger, anger, worry, or time constraints can make concentration difficult.
      (1) Students should attend class well rested and fed, and not do their homework during their classmates' speeches.
   c. Attitudes are strong positive or negative biases toward a listener or topic that can prevent us from receiving messages accurately.
      (1) Attitudes can distort incoming messages through filtering, assimilation, and contrast effects.
         (a) Filtering occurs when listeners fail to process incoming information that challenges preconceived notions.
         (b) Assimilation occurs when we perceive positions similar to our own as being more similar than they actually are.
         (c) A contrast effect occurs when we see positions that differ from ours as more different than they actually are.
      (2) Attitudes are not easy to control.
         (a) Listeners should strive to recognize their attitudes, listen to messages as objectively as possible, and delay judgment until they have heard the entire message.
         (b) Listeners should seek constructive value in messages, and should be willing to reevaluate their own positions.
   d. Many listening problems are simply the result of bad habits.
      (1) Television may lead us to favor messages that are fast-moving and entertaining.
      (2) Many people learn how to feign attention, which results in poor (if any) feedback.
      (3) Fear of failure can cause people to avoid listening to difficult material.
      (4) Some students are trained to listen only for facts, which blinds them to crucial nonverbal aspects of communication.
      (5) Overcoming bad listening habits requires effort. Listeners should:
         (a) remember their responsibility to provide appropriate feedback.
         (b) take notes of main ideas and supporting information.
         (c) attend nonverbal cues.
         (d) practice (using their listening logs) extending their attention spans.

III. Critical thinking and listening is an integrated process of examining information, ideas, and proposals. *(text pp. 81–85)*
   A. Critical thinking and listening involve:
      1. questioning and exploring messages, accepting nothing at face value.
      2. developing positions on issues by examining competing ideas.
      3. being receptive to new thoughts and new perspectives on old ideas.
      4. evaluating evidence and reasoning.
      5. discussing with others the meanings of events.
   B. Analyzing and evaluating messages is an inherent part of learning the art of public speaking.
   C. The following questions are basic to critical listening:

1. Does the speaker support ideas or claims with facts and figures, testimony, and examples or narratives?
2. Does the speaker use supporting materials that are relevant, representative, recent, and reliable?
   a. Facts and figures should be the most recent available.
3. Does the speaker cite credible sources?
   a. Ethical speakers specify the credentials of their sources.
4. Does the speaker clearly distinguish among facts, inferences, and opinions?
   a. Facts are verifiable units of information that may be confirmed by independent observation, whereas opinions add personal interpretations and/or evaluations.
5. Does the speaker use language that is concrete and understandable or purposely vague?
6. Does the speaker ask you to ignore reason?
   a. Demagogues rely exclusively on emotional appeals without regard to the accuracy or adequacy of their claims.
7. Does the speaker rely too much on facts and figures?
8. Does the speaker use plausible reasoning?
   a. Conclusions should follow from the points and supporting materials that precede them.
9. Does the message promise too much?
10. Does this message fit with what I already know?
11. What other perspectives might there be on this issue?

IV. Critical evaluations of speeches should be aimed at helping speakers improve. *(text pp. 85–93)*
   A. A speech critique should emphasize strengths as well as weaknesses.
   B. Speeches are generally evaluated in terms of overall considerations, substance, structure, and presentation.
      1. Overall considerations include commitment, adaptation, purpose, freshness, and ethics.
         a. Commitment comes across as speakers' belief in their ideas and concern for audience welfare, and is enhanced by substantive, structured, and well-delivered messages.
         b. Speakers should adapt their messages to the situation and to audience concerns.
            (1) General functions, such as to inform, to persuade, or to celebrate, are often specified by the nature of the situation.
            (2) Student speakers should adapt to the requirements of the assignment.
            (3) By appealing to audience interests and needs, speakers can enhance identification between a speaker, her or his speech, and an audience.
         c. A speaker's specific purpose entails what she or he wants listeners to learn, think, or do as a result of the speech.
            (1) Speakers usually make their specific purposes clear from the start to keep their presentations from drifting.
         d. Freshness entails the newness and interest value of messages.
            (1) Students addressing "old" topics should make sure that they have a fresh perspective.
         e. Speech ethics entails respect for the audience, responsible knowledge, and concern for the consequences of audience exposure to the message.
            (1) Respect for the audience entails a sensitivity to cultural differences and an effort not to offend audience members even while disagreeing with them.
            (2) Ethical speakers assess their sources of information and their own prejudices, and avoid confusing facts and inferences.
            (3) Ethical speakers think through the possible ramifications of their messages before presenting them.
      2. Substantive speeches develop well-chosen topics with facts and figures, testimony, and examples and/or narratives.
         a. Speakers can enhance the substance of their speeches by choosing topics they already know something about and by supplementing personal experience with quality research.

b. Speakers often combine different types of supporting materials to make their ideas more accessible to listeners.

3. A well-structured speech uses a carefully planned progression of ideas that is easily followed by an audience.
   a. Every message should have an introduction, body, and conclusion that serve their respective functions.
   b. The organization of the body's main ideas will vary with the speech's subject and purpose.
      (1) "How to" speeches should follow the order of the described process.
      (2) Categorical designs are useful when subjects break naturally into parts.
   c. Transitions, which link the various parts of a speech together, should be used between the introduction and the body, between the body and the conclusion, and between the main points of the body.

4. Speeches are not complete until they are effectively presented.
   a. The oral language of speeches must be instantly intelligible.
      (1) Sentences should be simple and direct, avoiding complex chains of dependent clauses.
      (2) Concrete words are generally preferable to abstract ones because they help listeners visualize messages.
   b. An extemporaneous presentation is carefully prepared and practiced, but not written out or memorized.
      (1) Extemporaneous speaking allows speakers to interact naturally with an audience by leaving room for them to adapt to the audience during a presentation.
   c. Effective speeches are thoroughly practiced.
      (1) Practice allows for last-minute adjustments.
      (2) Many speakers like to tape-record their presentations, and play them back later.
      (3) Supportive friends can listen to a speech and offer suggestions to clarify a speaker's purpose and main ideas.
      (4) Speakers should imagine their audience before them as they practice.
      (5) Speakers should acquaint themselves (if possible) with the actual physical environment in which they will speak.
   d. Nonverbal aspects are also an important part of an effective presentation. Speakers should:
      (1) speak loudly enough to be heard at the back of the room.
      (2) exhibit a relaxed posture.
      (3) use movements that seem natural and spontaneous.
      (4) use gestures that complement rather than compete with the message.

V. Listeners, like speakers, have important responsibilities in facilitating ethical public speaking. *(text pp. 93–94)*
   A. Ethical listeners do not prejudge a speech and keep an open mind.
      1. Listening to opposing positions benefits us by exposing us to new and sometimes better perspectives on issues, or by helping us to better understand why we believe as we do.
   B. Ethical listeners are receptive to the lifestyles and cultural backgrounds of others.
      1. Listeners should not allow prejudice to interfere with effective listening.
   C. Ethical listeners recognize that openness does not mean lowering our critical guard to possibly dangerous messages.
   D. Ethical listeners recognize the impact of their listening behaviors on others.
      1. Good listeners seek out the value of messages, and share a concern for these messages' impact on others.
      2. Good listeners extend our Golden Rule variation, "Listen to others as you would have them listen to you," to Bennett's Platinum Rule, "Listen to others as they would have you listen to them."

USING END-OF-CHAPTER ITEMS

Discussion *(text p. 95)*

1. Complete the "Listening Problems Check List" on [text] page 73 of this chapter. Working in small groups, discuss your listening problems with the other members of the group. Develop a listening improvement plan for the three most common listening problems in your group. Report this plan to the rest of the class.

    This exercise is intended for in-class use. You might duplicate the check list and distribute it for use with this exercise, or project a transparency of it and have your students write their responses on a separate sheet of scratch paper. Upon completion, have them present their responses to the class. Emphasize that this is not a quiz and encourage them to be forthright and honest with their answers. Demonstrate how the various problems illustrated in this exercise can be broken down according to the categories covered in the text: personal reactions, attitudes, and bad listening habits. Students should mark the three items that they believe cause their greatest listening problems, and develop strategies for dealing with them. Focus discussion on the most common problems that emerge, and the appropriateness and feasibility of proposed solutions.

2. List three positive and three negative trigger words that provoke a strong emotional reaction when you hear them. Have someone write these words on the chalkboard. Try to group the words into categories, such as sexist or ethnic slurs, political terms, ideals, and so forth. Discuss why these words have such a strong impact on you. How might you control their effect?

    This exercise works best for general class discussion. You might start things off by offering some of your own positive and negative trigger words. Some positive ones might include: freedom, progress, education, salvation, and charity. Negative trigger words might include any racial, ethnic, religious, or sexist slurs, or political terms such as *liberal* and *taxes*. Focus discussion on the reactions students have to such words and how they might interfere with critical listening. Further discussion might consider reasons for using trigger words, how listeners can avoid being distracted by them, and the ethical considerations of their use.

3. Identify a speaker outside your class to whom you have difficulty listening. Identify the sources of indifference in yourself that make it hard for you to listen. Do you feel that such indifference is justified?

    This exercise works as a short homework activity followed by in-class discussion. It provides a useful opportunity to have your students identify (rather than confessing) their own listening problems as they occur in practice. If you feel comfortable, you might have your students evaluate problems they might be having with your speaking skills. Otherwise, have them consider other teachers or speakers whom they have been obliged to hear, but have had trouble listening to. As an alternative, have your students critique a prominent political or religious leader whom they have trouble listening to, and offer constructive advice for improving that person's speaking skills. Try to steer class discussion toward the listening barriers and correctives offered in the text.

Application *(text p. 96)*

1. Review the notes you have taken in one of your lecture courses. Are you able to identify the main points, or have you been trying to write down everything that was said? Compare your note taking before and after studying listening behavior. Can you see any difference?

    This works best as homework followed by small-group and/or general class discussion. Note-taking ability is a valuable application of critical listening skills. You might provide a supplemental lecture on note taking based on the following material and the guidelines for taking notes on p. 75 of the text. Break your students into small groups to review each other's notes. If you have lectured the class for more than fifteen minutes prior to this activity, have them review the notes from that lecture so that they will have an equal basis for comparison. (This can provide quality insights into your strengths and weaknesses as a lecturer, and it keeps your students focused on your class materials.)

Students may have problems taking effective notes for several reasons (besides having poorly organized instructors). Some students try to write down everything a speaker says, which is virtually impossible. Others wait for speakers to say something that personally interests them before bothering to take notes. When they get around to reviewing their notes later, all they have is a collection of anecdotes or morsels of information that make little or no sense. Finally, students often wait too long to review class notes. Notes that make sense when taken often seem obscure a week or two later. Students should review notes quickly so that they can fill in blank spots from memory or ask appropriate questions for clarification at the beginning of the next class period. The following suggestions may help them take better notes.*

1. The best note-taking paper is "law school" paper. The left margin is indented about three inches, as opposed to the one- to one-and-one-quarter-inch margins common in most spiral notebooks. Students can make their own versions of "law school" paper by simply drawing in their own vertical margins in the proper place.

2. Take class notes in the right-hand column of the page, reserving the left-hand column for summaries, key words, or questions to be added as you review your notes.

3. Use a "telegraphic" writing style, omitting nonessential words. For example, instead of writing "I will arrive home promptly at seven o'clock tomorrow night," try "I arrive 7 P.M. tomorrow."

4. Distinguish between main ideas and supporting materials. Consider using a modified key-word outline format for taking notes. Leave blank lines between points, and use indention to distinguish main points and supporting materials. Consider the following lecture excerpt as an example:

   In selling, you can overcome a customer's objections to almost any product if you can come up with a good idea. Here are two examples: First, a man who objected to a square fly swatter bought it when the salesperson said, "These are square, sir, so that you can swat the flies when they get in the corners." Second, a woman who wanted round clothespins bought the square ones when the clerk told her, "They don't roll out of reach under the washer if you drop them." So don't sell the steak—sell the sizzle.

   Your notes on this passage might read:

   People buy ideas, not products.
       square fly swatter—gets in corners
       square clothespins—won't roll away
       don't sell steak—sell sizzle

5. Listen for transitions and signal words, which clarify relationships among main points and supporting materials, and help listeners track the overall organization of a message. Transitions may signal: supporting materials to follow ("for example"), a list listeners should know ("the four steps" or "five causes"), important time relationships ("prior to that," "subsequently," and "meanwhile"), causal relationships ("therefore" and "consequently"), contrasts and comparisons ("on the other hand"), emphasis ("most importantly" and "above all"), and simplification or paraphrase ("in other words" or "in short").

---

* Adapted from Walter Pauk, *How to Study in College*, 4th ed. (Boston: Houghton Mifflin, 1989), pp. 136–161. Used by permission

6. You should review your notes as soon as possible after taking them so that you can fill in blank spaces from memory. The left-hand column can be used to reduce notes to key words, paraphrase complicated material, summarize information, jot down questions, and add notes from the text that relate to lecture material.

2. **Read the following paragraph carefully:**

    Dirty Dick has been killed. The police have rounded up six suspects, all of whom are known criminals. All of them were near the scene of the crime at the approximate time that the murder took place. All had good motives for wanting Dirty Dick dead. However, Larcenous Lenny has been completely cleared of guilt.

    Now determine whether each of the following statements is true (T), false (F), or an inference (?).

T	F	?	1.	Larcenous Lenny is known to have been near the scene of the killing of Dirty Dick.
T	F	?	2.	All six of the rounded-up gangsters were known to have been near the scene of the murder.
T	F	?	3.	Only Larcenous Lenny has been cleared of guilt.
T	F	?	4.	The police do not know who killed Dirty Dick.
T	F	?	5.	Dirty Dick's murderer did not confess of his own free will.
T	F	?	6.	It is known that the six suspects were in the vicinity of the cold-blooded assassination.
T	F	?	7.	Larcenous Lenny did not kill Dirty Dick.
T	F	?	8.	Dirty Dick is dead.

    The answers are found following the Notes at the end of the chapter [text]. Were you able to distinguish between inferences and facts?

    This exercise is intended for in-class discussion to illustrate the differences between facts and inferences. Either read the passage and questions aloud or have your students write down their answers without looking at the key in the text, and then share them for a class discussion focusing on the differences between facts and inferences as evidenced in this exercise. Most of the items above are inferences not substantiated by the actual paragraph. You might note how connotative prefixes (see text Chapter 10) such as "Dirty," "Larcenous," and "cold-blooded" can entice people to make unsubstantiated inferences concerning situations about which they know very little. The following annotated key may help to guide class discussion.

    1. ?   Larcenous Lenny may or may not be one of the six convicts rounded up.
    2. T   This item is clearly stated in the paragraph.
    3. ?   The paragraph does not say whether anyone else has been cleared of guilt. Others may also have been cleared.
    4. ?   The police could know but not intend to announce it until the suspect is apprehended.
    5. ?   The paragraph mentions nothing about a confession.
    6. ?   The paragraph says only that Dirty Dick has been killed, not that it was a "cold-blooded assassination."
    7. ?   Although Larcenous Lenny has been "completely cleared," the possibility still exists that he could have done it.
    8. T   This item is clearly stated in the first sentence of the paragraph.

3. With your classmates, observe three minutes of silence. During this time, write down all sounds or distractions heard in the classroom. Compile a list of these distractions on the chalkboard. Discuss (a) how much of a problem each might be for both speakers and listeners, and (b) what speakers and listeners could do to minimize these distractions.

This is good for stimulating class discussion on potential classroom barriers to student speeches. Interesting variations might include asking your students at the beginning of class to write down all the distractions they recognize during a subsequent mini-lecture, and reserving the last five to ten minutes of class to discuss how these distractions might be dealt with or minimized for student speeches. In addition, you might have your students attend some sort of outside public speaking event (church, public lecture, etc.) and record distractions for class discussion. Steer that discussion toward common physical barriers to public speaking and different strategies for overcoming them.

4. **Use the guidelines on [text] page 87 of this chapter to evaluate a speech you view on tape in class. Discuss the strengths and weaknesses of the presentation. Consider what type of constructive oral feedback you might offer this speaker to improve his or her next presentation. Discuss both critical and supportive ways of presenting the same type of feedback.**

This is a good exercise for stimulating class discussion on critical and constructive listening skills. Students are commonly overly critical of taped speeches by other students they don't know, and tend to focus exclusively on presentation skills when making their first evaluations. Emphasize the importance of highlighting strengths as well as weaknesses in conducting speech critiques, as well as the complementary nature of critical and constructive listening skills in facilitating the transformative capacity of public communication. Push your students to follow negative criticisms with suggestions for improvement. You can also use this activity to teach the basics of a good speech as covered in this chapter of the text, and to familiarize your students with your own grading criteria.

ADDITIONAL ACTIVITIES

Listening Logs

Purpose: To engage your students in the critical and constructive evaluation of their classmates' in-class speeches.

Directions: This is a good way to keep your students attentive to their classmates' presentations on a regular basis throughout the semester. You might coordinate this with the Reading Logs activity in Chapter 1 of this IRM. During a given round of speeches, have your students make a certain number of entries in response to their classmates' presentations. Emphasize the value of critical and constructive listening skills, as well as applications for enhancing their own public speaking skills. Also push your students to engage a variety of public speaking variables, such as substance, structure, language use, and ethical considerations, as well as quality of presentation. Take these logs up periodically for quick evaluations and perhaps a minor grade.

Evaluating Student Speeches

Purpose: To engage your students' critical listening skills in the evaluation of other student speeches.

Directions: Distribute copies of the speech evaluation form from p. 122 or the form you will be using to grade student speeches. Show a videotape of student speeches, and have the students evaluate and "grade" them, taking notes on a separate sheet of paper. You might set up this activity by briefly explaining your own grading criteria. Watch the speeches ahead of time and prepare your own commentaries and grades as if they were presented in your class. For class discussion, critique the speeches between viewings, first soliciting your students' own reactions. Emphasize strengths as well as weaknesses to work on. Students should assign grades for each of the major areas covered on the form, and justify them with references to the actual speeches and the principles of effective public speaking covered in the text. For example, "Student X gets a C for his presentation because he looked at his notes too much, and eye contact is central to making an effective presentation." Try to move toward consensual critiques and grades. If time allows, do this with several speeches. This should fine-tune your students' critical appreciation for what makes a good speech, and give them a better understanding of what's expected of them when they make their own presentations. You may well discover that many of your students are considerably harsher critics of other student speeches than most instructors.

Constructive Speech Evaluation

Purpose: To give your students an opportunity to engage their constructive listening skills in the evaluation of other student speeches.

Directions: Use this to sharpen your students' constructive listening skills. As with the previous activity, "Evaluating Student Speeches," show a videotape of student speeches for in-class discussion. However, your students should emphasize their constructive rather than their critical listening skills. They should dispassionately consider the speaker's intended meaning, the likely implications and consequences of the messages, and the possible applications to their own lives. How might the speech help to draw speaker and audience together? Does the message stimulate them to think about the subject being discussed? What constructive role could your students play as listeners in the creations of a quality, responsible message reflecting a mutual concern for all those who might be affected by it? What ideas does the speech raise in your students' minds that the speaker may not have considered? Have your students jot down notes and ideas for class discussion between viewings. Project the transparency "Using Constructive Listening Skills" in conjunction with this activity.

Applying Critical Thinking Skills

Purpose: To provide students an opportunity to apply their critical thinking skills to speeches by well known public figures.

Directions: This is intended for in-class use, although it easily adapts to an outside writing assignment. Show a videotape of a public figure making a speech on an important contemporary issue, and have your students take notes for subsequent analysis and discussion. If necessary, review the text on critically evaluating speeches. Project the transparency "Using Critical Thinking Skills" to guide class discussion. Focus the discussion on responsible information use, distinguishing facts from opinions, concrete language use, the reasonableness of the speaker's claims, and the extent to which her or his message takes into account differing perspectives on the issue being addressed. You might note that prominent figures who have already developed their public ethos can get away with fewer citations of respected sources of information than can younger, unknown speakers. Emphasize for your students the differences between what's expected of "prominent speakers" and what's expected of them in your class.

Describing Speakers: Pros and Cons

Purpose: To get your students thinking about the way they habitually evaluate public speakers with respect to familiar exemplars.

Directions: This can be adapted for homework or a small-group activity followed by general class discussion. Have each student think of a person (public speaker, teacher, celebrity) to whom they like to listen, and another to whom they do not like to listen. They should then compile separate lists of adjectives to describe both persons. As an alternative, give them a list of public figures they are likely to be familiar with (Bill Clinton, Barbara Walters, Bob Dole, Jesse Jackson, etc.) and have your students brainstorm things they like or dislike about their speaking styles. Have them present their adjectives in class, and collate them on the chalkboard under the headings "good" and "poor" speakers. Adjectives that typically characterize "good" speakers might include dynamic, friendly, intelligent, informed, committed, honest, warm-hearted, considerate, cheerful, well-organized, interesting, and humorous. Adjectives that typically characterize "poor" speakers include dull, cold, indifferent, ignorant, uninformed, deceitful, and monotonous. You might further sort your students' adjectives into the major areas of speech as covered on a basic evaluation form (see this chapter, p. 122). Do your students seem preoccupied with presentation skills? How do their adjectives fit into the four basic categories of ethos: competence, integrity, likability, and forcefulness? For discussion, have your students qualify their adjectives with specific illustrations and reasons, and indicate what speakers might do to make themselves more enjoyable to listen to.

Listening Self-Evaluations

Purpose: To have your students spend an in-class speech day focusing exclusively on their own habitual listening behaviors.

Directions: This works well as an outside writing assignment, although it can be used for general discussion during the class period after a completed round of speeches. It's a good way to get your students to pay attention to their classmates' speeches, and to engage them in a constructive as well as critical manner. During your next round of class speeches, have your students choose a day in which they will attempt to be an especially exemplary listener. As they listen to their classmates' speeches, they should try to balance their critical and constructive skills, perceiving messages as they are intended, and seeking creative applications to their own lives. Have your students keep notes and write a short one- to two-page report on their experiences, focusing on their strengths and shortcomings as listeners on that particular day, as well as giving suggestions for improving their own performance. As you evaluate these, consider the extent to which your students balance critical comments with constructive rejoinders for improvement, as well as substance and structural concerns with their classmates' presentation skills.

Outside Speech Critique

Purpose: To have your students engage their critical and constructive listening skills in the evaluation of real-life public presentations.

Directions: Have your students attend and critique an outside speaking event. You might assign this early and have it due toward the end of the semester. Most larger college campuses sponsor lectures by well-known scholars and public officials, as well as lectures by their own more prominent faculty members. Have your students attend such a presentation and write a three- to five-page critique that addresses the following areas:

1. What was the nature of the public speaking situation or event? What was the general function and purpose of the speaker's presentations? Was it appropriate given that situation and the audience's likely expectations?

2. What were the speaker's main and main supporting ideas? Were they well supported with reasoning, a variety of supporting information, and effective language use?

3. Were the speaker's main ideas easy to follow? Were they organized using a coherent design scheme, and clearly distinguished by an effective use of transitions? Did they get your attention and involve your interest in the introduction, and provide a sense of closure in the conclusion?

4. Was the speaker's presentation effective? Did he or she appear to speak extemporaneously, from memory, or from a teleprompter or manuscript? Did the speaker make effective eye contact, and did movements and gestures complement the tone of the message? Does his or her voice project enough volume and variety to contribute meaningfully to the message?

5. In general, what do you think were the strongest and weakest aspects of your chosen speaker's presentations? What constructive advice would you give him or her for future presentations?

For a less time-consuming alternative, shorten the writing assignment and have your students respond to speeches presented on C-Span.

Observing Audiences

Purpose: To impress upon your students the variety of "real-world" audience listening behaviors.

Directions: Have your students attend a public speech or a large lecture on campus. Instead of attending to the speech or lecture, they should inconspicuously observe audience behaviors, remembering examples of good and poor listening and different types of feedback. You might have them write down their ideas in preparation for this activity. During the next class period, have them report their observations so that a class profile of good and poor listening behaviors can be compiled for discussion. You might have them focus specifically on audience behaviors that pose a significant challenge to effective speaking (heckling, talking and making other noises, coming and going, etc.), and focus discussion on alternative strategies for dealing with such challenges. To ensure that everyone participates in this exercise, take up their observations for a quick pass or fail–type evaluation.

The Infamous Pop Quiz

Purpose: To determine whether students are reading assigned material, and to refocus (as necessary) their attention.

Directions: By this time in the semester, many instructors begin to suspect that their students are no longer keeping up with assigned readings. In such cases, a "pop quiz" covering that day's assigned material may help to get their attention. You might allow your students to grade their own quizzes, discussing the answers in turn, and even give them the option of not counting this first one so long as your point is sufficiently made. Tell your students that there will probably be more "pop quizzes" in the future that will definitely be recorded.

Name _____ Section _____

True-False Quiz: Place a T or an F on the blank next to each statement.

_____ 1. Listening is an automatic physiological process.

_____ 2. Students who listen effectively earn better grades and achieve beyond what their intelligence levels suggest.

_____ 3. Heavy television viewing tends to increase one's attention span.

_____ 4. The usual public speaking rate is about 125 words per minute.

_____ 5. The usual rate at which people process information is about one hundred words per minute.

_____ 6. People tend to listen less critically to speeches that support their own positions.

_____ 7. Effective listeners pay attention only to the words that are spoken.

_____ 8. Connotation is a major criterion for the evaluation of speeches.

_____ 9. Trigger words have strong denotative meanings.

_____ 10. Critical listeners differentiate among facts, inferences, and opinions.

_____ 11. A critique of a speech consists of telling the speaker what he or she did wrong.

_____ 12. The speaker is solely responsible for the effectiveness of communication.

_____ 13. Critical thinking includes discussing your ideas with others to test and enrich your thinking.

_____ 14. When you engage in assimilation, you interpret positions similar to your own as being closer than they actually are.

_____ 15. Listening is the most pervasive and most well-developed communication activity in our lives.

Discussion Guide for True/False "Pop Quiz," Chapter 3

1. F   Hearing is involuntary. Listening is a conscious process that rewards according to the amount of effort expended. Critical listening includes paying attention, hearing, interpreting, comprehending, analyzing and evaluating, remembering, and responding to messages. *(text p. 69)*

2. T   Critical listeners also perform better at work and are less susceptible to unscrupulous leaders and misleading advertising appeals. *(text pp. 70–71)*

3. F   Most critics correlate heavy television viewing with ineffective listening habits. Heavy television viewers may develop shortened attention spans and focus more on the entertainment than on the informative or persuasive functions of communication. *(text p. 79)*

4. T   Move immediately to the next item and discuss the two together. *(text p. 75)*

5. F   The usual rate of processing information is approximately five hundred words per minute. The difference between the speed at which people talk and the speed at which people process ideas and information invites inattention. *(text p. 75)*

6. T   If a listener's feelings toward a speaker are especially positive, he or she may be more attentive, but he or she may also accept anything the speaker says without question. On the other hand, negative feelings tend to make listeners less attentive and less likely to accept the speaker's information or advice. Being attentive and being critical are two different (if often related) things. *(text p. 77)*

7. F   Listening only for facts is a bad habit that leads to ineffective listening. A person who listens only for words and tries to write down everything a speaker says may miss nonverbal nuances that can greatly affect the meaning of a message. *(text p. 80)*

8. F   Connotative meanings include the emotional or attitudinal reactions that certain words can arouse in listeners. *(text pp. 75–76)* Move on to the next question and continue the discussion of types of meaning.

9. F   The denotative meaning of a word is its dictionary definition. Trigger words have strong connotative meanings. They set off extreme emotional reactions that interfere with effective critical listening ability. *(text pp. 75–76)*

10. T   Facts are verifiable units of information that can be confirmed by independent observation. Inferences are projections based on facts. Opinions add interpretations or judgments to facts. *(text p. 83)*

11. F   A critique should be helpful and supportive, giving credit where it is due and pointing out strengths as well as weaknesses. When addressing weaknesses, include hopeful suggestions for improvement. Overly negative criticism can foster a competitive, even hostile communication environment that inhibits learning. *(text pp. 85–86).*

12. F   People who mistakenly assume that speakers are solely responsible for public communication usually become passive recipients in the process. The listener has a very important role in providing feedback to speakers to complete the dynamic circle of communication. *(text pp. 85–89)*

13. T   Critical thinking also involves questioning for clarification, reaching one's own conclusions or decisions after considering the options, being open to new ideas and new perspectives,

supporting personal views with reason and evidence, and demanding reasons and evidence from others before accepting what they have to say on an issue. *(text pp. 81–82)*

14. T   Assimilation is a basic form of listening distortion. Other related forms of distortion include filtering and contrast effects. *(text p. 78)*

15. F   Listening is the most pervasive, but *least*-developed communication activity in our lives. Adults spend approximately half of their communication time hearing, and college students even more. Unfortunately, most people retain less than 25 percent of what they hear. *(text p. 68)*

Craig Newburger (Christopher Newport University, Newport News, VA), "Testing Students' Ability to Distinguish Facts from Inferences," *SCT* (Winter 1994), 13–14.

Goal: To confront students with our susceptibility for perceiving inferential observations as being factual.

Students are told that one source of perceptual misinterpretation involves an individual's ability to make finite distinctions between what is factual and what is inferential. A **fact** is defined as *something that has been or can be objectively verified*, while an **inference** is defined as *a conclusion a person draws from some observation(s)*. Students are asked to listen carefully to the original story presented here without writing notes. After the story is presented, they are asked to indicate (on a piece of note paper, without discussion) whether statements about the story are factually or inferentially based. Their answers are tallied on the blackboard by the instructor. The correct answers are then presented and discrepancies are discussed.

Fact or Inference?

Bill had been laboring for the past two months on a project at work. He had just successfully completed the project and his employer was so pleased with his work that he gave him a ten day paid vacation as a bonus. Bill decided to just stay around the house and be lazy. Late in the day he noticed that it was getting dark outside so he decided to walk his dog while there was still light. His neighbor, Stephen Lewis, a young single doctor, just bought a new red Buick Regal. As Bill was walking down the street he noticed a new red Buick Regal parked in Mrs. Smith's (a professional model) driveway. He knew that Mrs. Smith's husband, Bob, was out of town on a business trip. Bill could hear shouting coming from her house, and later, just before he was done walking his dog, he saw Dr. Lewis speeding down the street in his car. Bill noticed there was no longer a car parked in Mrs. Smith's driveway. That evening Bill heard sirens, so he stepped out on his front porch to see what was going on. An ambulance was just pulling out of Mrs. Smith's driveway when a police officer introduced himself and informed Bill that he would like to ask a few questions about Mrs. Smith.

Questions

Write "F" for fact and "I" for inference.

1. It was dusk when Bill decided to walk his dog.

2. A red Buick Regal was parked in Mrs. Smith's driveway.

3. Bill could not hear what the man and Mrs. Smith were arguing about.

4. Bill did not know why Dr. Lewis was visiting Mrs. Smith.

5. Bill did not know why Mrs. Smith was attacked.

6. Until the police arrived, Bill did not have any reason to be concerned about Dr. Lewis' speeding.

7. Shouting was coming from Mrs. Smith's house.

8. Mrs. Smith's husband, Bob, was out of town on business.

9. Bill saw Dr. Lewis speeding down the street in his new red Buick Regal.

10. The story involves only the following characters: Bill, Bill's dog, Dr. Lewis, Mrs. Smith, Mrs. Smith's husband (Bob), a policeman, Bill's employer, and whoever was in the ambulance.

Correct Answers and Explanations

1. This statement is inferential. We do not know from the story how late in the day Bill embarked on his walk. The sky could have been overcast. He was on vacation, and his sense of time might have been distorted. All we know from the story was that "it was getting dark outside."

2. This statement is factual.

3. This statement is inferential. All we know from the story is that Bill could hear shouting coming from Mrs. Smith's house. We do not know whether the shouting involved a man and a woman, two women, one or more persons of unknown sex, or whether Mrs. Smith was even involved.

4. This statement is inferential. Dr. Lewis does not own the only new red Buick Regal in America. Further, we do not know whether the owner of the car was even in the house, or whether Mrs. Smith was home, for that matter. She may have just purchased her own new red Buick Regal.

5. This statement is inferential. Who was attacked? Was anyone taken away in the ambulance? If so, for what reason? Could it be that Mrs. Smith attacked someone? The story does not mention that anyone was attacked.

6. This statement is inferential. How did the story in any way implicate Dr. Lewis in some questionable activity? The story does not even directly place him at the premises of Mrs. Smith.

7. This statement is factual.

8. This statement is inferential. The story indicates that Bill "knew that Mrs. Smith's husband, Bob, was out of town on business," but was he? For all we know, he was inside the house shouting (another inference).

9. This statement is inferential. The new red Buick Regal may not be the only car that Dr. Lewis owned. The story did not provide a description of the car in which he was speeding down the street.

10. This statement is inferential. There exists the unknown factor of who was in Mrs. Smith's house doing the shouting.

SUPPLEMENTARY MATERIALS

Films and Videos

"Listening and Speaking," Films for the Humanities, color, 15 minutes.

"Listening Assertively," RMI Media Productions, 28 minutes.

"Many Hear—Some Listen," Coronet/MTI Film and Video, color, 12 minutes.

"The Power of Listening," CRM/McGraw-Hill, color, 26 minutes.

"Effective Listening," RMI Media Productions, 28 minutes.

"Receiving a Message," Films for the Humanities, color, 15 minutes.

"A Case Study for Critical Thinking: Vietnam," Insight Media, 52 minutes.

Student Speakers Videos to accompany *Public Speaking*.

"Listen to Communicate," CRM/McGraw-Hill, 40 minutes.

"Listen Well, Learn Well," Coronet, 11 minutes.

"The Art of Listening," Insight Media, 27 minutes.

"Study Skills: How to Listen Effectively," A Guidance Associates Video, 16 minutes.

"Listening: A Key to Problem Solving," Paramount, 16 minutes.

"Critical Thinking: Making Sure of the Facts," Coronet, 11 minutes.

"Critical Thinking: How to Evaluate Information and Draw Conclusions," Insight Media, 47 minutes.

"How to Listen Effectively," RMI Media Productions, 28 minutes.

"The Power of Listening," CRM/McGraw-Hill, 26 minutes.

"The Listening Process," RMI Media Productions, 28 minutes.

"You're Not Listening," Arthur Barr Productions, 21 minutes.

Software

"Critical Thinking I," Compris.

Transparencies and Handouts *(see following pages)*

Improving Your Listening Skills (Transparency 3.1)

Using Constructive Listening Skills (Transparency 3.2)

Using Critical Thinking Skills (Transparency 3.3)

Listening Problems Checklist

Speech Evaluation Form

IMPROVING YOUR LISTENING SKILLS

1. Be conscious of your own listening behaviors and problems.

2. Motivate yourself to listen constructively.

3. Be prepared to listen by paying attention and putting problems and bias aside.

4. Control your reactions.

   a. Recognize and control inattention.

   b. Identify your own trigger words.

   c. Postpone critical evaluations and judgment until all of a message has been heard.

5. Work to improve your listening skills by seeking to expand your attention span.

6. Listen for main ideas and information.

7. Focus on the message and not on extraneous factors.

USING CONSTRUCTIVE LISTENING SKILLS

1. Consider whether and how the speech draws you closer to the speaker or other members of the audience.

2. Consider the impact of the message on other people.

3. Does the message stimulate you to think?

4. How might the speech relate to your life?

5. What ideas or possibilities does the speech raise in your mind that the speaker may not have considered?

USING CRITICAL THINKING SKILLS

1. Are the speaker's claims supported by facts and figures, testimony, examples, or narratives?

2. Are supporting materials relevant, representative, recent, and reliable?

3. Are the sources of information cited credible?

4. Does the speaker distinguish among facts, inferences, and opinions?

5. Is the language clear and concrete, or does it seem purposely vague and incomprehensible?

6. Does the message ask you to ignore reason and appeal mainly to your emotions and attitudes?

7. Do the speaker's conclusions follow logically from the information that precedes them?

8. Does the speaker make outlandish promises or claims?

9. Does this message fit with what you already know about the topic?

LISTENING PROBLEMS CHECKLIST

_____ 1. I believe listening is an automatic process, not a learned behavior.

_____ 2. I stop listening and think about something else when a speech is uninteresting.

_____ 3. I find it hard to listen to speeches on topics about which I feel strongly.

_____ 4. I react emotionally to trigger words.

_____ 5. I am easily distracted by noises when someone is speaking.

_____ 6. I don't like to listen to speakers who are not experts.

_____ 7. I find some people too objectionable to listen to.

_____ 8. I nod off when someone talks in a monotone.

_____ 9. I can be so dazzled by a glib presentation that I don't really listen to the speaker.

_____ 10. I don't like to listen to speeches that contradict my values.

_____ 11. I think up counterarguments when I disagree with a speaker's perspective.

_____ 12. I know so much on some topics that I can't learn from most speakers.

_____ 13. I believe the speaker is the one responsible for effective communication.

_____ 14. I find it hard to listen when I have a lot on my mind.

_____ 15. I stop listening when a subject is difficult.

_____ 16. I can look like I'm listening when I am not.

_____ 17. I listen only for facts and ignore the rest of a message.

_____ 18. I try to write down everything a lecturer says.

_____ 19. I let a speaker's appearance determine how well I listen.

_____ 20. I often jump to conclusions before I have listened all the way through a message.

SPEECH EVALUATION FORM

SPEAKER _____ TOPIC _____ DATE _____

OVERALL CONSIDERATIONS

_____ Did the speaker seem committed to the topic?
_____ Did the speech meet the requirements of the assignment?
_____ Was the speech adapted to fit the audience?
_____ Did the speech promote identification among topic, audience, and speaker?
_____ Was the purpose of the speech clear?
_____ Was the topic handled with imagination and freshness?
_____ Did the speech meet high ethical standards?

SUBSTANCE

_____ Was the topic worthwhile?
_____ Had the speaker done sufficient research?
_____ Were the main ideas supported with reliable and relevant information?
_____ Was testimony used appropriately?
_____ Were the sources documented appropriately?
_____ Were examples or narratives used effectively?
_____ Was the reasoning clear and correct?

STRUCTURE

_____ Did the introduction spark your interest?
_____ Did the introduction adequately preview the message?
_____ Was the speech easy to follow?
_____ Could you identify the main points of the speech?
_____ Were transitions used to tie the speech together?
_____ Did the conclusion summarize the message?
_____ Did the conclusion help you to remember the speech?

PRESENTATION

_____ Was the language clear, simple, and direct?
_____ Was the language colorful?
_____ Were grammar and pronunciation correct?
_____ Was the speech presented extemporaneously?
_____ Were notes used unobtrusively?
_____ Was the speaker appropriately enthusiastic?
_____ Did the speaker maintain good eye contact?
_____ Did gestures and body language complement ideas?
_____ Was the speaker's voice expressive?
_____ Were the rate and loudness appropriate to the material?
_____ Did the speaker use pauses appropriately?
_____ Did visual aids make the message clearer or more memorable?
_____ Were visual aids skillfully integrated into the speech?
_____ Was the presentation free from distracting mannerisms?

READINGS FOR ENRICHMENT

See guide to journal abbreviations on p. 37.

* Items marked with an asterisk are suitable for student enrichment.

Listening

Ayres, Joe, A. Kathleen Wilcox, and Debbie M. Ayres. "Receiver Apprehension: An Explanatory Model and Accompanying Research." *CE* (July 1995), 223–235.

Baldridge, Letitia. "The Art of Listening." *Town & Country* (Aug. 1995), 54–55.

Barker, Larry L., and Kittie W. Watson. "Listening Behavior, Definition, and Management." In *Communication Yearbook VIII,* edited by Robert Bostrum, pp. 178–197. Beverly Hills, Calif.: International Communication Association, 1986.

Barker, Larry L., Kittie W. Watson, and Robert J. Kibler. "An Investigation of the Effect of Presentations by Effective and Ineffective Speakers on Listening Test Scores." *SSCJ* (Spring 1984), 309–318.

Bohlken, Bob. "Learning to Listen as You Listen to Learn." *SCT* (Winter 1994), 8–9.

Boileau, Don M. "Listening: Teaching and Research." *CE* (Oct. 1983), 442–447.

Borisoff, Deborah, and Michael Purdy, eds. *Listening in Everyday Life: A Personal and Professional Approach.* Lanham, Md.: University Press of America, 1991.

Bostrom, Robert N., ed. *Listening Behavior: Measurement and Application.* New York: Guilford, 1990.

Bostrom, Robert, and Carol Bryant. "Factors in the Retention of Information Presented Orally: The Role of Short-Term Listening." *WJSC* (Spring 1980), 137–145.

Caudill, Donald W., and Regina M. Donaldson. "Effective Listening Tips for Managers." *Administrative Management* (Sept. 1986), 22–23.

Coakley, Carolyn, and Andrew D. Wolvin, eds. *Experiential Listening: Tools for Teachers and Trainers.* New Orleans: Spectra, 1989.

Devine, Thomas G. "Listening: What Do We Know After Fifty Years of Research and Theorizing?" *Journal of Reading* (1978), 299.

Edwards, Richard T. "You Cannot Communicate Unless You Are a Good Listener." *American Salesman* (Oct. 1990), 28–29.

Fiumara, Gemma C. *The Other Side of Language: A Philosophy of Listening.* London: Routledge, 1990.

Floyd, James J. *Listening: A Practical Approach.* Glenview, Ill.: Scott, Foresman, 1985.

Forestieri, Mary. "Listening Instruction." *SCT* (Spring 1987), 14–15.

Galvin, Kathleen. *Listening by Doing.* Lincolnwood, Ill.: National Textbook Company, 1985.

Gordon, Ronald D. "Communicating Positive Feedback." *SCT* (Summer 1988), 7, 10.

* Goss, Blaine. "Listening as Information Processing." *CQ* (Fall 1982), 304–307.

Handel, Stephen. *Listening.* Cambridge, Mass.: MIT Press, 1989.

* Harris, Tom W. "Listen Carefully." *Nation's Business* (June 1989), 78.

Hunt, Gary T., and Louis P. Cusella. "A Field Study of Listening Needs in Organizations." *CE* (Oct. 1983), 393–401.

Hyde, Richard Bruce. "Council: Using a Talking Stick to Teach Listening." *SCT* (Winter 1993), 1–2.

* "Is Anyone Out There Listening?" Excerpted from March 1969 issue of *The Alcoa News,* Alcoa Aluminum Company of America. Reprinted in Marcus L. Ambrester and Faye D. Julian, eds., *Speech Communication Reader* (Prospect Heights, Ill.: 1983), 89–90.

Jenson, Marvin D. "Listening With the Third Ear: An Experience in Empathy." *SCT* (Summer 1989), 10–11.

Johnson, Marcia. "Student Listening Tests." *SCT* (Winter 1991), 5.

* Karush, Teri Lynn. "Are You Listening, Really Listening?" *Cosmopolitan* (Dec. 1995), 104–105.

* Kiechel, Walter, III. "Learn How to Listen." *Fortune,* 17 Aug. 1987, pp. 107–108.

* Lane, Margaret. "Are You Really Listening?" *Reader's Digest* (Nov. 1980), 183.

Loesch, Robert W. "Three Nonverbal Listening Styles: A Demonstration." *SCT* (Summer 1987), 4.

Lundsteen, Sarah W. *Listening.* Urbana, Ill.: ERIC Clearinghouse on Reading and Communication Skills, 1979.

McPeak, Judith L. "Listening Activities." *SCT* (Spring 1994), 15–16.

* Miller, Arthur R. "Are You a Lousy Listener?" *Industry Week*, 5 Aug. 1985, pp. 44–45.

* Nichols, Ralph G. "Do We Know How to Listen: Practical Helps in a Modern Age." In *Speech Communication Reader*, edited by Marcus L. Ambrester and Faye D. Julian, pp. 91–99. Prospect Heights, Ill.: 1983.

———. "Listening Is a Ten-Part Skill." *Nation's Business* (Sept. 1987), 40.

O'Brien, Patricia. "Why Men Don't Listen . . . and What It Costs Women at Work." *Working Woman* (Feb. 1993), 56–60.

Osborg, Sharon. "Advanced Listening, Speaking, and Pronunciation Video Demonstration" [for ESL Students]. Paper presented at the Annual Meeting of the Teachers of English to Speakers of Other Languages, Long Beach Calif., 1995. Available through ERIC.

Pavitt, Charles. "Biases in the Recall of Communicators' Behaviors." *CR* (Winter 1989), 9–15.

Rhodes, Steven C. "What the Communication Journals Tell Us About Teaching Listening." *CSSJ* (Spring/Summer 1985), 24–32.

Rubin, Donald L. "Instruction in Speaking and Listening: Battles and Options." *Educational Leadership* (Feb. 1985), 32.

Schwartz, Jackie. "Listening Is an Important Business Skill, Especially for Managers." *Office Administration and Automation* (Sept. 1985), 81–82.

* Steil, Lyman K. "Your Personal Listening Profile." In *Speech Communication Reader*, edited by Marcus L. Ambrester and Faye D. Julian, pp. 101–109. Prospect Heights, Ill.: 1983.

Steil, Lyman K., Larry L. Barker, and Kittie W. Watson. *Effective Listening*. New York: Random House, 1983.

* Strother, Deborah Burnett. "On Listening." *Phi Delta Kappan* (Apr. 1987), 625–628.

Sypher, Beverly Davenport, Robert N. Bostrom, and Joy Hart Seibert. "Listening, Communication Abilities, and Success at Work." *Journal of Business Communication* (1989), 293–303.

Valentin, Kristin B., Michael L. Hecht, Frederick Corey, and Janet L. Jacobsen. "Two Measures of Audience Response to Performance." *CR* (Summer 1995), 170–177.

Watson, Kittie W., and Larry L. Barker. "Listening Behavior: Definition and Measurement." In *Communication Yearbook 8*, edited by R. N. Bostrom and B. Westley, pp. 178–197. Beverly Hills, Calif.: Sage, 1984.

Weaver, Carl H. *Human Listening: Processes and Behavior*. Indianapolis: Bobbs-Merrill, 1972.

Wirkus, Tom E. "Creating Student-Generated Listening Activities." *SCT* (Winter 1993), 3–4.

Wolff, Florence L., Nadine C. Marsnik, William S. Tacey and Ralph G. Nichols. *Perceptive Listening*. Englewood Cliffs, N.J.: Prentice-Hall, 1983.

Wolvin, Andrew D., and Carolyn Gwynn Coakley. *Listening Instruction*. Urbana, Ill.: ERIC Clearinghouse on Reading and Communication Skills, 1979.

———. "A Survey of the Status of Listening Training in Some Fortune 500 Corporations." *CE* (Apr. 1991), 152–164.

———. *Listening*, 4th ed. Dubuque, Iowa: Wm. C. Brown, 1992.

* "Your Attention, Please," *Changing Times*, 40 (Oct. 1986), pp. 127–129.

Critical Thinking

Beal, Carol. "Challenging Your Convictions: Critical Thinking Speech Activities for Secondary Students." *SCT* (Spring 1994), 6–7.

Beall, Melissa L. "Thinking About Thinking." *SCT* (Summer 1991), 2–3.

Bozik, Mary, and Melissa Beall. "Modeling Metaphorical Thinking." *SCT* (Winter 1994), 1–2.

Chaffee, John. *Thinking Critically*, 2nd ed. Boston: Houghton Mifflin, 1988.

Faries, Liz. "The Upside Down Exercise." *SCT* (Summer 1992), 10.

Fritz, Paul A., and Richard L. Weaver II. "Teaching Critical Thinking Skills in the Basic Course: A Liberal Arts Perspective." *CE* (April 1986), 174–182.

Haehl, Anne. "An Exercise in Believability." *SCT* (Winter 1992), 2.

* Hayakawa, S. I., and Alan R. Hayakawa. "Reporters, Inferences, Judgments." In *Language in Thought and Action*, 5th ed. San Diego, Calif.: Harcourt Brace Jovanovich, 1990, 22–32.

Hiland, Leah F. "Information and Thinking Skills and Processes to Prepare Young Adults for the Information Age." *Library Trends* (Summer 1988), 56–62.

* "How to Analyze a News Story: Eight Guidelines for Reading Between the Lines." *Media & Values* (Summer 1990), 22.

* Hynds, Patricia. "Balance Bias with Critical Questions." *Media & Values* (Summer 1990), 5–7.

Katula, Richard A., and Celest A. Martin. "Teaching Critical Thinking in the Speech Communication Classroom." *CE* (Apr. 1984), 160–167.

Kidd, Virginia. "Introduction to Message Analysis Through Cereal Boxes." *SCT* (Summer 1989), 1–2.

Krapp, JoAnn Vergona. "Teaching Research Skills: A Critical-Thinking Approach." *School Library Journal* (Jan. 1988), 32–35.

Newburger, Craig. "Testing Students' Ability to Distinguish Facts from Inferences." *SCT* (Winter 1994), 13–14.

O'Keefe, Virginia P. *Affecting Critical Thinking Through Speech*. Urbana, Ill.: ERIC Clearinghouse on Reading and Communication Skills, 1986. Available through the Speech Communication Association, 5105 Backlick Road, Suite E, Annandale, Va. 22003.

Palmerton, Patricia R. "Teaching Skills or Teaching Thinking?" *ACR* (Aug. 1992), 335–341.

* Postman, Neil. "Critical Thinking in the Electronic Age." *National Forum* (Winter 1985), 4–8. Reprinted in *Selected Issues in Logic and Communication*, edited by Trudy Govier, pp. 11–18. Belmont, Calif.: Wadsworth, 1988.

Powell, Robert G. "Critical Thinking and Speech Communication: Our Teaching Strategies Are Warranted—Not!" *ACR* (Aug. 1992), 342–347.

Proctor, Russell E. II. "Using Feature Films to Teach Critical Thinking." *SCT* (Spring 1993), 11–12.

Rankin, Virginia. "One Route to Critical Thinking." *School Library Journal* (Jan. 1988), 28–32.

Reppert, James E. "Critical Thinking Strategies for Nontraditional Students." Paper presented at the Speech Communication Association Convention, Miami Beach, Fla., 1993. Available through ERIC.

* Roberts, Donald F., Peter Christenson, Wendy A. Gibson, Linda Mooser, and Marvin E. Goldberg. "Developing Discriminating Consumers." *JC* (Summer 1980), 94–105.

Roth, Michael S. "On the Limits of Critical Thinking." *Tikkun* (Jan.–Feb. 1996), 86–96.

Sanders, Judith A., Richard L. Wiseman, and Robert H. Gass. "Does Teaching Argumentation Facilitate Students' Critical Thinking?" *CR* (Winter 1994), 27–35.

Schumer, Allison. "Speech Communication Via Critical Thinking—'It's In the Bag.'" *SCT* (Summer 1991), 4–5.

Spicer, Karin-Leigh, and William E. Hanks. "Critical Thinking Activities for Communication Textbooks." *SCT* (Summer 1993), 6–7.

Stoebig, Joe. "Speech Logs with a Twist." *SCT* (Spring 1992), 13 (critical thinking)

* Weddle, Perry. "Distinguishing Fact from Opinion." In *Selected Issues in Logic and Communication*, edited by Trudy Govier. Belmont, Calif.: Wadsworth, 1988. Adapted from "Fact From Opinion." *Informal Logic* (Winter 1985).

Evaluating Speeches

Bitunjac, John. "Self-Analysis: A Step Towards Becoming a Skillful Public Speaker." *SCT* (Summer 1987), 4–5.

Bollinger, Lee. "Tough Self-Evaluators." *SCT* (Summer 1995), 14.

Book, Cassandra, and Katrina Wynkoop Simmons. "Dimensions and Perceived Helpfulness of Student Speech Criticism." *CE* (May 1980), 135–145.

Carlson, Robert E., and Deborah Smith-Howell. "Classroom Public Speaking Assessment: Reliability and Validity of Selected Evaluation Instruments." *CE* (Apr. 1995), 87–97.

Goulden, Nancy Rost, and Charles J. G. Griffin. "The Meaning of Grades Based on Faculty and Student Metaphors." *CE* (Apr. 1995), 110–125.

Hallmark, James R. "Using Your Computer to Evaluate Speeches." *SCT* (Winter 1994), 3–4.

Haynes, W. Lance. "Grading Student Speeches: An Experiential Approach." *SCT* (Fall 1989), 1–2.

Kramer, Cheris. "Women's and Men's Ratings of Their Own and Ideal Speech." *CQ* (Spring 1978), 2–11.

LaFleur, Gary B. "A Special Tool for Offering Criticism: The Post-Speech Transcript." *ACAB* (Oct. 1985), 63–64.

Mino, Mary, and Dale A. Bertelsen. "Critiquing Student Speeches: Two Approaches." *SCT* (Winter 1993), 15–16.

Mino, Mary, and Marilyn N. Butler. "Using Oral Self-Evaluations to Assess and Improve Public Speaking Skills." *SCT* (Spring 1995), 4.

Phillips, Gary. "Put Your Test on ICE." *SCT* (Summer 1991), 8–9.

Rollman, Steven A. "Leading Class Discussions Which Evaluate Student's Oral Performance." *SCT* (Spring 1992), 10–12.

Stahl, Michael G. "Critiques That Count." *SCT* (Summer 1994), 5–6.

Webb, Lynn. "A Student-Devised Evaluation Form." *SCT* (Spring 1989), 5–6.

Chapter 3 General

Gorg, Robert. "The Use of Model Speeches on Videotapes (or See, Your Friends Can Do This Too!)." *SCT* (Fall 1993), 11–12.

Richmond, Virginia P. *Nonverbal Communication in the Classroom*. Edina, Minn.: Burgess, 1992.

West, Richard, and Judy C. Pearson. "Antecedent and Consequent Conditions of Student Questioning: An Analysis of Classroom Discourse Across the University." *CE* (Oct. 1994), 299–311.

CHAPTER 4
Adapting to Your Audience and Situation

OBJECTIVES

- To help your students understand the dynamics of their audiences.

- To help your students adapt their messages to audience characteristics.

- To help your students meet the ethical challenges of diversity.

- To help your students adjust their speeches to the presentation situation.

SUGGESTIONS FOR TEACHING

Audience analysis is another vitally important area of public speaking that often, unfortunately, receives little more than lip service in our basic courses. If you do not emphasize its importance, your students may prepare and present their speeches in a vacuum, as if they were intended to be delivered at any time to any audience, which defeats a major purpose of the course. We give speeches to bring specific people together on specific situations for specific reasons, and a crucial step in preparing effective speeches is to learn as much as possible about these factors.

Audience and situational considerations should affect every aspect of planning, researching, composing, and presenting speeches, and they become progressively more important when trying to influence or persuade people on significant issues. There are activities and exercises in other chapters of this IRM that have your students address audience considerations when selecting topics and supporting materials, crafting arguments, using feedback, and engaging in other aspects of public speaking; many of these activities can be coordinated with the ones in this chapter. Here we offer activities that cover the use of sexist language and stereotypes, need-based or psychological appeals, selecting and adapting speech materials, adapting to problem situations, the integration of audience demographics and dynamics in making long-range adjustments, and the assumptions that speakers make about audiences when developing their messages. We also offer surveys and exercises to gather information about your own particular classroom audience for students to use when preparing their speeches. You might want to administer a survey to chart your classes' predominant values and social/political convictions early in the course in order to emphasize the importance of knowing these things from the first assignment. Finally, we offer activities in which your students customize basic surveys and audience analyses to fit their particular speech topics.

CHAPTER OUTLINE

I. The more speakers know about their audiences and speaking situations, the more likely they are to make effective presentations. *(text pp. 101–102)*

    A. Considerations of audience and situational factors affect every aspect of the craft. Audience analysis can help speakers:

        1. choose topics listeners will find interesting.

        2. assess how much audiences know and how they feel about a given topic.

        3. select supporting materials to strengthen their speeches.

        4. choose an overall design and structure for their speeches.

        5. choose techniques to help listeners understand and relate to their topics.

    B. The central ethical criterion for audience/situational adaptation is the speaker's motive—i.e., does she or he use adaptation techniques to disguise a position, or to reveal it most effectively to a particular audience?

        1. Adapting a message does not mean waffling, or changing its essence.

        2. Ethical adaptation entails tailoring to gain a fair hearing without compromising principle.

        3. Ethical adaptation begins with developing a sensitivity to audience and situation differences, and a respect for how the spoken word can affect the lives of others.

II. A basic understanding of audience dynamics, i.e., the motivations, attitudes, beliefs, and values that influence our behaviors, is crucial to developing a sensitivity that is crucial to audience adaptation. *(text pp. 102–109)*

    A. Motivation entails the basic needs and wants that explain why people behave as they do.

        1. People will listen, learn, and retain your message only if they can relate it to their needs, wants, or wishes.

        2. While the importance of specific motivations can vary among people and with situations, the following appeals are important to motivating audiences:

            a. personal comfort

            b. safety from fear

            c. friendship

            d. recognition

            e. change and variety

            f. control over our lives

            g. independence and self-sufficiency

            h. curiosity and the need to understand

            i. tradition and a sense of history

            j. success and accomplishment

            k. nurturing and helping others in need

            l. enjoyment and relaxation

        3. Abraham Maslow organized human needs into a hierarchy of five levels, each of which must be reasonably satisfied before we can ascend to the next.

            a. Our most basic physiological needs are for water, food, air, and comfort.

                (1) Speeches addressing environmental health hazards invoke physiological needs.

            b. The second level of Maslow's hierarchy is safety and security needs.

                (1) The desire for a sense of protection and predictability is often invoked in speeches addressing topics such as crime and punishment.

            c. Belongingness needs entail the desire to give and receive affection, companionship, loyalty, approval, and support.

                (1) Speeches addressing social activities often invoke belongingness needs.

            d. Esteem needs include the desire for self-respect, prestige, and the respect of others.

                (1) Speeches that show listeners how to improve their lives or instill in them a sense of pride commonly invoke esteem needs.

            e. Our highest self-actualization needs are to grow as people, to realize our potentials, and to find our identities.

                (1) Speeches addressed to idealistic persons or those whose identity is not yet firmly established commonly invoke self-actualization appeals.

        4. The specific ways people choose to satisfy their needs may be determined by their attitudes, beliefs, and values.

a. Attitudes are positive or negative feelings about something—whether we like or dislike, approve or disapprove of people, events, or ideas.
   (1) Understanding audiences' attitudes can suggest strategies for getting a fair hearing.
b. Beliefs include what we think we know about something, and how we are inclined to act toward it.
   (1) Speakers may need to provide new or better information to correct faulty beliefs or understandings.
c. Our important social attitudes are usually anchored by our *values*, how we think we should behave or what we regard as an ideal state of being.
d. There are many ways to gather information regarding an audience's values, beliefs, and attitudes.
   (1) Student speakers can learn about their classmates by observing their input in class speeches and activities.
   (2) Outside the classroom, speakers often obtain information about their audiences from the person who invites them to speak.
   (3) Survey information (if available) can provide advance knowledge of audience dynamics. When conducting surveys, speakers should:
      (a) use language that is concrete, clear, and easily understood.
      (b) keep questions short and to the point.
      (c) use simple rather than complex or compound sentences.
      (d) avoid words such as *all, always, none,* and *never.*
      (e) keep bias out of their questions to avoid skewing results.
      (f) provide room for comments.
      (g) keep their questionnaires short.

III. Audience demographics are those observable characteristics of listeners that are important to successful audience adaptation. *(text pp. 110–117)*
A. By combining demographic information with an understanding of audience dynamics, speakers can better assess what their audiences know and how they might feel or be predisposed to act toward a given topic.
B. Student speakers can combine in-class observations with broader public opinion surveys to make intelligent adaptations.
C. The relevance of the following demographic categories may vary from topic to topic.
   1. Since Aristotle, age has been recognized as a crucial category for audience analysis.
      a. Younger audiences are generally considered more open to change and new ideas.
      b. College students represent an increasingly diversified segment of society.
         (1) The percentage of nontraditional students over thirty-five years old has been rising steadily for years and is projected to keep doing so.
         (2) Although less politically active than those of years past, today's college-age students hold strong political and social attitudes. While this may not reflect your particular class, college students tend to support:
            (a) tougher measures to fight and punish crime.
            (b) stronger government efforts to protect the environment.
            (c) handgun control.
            (d) increased consumer protection.
            (e) energy conservation.
            (f) developing a national health care plan.
   2. The gender makeup of an audience is very important.
      a. In our society, notions of "gender-appropriate" roles and interests are changing rapidly.
      b. Some of the greatest changes have come in the areas of work, education, and politics.
      c. Once elected, women tend to be more concerned with social issues that affect families and children.

d. Speakers may use gender as an effective category for audience analysis by making sure that reported differences really make a difference, making sure that assumptions are based on current data, and avoiding sexism and gender stereotyping.

3. The education level of an audience is suggestive of audience knowledge and interests. Educated audiences:
   a. are generally well informed on current events.
   b. are more likely to be concerned with social and political issues.
   c. tend to have a broad range of interests, and like to learn about new ideas, things, and places.
   d. tend to be critically open-minded and willing to accept changes.
   e. will respect only speakers who are especially well informed, and who acknowledge all viable options and alternative viewpoints.

4. An audience's many group affiliations merit careful consideration.
   a. People tend to choose social groups that correspond to their interests, attitudes, and values.
   b. *Occupational groups* often share interests and concerns that may help speakers:
      (1) choose and focus topics that will interest their audiences.
      (2) select effective examples and illustrations.
      (3) suggest authoritative sources that the audience is likely to respect.
      (4) determine the appropriateness of technical language or jargon.
   c. Members of organized political groups are usually interested in problems of public life.
      (1) People with strong political convictions tend to make their feelings known.
   d. Knowledge of an audience's affiliations with religious groups can provide useful information regarding social and cultural attitudes and values.
      (1) While religious denominations often advocate specific social and political views and attitudes, speakers should realize that membership in a church does not always entail unquestioning support of that church's political positions.
      (2) As most people are sensitive of their religious convictions, speakers should be wary of unnecessarily alienating people with different convictions.
   e. Membership in social groups can be as important as any other kind of affiliation.
      (1) People choose their social groups based on their own interests.
      (2) Many social groups (i.e., business and environmental groups) have explicit social and political agendas.

5. Sociocultural background can include everything from the section of the country from which audience members hail to their racial and ethnic identities.
   a. People from different sociocultural backgrounds often have different experiences, interests, and ways of looking at things.
   b. As most college classes are increasingly diverse, speakers should strive to reach the majority without ignoring or offending the minority.
   c. With diverse audiences, speakers should invoke experiences, feelings, values, and motivations that people hold in common.
   d. Introductory speeches can offer valuable insights regarding differences in sociocultural background.

IV. Mass media technologies present speakers with the challenges and opportunities of addressing audiences of unprecedented diversity. *(text pp. 117–124)*
   A. In order to address multicultural audiences effectively, speakers must understand the power of stereotypes and bias: ethnocentrism, sexism, and racism.
   1. Stereotypes are rigid sets of beliefs and expectations that prepare and predispose us toward good or bad or desirable or undesirable encounters with others.
      a. Positive and negative stereotypes may be based on such visible characteristics as gender, race, or age, or on ethnic identity, religion, occupation, or place of residence.

  b. Sometimes stereotypes are based on direct experience, but more often they are formed indirectly through exposure to family, friends, school, church, and the media.

  c. While people inevitably use stereotypes in making sense of their interactions, such stereotypes can be disastrous and should not be allowed to dominate our thinking and obscure our appreciation for people as individuals.

  d. Stereotypes are difficult to give up, especially when they are reinforced by family and friends.

    (1) Individuals who break stereotypes can easily be regarded as exceptions to the rule.

 2. Ethnocentrism, sexism, and racism represent the most common types of problems that impede effective communication with a diverse audience.

  a. Ethnocentrism is the belief that our way of life is the "right" and superior way.

    (1) When ethnocentrism goes beyond pride in one's own group to rejection or derogation of others, it becomes a real problem in human relations and a formidable barrier to cross-cultural communication.

    (2) Speakers can control their ethnocentrism by recognizing any tendencies they have to devalue other cultures, and by seeking out and respecting a humanity in all people that transcends race and culture.

  b. Sexism occurs when we allow gender stereotypes to control our interactions with members of the opposite sex.

    (1) Gender stereotyping, which involves making broad generalizations about men or women based on outmoded assumptions, is especially troublesome when it is used to justify discrimination.

    (2) Sexist language involves making gender references in situations where the gender is unknown or irrelevant.

      (a) Speakers should consider adopting a gender neutral/plural language style.

  c. Racism is also a serious block to effective cross-cultural communication.

    (1) Whereas blatant racism and discrimination are no longer socially acceptable in most circles, more subtle forms of *symbolic racism* may belie lip service to the principles of racial equality.

    (2) Speakers should consider their own biases and stereotypes, and be sensitive about their use of language, representative examples, and humor.

  d. Marking means adding irrelevant references to gender, ethnicity, race, or sexual preference (e.g., a *woman* doctor).

B. The search for common ground poses a great but not insurmountable challenge for today's public speaker.

 1. Survey data suggest that, whereas most "white" people believe that minorities enjoy equality of opportunity, most minorities perceive themselves as victims of discrimination.

 2. Americans are increasingly learning to value cultural differences. Most Americans now:

  a. rate learning about alternative cultural experiences and lifestyles as important.

  b. express a willingness to work with one another to solve problems in their local communities and neighborhoods.

 3. The following universal human values may be useful for transcending cultural barriers:

a. power	f. security
b. achievement	g. unity
c. tradition	h. benevolence
d. enjoyment	i. conformity
e. self-direction	j. stimulation

V. The last vital stage of analysis includes considerations of timing, place, occasion, audience size, and the overall context of your speech. *(text pp. 124–129)*

A. The time of day, day of the week, time of the year, and amount of time allotted for speaking may all call for careful consideration.
1. Speakers scheduled early in the morning or at night risk facing tired, inattentive listeners.
2. The day of the week and even seasonal changes can affect audience mood.
3. Speakers must focus their materials well when they are allotted a short presentation period.
B. The place where the speech is delivered should affect your planning.
1. Outdoor presentations can present unpredictable distractions.
2. Indoor presentations may be affected by sources of noise, the size and layout of the room, the availability of lecterns and electronic equipment, etc.
3. Speakers should maintain their composure and take physical distractions in stride.
C. The occasion (reason for gathering) can impose audience expectations on a speaker.
1. Speakers should work extra hard to involve a captive audience.
D. The size of the audience raises important considerations.
1. Whereas smaller audiences allow for more audience interaction and invite a more casual presentation style, larger audiences call for more distinctive language use and a more emphatic presentation style.
   a. As larger audiences mean less direct feedback, speakers should pan back and forth to audience members in all sections of the room.
E. Anything that happens near the time of your presentation becomes part of the context of your speech.
1. Recent speeches can have a preliminary tuning effect on listeners, predisposing them to respond to your message in a given way.
   a. Good speeches can stimulate other speakers and audience members alike to be better communicators.
   b. Previous speeches can affect the emotional mood of an audience.
   c. Previous speeches can force speakers to adapt the content of their speeches.
2. The context of recent events can affect the way listeners react to your message.
   a. If you are not up on the latest news on your topic, your credibility may suffer.
   b. Sometimes unexpected last-minute events force speakers to improvise on-the-spot adjustments.

USING END-OF-CHAPTER ITEMS

Discussion *(text pp. 130–131)*

1. How might the following situations affect a speech you are about to give, and how would you adapt to them?

   a. You are the last speaker during the last class period before spring break.
   b. A lost student walks into the class right in the middle of your speech, looks around, says "Excuse me," and walks out.
   c. The speaker right before you gives an incredibly successful speech, which brings spontaneous applause from the class and high praise from the instructor.
   d. The speaker right before you bombs badly. The speech is poorly prepared, the speaker is very nervous and simply stops in the middle and sits down, visibly upset.
   e. (It rarely happens, but . . .) The speaker right before you gives a speech on the same topic, taking the same general approach.

These questions have no absolute answers. Focus discussion on the specific situation. Remember that as the instructor, you can and should help beginning students adapt to problematic situations. The following suggestions may help guide class discussion.

a.   Students are probably eager to leave campus, and attendance that day is often low. To get and sustain their audiences' attention, speakers might try an especially energetic presentation or, if appropriate, tie their topic to the upcoming vacation.

b.   Such interruptions are not unusual early in the semester and can be awkward. They can disrupt the flow of a speech, disorienting speaker and audience alike. Advise your students to pause on such occasions, perhaps even addressing the "lost" one with a nod or comment such as "no problem," take a breath to calm and reorient themselves, and then proceed. If needed, they might review a previous point or the point being made at the time of the interruption.

c.   Having to follow an especially strong presentation can be intimidating, especially for nervous first-timers. Reassure your students that they are not competing with one another, and that you are more concerned with their improvement over the course of the semester than with how polished they look the first time out. Instructors should not allow one exemplary speaker in a freshman-level class to set the standard by which others are evaluated.

d.   Audiences are usually made uncomfortable by watching a speaker bomb. Speakers should know that in such situations, the audience is probably tense and eager to see someone succeed. If later speakers maintain their composure, the audience will probably be especially warm and receptive. Speakers should not allow the anxiety of others to make them unduly nervous about their own presentations.

e.   Assure your students that even when two or more people speak on the same topic with the same general approach, this does not mean that they will be giving the same speech. However, this is definitely one of those situations calling for immediate adjustments. Speakers might acknowledge the previous speaker in the introduction as confirming the importance of their topic. If a speaker's planned examples and illustrations are identical to those used in the previous speech, he or she might substitute one from memory or simply allude to its previous use with a comment such as, "Remember the ____ Joe discussed; it applies to my point as well." Students should not try to revise their entire speeches at the last minute.

2.   **Rank the ten human universal values in [text p. 123] Figure 4.5 in terms of their importance to you. Discuss how the three values you ranked highest might make you susceptible to certain speech topics and approaches.**

This works well as a homework activity followed by in-class discussion, but it can easily be converted to a small-group or general class discussion piece. Have your students identify their three highest values from the list and relate each to at least three topics or appeals that might be addressed in public dialogue for class discussion. Encourage your students to explore and express their own separate reactions to these values. Discuss how speakers might (or might not) invoke them to transcend cultural and experiential barriers to effective public speaking. What implications do these "universal values" have for minority groups that have historically been excluded from meaningful participation in public life? Note that this is another discussion piece that is likely to prompt heated debates from your students. Again, try to avoid "taking sides" and do whatever you can to foster an atmosphere of respectful tolerance for intelligently voiced opposing positions.

3.   **Construct a demographic portrait of the average student at your school with respect to age, gender, educational background, group affiliations, and sociocultural background. What speech topics might this listener find most interesting? What motives, values, and attitudes might he or she bring to these topics?**

Much of the information needed to complete this activity—age, gender, race, place of residence, and majors—may be available through the registrar's office. However, your class may not conform to the college mean, and students should not get into the habit of relying on broad survey information to make assumptions about any particular audience. You might administer the "Audience Survey Form" (p. 143) early in the term and make the results available at this time, or use the exercise "The Importance of Knowing Your Audience" (p. 136) in conjunction with this activity. Discussion following self-introductory speeches can help suggest topics the audience might find interesting, as well as motives, values, and attitudes that a speaker should take into consideration. As an alternative, consider how this "average" student relates to minority students and groups on campus. How might their motives, values, and attitudes be brought into harmony or contradiction with one another? What topics and appeals might be used to bridge demographic barriers between the "average" student and the multicultural makeup of most collegiate student bodies?

4. Consider the following situation:

> A Boston couple decided to spend their vacation in Memphis, where they had grown up and had families. On their way they stopped at the Shiloh Civil War Battleground, where the guide extolled the virtues of the Northern forces in that battle. When their tour was finished, they thanked the guide and told her they wanted to get back home to Memphis before dark. She looked surprised and said, "From your license plate I assumed you were Yankees. I should have given you the 'Southern' tour."

Working in small groups, discuss the ethical ramifications of this "adaptation." Have a spokesperson for your group present your conclusions to the class as a whole.

You might preview this activity (which easily converts to general in-class discussion) with a short discussion of communication ethics and the sometimes transparent line between healthy audience adaptation and deceptive waffling. Emphasize, as does your text, that ethical evaluations must ultimately grapple with considerations of motive, as well as our own experiential backgrounds and biases. Whereas most Americans might recognize troubling overtones of regional chauvinism, southerners might well perceive a conciliatory if comic friendliness. Keep in mind that southerners historically perceive themselves as a culture under siege, and are typically ambiguous and defensive with regard to their regional identities. It can be difficult to draw meaningful lessons from experiences such as these. You might emphasize that what someone perceives as rational adaptation versus unethical waffling is largely a matter of that person's experiential background, and that we should be reflexive and cautious in our evaluations of other people's uses of strategic audience adaptation.

Application *(text pp. 131–133)*

1. Explain how you would tailor a speech on the general topic of recycling for an audience composed of:

   a. high school sophomores
   b. the local Chamber of Commerce
   c. your college administration
   d. your classmates

This can be used for homework or in-class discussion. For in-class use, divide your students into four small groups, designate one primary audience for each, and have them come up with specific purposes, thematic statements, two to three main points, and what types of supporting materials would be appropriate for each one. Novice speakers often ignore the audience analysis aspects of speech preparation and leap right into outlining major points. Before the groups begin working on this project, instruct them to consider:

1. The important dynamics and demographics of their audience relative to recycling
2. The inferences they are making based on these factors
3. How much they would expect the audience to know about recycling and environmental concerns
4. What aspects of the topic might be most relevant, important, or interesting to the audience

Suggestions for discussion:

a. While young people tend to be concerned with environmental issues, students this young may know little about recycling beyond what they've been taught in school. Most obviously live at home, and they may have yet to know the whats, whys, and hows of recycling.

b. Chamber of Commerce members would probably be interested in the potential public relations and economic benefits of recycling, and resistant to costly, adventuresome schemes.

c. Most college administrations are coming around to recycling. Certainly they have become conscious of their public images with respect to this and other popular political and social issues. Administrators may be interested in knowing how the school can save money through recycling, or how they can make recycling more accessible to students who live or spend much of their time on campus.

d. College students of all political persuasions are increasingly sensitive to environmental concerns and things like recycling. However, they typically lead hurried lifestyles (and hence excuses not to recycle are easy to come by), and they may need information on how to recycle efficiently on campus. They might also be interested in careers or entrepreneurial ventures in recycling.

2. **If you were to speak on the general topic of recycling, what kinds of examples might you develop to appeal to the following audience needs?**

   a. **safety**   c. **comfort**
   b. **nurturance**   d. **recognition**

This is useful for in-class discussion, or it may be expanded and used in conjunction with the previous application. It is useful for stressing the importance of concrete examples for invoking audience dynamics in support of a given thesis or claim. Note for your students that such appeals often do and should overlap in actual practice. The following suggestions may help to stimulate class discussion.

Suggestions for discussion:

a. Safety appeals: Hypothetical future examples suggesting negative health and environmental consequences of overflowing landfills and deforestation might be appropriate.

b. Nurturance appeals: You might suggest social activities with or the general attractiveness of people who are likewise involved. Perhaps you could give hypothetical examples of prospective significant others being turned off by seeing us throw out recyclable trash.

c. Comfort appeals: You might use examples similar to those for safety appeals, and identify them explicitly with threats to basic human physiological needs such as clean air and water.

d. Recognition appeals: Give examples of people recognized for recycling and other environmental efforts, hypothetical examples of audience members influencing recalcitrant neighbors to recycle, or examples suggesting the profitability of recycling.

3. Imagine for the moment that you are the speaker we mentioned at the beginning of this chapter. You are the president of Students for Environmental Action. To refresh your memory, you have been asked to attend an 8 A.M. meeting of new students at the soccer field and to introduce them to SEA. Your major goals will be to inform them about SEA's projects for the coming years and to recruit new members. That evening, you have been invited to address the Coahoma Country Industrial Development Board on "what you students are up to." Your task is to reassure them that SEA's work will help, not hinder, the business climate in the area. Like every good speaker, you have carefully constructed a demographic analysis of both groups and have also identified some pertinent situational factors. Your task is to analyze the data that follow in light of what we have said in this chapter in order to plan an overall speech strategy. Develop a one-page written report for each speech that will outline a plan for adaptation to each audience and situation.

This makes a good homework assignment followed by in-class discussion. Refer your students to pp. 110–117 of the text on relevant situational and demographic factors. Remember that topics pertinent to environmental preservation are generally disputed—especially by business communities that may have direct interests at stake. In these cases, you want to go beyond considering what your audience knows to where they stand and their specific concerns and interests. It's no secret that college students are generally sympathetic to environmental issues, but a captive audience outdoors at 8 A.M. presents definite situational challenges. A good speaker will plan to animate her or his presentation and speak loudly, and to involve the audience's values and interests from the beginning. Depending on audience size, she or he might want to arrange some sort of electronic amplification. College students are busy people, and they may need to be involved emotionally as well as rationally before they take action. As the speaker would be addressing a mixed audience, he or she might defend ends and means in terms of mainstream environmental arguments, and avoid needlessly alienating moderate students who might agree on ends but have trouble with certain means. Developers would obviously be more concerned with how prospective actions would influence the business community, and an intelligent speaker would express sympathy for their concerns and emphasize positive short- and long-term gains to offset their concerns.

ADDITIONAL ACTIVITIES

The Importance of Knowing Your Audience

Purpose: To make students aware of differences that may exist between their specific audiences and national survey information.

Directions: This works well in conjunction with major speaking assignments. Each January, the American Council on Education, in conjunction with the University of California—Los Angeles, releases the results of a survey of college freshmen. Survey highlights are usually reported in *USA Today* and other major newspapers. Prepare an audience questionnaire that covers the items reported from the national survey, distribute it to your students early in the term, and collate the results for comparison with the national data. See below for the results of the 1995 survey as well as a sample questionnaire constructed from those data.* You might combine this information with the results of a more general audience analysis using the "Audience Survey Form" from p. 143 of this IRM. Focus class discussion on the similarities and differences between your students' attitudes and those reported in the national survey. Explore possible reasons for the differences. Encourage your students to hold onto and consider this information when preparing their speeches.

Percent of college freshmen agreeing with the items on the 1995 survey: (1) 58%; (2) 79%; (3) 80%; (4) 88%; (5) 81%; (6) 42%; (7) 17%; (8) 58%; (9) 33%; (10) 72%; (11) 32%; (12) 23%; (13) 84%; (14) 20%; (15) 54%; (16) 64%.

---

* Adapted from UCLA's National Survey of College Freshmen. Reported in *U.S. News & World Report*, 15 Jan. 1996, p. 10.

Planning Long-Range Adjustments

Purpose: To give your students a chance to conduct an in-class audience analysis in preparation for their actual speeches.

Directions: This activity is ideal for use in preparation for the informative speaking assignment, although similar activities can and should be used in conjunction with persuasive and ceremonial presentations. Audience analysis works best if you have actual survey information to complement personal observations and broad demographic data, and this activity works well as a follow-up to an in-class survey activity. For homework in preparation for this activity, have your students prepare short responses to the speech environment and audience analysis questions with regard to their respective speech ideas (see pp. 145–146 of this IRM):

After the students have completed the homework assignment, break them into small groups and have them critique one another's ideas for their efficacy and mention ideas they may have missed. Impress upon students the necessity of approaching audience analysis systematically and knowing as much as possible about their particular audience. No matter how systematic our methods get, there is always an element of educated guesswork involved in ascertaining how particular audiences will react to particular messages. At this time, distribute whatever survey information you have gathered on your students and encourage them to consider it in making their observations. Students can also pick up valuable tidbits about their classmates' values and predispositions simply by observing their comments in class. Have them present their ideas for discussion and analysis. Encourage them to work their results into effective involvement strategies for their actual speeches.

Value Surveys

Purpose: To provide your students with information regarding their classmates' instrumental and terminal values.

Directions: The lists of instrumental and terminal values (see Value Surveys I and II on pp. 147–148 of this IRM) have been adapted from the work of Milton Rokeach. Administer each of the value questionnaires to the class and tabulate the results. Discuss the findings of the survey with the class in terms of its importance for topic selection, purpose, and the selection of supporting materials.

Preparing and Using An Audience Survey

Purpose: To give your students a chance to gather concrete information about their classmates' predispositions toward their topics through the administration of a customized audience analysis questionnaire.

Directions: In some situations it is not enough to make educated inferences about an audience's predisposition toward a given topic, especially when trying to influence or persuade them. Your students can pick up valuable cues simply by observing their classmates' comments and behaviors during class discussion. However, when possible, it is always better to get specific topic-related information through the administration of an audience analysis questionnaire. The "Sample Attitude Questionnaire" on p. 109 of the text can be adapted for classroom purposes. This sample questionnaire, on the topic of capital punishment, is designed to gather information about the audience's interest in and involvement with the topic, their knowledge of the subject, whether they favor capital punishment, and how they perceive different sources of evidence that could be used in a speech on the subject. A similar audience analysis questionnaire could be tailored for any topic by substituting that topic for capital punishment and changing the sources of information to those relevant to the newly chosen topic.

After administering the questionnaires, use the following conversions to score items 1 through 4: –3 = 1; –2 = 2; –1 = 3; 0 = 4; 1 = 5; 2 = 6; 3 = 7. To get the audience average for each item, total the responses for each item and divide this sum by the number of questionnaires. Remind your students to save the completed questionnaires in case they want to analyze any responses in more detail. Although such a questionnaire does not provide in-depth information about the knowledge and attitudes of an audience, it can serve as a good starting point for developing a speech. Students can use the results of audience analysis questionnaires to tailor speeches to a specific audience. Such questionnaires are time-consuming to administer and interpret, but the insights they provide are well worth the effort. Caution your students against contaminating their results by asking biased, leading, or closed questions. The following suggestions can help students develop high-quality attitude surveys.

1. Do not use statements that can be interpreted as factual.

2. Avoid wording statements so that they can be interpreted two ways.

3. Avoid statements irrelevant to the attitude in question.

4. Use language that is simple, clear, direct, and concrete.

5. Keep statements as short as possible.

6. Each statement should express only one thought.

7. Avoid words such as *all, always, none,* and *never*.

8. Use simple rather than complex or compound sentences.

9. Use language that is easily understood.

10. Avoid the use of double negatives.

Maslow's Hierarchy of Needs

Purpose: To introduce your students to a classic perspective on human motivation.

Directions: Many instructors are accustomed to teaching motivation using the ideas of Abraham Maslow. Refer your students to text pp. 103–107 in preparation for this exercise, and project the transparency "Maslow's Hierarchy of Needs." Briefly review Maslow on the five levels of psychological need. Then break your students into small groups to discuss how they could work appeals to each of the five levels of needs into given speech topics. Consider the adequacy of this scheme for characterizing need-based appeals in public speaking. Some students may comment that appealing directly or explicitly to such motives would often come across as self-centered and manipulative, especially when addressing timely issues that promise to affect all of us. That is, you wouldn't say, "Vote for this candidate, or we'll take your nurturance away!" Still, appeals to basic physical, security, belongingness, esteem, and self-actualization needs are implicit and vitally important elements of many effective and influential public messages. Have your students think of how they might work in two appeals for each level of needs. As an alternative, have your students critique chosen speeches or magazine articles in terms of the five levels of human needs.

Audience Adaptation in Contemporary Speeches

Purpose: To provide your students an opportunity to analyze a contemporary speech with respect to the assumptions it makes regarding its primary audience.

Directions: This activity works well as a written homework assignment, although you might show a videotaped speech for in-class discussion and analysis. See Appendix B for texts of contemporary speeches, or have your students select a speech from *Vital Speeches of the Day.* Have your students consider the following questions with respect to their chosen speeches:

1. Does the speaker make any direct reference to his or her audience or attempt to characterize them with respect to his or her topic and thesis? What attempts does the speaker make to adjust his or her topic and thesis to this particular audience?

2. Does the speaker make any direct reference to the occasion, setting, context, or timing? What?

3. What is the speaker's point and purpose with respect to the particular audience? Who do you suspect the speaker's primary audience is and why?

4. What assumptions does this speaker apparently make about his or her audience's attitudes and values concerning the topic? What level of knowledge is presumed? Is respect shown for the audience by making a balanced and responsible presentation?

Focus discussion on how these particular speeches might have been tailored to fit a particular audience and communication environment. Emphasize that this is not ethically troublesome, but a necessary part of effective speech making. Some critics argue that an image of audience rationality is implicit within all messages. Ethical considerations might address whether the speaker communicates in a responsible fashion that facilitates rational decision making on the part of the audience.

Exploring Cultures

Purpose: To increase your students' awareness of "deep culture."

Directions: Distribute the "Cultural Iceberg" handout on p. 149 of this IRM. Divide the class into small groups (no more than five students) to represent the various cultural groups represented in the class or in the locale. For example, you may have one group of Latinos, one group of African Americans, one group of Asian Americans, and one group of Native Americans. If the students in your class do not actually represent a variety of cultural groups, assign the students to cultural study groups. Have the students work through the cultural iceberg, identifying those factors that might influence public communication practices. As a homework assignment, have the students discover whatever they can about the deep culture of the group they are studying. This can be done through either library research or personal interviews. When the homework is completed, have the groups of students reconvene to share their information and make a summary report to the class as a whole.

Avoiding Sexist Language

Purpose: To increase your students' awareness of sexual stereotyping and sexist language, and to make them aware of options for avoiding sexist terminology.

Directions: Administer either of the two exercise forms ("Please Fill in the Blanks" or "Avoiding Sexist Language") found on pp. 150–151 of this IRM. The first promotes awareness of sexist stereotyping, and the second is a guide for avoiding sexist language. Have your students share their responses for class discussion. Focus on the effects that sexist language has on your students. Encourage them to freely share whatever feelings or reactions these items evoke in them. Some of your male students may be surprised by how offended their female counterparts are by these stereotypes—even those who do not consciously think of themselves as feminists. Are there significant differences between the responses of your male and female students? Why? Use this as an opportunity to make a basic point about stereotyping and communication. It is pointless to unnecessarily offend anyone, and, once done, it doesn't matter whether it was intentional or not. Speakers should be especially cautious about implied stereotypes relating to race, sex, religion, regional or cultural heritage, or personal lifestyle.

Suggested options for the second exercise: early humans, early people, our ancestors; humankind or people; mail-, repair-, business-, or chairperson; or Congressperson or representative; and human resources.

Advertising and Gender Stereotyping

Purpose: To engage your students with the social and ethical implications of social and gender stereotyping in advertising and public communication.

Directions: Have your students find and bring to class examples of magazine or newspaper advertising that they feel exemplifies gender or some other form of stereotyping. They should consider why such techniques are used and their social and ethical implications for those depicted. Who is the primary audience for such ads, and what assumptions do the ads imply about them? This makes a good opportunity to bring in Maslow's needs. For instance, ads for feminine beauty products commonly prey on women's fears of not living up to arbitrary standards of beauty and sexual attraction, and commonly use visuals to associate the use of these products with fulfilling fantasy lifestyles of material and sexual excess. Such ads typically include just enough text to introduce the products. Although many students may argue that such ads perpetuate demeaning stereotypes of men and women alike, try to facilitate tolerance for opposing positions. Business or advertising students might counter that the ads simply appeal to what most people want. Certainly, there are plenty of women who do not find such ads demeaning, or else they wouldn't buy the products. Steer discussion toward the differing roles and social responsibilities of advertisers as opposed to public speakers. Advertisers' chief concern is to sell a product, and they have few scruples about targeting specific audiences and excluding others. In conjunction with this exercise, you might show Jean Kilbourne's film *Still Killing Us Softly*, which explores the impact of advertising on popular gender stereotypes, or use the "Avoiding Sexist Language" materials on p. 151 of this IRM.

SUPPLEMENTARY MATERIALS

Films and Videos

"Still Killing Us Softly," Cambridge Documentary Films.

"American Tongues," Center of New American Media, 40 minutes.

"The Topic and the Audience," Films for the Humanities, color, 15 minutes.

"Managing Diversity," CRM Films, 22 minutes.

"Cross-Cultural Communication in Diverse Settings," Insight Media, 60 minutes.

"The Public Speaker and the Audience," RMI Media Productions, 28 minutes.

Transparencies and Handouts *(see following pages)*

Audience Demographics (Transparency 4.1)

Audience Survey Form

College Student Attitude Questionnaire

Assessing Your Speech Environment

Assessing Your Audience

Value Survey I

Value Survey II

The Cultural Iceberg

Please Fill In the Blanks (gender exercise)

Avoiding Sexist Language

AUDIENCE DEMOGRAPHICS

1. **Age:** Younger people are more open to change and new ideas, and easier to persuade.

2. **Gender:** Women may be more concerned with social issues that affect families and children. Notions of gender-appropriate behavior are changing rapidly.

3. **Education:** Educated audiences are more open to opposing viewpoints and new ideas, but are not easier to persuade. They expect speakers to be well informed, and to address all viable options.

4. **Group Affiliations:** Related to interests and values. Can suggest appropriate topics, examples and illustrations, and sources to cite.

5. **Sociocultural Background:** Suggests different experiences, interests, and ways of seeing things. Speakers can help bridge cultural barriers by stressing common interests and values, and by using examples and narratives.

AUDIENCE SURVEY FORM

Sex: M F   Age _____   Year: FR SO JR SR   GPA _____   Race _____

Marital Status _____   Religious preference _____

Major _____   State lived in longest _____

Current job (full- or part-time) _____   Hours per week _____

Career aspirations _____

Persons I admire most (male) _____ (female) _____

Politically, I consider myself: liberal, conservative, moderate;   Democrat, Republican, other
                                              (circle one)   (circle one)

If a presidential election were held next week, I would vote for _____

Group memberships (occupational, political, religious, or social)_____

_____

Father's occupation _____   Mother's occupation _____

Place of birth _____   Places lived _____

Travel (in USA) _____

Travel (outside USA) _____

Hobbies _____

_____

Positive "trigger words" _____

Negative "trigger words" _____

The most important thing in my life right now is _____

_____

Topics on which I would like to hear an informative speech (name 3) _____

_____

Topics on which I would like to hear a persuasive speech (name 3) _____

_____

COLLEGE STUDENT ATTITUDE QUESTIONNAIRE

Fall 1995

Respond to each of the following statements by placing the number of the option that best represents your position in the space before the item. Do not put your name on this questionnaire. All responses should be anonymous and will be kept confidential.

    5   I strongly agree with this statement.
    4   I agree with this statement somewhat.
    3   I have no opinion on this statement.
    2   I disagree with this statement somewhat.
    1   I strongly disagree with this statement.

_____ 1. I strive to keep up with political affairs.

_____ 2. The government should do more to control the sale of handguns.

_____ 3. There is too much concern in the courts for the rights of criminals.

_____ 4. Better education and more job opportunities would substantially reduce crime.

_____ 5. The government is not doing enough to control pollution.

_____ 6. If two people really like each other, it's all right for them to have sex even if they've known each other for only a very short time.

_____ 7. The activities of married women are best confined to the home and family.

_____ 8. Abortion should be legal.

_____ 9. It is important to have laws prohibiting homosexual relationships.

_____ 10. Wealthy people should pay a larger share of taxes than they do now.

_____ 11. Taxes should be raised to reduce the deficit.

_____ 12. Marijuana should be legalized.

_____ 13. Employers should be allowed to require drug testing of employees or job applicants.

_____ 14. Racial discrimination is no longer a major problem in America.

_____ 15. Affirmative action in college admissions should be abolished.

_____ 16. A national health care plan is needed to cover everybody's medical costs.

Thank you for your cooperation.

ASSESSING YOUR SPEECH ENVIRONMENT

1. Can you anticipate any problems with your particular presentations as a result of time or timing? Students should come up with at least one potential problem regarding their particular topic/purpose and timing.

2. What about the physical dimensions of the setting? How might the size of the room or the availability of special equipment affect your presentation?

3. How might audience expectations for this particular occasion affect your presentation? (Note that with most class speaking assignments, the occasional expectations are defined by the assignment. For instance, the audience would obviously not expect a spiritual sermon for the informative speech.)

4. Is there any late-breaking news that might affect the way your audience perceives your topic?

5. Is there a good chance that other speakers might address this topic before you? If so, how would you adjust to this?

6. How large and diverse is your particular audience? Who is your primary audience?

ASSESSING YOUR AUDIENCE

1. What beliefs, attitudes, needs, interests, or values do you share with the members of your primary audience? How might you build on this common ground to support your thesis?

2. What audience demographics (age, gender, education level, group and political affiliations, religion, sociocultural background) might be relevant to your topic and purpose/thesis statements? Can your audience be characterized with respect to predominant demographic characteristics?

3. How important is your topic to your audience? Do they already care about it? Why? If not, how can you motivate them to listen?

4. What aspects of your topic will be most relevant to them? How might you best gain and hold their attention from the beginning of your speech?

5. What do they already know about your topic? What do they want and need to know in order to establish your main points and assertions responsibly?

5. How do they feel about your topic? Would they be predisposed to act in a positive, neutral, or negative fashion? Can you think of any obvious reasons why they may not be open to your proposal or any other new ideas with respect to your topic and purpose?

VALUE SURVEY I

On this page are eighteen values listed in alphabetical order. Your task is to arrange them in the order of their importance to *you*. Study the list carefully and pick out the one value that is the most important for you. Write the *letter* of that value on the line next to number 1. Then pick out the value that is second most important and write the *letter* of that value on the line next to number 2. Continue to do the same for each of the remaining values. The value that is least important to you goes on the line next to number 18.

1. _____	A. A comfortable life
2. _____	B. An exciting life
3. _____	C. A sense of accomplishment
4. _____	D. A world at peace
5. _____	E. A world of beauty
6. _____	F. Equality
7. _____	G. Family security
8. _____	H. Freedom
9. _____	I. Happiness
10. _____	J. Inner harmony
11. _____	K. Mature love
12. _____	L. National security
13. _____	M. Pleasure
14. _____	N. Salvation
15. _____	O. Self-respect
16. _____	P. Social recognition
17. _____	Q. True friendship
18. _____	R. Wisdom

VALUE SURVEY II

On this page are eighteen values listed in alphabetical order. Your task is to arrange them in the order of their importance to *you*. Study the list carefully and pick out the one value that is the most important for you. Write the *letter* of that value on the line next to number 1. Then pick out the value that is second most important and write the *letter* of that value on the line next to number 2. Continue to do the same for each of the remaining values. The value that is least important to you goes on the line next to number 18.

1. _____	A. Ambitious
2. _____	B. Broadminded
3. _____	C. Capable
4. _____	D. Cheerful
5. _____	E. Clean
6. _____	F. Courageous
7. _____	G. Forgiving
8. _____	H. Helpful
9. _____	I. Honest
10. _____	J. Imaginative
11. _____	K. Independent
12. _____	L. Intellectual
13. _____	M. Logical
14. _____	N. Loving
15. _____	O. Obedient
16. _____	P. Polite
17. _____	Q. Responsible
18. _____	R. Self-controlled

THE CULTURAL ICEBERG*

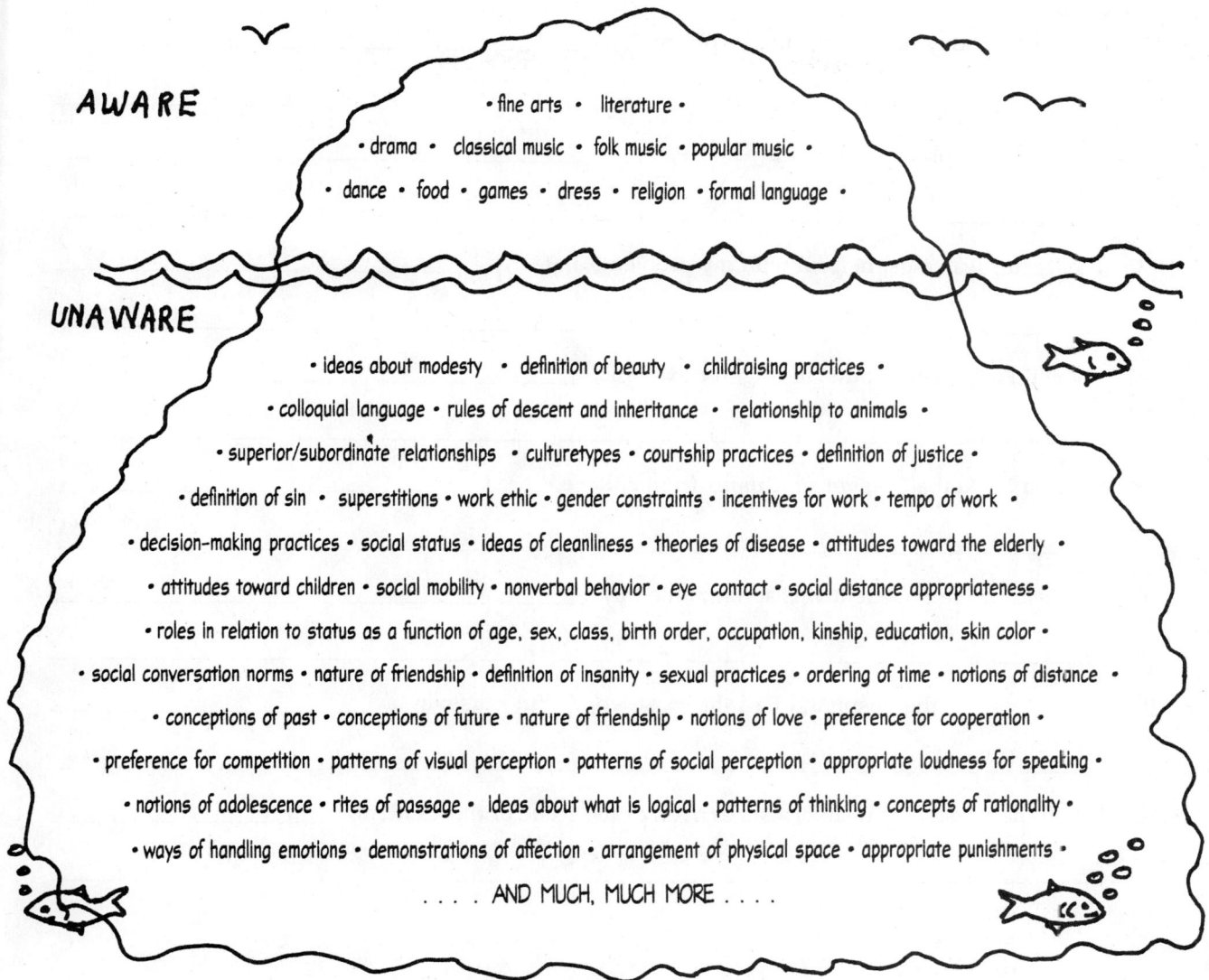

AWARE

- fine arts • literature •
- drama • classical music • folk music • popular music •
- dance • food • games • dress • religion • formal language •

UNAWARE

- ideas about modesty • definition of beauty • childraising practices •
- colloquial language • rules of descent and inheritance • relationship to animals •
- superior/subordinate relationships • culturetypes • courtship practices • definition of justice •
- definition of sin • superstitions • work ethic • gender constraints • incentives for work • tempo of work •
- decision-making practices • social status • ideas of cleanliness • theories of disease • attitudes toward the elderly •
- attitudes toward children • social mobility • nonverbal behavior • eye contact • social distance appropriateness •
- roles in relation to status as a function of age, sex, class, birth order, occupation, kinship, education, skin color •
- social conversation norms • nature of friendship • definition of insanity • sexual practices • ordering of time • notions of distance •
- conceptions of past • conceptions of future • nature of friendship • notions of love • preference for cooperation •
- preference for competition • patterns of visual perception • patterns of social perception • appropriate loudness for speaking •
- notions of adolescence • rites of passage • ideas about what is logical • patterns of thinking • concepts of rationality •
- ways of handling emotions • demonstrations of affection • arrangement of physical space • appropriate punishments •

. . . . AND MUCH, MUCH MORE . . . .

Just as most of an iceberg is out of sight, so is most of a culture out of conscious awareness.

---

* Adapted from *AFS Student Yearbook and the Arrival Orientation*, New York: American Field Service, p. 71.

Please Fill In the Blanks

1. After a hard day on the job, the secretary _____

_____

2. When the plumber arrived at my house, _____

_____

3. The doctor was most helpful with my problems, in fact, _____

_____

4. My child's teacher is outstanding; for example, _____

_____

5. When a basketball player graduates from college, _____

_____

6. On the tour the president was accompanied by _____

_____

7. While I was in the hospital, I had the most wonderful nurse; in fact, _____

_____

8. When the construction supervisor arrived at the scene of the accident, _____

_____

AVOIDING SEXIST LANGUAGE

What alternatives can you suggest for the following words?

Early man   _____

Mankind   _____

Mailman   _____

Manmade   _____

Congressman   _____

Chairman   _____

Repairman   _____

Businessman   _____

Manpower   _____

Susan Mitchell, "Younger Generations Are More Diverse," *Marketing Power* (Feb. 1996), 4.[*]

The United States is far more diverse today than it was half a century ago. The agent of that change is generational replacement. Due to immigration and higher fertility rates among some racial and ethnic groups, each age group is more diverse than the one preceding it. Only 65 percent of Americans under age 5 are non-Hispanic whites, for example, versus fully 87 percent of people aged 85 or older.

Overall, 85 percent of the members of the World War II generation are non-Hispanic white. Among boomers, this proportion is 75 percent. Among Generation X, 69 percent are non-Hispanic white. Only 8 percent of Americans aged 63 or older are non-Hispanic black, while 5 percent are Hispanic. But within Generation X, Hispanics (13.1 percent) are almost as numerous as non-Hispanic blacks (13.4 percent).

Within racial and ethnic groups, age distributions vary. The proportion of people under age 19 is greatest among Hispanics and Native Americans. It is lowest among non-Hispanic whites. Generation X makes 22 percent of the Hispanic population. In contrast Xers account for only 16 percent of the non-Hispanic white population.

The Baby-Boom generation is a slightly larger percentage of the Asian and Pacific Islander population than of any other racial or ethnic group. The World War II generation is proportionately twice as large among non-Hispanic whites than it is among Hispanics, Native Americans, and Asian and Pacific Islanders.

POPULATION BY GENERATION, RACE, AND ETHNIC ORIGIN, 1995

(percent distribution of population by generation, race, and ethnic origin, 1995; numbers in thousands)

	Total	White	Black	Islander	Nat. Am.	Hispanic
Total	100	73.6%	12.1%	3.5%	0.7%	10.1%
Children (< age 19)	100	66.8%	15.0%	3.9%	1.0%	13.3%
Generation X (aged 19–30)	100	68.5%	13.4%	4.2%	0.8%	13.1%
Baby Boom (aged 31–49)	100	74.9%	11.4%	3.7%	0.7%	9.3%
Swing (aged 50–62)	100	79.6%	9.8%	3.1%	0.6%	6.9%
World War II (aged 63 or older)	100	84.8%	8.1%	2.0%	0.4%	4.7%

[*] Susan Mitchell, "The Official Guide to the Generations" (Ithaca, New York: New Strategist Publications, Inc., 1995). Used by permission.

READINGS FOR ENRICHMENT

See guide to journal abbreviations on p. 37.

* Items marked with an asterisk are suitable for student enrichment.

Audience Analysis: General

Clevenger, Theodore. *Audience Analysis*. Indianapolis: Bobbs-Merrill, 1966.

Colbourn, C. William, and Sanford B. Weinberg. *An Orientation to Listening and Audience Analysis*. Chicago: Science Research Associates, 1980.

* Cowley, Geoffrey. "How the Mind Was Designed." *Newsweek*, 13 Mar. 1989, pp. 56–58.

Cronkhite, Gary L. "Perception and Meaning." In *Handbook of Rhetorical and Communication Theory*, edited by Carroll C. Arnold and John Waite Bowers, pp. 51–229. Boston: Allyn and Bacon, 1984.

Duran, Robert L. "Communicative Adaptability: A Measure of Social Communicative Competence." *CQ* (Fall 1983), 320–326.

Gibson, James W., and Michael S. Hanna. *Audience Analysis: A Programmed Approach to Receiver Behavior*. Englewood Cliffs, N.J.: Prentice-Hall, 1976.

Hecht, Michael L., Franklin J. Boster, and Sarah LaMer. "The Effect of Extroversion and Differentiation on Listener-Adapted Communication." *CR* (Winter 1989), 1–8.

Holtzman, Paula D. *The Psychology of Speaker's Audiences*. Glenview, Ill.: Scott, Foresman, 1970.

Mandeville, Mary Y. "Are Our Basic Speech Communication Courses Targeting Today's Diverse Student Audience? Teacher Perceptions of Course Rigidity and Its Effect on Student Learning." Paper presented at the Speech Communication Association Convention, 1994; available through ERIC.

* Menneer, Peter. "Audience Appreciation: A Different Story from Audience Members." *Journal of the Market Research Society* (July 1987), 241–263.

Nieto, Sonia. *Affirming Diversity: The Sociopolitical Context of Multicultural Education*. New York: Longman, 1992.

* Pavlik, John. "Audience Complexity as a Component of Campaign Planning." *Public Relations Review* (Summer 1988), 12–21.

Audience Analysis Activities

Bowers, Anne A., Jr. "When We Become They: Teaching Audience Awareness Skills." *SCT* (Summer 1994), 8–9.

Bozic, Mary. "Who Said That?" *SCT* (Summer 1988), 6.

Brunson, Deborah A. "A Perceptual Awareness Exercise in Interracial Communication." *SCT* (Fall 1994), 2–4.

Corey, James. "International Bazaar." *SCT* (Fall 1990), 5.

Downey, Sharon D. "Audience Analysis Exercise." *SCT* (Winter 1988), 1–2.

Ekachai, Daradirek "Gee." "Diversity Icebreaker." *SCT* (Spring 1996), 14–15.

Fuller, Linda K. "Participatory Audience Analysis: A Research Technique that Teaches About the Community." *SCT* (Summer 1994), 9–10.

Garbowitz, Fred. "Changing Classroom Populations Call for Increased Cultural Sensitivity." *SCT* (Summer 1990), 13–14.

Gschwend, Laura L. "Oral Webbing." *SCT* (Summer 1994), 1.

Halloway, Hal. "An Exercise in Audience Analysis." *CE* (Oct. 1984), 392–397.

Hankins, Gail Armstead. "Don't Judge a Book by Its Cover." *SCT* (Summer 1991), 8.

Hawkinson, Ken. "Through the Eyes of Djeli Baba Sissoko: The Malian Oral Tradition." *SCT* (Winter 1991), 1–2.

Hochel, Sandra. "An Exercise in Understanding Ethnocentrism." *SCT* (Summer 1994), 10–11.

Kaye, Tom. "Respecting Others' Point of View." *SCT* (Spring 1990), 12.

Langley, C. Darrell. "The Heckling Speech." *SCT* (Summer 1988), 7.

McClarty, Wilma. "Audience Analysis: Go and Tell." *SCT* (Fall 1993), 4–5.

McKinney, Bruce C. "Audience Analysis Exercise." *SCT* (Winter 1989), 6.

Neumann, David. "Selecting Messages: An Exercise in Audience Analysis." *SCT* (Summer 1990), 9.

Patterson, Brian R. "An Experiential Vehicle for Instruction on Human Perception." *SCT* (Fall 1994), 7–8.

Powell, Kimberly A. "Increasing Appreciation for Diversity Through the Group Culture Speech." *SCT* (Winter 1996), 3–4.

Robie, Harry. "A Native American Speech Text for Classroom Use." *SCT* (Summer 1991), 12.

Ross, Roseanna. "What Is in the Shoe Box?" *SCT* (Spring 1991), 12.

Schumer, Allison. "Custom Comparison Speeches." *SCT* (Fall 1989), 1.

Smith, Donald C. "Look Who's Listening: The Importance of Sub Audiences in Public Speaking." *SCT* (Summer 1995), 6.

Spicer, Karin-Leigh. "Stereotypes and Appearances." *SCT* (Winter 1995), 10.

Stern, Rick. "Audience Spinouts." *SCT* (Spring 1991), 7–8.

Thompson, Dawn, and Myra Cullen. Collidascope: An Intercultural Learning Experience," [a learning game]. Available from Collidascope, 188 Blakeslee Hill Road, Newfield, NY 14867.

Walter, Suzanne. "Introduction of a Speaker: Multipurpose and Multicultural." *SCT* (Spring 1993), 3.

———. "Experiences in Intercultural Communication." *SCT* (Summer 1995), 1–3.

Wilson, Susan, and Mark H. Wright. "From 'Animism' to 'Zeitgeist': Culturally Literate Assigned Topics." *SCT* (Winter 1991), 8–9.

Wilson, Wendy L. "Sex Role Stereotypes: What Do We See in Them?" *SCT* (Winter 1989), 15.

Yook, Eunkyong Lee. "Students Creating Intercultural Sensitizers: Storytelling and Attribution." *SCT* (Spring 1996), 11–12.

Demographic Factors

* Atlas, James. "Beyond Demographics." *The Atlantic Monthly* (Oct. 1984), 49–58.

* Baker, Ross K. "Cluster Busters." *American Demographics* (June 1989), 64.

Banks, Stephen P., and Anna Banks. "Translation as Problematic Discourse in Organizations." *ACR* (Nov. 1991), 223–241.

Barringer, Felicity. "Census Shows Profound Change in Racial Makeup of the Nation." *New York Times*, 11 Mar. 1991, p. A1.

* Bonvillian, Gary, and William A. Nowlin. "Cultural Awareness: An Essential Element of Doing Business Abroad." *Business Horizons* (Nov.–Dec. 1994), pp. 44–50.

Braus, Patricia. "Boomers Against Gravity." *American Demographics* (Feb. 1995), 50–57.

———. "The Baby Boom at Mid-Decade." *American Demographics* (Apr. 1995), 40–45.

Brown, William J. "Culture and AIDS Education: Reaching High-Risk Heterosexuals in Asian-American Communities." *ACR* (Aug. 1992), 275–291.

* Carnevale, Anthony P., and Susan C. Stone. "Diversity Beyond the Golden Rule." *Training and Development* (Oct. 1994), pp. 22–39.

Casale, Anthony M., and Philip Lerman. *USA Today: Tracking Tomorrow's Trends*. Kansas City, Mo.: Andrews, McMeel & Parker, 1986.

* Crispell, Diane. "Educated Americans." *American Demographics* (May 1994), 59.

* ———. "The Real Middle Americans." *American Demographics* (Oct. 1994), 28–35.

Delgado, Fernando Pedro. "Chicano Movement Rhetoric: An Ideographic Interpretation." *CQ* (Fall 1994), 446–455.

Donald, J., and A. Rattansi, eds. *'Race', Culture and Difference*. Newbury Park, Calif.: Sage, 1992.

Dunn, William. "The Eisenhower Generation." *American Demographics* (July 1994), 34–41.

* Eskin, Leah. "The Tonto Syndrome." *Scholastic Update*, 26 May 1989, pp. 21–22

Fayer, Joan M., ed. *Puerto Rican Communication Studies*. San Juan, P.R.: La Fundacion Arqueological, Antropologica e Historica de Puerto Rico, Inc., 1993.

* Francese, Peter. "America at Mid-Decade." *American Demographics* (Feb. 1995), 23–31.

From Melting Pot to Magnet: The New American Diversity. New York: American Demographics, 1994.

* Gardner, R. C. "Stereotypes as Consensual Beliefs." In *The Psychology of Prejudice: The Ontario Symposium*, vol. 7, edited by Mark P. Zanna and James M. Olson, pp. 1–32. Hillsdale, N.J.: Erlbaum, 1994.

Gill, Mary M. "Accents and Stereotypes: Their Effect on Perceptions of Teachers and Lecture Comprehension." *ACR* (Nov. 1944), 348–360.

Gill, Mary M., and Diane M. Badzinski. "The Impact of Accent and Status on Information Recall and Perception Formation." *CR* (Summer 1992), 99–106.

* Hajari, Nisid. "The Dark Side of the Sun: Stereotypes in 'Rising Sun.'" *Entertainment Weekly*, 6 Aug. 1993, pp. 26–28.

Hammer, Mitchell R., and Judith N. Martin. "The Effects of Cross-Cultural Training on American Managers in a Japanese-American Joint Venture." *ACR* (May 1992), 162–183.

Hart, Russell D., and David E. Williams. "Able-Bodied Instructors and Students with Physical Disabilities: A Relationship Handicapped by Communication." *CE* (Apr. 1995), 140–154.

Higgins, Mary Anne. "Bridging the Communication Gap Between Farmers and Nonfarmers." *ACR* (Aug. 1991), 217–222.

Kahan, Hazel, and David Mulrya., "Out of the Closet." *American Demographics* (May 1995), 40–47.

Kinder, Donald R., and David O. Sears. "Public Opinion and Political Action." In *The Handbook of Social Psychology*, vol. 2, edited by Gardner Lindzey and Elliot Aronson, pp. 659–741. New York: Random House, 1985.

Klopf, Donald W., and Catherine A. Thompson. *Communication in the Multicultural Classroom.* Edina, Minn.: Burgess, 1992.

Kondo, David Shinji. "Strategies for Reducing Public Speaking Anxiety in Japan." *CR* (Winter 1994), 20–26.

* Krafft, Susan. "¿Quien Es Numero Uno?: Hispanic Heroes." *American Demographics* (July 1993), 16–17.

Langer, Judith. "Eight Boomers Views." *American Demographics* (Dec. 1995), 34–41.

Lee, Wen Shu. "On Not Missing the Boat: A Processual Method for Intercultural Understanding of Idioms and Lifeworld." *ACR* (May 1994), 141–161.

Longino, Charles F., Jr. "Myths of an Aging America." *American Demographics* (Aug. 1994), 44–47.

Lu, Xing, and David A. Frank. "On the Study of Ancient Chinese Rhetoric/Bian." *WJC* (Fall 1993), 445–463.

Martin, Judith N., Mitchell R. Hammer, and Lisa Bradford. "The Influence of Cultural and Situational Contexts on Hispanic and Non-Hispanic Communication Competence Behaviors." *CQ* (Spring 1994), 160–195.

Mature Americans. New York: American Demographics, 1994.

McLaurin, Patrick. "An Examination of the Effect of Culture on Pro-Social Messages Directed at African-American At-Risk Youth." *CM* (Dec. 1995), 301–326.

* "Measuring Diversity: How Does Your State Rate?" *National Education Association Today* (Sept. 1992), p. 8.

* Meredith, Geoffrey, and Charles Schewe. "The Power of Cohorts." *American Demographics* (Dec. 1994), 22–31.

Miller, E. K. "Diversity and Its Management: Training Managers for Cultural Competence Within the Organization." *Management Quarterly* (Summer 1994), pp. 17–23.

Mitchell, Susan. *The Official Guide to the Generations.* New York: American Demographics, 1995.

———. "The Generations Quiz." *American Demographics* (Feb. 1996), 52–53.

———. "Younger Generations Are More Diverse." *Marketing Power* (Feb. 1996), 4.

Mogelonsky, Marcia. "Asian-Indian Americans." *American Demographics* (Aug. 1995), 32–39.

Munter, Mary. "Cross-Cultural Communication for Managers." *Business Horizons* (May–June 1993), pp. 69–78.

The 1995 Lifestyle Market Analyst. New York: American Demographics, 1995.

O'Hare, William P., William H. Frey and Dan Fost, "Asians in the Suburbs," *American Demographics* (May 1994), 32–39.

Olaniran, Bolanie A., and K. David Roach. "Communication Apprehension and Classroom Apprehension in Nigerian Classrooms." *CQ* (Fall 1994), 379–389.

Orbe, Mark P. "African American Communication Research: Toward a Deeper Understanding of Interethnic Communication." *WJC* (Winter 1995), 61–78.

Peterson, Karen S. "Midlife Marks Shift in Priorities." *USA Today*, 23 Jan. 1990, p. D1.

———. "Respect Spells Middle Age." *USA Today*, 23 Jan. 1990, p. A1.

Piirto, Rebecca. *Beyond Mind Games: The Marketing Power of Psychographics.* New York: American Demographics, 1991.

Ralston, Steven Michael, Robert Ambler, and Joseph N. Scudder. "Reconsidering the Impact of Racial Differences in the College Public Speaking Classroom on Minority Student Communication Anxiety." *CR*, 43–50.

Robey, Bryant. "The Impending Rise of Middle Agers: Maturing Baby Boomers." *Adweek's Marketing Week*, 16 Jan. 1989, p. 37.

Rossman, Marlene L. *Multicultural Marketing.* New York: American Demographics, 1994.

Russell, Cheryl. "The Baby Boom Turns 50." *American Demographics* (Dec. 1995), 22–33.

Sanders, Judith, Robert Gass, Richard Wiseman, and Jon Bruschke. "Ethnic Comparison and Measurement of Argumentativeness, Verbal Aggressiveness, and Need for Cognition." *CR* (Winter 1992), 50–56.

* Sandor, Gabrielle. "The 'Other' Americans." *American Demographics* (June 1994), 36–43.

Summerfield, E. *Crossing Cultures Through Film.* Yarmouth, Me.: Intercultural Press, 1993.

Suzuki, Shinobu, and Andrew S. Rancer. "Argumentativeness and Verbal Aggressiveness: Testing for Conceptual and Measurement Equivalence Across Cultures." *CM* (Sept. 1994), 256–279.

* Townsend, Bickley. "Psychographic Glitter: Demographics on Tastes, Attitudes, and Value Systems." *Across the Board* (Mar. 1986), 41–46.

Valdes, M. Isabel, and Marta H. Seoane. *Hispanic Market Handbook.* New York: American Demographics, 1995.

* Waldrop, Judith. "Markets with Attitudes." *American Demographics* (July 1994), 22–33.

* Wangerin, Walter, Jr. "A Matter of Being, and a Matter of Being Right: Speaking to Religious and Religionless People." *Christian Century*, 1 July 1987, 591–593.

Wood, Julia. "Diversity and Commonality: Sustaining Their Tension in Communication Courses." *WJC*, 367–380.

Zimmerman, Stephanie. "Perceptions of Intercultural Communication Competence and International Student Adaptation to an American Campus." *CE* (Oct. 1995), 321–335.

Information Specific to College Student Audiences

The American Freshman: National Norms for Fall 1995. Available from the Higher Education Research Institute, Graduate School of Education and Information Studies, University of California at Los Angeles, 3005 Moore Hall, Mailbox 951251, Los Angeles, CA 90095-1521 (telephone 310-825-1925). Issued annually in January.

"Colleges Come Back." *American Demographics* (May 1995), 4–6.

Dunn, William. *The Baby Bust: A Generation Comes of Age.* New York: American Demographics, 1993.

———. "The Baby Boomlet Heads for College." *American Demographics* (May 1994), 12–13.

Jorgensen-Earp, Cheryl R., and Ann Q. Stanton. "Student Metaphors for the College Freshman Experience." *CE* (April 1993), 123–141.

Miller, Eric. *In the Shadow of the Baby Boom.* New York: American Demographics, 1994.

Susan Mitchell, "The Next Baby Boom," *American Demographics*, October 1995, 22–31.

———. "Younger Generations are More Diverse." *Marketing Power* (Feb. 1996), 4.

Ritchie, Karen. "Marketing to Generation X." *American Demographics* (Apr. 1995), 34–39.

———. *Marketing to Generation X.* New York: American Demographics, 1995.

Stein, Alison. "What to Be When I Grow Up." *American Demographics* (June 1966), 17–19.

"Talking With Fewer Words," *American Demographics*, Apr. 1995, 13–14.

Walker, Chip. "Meet the New Vegetarian." *American Demographics* (Jan. 1995).

Zill, Nicholas, and John Robinson. "The Generation X Difference." *American Demographics* (Apr. 1995), 24–33.

* Zollo, Peter. "Talking to Teens." *American Demographics* (Nov. 1995), 22–28.

———. *Wise Up to Teens.* New York: American Demographics, 1995.

Gender

About Women, Inc. *Marketing to Women.* New York: American Demographics, 1995.

"Agency Takes Heat for 'Sexist' Ad," *Travel Weekly,* 25 July 1994.

Bate, Barbara. "Nonsexist Language Use in Transition." *JC* (Winter 1978), 139–149.

* Batstone, Matther. "Male Misgivings: Men in Advertising." *Marketing,* 20 Oct. 1994, pp. 20–21.

* Blair, Kristine. "Selling the Self: Women and the Feminine Seduction of Advertising." *Women and Language* (Spring 1994), 20–24.

Boddewyn, Jean J. "Controling Sex and Decency in Advertising Around the World." *Journal of Advertising* (Dec. 1991), 25–35.

Canary, Daniel J., and Kimberley S. Hause. "Is There Any Reason to Research Sex Differences in Communication?" *Communication Quarterly,* 41 (1993), 129–144.

* Cooper, Ann. "Meeting Ms. Right: Advertising and Images of Women," *Adweek (Eastern Ed.),* 30 Oct. 1995, pp. 26–31.

DeYoung, Susan, and F. G. Crane. "Females' Attitudes Toward the Portrayal of Women in Advertising: A Canadian Study." *International Journal of Advertising* (Summer 1992), 11–13.

DiMona, Lisa, and Constance Herndon, eds. *The 1995 Information Please Women's Sourcebook.* Boston: Houghton Mifflin, 1994.

Donagby, William C., and Becky Dooley. "Head Movement, Gender, and Deceptive Communication." *CR* (Summer 1994), 67–75.

Hersh, Amy. "The Image of Women in Ads Still Suffers: Stereotypes in Television Commercials." *Back Stage,* 7 June 1991, p. 26.

* Jaffe, Lynn J., and Paul D. Berger. "The Effect of Modern Female Sex Role Portrayals on Advertising Effectiveness." *Journal of Advertising Research* (July–Aug. 1994), 32–42.

Kent, Russell L., and Sherry E. Moss. "Effects of Sex and Gender Role on Leader Emergence." *Academy of Management Journal* (Oct. 1994), 1335–1346.

* Kilbourne, Jean. "Beauty and the Beast of Advertising." *Media and Values* (Winter 1989), 8–10.

Langer, Judith, & Associates. "Women and Technology." *American Demographics* (Apr. 1996), 19–20.

* Leo, John. "Madison Avenue's Gender War." *U.S. News & World Report,* 15 Oct. 1993, p. 25.

Lippert, Barbara. "Having It All . . . Not!" *Adweek (Eastern Ed.),* 14 June 1991, 29–31.

* ———. "Breaking the Bimbo Barrier," *Adweek (Eastern Ed.),* 4 Nov. 1991, p. 35.

———. "Age Before Beauty: Advertisers Are Deserting Loose Women for Grandmotherly Types." *Adweek (Eastern Ed.),* 25 May 1992, p. 20.

* Miller, Cyndee. "Michelob Ads Feature Women—And They're Not Wearing Bikinis." *Marketing News,* 2 March 1992, 2.

* ———. "Liberation for Women in Ads: Nymphettes, June Cleaver Are Out; Middle Ground Is In," *Marketing News,* 17 August 1992, 1–3.

* Mingo, Jack. "Men, Women, and Butts." *Canadian Business* (Nov. 1994), 59–61.

* Myers, Gerry. "Selling a Man's World to Women." *American Demographics* (Apr. 1996), 36–43.

Pearson, Judy Cornelia. *Gender and Communication.* Dubuque, Iowa: William C. Brown, 1985.

* Pearson, Judy C., Gerald R. Miller, and Margo-Marie Senter. "Sexism and Sexual Humor: A Research Note." *CSSJ* (Winter 1983), 257–259.

"Pressure Groups Put Squeeze on Sexist Tube Ads After Complaints." *Campaign,* 15 Feb. 1991, p. 4.

Randall, Phyllis R. "Sexist Language and Speech Communication Texts: Another Case of Benign Neglect." *CE* (Apr. 1985), 128–134.

Richmond, Virginia P., and Paula Dyba. "The Roots of Sexual Stereotyping: The Teacher as Model." *CE* (Oct. 1982), 265–273.

* Russell, Cheryl. "Glass Ceilings Can Break." *American Demographics* (Nov. 1995), 8.

* Salter, Marty M., Deborah Weider-Hatfield, and Donald L. Rubin. "Generic Pronoun Use and Perceived Speaker Credibility." *CQ* (Spring 1983), 180–184.

"Sexism in Ads: All Part of the Brotherhood of Man: Survey Results Show Practice Is Universal." *Adweek (Eastern Ed.),* 27 Apr. 1992, p. 10.

Shapiro, Evelyn, and Barry M. Shapiro. *The Women Say: The Men Say: Women's Liberation and Men's Consciousness: Issues in Politics, Work, Family, Sexuality, and Power.* New York: Dell, 1979.

Stewart, Lea P., Pamela J. Cooper, and Sheryl A. Friedley. *Communication Between the Sexes: Sex Differences and Sex-Role Stereotypes.* Scottsdale, Ariz.: Gorsuch Scarisbrick, 1986.

Tarvis, Carol. *The Mismeasure of Women.* New York: Simon & Schuster: 1992.

Time (Special Issue: Women: The Road Ahead), Fall 1990.

Trenholm, Sarah, and William R. Todd de Mancillas. "Student Perceptions of Sexism." *QJS* (Oct. 1978), 267–283.

Wheeless, Virginia Eman, and Robert L. Duran. "Gender Orientation as a Correlate of Communicative Competence." *SSCJ* (Fall 1982), 51–64.

* White, Barbie. "Sexist Advertisements: How to See Through the Soft Sell." *Media and Values* (Winter 1989), 10.

Wiles, Charles R., and Anders Tjernlund. "A Comparison of Role Portrayal of Men and Women in Magazine Advertising in the USA and Sweden." *International Journal of Advertising* (Summer 1991), 259–267.

"Women on Women: Special Report: Women and Advertising," *Adweek (Eastern Ed.),* 24 June 1991, pp. 32–33.

Wood, Julia T. *Gendered Lives: Communication, Gender, and Culture.* Belmont, Calif.: Wadsworth, 1994, p. 126.

Motivation

Atkinson, J. W. *Personality, Motivation and Action.* New York: Praeger, 1983.

* Braus, Patricia. "Everyday Fears." *American Demographics* (Dec. 1994), 32–37.

* Davidson, Andrew. "Striking the Right Key with Buyers." *Marketing,* 7 May 1987, pp. 30–31.

Fisher, Walter R. "A Motive View of Communication." *QJS* (Apr. 1970), 131–139.

* Fowles, Jib. "Advertising's Fifteen Basic Appeals." *Et Cetera* (Fall 1982). Reprinted in Robert Atwan, Barry Orton, and William Vesterman. *American Mass Media: Industries and Issues,* 3rd ed. New York: Random House, 1986, pp. 43–54.

* Hoffman, Edward. "The Last Interview of Abraham Maslow," *Psychology Today,* Jan.-Feb. 1992, pp. 68–74.

* George Leonard, "Abraham Maslow and the New Self." *Esquire* (Dec. 1983), 326–336.

Maslow, Abraham H. *Motivation and Personality,* 2nd ed. New York: Harper & Row, 1970.

* McDaniel, Thomas R. "The Ten Commandments of Motivation." *The Clearing House* (Sept. 1985), 19–23.

* Miller, Annetta, and Dody Tsiantar. "Psyching Out Consumers." *Newsweek,* 27 Feb. 1989, pp. 46–47.

Murray, Henry A. *Explorations in Personality.* New York: Oxford University Press, 1938.

Reykowski, Janusz. "Social Motivation." *Annual Review of Psychology* (1982), 123–154.

* Ross, Art. "More TV Motivators to Trigger Sales." *Back Stage,* 24 May 1985, pp. 43–44.

* ———. "Twenty-one Meaningful Motivational Messages." *Back Stage,* 31 Oct. 1986, p. 45.

Veroff, J., C. Depner, R. Kulka, and E. Douvan. "Comparison of American Motives: 1957 versus 1976." *Journal of Personality and Social Psychology* (1980), 1249–1262.

Weiner, B. "A Cognitive (Attribution)-Emotion-Action Model of Motivated Behavior." *Journal of Personality and Social Psychology* (1980), 186–200.

Attitudes and Values

* Edmondson, Brad. "Crime Crazy." *American Demographics* (May 1994), 2.

Edwards, Allen L. *Techniques of Attitude Scale Construction.* New York: Appleton-Century-Crofts, 1957.

Gleicher, F., and R. E. Petty. "Expectations of Reassurance Influence the Nature of Fear-Stimulated Attitude Change." *Journal of Experimental Social Psychology,* 28 (1992), 86–100.

Kidder, Rushworth M. *Shared Values for a Troubled World.* San Francisco: Jossey-Bass, 1994.

Krippendorff, Klaus. "The Expression of Value in Political Documents." *Journalism Quarterly* (Autumn 1970), 510–518.

Krosnick, J. A., and D. F. Alwin. "Aging and Susceptibility to Attitude Change." *Journal of Personality and Social Psychology*, 57 (1989).

* Lewis, Pierce, Casey McCracken, and Roger Hunt. "Politics: Who Cares?" *American Demographics* (Oct. 1994), 20–27.

McGuire, William J. "Attitudes and Attitude Change." In *The Handbook of Social Psychology*, vol. 2, edited by Gardner Lindzey and Elliot Aronson. New York: Random House, 1985.

* Moore, Thomas. "Idealism's Rebirth: JFK—Twenty-five Years Later." *U.S. News and World Report*, 24 Oct. 1988, pp. 37–39.

The National Conference of Christians and Jews. "Taking America's Pulse: A Summary Report of the National Conference Survey on Inter-Group Relations." Undated, available from The National Conference, 71 Fifth Avenue, New York, NY 10003.

Olson, James M., and Mark P. Zanna. "Attitudes and Attitude Change." *Annual Review of Psychology*, 44 (1993), 117–154.

* Robinson, John P., and Tibbett L. Speer. "The Air We Breathe." *American Demographics* (June 1995), 24–33.

Rokeach, Milton. *The Open and Closed Mind.* New York: Basic Books, 1960.

——. *Beliefs, Attitudes, and Values: A Theory of Organization and Change.* San Francisco: Jossey-Bass, 1970.

——. *The Nature of Human Values.* New York: Free Press, 1973.

* Rous, Gerald L., and Dorothy E. Lee. "Freedom and Equality: Two Values of Political Orientation." *JC* (Winter 1978), 45–51.

* Schelle, Henry Z. "Ronald Reagan's 1980 Acceptance Address: A Focus on American Values." *WSCJ* (Winter 1984), 51–62.

Schwartz, Shalom H., and Wolfgang Bilsky. "Toward a Theory of the Universal Content and Structure of Values: Extensions and Cross-Cultural Replications." *Journal of Personality and Social Psychology*, 58 (1990), 878–891.

Schwartz, Shalom H., Sonia Roccas and Lilach Sagiv. "Universals in the Content and Structure of Values: Theoretical Advances and Empirical Tests in Twenty Countries." *Advances in Experimental Social Psychology*, 25 (1992), 1–65.

Stark, Kenneth. "Values and Information Source Preference." *JC* (Mar. 1973), 74–85.

Steele, Edward D., and Charles Redding. "The American Value System: Premises for Persuasion." *WJSC* (Spring 1962), 83–91.

Thompson, Wayne N. "Barbara Jordan's Keynote Address: The Juxtaposition of Contradictory Values." *SSCJ* (Spring 1979), 223–232.

Tyler, T. R., and R. A. Schuller. "Aging and Attitude Change." *Journal of Personality and Social Psychology*, 61 (1991), 689–697.

Vanderford, Marsha L., David H. Smith, and Willard S. Harris. "Value Identification in Narrative Discourse: Evaluation of an HIV Education Demonstration Project." *ACR* (May 1992), 123–161.

Witte, Kim. "Fear Control and Danger Control: A Test of the Extended Parallel Process Model (EPPM)." *Communication Monographs*, 61 (1994), 113–134.

Witte, Kim, and Kelly Morrison. "Using Scare Tactics to Promote Safer Sex Among Juvenile Detention and High School Youth." *Applied Communication Research*, 23 (1995), 128–142.

CHAPTER 5
Selecting and Researching Your Topic

OBJECTIVES

- To help your students select and focus their speech topics.

- To help your students determine the general and specific purposes of their speeches.

- To help your students develop clear thesis statements.

- To help your students obtain responsible knowledge on their topics.

SUGGESTIONS FOR TEACHING

Getting your students to select and research substantive, original, and manageable speech topics can be a challenge. Many instructors like to personally approve their students' ideas in preparation for every major speaking assignment. This chapter offers numerous activities for choosing and critiquing topics and developing specific purpose and thesis statements. The ongoing "Topic Scrapbook" activity should help your students develop a variety of critiqued ideas for their major speaking assignments, and should prove invaluable in convincing your students that there are more timely and original topics to address than using condoms and the dangers of suntanning booths. Many students will choose areas that are clearly substantive, but that are way too broad for disciplined research and speech preparation, such as "AIDS research." There are activities here that have your students focus general topic areas and vague purpose and thesis statements. There are also small-group activities to have them discuss their own research overviews and topic/speech proposals.

Out of respect for the First Amendment, we suggest that you do not censor topics in a public speaking class. It is not unreasonable to ask your students to sit through speeches they do not agree with. Some basic principles of sound topic selection can help you steer students away from overheated and polarized issues, such as abortion, with which all your students are probably already familiar. If you and your students generate a code of ethics for speaking at the beginning or the term, suggest a clause forbidding raw and unsubstantiated hate messages.

Do not assume that freshmen know how to use the library. Many of them benefit from activities and assignments that have them engage library sources. We offer a choice of such exercises, including library trivia quizzes and "speech research strategies" for their own topic ideas. Many of those pertaining to research can be logically coordinated with the activities covering supporting materials in the next chapter. Exercises dealing with topic selection and generating specific purpose and thematic statements can be logically coordinated with those covering the generation of main ideas and speech structure in Chapters 7 and 8.

160

CHAPTER OUTLINE

I. Selecting meaningful and substantive speech topics is the first and sometimes the most difficult part of speech preparation. *(text pp. 142–147)*
   A. Good speech topics are important to both speakers and audiences, and can be handled responsibly in the time allotted for preparation and speaking.
      1. Topics should be important enough for speakers to develop a genuine sense of personal commitment.
      2. Topics should appeal to the dynamics and demographics of a given audience.
         a. Speakers should engage their listeners' interests and concerns from the introduction.
      3. The final test of a good topic is whether you can acquire the responsible knowledge needed to speak credibly about it.
         a. Given time constraints, speakers should select topics they already know something about, and focus on some manageable part of their topic for their presentations.
   B. Speakers should take a systematic approach to selecting their topics.
      1. Students might chart their own interests and compare them with those of their audiences in terms of places they find interesting, people they find fascinating, activities they enjoy, objects they find interesting, events foremost in their minds, long- and short-range goals, important values, problems that concern them, and campus concerns.
         a. Speakers should try to write down at least five brief responses to each question.
      2. Speakers can use media resources, such as newspapers, magazines, and news broadcasts, to stimulate ideas for their interest charts.
         a. Speakers should be careful not to commit plagiarism by summarizing the contents of a single article.
      3. Speakers can make similar charts of apparent audience interests from class discussions and their demographic analyses, and then compare these to their own interests to construct three-column topic area inventory charts.
   C. Speakers should develop a system of analysis for evaluating and focusing speech topics.
      1. Journalists are taught to focus topics in terms of Who? What? When? Where? Why? and How?
         a. This approach may be especially appropriate for informative speaking.
         b. Students should write down as many connections to their topic areas as possible, and look for where the best ideas seem to cluster.
         c. This system can be adapted to persuasive speeches addressing problems.
      2. Final choices on topics should be made in light of a speaker's purpose—what she or he hopes to accomplish for the benefit of her or his listeners.
   D. Once students have completed their interest charts and analyzed emerging topic areas, they should critique each resulting specific topic in terms of whether it fits the assignment, whether it can be covered in the available time, whether the students can learn enough about it to speak responsibly, and why they want to speak on this particular topic.

II. To answer why they want to speak on a given topic, speakers should know the general function of their speech, determine their specific purpose, and develop clear thesis and preview statements. *(text pp. 147–152)*
   A. The general functions of speaking (which sometimes overlap) are to inform, persuade, and/or celebrate.
      1. A speech to inform should share knowledge with listeners and expand their competence in an area.
      2. A speech to persuade offers reasons why listeners should believe or act a certain way.
      3. A speech to celebrate recognizes the importance of some occasion.
      4. For class speaking assignments, general purposes are usually stipulated.
      5. People who invite you to speak outside the classroom will usually stipulate some general expected function of your speech.

     a. Careful audience, subject, and situational analysis is warranted in cases where the general function is left to the speaker's discretion.

B. The specific purpose of a speech indicates what the speaker wants to accomplish in terms of audience understanding, belief, feelings, and actions. A good specific purpose should:
1. help guide research efficiently toward relevant information.
2. be stated as a simple, well-focused idea.
3. focus on ideas that will be interesting or relevant to the audience.
4. limit the topic so that it can be handled adequately in the allotted time.

C. A speaker's specific purpose is usually reflected in his or her thesis statement and preview.
1. A thesis statement clarifies the speaker's purpose by condensing the speaker's message into a single declarative sentence.
   a. Thesis statements are usually offered in the introduction of a speech.
   b. Speakers sometimes (rarely) leave their thesis statements unstated to create a dramatic effect as listeners discover the theses for themselves.
2. The thesis statement should be followed with a *preview* signaling the main points to be developed in the body of the speech.
3. Listeners should be aware that speakers are not always candid about their specific purposes.
   a. The greater the distance between a hidden specific purpose and the surfacing thesis statement, the more ethically suspect is the speech.

III. Once speakers have clarified their thesis statements, they should take a systematic approach to researching responsible knowledge. *(text pp. 152–167)*

A. Speakers do not have to be experts to gain the responsible knowledge that places them on solid ethical ground by allowing them to enrich the lives of their listeners. This knowledge includes:
1. information about the main issues or points of interest.
2. knowing what respected authorities have to say.
3. awareness of latest major developments.
4. local concerns or applications of special interest to the audience.

B. There are three major sources of supporting information for speeches.
1. Citing personal experience can add credibility, authenticity, and freshness to a speech.
   a. In some cases (e.g., interviews), speakers can arrange to acquire personal experience relating to their topic areas and ideas.
   b. Personal experience should always be supplemented with other forms of research.
2. For most topics, library research provides the broad perspective that extends and enriches personal experience and makes for responsible speaking.
   a. Technology is fast changing the nature of library research.
     (1) We suggest that students take the guided tours offered at the beginning of academic years at most colleges or universities to learn about the availability and use of on-line catalogues, reference areas, government documents, nonprint media archives, special collections, CD-ROM databases, computerized search services, holding areas, and interlibrary loan services.
     (2) Professional librarians are the most valuable source for finding appropriate sources of information.
   b. The reference area offers concentrated sources of information.
     (1) Encyclopedias can offer general background information.
     (2) Current facts can be located through periodical indexes or *Facts on File*.
     (3) The right indexes and abstracts (many of which are now on CD-ROM) can help researchers find in-depth information on their topics.
       (a) Most academic libraries carry or have access to the *Reader's Guide to Periodical Literature, Business Periodicals Index, Public Affairs Information Service, Congressional Information Service, Social Sciences Index*, and *Index to Journals in Communication Studies*.

      (4)   Atlases can provide geographically specific information regarding religious preferences, population density, and agricultural and industrial productivity in given areas or countries.

      (5)   Most reference areas offer multiple sources of popular biographical information.

      (6)   Most reference areas offer books of quotations that can be useful for speeches.

      (7)   Almanacs, yearbooks, and directories provide compilations of facts and figures on a wide range of topics.

      (8)   Many libraries have their own clippings from local information resources.

c.   The government documents area contains specialized publications (many of which are now on-line) issued by federal, state, or municipal government agencies.

d.   Electronic databases and computerized search services are now available in most libraries. Many libraries offer:

      (1)   on-line catalogs for accessing their own collections.

      (2)   computerized indexes such as *Lexis, Nexis,* and *Newsbank.*

      (3)   periodical indexes such as *ERIC* and the *Humanities Index.*

      (4)   the Internet, which is the most comprehensive source available.

          (a)   Through the Internet, researchers can conduct electronic conversations with others and retrieve countless sources of information.

          (b)   Researchers should be wary of information quality and always verify the credibility of sources.

      (5)   CD-ROM databases that store enormous amounts of data on disks that can easily be downloaded.

3. Interviews with qualified experts can add credibility to a message.

a.   The first step is to identify the right expert to interview.

      (1)   Speakers may locate experts through their library's clippings services, through local newspaper indexes, or over the Internet.

b.   The second step is establishing contact with the prospective interviewee.

      (1)   If time permits, speakers should write a letter requesting the interview and follow up with a telephone call to set a time and place; if there is not time, they may have to initiate the request by telephone. Speakers should:

          (a)   introduce themselves, explain their purposes, and indicate the types of questions to be asked.

          (b)   not be shy, as interview prospects are usually flattered by the request.

c.   Interviews should be designed to acquire the desired information through a series of questions. Speaker/interviewers should:

      (1)   plan open questions, inviting their experts to discuss their responses in detail.

      (2)   avoid closed questions that constrain answers to brief responses.

          (a)   Closed questions are good for follow-ups to clarify positions.

      (3)   avoid providing the answers they desire in their questions.

      (4)   always allow their experts to finish their thoughts before interrupting them and proceeding with the next question.

          (a)   Interviewers should be flexible enough to adapt to a spontaneous flow of conversation.

      (5)   avoid wording questions in a manner that is likely to provoke defensive responses.

d.   Interviews can be conducted in a responsible manner by:

      (1)   being thankful, courteous, prompt, and neatly dressed.

      (2)   establishing some sort of common ground before moving to planned questions.

      (3)   letting the expert do most of the talking while being alert to opportunities to follow up responses with probes, mirror questions, verifiers, and/or reinforcers.

          (a)   Probes are questions that ask the expert to elaborate on a response.

          (b)   Mirror questions reflect back part of a response to solicit elaboration.

          (c)   Verifiers confirm the meaning of something that has been said.

        (d)   Reinforcers are verbal or nonverbal encouragements to communicate further.

    (4)   as necessary, politely steering the respondent back on course with questions and transitional statements.

    (5)   not overstaying their welcome by making interviews tediously long.

    (6)   ending with a summary statement of vital points so that experts can check the interviewer's understanding of their testimony.

C. Many researchers record their information on index cards because they are easy to handle and sort by categories.

    1. Information cards are used to record ideas and material from an article or book, one item of information to a card.

       a. Each card should contain one piece of information and an abbreviated reference.

    2. Source cards contain precise identification of information sources, including the author, title, publisher, and place and date of publication.

    3. Speakers should evaluate researched information in terms of its reliability, thoroughness, recency, and precision.

USING END-OF-CHAPTER ITEMS

Discussion *(text p. 169)*

1. **Working in small groups, exchange your personal interest charts. Discuss the most promising areas for speech topics that emerge across these charts. Report these to the class.**

Have your students complete the "Personal Interest Inventory" (p. 180 of this IRM) for homework, and bring it to class for small-group discussion. Inventories should include at least three entries in each category: places, people, activities, objects, events, goals, values, problems, and campus concerns. Working in small groups, students should brainstorm possible speech ideas from one another's self-interest charts. Project the transparency "Topic Brainstorming Guidelines" (p. 183) with this phase of the exercise. After ten to fifteen minutes, have each student report his or her three most interesting prospects for class discussion. You might combine this with item 2 and have students critique their ideas as they present them.

2. **Using the system of analysis described in this chapter, analyze the most promising topic areas identified in item 1. As you consider these topic possibilities, discuss what general functions they might serve.**

Once your students have chosen their three most promising topic ideas, they should critique them following the topic analysis method outlined in the text (pp. 145–146). Project the transparency "Criteria for a Good Speech Topic" (p. 181) in conjunction with this phase of the exercise. Are the topics manageable and at least potentially meaningful to speaker and audience alike? What would the general purpose of these topic areas probably be? to inform? to persuade? to celebrate? Use this as an opportunity to stress the principles and importance of systematic topic selection.

3. **As a follow-up to items 1 and 2, develop specific purposes and thesis statements for the three topics that interest you most. Evaluate them in class, using the criteria for selecting good topics and determining specific purposes described in this chapter.**

This is good for homework and a next-day small-group discussion activity. Students should take their three most promising topic areas, and develop specific purpose and thematic statements for each one. They should present their choices in class to be evaluated in terms of the criteria for specific purpose and thematic statements. Project the transparency "Criteria for a Good Specific Purpose" (p. 182) for class discussion in conjunction with this phase of the exercise.

4. **In what ways might personal experience limit and distort your knowledge as well as enrich it? Discuss in class, drawing on examples from your own experience.**

You might have your students write down some ideas for homework in preparation for this exercise. Have them choose an issue or subject that is important to them, and consider the ways in which their personal experiences might both enhance and distort their understanding of that issue. In general, personal experience adds authenticity to messages, enhances speaker credibility, and adds an element of human interest. However, it can also create biases that blind us to alternative positions, and make us feel overconfident about our general knowledge of something when we actually have a very limited range of experience. Furthermore, people speaking from personal experience sometimes fail to explain themselves adequately and tend to rely on jargon that an audience may not understand. For class discussion, emphasize that personal experience is fine and can contribute to a quality speech. However, it is not the only or final measure of a good speech topic, and it should always be supplemented with responsible research.

Application *(text pp. 169–170)*

1. **Working in small groups, scan a variety of media resources to generate topic areas for speeches. Each group should be responsible for checking one of the following materials:**

   a. **a local Sunday newspaper**
   b. **a television news program over a week's time**
   c. **a recent issue of a weekly news magazine**
   d. **a recent issue of a general-interest magazine**

   In the first part of a class period, meet as groups to generate a list of topic ideas. Each group should select five topic ideas. In the second part of the class period, a representative should present each group's recommendations to the class and explain how and why the topics were chosen. Which kind of media resource produces the best speech topics? What are the strengths and limitations of each?

   You might use this as a peer-review group activity early in the semester before actually covering the materials on topic selection. For in-class use, have your students bring one or two media sources (excluding TV news programs) to class for this activity. Project the transparencies "Topic Brainstorming Guidelines" and/or "Criteria for a Good Speech Topic" (pp. 183 and 181) to help facilitate class discussion. Have your students present and defend their choices before the class, using the relevant criteria. What media sources seemed to produce the best topic ideas, and what are the relative strengths and weaknesses of each type? Use this as an opportunity to discuss the general principles of choosing and narrowing topics.

2. **Choose one of the topics you selected from Application 1 and identify the most likely sources of information you could use to develop it.**

   This works well as a written homework assignment to help students learn strategic topic research, as well as the importance of doing responsible research. Refer your students to the material on library resources in the text (text pp. 155–161) and have them prepare a research plan specifying resources to consult for additional information. You might have them go to the library and prepare five source cards identifying author, title, date of publication, and information regarding their topics or ideas. Require a variety of source types, including newspaper and magazine articles, encyclopedias, source-specific reference materials, books, government documents, etc.

3. **Take a walking tour of your library, locating the various resources described in this chapter. While you are there, try to find the answers to the following questions. Do not ask the librarian for assistance. Record the source of each answer.**

a. What was the population of the city in which you were born in the year of your birth?
b. What television show had the highest ratings when you were six years old?
c. What contemporary public figure do you admire most? When and where was he or she born? What is he or she most noted for?
d. Who won the Nobel Prize for literature in the year your most admired public figure (MAPF) was born? What was the author's nationality? most admired work(s)?
e. What actress won the Academy Award for best supporting actress the year your MAPF was born? What movie was she in?
f. Who were the U.S. senators of the state in which you were born during the year of your birth?
g. Who were the Republican presidential and vice-presidential candidates during the election held nearest the birth year of your MAPF?
h. What noteworthy event took place during the month and year of your birth? When and where did this happen?

You should warn research librarians of this assignment in advance, and you might consider providing them with a list of the questions distributed to your students. If they are willing to cooperate (they often are), request that they steer students in the right direction without giving them the answers. You might shuffle and distribute the following alternative questionnaires to compel students to do their own work.

Alternative Library Quiz 1

a. Who is the United States' wealthiest person, and how wealthy is he or she?

b. What television shows did Norman Lear produce?

c. Who is the curator of New York's Museum of Modern Art?

d. What ABC prime-time show was interrupted on October 17, 1989, and by what event?

e. What horse holds the record in the Belmont Stakes?

f. Which movie won the Academy Award for best picture in 1960?

g. Who said, "The only thing we have to fear is fear itself"?

h. What is the life expectancy for infants born this year in the United States, and how does this compare with fifty years ago?

i. How many grizzly bears are there estimated to be in the United States?

Alternative Library Quiz 2

a. What are the per capita incomes of residents of California, West Virginia, and Illinois?

b. What was Bill Cosby's first television show?

c. Who is the conductor of the Boston Pops?

d. What noteworthy event took place on November 22, 1963?

e. What was the name of the last horse to win racing's "Triple Crown"?

f. Who won the Academy Award for best actor in 1990?

g. Who said, "Old soldiers never die," and on what occasion was this said?

h. What is the population of Minneapolis, and how has it changed since 1980?

i. What national park has the most visitors each year?

Alternative Library Quiz 3

a. What are the median prices of houses in Hartford, Connecticut; Indianapolis, Indiana; and Sacramento, California?

b. What was the size of the largest earthquake ever to hit the continental United States? When and where did this occur?

c. Who was the composer of *Jesus Christ, Superstar* and how old was he at the time?

d. Who was assassinated on June 5, 1968?

e. Who holds the record for the most medals won in swimming competition in one year's Olympic games?

f. Who won the Nobel Prize in literature in the year you were born, and for what work was this prize awarded?

g. Who said, "I have nothing to offer but blood, toil, tears, and sweat," and when and where was this said?

h. In what year was a vaccine for polio first available to the public?

i. What is the northernmost city in the continental United States?

Alternative Library Quiz 4

a. What was the first state to enter the union after the original thirteen?

b. How many Academy Awards were given to *Gone With the Wind*, in what year, and what were they for?

c. Who is the director of the National Trust for Historic Preservation, and how would you contact him or her?

d. On what date was the first atomic bomb used in a war, who used it, and on what city was it dropped?

e. What country did the U.S. hockey team defeat to win the gold medal in the Lake Placid Winter Olympics, and in what year did this happen?

f. In what year did *USA Today* begin publishing, and how was it different from other daily newspapers?

g. What American president coined the term "the great society," and when did this happen?

h. What city in the United States has the highest population density?

i. What was the name of the most recent hurricane to hit the eastern seaboard of the United States, and when did this happen?

Alternative Library Quiz 5

a. What United States city has the highest per capita income? the lowest?

b. When was the first Lone Ranger movie produced, and who played the Lone Ranger?

c. Where is the Buffalo Bill Museum located, and what types of exhibits does it have?

d. What noteworthy event took place on August 18, 1920?

e. Who was/were the winner(s) of the 1986, 1987, and 1988 Iditarod? What is this event, and where is it held?

f. What were the first and most recent newspapers to win Pulitzer Prizes for meritorious public service?

g. Who said, "Ich bin ein Berliner," and on what occasion was this said?

h. How many children in the United States are afflicted with AIDS, and how do they usually contract this disease?

i. How many acres of national forest are there in the state of California?

4. Discuss the following thesis statements in terms of their effectiveness:

    a. You ought to protect yourself from date rape.
    b. The role of superstitions in our lives.
    c. Young children should not be admitted to horror movies.
    d. Weekend trips are preferable to long vacations.
    e. Nutritious meals you can cook in your dorm room.

Improve those that do not meet the criteria for effective thesis statements.

This exercise works well for in-class discussion, although you might have students write down some ideas in preparation as homework. Your students should consider how these thesis statements might be improved. Emphasize that a good thesis statement reflects a clear focus and purpose, and previews the actual message. You might have your students generate main points to develop in support of their revised thesis statements. The following suggestions may help guide class discussion:

a. **You ought to protect yourself from date rape.** This thesis statement is too general and does not summarize or preview the main points of the message. An improved version might read, "You should protect yourself from date rape by avoiding isolated encounters, staying sober, and having an alternative means of transportation."

b. **The role of superstitions in our lives.** This thesis statement is not worded as a complete declarative sentence. It is too general, and it does not adequately preview or review the main points of a coherent message. In fact, this thesis statement does not appear to reflect any specific purpose. It does not sufficiently limit the topic so that it could be handled in a short presentation. An improved version might read, "Superstitions often affect our social, professional, and family relationships." This improved thesis statement suggests the categorical design of the speech and, as a preview, would help the audience track the message more easily.

c. **Young children should not be admitted to horror movies.** This is inadequate as a thesis statement because it does not specify precisely what the speaker wants from the audience. It also makes a claim without previewing any sort of rationale to be developed in the message. An improved version might read, "To convince my audience that young children should not be admitted to horror movies because viewing them condones violence as a means of problem solving."

d. **Weekend trips are preferable to long vacations.** Again, although this statement is a complete, declarative sentence, it is too general for a good specific statement and does not adequately summarize or preview the main points of a message. An improved alternative might be phrased, "Weekend trips are preferable to long vacations because they are easier to plan, less expensive to take, and do not leave you exhausted."

e. **Nutritious meals you can cook in your room.** This phrase is not a complete declarative sentence, and it is once again too general. An improved option might read, "You can prepare nutritious meals in your dorm room with a microwave, a small electric skillet, or a small slow cooker." The improved thesis statement suggests that the speech will cover meals that can be prepared with three common small appliances.

ADDITIONAL ACTIVITIES

Topic Scrapbooks

Purpose: To start your students thinking early about topic ideas for informative and persuasive speeches.

Directions: This exercise is useful for compelling your students to read and explore a number of topic options, and should prove useful for later class activities and speaking assignments. You might coordinate it with the reading and listening logs described in Chapters 1 and 3 of this IRM. Early in the term, have your students begin keeping a "topic scrapbook" either with their class logs or in a small spiral notebook. Their scrapbook entries should be ideas for speech topics that they get from newspaper or magazine articles, television shows, or conversations with other students, or simply ideas that come to them out of the blue. Entries should include a rationale for why they want to speak on this issue and what they hope to accomplish. Have your students make at least three entries a week in their scrapbooks, and check them periodically throughout the semester. As an alternative to evaluating them yourself, you might break your students into their peer review groups before each major round of speeches to troubleshoot one another's ideas and explore possible new options.

Preparing Thesis Statements

Purpose: To provide your students with practice developing thesis statements.

Directions: Briefly review your criteria for a good thesis statement. For subsequent class discussion, have your students generate thesis statements for the following topic ideas:

  a. Describing a nearby tourist attraction
  b. Introducing a service available to students on campus
  c. Urging fellow students to contribute to a charity
  d. Urging fellow students to take a specific nonrequired course
  e. Telling fellow students how to study for tests
  f. Discussing the meaning of the Fourth of July

Each group should present their best ideas for a class discussion focusing on their adequacy in terms of (1) whether they are complete, declarative statements, (2) whether they reflect a clear sense of purpose, and (3) whether they adequately summarize and preview the main points of a coherent and meaningful message. Encourage your students to offer suggestions for improvement along with their critiques, and revise their statements as appropriate. A suggested answer for (a) might read "Elkbreath Park offers several fun-filled activities for the family vacation, including camping, hiking, fishing, and a deluxe lodge with restaurant and bar."

Nonspecific Purposes

Purpose: To provide students an opportunity to revise overly vague specific-purpose statements.

Directions: Briefly review the criteria for a good specific-purpose statement. For subsequent class discussion, have your class evaluate and revise the following vague specific-purpose statements:

  a. To inform the audience how to brush their teeth
  b. To inform the audience how to pop popcorn
  c. To inform the audience about nuclear physics
  d. To inform the audience about indoor and outdoor gardening
  e. To persuade the audience to boycott our stupid commencement ceremonies
  f. To inform the audience about horses
  g. To inform the audience how to register for classes

Focus discussion on the criteria for specific-purpose statements. Remember that a specific-purpose statement should clearly indicate what the speaker expects from his or her audience with regard to a well-focused topic.

Suggestions for discussion:

a. This specific-purpose statement promises little new or enriching information. It lacks ambition and would probably not be interesting. A better statement in the same general topic area might be to inform an audience about technological changes in modern toothbrushes or disagreements among dentists concerning the best types and brands.

b. This specific-purpose statement will also not enrich listeners, lacks ambition, and probably would not attract and sustain audience interest. A better specific-purpose statement might be to inform an audience of alternative ways to prepare and use popcorn—but no promises.

c. This specific-purpose statement is too ambitious for a short class speech. It is doubtful whether students could learn enough to make responsible presentations. The speaker should focus and limit the topic to some manageable aspect. A better specific-purpose statement might be to inform an audience about Einstein's theory of relativity or how the atom bomb was developed.

d. This specific-purpose statement is too vague and needs to be limited to some manageable aspect. A better specific-purpose statement might be, "To instruct my audience how to force bulbs for indoor winter blooms."

e. The phrasing of this specific topic has been made offensive by the insertion of one emotionally loaded word—*stupid*—that suggests (for most audiences) that the speaker is narrow-minded. A specific-purpose statement should be less passionate and more objective to avoid unnecessarily offending audiences.

f. This specific-purpose statement is vague, unfocused, and unmanageable. A better statement might read, "To inform my audience about how Tennessee Walking Horses are trained," or "To inform my audience how to have a good time at the tracks without blowing the family fortune."

g. This specific-purpose statement would not be likely to enrich the audience because most students would probably already know as much about the topic as the speaker does (or as much as they care to, for that matter). Unless the speaker has something truly original in mind, she or he should ditch this topic and pick something else. An improved specific-purpose statement might be, "To inform my audience of three foolproof ways to get through registration without the usual hassle."

Narrowing Topic Ideas

Purpose: To give your students practice in focusing on workable speech topics, given overly general subject areas.

Directions: You might use this to introduce your criteria for choosing and narrowing speech topics. All of the following subject areas might lead to substantive and manageable speech topics, but are as yet too general and unfocused for research and speech preparation to begin. Break your students into small groups, distribute the following list, and have them brainstorm and critique topic ideas for each subject area. What general purpose would these speeches probably serve? Emphasize the importance of topics that are important, manageable, original, and interesting. You might project the transparencies "Criteria for a Good Speech Topic" and/or "Topic Brainstorming Guidelines" (pp. 181 and 183) in conjunction with this activity. Have your students present their ideas for a general class discussion. As an alternative, the day before speech topic proposals are due, have your students volunteer their own speech topic ideas and open them up for class discussion.

    a.   Environmental protection
    b.   Family values
    c.   The drug war
    d.   Gun control
    e.   Animal testing
    f.   Political reform
    g.   AIDS and safe sex
    h.   Hunger

Suggestions for discussion:

a.   While very important, this is an extremely broad (global) topic area. It would probably lead to persuasive speech topics. Students might focus on a specific environmental issue or problem, pending legislation, or things individuals can do to get involved, such as recycling. They might localize the issue by focusing on a controversy in their particular area.

b.   This general topic area is extremely vague and could lead in many directions. Students might develop ceremonial or self-introductory speeches emphasizing what family values mean to them and the significance of these values in their lives. The topic area could also lead to persuasive speeches on "deadbeat dads" and the importance of taking care of your kids.

c.   We've been fighting this "war" for quite a while, and there are many issues and topics that students could derive from it—most of them informative and/or persuasive. They might focus on the latest programs for treatment or education, or the latest efforts at law enforcement and interdiction. They might inform us about a new "designer" drug we are not yet familiar with, or a piece of pending legislation. Impress upon your students that legalizing marijuana and other recreational drugs is a dead issue in our society; for all practical purposes it was settled a long time ago. It tends to result in extremely lame and uninspired presentations.

d.   Obviously a persuasive topic, gun control is a hot issue that is still not settled. However, it is also not very new and chances are your students are familiar with the Brady bill and arguments for and against waiting periods. To generate more interesting and original topics, they might consider alternative approaches to gun control and licensing, local statutes and laws, or the latest lobbying efforts of the NRA.

e.   This could be informative and/or persuasive. Animal testing is one of the all-time most used topics, in my experience. I generally tell students that most of us are aware that animals have been mistreated and killed in laboratories, and not always for medical progress. Certainly we are generally familiar with abuses by the cosmetic industry. Try to steer students toward something new in the same general topic area, such as new animal-friendly products to look for, abuses in other types of laboratories, or the feasibility of new computer technologies designed to render such testing unnecessary.

f.   This is an obviously persuasive issue that is becoming very fashionable in our country. Students might focus on different proposals for political reform that are currently being advocated, such as term limits, and further caps on campaign spending and PAC contributions.

g.   This would probably be a combination of informative and persuasive. Public education on this issue is obviously very important, and there are many dedicated activists working on the dissemination of this message today. As a result of their efforts and numerous public service announcements, most college students are aware of AIDS, its consequences, and how to use condoms. Therefore, this information would be too general for a graded assignment. However, both of these areas could be focused on excellent speech topics, so long as the speaker takes care to dig up something new and original, such as the latest research efforts, treatments, or differing prophylactic devices.

h. This is another global problem that, when focused, would probably lead to informative and/or persuasive speech topics. Students might localize hunger to one region of the world, or discuss associated conditions or causes. They might also localize it to their own particular area or region, or things the audience can do to get involved and make a difference.

Non-Mass Media Sources

Purpose: To increase student awareness of the availability of non-mass media sources of information for researching their speeches.

Directions: This activity combines library homework with in-class discussion. The typical undergraduate may not be aware of the wide range of interesting periodicals available to research their speeches. The handout "Non-Mass Media Sources" (p. 186 of this IRM) can introduce students to a wide variety of periodicals that take them beyond the world of *Time, Newsweek,* and *Reader's Digest.* You might compile your own list of non-mass media periodicals available in your college library, or have your students go to the library and thumb through back issues of three periodicals that they suspect may have published articles and information relating to their topic areas. They should start with the most recent issues and work their way back (remind your students that current periodicals usually have their own section at the library, whereas back issues may be in the stacks, binding, or on microfilm). Your students should prepare source and information notecards for these periodicals and speculate whether their articles (or the periodical) may be biased in any way. They should also include a general assessment of the periodicals' relative value for researching their topics. Have them share their information and evaluations for class discussion.

The Credibility of Sources

Purpose: To impress upon students the importance of considering a periodical's reputation, especially with respect to how it would be received by a specific audience if cited during a presentation.

Directions: Early in the term, have the class complete the "Source Credibility Questionnaire" on IRM p. 187. Collate the results of their assessments and make them available to the class along with other audience analysis information. Discuss the results of the survey with the class. You might compare the responses of your students with the responses to national surveys or surveys taken at other universities, and consider, in class discussion, what this particular audience's orientation to important and timely issues would likely be.

Seventy-seven students enrolled in public speaking classes at Indiana University and Memphis State University were asked to assess the credibility of popular periodicals using the "Source Credibility Questionnaire." The following list is a rank ordering of the periodicals in terms of their perceived credibility. For each periodical, the mean score is reported along with the number of students (N) who felt they were familiar enough with the periodical to assign it a credibility rating.

RATINGS OF SOURCE CREDIBILITY

PERIODICAL	MEAN	N
Wall Street Journal	4.644	76
New England Journal of Medicine	4.551	29
National Geographic	4.493	77
Time Magazine	4.441	77
U.S. News & World Report	4.375	72
Newsweek	4.350	77
New York Times	4.246	69
Harvard Business Review	4.222	27
USA Today	4.026	75
Today's Health (AMA)	4.000	46
Psychology Today	3.909	44
Sports Illustrated	3.815	76
Money	3.771	57
The New Yorker	3.744	42
Reader's Digest	3.714	77
The American Psychologist	3.571	21
Field and Stream	3.521	46
Changing Times	3.444	27
Popular Mechanics	3.425	54
Ladies' Home Journal	3.108	37
Ebony	3.090	33
Rolling Stone	3.000	63
People	2.891	74
TV Guide	2.861	72
Cosmopolitan	2.859	57
Esquire	2.785	42
Playboy	2.691	68
Ms	2.375	32
National Enquirer	1.287	73

Strategic Research Assignment

Purpose: To offer your students a chance to develop their library research skills in preparation for an actual class presentation.

Directions: This works well in conjunction with the first major research speech assignment. It is important to get beginning students into the library as early and as often as possible. Many are intimidated by the size and technological demands of using modern research libraries, and will greatly benefit from completing a thorough library research assignment. Project the transparency "Speech Research Strategies" (p. 184), and preface this with a short discussion of basic library materials and efficiently accessing topic-specific information. Many departments like to coordinate library assignments with the annual lectures or tours presented by professional librarians at most university libraries. Have your students go to the library and complete their own research strategies, using the "Strategic Research Work Sheet" (pp. 188–190 of this IRM). Encourage them to use the text chapter as a guide to finding their materials before consulting reference librarians. You might break your students into small groups and have them complete their research plans in class. Emphasize for your students the value of this assignment in getting them started on their actual speech research. Tell them it's all right if they have to broaden their topic areas (especially local ones) in order to complete then. As this assignment incorporates materials from the next chapter, refer your students to the major forms of supporting materials and the concept of an ideal model of support. Remind them not to deface library materials. This exercise will take time to complete, and you should take them up and evaluate them. If your students need their work sheets to work on their speeches, be sure to get them back to them as soon as possible.

SUPPLEMENTARY MATERIALS

Films and Videos

"The Topic and the Audience," Films for the Humanities, 15 minutes.

"Researching a Topic," McGraw-Hill, 11 minutes.

"Crediting Your Sources," RMI Media Productions, 30 minutes.

"Speakers and the Library," Films for the Humanities, 15 minutes.

"Learning from Others," Films for the Humanities, 15 minutes.

"Learning to Use the Library," RMI Media Productions, 30 minutes.

Computer Software

IdeaFisher, Fisher Idea Systems.

Transparencies and Handouts *(see following pages)*

Personal Interest Inventory

Criteria for a Good Speech Topic (Transparency 5.1)

Criteria for a Good Specific Purpose (Transparency 5.2)

Topic Brainstorming Guidelines (Transparency 5.3)

Speech Research Strategies (Transparency 5.4)

Interviewing for Information (Transparency 5.5)

Non-Mass Media Sources

Source Credibility Questionnaire

Strategic Research Work Sheet

PERSONAL INTEREST INVENTORY

Places	People	Activities
_____	_____	_____
_____	_____	_____
_____	_____	_____
_____	_____	_____
_____	_____	_____

Objects	Events	Goals
_____	_____	_____
_____	_____	_____
_____	_____	_____
_____	_____	_____
_____	_____	_____

Values	Problems	Campus Concerns
_____	_____	_____
_____	_____	_____
_____	_____	_____
_____	_____	_____
_____	_____	_____

CRITERIA FOR A GOOD SPEECH TOPIC

1. It should be meaningful and important to your audience.

2. It should be important and interesting to you personally.

3. It should be tailored to fit your audience, so that it is relevant to their interests and concerns.

4. It should be something on which you already have some knowledge.

5. It should be limited so that you can learn enough about it to make a responsible presentation.

6. It should be appropriate to the time, place, and occasion of the speech.

CRITERIA FOR A GOOD SPECIFIC PURPOSE

1. It should indicate what you want to accomplish in your speech.

2. It should identify what you want your listeners to understand, believe, or do.

3. It should focus on those aspects of your topic that are most relevant or interesting to your audience.

4. It should enrich your listeners by offering new ideas, information, or advice.

5. It should be ambitious and fresh instead of trivial and stale.

6. It should limit your topic so that it is manageable in the time available.

TOPIC BRAINSTORMING GUIDELINES

1. Select a recorder to write the topic ideas on the board under the headings of places, people, activities, objects, events, goals, values, problems, and campus concerns.

2. Each student in turn states an idea for a speech that he or she would like to hear or present, disregarding issues of practicality, plausibility, possibility, or legality. *No criticism of ideas is permitted at this step.* Go around the room until no one has any more ideas.

3. Evaluate each topic by considering whether it is relevant to the audience, interesting, substantive, meaningful, and important, and whether it can be handled within the time constraints. Suggest adaptations or eliminate topic possibilities that do not meet the criteria for good speech topics.

4. Determine a final list of topic ideas for each heading. Have students use this list to select their topics.

SPEECH RESEARCH STRATEGIES

1. **What types of information do I need?**

   Consider background, current, and in-depth information, local applications, facts and figures, expert testimony, and examples.

2. **What sources are likely to contain these types of information?**

   These include encyclopedias (general and subject-specific), almanacs, yearbooks, handbooks, atlases, abstracts, periodicals (popular and professional), books, and government publications.

3. **What tools are available to help locate this information?**

   In most libraries, these include on-line terminals and card catalogues covering the library's in-house collections; newspaper, periodical, and subject-specific indexes; and computer search services.

INTERVIEWING FOR INFORMATION

1. Select and contact a person with expertise in your topic area.

2. Research the topic so that you can prepare a list of intelligent questions.

3. Avoid questions that call for "yes" or "no" answers, leading questions, and questions that will make your expert defensive or angry.

4. Arrive on time, dress neatly, and be courteous.

5. Let the expert do most of the talking.

6. Follow up answers with probes, mirror questions, verifiers, and reinforcers.

7. Do not overstay your welcome. Summarize what you think you heard so that your expert can verify it. Thank the expert for his or her time and cooperation.

8. Review your notes as soon as possible so that you can fill in any holes.

NON-MASS MEDIA SOURCES*

Adapted from Howard Kahane, *Logic and Contemporary Rhetoric: The Use of Reason in Everyday Life* (4th ed.), © 1980 by Wadsworth, Inc. Reprinted by permission of the publisher.

Armed Forces Journal International. Prints details on military issues most others just skim.

Atlantic Monthly. Good; middle to left wing; long established.

Columbia Journalism Review. The best journalism rag.

Commentary. Neoconservative, formerly left wing; overrated; too establishment-oriented for some tastes.

Conservative Digest. One of the few reasonably interesting conservative magazines.

Discover. Popular science magazine.

Foreign Affairs. Establishment quarterly; very influential in government. Tends to be right wing or establishment-oriented.

Harper's. Center to left of center; very good lately. Has been published for over a hundred years.

Harvard Medical School Health Letter. Reasonably reliable medical news.

Inquiry. Libertarian: occasionally excellent.

Libertarian Review. Libertarian; will appear conservative to some, because of free enterprise, anti-big government view.

Matchbox. Amnesty International publication. Gives the gory details about atrocities by governments.

Mother Jones. Successor to *Ramparts*; left publication.

The Nation. One of the oldest political journals, and very good.

National Review. Bill Buckley's conservative magazine; occasionally interesting.

The New Republic. Very good, long-established liberal magazine.

Newsletter on Intellectual Freedom. American Library Association newsletter; contains lists of censored books.

New Yorker. The main long article in each issue sometimes stunningly good, although usually written in dull style.

New York Review of Books. Left-wing; very good (good reviews of non-mass-media books).

The Progressive. Interesting left-wing publication.

Psychology Today. With the demise of *Human Nature*, the best popular psychology magazine; getting better.

Science Digest. Fair to middling science magazine.

Science 91. Popular science magazine. Date in title changes yearly.

Science News. Weekly on what's new in science. Useful.

The Sciences. New York Academy of Science publication.

Scientific American. The best science journal; the trick for a lay reader is to learn how to glean knowledge from articles over one's head.

Skeptical Inquirer. Excellent debunking of pseudo-sciences.

Soviet Life. Interesting to read this slick, picture-filled propaganda product to see how schlock (the current Soviet system) can be made to appear wonderful.

Technology Review. Massachusetts Institute of Technology publication.

The Village Voice. Left-wing; more on New York than national scene, but filled with exposes by such as Jack Newfield and Nat Hentoff, plus Feiffer cartoons.

Wall Street Journal. The best of the business publications; chock full of interesting facts, figures, and ideas.

The Washington Monthly. This writer's favorite political magazine about how our system works.

World Press Review. News and views from the foreign press.

---

* Adapted from Howard Kahane, *Logic and Contemporary Rhetoric: The Use of Reason in Everyday Life* (4th ed.), Fourth Edition. © 1984, 1980 by Wadsworth, Inc. Reprinted by permission of the publisher.

SOURCE CREDIBILITY QUESTIONNAIRE

Students use a variety of sources in preparing classroom speeches. These sources may range from highly credible to barely believable. A highly credible source is one that is seen as *accurate, unbiased, trustworthy,* and *fair.*

The following is a list of sources frequently used in student speeches. Please indicate how credible you believe each source is, using the following scale:

> 5 = very high credibility
> 4 = high credibility
> 3 = average credibility
> 2 = low credibility
> 1 = very low credibility
> N = not familiar with this publication

Please circle the number that represents your estimate of the credibility of each of the following publications:

Time Magazine	5	4	3	2	1	N
Cosmopolitan	5	4	3	2	1	N
Changing Times	5	4	3	2	1	N
The New Yorker	5	4	3	2	1	N
Esquire	5	4	3	2	1	N
Today's Health (AMA)	5	4	3	2	1	N
Wall Street Journal	5	4	3	2	1	N
National Geographic	5	4	3	2	1	N
Reader's Digest	5	4	3	2	1	N
U.S. News & World Report	5	4	3	2	1	N
Sports Illustrated	5	4	3	2	1	N
Ladies' Home Journal	5	4	3	2	1	N
New England Journal of Medicine	5	4	3	2	1	N
National Enquirer	5	4	3	2	1	N
New York Times	5	4	3	2	1	N
People	5	4	3	2	1	N
Playboy	5	4	3	2	1	N
Newsweek	5	4	3	2	1	N
Psychology Today	5	4	3	2	1	N
Ms	5	4	3	2	1	N
TV Guide	5	4	3	2	1	N
Harvard Business Review	5	4	3	2	1	N
Field and Stream	5	4	3	2	1	N
Ebony	5	4	3	2	1	N
Popular Mechanics	5	4	3	2	1	N
The American Psychologist	5	4	3	2	1	N
Money	5	4	3	2	1	N
Rolling Stone	5	4	3	2	1	N
USA Today	5	4	3	2	1	N

AGE _____   SEX _____   RACE _____   CLASSIFICATION: Sr Jr Soph Fresh Other

Name: _____

STRATEGIC RESEARCH WORK SHEET

1. What is my topic? _____

2. What is my audience-related purpose for speaking on this topic? _____

_____

_____

3. What kind of information (facts, figures, testimony, examples) do I need to achieve this purpose? What sources and research tools will help me find this information? Name at least one of each. *For example, if you wanted to inform your audience on the rise of AIDS in the heterosexual community, you would probably want figures and expert testimony to substantiate that growth, and projections for future developments. Examples, on the other hand, of unsuspecting heterosexuals who have contracted the disease could provide concrete human illustrations.*

   a. Facts/figures: _____

   _____

   _____

   b. Testimony: _____

   _____

   _____

   c. Examples: _____

   _____

   _____

4. Look up items of background information and give the citations for two general or ready-reference sources, such as encyclopedias, almanacs, dictionaries, statistical indexes, etc. Enter your items and citations below.

   a. _____   b. _____

   _____   _____

   _____   _____

   _____   _____

5. Look up and cite at least two relevant periodical articles, using the on-line terminal, *Reader's Guide to Periodical Literature,* or another general periodical index.

   a. _____   b. _____

   _____   _____

   _____   _____

   _____   _____

6. Look up and cite at least two relevant newspaper articles, using the on-line terminal, *New York Times Index,* or another national or local newspaper index.

   a. _____   b. _____

   _____   _____

   _____   _____

   _____   _____

7. Find and cite at least one book, using the on-line terminal or card catalogue: _____

   _____

   _____

8. If available, run a computer search using CD-ROM or Internet technologies. Likely sources might include *Facts on File, Infotrac, National Newspaper Index,* and the *World Wide Web.* Enter two citations below.

   a. _____   b. _____

   _____   _____

   _____   _____

   _____   _____

9. If available, look for at least one local application through local newspaper indexes or the library's clippings service. Enter the citation below. _____

   _____

   _____

10. Now use the citations you have gathered to research the supporting materials that will help you meet your speaking purpose cited above. Fill in researched items of information with citations below.

   a. Two facts or figures that will help me achieve my speaking purpose:

   _____   _____

   _____   _____

   _____   _____

   _____   _____

   b. Two pieces of testimony that will help me achieve my speaking purpose (paraphrase if exceedingly long):

   _____   _____

   _____   _____

   _____   _____

   _____   _____

   c. Two "real-life" examples that will help me achieve my speaking purpose:

   _____   _____

   _____   _____

   _____   _____

   _____   _____

Score: _____

READINGS FOR ENRICHMENT

See guide to journal abbreviations on p. 37.

* Items marked with an asterisk are suitable for student enrichment.

Topic Selection

Dakos, Kalli Desmarteua. "What's There to Write About?" *Instructor* (Aug. 1987), 82.
Duffy, Susan. "Using Magazines to Stimulate Topic Choices for Speeches." *SCT* (Summer 1987), 2–3.
Flower, Linda, and John R. Hayes. "The Cognition of Discovery: Defining a Rhetorical Problem." *College Composition and Communication* (1980), 21–32.
Grainer, Diane. "Creativity vs. 'My Speech Is About Avocados.'" *SCT* (Winter 1990), 14–15.
* Gunther, Max. "When You Need a Nonfiction Idea." In *The Writer's Handbook,* edited by A. S. Burack, pp. 328–332. Boston: The Writer, Inc., 1980.
Holmbert, Carl B. "The Pedagogy of Invention as the Architectonic Production of Communication and Humanness." *CE* (July 1981).
Hugenberg, Lawrence W., and Daniel J. O'Neill. "Speaking on Critical Issue Topics in the Public Speaking Course." *SCT* (Fall 1987), 12–13.
Infante, Dominic A. "Motivation to Speak on a Controversial Topic: Value Expectancy, Sex Differences, and Implications." *CSSJ* (Summer 1983), 96–103.
Kneupper, Charles W. "A Modern Theory of Invention." *CE* (Jan. 1983), 39–50.
Logue, Cal M. "An Exercise in Inventive Analysis." *CE* (Apr. 1982), 149–150.
Smith, Robert E. "Clustering: A Way to Discover Speech Topics." *SCT* (Winter 1993), 6–7.
* Wilson, Sloan. "Explore Your Own World." In *The Writer's Handbook,* edited by A. S. Burack, pp. 3–8. Boston: The Writer, Inc., 1980.
Woodside, Daria. "Choosing Topics for Speeches: A Breath of Fresh Air (Earth, Water, and Fire)." *SCT* (Fall 1992), 1–2.

Creativity

* "The Anatomy of Genius: Research on Creativity." *U.S. News & World Report,* 25 Oct. 1993, p. 56.
* "The Art of Creativity: Riding the White Moment." *Psychology Today* (Mar.–Apr. 1992), 40–49.
Bacon, Donald C. "Brainstorming with Your Computer." *Nation's Business* (Dec. 1989), 34.
Ball, Charles H., Eunice Boardman, and Karen A. Hamblen. "A Symposium on Skills, Knowledge, and Creativity in the Curriculum." *Design for Arts in Education* (May–June 1989), 221–225.
* "Bricolage Among the Trash Cans: The Process of Creativity." *Society* (Jan.–Feb. 1993), 70–75.
* Calano, Jimmy, and Jeff Salzman. "Ten Ways to Fire Up Your Creativity." *Working Woman* (July 1989), 94–95.
Carr, Judy. "Creative Teaching: Creative Learning." *The Writer* (Apr. 1988), 7–8.
"Creativity Killers." *Industry Week,* 23 Jan. 1995, p. 63.
* Curry, Tom, John E. Gallagher, and William McWhirter. "Let's Get Crazy! Creativity Is the Buzz Word as Companies Try to Spark Daring New Ideas." *Time,* 11 June 1990, pp. 40–41.
* Dormen, Lesley, Peter Edidin, and Marjory Roberts. "Original Spin: Creativity Is Not Just for Geniuses and Artists." *Psychology Today* (July–Aug. 1989), 46–52.
* "Get Crazy! How to Have a Breakthrough Idea." *Working Woman* (Sept. 1990), 144–148.
"Great Ideas: How You Can Generate Breakthroughs." *Home Office Computing* (June 1994), 85–89. Includes creativity and problem-solving exercises and a list of hardcopy, software, and audio resources to stimulate creativity.
Grimes, Martha. "Seeing Around Curves." *The Writer* (Sept. 1987), 11–14.
* Hooper, Judith, and Dick Teresi. "Brain Stretches: Exercises, Games, and Apparatus for Brain Training." *Health* (April 1989), 55–67.
* "How to Think Differently." *Fortune,* 15 Jan. 1990, pp. 11–12.
* Hurt, Floyd. "Better Brainstorming." *Training and Development* (Nov. 1944), 57–59.

Hurt, H. Thomas, Katherine Joseph, and Chester D. Cook. "Scales for the Measurement of Innovativeness." *HCR* (Fall 1977), 58–65.

"The Idea Makers." *Technology Review* (Jan. 1993), 32–40.

Isaacs, William M. "Taking Flight: Dialogue, Collective Thinking, and Organizational Learning." *Organizational Dynamics* (Autumn 1993), 24–39.

Jablin, Frederic M. "Cultivating Imagination: Factors that Enhance and Inhibit Creativity in Brainstorming Groups." *HCR* (Spring 1981), 245–258.

Kay, Gail. "Effective Meetings Through Electronic Brainstorming." *Management Quarterly* (Winter 1994), 15–26.

Lizotte, Ken. "Think! (Creativity in Business)." *Boston Magazine* (Apr. 1987), 81–85.

McCarthy, Paul. "The Idea Bank," *Omni* (Sept. 1989), 24.

"Mind Mapping: A Tool for Creative Thinking." *Business Horizons* (Jan.–Feb. 1993), 41–46.

* Noring, Audrey. "Brainstorms and Bright Ideas," *Savvy* (July 1987), 20.

* "Pure Creative Joy: The Importance of Creative Thinking," *Forbes,* 8 Apr. 1996, p. 114.

* Raudsepp, Eugene. "More Creative Gamesmanship." *Psychology Today* (July 1980), 71–75, 88, 90.

———. *More Creative Growth Games.* New York: Putnam, 1980.

* Rice, Berkeley. "Imagination to Go." *Psychology Today* (May 1984), 48–56.

Sternberg, R. J., ed. *The Nature of Creativity.* Cambridge: Cambridge University Press, 1988.

Stewart, William J. "Stimulating Intuitive Thinking Through Problem Solving." *The Clearing House* (Dec. 1988), 175–176.

* Thiagarajan, Sivasailam. "Take Five for Better Brainstorming." *Training and Development Journal* (Feb. 1992), 37–42.

* Weisburd, Stefi. "The Spark: Personal Testimonies of Creativity." *Science News,* 7 Nov. 1989, pp. 298–300.

* Zemke, Ron. "In Search of Good Ideas." *Training* (Jan. 1993), 46–51.

Library Resources

Allen, Terre H., and Scott H. "New Media for the Communication Classroom." *SCT* (Winter 1996), 13–14.

Bahti, Cynthia L. "Library Trivial Pursuit." *SCT* (Winter 1989), 14.

* Baker, Robert K. *Doing Library Research: An Introduction for Community College Students.* Boulder, Colo.: Westview, 1981.

Benefiel, Candace R., and Joe Jaros. "Planning and Testing a Self-Guided Taped Tour in an Academic Library." *Reference Quarterly* (Winter 1989), 199–208.

Benson, Thomas W. "Electronic Network Resources for Communication Scholars." *CE* (Apr. 1994), 120–128.

* Berkman, Robert I. *Find It Fast: How to Uncover Expert Information on Any Subject.* New York: Harper & Row, 1987.

Boatman, Sara A. Introducing Communication Resources." *SCT* (Summer 1995), 7–8.

* Booth, Wayne C., Gregory G. Colomb, and Joseph M. Williams. *The Craft of Research.* Chicago: University of Chicago Press, 1995.

DeHart, Jean. "Self-Contained Library Tour." *SCT* (Summer 1994), 10.

"The Draper Gopher." *Online* (Mar.–Apr. 1995), 21–26.

"Electronic Reference Options: How They Stack Up in Research Libraries." *Online* (Mar. 1992), 22–28.

Engledinger, Eugene A. "Bibliographic Instruction and Critical Thinking: The Contribution of the Annotated Bibliography," *Reference Quarterly* (Winter 1988), 195–202.

* Gates, Jean Key. *Guide to the Use of Libraries and Information Sources,* 7th ed. New York: McGraw-Hill, 1994.

Hankins, Gail. "Gathering Materials: A Three Course Solution to a One Course Problem." *SCT* (Summer 1992), 1–2.

* Harris, Sherwood. *The New York Public Library Book of How and Where to Look It Up.* Englewood Cliffs, N.J.: Prentice-Hall, 1991

* Horowitz, Lois. *Knowing Where to Look: The Ultimate Guide to Research.* Cincinnati, Ohio: Writer's Digest Books, 1984.

Hugenberg, Lawrence W., and Daniel J. O'Neill. "Researching National Issues Forum Topics." *SCT* (Fall 1991), 1–2.

"The Information Professional: An Unparalleled Resource." *Special Libraries* (Winter 1990), 56–60.

Kane, Eileen. *Doing Your Own Research: Basic Descriptive Research in the Social Sciences and Humanities.* New York: Marion Boyars, 1990.

Katz, William A. *Introduction to Reference Work,* 5th ed. New York: McGraw-Hill, 1987.

* Krapp, JoAnn Vergona. "Teaching Research Skills: A Critical-Thinking Approach." *School Library Journal* (Jan. 1988), 32–35.

"Masterminding Tomorrow's Information: Creative Strategies for the '90s." *Special Libraries* (Winter 1991), 76–81.

McComb, Mary. "Benefits of Computer-Mediated Communication in College Courses." *CE* (Apr. 1994), 159–170.

McCormack, Mona. *The New York Times Guide to Reference Materials,* rev. ed. New York: Dorsett, 1988.

Rowland, Lucy M. "Libraries and Librarians on the Internet." *CE* (Apr. 1994), 143–150.

Russell, Tracy, and Randy Hensley. "Education for Bibliographic Instruction." *Research Quarterly* (Winter 1989), 189–195.

Ryan, Susan M. "Uncle Sam Online: Government Information on the Internet." *CE* (Apr. 1994), 151–158.

Schub, Sue. "Teaching Bibliographic Instruction," *Library Journal,* 1 Feb. 1988, pp. 39–40.

Sheehy, E. P., ed. *Guide to Reference Work,* 10th ed. Chicago: American Library Association, 1986.

* Slaughter, Frank G. "How to Be an Expert on Anything." In *The Writer's Handbook,* edited by A. S. Burack, pp. 147–150. Boston: The Writer, Inc., 1980.

Speer, Tibbett L. "I Sing the Library Electric." *American Demographics* (Oct. 1995), 19–21.

Vitale, Philip H. *Basic Tools of Research: An Annotated Guide for Students of English,* 3rd ed., rev. and enl. New York: Barron's Educational Series, 1975.

Walther, Joseph B. "Challenging the Pepsi Challenge." *SCT* (Fall 1992), 6–7.

"When One Database Isn't Enough: Creating Composite Bibliographies on DIALOG or BRS." *Online* (Jan. 1991), 82–86.

Willer, Lynda R. "Learning Research Skills . . . and Having Fun While Doing It." *SCT* (Winter 1995), 12–13.

Interviewing

Barone, Jeanne Tessier, and Jo Young Switzer. *Interviewing Art and Skill.* Boston: Allyn and Bacon, 1995, pp. 89–99.

Bowers, A. Anne, Jr. "The Telephone Interview." *SCT* (Summer 1993), 4–5.

* "Conducting Interviews," Speechwriter's Newsletter, 2 May 1986, p. 2.

* "Conducting the Sensitive Interview." *The Writer* (Jan. 1995), 18–20.

Douglas, Jack D. *Creative Interviewing.* Beverly Hills, Calif.: Sage, 1985.

* "The Foolproof Interviewer's Guide." *Inc.* (Dec. 1991), 127–130.

Garrett, Roger L. "Helping Students Discover Interviewing Skills." *SCT* (Summer 1987), 14–15.

Harding, David A. "Group Feud: Reinforcing Interviewing Skills." *SCT* (Spring 1995), 6–7.

Hunt, Gary, and William Eadie. *Interviewing: A Communication Approach.* New York: Holt, Rinehart, and Winston, 1987.

* "Inside Interviewing." *The Writer* (March 1993), 15–17.

* "Interviewing by Telephone." *The Writer* (May 1994), 27–28.

* "Inventing the Interview." *American Heritage* (Oct. 1994), 46–48.

Metzler, Ken. *Creative Interviewing.* Englewood Cliffs, N.J.: Prentice-Hall, 1977.

Patrick, Perry A. "The 'Perfect' Interview." *The Writer* (Dec. 1988), 18–21.

Sellnow, Timothy L. "An Oral History Exercise for the Self-Evaluation of Interview Skills." *SCT* (Winter 1992), 11.

* Simons, Mary Crescenzo. "The Q's and A's of Interviewing: Ask Questions That Require More than Yes-or-No Answers." *The Writer* (August 1988), 19–23.

Stewart, Charles J. "Teaching Interviewing." In *Teaching Communication: Theory, Research, and Methods,* edited by John A. Daly, Gustav W. Friedrich, and Anita L. Vangelisti, pp. 157–167. Hillsdale, N.J.: Erlbaum, 1990.

Stewart, Charles J., and William B. Cash, Jr. *Interviewing: Principles and Practices*, 6th ed. Dubuque, Iowa: W. C. Brown, 1991.

* "Successful Interviewing: It's All in the Preparation." *Writer's Digest* (Feb. 1996), 35–37.

* "Talking Quotes: Using Quotes Right Is One of the Greatest Challenges in Assembling an Article." *Writer's Digest* (Apr. 1995), 62–64.

* "Tips for Tough Interview Types." *Writer's Digest* (March 1995), 58–60.

Willer, Lynda R. "An Interdisciplinary Approach to Teaching Interviewing." *SCT* (Summer 1995), 10–11.

Wright, Mark H., and Susan R. Wilson. "An Interview Analysis Project for Public Speaking Courses," *SCT* (Spring 1993), 5–6.

* "Yakety-Yak: The Lost Art of Interviewing." *Columbia Journalism Review* (Jan.–Feb. 1995), 23–27.

Evaluating Information Sources

"Accuracy Rules." *New Statesman & Society*, 24 Mar. 1995, pp. 18–20.

* Atwater, Tony. "Editorial Policy of *Ebony* Before and After the Civil Rights Act of 1964." *Journalism Quarterly* (Spring 1982), 87–91.

* Boyer, John H. "How Editors View Objectivity." *Journalism Quarterly* (Spring 1981), 24–28.

Burgoon, Michael, Judee K. Burgoon, and Miriam Wilkinson. "Newspaper Image and Evaluation." *Journalism Quarterly* (Autumn 1981), 411–419.

* Davis, Junetta. "Sexist Bias in Eight Newspapers." *Journalism Quarterly* (Autumn 1982), 456–460.

* Fedler, Fred, Ron Smith, and Mike Meeske. "*Time* and *Newsweek* Favor John F. Kennedy, Criticize Robert and Edward Kennedy." *Journalism Quarterly* (Autumn 1983), 489–496.

Fredin, Eric S. "Assessing Sources: Interviewing, Self-Monitoring and Attribution Theory." *Journalism Quarterly* (Winter 1984), 866–874.

Hayes, John P. "City/Regional Magazines: A Survey/Consensus." *Journalism Quarterly* (Summer 1981), 294–296.

Hynds, Ernest C. "Business Coverage Is Getting Better." *Journalism Quarterly* (Summer 1980), 297–304.

"Just Think: Lack of Objectivity Among American Journalists." *New Perspectives Quarterly* (Summer 1994), 64.

* Luttbeg, Norman R. "News Consensus: Do U.S. Newspapers Mirror Society's Happenings?" *Journalism Quarterly* (Autumn 1983), 484–488.

* Maddox, William S., and Robert Robins. "How *People Magazine* Covers Political Figures." *Journalism Quarterly* (Spring 1981), 113–115.

Mosier, Nancy R., and Andrew Ahlgren. "Credibility of Precision Journalism." *Journalism Quarterly* (Autumn 1981), 375–381.

* Peterson, Robert A., Gerald Albaum, George Kozmetsky, and Isabella C. M. Cunningham. "Attitudes of Newspaper Business Editors and General Public Toward Capitalism." *Journalism Quarterly* (Spring 1984), 56–65.

* Peterson, Robert A., George Kozmetsky, and Isabella C. M. Cunningham. "Perceptions of Media Bias Toward Business." *Journalism Quarterly* (Autumn 1982), 461–464.

Riffe, Daniel. "Relative Credibility Revisited: How 18 Unnamed Sources Are Rated." *Journalism Quarterly* (Winter 1980), 618–623.

Schoenfeld, A. Clay. "Newspersons and the Environment Today." *Journalism Quarterly* (Autumn 1980), 456–462.

* ———. "The Environmental Movement as Reflected in the American Magazine." *Journalism Quarterly* (Autumn 1983), 470–475.

* Smith, Ron F., and Linda Decker-Amos. "Of Lasting Interest? A Study of Change in the Content of Reader's Digest." *Journalism Quarterly* (Spring 1985), 127–131.

* Tillinghast, William A. "Slanting the News: Source Perceptions After Changes in Newspaper Management." *Journalism Quarterly* (Summer 1984), 310–316.

"Whose Views?" *New Statesman & Society*, 24 Mar. 1995, pp. 14–15.

CHAPTER 6
Using Supporting Materials in Your Speech

OBJECTIVES

- To help your students understand the forms of supporting materials.

- To help your students select the best supporting materials for their speeches.

- To help your students learn to use supporting materials to best advantage.

- To teach your students how to evaluate supporting materials used in speeches.

SUGGESTIONS FOR TEACHING

It is hard to overemphasize the importance of the materials covered in this chapter. For it is the effective use of supporting materials—facts and figures, testimony, examples, and narratives—that distinguishes a substantive and reliable speech from a string of mere assertions. Most instructors like to emphasize the importance of strategically engaging a sufficient variety of supporting materials in informative and persuasive speaking assignments.

A crucial step in learning to use supporting materials effectively is to constructively criticize their use in other speeches and message forms, and this chapter offers many activities and exercises that have your students do that. We also have exercises to illustrate how "factual" information can be used to distort rather than enlighten audience perceptions (and not always unintentionally), to illustrate how supporting materials are used in conjunction with visual aids, and to determine what materials are most appropriate to support given statements and propositions. To emphasize the importance of using a variety of supporting forms and stressing the qualifications of sources, we offer a short speaking activity, "Supporting a Point," that has your students make and establish a claim using an ideal model of support.

CHAPTER OUTLINE

I. Supporting materials provide speeches with substance, strength, credibility, and appeal. (*text pp. 173–174*)
   A. They help to arouse audience interest, elaborate and explain the meaning of ideas, emphasize the importance of these ideas to listeners, and substantiate controversial or surprising statements.
   B. They may be gathered through personal experience, library research, and expert interviews.

II. Facts and figures are the most objective forms of supporting information. *(text pp. 174–181)*
  A. Facts are verifiable units of information that are highly respected by most audiences.
    1. While factual statements can stand alone, speakers usually must interpret their meaning.
      a. Speakers should be careful to distinguish "the facts" from their interpretive claims.
      b. Speakers should cite reputable sources in support of interpretive claims.
    2. Speakers should be cognizant of potential bias in their sources of factual information.
      a. Even seemingly neutral sources are colored by cultural environment.
      b. Even relatively objective sources are inherently selective and omit important materials.
  B. Figures or statistics are numerical facts that can describe the size of something, make predictions, illustrate trends, or show relationships.
    1. Speakers can help unpack the meaning of figures for audiences by providing brief explanations and examples and by using presentation aids.
  C. As most audiences find facts and figures highly credible, they are vital for speeches addressing unfamiliar or controversial issues.
  D. Speakers should evaluate researched sources of facts and figures in terms of relevance, recency, source credibility, and reliability.
    1. Speakers should avoid cluttering their speeches with interesting but irrelevant materials.
    2. Recency is especially important with topics on which there is a fast turnover of information.
    3. Scrutinize all "factual" sources and materials for potential bias, distortions, or omissions.
    4. Reliability is especially important with controversial topics.
      a. Speeches should not rely too heavily on a single source for facts and statistics.
    5. Speakers should not cite extraneous information, or ignore information that contradicts their claims.
    6. Speakers should remember that statistics represent probabilities, not certainties, and are often subject to willful misuse.
  E. Three devices for turning facts and figures into powerful supporting materials are definitions, explanations, and descriptions.
    1. Definitions help audiences understand unfamiliar ideas and concepts by translating them into familiar words.
      a. Persuasive definitions provide a given perspective on a controversial topic.
    2. Explanations combine facts and statistics to clarify a topic or demonstrate how it works.
      a. Explanations are longer and more detailed than definitions.
    3. Descriptions are "word pictures" that evoke vivid, mood-setting images in the mind of an audience to help them visualize information.
      a. Speakers should avoid descriptive overkill, and let their audiences participate by envisioning their own adjectives.

III. Speakers use testimony by citing the words and/or ideas of others in support of their messages. *(text pp. 181–184)*
  A. Speakers may use direct quotation (citing the words of others verbatim), or they may paraphrase materials in their own words.
    1. Regardless of the form, speakers should always cite their sources when quoting testimony.
  B. There are three types of testimony that can be used as supporting materials.
    1. Expert testimony comes from people who are qualified by training or experience to serve as authorities on a subject.
      a. Citing expert testimony allows the speaker to borrow ethos from well-respected sources.

      b. Expert testimony is crucial for supporting topics and ideas that are innovative, unfamiliar, technical, or controversial.

      c. Speakers should remember that expertise is area-specific, and should stress the credentials of their sources.

    2. The effective use of lay testimony can provide an understanding of the real-life consequences of issues.

      a. The voices of the "people" are generally highly regarded in our culture.

      b. Lay testimony can enhance identification between listeners and a message.

      c. Lay testimony cannot be used to establish the objective validity of ideas.

    3. Prestige testimony associates a message with the words of a respected public figure.

      a. By citing cultural heroes, speakers can invoke persuasion by mythos.

      b. The skill and subtlety with which speakers invoke prestige testimony is usually a determining factor of its effectiveness.

  C. Testimony used as supporting material should be carefully evaluated.

    1. Testimony should be relevant, seem free from bias, and be recent.

      a. Prestige testimony by cultural heroes often improves with age.

    2. Testimony should be appropriate to the speaker's purpose.

      a. Lay testimony can humanize a message and promote audience identification.

      b. Prestige testimony can enhance the distinction of both a speech and a speaker.

      c. Only expert testimony can demonstrate the factual validity of a statement.

    3. Speakers should avoid distorting the quoted source's meaning and intent when using his or her words out of context.

    4. To assure accuracy, speakers should write quotes out on note cards rather than memorizing them.

    5. Speakers should cite a variety of experts and stress their credentials when addressing controversial issues.

IV. Examples enliven an oral message by providing it with verbal illustrations. *(text pp. 184–189)*

  A. In addition to clarifying ideas, examples arouse and sustain audience attention by providing concrete applications of ideas.

    1. Personal examples can involve an audience and promote identification.

    2. Examples of common experiences, beliefs, or values can help bridge cultural barriers.

    3. Examples provide emphasis and help amplify your most important ideas.

  B. Examples take different forms, and these forms have different functions.

    1. A brief example mentions a specific instance to demonstrate a more general statement.

    2. An extended example contains more detail and allows the speaker to convey a mood through a single instance.

    3. A factual example provides strong support for ideas because it is based on an actual event or real person.

    4. A hypothetical example is a composite of actual people, situations, or events.

      a. While fictional, hypothetical examples should seem plausible.

      b. Hypothetical examples are useful when factual examples illustrating your ideas are not available, or when real examples might embarrass actual people.

      c. Hypothetical examples should be representative, and should not distort the truth just to make a point.

      d. Speakers should alert audiences to hypothetical examples with cues such as "imagine yourself" or "picture this."

  C. Speakers should be cautious in both evaluating and using examples.

    1. Examples should be evaluated in terms of relevance, representativeness, and believability.

    2. Examples should show taste and propriety with respect to the occasion.

V. Narratives illustrate a point by telling a story within a speech. *(text pp. 189–192)*

  A. Humans are story-telling animals who use narrative to order and make sense of experience.

1. Narratives can involve audiences in participative communication, facilitating the transformative capacity of ethical public speaking.
2. Personal narratives can promote identification and help transcend cultural barriers.

B. In speeches, narratives function much like examples in gaining and sustaining audience attention, clarifying abstract and technical ideas, and amplifying a point.
   1. A narrative functions as a speech within a speech, beginning with an attention-getting introduction, continuing with a body in which the story develops, and ending with a conclusion that reinforces the message.
   2. Narratives are effective tools for both introducing and concluding a speech.
   3. Speakers invoking narratives should use dialogue rather than paraphrase to promote a sense of immediacy with the audience.

C. Narratives should be evaluated in terms of relevance, audience predisposition, and originality.
   1. Speakers can present effective narratives by:
      a. clearly marking their narratives with transitional cues.
      b. using colorful, active language.
      c. creating a sense of anticipation that builds to a punch line or conclusion.
      d. pausing for effect or for laughter to subside.
      e. being less formal in tone.
      f. directing humor at themselves instead of at others.
      g. not overusing them in their speeches.

VI. Much of the art of crafting speeches from supporting materials depends upon the wise use of three major techniques. *(text pp. 193–195)*
   A. A comparison makes an unfamiliar or controversial idea more understandable or acceptable by pointing out its similarities to something the audience already understands or accepts.
      1. Comparisons strengthen all the supporting forms of information by connecting them with each other.
      2. Comparisons can take the strangeness out of new and sometimes radical proposals.
      3. Speakers should ask themselves three questions before deciding to use a comparison:
         a. Are there enough similarities to justify the comparison?
         b. Are the similarities significant to the idea you wish to support?
         c. Are there important differences that might invalidate the comparison?
   B. A contrast can provide sharp relief by emphasizing the difference between things.
      1. Speakers should ask themselves three questions before using a contrast.
         a. Is the sense of contrast dramatic enough to help my case?
         b. Is the difference relevant to the point I wish to make?
         c. Are there other points of difference that might invalidate the point?
   C. An analogy combines the principles of both comparison and contrast by pointing out similarities between things or concepts that are essentially dissimilar.
      1. Literal analogies are similar to comparisons in that they tie together subjects from the same realm of experience to reinforce a point.
      2. Figurative analogies combine subjects from different realms of experience.
      3. Speakers should ask themselves three questions before using analogies in their speeches:
         a. Will the analogy help me make some fundamental point about my subject?
         b. Will the analogy distract my listeners?
         c. Does the analogy establish a beneficial association for my subject?

VII. It is important that students choose the right supporting materials. *(text p. 196)*
   A. The following guidelines can help speakers select their materials wisely.
      1. If an idea is controversial, rely primarily on facts, statistics, factual examples, or expert testimony from sources that the audience will respect and accept.
      2. If your ideas or concepts are abstract, use examples and narratives to bring them to life. Use comparisons, contrasts, or analogies so that your listeners grasp your ideas and develop appropriate feelings about them.

3. If an idea is highly technical, supplement facts and statistics with expert testimony. Use definitions, explanations, and descriptions to aid understanding. Use examples, comparisons, contrasts, and analogies to help listeners integrate information.
4. If you need to arouse emotions, use lay and prestige testimony, examples, or narratives. Excite listeners by using contrast and analogy.
5. If you need to defuse emotions, emphasize facts and statistics and expert testimony. Keep the focus on definitions and explanations.
6. If your topic is distant from the lives of your listeners, draw it closer to them through information, examples, and narratives, activated by descriptions, comparisons, and analogies with which they can identify.

B. While different topics and audiences will suggest different types of supporting materials, speakers, in general, should:
1. support each main point with the most important and relevant facts and statistics available.
2. clarify each main point with testimony, definitions, explanations, and descriptions.
3. illustrate each main point with at least one interesting example or narrative.

USING END-OF-CHAPTER ITEMS

Discussion *(text p. 198)*

1. **Read a speech from a recent issue of *Vital Speeches of the Day*, looking closely for examples of statistics used as supporting materials. Were you convinced by the statistics? Did the speaker use definitions, explanations, or descriptions to increase their effectiveness? Apply the test of relevance, recency, credibility, and reliability to determine whether the statistics might have been more convincing. Report your observations and conclusions in class.**

    This is intended for homework followed by in-class discussion, although it can be easily converted to a small-group discussion piece. You might also have your students critique the same speech, or a speech out of the appendix. You preview class discussion with a short discussion of the various forms, functions, and criteria for evaluation of statistical information. You may wish to use the transparency "Evaluating Facts and Figures" on p. 207 of this IRM as you lead this discussion. Emphasize that figures must be interpreted if they are to be meaningful for an audience, and that they are generally more effective when used in conjunction with other forms of supporting materials. You might consider forms of statistics that the speaker might have used to make her or his case more effective. Caution your students that statistics are often abused to distort events, especially in addressing controversial issues. Encourage your students to explore their own biases in considering why they may be willing to accept questionable numbers in some situations and refuse to accept impressive correlations in other situations. Try to push your students to evaluate their statistics in terms of the criteria offered above.

2. **In the same speech you examine for item 1, evaluate the use of testimony. Can you find instances in which the kind of testimony was inappropriate, or when testimony of a different or additional sort might have helped the speakers realize their purposes? Do these speakers establish adequately the credentials of those whom they quote or cite? Report your discoveries in class.**

    You might follow the same general approach, or even combine this activity with Discussion item 1. You may wish to use the transparency "Evaluating Testimony" from p. 208 of this IRM as you lead this discussion. Focus discussion on the appropriate uses of testimony to support differing types of assertions, and the various criteria used for evaluating the various forms of testimony discussed in the text. Solicit audience input on the different types of testimony used, as well as forms of testimony that might have made the speech more effective.

3. Evaluate the use of supporting materials in one of the student speeches in Appendix B. Consider the following questions: Is there sufficient supporting material? What types are used? Are they appropriate to the purpose? Do they make the speech more effective for you? How and why?

This works well for homework or as a small-group activity followed by in-class discussion. You might quickly review the forms and functions of supporting materials, as well as the value of using a variety of supporting forms of information to back up a speech's main assertions. Solicit positive and negative criticisms of the chosen speech. You may wish to use the handout "Evaluation of the Use of Supporting Materials" (p. 212) with this discussion item. Focus discussion on the uses (or lack thereof) of adequate supporting materials, as well as on how the speech might have been made more effective.

4. Look in newspapers or magazines for recent statements by public officials that purport to be factual but may actually contain distortion. What tips you off to the distortion? Would most people be likely to detect this bias?

This exercise works well as a homework assignment followed by a small-group and/or general class discussion. Alternatively, you might find and photocopy the statements yourself. If you send your students to the library, have them photocopy their chosen statements and underline the references that contain distortion. They should consider what types of information are used and how it distorts the situation or issue at hand. They should watch out for unbelievable figures from obscure and/or biased sources, misleading testimony taken out of the context of its intended meaning, the use of incomparable percentages, etc. What conscious or unconscious motives or biases (political, cultural, economic, personal) on the speaker's part might account for the distortion? What is the speaker presuming about his or her primary audience, and what kinds of people would be likely to detect this distortion? Finally, what forms of information might be used to successfully contradict or "undistort" the speaker's position?

Application *(text pp. 198–199)*

1. Develop a hypothetical example or narrative to illustrate one of the following abstract concepts:

   love
   pain
   compassion
   justice
   peace

This exercise can be used for homework or as a small-group discussion piece. Divide your students into five groups, and have each group develop both a hypothetical example and a narrative for one of the abstract concepts. To extend this exercise, simply have each group work on more than one of the concepts. Have your students present their ideas to the class. Focus discussion on relevance to the concept, how authentic or believable they seem, whether or not they would be likely to involve the audience and enhance identification, and whatever alternative ideas you and your students can come up with. You might prepare in advance by generating a list of your own examples for each concept to help stimulate class discussion.

2. Note how television advertisements often give facts and statistics, testimony, examples, or narratives in combination with presentation aids. Using the criteria provided in this chapter and in Chapter 9, analyze and evaluate a current TV ad with respect to the techniques used.

This exercise works well as a homework assignment followed by an in-class discussion. For a shortened alternative, videotape ads for in-class viewing and discussion, or bring an assortment of commercial magazine ads that combine visual aids with supporting information. You will soon discover that facts and figures from obscure sources are commonly abused in television and print ads. Expert testimony is often presented secondhand, such as in commercials citing "scientific" studies and surveys. Prestige testimony using celebrity endorsements is also common in modern advertising. You might consider what form of ethos qualifies Penny Hardaway to represent Nike, or Dionne Warwick, the Psychic Friends' Network. Lay testimony is frequently used to convey the trust of "common people" in a product. Consider, for example, ads for insurance highlighting grateful "victims" of natural disasters being promptly taken care of. The use of truncated narratives and brief examples is also common, and these are often used in conjunction with lay testimony. Such ads may invoke popular beliefs and mythos (see text Chapter 14) to sell their products. How are visual images used in conjunction with other forms of information to enhance or strengthen the ads' central thesis or purpose? Often, ads offer visual illustrations of their products being used at work (or play), or of human problems, to arouse the emotional involvement of primary audiences. Some argue that visuals are used to circumvent the process of rationally perceiving and interpreting examples and information. For instance, a montage format (common for beer, car, MTV, and other ads targeting younger audiences) may force receivers out of a diachronic or linear mode of consciousness and into a synchronic mode, which is generally more emotive and reactionary.

Students might use the following questions to guide their evaluations. Are the visual aids used in conjunction with verbal information? What kinds? Do they facilitate a rational comprehension of the message and its purpose? Can you think of visual aids that might be more appropriate or effective to support the message? How might these visual aids be adapted for use in your students' speeches?

3. **Determine which types of testimony might best support the following statements:**

   a. **Native Americans don't get a square deal in the United States.**
   b. **Campus security measures are inadequate.**
   c. **AIDS is rapidly spreading in the heterosexual community.**
   d. **America should return to a system of open immigration.**
   e. **Asian immigrant children are outperforming American-born children in public schools.**

   Defend your choices in class.

   This exercise can be used as homework, for a small-group or general class discussion, or for both. Remind your students that their choice of testimony should be determined in part by the statement they wish to advance and the characteristics of their primary audience. Have them present their ideas for a general class discussion.

Suggestions for discussion:

   a. All three forms of testimony could help establish the validity of this claim. Experts (scholars, public officials, and professionals involved with Native American affairs) could offer the hard facts and figures, and the lay testimony of Native Americans could help promote audience involvement. Finally, the testimony of celebrity activists such as Jane Fonda, Marlon Brando, and Robert Redford can help to raise popular consciousness with such issues of public moral concern.

   b. Both expert and lay testimony would be appropriate. Expert testimony from law enforcement officials or organizations could help verify the rising crime rate on college campuses. Testimony from the director of campus security at *your* college or university would help to localize the problem, making it more relevant to your direct audience. Lay testimony from a victim could help enhance audience identification with the problem. Lay testimony based on personal experience might be especially effective.

   c. Depending on your purpose and audience, all three forms could be used to establish this claim. Expert testimony could help develop the factual validity, lay testimony could help provide human illustrations, and celebrity activists can and have helped to spread the word on AIDS in all human communities.

d.   While celebrity testimony could help with consciousness raising, expert and lay testimony would probably be the two most effective forms of testimony for supporting this statement. Speakers might use expert testimony to counter concerns that increased immigration might increase unemployment or hurt the economy, or they might use the lay testimony of immigrants or prospective immigrants.

e.   Expert testimony would be most appropriate for this claim. It should come from qualified sources that the audience would be likely to respect, such as the secretary of education, respected academics or school board administrators, or experienced and well-respected teachers.

ADDITIONAL ACTIVITIES

Evaluating Supporting Material

Purpose: To provide your students an opportunity to evaluate the use of supporting materials in actual presentations.

Directions: This works well for general class discussion. Distribute the "Evaluation of the Use of Supporting Materials" form (p. 212). Review the items and the rating scale with the students: 5 = excellent, 4 = very good, 3 = average, 2 = below average, 1 = poor. Play a videotape of informative or persuasive student speeches. Try to find speeches that are both really strong and really weak for contrast, and have your students take notes while viewing them. They should then complete the evaluation form. To extend this activity, show several speeches and have your students evaluate them on separate pieces of scratch paper, using the evaluation form as a guide. For class discussion, have your students justify the ratings they assigned. Prepare your own evaluations in advance and offer them as necessary to stimulate class discussion. Use this as an opportunity to let your students know how you will evaluate and grade the use of supporting materials in their speeches. Emphasize the need for a variety of supporting forms. This can be used in conjunction with the next activity or adapted for an outside writing assignment.

Choose That Form

Purpose: To give your students practice in determining what forms of supporting information would be most appropriate for given topics or propositions.

Directions: This works well for in-class discussion. Read the following statements to your students and solicit input from them as to what materials would be most appropriate for supporting them in speeches. Impress upon them that different topics and messages require different forms and combinations of information to support them, and that controversial claims need a balanced model of supporting information.

1.   A statement addressing homelessness in your local area
2.   A statement on how AIDS is acquired
3.   To emphasize the value and significance of the Internet
4.   A statement urging people to support or not support gun control efforts
5.   An informative speech on the effects of acid rain on northern timberlands
6.   A speech urging people to contribute money for needy urban kids
7.   An informative speech on the evolution of personal computers since the 1970s
8.   What to do should you become the victim of a sexual assault
9.   A statement for or against open immigration policies

Suggestions for discussion:

1. Facts and figures on the extent of the problem and its relative rise or decline in recent years, to substantiate attributions of causation or effects; testimony from experts (scholars, government and social workers, activists), and from lay persons (homeless people); examples of local homelessness and adverse effects, such as crime or loss of business revenues.

2. Facts and expert testimony from scientists and activists; celebrity testimony to help spread the word on popular messages such as wearing condoms; and examples of people contracting AIDS and their lay testimony to provide concrete human illustrations.

3. Basic facts about what the Internet is for most audiences; expert testimony on its uses and practical applications; maybe examples of everyday beneficiaries and their lay testimony.

4. Facts, figures, and expert testimony relating to crime rates, correlations between the availability of guns and crime, the feasibility of gun control, new plans for gun control, the success or failure of past plans; examples and lay testimony concerning accidents due to kids getting hold of guns, or victims who were not sufficiently armed to protect themselves.

5. Facts, figures, and expert testimony from scientists, forestry workers, or activists on the extent and growth of the problem in recent times (if this is a politically volatile issue, there are probably well-paid experts advocating contrary positions); examples of negative environmental effects; and maybe celebrity testimony from activists.

6. Facts, figures, and expert testimony from reliable sources to stress the problem or need; celebrity testimony, which would probably be very effective on this well-known issue; examples of problems caused by urban neglect; lay testimony from parents and kids affected by the problems.

7. This topic is really too general to begin substantive research. Students could probably find sufficient general background information by consulting a basic survey text on computer literacy.

8. Facts and figures on types and frequency of sexual assault, laws concerning date and other forms of rape, the extent of the problem and its relative growth or decline in our times; expert testimony from police or social workers on what to do should you be victimized by this crime; and examples of victims and their lay testimony.

9. Facts on current immigration laws and quotas; figures on immigration rates and projections for future developments; expert testimony (social workers, immigration experts, politicians, economists, etc.) on the social and economic implications of increased immigration; and examples of common people who stand to be affected in positive or negative ways and their lay testimony.

Narrative and the "Great Communicator"

Purpose: To give your students a chance to study the use of narrative in the speeches of a prominent contemporary public figure.

Directions: This works well for homework or as a small-group discussion piece followed by general class discussion. You may wish to use the transparencies "Evaluating Narratives" and "Using Narratives," pp. 210 and 211 of this IRM, as you lead this discussion. Narratives can establish moods, shape perceptions, enhance the perceived likability of speakers, and promote identification with the audience. Many critics believe that narrativity is basic to human nature. Our early ancestors used campfire narratives to transmit basic cultural "truths" and behavioral norms to their young.

Similarly, politicians and other opinion leaders use narratives to reaffirm and reinterpret our basic beliefs and values. Former President Ronald Reagan is commonly cited for his masterly use of narrative. Find examples of his speeches, and have your students study his use of narrative as a supporting material. Critical exemplars might include his inaugural addresses, his "Star Wars" address, his Challenger disaster eulogy, and his farewell address, among others. You might preview this activity with some basic comments about Reagan as a rhetorical president. Evaluate Reagan's use of narrative in terms of the criteria offered in the text. What functions did narrative play in strengthening his appeal? Did he rely too heavily on the form? What are the likely social and ethical implications of his narrative vision? You should remember that Reagan remains a hero to many American conservatives, and go out of your way to foster an atmosphere of tolerance for differing opinions when evaluating his use of narrative. You might use this activity to introduce the concepts of proof by mythos and ceremonial speaking, discussed in Chapters 14 and 15, respectively. What America is characterized in his stories, and what are its values and imperatives?

Developing Supporting Material

Purpose: To provide students with an opportunity to develop a variety of forms of supporting material from newspaper and magazine articles.

Directions: Select five or six topics that are currently seen as newsworthy and prepare an information folder for each topic. Each information folder should contain a local newspaper account of the topic, a national (e.g., *USA Today*) news story on the topic, and at least two magazine articles (from sources such as *Time, Newsweek, U.S. News & World Report,* etc.) on the topic. List the topics on the chalkboard and have the students indicate which topics they prefer. Divide the class into groups of three to five students to work on developing supporting materials from the information folders. Each group should prepare at least one example or narrative, and find factual data and testimony that could be used in a speech. Allow the groups approximately twenty minutes to develop their materials. Reconvene the class as a whole for the groups to share their results.

Telling a Story

Purpose: To provide your students with an opportunity to polish their story-telling skills before using them in a major speaking assignment.

Directions: This works well as a homework assignment. Distribute the "Possible Topics for Stories" handout from p. 213 of this IRM. As you discuss the use and evaluation of narratives with your students, you may wish to use the transparencies "Using Narratives" and "Evaluating Narratives" on pp. 211 and 210 of this IRM, or you may wish to make these transparencies into handouts to distribute along with the "Possible Topics for Stories" handout. Have the students prepare a one- to two-minute story presentation to be made during the next class period.

James Kauffman (Indiana University Southeast, New Albany, Ind.), "Collecting and Evaluating Evidence," *SCT* (Winter 1992), 12.

Goal: To teach students how to collect and then evaluate evidence.

Students in the basic course often have difficulty collecting and evaluating evidence. I have developed an exercise for evaluating sources which involves the hypothetical purchase of an automobile and the research required to make an intelligent selection. The exercise offers the following benefits: 1) students become actively involved; 2) students receive practice in critical thinking; 3) students perceive the exercise as directly applicable to their lives, thereby increasing their interest and motivation; 4) the instructor can use the exercise as a springboard to teach other skills like organizing a speech, citing sources, and constructing bibliographies.

I begin the exercise by asking the students to imagine that they win $15,000 in the lottery and they decide to use it to purchase a new car. They have been thinking about purchasing a car for some time and like the looks of two automobiles: a Honda Accord and a Toyota Corolla. I instruct the class to brainstorm all possible sources of information about the cars which would help them in making their decision. I suggest they think in terms of people and publications. I remind them that the object of brainstorming is to generate as many ideas as possible, not to evaluate the sources.

As students call out possible sources of information, I write them on the board. Students' submissions usually include the following: owners, mechanics, dealers, friends, family members, car salespersons, newspapers, government reports, automotive books, *Consumer Reports, Road and Drive, Car and Track,* and other similar magazines.

Once they have named all the sources they can think of, I explain that not all sources are of equal value. Clearly, some sources of information are better than others. To evaluate sources, one should apply tests of evidence. I introduce the following tests from Patricia Bradley Andrews' *Basic Public Speaking* (New York: Harper & Row, 1985): reliability, recency, accuracy, and completeness. I then briefly explain each, writing them on a separate portion of the board.

The *reliability* test holds that sources should be objective and competent. One should be skeptical of sources which are self-interested, sources who might have something to gain from espousing a particular point of view. The source also should be in a position to know about the subject at hand. The source should be competent to judge or comment on the specific issue, item, or idea. The *recency* test holds that one should strive for the most recent information possible. The two final tests are closely related to one another. The *completeness* criterion holds that one should consult as many sources as possible to receive a complete view (not that one can ever know everything there is to know about a topic). Doing so will allow the testing of evidence for *accuracy*. Accurate information is redundant and verifiable. One should be able to find similar information when consulting a variety of sources. If not, one should be skeptical of the aberrant figure or idea.

Next, I ask the students to use the tests of evidence to evaluate the possible sources of information about the two cars. For example, I point to "car salesman" and ask which of the tests would apply. Invariably they point out that the salesperson's reliability is questionable since he or she has a vested interest in selling a car. If I point to "mechanics," students usually point out that some mechanics are more trustworthy than others. A few leading questions about the initial sources are usually enough to make students aware of how to apply the evidence tests.

Similarly, when I ask about magazines, newspapers, books, and government reports, the students apply the pertinent tests of evidence and make their evaluation. I also stress the inherent strengths and weaknesses of certain types of printed sources. For example, newspapers can rate high in recency, but low in completeness of information. Newspapers may be an excellent source of information about automobiles which recently have been recalled by the dealer. Books, on the other hand, can rank high on completeness, but because of the long time it takes to publish a book, the information will not be as recent as that of a newspaper.

After asking the students to test various sources listed on the board, I point out the advantages of consulting numerous sources of information. The researcher should find similar information about the price, gas mileage, and service record from more than one reliable source before drawing even tentative conclusions. Moreover, consulting numerous sources can minimize the possible biases of some sources. For example, different individuals, groups, and organizations may rate automobiles differently based on weightings of one or more of the following criteria: price, safety, performance, handling, maintenance, comfort, styling, and gas mileage.

In the four years I have used the exercise, I have found that students become actively involved because they already have some knowledge they can contribute and they perceive the topic as one which is relevant to them. Moreover, I have found that most of my students become quite adept at testing evidence. Frequently, they question the evidence of fellow students in their written critiques of student speeches. I like to believe that students take these skills outside the classroom, becoming more critical consumers of all messages.

SUPPLEMENTARY MATERIALS

Films and Videos

"Promises," RAM film, 21 minutes.

Videos to accompany *Public Speaking,* Houghton Mifflin.

"Crediting Your Sources," RMI Media Productions, 30 minutes.

"Critical Thinking: How to Evaluate Information and Draw Conclusions," Insight Media, 47 minutes.

Computer Software

"Speech Designer," Houghton Mifflin, 1997.

Transparencies and Handouts *(see following pages)*

Evaluating Facts and Figures (Transparency 6.1)

Evaluating Testimony (Transparency 6.2)

Evaluating Examples (Transparency 6.3)

Evaluating Narratives (Transparency 6.4)

Using Narratives (Transparency 6.5)

Evaluation of the Use of Supporting Materials

Possible Topics for Stories

EVALUATING FACTS AND FIGURES

1. Is the information relevant to the issue?

2. Is the information up-to-date?

3. Is the information reliable? Would an independent expert confirm it?

4. Have the sources and dates of the information been identified?

5. Are the sources of information competent, trustworthy, and unbiased?

6. Is the information complete and sufficient? Has anything been purposely withheld?

7. Has the information been distorted or made unintelligible with jargon?

8. Is this information or opinion?

9. Are statistics passed off as representing certainty rather than probability?

10. Do statistical differences represent actual differences?

EVALUATING TESTIMONY

1. Is the testimony relevant to the issue?

2. Is the testimony representative of the source's position?

3. Has the proper type of testimony been used?

4. Have the credentials of the source been presented?

5. Has the source been quoted or paraphrased accurately?

6. If expert testimony is used, is the source an authority on the subject?

7. Is the source objective and unbiased?

8. Is the testimony recent or out-of-date?

EVALUATING EXAMPLES

1. Are the examples relevant to the issue?

2. Do the examples help clarify the subject?

3. Are the examples representative of the situation or exceptions to the rule?

4. Are the examples believable, or do they seem far-fetched?

5. Are the examples fresh and interesting?

6. Do the examples fit the mood and spirit of the occasion?

7. Are the examples in good taste?

8. Are factual and hypothetical examples clearly differentiated?

EVALUATING NARRATIVES

1. Are the narratives relevant to the points they support?

2. Are the narratives believable and realistic?

3. Do the narratives create a mood consistent with the topic?

4. Are the narratives fresh and interesting?

5. Do the narratives involve the audience and create identification?

6. Are the narratives in good taste?

USING NARRATIVES

1. Set the narrative off from the rest of your speech with oral or physical punctuation marks.

2. Strive for an intimate style of presentation.

3. Use colorful, concrete, and active language.

4. Use dialogue whenever possible rather than paraphrasing an idea.

5. Present the story linearly from beginning to end. Avoid digressions.

6. Create a sense of anticipation and suspense as you build toward the conclusion of the story.

7. Keep your stories short and to the point.

8. Save narratives for special moments in your speech.

EVALUATION OF THE USE OF SUPPORTING MATERIALS

NAME _____   SECTION _____

Factual information or statistics

Relevance to point	5	4	3	2	1
Recency of information/statistics	5	4	3	2	1
Sources/dates identified	5	4	3	2	1
Credibility of sources	5	4	3	2	1
Freedom from distortion	5	4	3	2	1
Facts differentiated from opinions	5	4	3	2	1
Sufficient information/statistics provided	5	4	3	2	1

Testimony

Relevance to point	5	4	3	2	1
Recency of testimony	5	4	3	2	1
Proper type of testimony used	5	4	3	2	1
Qualifications specified	5	4	3	2	1
Accuracy of quote or paraphrase	5	4	3	2	1

Examples or Narratives

Relevance to point	5	4	3	2	1
Representative of situation/point	5	4	3	2	1
Plausibility	5	4	3	2	1
Interest value	5	4	3	2	1
Sufficient number of examples/narratives	5	4	3	2	1

General

Use of transitions to integrate	5	4	3	2	1
Extemporaneous presentation	5	4	3	2	1

Comments

Possible Topics for Stories

The most exciting day of my life.

The worst day of my life.

How I met the person I am dating/married to.

A story my mother/father told me.

A story I want to tell my children.

A story that reflects my cultural background.

The scariest dream I ever had.

The wildest dream I ever had.

The sweetest dream I ever had.

How I learned how to laugh at myself.

How I learned the importance of telling the truth.

How I bought my first _____.

How I got taken for a sucker.

The story of my bravest hour.

How I decided on my major.

The funniest thing my pet ever did.

The funniest thing a family member of mine ever did.

The funniest thing I ever did.

The dumbest thing I ever did.

The smartest thing I ever did.

How I overcame a problem with _____ .

The nicest thing anyone ever did for me.

The meanest thing anyone ever did to me.

READINGS FOR ENRICHMENT

See guide to journal abbreviations on p. 37.

* Items marked with an asterisk are suitable for student enrichment.

Supporting Material: General

Baxter, Leslie A., and Lee West. "On 'Whistler's Mother' and Discourse of the Fourth Kind." *WJC* (Winter 1996), 92–100.

* Crossen, Cynthia. *Tainted Truth: The Manipulation of Fact in America.* New York: Simon & Schuster, 1994.

* Deighton, J. "The Interaction of Advertising and Evidence." *Journal of Consumer Research* (1984), 763–770.

"The Dialogue of Evidence: A Topic Revisited." *WJC,* Special Issue, Winter 1994.

Durham, Weldon B. "Kenneth Burke's Concept of Substance." *QJS* (Dec. 1980), 351–364.

Grainer, Diane. "What's Evidence?" *SCT* (Winter 1993), 10–11.

Hollihan, Thomas A. "Evidencing Moral Claims: The Activist Rhetorical Critic's First Task." *WJC* (Summer 1994), 229–234.

Kakzkoleas, Dean C. "A Comparison of the Persuasive Effectiveness of Qualitative versus Quantitative Evidence: A Test of Explanatory Hypotheses." *CQ* (Winter 1993), 40–50.

Kauffman, James. "Collecting and Evaluating Evidence." *SCT* (Winter 1992), 12.

* Kellerman, Kathy. "The Concept of Evidence: A Critical Review." *JAFA* (Winter 1980), 59–72.

McCroskey, James C. "A Summary of Experimental Research on the Effects of Evidence in Persuasive Communication." *QJS* (Apr. 1969), 169–176.

Nakayama, Thomas. "Disciplining Evidence." *WJC* (Spring 1995), 171–175.

Newman, Robert, and Dale Newman. *Evidence.* Boston: Houghton Mifflin, 1969.

Phillips, Terilyn Goins. "Name That Analogy: The Communication Game." *SCT* (Winter 1996), 10–11.

Reinard, John C. "The Empirical Study of the Persuasive Effects of Evidence: The Status After Fifty Years of Research." *HCR* (Fall 1988), 3–59.

Reynolds, Rodney A., and Michael Burgoon. "Belief Processing, Reasoning, and Evidence." In *Communication Yearbook 7,* edited by Robert N. Bostrom, pp. 83–104. Beverly Hills, Calif.: Sage, 1983.

Schuetz, Janice. "Legal and Research Evidence and the O.J. Simpson Trial." *WJC* (Fall 1995), 347–354.

Sigman, Stuart J. "Question of What? Answer: Communication." *WJC* (Winter 1995), 79–84.

Whaley, Bryan B., and Austin S. Babrow. "Analogy in Persuasion: Translator's Dictionary or Art?" *CS* (Fall 1993), 239–253.

Narratives

Badzinski, Diane M. "Message Cues and Narrative Comprehension: A Developmental Study." *CQ* (Summer 1992), 228–238.

Baesler, E. James. "Construction and Test of an Empirical Measure for Narrative Coherence and Fidelity." *CR* (Summer 1995), 97–101.

Bartsch, Elmar. "How to Explain Terms: By Narrating or by Defining?" In *On Narratives,* edited by Hellmut Geissner, pp. 33–41. Frankfurt am Main: Scriptor, 1987.

Brown, Mary Helen. "Defining Stories in Organizations: Characteristics and Functions." In *Communication Yearbook 13,* edited by James A. Anderson, pp. 162–190. Newbury Park, Calif.: Sage, 1990.

Bruner, Jerome S. *Acts of Meaning.* Cambridge, Mass.: Harvard University Press, 1990.

———. "The Narrative Construction of Reality." *Critical Inquiry,* 18 (1991), 1–21.

* Coles, Robert. *The Call of Stories.* Boston: Houghton Mifflin, 1989.

Comisky, Paul, and Jennings Bryant. "Factors Involved in Generating Suspense." *HCR* (Fall 1982), 49–58.

Deetz, Stanley. "Narrative Accounts as Everyday Legitimating Practices in Organizations." In *On Narratives*, edited by Hellmut Geissner, pp. 91–97. Frankfurt am Main: Scriptor, 1987.

Fisher, Walter R. "Narration as Human Communication Paradigm: The Case of Public Moral Argument." *CM* (March 1984), 1–22.

———. "The Narrative Paradigm: In the Beginning." *JC* (Autumn 1985), 74–89.

———. "The Narrative Paradigm: An Elaboration." *CM* (Dec. 1985), 347–367.

———. "Clarifying the Narrative Paradigm." *CM* (March 1989), 55–58.

———. *Human Communication as Narration: Toward a Philosophy of Reason, Value, and Action.* Columbia, S.C.: University of South Carolina Press, 1989.

* Geissner, Hellmut. "Commercials as Narratives." In *On Narratives*, edited by Hellmut Geissner, pp. 297–303. Frankfurt am Main: Scriptor, 1987.

* Goodman, Nelson. "Twisted Tales; or, Story, Study, and Symphony." In *On Narrative*, edited by W. J. T. Mitchell, pp. 99–116. Chicago: University of Chicago Press, 1981.

Gruner, Charles R. "Advice to the Beginning Speaker on Using Humor—What the Research Tells Us." *CE*, 34 (1985), 142–147.

* Hernadi, Paul. "On the How, What, and Why of Narrative." In *On Narrative*, edited by W. J. T. Mitchell, pp. 197–199. Chicago: University of Chicago Press, 1981.

Hollihan, Thomas A., and Patricia Riley. "The Rhetorical Power of a Compelling Story: A Critique of a 'Toughlove' Parental Support Group." *CQ* (Winter 1987), 13–25.

Kaplan, Robert M., and Gregory C. Pascoe. "Humorous Lectures and Humorous Examples: Some Effects upon Comprehension and Retention." *Journal of Educational Psychology*, 69 (1977), 61–65.

Kirkwood, William G. "Storytelling and Self-Confrontation: Parables as Communication Strategies." *QJS* (Feb. 1983), 58–74.

———. "Parables as Metaphors and Examples." *QJS* (Nov. 1985), 422–440.

Langellier, Kristin M. "Personal Narratives: Perspectives on Theory and Research." *TPQ* (Oct. 1989), 243–276.

* LeGuin, Ursula K. "It Was a Dark and Stormy Night; or, Why Are We Huddling About the Campfire?" In *On Narrative*, edited by W. J. T. Mitchell, pp. 187–196. Chicago: University of Chicago Press, 1981.

Lewis, William F. "Telling America's Story, Narrative Form and the Reagan Presidency." *QJS* (Aug. 1987), 280–302.

Lucaites, John Louis, and Celeste Michelle Condit. "Re-Constructing Narrative Theory: A Functional Perspective." *JC* (Autumn 1985), 90–108.

McGee, Michael Calvin, and John S. Nelson. "Narrative Reason in Public Argument." *JC* (Autumn 1985), 139–155.

* McGuire, Michael. "Narrative Persuasion in Rhetorical Theory." In *On Narratives*, edited by Hellmut Geissner, pp. 163–178. Frankfurt am Main: Scriptor, 1987.

Smith, Barbara Hernstein. "Narrative Versions, Narrative Theories," In *On Narrative*, edited by W. J. T. Mitchell, pp. 209–232. Chicago: University of Chicago Press, 1981.

Smith, Christie McGuffee, and Larry Powell. "The Use of Disparaging Humor by Group Leaders." *SSCJ*, 53 (1988), 279–292.

Speer, Jean Haskell. "Commodifying Culture: Selling the Stories of Appalachian America." In *On Narratives*, edited by Hellmut Geissner, pp. 56–73. Frankfurt am Main: Scriptor, 1987.

Stuckey, Mary E. "Anecdotes and Conversations: The Narrational and Dialogic Styles of Modern Presidential Communication." *CQ* (Winter 1992), 45–55.

Vanderford, Marsha L., David H. Smith, and Willard S. Harris. "Value Identification in Narrative Discourse: Evaluation of an HIV Education Demonstration Project." *ACR* (May 1992), 123–161.

White, Hayden. "The Value of Narrativity in the Representation of Reality." In *On Narrative*, edited by W. J. T. Mitchell, pp. 1–24. Chicago: University of Chicago Press, 1981.

Examples

Consigny, Scott. "The Rhetorical Example." *SSCJ* (Winter 1975), 121–132.

Taylor, S. E., and S. C. Thompson. "Stalking the Elusive 'Vividness' Effect." *Psychological Review* (1982), 155–181.

Statistics

* Gould, Stephen Jay. "Of Crime, Cause, and Correlation." *Discover* (Dec. 1983). Reprinted in *Selected Issues in Logic and Communication*, edited by Trudy Govier, pp. 178–183. Belmont, Calif.: Wadsworth, 1988.

* Huff, Darrell. *How to Lie with Statistics.* New York: Norton, 1954.

* Johnson, Ralph. "Poll-ution: Coping with Surveys and Polls." In *Selected Issues in Logic and Communication*, edited by Trudy Govier, pp. 163–177. Belmont, Calif.: Wadsworth, 1988.

* McKean, Kevin. "The Fine Art of Reading Voters' Minds." *Discover* (May 1984), 66–69.

Paulos, John Allen. *Innumeracy: Mathematical Illiteracy and Its Consequences.* New York: Hill & Wang, 1988.

————. "Counting on Dyscalculia." *Discover* (Mar. 1994), 30–36.

* Runyon, Richard P. *How Numbers Lie: A Consumer's Guide to the Fine Art of Numerical Deception.* Lexington, Mass.: Lewis, 1981.

* Spiker, Barry K., Tom D. Daniels, and Lawrence M. Bernabo. "The Quantitative Quandry in Forensics: The Use and Abuse of Statistical Evidence." *JAFA* (Fall 1982), 87–96.

Yalch, R. F., and R. Elmore-Yalch. "The Effect of Numbers on the Route to Persuasion." *Journal of Consumer Research* (1984), 522–527.

Testimony

Arnold, William E., and James C. McCroskey. "The Credibility of Reluctant Testimony." *CSSJ* (May 1967), 97–103.

* Cederblom, Jerry, and David Paulsen. "Making Reasonable Decisions as an Amateur in a World of Experts." *Critical Reasoning*, 2nd ed. Belmont, Calif.: Wadsworth, 1986. Reprinted in *Selected Issues in Logic and Communication*, edited by Trudy Govier, pp. 138–149. Belmont, Calif.: Wadsworth, 1988.

* Hardwig, John. "Relying on Experts." Adapted from "Epistemic Dependence." *Journal of Philosophy* (July 1985), 335–349. In *Selected Issues in Logic and Communication*, edited by Trudy Govier, pp. 125–137. Belmont, Calif.: Wadsworth, 1988.

Loftus, Elizabeth F. *Eyewitness Testimony.* New Haven, Conn.: Harvard University Press, 1980.

* ————. "Eyewitnesses: Essential but Unreliable." *Psychology Today* (Feb. 1984), 22–27.

McGee, Michael Calvin. "In Search of the People: A Rhetorical Alternative." *QJS* (1975), 235–249.

CHAPTER 7
Structuring Your Speech

OBJECTIVES

- To help your students structure speeches that are simple, balanced, and orderly.

- To help your students shape and arrange their main points in a sensible fashion.

- To help your students use transitions to make their speeches flow smoothly.

- To help your students prepare effective introductions and conclusions for their speeches.

SUGGESTIONS FOR TEACHING

Structuring effective and comprehensible messages is a crucial phase in speech preparation relevant to all major speaking assignments. With this in mind, many instructors like to start teaching the basics of structure and form with their first speech activities, and continue to emphasize their importance throughout the course. Your students will benefit from learning how to move systematically from a research overview and thematic statement to the generation and construction of their actual speeches.

We place structuring of speeches between research and topic selection, and outlining, but in reality these processes usually overlap. Hence the materials in these chapters can and probably should be coordinated for effective teaching. You might want to give a quick lecture on key points, but these skills are more effectively taught through applied learning. In this chapter we offer numerous activities to have your students critique the structure of various message types, generate and critique speech materials from their research overviews, choose appropriate design strategies for given topics and materials, and structure and critique their own messages. Your students will encounter more specific materials for structuring their informative and persuasive speeches later on in the course.

CHAPTER OUTLINE

I. A well-organized message is crucial for successful public speaking. *(text pp. 203–204)*
   A. Well-organized speeches are easier for listeners to understand and remember.
   B. Well-organized speeches increase the speaker's competence dimension of ethos.

II. Three basic principles of good form reflect the ways in which people naturally perceive and interpret ideas and information. *(text pp. 204–208)*
   A. Simplicity of arrangement is generally preferred over elaborate, complicated design schemes.

1. Short speeches should develop no more than four main points, and longer ones no more than five.
2. Main points and ideas should be worded in a simple and direct fashion.
    a. Whenever possible, speakers should use parallel phrasing.
3. According to the principles of simplicity, a speech's specific purpose, thesis statement, and main points should be very clear.

B. Balance means that all the major parts of your speech—the introduction, body, and conclusion—should receive the right amount of emphasis and development.
1. The body should be the longest part of a speech.
2. Emphasis should be allocated according to a speaker's topic and audience. Speakers might:
    a. give each main point about the same amount of development.
    b. arrange their main ideas in either a descending or an ascending order of importance.
3. Introductions and conclusions should be approximately equal in length.
    a. For a five-minute speech, their combined length should rarely exceed one minute.

C. Orderliness can be achieved by following a consistent pattern of development.
1. The introduction, body, and conclusion of a speech should work together.
2. Orderly design schemes, such as the problem-solution, arrange the main points of a speech's body in a sensible fashion.

III. The first step is structuring the speech's body. *(text pp. 208–215)*
A. The main points of the body should develop the speaker's central thesis or idea.
B. Speakers face three tasks in developing and structuring the main points of a body.
1. First, speakers should determine their main points of focus. Speakers:
    a. should generate main points by considering researched information in terms of their specific purposes, their thesis statements, and the needs/interests of their audiences.
    b. may need to define key terms and explain key concepts, depending on their topics.
2. Second, main points should be arranged in a manner that is appropriate to the audience, that fits the speaker's materials, and that serves her or his purpose. The following principles of good form fit the patterns by which we habitually process incoming ideas and information.
    a. The principle of similarity leads people to group together things that seem alike.
        (1) A categorical design may represent the natural divisions of a subject, or customary ways of thinking about something.
    b. The principle of proximity suggests that things that occur close together in time or space should be presented in the order in which they normally occur.
        (1) A sequential design presents the steps of a process in the order to be followed, or explains events in the order in which they occurred.
        (2) A spatial design is used to describe the physical dimensions of a scene based upon physical relationships.
    c. The principle of closure suggests that people like to see patterns completed.
        (1) The cause-effect and problem-solution design schemes reflect the need to perceive a comprehensible and controllable world.
            (a) Cause-effect designs may be used to attribute past causes for a present situation, or to predict future developments based on present causes.
            (b) Problem-solution designs focus on problems and offer solutions, and often invoke emotional appeals.
    d. These three principles can help speakers choose appropriate designs, which in turn can help them determine and arrange main ideas.
3. Finally, speakers should select supporting materials for each main point of their speeches.
    a. Speakers should consider whether they need to divide main points into subpoints to provide the support listeners may need before understanding or accepting an assertion.

      b. Supporting points answer practical concerns that doubtful listeners might raise, such as:

        (1) What is the basis of that idea? (facts and statistics)

        (2) How do you know? Who else says so? (testimony)

        (3) How does it work? Where is it true? (examples)

        (4) So what? Why should I care? (narratives)

      c. An ideal model of support consists of the most relevant facts and statistics, the most authoritative judgments made by sources the audience respects, and at least one interesting story or example.

IV. Transitions are short phrases, words, or extended phrases that link the major parts and ideas of a speech and help listeners grasp its overall direction. *(text pp. 215–217)*

  A. Transitions can suggest that speakers are expanding on a previous point; that they are setting up comparisons and contrasts, cause and effect relationships, and spatial relationships; and that they are bringing their messages to a close.

  B. Internal summaries brief listeners on points previously made before moving on to a subsequent part of a speech.

  C. A lack of well-planned transitions is apparent when speakers over-rely on such fillers as "well," "you know," and "okay."

    1. Speakers should plan a variety of transitions and work them into their outlines to ensure their speeches flow smoothly.

V. The basic functions of an effective introduction answer for the audience why it should listen to this speech and to this speaker. *(text pp. 218–228)*

  A. Introductions should capture the audience's attention. Speakers can:

    1. involve their audiences through sincere, well-deserved compliments, relating their topics directly to their lives, and using inclusive pronouns.

    2. relate their subjects to personal experience.

      a. Citing personal experience can help enhance common ground with listeners.

    3. ask rhetorical questions to arouse curiosity and focus audience attention.

    4. arouse curiosity and anticipation by developing suspense.

    5. tell stories that educate, entertain, and tap into a sense of shared heritage.

      a. Narratives can help establish a desired mood for a message.

    6. use humor effectively to create a receptive mood.

      a. Humor that is not fresh and pertinent to the situation is rarely effective.

      b. Inappropriate humor can be disastrous.

      c. Irrelevant humor can upstage the actual message.

    7. open with striking quotes to enhance their ethos and arouse audience interest.

      a. Effective quotes are brief and to the point.

      b. Compilations (many now on CD-ROM) are often indexed by subject.

    8. startle their audiences with unusual information.

  B. Introductions should help strengthen the speaker's credibility in terms of the competence, trustworthiness, and likability dimensions of ethos.

    1. Speakers can enhance competence by citing personal experience and/or research, and by delivering well-organized and practiced speeches.

    2. Speakers with integrity come across as straightforward, sincere, and concerned with the consequences of their words.

    3. Likable and forceful speakers come across as pleasant, tactful, open, modest, and self-confident.

    4. Establishing ethos creates ground for generating identification—sharing thoughts and feelings despite personal and cultural differences—with an audience.

  C. Introductions should focus and preview messages for audiences.

    1. A preview statement presents the speech's message in concentrated form, and previews main ideas to be developed.

      a. Preview statements should follow thesis statements near the end of the introduction.

  D. A smooth introduction can help allay stage fright.

     1. Speakers should plan to make eye contact from the start and avoid reading their introductions.

  E. The following tips can help speakers develop effective introductions. Speakers should:

     1. consider their audiences' moods and interests.

     2. consider the mood they want to establish.

     3. consider time constraints.

     4. do what they do best.

VI. An effective conclusion meets an audience's need for closure by summarizing main ideas and offering concluding remarks. *(text pp. 228–232)*

  A. Conclusions should begin with transitional summary statements of main ideas covered.

  B. Many of the same techniques used to open a message can be used to give concluding remarks. Speakers can:

     1. involve their audiences by relating their messages directly to their lives.

     2. ask rhetorical questions.

       a. Rhetorical questions can enhance a climactic call to action.

     3. close with a narrative.

     4. close with a quote that captures the essence of their messages.

     5. use a striking metaphor.

       a. Metaphor often complements narrative.

     6. create a sense of balance by using the same technique to open and close a speech.

     7. make sure their concluding devices deliver on what was promised in the introduction.

USING END-OF-CHAPTER ITEMS

Discussion *(text pp. 233–234)*

1. **Working in small groups, share your research overviews for your next speeches. What major themes emerge, and how might these be framed into main points in light of the function and purpose of your speech? Defend your analysis and your selection of main points.**

This exercise is especially useful in conjunction with informative and persuasive speech assignments. Have each of your students complete a research overview (for form, see p. 234 of this IRM) and bring it for class discussion. To the right of the overviews, students should write out prospective main points based on their information. Break your students into small groups and have them review one another's ideas, offering suggestions for improvement, before the ideas are presented for class discussion. You might preface class discussion by quickly reviewing the text on generating main ideas from research overviews. Focus on simplifying wording, eliminating extraneous ideas, points that need more support, and points the speaker may be missing.

2. **Share the organizational plan of your next speech with a classmate so that you become consultants for each other. Help each other come up with alternative patterns for the main points, and optional introductions and conclusions. After the speeches are presented, each consulting team should explain the options it considered and why it chose the particular structures used for each speech.**

This exercise can be used in conjunction with Discussion item 1. After they have identified the main points of their speeches, have your students arrange these points for maximum effectiveness. For homework, they should choose a design (or combination of designs) for arranging their main points and suggest strategies for introducing and concluding their speeches. Push your students to explore a variety of strategies and to avoid locking into one prematurely.

Focus discussion on the appropriateness of suggested designs in relation to given topics and generated speech materials.

Application *(text pp. 234–235)*

1. Select a speech from Appendix B and write a thorough critique of its structure. Consider the following questions in your assessment:

    A. Did this speech satisfy the requirements of "good form?" Did it meet the needs of simplicity, balance, and order?

    B. What kind of speech design did it use? Did this satisfy the principles of similarity, proximity, and closure?

    C. Was supporting material used effectively to strengthen the main points and subpoints?

    D. Did transitions keep the message in focus for listeners as the speech developed?

    This works well for homework followed by in-class discussion. The following sample analysis of "Secondhand Smoke" may help to stimulate and guide class discussion.

    A. Good form

        1. *Simplicity:* The speech develops three main points: (1) the speaker's personal reasons for banning smoking in public areas, (2) statistical reasons linking secondhand smoke to health problems in adults and children, and (3) recognition and refutation of the counterargument on smokers' rights. The specific purpose, thesis statement, and main points are very clearly stated.

        2. *Balance:* The introduction, body, and conclusion of the speech are well balanced in terms of emphasis and development. The body is the longest part of the speech. The main points receive approximately the same amount of emphasis and development.

        3. *Order:* The speech flows nicely from the introduction to the body to the conclusion. Additionally, the main points are arranged so that they are easy to follow.

    B. The speech uses a categorical design in terms of why the speaker advocates banning smoking in public places, with the final category being the recognition and refutation of one major counterargument. This design is based on the principle of similarity. The conclusion provides a nice sense of closure to the speech.

    C. The two major forms of supporting materials used in the speech are personal examples and statistics. The speaker blends these artfully into her presentation. The statistics come from sources the audience should know and accept as credible.

    D. The speaker uses transitions to connect the introduction to the body of the speech, to connect the main points of the speech, and to bridge from the body of the speech to the conclusion.

2. What kinds of introductory and concluding techniques might be most effective for speeches based on the following specific purpose statements?

    To inform my audience of the dangers of tanning salons.
    To persuade my audience that it is better to marry than to live together.
    To inform my audience of the signs of domestic abuse.
    To persuade my audience that televising trials subverts the system of justice.

This can be used for homework, or as a small-group activity followed by in-class discussion. You might preview this with a short lecture on the functions and techniques of effectively introducing and concluding speeches. While there are no absolute right and wrong answers, some suggestions will probably be more effective than others. Break your students into small groups and have them come up with first and second alternative techniques for introducing and concluding speeches for each statement to be shared with the class. For class discussion, they should justify their chosen techniques, offering illustrative examples. Emphasize the value of "bookends," or using concluding techniques that refer back to introductory, attention-getting techniques. Focus on the appropriateness and likely effectiveness of your students' contributions, and try to move the class toward a consensus on the most effective strategies for each statement.

Suggestions for discussion:

a. Examples and/or lay testimony of victims of premature aging or skin cancer could help gain audience attention and provide a sense of closure for the conclusion. A rhetorical question might also be very effective. Speakers might establish credibility by citing testimony and/or statistical information on the relation of skin disorders to regular use of tanning booths. Citing personal experience or examples of personal friends could help enhance identification.

b. As this is essentially a moral issue, younger speakers addressing younger audiences would probably want to avoid sounding "preachy." They might enhance identification by soliciting some sort of direct audience participation. Testimony from respected moral and/or religious figures, psychologists, and/or family counselors could also help to enhance credibility. Similarly, speakers might close with testimony, or perhaps a rhetorical question to leave audiences thinking.

c. Examples (real or hypothetical) of abused children and their lay testimony could help gain audience attention and enhance emotional identification with this problem. Statistics on the rise and demographics of child abuse rates in recent years, or on how widespread the problem is, could startle the audience and help to gain its attention. Relevant personal experience could obviously help to enhance the speaker's credibility and audience identification. Referring back to cited examples or the attention-gaining strategies would probably make an effective conclusion.

d. Examples of widely viewed trials, such the O. J. Simpson double murder case, combined with a rhetorical question or expert testimony regarding the encroachment of show business into our legal system, could be very effective for introducing and/or concluding this speech. Perhaps statistical information on the growth and effects (costs, length, conviction rates) of cameras in the court could also help to gain the audience's attention.

3. **The following introduction was used in a speech presented at an honor society recognition conference. Evaluate this introduction in light of the guidelines for preparing effective introductions presented in this chapter and explain how you would revise or reorganize this material to make it more effective.**

> Today I'm going to talk about the technology of the future. The theme for your conference is "Preparing for the 21st Century," and getting a grip on the technological changes ahead of us is the best way to prepare for the next century. I'll also tell you a little about Battelle [the speaker's company], and I'll make a few predictions about what our world will be like over the next 10 to 50 years. That has me a little nervous, because, any time you start making predictions, you hope no one nearby has a tape recorder.

Here's an example of what I mean. At the Chicago World's Fair way back in 1893, a group of 74 social commentators got together to look 100 years into the future—at the world of 1993. Here are some of their predictions. Many people will live to be 150. The government will have grown more simple, as true greatness tends toward simplicity. Prisons will decline and divorce will be considered unnecessary. The Nicaraguan canal is as sure to be built as tides are to ebb and flow and the seasons to change.

This works well for homework or as a small-group activity followed by general class discussion. You might preview this by quickly discussing the functions of effective introductions and techniques for constructing them. You can extend this activity by having your students construct alternative introductions and defend their relative superiority in class discussion. As for this particular introduction, it has most of the right ingredients, but the order in which they are presented is somewhat dry and hard to follow. For instance, what would be an effective attention-getting analogy follows the preview statement, which is confusing. As this is a technical topic, the speaker might have alluded to his or her credibility to address it. In addition, a more explicit involvement strategy to gain audience attention might also be in order. The following alternative introduction may help stimulate class discussion.

Predicting the future is a precarious endeavor. At the Chicago World's Fair in 1893, a group of social "experts" gathered to offer their predictions for a hundred years into the future. Among other things, people would live to be 150. Government would grow more simple, as greatness tends in that direction. A canal would be built across Nicaragua, and both prisons and divorce would decline. [Pause] Therefore I'm a little nervous about my responsibility in speaking before you here today, as any time you start predicting the future, you hope that no one nearby has a tape recorder!

The title of your conference, "Preparing for the 21st Century," suggests that you are intelligent, future-oriented, and ambitious people. Mastering the technologies of tomorrow is the key to making your dreams a reality. As research coordinator of Battelle [the speaker's company], it is my responsibility to know where tomorrow's technologies are headed. Today, I'm going to tell you a little about our company, and then offer some predictions as to what our world will look like over the next ten to fifty years.

ADDITIONAL ACTIVITIES

Impromptu Structuring

Purpose: To provide your students an opportunity to generate and arrange the main points of a speech, using topics that are provided for them.

Directions: This works well for homework or as a small-group activity followed by class discussion. Write an assortment of speech topics on small pieces of paper, place them folded in a container, and have representatives for each group draw two to three slips from which to choose one for use in this exercise (for a list of potential topics, see IRM p. 235). Each student or group should generate and critique two to three main points to be covered in a speech on their topic, select and defend a design strategy, and consider how the introductions and conclusions might be developed. Allow ten to fifteen minutes for students to complete this phase of the exercise, before presenting their ideas to the class. Focus critiques on the structural principles of balance, simplicity, orderliness, and appropriateness of design strategies. This readily combines with the activity "Impromptu Outlining" in Chapter 8.

Optional Introductions and Conclusions

Purpose: To provide your students an opportunity to prepare optional introductions and/or conclusions for given speeches.

Directions: For work on introductions, divide your class into small groups, assigning each a short student speech from Appendix B. Have each group spend ten to fifteen minutes developing alternative introductions for the assigned speech, using different techniques, and then present them in class. To save time, you might simply outline the two or three main points of a chosen speech for your students. Preview the text on effective introductions and conclusions in preparation for this exercise. Focus class discussion on evaluating introductions in terms of appropriateness to the topic, thesis, and specific purpose; clarity of preview statement; and attention/involvement-gaining and ethos-establishing potential. For conclusions, have your students follow the same steps for generating and critiquing their ideas, and presenting them for class discussion.

Identifying Transitions

Purpose: To emphasize the importance of effective transitions by having your students locate and critique them in other student speeches.

Directions: This exercise works well for homework or small-group discussion. Preview this by discussing the functions of transitions and their various forms. Have your students select one of the short speeches from Appendix B of the text. They should locate and critique all of the transitions (including previews and internal summaries) in the speech, offering alternatives or suggestions for improvement. Have them focus especially on places where additional transitions, previews, or internal summaries would help make the speech flow more smoothly. To use this as a small-group activity, break your students into small groups, assigning each group one or two speeches for analysis, and have them present their ideas for subsequent class discussion.

Structural Speech Analysis

Purpose: To provide your students an opportunity to critique the structure of sample student speeches.

Directions: This exercise should be completed individually in class upon the viewing of short videotaped speech samples. It can also be converted to homework by having your student analyze one of the student speeches in Appendix B. Distribute the "Work Sheet for Structural Analysis" on p. 239. Have your students take notes while viewing the speeches for class discussion. You might preview this activity by discussing the basic principles of balance, simplicity, and orderliness. Use the work sheet as a format for discussion, focusing on the adequacy of introductions, clarity and appropriateness of the speech's structure, use of transitions, and effectiveness of conclusions. Do all the major parts of the speech develop the same idea in a sensible fashion? Relatively speaking, do they all receive an appropriate amount of support and development? As always, emphasize what you will be looking for in student speeches. If time allows, watch several speeches for discussion and analysis, and offer some of your own critiques to get your students warmed up.

We include here two sample structural analyses of speeches in Appendix B that may serve as guidelines for this exercise:

Structural Analysis of Rodney Nishikawa's "Free at Last"

Introduction:

Attention material: Personal example of previous speaking experience and tie-in to Martin Luther King's birthday.
Establishment of ethos: Cites personal experience.

Preview or transition: "You should understand what . . ." would have been better if he had worked this into the introduction as a preview.

Length (in relation to body and conclusion): 128 words. The inclusion of a preview would have more fully developed the introduction.

Body:

Main point 1: Encounter with prejudice.
   Type and amount of support: Personal narrative.
   Transition to point 2: "Of course, . . . [continues narrative].
   Length (relative to other main points): 192 words.
Main point 2: How parents helped.
   Type and amount of support: Narrative.
   Transition to point 3: "From my early encounter. . ."
   Length (relative to other main points): 321 words.
Main point 3: How what he learned has helped him in life.
   Type and amount of support: Examples.
   Transition to conclusion: "Although. . ."
   Length (relative to other main points): 184 words. Too short—most important main point the least developed. Speech would have been more effective if the main points had increased proportionately in length.

Conclusion:

Summary of message: None provided. Speech would have been improved by a short summary of what he learned about prejudice and life from his experience.
Concluding material: Personal example.
Length (in relation to body and introduction): 60 words. Too short; inclusion of a summary and a more specific personal example would have improved the speech.

Structural Analysis of Cecile Larson's "The 'Monument' at Wounded Knee"

Introduction:

Attention material: Startle technique. Created a mood of pride and then abruptly destroyed it with the word "massacre."
Establishment of ethos: Personal experience.
Preview or transition: No preview, but a clear transition. Speech short and easy to follow.
Length (in relation to body and conclusion): 55 words. Possibly rather short, but it is effective because of its dramatic impact.

Body:

Main point 1: Background on history and location sets the scene for descriptive point 2.
   Type and amount of support: Examples and richly vivid language.
   Transition to point 2: "When we finally arrived. . ."
   Length (relative to other main point): 224 words. Appropriate length.
Main point 2: Description of the monument.
   Type and amount of support: Examples and richly vivid language.
   Transition to conclusion: "Yes, we Americans. . ."
   Length (relative to other main point): 310 words. Appropriate length.

Conclusion:

Summary of message: Brief. Echoes the introduction and provides closure.

Concluding material: "Only when it makes us feel good."
Length (in relation to body and introduction): 31 words. The shortness and abruptness of the conclusion add to its dramatic impact and echo the abruptness of the change of mood in the introduction.

The Structure of Advertisements

Purpose: To give your students an opportunity to apply the principles of speech structure to mass media advertisements.

Directions: This works well for homework or as a small-group activity followed by in-class discussion. For in-class use, videotape a number of ads, show them in class, and have your students critique them in terms of the structural dynamics discussed in the text. You might also clip full-page ads from magazines for use with this activity. What strategies do the ads use to gain audience attention and establish credibility? Do they seem to follow any sort of noticeable design strategy? Do concluding remarks refer back to introductory ones? Commercials commonly open with rhetorical questions, maxims or quotes, "startling" pieces of information, or examples to get attention and invoke audience involvement. They often invoke the pseudo-credibility of actors giving expert advice on topics ranging from personal hygiene to legal and financial services. They also typically use a basic problem-solution format to associate their products with fulfilling audience needs or concerns. Note that many of the techniques used in television advertising would not usually work in public speaking. Commercials commonly rely on cinematic and visual techniques, music, or action scenes to arouse audience attention, and explicitly associate their products with fulfilling fantasy lifestyles of physical and material excess. Focus discussion on the differences and similarities between public speaking and advertising, and what observed advertising techniques might be usefully employed in your students' speeches.

Choosing Appropriate Design Strategies

Purpose: To familiarize your students with the process of choosing appropriate design strategies (or combinations thereof), given a general focus or thesis statement.

Directions: This works well as a general class discussion piece following a brief lecture on the major design strategies and their functions. Emphasize that different speech topics and research overviews should suggest their own designs or design combinations. After finishing your mini-lecture, simply read the following speech ideas and solicit student input as to which designs would be most appropriate. Keep in mind that there may be more than one correct answer to each idea, and try to solicit first and second alternatives as you move your class to consensus.

1.   To inform an audience about the five most important locations to know on campus.
2.   To inform an audience as to how to change the oil in their cars.
3.   To inform an audience about sexist advertising practices.
4.   To inform an audience as to how Prohibition came about and what eventually defeated it.
5.   To inform a student audience about the ideal way to prepare for an exam.
6.   To describe for an audience the complexities of the human circulatory system.
7.   To explain for an audience why consumer confidence has risen or declined over the past year.
8.   To persuade an audience to vote in the next election.
9.   To persuade an audience to vote for one particular party in the next election.
10.   To provide your audience a detailed recollection of an event witnessed this morning.

Suggested answers:

1.   Spatial, categorical
2.   Sequential
3.   Categorical, cause-effect

4. Sequential, cause-effect, perhaps categorical
5. Sequential, comparison and contrast
6. Spatial, comparison and contrast (note that an analogy to a city traffic system might be effective with an obscure or complex subject such as this)
7. Sequential, cause-effect, categorical
8. Problem-solution, sequential, perhaps categorical
9. Problem-solution, refutative, categorical
10. Sequential

Supporting a Point

Purpose: To provide your students an opportunity to develop an ideal model of support for a major point or claim before the class.

Directions: Inform your students that during the next class meeting they will make a one- to two-minute presentation supporting a single statement or claim. Distribute copies of the "Outline Format for Supporting a Point" (see p. 236). You might also distribute the "Check List for Supporting a Point" (p. 238) and the "Evaluation of One-Point Presentation" (see p. 237). Have your students state their points and support them with (1) facts and figures, (2) testimony, and (3) an example or narrative. They should also cite and evaluate their sources of information. Tell them to follow the outline format for making their presentations, and not to bother with developing introductions and conclusions. Encourage them to find information to support a point relevant to their next major speaking assignment. The completed outline format should be turned in prior to their presentations. Bibliographies should contain at least three references, only one of which may be an encyclopedia or dictionary. You may want to go over the evaluation form with your students so that they understand clearly what is expected of them. Offer oral critiques of their presentations, focusing on the quality and adequacy of their supporting forms and on the need for a variety of supporting forms. Emphasize what you will be looking for in their actual speeches.

Mary Mino (Penn State University, DuBois Campus), "Structuring: An Alternate Approach for Developing Clear Organization," *SCT* (Winter 1991), 14–15.

One of the instructor's most crucial objectives when teaching the basic public speaking course centers on organization. Outlining, one method of organization, has been described in numerous speech communication textbooks and is incorporated in a majority of speech communication classrooms. Although outlining is a useful approach to organization, students often develop the outline after the fact. Thus, speech organization leaves much to be desired. Structuring, an alternate approach, requires that the student formulate a residual message—the one idea the speaker wants the audience to remember at the end of the speech. Then, based on that residual message, the student constructs diagrams that contain each main point and further develops subpoints or substructures through the creation of additional diagrams. A structured speech presents ideas in a logical order—a progression of thoughts that helps the audience understand the whole idea.

Developed by Gerald Phillips, structuring's major benefit lies in its visualization component. That is, students are better able to analyze their ideas, see the speech's strengths and weaknesses, decide where evidence works best, uncover information needed to organize the introduction and conclusion, and remember their material. Another benefit is that structuring enables reticent students to focus on the management and manipulation of ideas, rather than on public speaking anxieties.

Although Phillips' explanation of structuring can be complex, understanding and using this approach is relatively simple. Because people have orderly minds, structuring helps students to organize ideas into patterns they and their audience can easily identify and understand. After formulating the residual message (When I am done with my speech, I want my audience to know or believe that . . .), the student chooses one of the seven structures by which to organize the speech. However, for the sake of explanation, I use an example that illustrates how structuring works by focusing on information-giving. This example incorporates a simplistic, general topic area (cakes). The instructor can use any topic with which he or she feels comfortable.

Time—series of events or steps in a process; events or steps must follow a specific order.

Residual Message: When I am done with my speech, I want my audience to know that baking a cake is a simple process.

>Buy ingredients
>Mix ingredients
>Bake ingredients

Space—parts of something and how they fit to form the whole, either literally or figuratively.

Residual Message: When I am done with my speech, I want my audience to know that there are three parts to a cake.

>Layer
>Layer
>Plate

Classification—information-giving is the speaker's primary goal; categories must be comprised of relatively equal, non-overlapping main points.

Residual Message: When I am done with my speech, I want my audience to know that there are three superior cake mixes.

>Betty Crocker
>Pillsbury
>Duncan Hines

Comparison—comparing things by showing their similarities.

Residual Message: When I am done with my speech, I want my audience to know that cakes and pies are similar in two ways.

>Cakes   Pies
>Dessert   Dessert
>Rich   Rich

Contrast—comparing things by showing their differences.

Residual Message: When I am done with my speech, I want my audience to know that cakes and poles are different in two ways.

>Cakes   Poles
>Eat   Build
>Batter   Wood

Cause-Effect—the speaker establishes a relationship between two events or a certain result(s) is the product of a certain event(s).

Residual Message: When I am done with my speech, I want my audience to know that when a person celebrates a birthday he or she usually receives a cake.

>Cause   Effect
>Birthday Celebration   Cake

Problem Solution—the speaker outlines a problem(s), offers a feasible solution(s) and illustrates the advantages of the solution or how the solution solves the problem.

> *Residual Message:* When I am done with my speech, I want my audience to know that the problem of eating too much cake is weight gain which can be solved through decreased cake consumption.

Problem	Solution	Advantage
Weight Gain	Decreased Consumption	Decreased Weight

After explaining structuring, it is important to illustrate how to further develop each main point. Here, substructuring is used. The student examines each main point and, based on that point, chooses one of the seven structures to develop these ideas, as illustrated in the following example.

> *Residual Message:* When I am done with my speech, I want my audience to know that baking a cake is a simple process.

Time Structure:

Buy ingredients
    Solids
    Liquids

Mix ingredients
    First do this
    Then do this
    Next do this

Bake ingredients
Baking times
Ready test

Substructures Used:

Main Point One—Classification
Main Point Two—Time
Main Point Three—Classification

Through the use of this example, students catch on to structuring very quickly. To be sure students understand and can apply all seven structures to different topic areas, divide them into groups. Give each group a broad, general subject area. Groups are asked to formulate a residual message and structure that corresponds to each of the seven structures. Each group presents this material in class. The lecture is reinforced through the opportunity the instructor has to correct any structural mistakes.

After using structuring as an alternate approach to outlining in my public speaking classes for ten years, I am convinced that students better understand the concept of clear organization.

Author's Note: See Structuring Work Sheet, pp. 240–241 of this IRM.

SUPPLEMENTARY MATERIALS

Films and Videos

"Basic Patterns of Organization," University of Iowa, 30 minutes.

"Organizing the Speech," RMI Media Productions, 28 minutes.

"Organizing Your Message," Agency for Instructional Television, color, 15 minutes.

"Planning Your Speech," Coronet/MTI Film and Video, color, 13 minutes.

"Be Prepared to Speak," Kantola-Skeie Productions, 27 minutes.

Videos to accompany *Public Speaking:* "Student Speeches, Vol. 1," "Student Speeches, Vol. 2, with Analysis," "Prominent Speakers," Houghton Mifflin, 1991.

Transparencies and Handouts *(see following pages)*

Principles of Good Form

Structural Principles and Speech Designs

Preparing Your Introduction

Research Overview Form

Topic Ideas for Impromptu Structuring Exercise

Outline Format for Supporting a Point

Evaluation of One-Point Presentation

Check List for Supporting a Point

Work Sheet for Structural Analysis

Structuring Work Sheet

PRINCIPLES OF GOOD FORM

Simplicity

Limit the number of main points.

Phrase main points clearly and succinctly.

Use parallel phrasing for emphasis.

Balance

The body should be the longest part of the speech.

Main points should be balanced:

All may be equal in importance and length.
They may increase or decrease in importance and length.

Introduction and conclusion should be nearly equal in length.

Orderliness

Open with an introduction.

Develop main ideas in the body of your speech.

End with a conclusion.

Follow a consistent pattern of development.

STRUCTURAL PRINCIPLES AND SPEECH DESIGNS

Principle of proximity:

Sequential
Spatial

Principle of similarity:

Categorical

Principle of closure:

Causation
Problem-solution

PREPARING YOUR INTRODUCTION

1. Use material that will capture your audience's attention.

2. Tie your topic to your audience's needs, interests, or well-being. Give people a reason to listen to your message.

3. Consider the mood you want to set.

4. Establish your credibility to speak on this topic. Give your audience a reason to listen to you as a speaker.

5. Keep your time constraints in mind.

6. Preview your message to make it easier for listeners to follow.

RESEARCH OVERVIEW FORM

Source:

_____

_____

_____

Main Points:

_____

_____

_____

_____

Source:

_____

_____

_____

Main Points:

_____

_____

_____

_____

Source:

_____

_____

_____

Main Points:

_____

_____

_____

_____

_____

TOPIC IDEAS FOR IMPROMPTU STRUCTURING EXERCISE

The best summer jobs for students	The worst summer jobs for students
How to leave your lover	How to make up with your lover
The cheapest places for dates	The most expensive places for dates
The best restaurants in town	The worst restaurants in town
Why exercise is good for you	Why exercise is bad for you
The best shows or movies	The worst shows or movies
Why women are superior	Why men are superior
The American dream	The American nightmare
The best things about our school	The worst things about our school
Why college is fun	Why college is a drag
The joys of leaving home	The joys of staying home
My favorite class	My least favorite class
The best vacation of my life	The worst vacation of my life
The best job I ever had	The worst job I ever had
The best part-time jobs for a student	The worst part-time jobs for a student
What makes me happy	What makes me sad
Inexpensive presents for dad	Inexpensive presents for mom
The best things in life are expensive	The best things in life are free
How to manage your work time efficiently	How to relax and reduce stress

OUTLINE FORMAT FOR SUPPORTING A POINT

NAME _____ SECTION _____

Statement: _____

    Transition into facts or statistics:_____

      1. Factual information or statistics to support statement: _____

      _____

      _____

    Transition into testimony: _____

      2. Expert, prestige, or lay testimony to support statement: _____

      _____

      _____

    Transition into example or narrative:_____

      3. Example or narrative to support statement: _____

      _____

      _____

    Transition into restatement: _____

Restatement of original assertion: _____

    _____

Bibliography

EVALUATION OF ONE-POINT PRESENTATION

NAME _____ SECTION _____ GRADE _____

Factual information or statistics:

Relevance to point	5	4	3	2	1
Recency of information/statistics	5	4	3	2	1
Source/date identified	5	4	3	2	1
Credibility of source	5	4	3	2	1
Freedom from distortion	5	4	3	2	1
Facts rather than opinions	5	4	3	2	1

Testimony:

Relevance to point	5	4	3	2	1
Recency of testimony	5	4	3	2	1
Proper type of testimony used	5	4	3	2	1
Qualifications specified	5	4	3	2	1
Accuracy of quote or paraphrase	5	4	3	2	1

Example or narrative:

Relevance to point	5	4	3	2	1
Representativeness of situation	5	4	3	2	1
Plausibility	5	4	3	2	1
Interest value	5	4	3	2	1

General:

Use of transitions to integrate	5	4	3	2	1
Extemporaneous presentation	5	4	3	2	1

Comments:

CHECK LIST FOR SUPPORTING A POINT

_____   The statement presents an unfamiliar fact or assertion that must be supported.

_____   The facts or statistics come from a credible source.

_____   The source of the information has been noted.

_____   The proper type of testimony has been chosen.

_____   The source of the testimony has been introduced and his or her credentials established.

_____   The example or narrative focuses attention on the most important aspect of the statement or assertion.

_____   The restatement summarizes the meaning of the support and paraphrases the original statement or assertion.

_____   Transitions have been provided to make the presentation flow smoothly.

_____   The bibliography contains at least three references, only one of which is from an encyclopedia or dictionary.

WORK SHEET FOR STRUCTURAL ANALYSIS

Introduction:

Attention material _____

Establishment of ethos _____

Preview or transition _____

Length (in relation to body and conclusion) _____

Body:

Main point 1 _____

    Type and amount of support _____

    Transition to point 2 _____

    Length (relative to other main points) _____

Main point 2 _____

    Type and amount of support _____

    Transition to point 3 _____

    Length (relative to other main points)_____

Main point 3 _____

    Type and amount of support _____

    Transition to conclusion _____

    Length (relative to other main points)_____

Conclusion:

Summary of message _____

Concluding material _____

Length (in relation to body and introduction)_____

STRUCTURING WORK SHEET

Name _____ Topic _____

Time—series of events or steps in a process; events or steps must follow a specific order.

Residual Message: When I am done with my speech, I want my audience to know that

_____

_____

_____

_____

Space—parts of something and how they fit to form the whole, either literally or figuratively.

Residual Message: When I am done with my speech, I want my audience to know that

_____

_____

_____

_____

Classification—information giving is the speaker's primary goal; categories must be made up of relatively equal, nonoverlapping main points.

Residual Message: When I am done with my speech, I want my audience to know that

_____

_____

_____

_____

Comparison—comparing things by showing their similarities.

Residual Message: When I am done with my speech, I want my audience to know that

_____

_____

_____

_____

STRUCTURING WORK SHEET (page 2)

Contrast—comparing things by showing their differences.

Residual Message: When I am done with my speech, I want my audience to know that

_____

_____

_____

_____

Cause-Effect—the speaker establishes a relationship between two events or a certain result(s) is the product of a certain event(s).

Residual Message: When I am done with my speech, I want my audience to know that

_____

_____

Cause(s)   Effect(s)

_____   _____

_____   _____

_____   _____

Problem Solution—the speaker outlines a problem(s), offers a feasible solution(s), and illustrates the advantages of the solution or how the solution solves the problem.

Residual Message: When I am done with my speech, I want my audience to know that

_____

_____

Problem   Solution   Advantage

_____   _____   _____

_____   _____   _____

_____   _____   _____

READINGS FOR ENRICHMENT

See guide to journal abbreviations on p. 37.

* Items marked with as asterisk are suitable for student enrichment.

Attention

Bower, Bruce. "Brain Scans Track Down Attention Systems." *Science News,* 14 Sept. 1991, p. 166.

Brown, William R. "Attention and the Rhetoric of Social Intervention." *QJS* (Feb. 1982), 17–27.

Cartier, F. A., and K. A. Harwood. "Some Questions About Attention." *JC* (Autumn 1958), 106–110.

* Celsi, Richard L., and Jerry C. Olson. "The Role of Involvement in Attention and Comprehension Processes." *Journal of Consumer Research* (Sept. 1988), 210–224.

Kittross, John M. "Some Attempts to Develop an Index of Interest." *JC* (Dec. 1962), 225–233.

Kliem, Ralph L. "Making Presentations That Command Attention." *Machine Design,* 9 Apr. 1987, pp. 143–147.

Krugman, E. "Points of View: Limits of Attention to Advertising." *Journal of Advertising Research* (Oct.–Nov. 1988), 47–50.

Levin, Stephen R., and Daniel R. Anderson. "The Development of Attention." *JC* (Spring 1976), 126–135.

Lynch, Mervin D., Brian D. Kent, and Richard P. Carlson. "The Meaning of Human Interest: Four Dimensions of Judgment." *JQ* (Winter 1967), 673–678.

Lynch, Mervin D., Hazel M. Nettleship, and Richard P. Carlson. "The Measurement of Human Interest." *JQ* (Summer 1968), 226–234.

* Runkel, Howard W. " How to Select Material That Will Hold Attention." *CQ* (Sept. 1960), 13–14.

Stauffer, John, Richard Frost, and William Rybolt. "The Attention Factor in Recalling Television News." *JC* (Winter 1983), 29–37.

* Stevens, Walter W. "Attention Through Language." *CQ* (Nov. 1963), 23–25.

* Vohs, John L. "An Empirical Approach to the Concept of Attention." *CM* (Aug. 1964), 355–360.

Wise, Stephen P., and Robert Desimone. "Behavioral Neurophysiology: Insights into Seeing and Grasping." *Science,* 4 Nov. 1988, pp. 736–741.

Introductions and Conclusions

* Anderson, Kevin J. "Getting Readers in the Mood," *Writer's Digest* (June 1995), 34–35.

* Jane Bosveld, "Wonderlust: Kindling a Sense of Wonder in Humans," *Omni* (Jan. 1989), 33.

Bowers, John Waite, and Michael Osborn. "Attitudinal Effects of Selected Types of Concluding Metaphors in Persuasive Speeches." *SM,* 33 (1966), 148–155.

* Boyd, Stephen D. "Creating a Quality Conclusion." *Public Relations Journal* (Sept. 1990), 34–35.

* Comisky, Paul, and Jennings Bryant. "Factors Involved in Generating Suspense." *HCR* (Fall 1982), 49–58.

Daniels, Tom D., and Richard F. Whitman. "The Effects of Message Introduction, Message Structure, and Verbal Organizing Ability Upon Learning of Message Information." *HCR* (Winter 1981), 147–160.

* Dunn, Don. "How to Grab—and Hold—an Audience." *Business Week,* 3 Apr. 1989, p. 118.

Hibben, Jean. "Eliminating the 'My Speech Is About' Introduction." *SCT* (Fall 1992), 11.

Knapp, Mark L., Robert Hopper, and Robert A. Bell. "Compliments: A Descriptive Taxonomy." *JC* (Autumn 1984), 12–31.

* Magee, Mary F., and Melinda M. Davies. "Crafting a Powerhouse Introduction." *Training and Development Journal* (Oct. 1989), 25–27.

Miller, Edd. "Speech Introductions and Conclusions." *QJS* (Apr. 1946), 181–183.

Overton, Julia. "Introductions and Conclusions: Helping Public Speaking Students Write Effective Beginnings and Endings." *SCT* (Fall 1994), 4.

* Reinhardt, Christine. "A Thousand Points to Write: Peggy Noonan on Getting a Speech Started—and Keeping It Going." *Working Woman* (Nov. 1990), 120–122.

Ryan, Earl H. "That First Awful Minute," *CQ* (Oct. 1953), 16–17.

* "What Triggers Negative Reactions." *USA Today* (magazine) (Apr. 1993), 14.

Organization

Anderson, Loren J. "A Summary of Research on Order Effects in Communication." In *Concepts in Communication,* edited by Jimmie D. Trent, Judith S. Trent and Daniel J. O'Neill, pp. 129–130. Boston: Allyn & Bacon, 1973.

Anderson, N. H., and A. A. Barrios, "Primacy-Effects in Personality-Impression Formation." *Journal of Abnormal and Social Psychology* (1961), 346–350.

Baird, John E. "The Effects of Speech Summaries upon Audience Comprehension of Expository Speeches of Varying Quality and Complexity." *CSSJ* (Summer 1974), 119–127.

Baker, Eldon E. "The Immediate Effects of Perceived Speaker Disorganization on Speaker Credibility and Audience Attitude Change in Persuasive Speaking." *WJSC* (Summer 1965), 148–161.

Bantz, Charles R., and David H. Smith. "A Critique and Experimental Test of Weick's Model of Organizing." *CM* (Aug. 1977), 171–184.

Beighley, Kenneth C. "An Experimental Study of the Effect of Four Speech Variables on Listener Comprehension." *CM* (Nov. 1952), 249–258.

——. "A Summary of Experimental Studies Dealing with the Effect of Organization and the Skill of Speaker on Comprehension." *JC* (Nov. 1952), 58–65.

——. "An Experimental Study of the Effect of Three Speech Variables on Listener Comprehension." *CM* (Nov. 1954), 248–253.

* Bertrand, Kate. "Speak Now, or. . . : In Presentation Training, Flair is Nice, but Discipline Wins Applause." *Business Marketing* (Jan. 1990), 68–70.

* Bowman, Sally-Jo. "How to Write the Informational Article." *Writer's Digest* (Apr. 1995), 34–36.

Callaghan, J. Calvin. "Testing the Ability to Organize Ideas." *CE* (Sept. 1964), 225–227.

Daniels, Tom D., and Richard F. Whitman. "The Effects of Message Introduction, Message Structure, and Verbal Organizing Ability upon Learning of Message Information." *HCR* (Winter 1981), 147–160.

* Dickson, Carolyn. "You Can't Write a Speech." *Training and Development Journal* (Apr. 1987), 70–72.

Gilkinson, Howard, Stanley F. Paulson, and Donald E. Sikkink. "Effects of Order and Authority in an Argumentative Speech." *QJS* (Apr. 1954), 183–192.

Gulley, Halbert E., and David K. Berlo. "Effect of Intercellular and Intracellular Speech Structure on Attitude Change and Learning." *CM* (Nov. 1956), 288–297.

Hauser, Margaret Fitch. "Message Structure, Inference Making, and Recall." In *Communication Yearbook 8,* edited by Robert N. Bostrom and Bruce Westley, pp. 278–292. Beverly Hills, Calif.: Sage, 1984.

Hoffman, Regina M. "Temporal Organization as a Rhetorical Resource." *SSCJ* (Spring 1992), 194–204.

Horowitz, Milton W. "Organizational Processes Underlying Differences Between Listening and Reading as a Function of Complexity of Material." *JC* (Mar. 1968), 37–46.

Hovland, C., W. Mandell, E. Campbell, T. Brock, A. Luchins, A. Cohen, W. McGuire, I. Janis, R. Feierabend, and N. Anderson. *The Order of Presentation in Persuasion.* New Haven: Yale University Press, 1957.

Johnson, Arlee. "A Preliminary Investigation of the Relationship Between Message Organization and Listener Comprehension." *CSSJ* (Summer 1970), 104–107.

Klein, Andy. "How Telecast's Organization Affects Viewer Retention." *JQ* (Summer 1978), 356–359.

Knapp, Mark L., and James C. McCroskey. "The Siamese Twins: Inventio and Dispositio." *CQ* (Apr. 1966), 17–18.

McClish, Glen. "The 'Authorial Conversion' Structure in Oral Argument." *SCT* (Spring 1993), 10–11.

McCroskey, James C., and R. Samuel Mehrley. "The Effects of Disorganization and Nonfluency on Attitude Change and Source Credibility." *CM* (Mar. 1969), 13–21.

Miller, N., and D. T. Campbell. "Recency and Primacy in Persuasion as a Function of the Timing of Speeches and Measurements." *Journal of Abnormal and Social Psychology* (1959), 250–253.

Mino, Mary. "Structuring: An Alternate Approach for Developing Clear Organization." *SCT* (Winter 1991), 14–15.

Muir, Star A. "Organizing and Critiquing Ideas." *SCT* (Spring 1995), 8–10.

* Olson, Donald O. "Confusion in Arrangement." *CE* (Sept. 1964), 216–219.

Parker, John P. "Some Organizational Variables and Their Effect upon Comprehension." *JC* (Mar. 1962), 27–32.

Pasma, Kristen. "Transitional Stories." *SCT* (Summer 1991), 15.

Schnell, Jim. "The Developmental Speech Sequence Model (DSSM)." *SCT* (Winter 1987), 15–16.

Sharp, Harry, Jr., and Thomas McClung. "Effect of Organization on the Speaker's Ethos." *CM* (June 1966), 182–183.

Sikkink, Donald. "An Experimental Study of the Effects on the Listener of Anticlimax Order and Authority in an Argumentative Speech." *SSCJ* (Winter 1956), 73–78.

Spicer, Christopher, and Ronald E. Bassett. "The Effect of Organization on Learning from an Informative Message." *SSCJ* (Spring 1976), 290–299.

Sponberg, Harold. "The Relative Effectiveness of Climax and Anti-Climax Order in an Argumentative Speech." *CM*, No. 1 (1946), 35–44.

* Sussman, Lyle. "Managing to Speak by Managing the Speech." *Personnel* (Dec. 1988), 60–64.

Thompson, Ernest. "An Experimental Investigation of the Relative Effectiveness of Organizational Structure in Oral Communication." *SSCJ* (Fall 1960), 59–69.

———. "Some Effects of Message Structure on Listener Comprehension." *CM* (Mar. 1967), 51–57.

Turner, Frederick H. "The Effect of Speech Summaries on Audience Comprehension." *CSSJ* (Spring 1970), 24–29.

Vickre, James F., Jr., "An Experimental Investigation of the Effect of 'Previews' and 'Reviews' on Retention of Orally Presented Information." *SSCJ* (Spring 1971), 209–219.

Whitman, Richard F., and John H. Timmis. "The Influence of Verbal Organizational Structure and Verbal Organizing Skills on Select Measures of Learning." *HCR* (Summer 1975), 293–301.

CHAPTER 8
Outlining Your Speech

OBJECTIVES

- To help your students appreciate the importance of outlining their speeches.

- To help your students understand the process of effective outlining.

- To teach your students how to develop working outlines to structure their speeches.

- To teach students how to prepare formal outlines with proper coordination and subordination.

- To teach students how to break formal outlines down to key-word outlines for their presentations.

SUGGESTIONS FOR TEACHING

Impressing upon freshmen the value of outlining in organizing, structuring, and revising their speeches can be a challenge. Nonetheless, it remains an extremely important part of building effective messages. Closely related to generating main points, choosing appropriate design strategies, and adapting speech materials, outlining is the process by which speakers develop their ideas and materials into something that is structurally sound and comprehensible. Like other compositional activities, it is more effectively taught through demonstration and application than through lecture alone.

Most of the exercises in this chapter focus on having your students construct, revise, and even "unjumble" outlines to make them more meaningful, using the principles of coordination and subordination. Many of them can be logically coordinated with those of Chapter 7, on speech structure. There is also an interesting discussion piece bringing in insights on metaphor to help students envision the structure and outline of a coherent speech. This chapter contains work sheets and check lists for both working and formal outlines. Outline formats, check lists, and sample speech outlines for informative and persuasive speech designs are given in IRM Chapters 12 and 13. All of these aids are also available in the "Speech Designer" computer software.

CHAPTER OUTLINE

I. Outlining is an crucial part of developing well-structured and well-organized messages. (*text pp. 240–241*)
   A. It helps speakers control, order, and support their thoughts in a simple, balanced, and orderly fashion. It allows speakers to catch potential mistakes before presenting them in their speeches. Speakers should consider:

1. the adequacy of their research.
2. the relevance of main and supporting ideas.
3. the overall structure and balance of their speeches.
4. the appropriateness of their chosen design schemes.
5. where they need transitions.
6. their introductions and conclusions with respect to the bodies of their speeches.

  B. Computers are making systematic outlining progressively more convenient.

  C. Outlining is a process that evolves from initial working outlines to a formal full-sentence outline to a key-word outline you can use as a prompt during presentation.

II. A working outline should be developed as a tentative plan for a speech. *(text pp. 241–248)*

  A. Working outlines give speakers an opportunity to explore the relationships among their ideas and to identify potential trouble spots.

    1. Speakers may go through several rough working outlines in developing a speech.

    2. Speakers should consider the relative importance of ideas, their logical interrelationships, and probable audience impact.

    3. Preparing working outlines often stimulates moments of creative inspiration that give speeches originality.

  B. There are several steps in developing working outlines. Speakers should:

    1. first write their topics, specific purposes, and thesis statements.

    2. develop and arrange main points in light of their speaking purposes, audience needs, and time constraints.

      a. Speakers should critique their main points in terms of the following questions:

        (1) Will these main points make my message clear to my audience?

        (2) Is this the right order in which to develop them?

        (3) Have I left out anything important?

    3. identify and support subpoints. Speakers should critique their own main points in terms of what these points mean for their audiences, why the audiences should care, and how the audiences know these points are true.

      a. Speakers should examine their subpoints in terms of how they relate to each other, and whether they should be collapsed or expanded into more detailed sub-subpoints.

      b. Once they have developed each main point, speakers should review the body of their working outline in terms of whether it fulfills their thesis statement for their listeners, and whether it can be covered in the time available.

      c. Before moving on, speakers should make sure that their ideas are organized in an orderly fashion, that each subpoint relates directly to the main point above it, and that they have sufficient supporting information.

    4. complete their working outlines by sketching an introduction and conclusion, and adding transitions.

    5. critique their completed working outlines in terms of the:

      a. following "Checklist for a Working Outline" *(see text p. 248)*.

        (1) My topic, specific purpose, and thesis statement are clearly stated.

        (2) My introduction contains attention-getting material, establishes my credibility, and focuses and previews my message.

        (3) My main points represent the most important ideas on my topic.

        (4) I have an appropriate number of main points to cover my material in the time allotted.

        (5) Each subpoint breaks its main point into more specific detail.

        (6) My conclusion contains a summary statement and concluding remarks that reinforce and reflect upon the meaning of my speech.

        (7) I have planned transitions to use between the introduction and body, between each main point, and between the body and conclusion of my speech.

      b. following audience-centered questions.

(1) Are my main points arranged so that they will be easily understood and remembered?

(2) Do I have enough supporting material for each main point to satisfy critical listeners?

(3) Do I have a variety of types of supporting materials to make my speech interesting?

III. A formal outline is the last polished product, often required as part of formal speaking assignments. *(text pp. 248–263)*

  A. Formal outlines generally follow such established conventions as:

   1. the identification of speech topics, specific purposes, and thesis statements.

   2. the separation of main parts: introduction, body, and conclusion.

    a. Speakers should usually memorize introductions and conclusions.

   3. a system of numbering and lettering that displays coordination and subordination.

    a. Coordination requires that all statements at a given level belong to the same order and be similar in terms of importance.

    b. Subordination requires that related materials descend in importance from the more general and abstract main points to the more concrete and specific subpoints and sub-subpoints related to them.

   4. wording main points and subpoints as declarative sentences.

    a. Breaking clauses into sub- and sub-subpoints helps to simplify the structure and logic of a speech.

    b. Using parallel construction can also help to clarify sentence structure, as well as making messages easier to follow.

   5. having a title.

    a. Outside the classroom, titles function to attract audiences.

    b. Titles should not promise too much or deceive an audience.

   6. having a list of major sources consulted.

    a. For (MLA form) citations, see text pp. 260–262; for APA format, see pp. 267–268 of this IRM.

   7. indicating supporting materials and source citations at critical points in the outline.

    a. Speakers should have enough supporting materials to be effective for their particular audience.

    b. Internal citations should be brief and clear cues to the bibliography.

    c. Speakers should plan oral citations in their actual presentations.

IV. Once they have developed their formal outlines, speakers should prepare key-word outlines for use in their presentations. *(text pp. 263–266)*

  A. Key-word outlines reduce a formal outline to a few essential words that will jog a speaker's memory and remind him or her of the sequence of main points.

  B. Key-word outlines should fit on a few pieces of paper or index cards.

  C. Key terms should be large enough to be read at a glance.

  D. Speakers should use the same system of lettering and indention.

  E. Speakers may want to expand and alter their source citations and write down quotes verbatim so that they can be presented accurately.

  F. Speakers should practice their presentations from formal outlines a few times before developing and practicing from key-word outlines.

USING END-OF-CHAPTER ITEMS

Discussion *(text p. 267)*

1. Working in small groups, share a working outline for your next speech. Explain the strategy of your structure and show how your outline satisfies the principles of coordination and subordination. Demonstrate that your supporting materials will be adequate. Revise as appropriate in light of the discussion that follows.

    This exercise combines outside speech preparation with in-class discussion. Have your students prepare rough working outlines for homework, and bring them to class for discussion and analysis. Break the students into small groups to critique one another's outlines with respect to overall structure and the principles of coordination and subordination. You might combine this exercise with Discussion item 2 from Chapter 7 (IRM pp. 220–221) and have your students critique one another's introductions, transitions, conclusions, and supporting materials. You might also distribute the "Working Outline Work Sheet" (pp. 260–261) and "Working Outline Check List" (p. 262) for students to use as guides for this exercise. The Houghton Mifflin software program. "Speech Designer" also contains a format, check list, and guidelines for developing working outlines. Students should offer one another suggestions for improvement, and revise their outlines as appropriate.

2. Select one of the speeches from Appendix B and prepare a formal outline of it. Does this outline make clear the structure of the speech? Does it reveal any structural flaws? Can you see any different ways the speaker might have developed the speech? Present your thoughts on these questions in class discussion.

    This exercise may be used for homework or for in-class group analysis and discussion. It is good for illustrating how outlining can help clarify the structure and flow of a speech. For use in class, break your students into small groups, assigning each group one of the speeches for analysis. You might combine this exercise with Application item 1, Chapter 7, which provides more specific directions for the structural analysis of speeches. Distribute the "Formal Outline Work Sheet" (pp. 263–264) and "Formal Outline Check List" (p. 265) to help students complete this exercise. The following sample outline of "The 'Monument' at Wounded Knee" may be used to serve as a guide for your students.

Sample Outline of "The 'Monument' at Wounded Knee," by Cecile Larson

Introduction

   I.   We Americans are big on monuments.
      A. We erect monuments for heroes.
      B. We erect monuments to honor martyrs.
      C. Sometimes we erect monuments to commemorate victims.
  II.   Last summer I visited the "monument" at Wounded Knee.

Body

   I.   Let me tell you about Wounded Knee.
      A. Between 200 and 300 Sioux were massacred at Wounded Knee.
          1.   More than two-thirds were women and children.
          2.   Their remains share a common grave.
      B. Wounded Knee is located in the Pine Ridge Reservation in South Dakota.
          1.   The reservation is near Mount Rushmore.
          2.   The reservation is directly south of the Badlands National Park.
          3.   The monument is difficult to find.
  II.   There is no historic marker or official monument at Wounded Knee.
      A. There is a crudely lettered, hand-painted sign.
      B. The grave site is not well maintained.
      C. The "monument" is an old-fashioned granite cemetery marker.
          1.   It was erected by the families of the deceased.
          2.   Weeds surround the base.
      D. The adjacent cemetery is simple and poorly maintained.

Conclusion

   I.   We Americans are big on monuments.
  II.   But only when it makes us feel good.

Application *(text pp. 267–268)*

1. **Assume that the speeches you give in class this semester will be advertised in the campus newspaper. Develop titles that might help attract an audience.**

   A good speech title (outside the classroom) should both attract prospective audience members and orient them to a speech's topic and general purpose. For homework in preparation for this exercise, have your students develop titles for their next speeches, and write them on a sheet of scratch paper along with a topic and specific-purpose statement. Take them up, shuffle them, and read them aloud, having the rest of your students try to guess the speaker's topic and purpose. If they cannot guess it correctly, give them the topic and purpose and solicit suggestions for improved alternatives. Students might also constructively critique the titles' interest/ attention value, or lack thereof.

2. **See if you can "unjumble" the following outline of the body of a speech using coordination and subordination appropriately. What title would you suggest for this speech? (see text p. 268 for jumbled outline)**

   This exercise can be used to teach the principles of coordination and subordination, as well as coherently arranging the main ideas and supporting materials of speeches. The outline as given is excessively flawed in these respects. Break your students into groups and have them "unjumble" it. As there are so many points and subpoints, students may have trouble getting started, and you might consider giving them the main ideas to work with, or explaining the general flow of the message (how to hunt deer with a camera followed by its gratifications). Students might come up with any number of titles, such as "Hunting Without Killing." The following is an example of how the material might be more sensibly arranged. Emphasize that there may be other ways to arrange the material (especially sub- and sub-subpoints), and encourage your students to offer and defend alternative suggestions. Consider the principles of coordination and subordination with respect to arranging the various parts of this speech.

   Thesis statement: Deer hunting with a camera can be an exciting sport.

   I. Not all hunters are killers: the film-hunter celebrates life, not death.
      A. When deer appear, they always surprise you.
         1. Presents example of big doe walking under my tree stand.
         2. Presents example of coming upon a big buck after a long walk.
      B. The film-hunter becomes part of a beautiful scene.
         1. There is a profound quiet, a sense of mystery.
         2. Dawn is especially lovely in the woods.
         3. The woods in late fall are enchanting.
   II. Selecting the right camera for film-hunting is essential
      A. Certain features—like zoom lens—are required.
      B. The right camera can be no more expensive than a rifle.
   III. There are two main ways to hunt with a camera.
      A. Hunting from a stand can be a good way to capture a deer on film.
         1. Stands offer elevation above the line of sight and the line of scent.
         2. You need to arrange for a stand.
            a. You need to determine where to locate your stand.
            b. You can build a stand from scrap lumber.
            c. You can buy a portable stand.
      B. The stalk method is another way to hunt with a camera.
         1. Hunt into the wind and move slowly.
         2. Learn to recognize deer signs.
            a. Learn to recognize tracks and droppings.
            b. Learn to recognize rubs on trees and scrapes on the ground.

IV. Film hunting allows you to collect "trophies" you can enjoy forever.
    A. Display slide of the doe and discuss where and how it was shot.
    B. Display slide of the buck and discuss where and how it was shot.

ADDITIONAL ACTIVITIES

Scrambled Outlines

Purpose: To give your students an opportunity to distinguish and arrange the main points, subpoints, and supporting materials of a speech provided for them.

Directions: Break your students into small groups, and distribute the "Scrambled Outline" that follows. They should identify a thesis statement, a specific-purpose statement, an attention-getting/involvement strategy, a credibility strategy, a preview statement, two main points, six sub-points, three sub-subpoints, a summary statement, and a concluding device. The point of this exercise is to drill your students in the basic dynamics of outlining, and to illustrate how the different parts of a speech should fit together as a coherently structured message, using a simple design strategy and the principles of coordination and subordination. Your students should quickly recognize that this speech follows a basic problem-solution design strategy. There may be legitimate variations of the sample answer that follows (especially with sub- and sub-subpoints), and your students should be encouraged to offer and defend alternative positions for class discussion.

Scrambled Outline

1. There are existing organizations that students can support to help curb sexual assault rates.
2. Student crime watch patrols could help curb rates of theft and assault at night.
3. The per capita rate of sexual assault is higher on campus than in many of our larger cities.
4. Today we've discussed the growing problem of crime on campus, and what we, as students, can do about it.
5. Only you can lessen the chances that someday you or someone you love might become another victim.
6. As a victim of campus crime myself, I've become intimately concerned with this issue.
7. Only organized student involvement can help stem the tide of crime on campus.
8. We students should conduct a campaign again campus crime.
9. Last year seven cars and forty-two bicycles were stolen on campus.
10. "Take Back the Night" has been working to raise awareness of rape and its effects on women for years.
11. The problem of campus crime has been growing steadily for years.
12. Can anyone imagine being robbed or even raped at gunpoint in your own dorm building?
13. Student representatives could help pressure the administration to tighten campus security measures.
14. Rates of physical and violent assaults reported have increased 17% since 1990.
15. Today, I'm going to talk to you about the growing problem of crime on campus, and offer some actions we can take to help stem the tide.
16. "Men Against Rape" needs volunteers to escort women on campus during evening hours.
17. Students could form a campuswide "crime watch" program that works in cooperation with campus security.
18. To persuade my audience to conduct a campaign against campus crime.

Unscrambled Outline

8. *Thesis statement:* We students should conduct a campaign again campus crime.
18. *Specific purpose:* To persuade my audience to conduct a campaign against campus crime.

Introduction

12. *Attention strategy:* Can anyone imagine being robbed or even raped at gunpoint in your own dorm building?
6. *Credibility strategy:* As a victim of campus crime myself, I've become intimately concerned with this issue.
15. *Preview:* Today, I'm going to talk to you about the growing problem of crime on campus, and offer some actions we can take to help stem the tide.

Body

11. I. The problem of campus crime has been growing steadily for years.
14. A. Rates of physical and violent assaults reported have increased 17% since 1990.
9. B. Last year seven cars and forty-two bicycles were stolen on campus.
3. C. The per capita rate of sexual assault is higher on campus than in many of our larger cities.

7. II. Only organized student involvement can help stem the tide of crime on campus.
13. A. Student representatives could help pressure the administration to tighten campus security measures.
17. B. Students could form a campuswide "crime watch" program that works in cooperation with campus security.
2. 1. Student crime watch patrols could help curb rates of theft and assault at night.
1. C. There are existing organizations that students can support to help curb sexual assault rates.
10. 1. "Take Back the Night" has been working to raise awareness of rape and its effects on women for years.
16. 2. "Men Against Rape" needs volunteers to escort women on campus during evening hours.

Conclusion

4. *Summary statement:* Today we've discussed the growing problem of crime on campus, and what we, as students, can do about it.
5. *Concluding remarks:* Only you can lessen the chances that someday you or someone you love might become another victim.

Impromptu Outlining

Purpose: To provide your students an opportunity to prepare impromptu outlines of given subjects.

Directions: This exercise works well as a small-group or general class discussion piece, and may be used in conjunction with the "Impromptu Structuring" activity in Chapter 7, p. 223. You might distribute either the "Working Outline Work Sheet" (pp. 260–261) or the "Formal Outline Work Sheet" (pp. 263–265) and "Formal Outline Check List" (p. 266) for use as a guide. Write an assortment of impromptu speech topics on small pieces of paper, place them in a bag or container, and have representatives of each group draw two or three from which to choose one for use in this exercise (for a list of potential topics, see Chapter 7 of this IRM, on p. 235). The groups should outline a speech around their chosen topic that follows a coherent design with two or three main points, and that follows the principles of coordination and subordination. They should include specific purpose and thematic statements, strategies for introductions and conclusions, and suggestions for appropriate supporting materials. Allow ten to twenty minutes for the students to complete this phase of the exercise, before presenting their outlines for class discussion.

Outlining Specific Speech Designs

Purpose: To provide your students an opportunity to develop outlines for speeches following specific design strategies.

Directions: This exercise is good for emphasizing the strengths and weaknesses of the different design patterns for different topics and specific purposes, as well as the basic principles of outlining. Follow the directions for the preceding "Impromptu Outlining" exercise, except assign each group three design strategies to use from the following list. The patterns listed below are covered in Chapters 12 and 13 of the text and in the "Speech Designer" computer software program. Have each group spend ten to twenty minutes working on these before presenting their ideas for class discussion. Students should consider the relative strengths and weaknesses of their assigned designs for their topic, as well as other designs or combinations of designs that might be more effective and why. If time allows, have them develop rough key-word outlines following an appropriate design. A list of the major speech designs follows (the outline formats for these designs may be found where indicated).

1. Spatial design   (Chapter 12, this IRM, pp. 358–360)
2. Sequential design   (Chapter 12, this IRM, pp. 363–365)
3. Categorical design   (Chapter 12, this IRM, pp. 368–370)
4. Comparative design   (Chapter 12, this IRM, pp. 373–375)
5. Causation design   (Chapter 12, this IRM, pp. 378–380)
6. Problem-solution design   (Chapter 13, this IRM, pp. 400–402)
7. Motivated sequence design   (Chapter 13, this IRM, pp. 412–415)
8. Refutative design   (Chapter 13, this IRM, pp. 418–422)

The Metaphors of Outlining

Purpose: To give your students an alternative approach to the significance of effective outlining.

Directions: This exercise is useful for homework or as a small-group activity followed by in-class discussion. It employs insights on metaphor to help your students visualize the significance of outlining coherent and structurally sound speeches. You might review some basics on metaphor (text Chapter 10), emphasizing its potential for shaping and illuminating abstract/complex ideas and propositions. Public speaking teachers have long used a variety of metaphorical images, such as bodies, pyramids, wagon wheels, flow charts, trees, and even combat formations, to effectively describe and teach the process of structuring effective messages.

In Chapter 7 we argue that an effectively structured speech can be likened to a bridge of meaning that joins speakers with listeners. If this is so, how would your students describe the importance of a speech's outline in facilitating effective public communication? For instance, if a speech is like a bridge, students may compare its outline to either an architectural blueprint or a steel frame that supports the bridge and holds its parts together despite the presence of physical distractions. The major sections of the bridge might represent main ideas, building materials its supporting information, and stress relief points between main sections its transitions. The road traveling across the bridge might represent the central thesis that gives meaning, direction, and purpose to a speech. Two land masses separated by "troubled waters" (communication barriers and distortions) could represent the separate experiential fields of speakers and their audiences, to be joined by the process of successful communication. Finally, the fact that bridges can be crossed by both sides can help to emphasize the stake and responsibility of all participants in the process. Encourage your students to be creative and stretch their imaginations. Have them develop their own alternative images that they think may better capture the process of structuring speeches and explain why. Following the analysis, they should share their ideas in a class discussion focusing on their relative strengths and weaknesses. You might have the class decide on favorite consensus images to illustrate the various aspects of outlining and its role in effective public communication.

Idea Maps

Purpose: To provide students with an alternative method of organizing ideas for a speech.

Directions: Provide students with a copy of the idea-mapping handout on the next page. Have them select a general topic area and write it in a circle on the middle of a sheet of paper. Next, have them free-associate to come up with words related to the general topic area and enter them on the paper in circles. The more general words should be close to and connected to the general topic; the more specific words should be further from the general topic and connected to the words with which they most closely fit. Advise students that they may have to make several maps to develop the structure of their speech. Have them review their original maps and correct the connections so that they make the most sense to them. You may also wish to take one segment of the "collecting antiques" sample and have them further elaborate on it. For example, you could take the "textiles" segment and have them work breakouts for the four entries connected to it (e.g., "quilts" might be broken out into "patchwork quilts," "crazy quilts," and "appliqued quilts").

Mind Mapping Diagram

mind mapping

- *helps* → **ideas**
  - *come to* → **mind**
- *reduces your* → **message**
  - *to its* → **essence**
- *helps show* → **organization**
  - *and* → **framework**
    - for your ideas
- *promotes* → **critical thinking**
  - *by revealing* → **gaps in logic**

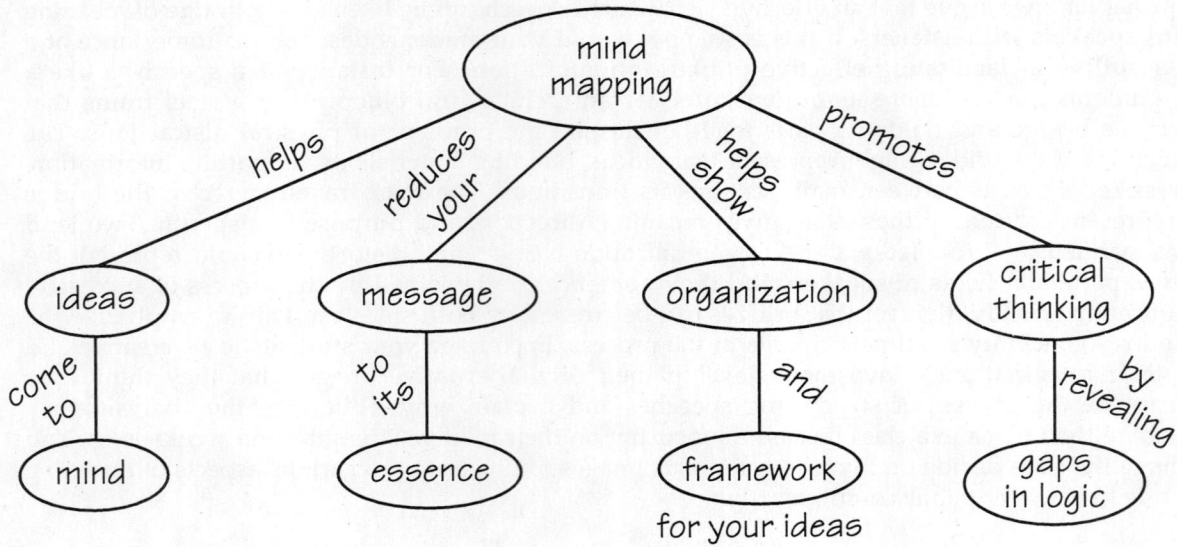

Adapted from Dave Ellis, *Becoming a Master Student*, Seventh Edition, p. 125. Copyright © 1994 by Houghton Mifflin Company. Used by permission.

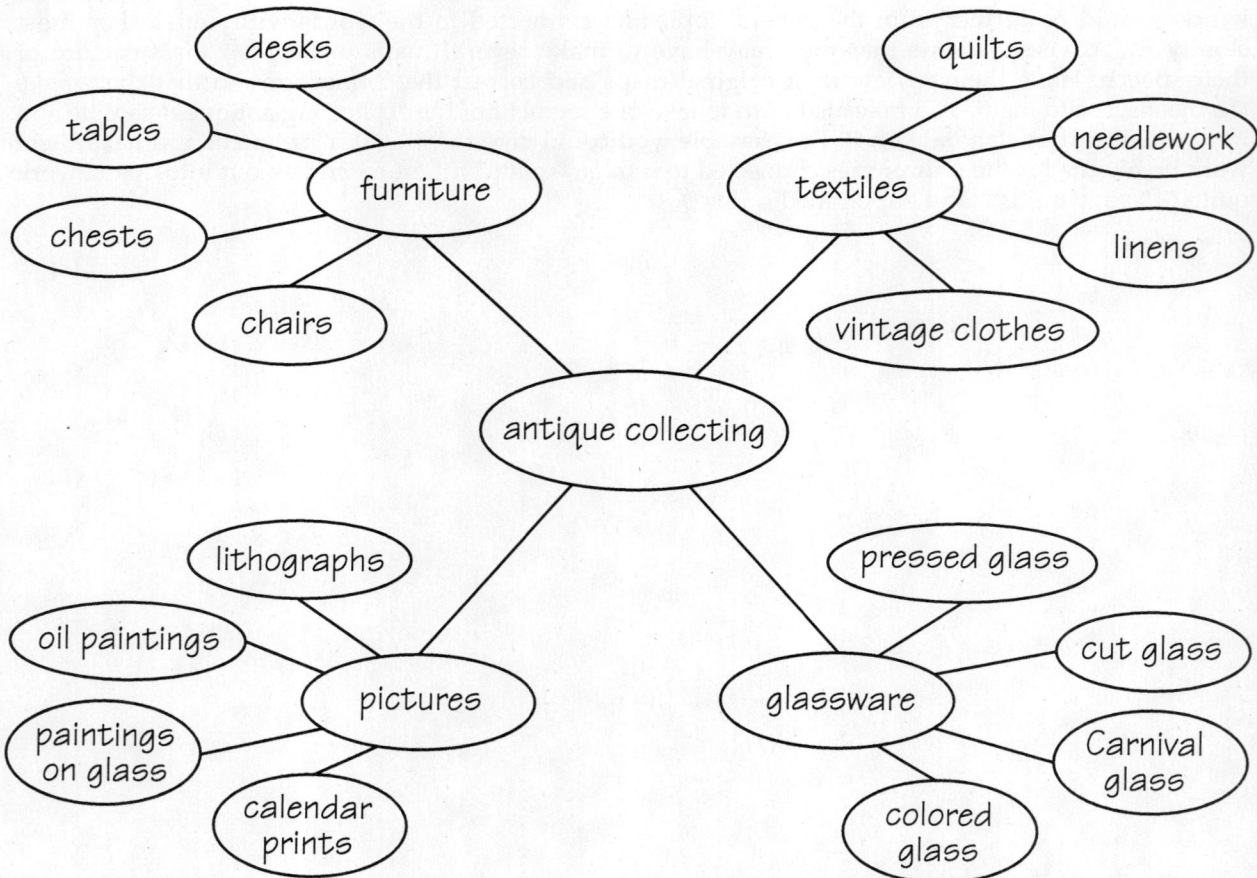

Antique Collecting Diagram

antique collecting

- **furniture**
  - desks
  - tables
  - chests
  - chairs
- **textiles**
  - quilts
  - needlework
  - linens
  - vintage clothes
- **pictures**
  - lithographs
  - oil paintings
  - paintings on glass
  - calendar prints
- **glassware**
  - pressed glass
  - cut glass
  - Carnival glass
  - colored glass

SUPPLEMENTARY MATERIALS

Films and Videos

"Organizing Your Message," Agency for Instructional Television, color, 15 minutes.

"The Outline," Films for the Humanities, color, 15 minutes.

"Planning Your Speech," Coronet/MTI Film and Video, color, 13 minutes.

Computer Software

"Speech Designer" Houghton Mifflin, 1991.

"Inspiration," Inspiration Software, 1994.

Transparencies and Handouts

Preparing a Key-Word Outline (Transparency 8.1)

Numbering and Lettering an Outline (Transparency 8.2)

Working Outline Work Sheet

Working Outline Check List

Formal Outline Work Sheet

Formal Outline Check List

APA Reference Formats

PREPARING A KEY-WORD OUTLINE

1. Underline all key words or phrases in your formal outline.

2. Copy the key words or phrases onto a single sheet of paper or note cards, using the same format as in your formal outline.

3. If using note cards, have one for your introduction, one for each main point, and one for your conclusion.

4. Include citations on your outline where needed.

5. Do not use full sentences in your key-word outline unless you must read a quote.

6. Cut anything you can remember easily.

7. If using note cards, number them in case you drop them.

8. Print or type your outline using large letters that you can read without straining.

NUMBERING AND LETTERING AN OUTLINE

I. First main point.

A. Subpoint 1: Supports I, equal to B.

1. Sub-subpoint 1: Supports A, equal to 2.
   a. Sub-sub-subpoint 1: Supports 1, equal to b.
   b. Sub-sub-subpoint 2: Supports 1, equal to a.

2. Sub-subpoint 2: Supports A, equal to 1.
   a. Sub-sub-subpoint 1: Supports 2, equal to b.
   b. Sub-sub-subpoint 2: Supports 2, equal to a.

B. Subpoint 2: Supports I, equal to A.

1. Sub-subpoint 1: Supports B, equal to 2.
   a. Sub-sub-subpoint 1: Supports 1, equal to b.
   b. Sub-sub-subpoint 2: Supports 1, equal to a.

2. Sub-subpoint 2: Supports B, equal to 1.
   a. Sub-sub-subpoint 1: Supports 2, equal to b.
   b. Sub-sub-subpoint 2: Supports 2, equal to a.

II. Second main point . . .

WORKING OUTLINE WORK SHEET
(page 1)

Topic: _____

Specific purpose: _____

_____

Thesis statement: _____

_____

INTRODUCTION

Attention-getting material: _____

_____

Credibility material: _____

_____

Preview: _____

_____

(Transition to body of speech)

_____

BODY

First main point: _____

   Subpoint: _____

   Subpoint: _____

(Transition to second main point)

_____

WORKING OUTLINE WORK SHEET
(page 2)

Second main point: _____

    Subpoint: _____

    Subpoint: _____

(Transition to third main point)

_____

Third main point: _____

    Subpoint: _____

    Subpoint: _____

(Transition to fourth main point)

_____

Fourth main point: _____

    Subpoint: _____

    Subpoint: _____

(Transition to conclusion)

_____

CONCLUSION

Summary: _____

_____

Concluding remarks: _____

_____

WORKING OUTLINE CHECK LIST

_____ 1. My topic, specific purpose, and thesis statement are clearly stated.

_____ 2. My introduction contains attention-getting material, establishes my credibility, and previews my message.

_____ 3. My main points represent the most important ideas about my topic.

_____ 4. I have an appropriate number of main points to cover my material in the time allotted.

_____ 5. Each subpoint breaks its main point into more specific detail.

_____ 6. My conclusion contains a summary and concluding remarks that reinforce and reflect upon the meaning of my speech.

_____ 7. I have planned transitions to use between the introduction and body, between each pair of main points, and between the body and conclusion of my speech.

FORMAL OUTLINE WORK SHEET
(page 1)

TITLE: _____

Topic: _____

Specific purpose: _____

_____

Thesis statement: _____

_____

INTRODUCTION

Attention-getting material: _____

_____

Credibility material: _____

_____

Preview: _____

_____

(Transition to body of speech)

_____

BODY

I. First main point: _____

    A. Subpoint or supporting material: _____

_____

    B. Subpoint or supporting material: _____

_____

FORMAL OUTLINE WORK SHEET
(page 2)

(Transition to second main point)

_____

II. Second main point: _____

    A. Subpoint or supporting material: _____

_____

    B. Subpoint or supporting material: _____

_____

(Transition to third main point)

_____

III. Third main point: _____

    A. Subpoint or supporting material: _____

_____

    B. Subpoint or supporting material: _____

_____

(Transition to fourth main point)

_____

FORMAL OUTLINE WORK SHEET
(page 3)

IV. Fourth main point: _____

    A. Subpoint or supporting material: _____

_____

    B. Subpoint or supporting material: _____

_____

(Transition to conclusion)

_____

CONCLUSION

Summary: _____

_____

_____

Concluding remarks: _____

_____

_____

Works Consulted:

FORMAL OUTLINE CHECKLIST

_____ 1. My topic and specific purpose are clearly stated.

_____ 2. My thesis statement is written as a complete, declarative sentence.

_____ 3. My introduction contains material to create attention, establish my credibility, and preview my message.

_____ 4. My main points represent the most important ideas about my topic.

_____ 5. My main points are approximately equal in importance.

_____ 6. My main points are stated as complete, declarative sentences.

_____ 7. Each main point is supported by facts, statistics, testimony, examples, or narratives.

_____ 8. My subpoints are divisions of the main points they follow.

_____ 9. My subpoints are more specific than the main points they follow.

_____ 10. My conclusion contains a summary that reinterprets my message and concluding remarks that reflect on the meaning and significance of my speech.

_____ 11. I have provided transitions where they are needed to make my speech flow smoothly.

_____ 12. I have compiled a list of works consulted in the preparation of my speech.

APA REFERENCE FORMATS

Books. For a book by one author, list the author's name (last name first), date of publication, book title, and publication information. For example:

> Damasio, Antonio. (1944). *Descartes' error.* New York: Putnam.

If the book has two or three authors, list the lead author's name (last name first), followed by the second and third authors' names (last names first), date of publication, title, and publication information.

> Combs, J. E., & Dan Nimmo, D. (1993). *The new propaganda.* White Plains, NY: Longman.

If the book has a corporate author, use the name of the corporation in place of the given name of an author: For example:

> Boston Women's Health Book Collective. (1973). *Our bodies, ourselves.* New York: Simon & Schuster.

If your material comes from a signed article in a reference book, list the author's name (last name first), date of publication, the title of the article, the title of the reference book preceded by "In," the volume and/or edition, and publication information. For example:

> Tobias, Richard. (1991). James Thurber. In *Encyclopedia Americana.* (Vol. 20, pp. 246–250). New York: Encyclopedia Americana.

If your material comes from an unsigned article in a reference book, list the title of the article, the date of publication, the title of the reference book preceded by "In," and the publication information. For example:

> Twyla Tharp. (1992). In *Who's who of American women.* 17th ed. New York: Who's Who.

If your material comes from a government document, list the source of the document, the date of publication, the title of the document, the edition (if given), and publication information. For example:

> United States Cong. House Committee on the Judiciary. (1980). *Immigration and nationality act with amendments and notes on related laws.* 7th ed. Washington: U.S. Government Printing Office.

Periodicals. The general format is the same for all periodicals. List the author's name (last name first), followed by the date of publication, title of the article, name of the periodical, volume number if applicable, and page numbers. For example:

> Wall, Dennis. (1995, November). Chimayó weavers. *New Mexico,* 40–47.

If the author of the article is not specified, begin with the title of the article, then follow the same general format. For example:

> Ozone Mystery Solved. (1995, April/May). *National Wildlife,* 6.

Materials taken from daily newspapers should include the edition of the paper if applicable, full date of publication, and the section as well as the page numbers. For example:

> Perrusquia, Marc. (1995, November 5). Farewell to innocence: School kids take up arms. *Memphis Commercial Appeal,* final ed. A: 1.

CD-ROMs, Online Databases, and Computer Networks. When citing material from these sources, you should provide the following types of information: author's name (last name first), date of publication, article title, periodical title (if appropriate), inclusive pages, publication medium (e.g., CD-ROM, online database), and name of vendor or computer service. The formats for referencing such sources are in a state of flux because they are so new.

If your material comes from a CD-ROM, use the following format:

> Hughes, Robert. (1992, February 3). The fraying of America. *Time*, 44–53. *Time Almanac*. CD-ROM. Compact, 1994.

If your material comes from an online database, use the following format:

> Gray, John. (1992, October 5). The virtues of toleration. *National Review*, 28–33. *Magazine Database Plus*. On-line. Compuserve.

If your material comes from a computer network electronic journal, newsletter, or conference, use the following format:

> Schreibman, Vigdor. (1993, March 8). Closing the 'values gap.' *FINS*. n.pag. On-line. Internet.

If your material comes from a computer network electronic mail, use the following format:

> Pierson, Michael. (1995, April 30). "Internet Freedom." On-line posting: alt.culture. Internet. *Usenet*.

Miscellaneous References. You may use other sources of information in your speech, such as radio or television programs, films, interviews, advertisements, lectures, or speeches.

For a radio or television show or film, use the following format:

> Tatge, Catherine (Executive Producer). (1988, May 23). *Moyers: Joseph Campbell and the Power of Myth*. New York: Public Broadcasting Service.

For an interview, use the following format:

> Frentz, C. R. (1991, July 25). Telephone interview.

For an advertisement, use the following format:

> Chevrolet. (1995, July). Send yourself to camp. Advertisement. *National Geographic*. 142–143.

For a speech or lecture, use the following format:

> Webb, Lynn. (1996, March). "Presidential Address." Presented at the meeting of the Southern States Communication Association, Memphis, TN.

READINGS FOR ENRICHMENT

See guide to journal abbreviations on p. 37.

Avadian, Brenda, and Marilyn Thanos. "Speechmapping: The Road Through Speech Preparation and Delivery." *SCT* (Spring 1988), 14–15.

Boyd, Stephen D., and Mary Ann Renz. *Organization and Outlining: A Workbook for Students in a Basic Speech Course.* Indianapolis: Bobbs-Merrill, 1985.

Brown, Kevin James. "'Spidergrams': An Aid for Teaching Outlining and Organization." *SCT* (Spring 1990), 4–5.

Ensign, Russell L. "The 'Arrow Through Ass's Ribs' Outline: A Teaching Aid for the Basic Course." *SCT* (Fall 1993), 10–11.

Gschwend, Laura L. "Outlining Relay." *SCT* (Fall 1995), 8–10.

Hufman, Melody. "The Maze as an Instructional Instrument for Public Speaking," *CE* (Jan. 1985), 63–68.

Logue, Cal M. "An Exercise in Inventive Analysis." *CE* (Apr. 1982), 149–150.

Mayhew, Virginia. "Outline the Pictures." *SCT* (Winter 1987), 4.

Schiff, Roselyn L., et al. *Communication Strategy: A Guide to Speech Preparation.* Glenview, Ill.: Scott, Foresman, 1981.

West, Valerie Y. "Newspaper Outlines." *SCT* (Summer 1995), 12.

CHAPTER 9
Presentation Aids

OBJECTIVES

- To help your students appreciate the advantages of using presentation aids in their speeches.

- To help your students understand what types of presentation aids work best in different situations.

- To teach your students how to use presentation aids.

- To help your students learn to plan, design, and prepare presentation aids.

SUGGESTIONS FOR TEACHING

Most instructors require the use of presentation aids with at least one of their major speaking assignments. Their use is best taught through a combination of lecture and demonstration [see Bohn and Jabusch, "The Effect of Four Methods of Instruction on the Use of Visual Aids," *WJSC* (Summer 1982), 252–265]. We've included an overhead projection, "Graphic Messages," and handout, "Check List for Using Presentation Aids," to help guide discussion of the aids many of your students will be using (IRM, pp. 283 and 284). We offer a short video on using presentation aids as part of our ancillary package for adopters.

   We suggest that you begin accumulating an assortment of aids used by students in your classes. Most are more than willing to part with them after they have finished their speeches (often they simply throw them out). For contrast, collect presentation aids that are both very effective and very poor, using the latter for discussions of how they could be improved. They should prove useful for demonstrating why pastel colors are not suited for lettering and why you shouldn't cram too much onto one presentation aid. In addition to teaching about the various types of aids, their appropriate uses, and how to construct them, impress upon your students that these aids should be used to illustrate and emphasize their most important ideas and information. Remind them that cute drawings and ornamental afterthoughts may be more of a distraction than an aid to understanding because they will distract audiences from the important parts of their messages. There are many exercises and activities in this chapter to illustrate the appropriateness of different aids for different messages. Some have your students propose their own ideas for discussion and analysis. Others have them consider problem situations and solutions for dealing with them, and critique the use of visuals in advertising. We also offer a short speaking activity to provide your students with an opportunity to practice integrating presentation aids into their actual presentations. Finally, we suggest small-group consultations in which your students can critique one another's ideas for presentation aids to be used in upcoming speaking assignments.

CHAPTER OUTLINE

I. Presentation aids can increase the clarity and effectiveness of a speech. *(text pp. 274–276)*
   A. Presentation aids can supplement abstract verbal messages with sensory representations. Presentation aids help speeches in the following ways:
      1. Presentation aids enhance understanding.
      2. Presentation aids add authenticity.
      3. Presentation aids add variety.
      4. Presentation aids may improve your delivery skills.
      5. Presentation aids help your speech have lasting impact.
      6. Neat, attractively designed presentation aids enhance credibility.
   B. Presentation aids are almost mandatory in most organizational settings.

II. The kinds of presentation aids available are limited only by the speaker's imagination. *(text pp. 276–288)*
   A. People can function as presentation aids.
      1. The speaker is the first presentation aid an audience sees.
         a. Gestures and actions can help illustrate ideas.
         b. Dress and personal grooming can enhance a presentation.
      2. Other people can be used as presentation aids.
         a. They can demonstrate described actions.
         b. They must be willing and know what is expected of them.
   B. Objects and models can function as effective presentation aids.
      1. Any object used should be small enough to carry and large enough to be easily seen by everyone in the audience.
         a. If possible, objects should be kept out of sight until they are needed to prevent them from distracting the audience's attention.
         b. Inanimate objects generally make better presentation aids than living things.
         c. Speakers should be wary of dangerous, illegal, or potentially offensive objects.
         d. Objects are often appropriate for speeches of demonstration.
      2. Models are useful when subjects are unavailable, too large, too small, too valuable, or too fragile to risk bringing to class. They should be:
         a. representative and made to scale.
         b. easy for everyone to see and understand.
   C. Graphics include sketches, maps, graphs, charts, and textual materials.
      1. Sketches or diagrams can offer simplified representations of items and ideas.
      2. Maps are good for spatial descriptions.
         a. They should be simple and free of any extraneous information.
         b. They should be carefully worked into a presentation.
      3. Graphs can help make statistical information more understandable.
         a. Pie graphs show the size of a subject's parts in relation to one another, and to the whole.
         b. Bar graphs show comparisons and contrasts between two or more items or groups.
         c. Line graphs help to demonstrate changes over time and are especially useful for indicating trends of growth or decline.
            (1) When plotting more than one line, be certain listeners can distinguish the lines.
         d. Mountain graphs are variations of line graphs that use different colors to fill in the areas.
      4. Charts can provide convenient (if sometimes oversimplified) summaries of processes and relationships.
         a. Flow charts may be used to show power and responsibility relationships, or the steps of a process.
         b. When speakers feel tempted to clutter up a flow chart too much, they might resort to sequence charts shown in succession.

      c.   Charts often use pictographs or visually symbolic representations.

    5.   Textual graphics are lists of phrases, words, or numbers.

      a.   Key terms can help audiences follow complicated speeches.

      b.   Bulleted lists of information are frequently used textual graphics.

      c.   Acronyms use the initial letters of words to implant ideas in the minds of an audience so that messages are more memorable.

D. Pictures as presentation aids have advantages and disadvantages.

    1.   While they help authenticate a point, they often contain distracting details, are too small to be seen clearly, and will distract audiences if circulated during a speech.

    2.   Speakers should make enlargements of photographs.

    3.   As with all presentation aids, speakers should display them as needed then put them away.

III. Many media are available for developing presentation aids. *(text pp. 288–297)*

A. A flip chart is a large, unlined tablet used on an easel.

    1.   Flip charts are cheap, convenient, good for presenting a series of aids, and easy to display.

    2.   They can be prepared in advance, or used for spontaneous aids and sequence presentations.

    3.   Speakers should keep each page as simple as possible.

B. Poster board is frequently used to make presentation aids.

    1.   It is well suited for sketches, maps, charts, or graphs.

    2.   Speakers should plan and practice how they will display their posters.

      a.   Posters should be concealed until used.

      b.   Speakers should use transitions to introduce and conclude references to presentation aids.

C. Handouts are useful when subjects are complex, when lots of statistical information is presented, or when speakers introduce new vocabularies.

    1.   Handouts should be distributed before a presentation only when they are to be referred to during the presentation itself.

    2.   Handouts should never be distributed during a presentation.

D. Chalk- or marker boards are available in most classrooms and conference rooms.

    1.   Spelling key terms can help focus audience attention.

    2.   They can help with spontaneous adaptations to audience feedback.

    3.   Speakers should write in letters large enough to be read from the back of the room.

    4.   Speakers should not overuse the chalkboard.

E. Overhead projections and slides make graphics easier to see.

    1.   Slides are more effective with larger audiences.

    2.   Speakers using transparencies:

      a.   do not have to completely darken the room.

      b.   can revise them while showing them.

      c.   can make eye contact with their audiences more easily while using them.

    3.   Unless equipment is remote-controlled, projections and slides force a speaker to stand next to the equipment.

    4.   Speakers should always check equipment ahead of time and be familiar with its operation.

    5.   Speakers should not substitute slides or transparencies for an actual presentation.

F. Video- and audiotapes can authenticate a speech, adding variety to a presentation.

    1.   Videos can help transport audiences to distant, dangerous, or otherwise unavailable locations.

      a.   They should be short and carefully cued and edited.

    2.   Speakers should check the availability of equipment.

G. Computer-generated materials and computer-assisted presentations are becoming the norm in academic and business settings.

1. Most personal computers can now be used to generate sketches, maps, graphs, charts, textual graphics for handouts, transparencies, and slides.
   a. More sophisticated computers can reproduce pictures, add animation, and edit videotapes.
2. To make effective presentation aids, students need access to spreadsheet, word processing, graphics, and/or presentation software.
   a. *Media View* is in the public domain and can be downloaded from the World Wide Web.
3. Computer-assisted presentations can bring together texts, pictures, and artwork into slides, videos, animations, and audio materials.
4. Speakers should not let showing off their fancy hardware take the place of substantive presentations.
H. Because of their power to deceive, presentation aids raise important ethical questions.
   1. Modern technology is increasing our capacity to deceive using visuals.
   2. As most people are prone to believe what they see, our ethical position is:
      a. Speakers should alert listeners when they are manipulating images to forcefully bring home a point.
      b. Speakers should be ready to defend their illusions as representative of some underlying truth.
      c. Listeners should cultivate a healthy skepticism of visual images.
      d. Listeners should always request further confirmation when visual images are used to support important claims.

IV. Speakers should carefully plan, design, prepare, and practice using presentation aids. *(text pp. 297–302)*
   A. Presentation aids should adhere to basic principles of design.
      1. They must be easily visible to the entire audience.
         a. Letters should be large and in dark colors.
      2. They should emphasize the central ideas and information that a speech emphasizes.
      3. They should be balanced and pleasing to the eye.
         a. A focal point should balance graphic and textual materials.
         b. There should be adequate margins around the material.
      4. Designs present ethical concerns because they can misrepresent reality.
         a. Speakers should cite sources of information on their actual aids.
   B. Some basic principles of color can also enhance presentation aids.
      1. Color can arouse attention and interest.
      2. Color can influence moods and impressions.
         a. Red tends to excite, whereas blue suggests power and stability.
      3. Combining colors can convey subtle nuances of meaning.
         a. Analogous color schemes (adjacent on the color wheel) suggest compatible differences.
         c. Complementary color schemes (opposite on the color wheel) suggest tension and contrast.
      4. Colors should stand out from the background.
   C. Preparing effective presentation aids takes time.
      1. Rough drafts allow speakers to see how presentation aids will look.
      2. Speakers should avoid cluttering one presentation aid with too much information.
      3. Speakers should practice using their rough drafts.

V. The following guidelines can help speakers prepare and use presentation aids effectively. *(text pp. 302–303).*
   A. Practice using your aid. Integrate it smoothly into your message.
   B. Go to the room where you will be speaking to decide where you will place your aid before and during your speech. Determine what will be needed to display it.

   C. Check out any electronic equipment to be used in advance. Be sure that you can operate it and that it is working properly.

   D. Do not display your aid until you are ready to use it. When you are finished using it, cover or remove it so that it does not distract from your presentation.

   E. Do not stand directly in front of your presentation aid. Stand to the side and maintain eye contact with your listeners. You want both yourself and your aid to be visible.

   F. When using the aid, point to what you are talking about. Don't leave your audience searching.

   G. Do not distribute materials during your speech. Distribute handouts before or after.

   H. Do not use too many presentation aids in a single speech.

USING END-OF-CHAPTER ITEMS

Discussion *(text pp. 304–305)*

1. **Watch news programs on television or read *USA Today* for several days and observe how graphics and pictures are combined with words to convey meaning. What techniques are most and least useful? Be prepared to discuss examples of effective and ineffective usage in class.**

This exercise works well as a combined homework and in-class discussion activity, or you might collect samples yourself and bring them to class. The news media commonly use video, still photographs, textual graphics, charts, graphs, and maps to supplement or even confirm an oral commentary. Focus discussion on the appropriateness of presentation aids for making messages more comprehensible and memorable, the types of information illustrated most often (statistics, visual examples, textual information), and how TV anchorpersons integrate references into their presentations and deal with technical mishaps. You might also consider the similarities and differences between the news media and public speaking with respect to using presentation aids, and how observed strategies might be adapted for use in your students' speeches.

2. **Recall classes in which your instructors used presentation aids. Did these aids serve one or more of the basic functions discussed in this chapter:**

    • **Did they aid your understanding?**
    • **Did they authenticate a point?**
    • **Did they enhance your instructors' presentation skills?**
    • **Did they enhance their credibility?**
    • **Did they add variety?**
    • **Did they give more impact to messages?**

Why or why not?

The experiences of students in your class may vary widely. Most will have had instructors who used the chalkboard poorly, or who did not know how to properly operate technical equipment. Students should be discouraged from simply trashing professors they do not like, and steered toward the lessons that can be learned from them—for example, the importance of eye contact, legible presentation aids, knowledge of operating equipment, and cueing up videotapes before a presentation. Positive examples might include the sparing use of the chalkboard to note important words and phrases, projections of outlines that help students follow complicated lectures, handouts that are useful for studying, and the use of scale models. Try to discuss these in terms of what made them effective and what students might learn from them to improve the quality of their own presentation aids.

3. **Describe situations in which speakers either would or would not be effective visual aids for their own speeches. Have you ever seen examples outside your classroom in which the appearance of speakers worked against their message?**

Speakers are not effective visual aids when they send mixed messages to an audience. For example, a person who is obviously out of shape would make a poor visual aid for a message on physical fitness. A speaker's appearance should not detract from his or her message. Gaudy jewelry or loud, inappropriate clothing can impair the ethos of the speaker and compete with his or her messages for audience attention. Speakers are effective visual aids for their messages when their appearance is consistent with and reinforces what they have to say. They should dress in consideration of the expectations and conventions of their audiences and specific speaking occasions.

4. **Look through a recent popular magazine and analyze the advertisements according to the principles of design discussed here. Do the visual aspects of the ads work in concert with the words to emphasize the message? Which of the ads seem most balanced and pleasing to the eye? Do any of the ads violate the rules of simplicity and ease of comprehension? Which of the ads use color most and least effectively? Bring the most interesting ads to class and discuss your findings.**

This exercise may be used for in-class group discussion or homework. You might have your students each find three or four appropriate ads for homework, or you might preselect them yourself for class discussion. If you use this for homework, remind your students to make photocopies, and not to deface library materials.

Advertisements are designed by professionals—they tend to be well balanced and simple. They often use visual illustrations of their products or "happy customers" along with textual information, and sometimes they use graphic representations. There are important differences between the presentation aids used in advertising and those used effectively in speeches. Magazine ads rely more heavily on photographs, and can pack in a lot more information. Many of them purposely violate basic principles of form and message agreement for dramatic effect. You might ask students to find ads that violate any of the principles of design or color, and offer suggestions for improvement. You might also have them consider how the visual formats of ads might be adapted for use in constructing presentation aids for their own speeches, and what types of messages (besides selling a product) they might be used to illustrate.

Application *(text p. 305)*

1. **Select a speech from Appendix B and prepare the rough draft of a presentation aid that might have been used with it. Would the aid have helped the speech? What other options did you consider?**

This works well for homework or for small-group discussion. The purpose of this exercise is to demonstrate that some speeches would not benefit from presentation aids, and that more than one type of presentation aid may be appropriate for any given speech. Before drawing up any rough drafts, your students should spend time discussing (1) whether presentation aids would really be appropriate and effective for this particular speech, and (2) what various alternatives or combinations of presentation aids might be more effective. Although your students should come up with their own suggestions, here are some possibilities with the student speeches from the appendix.

Rod Nishikawa, "Free at Last." Presentation aids are rarely used in speeches of introduction.

Laura Haskins, "The Magnificent Juggler." Although presentation aids are rarely used in speeches of introduction, if she had managed to juggle three balls while making her introductory "spiel," the effect would have been very dramatic.

Cecile Larson, "The 'Monument' at Wounded Knee." This speech paints vivid word pictures, and the introduction of a presentation aid could disrupt its flow. Enlarged photographs of slides of the gravesite might have been used in the background to reinforce her descriptive language. She might also have used a simplified map showing the location of Wounded Knee.

Stephen Lee, "The Trouble with Numbers." Although most speeches dealing with statistics can benefit from the use of charts or graphs, this particular speech criticizes the misuse of numbers but does not try to explain numerical data. The only place at which a presentation aid might have been effective is in the introduction: The statistical profile of the "average American" could have been presented as a textual graphic on a poster, transparency projection, or slide.

Bonnie Marshal, "Living Wills: Insuring Your Right to Choose." The material near the end of this speech on how to insure your personal right to choose might have been summarized in a handout to be distributed after the conclusion of the speech. The handout would have assured that the audience knew where they could write for more information on living wills.

Gina Norman, "Secondhand Smoke." In this speech, Gina used a visual aid that shows the statistical data on the effects of environmental tobacco smoke.

John Scipio, "Martin Luther King at the Mountaintop." This speech might have benefited from the use of some short video clips of King speaking or scenes from civil rights activities of the 1960s.

2. **What kinds of presentation aids might be most useful for the following speech topics?**

   a. **Nuclear waste disposal sites in the United States**
   b. **What to do in case of snakebite**
   c. **History of the stock market over the last decade**
   d. **How the federal budget is divided into major categories**
   e. **Administering your university: Who has the power to do what to whom?**
   f. **How we got the modern telephone: The growth of an invention**
   g. **Hunger in Africa: The human story**
   h. **The sounds of navigation and what they mean**

Suggestions for discussion:

   a. A simplified outline map of the United States (or the immediate state or area) showing nuclear waste disposal sites in red or with pictographic skulls and crossbones.

   b. A snakebite kit and/or textual chart showing the sequence of steps to be taken in case of snakebite. Commercial charts are available, but they typically contain too much detail for use in a speech. Students might also distribute a detailed handout upon completion of their speeches.

   c. A line graph showing growth over time. Different lines on the same graph could illustrate the comparative growth of different types of stocks over the past decade. Bar graphs might help represent their comparative overall growth during the same period as well.

   d. A pie graph showing the major categories in different colors would be perfect. Comparative bar graphs might work as well.

   e. A flow chart illustrating the administration hierarchy would be the obvious choice here.

   f. Sequence charts or a poster containing sketches of telephones from different periods. Although timelines are not covered in the text, thoughtful students might propose a timeline highlighting key inventions and developments.

g. Visual representations (photos, video, etc.) of actual victims (preferably children) could help involve audiences emotionally with this topic. Various graphs could help illustrate overall figures pertaining to famine, starvation, and infant mortality rates, or the comparison of these rates to those in other parts of the world. Textual information or handouts concerning how to get involved or where to send contributions might also be appropriate.

h. A chart listing signals and meanings, or a boat horn or bell for actual demonstration.

ADDITIONAL ACTIVITIES

Presentation Aid Adaptations

Purpose: To give your students practice in finding solutions to problems they may encounter when preparing or using presentation aids.

Directions: This exercise works best as an in-class small-group discussion piece. Break your students into small groups and give them ten to fifteen minutes to discuss and brainstorm solutions for dealing with the following problem situations. They should present their solutions for class discussion. Critique their likely effectiveness relative to possible alternatives.

Problem situations:

1. You have found a photograph that is perfect but too small.

2. You have a commercially prepared map of an area you wish to describe in your speech.

3. Your speech on the treasure ship Atocha needs an aid showing where the ship was located and illustrating its treasures. You have found a map in a book that provides the location, and small pictures of its treasures.

4. You are the first speaker scheduled for the day, and the second speaker has already drawn on the chalkboard.

5. The speaker before you leaves material drawn on the chalkboard.

6. You are planning to use a posterboard presentation aid, and you notice that previous speakers have been having problems with them falling off chalkboard ledges.

7. You plan to display several small objects, one at a time, in the middle of a speech, and you want to make sure they can be reached easily and quickly at the appropriate times.

Suggestions for discussion:

1. Have the photograph enlarged to at least 11 by 17 inches and mount it on posterboard. Remind students not to pass photographs around during their speeches.

2. Trace the map onto a posterboard, including only relevant details.

3. Trace the map onto a posterboard or have an 11-by-17-inch enlargement produced. Enlarge any photographs for use; once again, avoid passing small pictures around during the course of a presentation.

4. Confer with the instructor and student involved to see if you can switch speaking orders. If this cannot be done, pull a projection screen down over the aid if one is available.

5. Say "Excuse me for a moment" to your audience and erase the chalkboard.

6. Chalkboard ledges were not made to hold presentation aids. Ask your instructor if an easel is available, or bring masking tape to secure your aid. Be sure to remove presentation aids when you have finished.

7. Place the articles on a tray and cover them with a cloth. Put them inside the lectern so that they can easily be retrieved as needed. They should not be lined up in full view in front of a lectern, and speakers should not distribute them for observation during the course of a presentation.

Impromptu Presentation Aids

Purpose: To provide students an opportunity to generate and critique rough drafts of presentation aids for given topic proposals.

Directions: This works well for in-class discussion. Divide your class into small groups, and have them spend fifteen to twenty minutes generating prospective presentation aids for the following topic areas. They should draw up rough drafts of their recommendations, and present them to the class. Focus discussion on their appropriateness, alternative ideas and designs, and any problems speakers might encounter in constructing and using them. For an alternative homework assignment, have your students choose a newspaper or magazine article (or another speech) and design a presentation aid to accompany it for class discussion.

Topic areas:

1. The perils of the Oregon Trail
2. How to housebreak a puppy
3. Comparative crime rates in major U.S. cities.
4. The superiority of compact discs over cassettes and records
5. Massaging away tensions
6. Budget appropriations for the major schools in your university
7. The importance of using sunscreen
8. Comparing tourism rates and revenues of Florida, Texas, California, and New York
9. County emergency services
10. The correlation between economic growth ratings and a President's general approval ratings over the course of a year

Suggestions for discussion:

1. A map showing the trail, with symbols to indicate major perils, or a pie chart showing the major causes of pioneer deaths on the trail.

2. Instead of showing up with an untrained puppy and newspapers, students might prepare a posterboard textual graphic outlining the steps in housebreaking a puppy, or bring samples of materials that are useful for training puppies.

3. Bar graphs illustrating comparative rates would work well with this message.

4. Speakers might bring compact disc and cassette players for a demonstrated comparison. Speakers might also use graphs to contrast the differences in audible range and sound quality.

5. A "trained model" who has been coached not to upstage the presentation with groans and comments as techniques are demonstrated.

6. Although a flow chart separating the various schools on campus might work, pie or bar graphs would be more effective for emphasizing the comparative sums allocated to each school in a yearly budget.

7. Graphs or charts showing skin cancer incidence, enlarged photographs of skin cancer lesions, brochures from the American Cancer Society to distribute after the speech.

8. Bar graphs measuring comparative round sums of revenues and estimated visitors per year, or bar graphs illustrating and comparing estimates of how much money gets spent per tourist or per vacation in each of these states.

9. A handout or textual graphic listing available services and hot lines to call in case of an emergency.

10. A line graph correlating the president's major approval ratings and economic growth reports over the same period of time.

Grab Bag Impromptu Speeches

Purpose: To provide students with an opportunity to practice using a presentation aid.

Directions: Assemble assorted common household items in a large box, and have each student select one. Give students five to ten minutes to prepare a one- to two-minute speech demonstrating how the item selected could be used as a presentation aid. Remind your students to design their messages around their presentation aid, and to integrate them into their actual presentations. Also push them to maintain quality eye contact and audience interaction.

Small-Group Consultations for Presentation Aids

Purpose: To give your students a chance to present their ideas for presentation aids for peer analysis and review before using them in their actual speeches.

Directions: This is intended for use in preparation for a speech assignment requiring the use of a presentation aid. No matter how thoroughly you cover the ideas in this chapter through lecture and exercises, many students will still benefit from having their proposals critiqued before they actually construct their presentation aids. As with group consultations for their speeches, break your students up into small groups and give them the last ten to fifteen minutes of class to discuss one another's ideas. In preparation for this activity, students should bring rough drafts of their first and second alternatives to class with them. Obviously, they should be roughly familiar with their speeches in order to know what presentation aids would be most appropriate. For discussion, they should consider the appropriateness of one another's proposals with respect to their overall messages, as well as alternative ideas that might be more effective. Have the speakers chosen the right information to illustrate? Have they chosen the right form of aid to illustrate it?

Mary Ann Danielson (Creighton University, Nebraska), "A Critical Thinking Approach to the Use of Visual Aids," *SCT* (Winter 1996), 8–9.

Goal: To introduce the student to the critical thinking (choice making) process inherent in deciding *when* to use a visual aid.

Most speech textbooks discuss the types of visual aids that may be used and provide guidelines for their effective use. Unfortunately, most texts do not discuss *when* one can or should use a visual aid; texts do not teach the students *how to decide when* to use a visual aid. This consciousness of one's own thinking process and that of others characterizes critical thinking (Rehner, 1994).

Critical thinking

- Encourages one to examine carefully the steps followed and activities engaged in when one thinks,
- Is developmental (i.e., by becoming aware of what you do or might not do when you think, you can learn and practice skills that will improve your thinking),
- Requires active participation (p. 61).

To the extent that critical thinking encourages us to carefully examine our choices and actions, a critical thinking approach to the selection of visual aids appears beneficial.

Activities which promote critical thinking include:

- Asking pertinent questions.
- Viewing a situation from a variety of perspectives.
- Trying to generate alternatives.
- Being open to new ideas.
- MacNeal's (1984) concept of alternaquencing encompasses many of these activities.

Coined by MacNeal, alternaquencing refers to alternatives-with-its-consequences. MacNeal believes that all alternatives have consequences, and as we cannot separate a course of action from its consequences, we should not consider a decision without first weighing the consequences. This exercise, involving an interactive discussion among the instructor and students, explores a critical thinking process (i.e., alternaquencing) for knowing when to use visual aids.

Instructions

Begin the exercise by arranging the students in a circle or some other physical arrangement that facilitates discussion. Using a flip chart or a chalkboard, the instructor will begin the discussion by asking some questions concerning visual aids. These initial questions are designed to focus the students' attention on visual aids and their experiences (if any) with using visual aids.

What are visual aids?
Has anyone ever used a visual aid in a speech?
Can someone give me an example of a visual aid?
Can someone share an example of a speech in which they used a visual aid?

Once you have the students sharing descriptions, definitions, and/or experiences, ask them to explain how they knew *when* to use visual aids (e.g., When do we use visual aids?) Go beyond answers like "in an informative speech." Ask them follow-up (probing) questions such as: Do we always use visual aids with informative speeches? Do we ever (never) use visual aids with persuasive speeches?

This discussion will probably lead to the conclusion that using visual aids *depends* on a number of factors. Prompt the students to provide you with criteria or factors for their use or nonuse. Their responses may include the purpose, audience, speech topic, time limits, facilities, requirements of the presentation, which all determine whether or not one uses a visual aid. Once the students realize that a number of factors are involved in the decision whether or not to use a visual aid, the class is ready to advance the discussion toward creating alternatives (e.g., yes, use the visual aid, or, no, don't use the visual aid) and alternaquences.

What happens if we use the visual aid? What happens if we choose not to use a visual aid? Let's explore the possibilities. *If* we use visual aids, *then* what happens? Let the students brainstorm possibilities. Prompt the students to look at both positive and negative consequences. Nothing is too far-fetched. MacNeal refers to this process of connecting consequences with alternatives as alternaquencing.

* * * * *

The students have just completed an alternaquencing exercise. To give the students additional practice in alternaquencing, have them select an occasion and determine whether or not to use a visual aid. This extension of the original exercise can be completed as a class or in smaller groups.

Each group, or the class as a whole, must select a speaking occasion (e.g., application for funding from their student government body), identify their alternatives (e.g., yes-no), alternaquence, decide on whether or not they will use a visual aid, and defend their decision (to you or the rest of the class). Upon completing this exercise, make sure that you review what has been learned.

This exercise was designed to provide the student with the knowledge necessary to (a) explain what is meant by the term alternaquencing, (b) describe the decision making process associated with selecting a visual aid, (c) identify various situations where the use of a visual aid would be appropriate, and (d) defend one's choice of whether or not to use a visual aid in a given situation. It is hoped that upon completion of this exercise, the student has a better understanding of the critical choices inherent in deciding when to use visual aids.

Readings

MacNeal, E. (1984). The flaw. *Et cetera,* 41(3), 290–298.

Rehner, J. (1994). *Practical Strategies for Critical Thinking.* Boston: Houghton Mifflin.

SUPPLEMENTARY MATERIALS

Films and Videos

"Aids to Speaking," Coronet/MTI Film and Video, 15 minutes.

"Choosing the Audio-Visual Dimension," Films for the Humanities, 15 minutes.

"How to Get Your Point Across in 30 Seconds or Less," Coronet/MTI Film and Video, 30 minutes.

"Producing Your Presentation," Films for the Humanities, 15 minutes.

Computer Software

"Chart-Master," "Diagram-Master," "Map-Master," and "Sign-Master," Ashton-Tate.

"Diagraph" and "Picture Perfect," Computer Support Corporation.

"Freelance Plus," Lotus.

"The Graphics Gallery," Hewlett-Packard.

"Graph Plus" Micrografx.

"Harvard Graphics," Software Publishing Corporation.

"Illustrator 88," Adobe.

"MacPaint," "MacDraw," "MacDraft," Apple.

"Microsoft Chart," Microsoft.

"Pagemaker," Aldus.

"Pixie," and "Mirage," Zenographic.

Transparencies and Handouts

Graphic Messages

Check List for Using Presentation Aids

GRAPHIC MESSAGES

1. *Sketches:* simplified representations of items and ideas.

2. *Maps:* good for describing spatial locations.

3. *Graphs:* help to illustrate complex numerical descriptions.

   a. *Pie Graphs:* to show the size of parts relative to one another and to the subject as a whole.

   b. *Bar Graphs:* to compare and contrast items and information.

   c. *Line Graphs:* to illustrate changes or growth rates over time.

   d. *Mountain Graphs:* effective when there are extreme variations in data.

4. *Charts:* help to summarize processes and relationships.

   a. *Flow Charts:* steps of a process, or power/responsibility relationships within a hierarchy.

   b. *Sequence Charts:* presented as a series.

5. *Textual Graphics:* use words to illustrate crucial information.

   a. *Bulleted Lists:* have no more than six words to a line and no more than six lines.

   b. *Acronyms:* use initial letters to help audience remember.

   c. *Statistical Charts:* have no more than three columns and six rows of data.

CHECK LIST FOR USING PRESENTATION AIDS

_____ Will my presentation aid enhance understanding?

_____ Is my presentation aid easy to understand?

_____ Is there enough information on my presentation aid?

_____ Is there too much information on my presentation aid?

_____ Is my presentation aid neat?

_____ Is the print on my presentation aid large enough for all audience members to read?

_____ Is everything on my presentation aid drawn to scale?

_____ Do I have the necessary equipment to use my presentation aid?

_____ Do I know how to use the equipment?

_____ Will I need tape or thumbtacks to position my presentation aid?

_____ Have I practiced presenting my speech using my presentation aid?

_____ Could I give my speech just as well, if not better, without my presentation aid?

READINGS FOR ENRICHMENT

See guide to journal abbreviations on p. 37.

* Items marked with an asterisk are suitable for student enrichment.

Antonoff, Michael. "Presentations That Persuade." *Personal Computing* (July 1990), 60–68.

Arnheim, Rudolph. *Visual Thinking.* Berkeley, California: University of California Press, 1969.

"The Art of Business Presentations." *Managing Office Technology* (Mar. 1994), 83.

Baird, Russell N., Arthur T. Turnbull, and Duncan McDonald. *The Graphics of Communication: Media, Methods, and Technology*, 6th ed. Fort Worth, Tex.: Harcourt Brace Jovanovich, 1993.

Barrier, Michael. "How He Helps Jurors Stay Awake by Turning Trials into 'Multimedia Events.'" *Nation's Business* (Oct. 1991), 18.

Batiste, Stephen. "Sound Barrier: Audio-Visual Aids in Business Meetings." *Marketing*, 28 May 1987, pp. 59–61.

* Bishop, Philip. "The World on a Silver Platter: Bring New Power and Flexibility to Your Business with Multimedia." *Home Office Computing* (June 1993), 61–63.

Bohn, Emil, and David Jabusch. "The Effect of Four Methods of Instruction on the Use of Visual Aids in Speeches." *WJSC* (Summer 1982), 252–265.

* Borger, Gloria. "The Story the Pictures Didn't Tell." *U.S. News & World Report*, 22 Feb. 1993, pp. 6–7.

* Boroughs, Robert. "New Teaching, New Learning." *Electronic Learning* (Jan. 1990), 52–54.

Bottoms, David T. "Multimedia Delivers the Message: Interactivity Livens Up Training, Presentations, and the Budget at TRW." *Industry Week*, 4 Apr. 1994, pp. 70–71.

Brody, Marjorie, and Shawn Kent. *Power Presentations: How to Connect with Your Audience and Sell Your Ideas.* New York: Wiley, 1993.

* Bruder, Isabelle. "Multimedia: How It Changes the Way We Teach and Learn." *Electronic Learning* (Sept. 1991), 22–26.

* Brunner, Cornelia. "Teaching Visual Literacy." *Electronic Learning* (Nov.–Dec. 1994), 16–17.

* Bunzel, Tom. "Content—Not Technology—Is What Counts." *Computer Pictures* (May–June 1993), 23.

* Burge, Stewart L. "Audiovisuals." In *Inside Organizational Communication*, edited by Carol Reuss and Donn Silvis, pp. 187–204. New York: Longman, 1985.

Danielson, Mary Ann. "A Critical Thinking Approach to the Use of Visual Aids." *SCT* (Winter 1996), 8–9.

D'Arcy, Jan. *Technically Speaking: Proven Ways to Make Your Next Presentation a Success.* New York: American Management Association, 1992.

Dwyer, F. M. "Exploratory Studies in the Effectiveness of Visual Illustrations." *AV Communication Review* (1970), 235–240.

Feliciano, G. D., R. D. Powers, and B. E. Kearle. "The Presentation of Statistical Information." *AV Communication Review* (1963), 32–39.

Gardano, Anne C. "Cultural Influence on Emotional Response to Color: A Research Study Comparing Hispanics and Non-Hispanics." *American Journal of Art Therapy* (May 1986), 119–124.

* Goldsmith, Arthur. "Digitally Altered Photography: The New Image Makers." *Britannica Book of the Year: 1995.* Chicago: Encyclopaedia Britannica: 1995, p. 135.

* Grice, George L., and John F. Skinner. "Prepare to Enter the Visual Dimension." *Management World* (Jan.–Feb. 1989), 11–12.

* Hatch, Ripley. "Making the Best Presentations." *Nation's Business* (Aug. 1992), 37–38.

Heidt, E. *Instructional Media and the Individual Learner.* New York: Nichols, 1976.

Holcombe, Marya W., and Judith K. Stein. *Presentations for Decision Makers: Strategies for Structuring and Delivering Your Ideas.* Belmont, Calif.: Lifetime Learning Publications, 1983.

Hull, William W. "When You're in Prime Time." *The American Salesman* (Mar. 1989), 16–20.

Itten, Johannes. *The Art of Color*, translated from Ernst van Haagen. New York: Van Nostrand Reinhold, 1973.

* Johnson, Virginia. "Picture Perfect Presentations." *The Toastmaster* (Feb. 1990), 7.

Jurek, Ken. "Portable Computers: Compact Presentations Receive Rave Reviews." *Presentation Products* (Dec. 1992), 32–38.

Kaufmann, R., and M. O. O'Neill. "Color Names and Focal Colors on Electronic Displays." *Ergonomics* (Aug. 1993), 881–890.

Kennedy, John M. *A Psychology of Picture Perception.* San Francisco: Jossey-Bass, 1974.

* Kern, Richard. "Making Visual Aids Work for You." *Sales and Marketing Management* (Feb. 1989), 45–48.

King, Thomas R. "Visual Aids: Moving into the 21st Century." Southern States Communication Association Convention, New Orleans, April 1995.

Lamberski, R. J., and F. M. Dwyer. "Exploratory Studies in the Effectiveness of Visual Illustrations." *AV Communication Review* (1970), 235–240.

Lefferts, Robert. *Elements of Graphics: How to Prepare Charts and Graphs for Effective Reports.* New York: Harper & Row, 1981.

* Leo, John. "Lapse or TV News Preview?" *The Washington Times,* 3 Mar. 1993, p. G3.

* LeRoux, Paul. "The Fine Art of Show and Tell." *Working Woman* (Sept. 1985), 126–130.

Lester, P. M. *Visual Communication: Images with Messages.* Belmont, Calif.: Wadsworth, 1995.

* Lindstrom, Robert L. "The Presentation Power of Multimedia." *Sales and Marketing Management* (Sept. 1994), 51–57.

"The Low-Down on A-V Use." *Sales and Marketing Management* (Aug. 1991), 25.

McGivney. James J. "Multimedia Educational Systems." *The FBI Law Enforcement Bulletin* (Feb. 1993), 6–9.

* Meilach, Dona Z. "Visually Speaking." Special Advertising Section, *Presentation Products Magazine* (June 1993), J–L.

* ———. "Even the Odds with Visual Presentations." *Inc. Annual* (1994), 1–6.

O'Malley, Christopher. "Making Quick Presentations: How to Get Better Visuals in Minutes." *Personal Computing* (Dec. 1985), 76–83.

Oppenheimer, Todd. "Exploring the Interactive Future: Newsweek's Voyage through Cyberspace." *Columbia Journalism Review* (Nov.–Dec. 1993), 34–37.

* Ozer, Jan. "Presentations Come to Life." *Home Office Computing* (Dec. 1994), 74.

* Peterson, L. V., and Wilbur Schramm. "How Accurately Are Different Kinds of Graphs Read?" *AV Communication Review* (1955), 178–189.

Phillips, John T., Jr. "Professional Presentations." *Records Management Quarterly* (Oct. 1994), 44–46.

* "Presentation Graphics Should Help Audiences Get the Picture." *PC Week,* 8 Dec. 1987, p. 56.

Presentation Products Magazine, available from the Circulation Department, Presentation Products Magazine, 23410 Civic Center Way, Suite #-10, Malibu, CA 91320.

Rabb, Margaret Y. *The Presentation Design Book: Tips, Techniques, and Advice for Creating Effective, Attractive Slides, Overheads, Multimedia Presentations, Screen Shows, and More,* 2nd ed. Chapel Hill, N.C.: Ventana Press, 1993.

Rand, Paul. *Design, Form, and Chaos.* New Haven, Conn.: Yale University Press, 1993.

Rigden, John S. "The Lost Art of Oratory: Damn the Overhead Projector." *Physics Today* (Mar. 1990), 73–75.

Salomon, Gavriel. *Interaction of Media, Cognition, and Learning.* San Francisco: Jossey-Bass, 1979.

Satterthwaite, Les. *Using Graphics: Skills, Media, and Materials,* 3rd ed. Dubuque, Iowa: Kendall/Hunt, 1977.

* Scoville, Richard. "Ten Graphs (and How to Use Them)." *PC World* (Sept. 1988), 217.

Seiler, William J. "The Effects of Visual Materials on Attitudes, Credibility, and Retention." *CM* (Nov. 1971), 331–334.

Selby, Peter H. *Using Graphs and Tables: A Self-Teaching Guide.* New York: Wiley, 1979.

Smeltzer, Larry R., and Charles M. Vance. "An Analysis of Graphic Use in Audio-Graphic Teleconferences." *Journal of Business Communication* (Spring 1989), 123–131.

Studt, Tim. "Multimedia Allows Researchers to Interact with Their Data." *R&D* (July 1994), 35–36.

Talman, Michael. *Understanding Presentation Graphics.* Almeda, Calif.: SYBEX, 1992.

Treece, Malra. *Communication for Business and the Professions,* 6th ed. Boston: Allyn & Bacon, 1993.

Tufts, Edward R. *The Visual Display of Quantitative Information.* Cheshire, Conn.: Graphics Press, 1983.

* "Use Simple Audio-Visual Techniques to Liven Up Speeches and Meetings." *Sales and Marketing* (Aug. 1989), 19.

Vernon, M. D. "Presenting Information in Diagrams." *AV Communication Review* (1953), 147–158.

* "Vivid Colors Enhance In-House Presentations: Lectures or 'Chalk-Talks' Were Once Enough, but Quality Visuals Hold Audiences Much Longer." *The Office* (Feb. 1989), 76–77.

Vogel, Douglas R., Gary W. Dickson, and John A. Lehman. "Persuasion and the Role of Visual Presentation Support: The UM/3M Study." 3M Corporation, 1986.

Weichselgartner, Erich, and George Sperling. "Dynamics of Automatic and Controlled Visual Attention." *Science*, 6 Nov. 1989, pp. 778–780.

Wilks, Dorothy. "Two Birds with One Stone." *SCT* (Winter 1991), 12.

Williams, Robin. *The Non-Designer's Design Book: Design and Typographic Principles for the Visual Novice.* Berkeley, Calif.: Peachpit Press, 1994.

Worth, Sol. "Pictures Can't Say Ain't." *Versus* (Dec. 1975), 85–108.

* Wyucoff, Edgar B. "Why Visuals?" *AV Communication Review* (1977), 39, 59.

Zayas-Baya, E. P. "Instructional Media in the Total Language Picture." *International Journal of Instructional Media* (1977–78), 145–150.

Zelazny, Gene. *Say It with Charts: The Executive's Guide to Successful Presentations in the 1990s,* 2nd ed. Burr Ridge, Ill.: Irwin Professional Publishing, 1991.

CHAPTER 10
Using Language Effectively

OBJECTIVES

- To help your students understand the power of words.

- To help your students express their thoughts clearly, simply, and correctly.

- To help your students enliven their ideas through powerful images.

- To help your students use symbols to bring their audiences together.

- To help your students choose words that can move an audience to action.

SUGGESTIONS FOR TEACHING

Effective language use occupies an important and time-honored place within the discipline of public speaking. In fact, language style was one of the original five canons of rhetoric. However, some instructors have difficulty working the subject into their lesson plans. This is not surprising considering the profusion of ideas about the significance of language in our times. Until recently, scholars tended to treat the use of such language forms as metaphor, antithesis, irony, repetition, and climax as ornamental afterthoughts intended to make substantive messages more aesthetically pleasing to the ear. However, lately it has become apparent that words are inseparable from the substance and meaning of ideas, and we suggest that you teach these materials as an integral part of creating meaningful messages.

Some of your students may be overwhelmed at first by the wealth of terms and ideas in this chapter, and, while you may need to quickly review ideas to set up activities, these skills are once again best learned through critique and application. In this chapter, we offer plenty of activities that illustrate the rhetorical significance of language and the play and interplay of different language forms and appeals in actual messages. We also have activities and applications that should help your students assess and improve their oral language skills by practicing the forms and techniques offered in the text.

CHAPTER OUTLINE

I. It is important to understand the power of language to influence attitudes and behavior. *(text pp. 309–310)*
   A. Effective language use establishes for listeners the reality and truth of a situation.

288

B. Just as speakers learn to climb the barriers that separate them from their listeners and to build the structures of their speeches, they must learn to weave a fabric of words that give their ideas maximum clarity, beauty, and power.

II. Understanding the power of the spoken word begins with distinguishing oral from written language. *(text pp. 310–319)*
   A. Oral language is more spontaneous, colorful, and intense, and less formal.
   B. Oral language relies on audience involvement for its effectiveness.
   C. Oral language uses pauses and vocal emphasis/variations as punctuation marks.
   D. There are three significant temporal differences between oral and written language.
      1. Speakers should spend more time explaining simpler ideas through repetition.
      2. More impressive ideas should be developed at the end of sentences.
      3. The flow and beat of syllabic rhythm is more important in oral language.
   E. The skillfully used spoken word can reach others in four ways.
      1. The power of language to make people see can transcend communication barriers.
         a. This is especially important when addressing unfamiliar or unusual subjects.
         b. Words can also distort or disguise reality.
      2. The power of language to awaken feelings can help speakers overcome time, distance, and apathy barriers.
         a. Time barriers increase the emotional distance between people and topics.
         b. Distance barriers can insulate people from emotional involvement.
         c. Apathy barriers interfere with emotional responses.
         d. Speakers can help overcome emotional barriers by using narratives, examples, and vivid images, and invoking common values and experiences.
         e. Emotional appeals are subject to abuse; they can be allowed to substitute for reasoning and evidence.
      3. Language can help bring listeners together for collective action by emphasizing the importance of group membership.
         a. Speakers can unite audiences by invoking heroes and enemies, common goals, and shared values, and using metaphors of inclusion.
         b. Speakers should take care, as language can divide as well as unite audiences.
      4. Language can help speakers encourage action.
         a. Audience members may not accept the soundness of a proposal, or that action is either necessary or practical.
         b. Speakers should depict real-life dramas that reveal what is at stake and the listener's role.
            (1) While such scenarios draw clear lines between right and wrong, speakers should avoid distorting reality with good-versus-evil depictions.

III. A number of techniques can help speakers use the power of language effectively. *(text pp. 319–327)*
   A. There are many barriers speakers may face in shaping audience perceptions.
      1. Abstract subjects (such as justice) cannot be accessed through direct sensory perception.
         a. Speakers might point out relationships to concrete objects of comparison.
            (1) Similes set up comparisons using *like* or *as*.
         b. Another means of handling abstraction is through the replacement of expected words with unexpected words in the form of a metaphor.
            (1) Metaphors perform a constructive, informative function by inviting speakers to explore unusual connections of ideas.
            (2) Metaphors can involve audiences and are prominent in speeches of celebration.
            (3) Because of their power, they should be carefully selected and used in moderation.
               (a) Mixed, trite, and overused metaphors can damage a speaker's ethos.
      2. Complex subjects can be difficult to effectively describe.
         a. Synecdoche focuses on part of the subject as a representation of it.

  b. Sharp moral contrast can also be used to simplify complex issues, although speakers should be aware of the ethical implications of distorting situations.

B. The following language techniques can help speakers arouse audience feelings.
 1. Denotative language is purposefully objective and neutral, and tends to detach audiences.
 2. Connotative language invests a subject with strong emotional associations.
  a. Simile and metaphor can kindle feelings by the relationships/similarities suggested.
  b. Synecdoche can focus and arouse feelings.
  c. Metaphoric images can help arouse emotions.
  d. Onomatopoeia, the tendency for certain words to imitate through sound the objects or actions signified, can be very effective.
  e. Hyperbole (exaggeration) can help force listeners to confront moral problems.
  f. Personification helps arouse emotional involvement by investing inanimate subjects and concerns with human qualities.
 3. Speakers should be wary of the ethical implications of using emotional appeals.
  a. Perceived abuse of emotional appeals can backfire and damage ethos.
  b. Euphemisms are words used to numb feelings by hiding rather than revealing reality.

C. Several language techniques can help speakers bring people together.
 1. Inclusive pronouns such as "our" and "we" can promote identification.
 2. Special words or culturetypes reaffirm group identity by stressing shared values and goals.
  a. Speakers may invoke culturetypes by citing heroes and enemies or god and devil terms.
  b. Culturetypes are specific to a particular group identity and may change over time.
  c. Ideographs express and support a group's predominant political beliefs.
  d. Culturetypes add strength to a speech when used ethically, but are easily abused.
   (1) Speakers should demonstrate the relevance of a culturetype to their topics, and respect those who reject their invitations to group identity.
 3. Universal symbols are extremely potent symbolic forms that transcend time and culture.
  a. Archetypal metaphors are the most frequently used universal symbols in speeches.
   (1) Archetypal metaphors might include light/dark, storms and the sea, disease and cure, structure, verticality, family, and spatial images.

D. The following language techniques can help encourage action.
 1. Taking collective action entails time, risk, and trust in a given speaker.
  a. Speakers should use hyperbole, imagery, personification, synecdoche, archetypal metaphors, and other techniques to arouse the feelings that are necessary to spur action.
 2. The following techniques can help move audiences to action and enhance speaker ethos.
  a. Alliteration (repetition of initial consonant sounds in closely connected words) can be very effective in the introductions and conclusions of action-oriented speeches.
  b. Parallel construction (repetition of the same initial words in a sequence of phrases or sentences) can be very effective with emphatic final calls to action.
 3. Inversion (changing expected word sequences) can help make a point more memorable and emphatic.
 4. Antithesis (juxtaposing opposing views within the same or adjoining sentences) can suggest a clear grasp of alternative options.

IV. Rhetorical style concerns the unique way speakers choose and arrange words. The following "six Cs" provide useful standards for effective language use. *(text pp. 327–334)*
A. Clarity is the first standard of effective language use. Speakers should:
 1. use lay terms rather than jargon or needlessly overblown language for most audiences.
  a. Sometimes deceptive speakers hide behind a smokescreen of jargon.
 2. use strategic amplification (rephrasing and supporting) to clarify important ideas.

B. Color refers to the emotional intensity, vividness, and memorability of language.
   1. Speakers should use well-chosen descriptive adjectives sparingly.
   2. Used effectively, colorful language use reflects commitment and enhances ethos.
C. The language of speeches should be specific and concrete.
   1. Concrete language is more interesting, less ambiguous, and easier to remember.
   2. Listeners tend to lose interest when language is overly abstract, vague, or general.
D. The language of speeches should be correct.
   1. Incorrect or inappropriate language use can damage a speaker's perceived competence.
   2. Speakers should look up unfamiliar words, and avoid using long words that they do not really know.
   3. Malapropisms occur when speakers use wrong words that sound similar.
E. The language of speeches should be concise and to the point.
   1. Long-drawn-out speeches and expressions are generally ineffective. Speakers should:
      a. strive for simple, direct expression.
      b. use comparisons to explain complex issues.
      c. use maxims to convey collective reasoning, not as substitutes for substantive speeches.
F. Cultural sensitivity is also an important standard for effective language use.
   1. Although classroom audiences are increasingly more diverse, speakers should not try to be what they are not.
   2. A lack of cultural sensitivity usually has negative consequences for speakers.
      a. Audience reactions may range from mild offense to rejecting speakers and their messages.
   3. Developing cultural sensitivity begins with being attuned to audience diversity, appreciating differences, and being careful about the words chosen to refer to other people who may be different.
      a. Speakers should be cautious of stereotyping others as inferior, and avoid racial, ethnic, religious, or gender-based humor—or anything else that others might interpret as racist or sexist.

USING END-OF-CHAPTER ITEMS

Discussion *(text pp. 335–336)*

1. **The example that opens this chapter presents arguments for and against whiskey, using connotative language. Rephrase these arguments, using denotative language. How does this change affect the power of the appeals? Which speech situations call for more denotative speech? How can connotative words be misused? Under what circumstances are they most appropriate?**

This works well for homework followed by in-class discussion. The passage from the beginning of the text chapter reads:

A legislator was asked how he felt about whiskey. He replied, "If, when you say whiskey, you mean the Devil's brew, the poison scourge, the bloody monster that defiles innocence, dethrones reason, creates misery and poverty—yes, literally takes the bread from the mouths of little children; if you mean the drink that topples Christian man and woman from the pinnacle of righteous, gracious living into the bottomless pit of degradation, despair, shame and helplessness, then certainly I am against it with all my power.

"But if, when you say whiskey, you mean the oil of conversations, the philosophic wine, the ale that is consumed when good fellows get together, that puts a song in their hearts and the warm glow of contentment in their eyes; if you mean Christmas cheer; if you mean the stimulating drink that puts the spring in an old gentlemen's step on a frosty morning; if you mean that drink, the sale of which pours into our treasury untold millions of dollars which are used to provide tender care for our crippled children, our blind, our deaf, pitiful, aged and infirm, to build highways, hospitals, and schools, then certainly I am in favor of it.

"That is my stand, and I will not compromise."

The same material rephrased in more denotative language is obviously less vivid and less likely to arouse an audience emotionally:

A legislator was asked how he felt about alcohol. He replied, "If, when you say alcohol, you mean that beverage that causes people to act irrationally and that disrupts family relationships because of the money that is spent on it, that makes people behave in undesirable ways, that keeps people from maintaining a decent standard of living, then certainly I am against it with all my power.

"But if, when you say alcohol, you are referring to that social beverage that helps people relate better with one another, that is used on special, festive occasions, and that brings in needed state revenues through the taxes on it, which are used to fund social services and amenities for our citizens, then certainly I am in favor of it."

Denotative language is appropriate in situations in which precision is important, such as legal or medical documents. It can also be useful for tempering audience emotions. Sometimes connotative language can reduce public discussion of volatile issues to name calling. Speakers often misuse connotative language to short-circuit the reasoning process or direct attention away from crucial aspects of a topic. Connotative language is appropriate when it helps audiences to see and feel the impact of situations as they exist. The "Whiskey Speech," a legend of Southern politics, was originally presented by the late Judge N. S. (Soggy) Sweat, Jr., of Corinth, Mississippi, when he ran for governor of that state during the Prohibition era. He had managed to get through most of his campaign without taking a stand on the "whiskey issue," until he was finally confronted during a rally. His response, using hyperbole and extremely connotative language to carry arguments to their most ridiculous extreme, exemplifies what Morris Udall has called "the art of the waffle." See Udall, *Too Funny to Be President* (New York: Henry Holt, 1988).

2. **In the 1950s, Richard Weaver suggested that *progress* was the prime culturetype of American society. What words do you nominate as culturetypes in contemporary society? Why? How are they used now in public communication? Find and share examples from speeches, essays, editorials, cartoons, or advertisements.**

This works well for homework followed by small-group or general class discussion. As an alternative, collect the artifacts yourself and bring them to class for discussion and analysis. Have your students suggest terms or phrases that serve as "god terms" and "devil terms" in American culture. Students may come up with many original examples, some specific to their region or subcultural identity. Presidential rhetoric is a good source of political culturetypes or ideographs. Critics commonly credit Reagan with revitalizing the Western and Horatio Alger myths as primary "god terms" in American politics. Some enduring "devil terms" in Reagan's speaking included "big government," "welfare," and "liberalism."

3. **Look for examples of the use and abuse of specific language techniques in public communication. Report in class and explain how they work.**

Use this for homework or as a small-group activity followed by in-class discussion. Remind students that language abuse is often unintentional. Advertisements, especially those in sensationalist tabloids, are a good source of deliberate language manipulations. Letters to the

Edwin R. Rowley (Indiana State University, Terre Haute, Indiana), "More than Mere Words," *SCT* (Fall 1992), 5.

Goal: Students will be made aware that language creates social reality, and become more appreciative of the potential of communication.

Some students enter a beginning speech course with a "speech as solo performance" mentality. Others may have a slightly cynical attitude toward the potential effectiveness of the strategic use of language. After this exercise I've had students remark on how they came to value the transactional nature of communication and had better insight on how words influence their lives.

This exercise is best done early in the term, particularly when considering the process or nature of communication. The students are asked to take out three slips of paper. In quick succession the instructor asks the students to:

1. Take the first piece of paper and draw a picture of an ugly creepy insect.

2. Take the second piece of paper and write the name of or draw a picture of a least favorite food. Vegetables appear regularly.

3. Take the third piece of paper and write the name they use to address their mother.

4. Take the first piece of paper, put it on the floor, and step repeatedly and enthusiastically on the bug.

5. Take the second piece of paper, put it on the floor and step on that horrid food.

6. Place the third piece of paper on the floor and stomp on it.

At this point students hesitate, groan, and think you are a candidate for the first piece of paper. I immediately tell them to stop but ask why they objected. Students agree that the third piece of paper with its inscription of "Mom" is not their mother but also come to realize the power of words/symbols. I specifically indicate the point of the exercise was to demonstrate that language creates social reality and that through the study of communication we can influence the world in which we live. I also ask them to pick up the product of their human symbolic activity and dispose of it properly on the way out of class.

SUPPLEMENTARY MATERIALS

Films and Videos

"Style in Language," Films for the Humanities, color, 15 minutes.

"Choosing the Ideas and Words," RMI Media Productions, 28 minutes.

"The Language of Leadership: The Winston Churchill Method," Films for the Humanities, 60 minutes.

"Sexism in Language," Films for the Humanities, 20 minutes.

"Language," Insight Media, 30 min.

"Words and Meaning," Films for the Humanities, color, 15 minutes.

"Verbal Communication: The Power of Words," CRM Films, 22 minutes.

"Language and Communication," Insight Media, 30 minutes.

"What Do You Mean?" Insight Media, 30 minutes.

Videos to accompany *Public Speaking*, Houghton Mifflin.

Transparencies and Handouts

Language Techniques (Transparency 10.1)

Oral vs. Written Language (Transparency 10.2)

Guidelines for Language Use (Transparency 10.3)

Guaranteed Effective All-Occasion Non-Slanderous Political Smear Speech

Guide for Decoding Academic Jargon

Numbers Work Sheet: How Much Is . . . ?

New Adages for Old

Check List for Language Analysis

LANGUAGE TECHNIQUES

1. **To help audiences see things, use:**
   a. Similes or metaphors
   b. Synecdoche
   c. Metonymy
   d. Contrast
   e. Representative examples

2. **To arouse emotions, use:**
   a. Connotative language
   b. Images
   c. Onomatopeia
   d. Hyperbole
   e. Personification

3. **To temper emotions, use:**
   a. Denotative language
   b. Facts and figures
   c. Euphemisms

4. **To promote identification, use:**
   a. Inclusive pronouns
   b. Narratives
   c. Culturetypes and ideographs
   d. Archetypal metaphors

5. **To move people to action, use:**
   a. The techniques used to arouse emotions
   b. Alliteration
   c. Parallel construction
   d. Inversion
   e. Antithesis

ORAL VS. WRITTEN LANGUAGE

"A speech is not merely an essay standing on its hind legs."
James A. Winans, 1931

In comparison with written language, oral language uses:

1. More words that refer to human beings and human relationships.

2. More personal pronouns such as "I," "you," "we," and "our" to help build identification.

3. Shorter thought units, sentence fragments, and interjections.

4. More repetition of words, phrases, and sentences.

5. Shorter words and more contractions.

6. More familiar words or colloquial words.

GUIDELINES FOR LANGUAGE USE

1. Be clear.
    a.   Use repetition, paraphrasing, and examples.

    b.   Use lay language.

2. Be colorful.
    a.   Use vivid and intense words.

    b.   Evoke vivid sensory images.

3. Be concrete.
    a.   Avoid abstractions.

    b.   Use specific examples.

4. Be correct.
    a.   Look up unfamiliar words.

    b.   Pronounce words properly.

5. Be concise.
    a.   Use simple, direct sentences.

    b.   Avoid redundancy.

6. Be culturally sensitive.
    a.   Respect the diversity of your audience.

    b.   Don't use language that may offend listeners.

GUARANTEED EFFECTIVE ALL-OCCASION NON-SLANDEROUS POLITICAL SMEAR SPEECH*

by Bill Garvin

My fellow citizens, it is an honor and a pleasure to be here today. My opponent has openly admitted he feels an affinity toward your city, but I happen to *like* this area. It might be a salubrious place to him, but to me it is one of the nation's most delightful garden spots.

When I embarked upon this political campaign I hoped that it could be conducted on a high level and that my opponent would be willing to stick to the issues. Unfortunately, he has decided to be tractable instead—to indulge in unequivocal language, to eschew the use of outright lies in his speeches, and even to make repeated veracious statements about me.

At first I tried to ignore these scrupulous, unvarnished fidelities. Now I do so no longer. *If my opponent wants a fight, he's going to get one!*

It might be instructive to start with his background. My friends, have you ever accidentally dislodged a rock on the ground and seen what was underneath? Well, exploring my opponent's background is dissimilar. All the slime and filth and corruption you can possibly imagine, even in your wildest dreams, are glaringly nonexistent in this man's life. And even during his childhood!

Let us take a very quick look at that childhood. It is a known fact that, on a number of occasions, he emulated older boys at a certain playground. It is also known that his parents not only permitted him to masticate excessively in their presence, but even urged him to do so. Most explicable of all, this man who poses as a paragon of virtue exacerbated his own sister when they were both teenagers.

I ask you, my fellow Americans: is this the kind of person we want in public office to set an example for our youth?

Of course, it's not surprising that he should have such a typically pristine background—no, not when you consider the other members of his family:

His female relatives put on a constant pose of purity and innocence, and claim they are inscrutable, yet every one of them has taken part in horatory activities.

The men in the family are likewise completely amenable to moral suasion.

My opponent's second cousin is a Mormon.

His uncle was a flagrant heterosexual.

His sister, who has always been obsessed by sects, once worked as a proselyte outside a church.

His father was secretly chagrined at least a dozen times by matters of a pecuniary nature.

His youngest brother wrote an essay extolling the virtues of being a homo sapiens.

His great-aunt expired from a degenerative disease.

His nephew subscribes to a phonographic magazine.

---

* Reprinted by permission of *Mad Magazine.*

His wife was a thespian before their marriage and even performed the act in front of paying customers.

And, his own mother had to resign from a women's organization in her later years because she was an admitted sexagenarian.

Now what of the man himself?

I can tell you in solemn truth that he is the very antithesis of political radicalism, economic irresponsibility and personal depravity. His own record proves that he has frequently discountenanced treasonable, un-American philosophies and has perpetrated many overt acts as well.

He perambulated his infant son on the street.

He practiced nepotism with his uncle and first cousin.

He attempted to interest a 13-year-old girl in philately.

He participated in a seance at a private residence where, among the odd goings-on, there was incense.

He has declared himself in favor of more homogeneity on college campuses.

He has advocated social intercourse in mixed company—and has taken part in such gatherings himself.

He has been deliberately averse to crime in our streets.

He has urged our Protestant and Jewish citizens to develop more catholic tastes.

Last summer he committed a piscatorial act on a boat that was flying the American flag.

Finally, at a time when we must be on our guard against all foreign isms, he has coolly announced his belief in altruism—and his fervent hope that some day this entire nation will be altruistic.

I beg you, my friends, to oppose this man whose life and work and ideas are so openly and avowedly compatible with our American way of life. A vote for him would be a vote for the perpetuation of everything we hold dear.

The facts are clear; the record speaks for itself.

Do your duty.

GUIDE FOR DECODING ACADEMIC JARGON

What they say	*What they mean*
It has long been known that	I didn't bother to look up the original reference
Of great theoretical importance	Interesting to me
Three of the samples were chosen for detailed study	The results on the others didn't make sense and were ignored
Typical results are shown	The best results are shown
The agreement with the predicted curve is excellent	The agreement with the predicted curve is fair
The agreement with the predicted curve is fair	The agreement with the predicted curve is imaginary
It is believed that	I think
It is generally believed that	A couple of my friends think so too
It is clear that much additional work will be necessary before a complete understanding	I don't understand it
A comprehensive theory to account for these effects has not been formulated	Neither does anyone else
We are making a survey	We need more time to think of an answer
Will advise in due course	If we ever figure it out, we'll let you know
A study is being made	We haven't got started on it yet
It is under consideration	I never heard of it
It is under active consideration	We are looking in the files for it
Note and initial	Let's spread the blame

NUMBERS WORK SHEET: HOW MUCH IS . . .

a few?   _____

some?   _____

a lot?   _____

a little?   _____

a whole lot?   _____

scads?   _____

a trifle?   _____

just a tad?   _____

many?   _____

a good many?   _____

several?   _____

not many?   _____

NEW ADAGES FOR OLD

Where there's a will _____

Don't put all your eggs _____

Where there's smoke _____

Time and tide _____

Don't put the cart _____

A rolling stone _____

A bird in the hand _____

A stitch in time _____

He/she who hesitates _____

Look before you _____

CHECK LIST FOR LANGUAGE ANALYSIS

_____ Was my language clear and simple?

_____ Did I translate technical terms into lay language?

_____ Was I guilty of resorting to jargon?

_____ Was my language colorful and vivid?

_____ Did I create images for my audience?

_____ Was my language appropriately concrete?

_____ Did I use words correctly?

_____ Did I use strategic repetition?

_____ Did I avoid unnecessary repetition?

_____ Did I use any figures of speech?

Specify: _____

_____ Did my language foster identification with the audience?

Specify: _____

_____ Did I use connotative language ethically and effectively?

Specify: _____

_____ Did I use culturetypes ethically and effectively?

Specify: _____

_____ Did I use archetypal metaphors ethically and effectively?

Specify: _____

READINGS FOR ENRICHMENT

See guide to journal abbreviations on p. 37.

* Items marked with an asterisk are suitable for student enrichment.

Figurative Language

Anderson, Timothy. "A Hard Nut to Crack: Evolving English Metaphors for Insanity in Social-Historical Context." *American Imago* (Spring 1993), 111–130.

Ayim, Maryann. "Violence and Domination as Metaphors in Academic Discourse." In *Selected Issues in Logic and Communication*, edited by Trudy Govier, pp. 184–195. Belmont, Calif.: Wadsworth, 1988.

* Bineham, Jeffery L. "Some Ethical Implications of Team Sports Metaphors in Politics." *CR* (Winter 1991), 35–42.

* Boorstin, Daniel J. "Metaphors Should Be Made at Home: The Idea of Progress: Progress to What?" *UNESCO Courier* (Dec. 1993), 13–14.

Bugeja, Michael J. "Personification Lives!" *Writer's Digest* (Aug. 1995), 14–16.

Crable, Richard E., ed. "On Mythic Criticism: The Conversation Continues." *CS* (Winter 1990), 278–298.

* Denton, Robert E., Jr. "The Rhetorical Effect of Slogans: Classifications and Characteristics." *CQ* (Spring 1980), 10–18.

Dorsey, Leroy G. "The Frontier Myth in Presidential Rhetoric: Theodore Roosevelt's Campaign for Conservation." *WJC* (Winter 1995), 1–19.

Fienup-Riordan, Ann. "Clearing the Path: Metaphors to Live By in Yup'ik Eskimo Oral Tradition." *The American Indian Quarterly* (Winter 1994), 61–70.

Goulden, Nancy Rost, and Charles J. G. Griffin. "The Meaning of Grades Based on Faculty and Student Metaphors." *CE* (Apr. 1995), 110–125.

Hardy-Short, Dayle C., and C. Brant Short. "Fire, Death, and Rebirth: A Metaphoric Analysis of the 1988 Yellowstone Fire Debate." *WJC* (Spring 1995), 103–125.

Ivie, Robert L. "Images of Savagery in American Justifications for War." *CM* (Nov. 1980), 279–294.

* Ivins, Molly. "What About Apple Pie?" *The Progressive* (Nov. 1988), 37.

Jordan, William J., Lyndia L. Flanagan, and Ronald W. Wineinger. "Novelty and Recall Effects of Animate and Inanimate Metaphorical Discourse." *CSSJ* (Spring 1975), 29–33.

Jorgensen-Earp, Cheryl R., and Ann Q. Stanton. "Student Metaphors for the College Freshman Experience." *CE* (April 1993), 123–141.

* Lakoff, George, and Mark Johnson. *Metaphors We Live By*. Chicago: University of Chicago Press, 1980.

McGee, Michael Calvin. "The 'Ideograph': A Link Between Rhetoric and Ideology." *QJS* (Feb. 1980), 1–16.

———. "The Origins of 'Liberty': A Feminization of Power." *CM* (March 1980), 23–45.

———. "Power to the <People>." *CSMC* (Dec. 1987), 432–437.

* "Metaphorically Speaking." *Sales & Marketing Management* (Aug. 1991), 30.

Moore, Mark P. "Life, Liberty and the Handgun: The Function of Synecdoche in the Brady Debate." *CQ* (Fall 1994), 434–447.

Morrow, Lance. " Metaphors of the World, Unite!" *Time*, 16 Oct. 1989, p. 96.

"On Mythic Criticism." *CS* [Special Section] (Summer 1990), 101–160.

Osborn, Michael. "Archetypal Metaphor in Rhetoric: The Light-Dark Family." *QJS* (Apr. 1967), 115–126.

———. "The Evolution of the Archetypal Sea in Rhetoric and Poetic." *QJS* (Dec. 1977), 347–363.

———. "Rhetorical Depiction." In *Form, Genre, and the Study of Political Discourse*, edited by Herbert W. Simons and Aram A. Aghazarian. Columbia: University of South Carolina Press, 1986.

* ———. "In Quest of Metaphor: The Story of an Odyssey." *The Florida Communication Journal* (1989), 1–9.

* Peretz, Martin. "Symbolic Politics." *The New Republic,* 24 Oct. 1988, p. 50.

 Petersen, David. " Add Spice to Your Writing: Using Figurative Language." *Writer's Digest* (July 1994), 40–41.

* "Playing with Words: Sports Metaphors." *The Economist,* 30 July 1994, p. 78.

Procter, David E. "Bridging Social Change Through Mythic Regeneration." *CS* (Fall 1992), 171–181.

Quinn, Arthur. *Figures of Speech: Sixty Ways to Turn a Phrase.* Salt Lake City: Gibbs M. Smith, 1982.

* Reich, Robert B. "Remembering Pearl Harbor—Too Often: Use of War Metaphors." *Harper's* (Jan. 1992), 20–22.

Reinsch, N. L., Jr. "Figurative Language and Source Credibility." *HCR* (Fall 1974), 75–80.

* Rubin, John. "Anatomy of Analogy." *Psychology Today* (Feb. 1988), 12.

Siddens, Paul L., III. "Figures of Speech in Poetic and Everyday Discourse." *SCT* (Spring 1994), 13–14.

Siltanen, Susan A. "The Persuasiveness of Metaphor: A Replication and Extension." *SSCJ* (Fall 1981), 67–83.

Sontag, Susan. *Illness as Metaphor.* New York: Vintage Books, 1979.

———. *AIDS and Its Metaphors.* New York: Farrar, Straus, and Giroux, 1988.

* Sweet, Robert Burdette. "Creatures of the Metaphor: The Importance of Art and Metaphor to Society." *The Humanist* (Nov.–Dec. 1995), 26–29.

Ullman, Montague. "The Role of Imagery." *JC* (Winter 1975), 162–172.

von Baeyer, Hans Christian. "The Ocean, the Stars, and the Kitchen Sink: Analogies in Natural Systems." *Discover* (Mar. 1994), 82–87.

* Weaver, Richard. "Ultimate Terms in Contemporary Rhetoric." In *The Ethics of Rhetoric.* Chicago: Henry Regnery, 1953, 211–232.

Whaley, Bryan B., and Austin S. Babrow. "Analogy in Persuasion: Translator's Dictionary or Art?" *CS* (Fall 1993), 239–253.

General

"Babel Revisited." *The Economist,* 7 July 1990, p. 20.

* Baker, Ross K. "Lincoln on a Computer: Revised Version of the Gettysburg Address." *American Demographics* (June 1987), 72.

Bosmajian, Haig. *The Language of Oppression.* Washington, D.C.: Public Affairs Press, 1974.

Bowers, John Waite. "Language Intensity, Social Introversion and Attitude Change." *CM* (Nov. 1963), 345–352.

———. "Some Correlates of Language Intensity." *QJS* (Dec. 1964), 415–420.

Burke, Kenneth. *Language as Symbolic Action: Essays on Life, Literature, and Method.* Berkeley: University of California Press, 1966.

Carbone, Tamara. "Stylistic Variables as Related to Source Credibility: A Content Analysis Approach." *CM* (June 1975), 99–106.

Colquit, Jesse L. "The Student's Right to His Own Language: A Viable Model or Empty Rhetoric?" *CQ* (Fall 1977), 177–120.

* Ewart, Neil. "Saved by What Bell? Origins of Common Phrases." *Reader's Digest* (May 1989), 165–167.

Franzwa, Helen H. "Psychological Factors Influencing Use of Evaluative-Dynamic Language." *CM* (June 1969), 103–109.

Gelderman, Carol. "All the Presidents' Words." *The Wilson Quarterly* (Spring 1995), 68–79.

* "The Gift of the Gab: Rhetoric and Speech-making Were an Essential Part of Ancient Grecian Democracy, Education." *The Economist,* 2 Sept. 1995, p. 80.

Gozzi, Raymond, Jr. *New Words and a Changing American Culture.* Columbia: University of South Carolina Press, 1990.

* Hagege, Claude. "The Powers of Language." *UNESCO Courier* (Mar. 1986), 18–21.

Halloran, S. Michael. "Eloquence in a Technological Society." *CSSJ* (Winter 1978), 221–227.

Hamilton, Mark A., and Becky L. Stewart. "Extending an Information Processing Model of Language Intensity Effects." *CQ* (Spring 1993), 231–246.

Hensley, Carl Wayne. "Speak with Style and Watch the Impact." *Vital Speeches of the Day,* 1 Sept. 1995, pp. 701–704.

Infante, Dominic A. "Effects of Opinionated Language on Communicator Image and in Conferring Resistance to Persuasion." *WJSC* (Spring 1975), 112–119.

Jackson, Sally. "How to Do Things to Words: The Experimental Manipulation of Message Variables." *SCJ* (Winter 1993), 103–114.

Jensen, Marvin D. "Revising Speech Style." *SCT* (Summer 1988), 3–4.

Joshi, Aravind K. "Natural Language Processing." *Science*, 13 Sept. 1991, pp. 1242–1249.

Kauffman, Charles. "Names and Weapons." *CM* (Sept. 1989), 273–285.

* "The Lost Art of Speechmaking: Four Veteran Wordsmiths Reveal the Secrets of Writing and Delivering Effective Speeches." *Campaigns & Elections* (June–July 1993), 48–49.

* Lyons, Lois J. "A Weary Listener's Plea for Eloquence." *National Underwriter Property and Casualty-Employee Benefits Edition*, 4 May 1987, pp. 37–38.

McNally, David. "Language, History, and Class Struggle." *Monthly Review* (July–Aug. 1995), 13–30.

Muhlhausler, Peter. "Babel Revisited." *UNESCO Courier* (Feb. 1994), 16–21.

Osborn, Michael. *Orientations to Rhetorical Style*. Chicago: Science Research Associates, 1976.

* "Probable Uncertainty: What Probability Terms Mean to Different People." *Psychology Today* (Feb. 1988), 12–13.

Rogan, Randall G. "Language Intensity: Testing a Content-based Metric." *CR* (Summer 1995), 128–135.

Sanders, Robert E. "Style, Meaning, and Message Effects." *CM* (June 1984), 154–167.

Sayer, James Edward. "The Student's Right to His Own Language: A Response to Colquit." *CQ* (Winter 1979), 44–46.

Schiappa, Edward. "The Rhetoric of Nukespeak." *CM* (Sept. 1989), 252–272.

* Smith, Larry. "The Borders of Words." *The Humanist* (Nov.–Dec. 1995), 30–32.

* Smith, Wen, and Don Trawin. "Let's Hear It for Rhetoric!" *Saturday Evening Post* (May–June 1995), 22–24.

Tanenhaus, Michael K., Michael J. Spivey-Knowlton, Kathleen M. Eberhard, and Julie C. Sedivy. "Integration of Visual and Linguistic Information in Spoken Language Comprehension." *Science*, 16 June 1995, pp. 1632–1634.

* "'To Be' in Their Bonnets: A Matter of Semantics." *Atlantic* (Feb. 1992), 20.

* West, Paul. "The stylist's revenge." *Harper's* (Apr. 1994), 35.

Williams, M. Lee. "The Effect of Deliberate Vagueness on Receiver Recall and Agreement." *CSSJ* (Spring 1980), 30–41.

* Wurm, Stephen. " The Gift of Tongues." *UNESCO Courier* (Feb. 1994), 10–14.

Language and Gender

Cameron, Deborah, ed. *The Feminist Critique of Language: A Reader*. London: Routledge, 1990.

Decure, Nicole. "The Difficulties of Teaching a 'Man-made Language.'" *Women and Language* (Spring 1994), 36–37.

Goueffic, Louise. "Reflecting Changing Social Realities Through the Word." *Women and Language* (Fall 1993), 38–39.

Hardman, M. M. "Gender Through the Levels." Women and Language (Fall 1993), 42–49.

Ivy, Diane K., and Phil Backlund. *Exploring Gender-Speak: Personal Effectiveness in Gender Communication*. New York: McGraw Hill, 1994.

* Kohn, Alfie. "Girl Talk, Guy Talk: Do Men and Women Really Have Distinctive Conversational Styles?" *Psychology Today* (Feb. 1988), 65–66.

Maggio, Rosalie. *The Bias-Free Word Finder: A Dictionary of Nondiscriminatory Language*. Boston: Beacon Press, 1991.

Penelope, Julia. "Grammar Is Sex; Language Is a Woman." *Women and Language* (Fall 1993), 53–56.

Peterson, Eric E. " Nonsexist Language Reform and 'Political Correctness.'" *Women and Language* (Fall 1994), 6–10.

Shurbutt, Sylvia Bailey. "Creating a Woman's Wife Through Words: A Language of Their Own." *Women and Language* (Spring 1994), 38–41.

Valentine, Kristin Bervig, and Eugene Valentine. "Metaphors in the University, or I Never Promised You an Ivory Tower." *Women and Language* (Fall 1994), 11–17.

Wood, Julia T. *Gendered Lives: Communication, Gender, and Culture.* Belmont, Calif.: Wadsworth, 1994.

Yusuf, Yisa Kehinde. "From 'Motherless Babies' to 'Babiless Mothers': A Sexist Metaphorical Transition of Female Undergraduates." *Women and Language* (Fall 1994), 30–33.

Teaching Techniques

Feezel, Jerry D. "Means-to-Me: A Word Game Without Winning or Losing." *CE* (Apr. 1982), 159–162.

Gschwend, Laura L. "Acquiring the Artful Use of Antithesis." *SCT* (Winter 1995), 2–3.

Hochel, Sandra. "Language Awareness and Assessment." *SCT* (Winter 1990), 4–5.

Jensen, Marvin D. "Revising Speech Style." *SCT* (Summer 1988), 3–4.

———. "The Gettysburg Address: Exploring Lincoln's Second Thoughts." *SCT* (Summer 1990), 10.

Kassing, Jeffrey W. "The Color of Perception." *SCT* (Summer 1994), 4–5.

Lamoureux, Edward Lee. "Practicing Creative Word Choice with Dialogic Listening." *SCT* (Summer 1990), 4–5.

McGrath, Richard. "The Slang Game." *SCT* (Fall 1987), 5.

Phillips, Terilyn Goins. "Name That Analogy: The Communication Game." *SCT* (Winter 1996), 10–11.

Ringer, Jeffery R. "Simply Jargon." *SCT* (Fall 1994), 11.

Rowley, Edwin N. "More than Mere Words." *SCT* (Fall 1992), 5.

Siddens, Paul L., III. "Figures of Speech in Poetic and Everyday Discourse." *SCT* (Spring 1994), 13–14.

Snyder, Lee. "How to Make a World." *SCT* (Winter 1989), 4–5.

Zizik, Catherine H. "Powerspeak: Avoiding Ambiguous Language." *SCT* (Summer 1995), 8–9.

Oral Style

Blankenship, Jane. "A Linguistic Analysis of Oral and Written Style." *QJS* (Dec. 1962), 419–422.

Einhorn, Lois. "Oral and Written Style: An Examination of Differences." *SSCJ* (Spring 1978), 302–311.

Fallows, James. " Who's a Snob and Who's Not." *Washington Monthly* (Feb. 1989), 34–35.

"From the Desk of Peggy Noonan—To: Bob Dole; Date: May 27, 1996." *Time,* 27 May 1996, p. 88.

Gibson, James W., Charles R. Gruner, Robert J. Kibler, and Francis J. Kelly. "A Quantitative Examination of Differences and Similarities in Written and Spoken Messages." *CM* (Nov. 1966), 444–451.

"Keep It Simple, Bill." *The Economist,* 11 July 1992, p. 32.

* "Southern-speak: Clinton Uses It Well." *Norfolk Virginian-Pilot and the Ledger-Star,* 10 Apr. 1994, p. A6.

* Tarver, Jerry. "Words in Time: Some Reflections on the Language of Speech." *Vital Speeches of the Day,* 15 Apr. 1988, pp. 410–412.

DeVito, Joseph A. "Comprehension in Oral and Written Discourse." *CM* (June 1965), 124–128.

Misuse

Dieterich, Daniel, ed. *Teaching About Doublespeak.* Urbana, Ill.: National Council of Teachers of English, 1976. A collection of essays designed to help instructors develop student abilities to understand and ethically evaluate political and commercial doublespeak. Available only from NCTE, 1111 Kenyon Road, Urbana, IL 61801, $5.00 postpaid.

* "Fertilizer of Hate [Oklahoma City federal building bombing]." *The Progressive* (June 1995), 46.

"Flat Earthers [satire of free trade jargon]." *The Economist,* 11 July 1992, p. 20.

Fotheringham, Alan. "The Word They Dare Not Speak: Military Doublespeak." *Maclean's,* 19 Feb. 1991, p. 56.

* "The Gobblies at the Gate [column on abuse of the English language]. *The Economist,* 21 Nov. 1992, p. 104.

* Grant, Eleanor. "A Pen by Any Other Name? Labeling Objects Hinders Creativity." *Psychology Today* (Feb. 1988), 16.

* Hale, Robert D. "Musings: On Keeping Writing Free of Potentially Offensive Words and Phrases." *The Horn Book Magazine* (May–June 1993), 363–364.

* "Health-Care Double-Speak." *The Progressive* (Sept. 1994), 46.

* Lapham, Lewis H. " Reactionary Chic: How the Nineties Right Recycles the Bombast of the Sixties Left." *Harper's* (Mar. 1995), 31–42.

Lutz, William. *Doublespeak*. New York: Harper & Row, 1989.

* Lutz, William, and Don Trawin. " How's That Again? Doublespeak." *Saturday Evening Post* (Mar. 1990), 64–66.

* "The Meaning of Mean: Usage of the Term 'Mean-spirited' in Politics." *Fortune,* 25 Dec. 1995, p. 231.

* Motley, Michael T. "What I Meant to Say: Sometimes Embarrassing, Sometimes Hilarious, Verbal Slips May Reflect Linguistic Confusion or Freudian Mix-Ups." *Psychology Today* (Feb. 1987), 24–28.

* Pacentrilli, Paul. "How to Sound Erudite." *World Press Review* (Aug. 1993), 26.

"Psychobabble Rising, but We Feel the Pain." *Insight on the News,* 18 Dec. 1995, pp. 23–24.

* Satchell, Michael. "Could You, er, Say That Again: Doublespeak." *U.S. News & World Report,* 20 April 1987, p. 71.

* Smith, Wen. "Silver spoonerisms." *Saturday Evening Post* (Jan.–Feb. 1992), 14–15.

* "Stamp Out 'Doublespeak.'" *Parade,* 10 Jan. 1988, p. 16.

* Udall, Morris K. "Stalking the Elusive Malaprop." *Saturday Evening Post* (Oct. 1988), 38–41.

* Visser, Margaret. "Tips of the Slongue." *Saturday Night* (Sept. 1988), 73.

Wallace, Bruce. "Politics of Abuse: Harsh Language Is Under Widespread Attack." *Maclean's,* 26 Nov. 1990, p. 64.

* "What's In a Name? [political labeling]." *Scholastic Update,* 7 Oct. 1994, pp. 18–19.

CHAPTER 11
Presenting Your Speech

OBJECTIVES

- To help your students understand what makes an effective presentation.

- To teach your students the four major methods of presentation.

- To help your students understand how to adapt to video presentations.

- To help your students learn how to respond to audience feedback.

- To teach your students how to participate in question-and-answer sessions.

- To improve your students' speaking voices.

- To improve your students' use of body language.

- To teach your students how to practice effectively.

SUGGESTIONS FOR TEACHING

Teaching and grading presentation skills can be very challenging. Presentation is a crucial part of the art that imparts a speaker's ideas and proposals. Yet while there are general principles of effective delivery—speakers should speak extemporaneously and loud enough to be heard—there are few absolute rules that "great" speakers do not defy from time to time. Winston Churchill, for instance, spoke with a lisp, and Abraham Lincoln is said to have spoken in a whiny, high-pitched voice.

The challenge of teaching presentation skills is to teach those basic principles without discouraging beginning speakers from developing their own unique styles. Like most communication skills, presentation skills are most effectively learned through critique and application, and it is crucial that you establish a supportive, nonthreatening classroom atmosphere in which your students can participate and develop their skills uninhibited. Get your students in front of the class for short, ungraded speaking activities as often as possible. Always be constructive with suggestions for improvement, and be willing to break the ice by going first. If necessary, refer your students back to Chapter 2 on dealing with communication apprehension.

Some instructors emphasize presentation skills heavily in their grading, while others focus more on the speech itself, especially with earlier presentations. Avoid rewarding "slick" speakers with nothing to say while punishing people with severe communication apprehension. Emphasize that students who force themselves to speak extemporaneously will improve with every presentation, and look for and recognize effort and improvement over the course of the semester.

In this chapter we offer exercises to impress upon your students the importance of nonverbal factors in presentations, the relationship between ethos perceptions and presentation skills, and multiple activities for assessing and improving your students' speaking voices, spotlighting ideas, animating expressions, and other basic skills covered in the text. There are also exercises that have your students critique themselves, one another, and other student and "expert" speakers to help sharpen their general appreciation for what makes for effective presentation skills.

CHAPTER OUTLINE

I. An effective presentation concerns the "how" as opposed to the "what" of public speaking. Effective presentations: *(text pp. 342–343)*
   A. allow speakers and audiences to share ideas and feelings.
   B. reflect enthusiasm and commitment.
   C. do not call attention to themselves or distract from the message.
   D. sound natural, spontaneous, and conversational.
      1. Immediacy is a sense of closeness experienced by speakers and audiences. Speakers should:
         a. try to overcome barriers between themselves and their audiences by moving closer, smiling, and making eye contact.
         b. appear controlled to their listeners, even if they don't feel that way.
      2. An expanded conversational style preserves the directness and spontaneity of conversation, is colorful, and is tuned to the responses of listeners.

II. There are several ways of presenting speeches. *(text pp. 343–354)*
   A. Impromptu speaking is appropriate when time for preparation and practice is limited.
      1. Speakers should first determine their purposes, then determine main points (no more than three), write out key words (if possible), stick to and enumerate main points, keep their presentations short, and end with a summary of main points.
         a. Speakers using the PREP formula state their points, offer a reason or example, and then restate their points.
         b. When impromptu speeches are presented in a series, speakers should adapt to the immediate context that emerges in the other speeches.
   B. Memorized text presentations are written out, committed to memory, and delivered word for word.
      1. You should memorize only key parts of a speech (introduction, conclusion, and transitions) and the order of main points.
      2. You may wish to memorize short presentations, such as toasts.
      3. Beginning speakers rarely make effective memorized presentations.
         a. Memorized speeches often sound stilted.
         b. Being bound to a text inhibits eye contact and response to feedback.
      4. When making memorized presentations, speakers should:
         a. know the speech well enough to concentrate on the audience.
         b. use repetition to talk their way through mental blocks.
   C. In a manuscript presentation, a written text is either read from a paper script or a teleprompter.
      1. Manuscript presentations pose many of the same challenges as memorized ones.
         a. Most untrained speakers do not read effectively.
      2. Manuscript presentations are appropriate when exact wording or timing is important.
      3. Speakers should read extended quotes or complex information.
      4. When reading from a manuscript, speakers should use large print that can be read without straining, use pastel paper to reduce glare, double- or triple-space the manuscript, mark pauses with slashes, highlight materials to be emphasized, and practice sufficiently so that they can maintain eye contact.

    D. Extemporaneous speaking is prepared and practiced, but not written out or memorized. Speakers should:
1. thoroughly prepare and practice their presentations.
2. word their speeches slightly differently each time they practice.
3. respond to feedback from the audience. Speakers should learn to recognize:
    a. feedback that signals misunderstanding.
    b. feedback that signals loss of interest.
    c. feedback that signals disagreement.

    E. Most of us may be asked to make video presentations at some time.
1. Television amplifies the visual to bring speakers close to listeners. Speakers should:
    a. dress conservatively and coordinate with the backdrop color.
    b. use makeup and avoid tinted glasses.
    c. strive for an intimate, conversational voice.
    d. avoid abrupt changes in vocal and facial expressions.
    e. emphasize precise timing.
    f. develop rapport and be cooperative with studio technicians.
    g. always assume the camera is live and address it as if it were a friendly face.
    h. relax and be prepared to start on cue.
    i. practice thoroughly.

    F. The following suggestions can help speakers prepare for question-and-answer sessions.
1. Anticipate and prepare for questions in advance.
2. Repeat questions and paraphrase what you heard.
3. Maintain eye contact with the audience as you answer.
4. Defuse hostile or emotional questions by rewording them in more objective language and not responding in kind.
5. Keep answers short and to the point.
6. Handle nonquestions politely by waiting for pauses to reassume control of the speaking situation.
7. Bring question-and-answer sessions to a close by calling for final questions and summarizing your message.

III. A good speaking voice helps convey meaning and feeling and enhances ethos. *(text pp. 354–364)*
    A. Minor improvements can help make most speakers more effective.
1. Record your voice and critique it in terms of whether it conveys your meaning, whether you like listening to it, and whether it presents you at your best.
2. Speakers may need to work on their voices in terms of pitch, rate, loudness, variety, articulation, enunciation, pronunciation, or dialect.
3. Speakers with serious speech impediments should seek professional treatment.

    B. Pitch refers to placement of your voice on a musical scale.
1. Habitual pitch is the level at which you usually speak.
2. Optimum pitch is the level that allows variation with minimal effort.
3. Stress often causes people to speak at a higher pitch.

    C. Rate refers to the speed at which words are uttered.
1. Serious topics call for a slow, deliberate rate, and lighter topics, a faster one.
2. Variations of rate patterns, or rhythm, should reflect changes in your material.
3. Beginning speakers typically speak too fast.
4. Pauses are oral punctuation marks that add emphasis and give listeners time to contemplate what has been said.
5. Vocal distractions such as "er," "um," and "you know" should be avoided.
6. Different cultures and subcultures have their own speech rhythms.

    D. Loudness is important because listeners must be able to hear a presentation.
1. Speakers generally should talk louder than in casual conversation.
2. Different cultures have different norms regarding appropriate loudness.
3. Loudness variations can help convey emotions.

    E. Variety of pitch, rate, and loudness can bring a presentation to life.

F. People are often judged by their articulation, enunciation, pronunciation, and dialect.
    1. Articulation refers to the production of individual speech sounds.
    2. Enunciation refers to how we pronounce words in context.
    3. Pronunciation involves saying words correctly.
    4. Dialects are speech patterns associated with a particular region or ethnic group.

IV. Body language consists of the nonverbal communication that accompanies a speech. *(text pp. 364–368)*
    A. Nonverbal messages should complement and reinforce verbal messages.
    B. Facial expression and eye contact affect the way audiences perceive a speaker.
        1. Speakers who avoid eye contact may be seen as dishonest, indifferent, or nervous.
        2. Speakers should establish and maintain eye contact with their entire audience.
    C. Movement and gestures should complement the speaker's message.
        1. Random movements distract attention from the message.
        2. Speakers should not assume a universal language of gestures.
        3. Proxemics, the study of how space is used in communication, suggests two principles of effective movement during speeches.
            a. Moving closer to audiences while speaking can enhance feelings of closeness.
            b. Presenting speeches from an elevated position can inhibit identification.
    D. Dress and grooming should complement a message and be appropriate to the occasion.

V. Practicing is crucial to making effective presentations. *(text pp. 368–370)*
    A. It takes a lot of practice to sound natural.
        1. Speakers should practice until they can respond fully to their ideas as they present them.
        2. Speakers should rehearse nonverbal as well as verbal aspects of their presentations.
        3. Speakers should try out different techniques during practice.
    B. Speakers should simulate the actual speaking situation for practice.
    C. Speakers should practice their speeches first from formal and then from key-word outlines.
    D. Speakers should record and critique themselves, using video- or audiotape.
    E. Practicing before others can provide valuable feedback.

USING END-OF-CHAPTER ITEMS

Discussion *(text p. 372)*

1. Be part of an audience for a lecture or political speech. Did the speaker read from a manuscript, make a memorized presentation, or speak extemporaneously? Was the speaker's voice effective or ineffective? Why? How would you evaluate the speaker's body language? Discuss your observations with your classmates.

    Provide your students with the "Guide for Evaluating a Presentation" (p. 331). Have your students attend a speech and report their ideas in class. This assignment can also be completed in class, using videotaped speeches. On C-Span, you can often find speakers whose presentations are read with little preparation. Use these to demonstrate what you will be looking for in student presentations, as well as the relative strengths and weaknesses of different presentation styles.

2. Comedians often capture the personalities of public figures by accentuating their verbal and gestural characteristics in comic impersonations. Be alert for such impersonations on late-night television. Which identifying characteristics do the comedians exaggerate? What might this indicate about the "real" speaker's style and ethos? Contribute your observations to a class discussion.

This is intended for in-class discussion, and offers an interesting change of pace that your students should appreciate. Many late-night personalities do political impersonations, but perhaps none better than the cast members of NBC's *Saturday Night Live*. Who could forget Chevy Chase's treatment of Jerry Ford, or Dan Aykroyd doing Richard Nixon and Jimmy Carter? Dana Carvey and Phil Hartman have helped to keep the tradition alive with their impressions of George Bush and Bill Clinton. What aspects of the speaker's delivery style get magnified and exaggerated in the comic impersonations? You might note that such attention is inevitable and not always hurtful. The grace with which politicians react to such treatment can influence the way audiences perceive them.

3. **You have been invited to present your most recent classroom speech on local public television. How would you adapt your message to that medium? Report your ideas in class. What general conclusions can you draw about the impact of video presentations on public communication?**

This works well as a homework assignment followed by in-class presentations. If you have access to video equipment, make tapes of the presentations. Conduct impromptu critiques for in-class discussion between presentations. You might project the transparency "Speaking on Television" (p. 330) in conjunction with these presentations as a guide for critiquing them.

4. **Make a list of questions you think you might be asked following your next speech. Plan and prepare answers to those questions. Working in small groups, distribute your questions to group members to ask of you. Invite them to evaluate your responses.**

This can be used either for homework or as a small-group activity followed by general class discussion just prior to a round of planned speeches. It helps to force students to focus their thinking in terms of audience predisposition. Obviously, students should know their topics and have a good idea of their specific-purpose and thesis statements. In preparation for class discussion, they should try to anticipate likely misunderstandings, concerns, and objections, and roughly outline responses to probable questions that might be asked. Focus class discussion on the adequacy of planned responses, and questions the speaker might have missed.

Application *(text pp. 372–373)*

1. **Exchange your self-evaluation tape with a classmate and write a critique of the other person's voice and articulation. Emphasize the positive, but make specific recommendations for improvement. Work on your classmate's recommendations to you, and then make a second tape to share with your partner. Do you hear signs of improvement in each other's performance?**

This exercise helps to get students thinking about what makes an effective voice and improving their own voices. It can also help students deal with communication apprehension. You might combine it with "Creating a Supportive Classroom Climate" in Chapter 2, IRM p. 82. Remind students to criticize in a constructive manner, emphasizing strengths as well as weaknesses and offering suggestions for improvement. You might distribute the "Guide for Evaluation of Voice and Articulation" (p. 332) to help guide their evaluations.

2. **Make a list of words you often mispronounce. Practice saying these words correctly each day for a week. See if you notice any carryover of these changes into social conversation.**

This can be used for homework. Students might ask friends to help them develop of list of five words they often mispronounce. They should include representations of how they mispronounce the words and correct pronunciations. You might start the exercise by revealing your own troublesome words, and then ask the students to share their examples. After a week, have each student pronounce her or his words before the class. As an alternative, have your students look especially for mispronounced words during one another's presentations in conjunction with any type of short speaking activity. At the end of each speech, compile a list of mispronounced words for each student for class discussion. Although you might include considerations of articulation and enunciation, keep students focused on constructive criticism.

3. **Experiment with reading the same material aloud at different rates of speed and with varying loudness. Do these differences seem to affect the meaning of the material?**

   A good way to handle this exercise is to have your students bring short poems, prose readings, or speech passages to class. Have them make four fifteen-second presentations of the same material in which they purposefully speak too fast, too slow, too loud, and too soft. Then have them read the material again with what they perceive to be the proper rate, volume, pitch, and variation. Emphasize the importance of vocal variation in giving expressive meaning to spoken ideas. You might also use this as an opportunity to assess your students' habitual and optimal pitches. Elicit class reactions to the different readings. Be enthusiastic and encourage your students to exaggerate their presentations. This exercise can be a fun icebreaker for approaching the subject of voice and articulation, as well as for helping students to deal with communication apprehension.

4. **As you practice your next speech, deliberately try to speak in as dull a voice as possible. Stifle all impulses to gesture. Then practice speaking with as colorful a voice as possible, giving full freedom to movement and gesture. Notice how a colorful and expressive presentation makes your ideas seem more lively and vivid as you speak.**

   This can be used for homework or as an in-class short speaking activity. If it is used as homework, have your students tape their practice presentations and bring them to class. Or, have them take center stage to practice a chosen part of their speech (no more than one minute) in class. Emphasize the importance of a lively presentation that complements the tone and meaning of a message. Again, it is important to be enthusiastic in order to get students to participate in activities such as this. Encourage them to purposefully exaggerate their presentations.

5. **Form small groups and conduct an impromptu speaking contest. Each participant should supply two topics for impromptu speeches, and participants should then draw two topics (not their own). Participants have five minutes to prepare a three-minute speech on one of these topics. Each student then presents the speech to the group, which selects a winner.**

   Project the transparency "Making Impromptu Presentations" (p. 327). Have students work in small groups, preparing and presenting their speeches. Each group should nominate a best speech to be presented to the class, which will subsequently vote on a winner. As an alternative, schedule a classroom round of impromptu speeches. The list of quotations in this chapter (pp. 333–334) may be used as subjects. Cut and fold the individual quotations and place them in a container. Have students pull two quotations from the container, choose one, and return the other to the container. (See Chapter 7 for another list of impromptu subjects, p. 235.) Evaluate their speeches using the "Guide for Evaluating Impromptu Presentations," p. 335.

ADDITIONAL ACTIVITIES

Observing Nonverbals in Public vs. Interpersonal Communication

Purpose: To get your students thinking about the different requirements of effective "body talk" in public and private settings.

Directions: This exercise works well as a combined homework/in-class discussion piece. For in-class use, show videotapes of interpersonal discussions and clips of well-known speakers. Your students will probably notice that effective public speakers tend to be a lot more expressive and dramatic in their nonverbal behaviors. Many novice speakers are ineffective in nonverbal aspects of public speaking because (in addition to being nervous) they have developed their nonverbal skills in small interpersonal settings. In such intimate settings, subtlety is usually the key, and exaggerated face, eye, and vocal gestures are more often perceived as overbearing and rude. Yet understated inflections of voice and facial gestures are usually imperceptible to most members of larger audiences, and so such animation is not only acceptable, but crucial to an effective and dynamic presentation. Emphasize that beginning speakers should constantly seek to animate their nonverbal expressions when addressing larger audiences, and remind your students of this throughout the term during short speaking activities.

Expressive Reading

Purpose: To provide a nonthreatening environment in which students can practice expressive reading skills.

Directions: In a container, place an assortment of nonexpressive reading materials: printed matter from cereal boxes, toothpaste containers, cartons, wrappers, etc. In a second container, provide small folded pieces of paper with words describing emotions written on them, such as:

anger	fear	surprise
suspense	resignation	disgust
love	jealousy	disappointment
contentment	joy	contempt

Be sure you have enough pieces of paper for all students. Duplications are acceptable. Each student should draw one slip from each container. Have students read the material expressing the stipulated emotion, without telling the class which one they are trying to convey. If the class cannot tell, focus discussion on what the student might have done vocally or with gestures to convey the proper emotion more effectively.

Question-and-Answer Sessions

Purpose: To provide students with experience combining extemporaneous and impromptu speaking.

Directions: This exercise works well in conjunction with a major speech assignment, and is an excellent means of getting your students to engage one another's speeches as critical and constructive audience members. Follow your usual instructions for the assignment, but inform your students that there will be a three- to five-minute question-and-answer session following their presentations. Distribute "Handling Questions and Answers" (p. 329) when making the speaking assignment. You might also distribute the "Evaluation Form for Question-and-Answer Sessions" (p. 336). Instruct your students to jot down (during the speeches) at least two questions they would like to ask each speaker following the conclusion of his or her presentation. The speakers should then lead the question-and-answer sessions and bring them to a conclusion when the allotted time has elapsed.

Speak Up!

Purpose: To force your students to use their optimal voices to overcome physical noise barriers to effective public speaking.

Directions: Every semester instructors have students who obviously work hard preparing their speeches, but never manage to present them clearly or forcefully enough to be really effective. This will hinder them, especially in "real-world" contexts in which audiences are not captive and there are competing sources of noise. It can be hard to simulate some real-world challenges in the classroom, but physical noise barriers are easy to create. Ask your students to read the lyrics of a favorite song, poem, piece of literature, etc., that takes about one minute to present. Bring a radio and set it up at the front of the class so that students will have to compete with it directly. Don't turn it up so high that it disturbs adjacent classes or that your students have to scream to be heard, just high enough so that they have to speak loudly and clearly in order to be understood. Stress the importance of animating your voice (volume and pitch variation) and gestures in public speaking as opposed to everyday conversation. You might preface this activity by noting that the Greeks trained their students by having them speak over the sound of crashing waves. If you have an auditorium or outdoor setting, take the opportunity to get your students outside for speaking activities that require them to use their voices more effectively to take charge of the larger and noisier settings.

Spotlighting and Animating Ideas

Purpose: To give your students an opportunity to practice their expressive presentations skills using a prepared text.

Directions: This speaking activity can be coordinated with "Speak Up!" and Application item 3. Have your students choose text samples to interpret for this exercise. Students should become familiar with their samples for homework, and "spotlight" the ideas as they present them to the class. Don't let them just read their passages quickly without making eye contact and then sit down. Push them to animate their moves, gestures, and voices to help convey their messages as clearly as possible, and to maintain eye contact with their audience. Be enthusiastic and constructive with your critiques. Activities such as this can be very effective at reducing inhibitions. You might start things off by going first yourself. Impress upon students the differences between face-to-face communication and public speaking, and the need for an animated presentation.

Finding Your Best Voice

Purpose: To help your students determine their habitual and optimal vocal pitch.

Directions: This can be used as a short speaking activity, or as a small-group discussion piece in conjunction with Application item 1. Some people never reach their potential as public speakers because they habitually speak at a pitch that is inconsistent with their maximum potential in terms of pitch variability. Communication apprehension may well be a contributing factor, but people who speak at too low or too high a pitch commonly do not project their voices clearly and effectively. This is also true of people who speak too fast, too slow, or in a lifeless monotone. Combine this with any type of short speaking activity. You might have students interpret a prepared text or read from a past speech outline. Have your students speak for about thirty seconds using their everyday pitch and voice, and then stop them for class discussion. Emphasize that they should not try to consciously change or "fix" their voices simply to get through this exercise unscathed, which would defeat its purpose. Ask if they feel they are using their optimal or strongest voices. What do their classmates think? Do they need to speak at a higher or lower pitch? Then have them interpret the same text at a consciously higher and lower pitch for ten to fifteen seconds. Does either of these feel more comfortable or sound more effective? You may adapt this exercise for variations of rate and volume. As with all speaking activities, be enthusiastic and constructive with your critiques. No one will magically transform her or his voice immediately, but the conscious recognition of such problems is a crucial first step in dealing with them. Encourage your students to further explore their most effective public voices on their own.

Critiquing Student Speeches

Purpose: To give your students a chance to critique the presentations of other student speakers.

Directions: This is intended for in-class viewing and general class discussion. Show a videotape of student speeches, and conduct impromptu critiques for class discussion between viewings. Start with basics. Do the students make extemporaneous presentations, or are they reading notes or reciting from memory? Do they establish and maintain eye contact? Do they speak loudly and clearly enough to be heard? Do they speak with a natural pitch variation that complements the tone and flow of the message, or do they speak in a weak and monotone voice? Is there anything about the nature of their vocal patterns and gestures that seems mechanical and arbitrary (pacing, hair or mustache curling), and distracts attention from the actual message? Sometimes students consciously sound every syllable, resulting in a mechanical vocal pattern that can erect barriers to identification. Encourage all your students to offer comments and observations. This provides another opportunity to let them know what you will look for when grading their presentations.

The Impact of a Little Drama on Presentation Skills*

Goal: To help students realize how a little drama can help their presentations.

Directions: Professor Unger supplied us with the following account of how one of his students injected an element of drama into a presentation. When we first heard the account of this presentation, our response was simply, "Wow!" You may wish to share this with your students in the hopes that this example might serve as a model and start them thinking about similar ways they can inject some drama into their presentations.

A couple of years ago a student of mine took me up on my suggestion that he use a little drama as part of his hook to capture the interest and attention of the audience in his Introduction to Public Speaking course.

He had made arrangements with the instructor that a friend could pass a card to each student ahead of time so as not to spoil the effect of his foreboding entrance. There was a card for each student, and each contained the name of a common profession that was practiced at the time of the Black Plague of Europe, such as clergyman, sailor, farmer, merchant, and so on, in roughly the proportions that they represented in that society.

When his name was called, the student entered the door in the back of the room with a measured gait, wearing an oversized black sweatshirt, hood up, and cinched around the waist with a length of sash cord. His opening statement was delivered in somber tones in which he identified his topic as the Black Plague, established his credibility by telling the audience in arcane language that he had just completed study for a term paper on the subject, and asked the rhetorical question, "If the disease were to strike the community in which Kutztown University is located today, given the same medical limitations, how many do you think would survive?" He then asked all of the students in the audience to stand up.

After a long dramatic pause, during which his eyes slowly moved from student to student in the room, he said in sepulchral tones, "Will all those with a card reading 'physician' please sit down. In tending the sick, you have come in contact with the disease and have become one of its victims." A student took her seat. He followed with, "Will all those identified as 'sailor' or 'merchant' please be seated. You have traveled about the country or the world and so have also come close to other victims and have sealed your fate." Five other students sat down. He then called out such categories of medieval society as clergy, city dweller, dock worker, soldier, and others who would have had occasion to be exposed to the disease.

By the time he was finished reading the list of those who had been must susceptible to the disease, there were only five students still standing in the class of 24. He then finished his introduction with an explanation that had the plague struck the university town with the relentless ferocity of the European version, all who were seated would have been victims, leaving the remaining five students with the task of rebuilding European society.

---

* The material in this exercise was supplied by Professor Reno C. Unger, Kutztown University. Used with permission.

Pamela Hayward (University of Illinois at Urbana-Champaign), "Delivery Cards," *SCT* (Spring 1994), 3.

Goal: To help students understand how ineffective delivery can negatively impact the message they are trying to convey.

This activity, which stresses delivery skills, can be used in a variety of different instructional siutations. I have had success using this exercise during a leadership workshop for high school students, in a university-level introductory speaking course, and in a workshop for bank employees. The key to utilizing the activity successfully lies in providing a comfortable and constructive atmosphere for the participants.

Often it can be difficult to cover the basic elements of speech delivery, particularly when there is little time allocated in the curriculum to do so. The topic of delivery is a complex one and can rarely be treated well by merely listing a series of "prescriptions" on the board. I found that instead of giving a lecture to students on what they *should* do in terms of delivery, it has been much more effective for me to let them discover what they *shouldn't* do. The "Delivery Cards" activity helps stress the idea that different topics call for different modes of delivery—that there is not one perfect delivery style. And, if this activity is used early in your unit on presentational skills, it can have the serendipitous effect of breaking the tension of public speaking for students, since it allows them to purposely break rules of delivery and live out their "worst case scenarios" in a relaxed and constructive environment.

After introducing the subject of speech delivery to your students, explain that you will be engaging them in an activity that will demonstrate the impact that poor delivery skills can have on a particular speech topic. Ask for nine volunteers from the class. If students are particularly apprehensive, you may want to demonstrate the activity first. Give each of the nine volunteers a "delivery card" you have chosen at random from the pack. The volunteer is not to share the card with anyone else.

Each delivery card has two pieces of information. The top of the card describes a poor delivery style (such as speaking too quickly). The bottom of the card gives a topic for an impromptu speech (for example, "how to register for classes"). Tell the volunteers that they should present a one-minute impromptu speech on the topic provided, incorporating the ineffective delivery technique that is also on the card. Give them a minute to prepare.

Then have each volunteer present their topic to the class. After a speaker has spoken for a minute, stop her or him and ask the class what was wrong in terms of the delivery. Take a minute to have the class discuss why communication about that particular topic was hindered by the delivery style. For example, information about how to register for classes would be largely incomprehensible if delivered too quickly. Continue the activity until all the volunteers have presented.

I make sure that I hand out the cards randomly so volunteers don't think I have targeted them for having a particular problem. You will find that students end up having a lot of fun with this activity, especially if the volunteers "ham it up" a bit. By the end of the activity, the group should have a clearer idea of how delivery can impact even the best of messages and how each topic brings with it specific delivery demands. Sample delivery card ideas that are presented here can certainly be adapted to fit the topic areas your group may cover in their future assignments.

Sample "Delivery Cards"

Style: Speak too quickly
Topic: Explain how to register for classes at the university

Style: Use unnatural, overdone hand gestures
Topic: Discuss the importance of registering to vote

Style: Avoid eye contact with the audience
Topic: Discuss the importance of making friendships

Style: Speak too softly
Topic: Discuss the importance of equal rights for women in the workplace

Style: Speak too slowly
Topic: Tell audience about an exciting moment in sports history

Style: Don't use any pauses
Topic: Explain a technical, mathematical, or scientific theory

Style: Fidget with the card while speaking
Topic: Give tips on how to stay calm before an exam

Style: Use too many pauses
Topic: Tell us about a scene from your favorite action movie

Style: Speak in a monotone
Topic: Tell us about the excitement involved in riding a motorcycle.

SUPPLEMENTARY MATERIALS

Films and Videos

"Aids to Speaking," Coronet/MTI, 15 minutes.

"Communicating Correctly," McGraw-Hill, 16 minutes.

"A World of Gestures," University of California Extension Center for Media and Independent Learning, 28 minutes.

"Communication by Voice and Action," Coronet/MTI, 14 minutes.

"Presentation Excellence," Video Publishing House, 77 minutes.

"Nonverbal Communication," Insight Media, 27 minutes.

"Communication: The Nonverbal Agenda," CRM/McGraw-Hill, 30 minutes.

"American Tongues," Center for New American Media, 40 minutes.

"Impromptu Speaking," Films for the Humanities, 15 minutes.

"Speak for Yourself: A Dynamic Vocal Workout, Insight Media, 25 minutes.

"Nonverbal Communication: Eye Contact and Kinesics," RMI Media Productions, 28 minutes.

"Nonverbal Communication: Paralanguage and Proxemics," RMI Media Productions, 28 minutes.

"Improve Your Pronunciation," Coronet/MTI, 11 minutes.

"The Human Voice," University of California Extension Center for Media and Independent Learning, 30 minutes.

"Body Language," Insight Media, 30 minutes.

"Sending a Message," Films for the Humanities, 15 minutes.

Student Speeches to Accompany *Public Speaking*, Houghton Mifflin.

"Delivering the Speech," RMI Media Productions, 28 minutes.

"Making Your Point Without Saying a Word," Insight Media, 27 minutes.

Transparencies and Handouts

Extemporaneous Speaking (Transparency Master 11.1)

Practicing for Extemporaneous Presentations (Transparency Master 11.2)

Making Impromptu Presentations (Transparency Master 11.3)

Making Manuscript Presentations (Transparency Master 11.4)

Handling Questions and Answers (Transparency Master 11.5)

Speaking on Television (Transparency Master 11.6)

Guide for Evaluating a Presentation

Guide for Evaluation of Voice and Articulation

Quotations for Impromptu Speech Assignments

Guide for Evaluating Impromptu Presentations

Evaluation Form for Question-and-Answer Sessions

Evaluation Form for Televised Presentations

EXTEMPORANEOUS SPEAKING

1. Speak naturally and spontaneously.

2. Respond to audience feedback.

3. Establish and maintain eye contact.

4. Let your wording differ during practice.

5. Practice from your key-word outline.

6. Practice gestures and movement.

PRACTICING FOR EXTEMPORANEOUS PRESENTATIONS

1. Practice until you can fully respond to your ideas.

2. Practice where you will be speaking.

3. Practice gestures and visual aids.

4. Begin with your formal outline, then switch to a key-word outline and practice some more.

5. Critique yourself by speaking in front of a mirror or making a recording.

6. Practice before friends.

MAKING IMPROMPTU PRESENTATIONS

1. Determine your main ideas.

2. Arrange your ideas so that they are easy to follow.

3. Open with an example or story.

4. Preview the ideas you will cover.

5. Enumerate your ideas as you speak.

6. Use examples, narratives, or information to support your ideas.

7. Summarize what you have covered.

8. End with remarks that reflect on the meaning of your message.

MAKING MANUSCRIPT PRESENTATIONS

1. Write your speech in good oral style.

2. Triple-space the manuscript in large type.

3. Underline or highlight words you will emphasize.

4. Mark pauses and gestures.

5. Practice as much as you would for an extemporaneous presentation.

6. Practice with the manuscript copy you will use during presentation.

7. Know your manuscript well enough to maintain eye contact with the audience.

HANDLING QUESTIONS AND ANSWERS

1. Anticipate questions and plan answers.

2. Repeat or rephrase each question before answering it.

3. Make eye contact with the audience, not just the person who asked the question.

4. Defuse loaded questions by rephrasing them objectively.

5. Keep your answers short and to the point.

6. Maintain control of the situation, but be polite.

7. Close the session by recapping your original message.

SPEAKING ON TELEVISION

1. Time your presentation exactly.

2. Write your speech in good oral style.

3. Use colorful, memorable language.

4. Be neat, well groomed, and appropriately dressed.

5. Practice your speech before going to the studio.

6. Familiarize yourself with production cues.

7. Supply the director with a manuscript.

8. Practice using the microphone and teleprompter.

9. Let your posture convey relaxed alertness.

10. Maintain eye contact with the camera.

11. Speak conversationally, as though talking with a small group in an intimate setting.

12. Scale down your gestures and movement.

13. Keep going even if you make a mistake.

14. Do not assume you are off camera until you are so advised.

GUIDE FOR EVALUATING A PRESENTATION

Write a short (two- to three-page) evaluation of a speech you attended, covering the following items:

1. Name, title, and/or position of speaker

2. Subject, date, and time of speech

3. Occasion for speech, including sponsoring group

4. Location and physical setting of speech

5. Mode of presentation (impromptu, memorized, manuscript, extemporaneous)

6. Discussion of appropriateness and effectiveness of mode of presentation

7. Description and discussion of speaker's voice

8. Discussion of appropriateness and effectiveness of rate of speaking (including the use of pauses)

9. Discussion of appropriateness and effectiveness of loudness (including any problems with equipment such as microphone squeal)

10. Discussion of speaker's vocal variety

11. Discussion of speaker's articulation, enunciation, pronunciation, or dialect

12. Discussion of speaker's use of body language (including facial expressions, eye contact, movement, gestures, and appearance)

13. Suggestions you would give this speaker for improving presentation skills

GUIDE FOR EVALUATION OF VOICE AND ARTICULATION

Speaker's Name _____ Evaluated by _____

1. What did you feel was the most effective aspect of the speaker's voice and articulation?

   _____

   _____

2. What did you feel was the least effective aspect of the speaker's voice and articulation?

   _____

   _____

3. Should the speaker try to raise or lower his or her habitual pitch? _____

4. Does the speaker tend to speak too rapidly or too slowly? _____

5. Does the speaker use pauses effectively? _____

6. Does the speaker speak too quietly or too loudly? _____

7. Does the speaker have enough vocal variety? _____

8. Does the speaker have acceptable articulation and enunciation? _____

9. Are any words mispronounced? _____

10. Is the speaker's dialect acceptable? _____

11. What recommendations would you make for improvement? _____

    _____

    _____

QUOTATIONS FOR IMPROMPTU SPEECH ASSIGNMENTS

"Ability is the art of getting credit for the home runs somebody else hits." *Casey Stengel*

"Do what you can, with what you have, where you are." *Theodore Roosevelt*

"It may be those who do most, dream most." *Stephen Leacock*

"Ability without education is like a tree without fruit." *Aristippus*

"Advertising is the science of arresting human intelligence long enough to get money from it." *Stephen Leacock*

"You can tell the ideals of a nation by its advertisements." *Norman Douglas*

"I have found the best way to give advice to your children is to find out what they want and then advise them to do it." *Harry S. Truman*

"America is a country that doesn't know where it's going but is determined to set a speed record getting there." *Laurence J. Peter*

"The American Revolution was a beginning, not a consummation." *Woodrow Wilson*

"The worst sin towards our fellow creatures is not to hate them, but to be indifferent to them: that's the essence of inhumanity." *George Bernard Shaw*

"The most powerful stimulus for changing minds is not a chemical. Or a baseball bat. It is a word." *George A. Miller*

"The man who does not read good books has no advantage over the man who can't read them." *Mark Twain*

"All the men on my staff can type." *Bella Abzug*

"When all else fails, read the directions." *Anonymous*

"If you think education is expensive, try ignorance." *Derek Bok*

"Whoever said, 'Money can't buy happiness,' didn't know where to shop. *Anonymous*

"A woman does not become interesting until she is over forty." *Coco Chanel*

"Taking life in the fast lane gets you to the other end quicker." *Anonymous*

"The light at the end of the tunnel may be an oncoming truck." *Anonymous*

"I hate small towns because once you've seen the cannon in the park there's nothing else to do." *Lenny Bruce*

"If you can't get rid of the family skeleton, you might as well make it dance." *George Bernard Shaw*

"I am not young enough to know everything." *James M. Barrie*

If A equals success; then the formula is A equals X plus Y plus Z, with X being work, Y being play, and Z keeping your mouth shut." *Albert Einstein*

"Worry is interest paid on trouble before it is due." *William Inge*

"A classic is something everybody wants to have read and nobody wants to read." *Mark Twain*

"Few minds wear out, more rust out." *Christian Nestell Bovee*

"The best way to keep the wolf from the door is with a sheepskin." *Laurence J. Peter*

"One man with courage makes a majority." *Andrew Jackson*

"Not to decide is to decide." *Harvey Cox*

"TV is chewing gum for the eyes." *Frank Lloyd Wright*

"He can compress the most words into the smallest idea of any man I ever met." *Abraham Lincoln*

"Separate your dark and light clothes before you put them in the washer." *Mother*

"The louder he talked of his honor, the faster we counted our spoons." *Ralph Waldo Emerson*

"Some politicians believe that when they have coined a slogan, they have solved a problem."
     Morris Udall

"Do I not destroy my enemies when I make them my friends?" *Abraham Lincoln*

"Even Albert Einstein needed help on his 1040 form." *Ronald Reagan*

"Because life is not a spectator sport. . . ." *Reebok advertisement*

"Man does not live by words alone, despite the fact that sometimes he has to eat them."
     Adlai E. Stevenson

"A fanatic is one who can't change his mind and won't change the subject." *Winston Churchill*

"About the time we can make ends meet, somebody moves the ends." *Herbert Hoover*

"The greatest obstacle to discovery is not ignorance—it is the illusion of knowledge." *Daniel Boorstin*

"Two things are bad for the heart—running uphill and running down people." *Bernard Gimbel*

GUIDE FOR EVALUATING IMPROMPTU PRESENTATIONS

Speaker _____ Topic _____ Date _____

5 = excellent   4 = good   3 = average   2 = below average   1 = poor

Opened with an introduction	5	4	3	2	1
Main ideas were previewed	5	4	3	2	1
Main ideas were easily identified	5	4	3	2	1
Main ideas were adapted to audience	5	4	3	2	1
Main ideas were properly supported	5	4	3	2	1
Main ideas were easy to follow	5	4	3	2	1
Main ideas were summarized	5	4	3	2	1
Concluding remarks reflected on meaning	5	4	3	2	1
Speaker maintained good eye contact	5	4	3	2	1
Gestures were used effectively	5	4	3	2	1
Rate of speaking was appropriate	5	4	3	2	1
Loudness level was appropriate	5	4	3	2	1
Vocal variety was appropriate	5	4	3	2	1

Comments: _____

_____

_____

_____

_____

_____

Grade: _____

EVALUATION FORM FOR QUESTION-AND-ANSWER SESSIONS

Speaker _____ Topic _____ Date _____

5 = excellent   4 = good   3 = average   2 = below average   1 = poor   NA = not appropriate

Actively encouraged questions	5	4	3	2	1	NA
Was well prepared to answer questions	5	4	3	2	1	NA
Repeated or paraphrased questions	5	4	3	2	1	NA
Maintained eye contact with audience	5	4	3	2	1	NA
Kept answers short and to the point	5	4	3	2	1	NA
Defused loaded questions	5	4	3	2	1	NA
Handled nonquestions appropriately	5	4	3	2	1	NA
Maintained control	5	4	3	2	1	NA
Observed time limits	5	4	3	2	1	NA
Concluded by refocusing on main points of prepared message	5	4	3	2	1	NA

Comments: _____

_____

_____

_____

_____

_____

Grade: _____

EVALUATION FORM FOR TELEVISED PRESENTATIONS

Speaker _____ Topic _____ Date _____

5 = excellent	4 = good	3 = average	2 = below average	1 = poor	NA = not appropriate

Speech appropriately timed	5	4	3	2	1	NA
Manuscript written in good oral style	5	4	3	2	1	NA
Colorful, memorable language	5	4	3	2	1	NA
Point, reason/example, restatement	5	4	3	2	1	NA
Sufficient previews and summaries	5	4	3	2	1	NA
Neat, well-groomed appearance	5	4	3	2	1	NA
Appropriate attire	5	4	3	2	1	NA
Good posture	5	4	3	2	1	NA
Conversational presentation	5	4	3	2	1	NA
Good use of vocal variety	5	4	3	2	1	NA
Eye contact through camera	5	4	3	2	1	NA
Gestures appropriately restrained	5	4	3	2	1	NA
Maintained demeanor through fade-out	5	4	3	2	1	NA

Comments: _____

_____

_____

_____

_____

Grade: _____

READINGS FOR ENRICHMENT

See guide to journal abbreviations on p. 37.

* Items marked with an asterisk are suitable for student enrichment.

General

Ailes, Roger. *You Are the Message: Getting What You Want by Being Who You Are.* New York: Doubleday, 1988.

Buller, David B., Beth A. LePoire and R. Kelly Aune. "Social Perceptions as Mediators of the Effect of Speech Rate Similarity on Compliance." *HCR* (1992), 286–311.

* Cavanagh, Michael E. "Make Effective Speeches." *Personnel Journal* (Mar. 1988), 51–55.

Crannell, Kenneth C. *Voice and Articulation,* 2nd ed. Belmont, Calif.: Wadsworth, 1991.

*Deitzer, Bernard A., and Alan G. Krigline. "When Making That Presentation." *Management Solutions* (Dec. 1987), 34–39.

Douglis, Carole. "The Beat Goes On: Social Rhythms Underlie All Our Speech and Actions." *Psychology Today* (Nov. 1987), 36(6).

* Feudo, John A. "How to Build Your Speaking Power." *American Salesman* (Feb. 1987), 7–11.

* Franchetti, Jack, George McCartney, and Bertha Kainen. "How to Wow 'Em When You Speak." *Changing Times* (Aug. 1988), 28–31.

* Giallourakis, Michael C. "Management Presentations." *The Woman CPA* (Apr. 1986), 20–25.

Gunderso, D. F., and Robert Hopper. "Relationships Between Speech Delivery and Speech Effectiveness." *CM* (June 1976), 158–165.

Hosman, Lawrence A., and John W. Wright. "The Effects of Hedges and Hesitations on Impression Formation in a Simulated Courtroom Context." *WJSC* (Spring 1987), 173–188.

* Inglis, Scott, and Joane Kozubska. "Making Presentations." *Management Decision* (May 1987), 3–10.

Jones, John A. "Preparing Contingency Plans for Public Speaking Situations." *CE* (Oct. 1981), 423–425.

* Lau, Barbara. "Communicating Under Fire." *Management Quarterly* (Spring 1987), 17–20.

* ———. "Imaging Your Path to Success." *Management Quarterly* (Spring 1989), 30–32.

Lawrence, Samuel G., and Mike Watson. "Getting Others to Help: The Effectiveness of Professional Uniforms in Charitable Fund Raising." *ACR* (Aug. 1991), 170–185.

* Leeds, Dorothy. "Power Speak." *Cosmopolitan* (Sept. 1988), 170–172.

* Marken, G. A. "Many Executives Must Learn How to Speak." *Marketing News,* 19 Jan. 1988, pp. 8–9.

* Mayer, Kenneth R. "Developing Delivery Skills in Oral Business Communication." *American Business Communication Association Bulletin* (Sept. 1980), 21–24.

* Osgood, Charles. "Standing Tall." *Sales and Marketing Management* (Mar. 1988), 16–17.

* Randall, J. "Voice Power: How to Sound as Professional as You Look." *Executive Female* (Mar.–Apr. 1988), 51–53.

Ray, George B. "Vocally Cued Personality Prototypes: An Implicit Personality Theory." *CM* (Sept. 1986), 266–276.

Safire, William. "Impregnating the Pause." *New York Times Magazine,* 16 June 1991, p. 8.

* Schwartz, Andrew E. "Rehearsing: Key to Avoiding Training Chaos." *Training and Development Journal* (Aug. 1988), 15–17.

* Sherman, Jean. "The Sounds of Success." *Working Woman* (Dec. 1987), 72.

* Shulman, Susan. "Exercises for Specific Vocal Problems." *American Salesman* (Feb. 1987), 12–13.

* Smith, Homer. "Deliver Your Talk Like a Pro." *Sales and Marketing Management,* 11 Mar. 1985, 130–134.

* Wiener, Leonard. "Honing Your Speaking Skills." *U.S. News & World Report,* 12 Jan. 1987, p. 56.

Teaching Techniques and Activities

Adams, Lori. "Two Takes on Impromptu Speaking Topics: Retiring the Hat (Take Two)." *SCT* (Winter 1994), 5–6.

Armstrong, Lindsley F., and Peter M. Kellett. "Teaching Public Speaking Principles Through Impromptu Speaking." *SCT* (Winter 1995), 5.

Beauchene, Kathleen. "Using Quotations As Impromptu Speech Topics." *SCT* (Fall 1988), 10.

Bytwerk, Randall. "Impromptu Speaking Exercise." *CE* (Apr. 1985), 148–149.

————. "The 'Just a Minute' Impromptu Exercise." *SCT* (Winter 1991), 3.

Ehrler, Rhonda. "Extemporizing Through Humor and Repetition." *SCT* (Summer 1988), 2–3.

Friedley, Sheryl A. "A Coaching Tip for Impromptu Speaking." *SCT* (Summer 1987), 3.

Gaulard, Joan M. "To Read, To Memorize, or To Speak." *SCT* (Spring 1991), 11.

Gordon, Ronald D. "Re-Discovering Impromptu Speaking." *SCT* (Fall 1986), 10–11.

Hayward, Pamela. "Delivery Cards." *SCT* (Spring 1994), 3.

Holt, John R. "Speaker's Roulette." *SCT* (Summer 1994), 7–8.

Johnson, Craig. "*People's Court* Comes to the Classroom." *SCT* (Fall 1987), 10.

McKinney, Bruce C. "The 'Jeopardy' of Impromptu Speaking." *SCT* (Fall 1987), 14–16.

Mills, Daniel D. "Tag Team Championship: Improving Delivery Skills." *SCT* (Winter 1991), 10–11.

Murray, Patricia. "The Objective Game." *SCT* (Summer 1991), 15.

Myers, Scott A. "The Extempu Speech." *SCT* (Winter 1995), 14–15.

Purdy, Ed. "Painless Impromptu Speaking." *SCT* (Spring 1988), 1–2.

Stahl, Michael G. "Two Takes on Impromptu Speaking Topics: Retiring the Hat (Take One)." *SCT* (Winter 1994), 4–5.

Sugimoto, Naomi. "Impromptu Fortune-Telling Exercise." *SCT* (Fall 1993), 5.

Sutton, David L. "Impromptu Speaking Exercise: Academy Award Acceptance Speeches." *SCT* (Fall 1994), 15.

Valentine, Carol Ann, and William E. Arnold. "Nonverbal Scavenger Hunt." *SCT* (Winter 1992), 14–15.

Wall, Jeanette. "Me? Give an Impromptu Speech? No Way!" *SCT* (Fall 1988), 11, 15.

Dialects

Delia, Jesse G. "Regional Dialect, Message Acceptance, and Perceptions of the Speaker." *CSSJ* (Fall 1975), 188–194.

Gill, Mary M. "Accents and Stereotypes: Their Effect on Perceptions of Teachers and Lecture Comprehension." *ACR* (Nov. 1944), 348–360.

Gill, Mary M., and Diane M. Badzinski. "The Impact of Accent and Status on Information Recall and Perception Formation." *CR* (Summer 1992), 99–106.

Griffith-Roberts, Carolanne. "Let's Talk Southern." *Southern Living* (Feb. 1995), 82.

Harple, Charles H. "ERIC Report: Nonstandard Speech." *CE* (Sept. 1975), 226–231.

Johnson, Fern L., and Richard Buttny. "White Listeners' Responses to 'Sounding Black' and 'Sounding White': The Effects of Message Content on Judgments About Language." *CM* (Mar. 1982), 33–49.

Miller, Dale T. "The Effect of Dialect and Ethnicity on Communicator Effectiveness." *CM* (Mar. 1975), 69–74.

Mulac, Anthony. "Evaluation of the Speech Dialect Attitudinal Scale." *CM* (Aug. 1975), 184–189.

————. "Assessment and Application of the Revised Speech Dialect Attitudinal Scale." *CM* (Aug. 1976), 238–245.

Mulac, Anthony, and Mary Jo Rudd. "Effects of Selected American Regional Dialects upon Regional Audience Members." *CM* (Aug. 1977), 183–195.

NBC Handbook of Pronunciation, 4th ed. New York: Harper, 1991.

Types of Presentations

Benson, James A. "Extemporaneous Speaking: Organization Which Inheres." *JAFA* (Winter 1978), 150–155.

Dornbusch, Joan P. "The Business of Reading a Paper Aloud." *American Business Communication Association Bulletin* (June 1980), 18–20.

* Hannaford, Peter. "Why Off the Cuff Is Off the Mark." *Nation's Business* (May 1984), 28.

Television and Radio Presentations

* Blotnick, Srully. "So You're Going to Be on TV?" *Forbes*, 27 Jan. 1986, pp. 118–119.

Blythin, Evan, and Larry A. Samovar. *Communicating Effectively on Television.* Belmont, Calif.: Wadsworth, 1985.

Flick, Hank. "Media Interviewing Eduction for Soon to Be Executives and Company Representatives." *SCT* (Fall 1995), 12–14.

Haynes, W. Lance. "Public Speaking Pedagogy in the Media Age." *CE* (Apr. 1990), 89–102.

Horwitz, Simi. "After the Fall: Television Interview Consultants." *Channels: The Business of Communications* (Nov. 1986), 16.

Hyde, Stewart W. *Television and Radio Announcing*, 6th ed. Boston: Houghton Mifflin, 1991, pp. 80–85.

Jamieson, Kathleen Hall. *Eloquence in an Electronic Age.* New York: Oxford University Press, 1988.

* Janner, Greville. "Effective Presentation for Television and Radio." *Accountancy* (May 1989), 138–139.

* Lynn, Terri. "Facing the Camera." *Audio-Visual Communications* (May 1987), 46–48.

Maher, Thomas M. "TV or Not TV? Not the Question at I. I. I. Studio." *National Underwriter Property and Casualty-Employee Benefits Edition*, 18 Apr. 1988, pp. 73–74.

Pfau, Michael, and Jong Geun Kang. "The Impact of Relational Messages on Candidate Influence in Televised Political Debates." *CS* (Summer 1991), 114–128.

Schram, Sanford F. "The Post-Modern Presidency and the Grammar of Electronic Electioneering." *CSMC* (June 1991), 210–216.

White, Sylvia E. "A Content Analytic Technique for Measuring the Sexiness of Women's Business Attire in Media Presentations." *CRR* (Fall 1995), 178–185.

Question-and-Answer Sessions

* Boyd, Stephen D. "Nine Steps to a Successful Question and Answer Session." *Management Solutions* (May 1988), 16–17.

Brady, Teresa. "Fielding Abrasive Questions During Presentations." *Supervisory Management* (Feb. 1993), 6.

* Mandel, Steve. "Getting Questions and Giving Answers: How to Make It Easier." *Management Quarterly* (Fall 1987), 13–15.

* Rafe, Stephen C. "Avoid the Question Quagmire: Learn How to Answer Questions Following Your Agenda—Not the Questioner's." *Association Management* (Aug. 1989), 173–175.

Ragsdale, J. Donald, and Alan L. Mikels. "Effects of Question Periods on a Speaker's Credibility with a Television Audience." *SSCJ* (Spring 1975), 302–312.

* Zaremba, Alan. "Q and A: The Other Part of Your Presentation." *Management World* (Jan.–Feb. 1989), 8–10.

Nonverbal Communication

* "Anatomy of a Lying Smile." *Science News*, 19 Mar. 1988, p. 187.

Andersen, Peter A. "Nonverbal Immediacy in Interpersonal Communication." In *Multichannel Integrations of Nonverbal Behavior*, edited by A. W. Siegman and S. Feldstein. Hillsdale: Erlbaum, 1985.

Baglan, Thomas, and Dorris J. Nelson. "A Comparison of the Effects of Sex and Status on the Perceived Appropriateness of Nonverbal Behaviors." *WSC* (Spring 1982), 28–38.

* Bassett, Ronald E., Ann Q. Stanton-Spicer, and Jack L. Whitehead. "Effects of Source Attire on Judgments of Credibility." *CSSJ* (Fall 1979), 282–285.

* Bower, Bruce. "The Face of Emotion." *Science News*, 128 (6 July 1985), pp. 12–13.

* ———. "Faces of Emotion: Social or Innate?" *Science News*, 5 Sept. 1987, p. 150.

Buller, David B. "Patterns and Functions of Nonverbal Communication: An Introduction." *SCJ* (Winter 1991), 81–82.

Burgoon, Judee K., Thomas Birk, and Michael Pfau. "Nonverbal Behaviors, Persuasion, and Credibility." *HCR* (Fall 1990), 140–169.

Burgoon, Judee K., David B. Buller, and W. Gill Woodall. *Nonverbal Communication: The Unspoken Dialogue*. New York: HarperCollins, 1990.

* Browne, Malcolm W. "A Smile or a Grimace? Ask a Pigeon's Opinion." *The New York Times*, 2 May 1989, p. B10.

De Klerk, Vivian. "Expletives: Men Only?" *CM* (June 1991), 156–169.

DeVito, Joseph, and Michael L. Hecht, eds. *The Nonverbal Communication Reader*. Prospect Heights, Ill.: Waveland, 1990.

Donagby, William C., and Becky Dooley. "Head Movement, Gender, and Deceptive Communication." *CR* (Summer 1994), 67–75.

Ekman, Paul. "Movements with Precise Meanings." *JC* (Summer 1976), 14–26.

* "Gestures: Are They Saying More Than You Mean?" *Teen Magazine* (Oct. 1985), 70–71.

Goldman, Alan. "A Rhetorical Lesson for Communication Theorists: Learning Nonverbal Performance from Elocutionists." *CR* (Summer 1991), 136–137.

Hall, Judith A. "Voice Tone and Persuasion." *Journal of Personality and Social Psychology* (June 1980), 924–936.

Knapp, Mark. *Essentials of Nonverbal Communication*. New York: Holt, Rinehart, & Winston, 1980.

———. "Teaching Nonverbal Communication." In *Teaching Communication: Theory, Research, and Methods*, edited by John A. Daly, Gustav W. Friedrich, and Anita Vangelisti, pp. 129–144. Hillsdale, N.J.: Erlbaum, 1990.

Knapp, Mark, and Judith A. Hall. *Nonverbal Communication in Human Interaction*, 3rd ed. Fort Worth, Tex.: Holt, Rinehart & Winston, 1992.

* Landau, Terry. "No Fooling: How to Know What's Going On Behind the Faces Close to You." *Health* (May 1989), 49–53.

Manusov, Valerie. "Perceiving Nonverbal Messages: Effects of Immediacy and Encoded Intent on Receiver Judgments." *WJSC* (Summer 1991), 245–253.

* Meer, Jeff. "Reagan's Facial Teflon." *Psychology Today* (Jan. 1986), 18.

Nelson, Audrey A. "Sex and Proxemics: An Annotated Bibliography." *WSC* (Summer 1978), 16–28.

———. "Women's Nonverbal Behavior: The Paradox of Skill and Acquiescence." *WSC* (Fall 1981), 18–31.

Patterson, Miles L., Mary E. Churchill, Gary K. Burger, and Jack L. Powell. "Verbal and Nonverbal Modality Effects on Impressions of Political Candidates: Analysis from the 1984 Presidential Debates." *CM* (Sept. 1992), 231–242.

Randall, Phyllis. "Re-examining the Smiles of Women." *WSC* (Spring 1985), 1–10.

Richmond, Virginia P., James C. McCroskey, and S. K. Payne. *Nonverbal Behavior in Interpersonal Relations*, 2nd ed. Englewood Cliffs, N.J.: Prentice-Hall, 1991, pp. 208–228.

* Rohr, Wendy Joi. "Facial Gestures." *Teen Magazine* (Apr. 1987), 20–21.

Rollman, Stephen A. "Classroom Exercises for Teaching Nonverbal Communication." *SCT* (Spring 1988), 13.

*Rosenfeld, Lawrence B., and Timothy G. Plax. "Clothing as Communication." *JC* (Spring 1977), 24–31.

Schnell, James. "Experiential Learning of Nonverbal Communication in Popular Magazine Advertising." *SCT* (Summer 1988), 1–2.

Segrin, Chris. "The Effects of Nonverbal Behavior on Outcomes of Compliance Gaining Attempts." *CS* (Fall 1993), 169–187.

Streek, Jurgen. "Gesture as Communication I: Its Coordination with Gaze and Speech." *CM* (Dec. 1993), 275–299.

* Townsend, John. "Paralinguistics: It's Not What You Say It's the Way That You Say It." *Management Decision* (May 1988), 36–40.

* Trimby, Madeline J. "What Do You Really Mean? Nonverbal Communication." *Management World* (July–Aug. 1988), 12–13.

Valentine, Carol Ann, and William E. Arnold. "Nonverbal Scavenger Hunt." *SCT* (Winter 1992), 14.

White, Sylvia E. "A Content Analytic Technique for Measuring the Sexiness of Women's Business Attire in Media Presentations." *CRR* (Fall 1995), 178–185.

* Zajonc, R. B. "Emotion and Facial Efference: A Theory Reclaimed." *Science*, 228, 5 Apr. 1985, 15–19.

Zinner, Carol Dolphin. "Beyond Hall: Variables in the Use of Personal Space." *Howard Journal of Communication* (Spring 1988), 23–38.

Cultural Variations

Axtell, Roger. *Gestures: The Do's and Taboos of Body Language Around the World*. New York: Wiley. 1991.

Ferrieux, Emmanuelle. "Hidden Messages: A Different Kind of Babel [meanings of gestures in different countries]." *World Press Review* (July 1989), 39.

Gudykunst, Willaim B., et al. "Language and Intergroup Communication." In *Handbook of International and Intercultural Communication*, edited by Molefi Kete Asante and William B. Gudykunst, pp. 145–162. Newbury Park, Calif.: Sage. 1989.

Hall. E. *Understanding Cultural Differences*. Yarmouth, Me.: Intercultural Press, 1990.

Hecht, Michael L., Peter A. Andersen, and Sidney A. Ribeau. "The Cultural Dimensions of Nonverbal Communication." In *Handbook of International and Intercultural Communication*, edited by Molefi Kete Asante and William B. Gudykunst, pp. 163–185. Newbury Park, Calif.: Sage. 1989.

Ishii, S. "Characteristics of Japanese Nonverbal Communication Behavior." *Communication* (Summer 1973), 163–180.

Matsumoto, David. "Cultural Influences on Facial Expressions of Emotion." *SCJ* (Winter 1991), 128–137.

Mole, J. *When in Rome . . . A Business Guide to Cultures and Customs in Twelve European Nations*. New York: AMACOM, 1991.

Munter, Mary. "Cross Cultural Communication for Managers." *Business Horizons* (May–June 1993), 69(10).

Ricks, D. *Big Business Blunders*. Homewood, Ill.: Dow Jones-Irwin, 1983.

Samovar, Larry A., and Richard E. Porter. *Communication Between Cultures*. Belmont, Calif.: Wadsworth, 1991.

Shuter, Robert. "A Field Study of Nonverbal Communication in Germany, Italy, and the United States." *CM* (Nov. 1977), 298–305.

Storti, C. *The Art of Crossing Cultures*. Yarmouth, Me.: Intercultural Press. 1990.

"Understanding Culture: Don't Stare at a Navajo." *Psychology Today* (June 1974), 107.

* Young, Patrick. "The Nature and Nurture of Emotions: Universality of Facial Expressions." *Science News*, 28 Jan. 1989, p. 59.

Memory

* "The Anatomy of Memory Loss." *Science News*, 23 Sept. 1989, p. 204.

* Baddeley, Alan. "Working Memory." *Science*, 31 Jan. 1992, pp. 556–559.

Best, Deborah L. "Inducing Children to Generate Mnemonic Organizational Strategies: An Examination of Long-term Retention and Materials." *Developmental Psychology* (Mar. 1993), 324–336.

Bogartz, Richard S. "Evaluating Forgetting Curves Psychologically." *Journal of Experimental Psychology: Learning, Memory and Cognition* (Jan. 1990), 138–148.

* Bower, Bruce. "Gone but Not Forgotten: Scientists Uncover Pervasive, Unconscious Influences on Memory." *Science News*, 17 Nov. 1990, pp. 312–314.

Brown, Norman R. "Organization of Public Events in Long-term Memory: Historical Memory." *Journal of Experimental Psychology: General* (Sept. 1990), 297–314.

Carlson, Richard A., David H. Lundy, and Robin G. Yaure. "Syllogistic Inference Chains in Meaningful Text." *American Journal of Psychology* (Spring 1992), 75–99.

Dagenbach, Dale, Sonia Horst, and Thomas H. Carr. "Adding New Information to Semantic Memory: How Much Learning Is Enough to Produce Automatic Priming?" *Journal of Experimental Psychology: Learning, Memory and Cognition* (July 1990), 581–591.

Fabiani, Monica, and Emanuel Donchin. "Encoding Processes and Memory Organization: A Model of the von Restorff Effect." *Journal of Experimental Psychology: Learning, Memory and Cognition* (Jan. 1995), 224–240.

Greene, Robert L. "Spacing Effects on Implicit Memory Tests." *Journal of Experimental Psychology: Learning, Memory and Cognition* (Nov. 1990), 1004–1011.

Greene, Robert L., and Rebecca Lasek. "Category-order Effects in Memory Span." *Journal of Experimental Psychology: Learning, Memory and Cognition* (Nov. 1994), 1391–1396.

Hanson, Catherine, and William Hurst. "On the Representation of Events: a Study of Orientation, Recall, and Recognition." *Journal of Experimental Psychology: General* (June 1989), 136–147.

Hassebrock, Frank, Paul E. Johnson, Peter Bullemer, Paul W. Fox, and James H. Moller. "When Less Is More: Representation and Selective Memory in Expert Problem Solving." *American Journal of Psychology* (Summer 1993), 155–189.

Hirshman, Eliot, Dawn Trembath, and Neil Mulligan. "Theoretical Implications of the Mnemonic Benefits of Perceptual Interference." *Journal of Experimental Psychology: Learning, Memory and Cognition* (May 1994), 608–620.

Hulme, Charles, Steven Roodenrys, Gordon Brown, and Robin Mercere. "The Role of Long-Term Memory Mechanisms in Memory Span." *British Journal of Psychology* (Nov. 1995), 527–536.

Koriat, Asher, and Morris Goldsmith. "Memory in Naturalistic and Laboratory Contexts: Distinguishing the Accuracy-oriented and Quality-oriented Approaches to Memory Assessment." *Journal of Experimental Psychology: General* (Sept. 1994), 297–315.

Milikowski, Marisca, and Jan J. Elshout. "What Makes a Number Easy to Remember?" *British Journal of Psychology* (Nov. 1995), 537–547.

* Neimark, Jill. "The Diva of Disclosure: Memory Researcher Elizabeth Loftus." *Psychology Today* (Jan.–Feb. 1996), 48–54.

Paivio, Allan, Mary Walsh, and Trudy Bons. "Concreteness Effects on Memory: When and Why?" *Journal of Experimental Psychology: Learning, Memory and Cognition* (Sept. 1994), 1196–1204.

* Perry, Susan. "Mind Over Matter: Memory." *Current Health* (May 1987), 22–23.

* Roach, Mary. "Thanks for the Memories: Memory Training Humor." *Health* (Jan.–Feb. 1993), 30–31.

Scruggs, Thomas E., and Margo Mastropieri. "Classroom Applications of Mnemonic Instruction: Acquisition, Maintenance, and Generalization." *Exceptional Children* (Dec.–Jan. 1991), 219–229.

Sechler, Elizabeth S., and Michael J. Watkins. "Learning to Reproduce a List and Memory for the Learning: Memorization of Verbal Items Immediately Following Presentation." *American Journal of Psychology* (Fall 1991), 367–394.

Sehulster, Jerome R. "Memory Styles and Related Abilities in Presentation of Self." *American Journal of Psychology* (Spring 1995), 67–88.

Squire, L. R., B. Knowlton, and G. Musen. "The Structure and Organization of Memory." *Annual Review of Psychology* (1993), 453–497.

* Tulving, Endel, and Daniel L. Schacter. "Priming and Human Memory Systems." *Science,* 19 Jan. 1990, 301–306.

* Witsman, Karl. "No More What's His Name Again: Memory Exercises for Salesmen." *American Salesman* (Feb. 1987), 24–25.

CHAPTER 12
Informative Speaking

OBJECTIVES

- To help your students understand the basic functions of informative speaking.

- To help your students apply the principles of motivation and attention in their informative speeches.

- To make your students familiar with the different types of informative speeches and the designs most appropriate to each.

- To help your students prepare and present effective informative speeches.

SUGGESTIONS FOR TEACHING

Often questions arise about the distinction between informative and persuasive speaking. Our position is that, although pure objectivity may be an impossible ideal, there are both practical and ethical benefits to teaching students to present ideas and information in a balanced and responsible fashion. Certainly, there are "real-life" situations in which your students will be expected to provide their audiences with the information they need to make their own decisions rather than pushing them to think or act a certain way. Consider the functions of teachers, news reporters, or corporate executives making boardroom presentations.

For informative assignments, students should select topics of social/political significance (defined by potential importance to the lives of audience members), obtain responsible knowledge, and make balanced presentations that incorporate effective learning principles without "taking sides" or engaging opposing views. Be specific about what you expect from your students. If this is the first major speaking assignment, you might check working outlines in advance, and specify the number and type of references required.

The primary emphasis in this chapter is on structuring informative speeches. Skeleton outline formats and check lists for the major informative designs may be found on pp. 357 to 381 of this manual. The material is also available in the "Speech Designer" computer software. There are exercises to demonstrate the often fuzzy line between persuasion and information, and to have your students consider the principles of learning in their own speeches and in others'. Other exercises have them construct and critique their own short informative messages. Many of the materials here logically coordinate with those in Chapters 5, 6, and 7, on research, supporting materials, and speech structure.

CHAPTER OUTLINE

I. Informative speaking is about sharing knowledge and ideas to enhance mutual understanding. *(text p. 377–378)*
   A. Sharing ideas and information is an integral part of human communication.
      1. Only humans have the linguistic ability to accumulate and transmit knowledge.
      2. Shared information is essential to human progress and survival.
      3. Information is a powerful commodity for individual success.

II. Speeches that are primarily informative perform four basic functions. *(text pp. 378–381)*
   A. Informative speeches share information and ideas to teach and enhance understanding.
      1. Informative speakers do not try to change values or enact reforms.
      2. Speakers must have responsible knowledge to share information effectively.
      3. The value of informative speaking can be considered in terms of how much new information or understanding is provided for the audience. Speakers should ask themselves:
         a. if their topics are significant enough to merit an informative speech.
         b. what their listeners already know about their topics.
         c. what more their audiences need to know.
         d. whether they have sufficient understanding of their topics to help listeners understand.
      4. Informative speakers function as teachers by adapting information to listeners.
   B. Informative speeches can influence listeners by shaping perceptions.
      1. As citing information is inherently selective, it can serve a prepersuasive function by favoring certain interpretations over others.
      2. Informative speakers should strive to be objective and avoid presenting distorted perspectives when selecting and interpreting information.
   C. Informative speeches set agendas of public concern by creating hierarchies of importance among subjects and issues that can prepare listeners for later persuasive attempts.
   D. Informative speeches can clarify options to facilitate thoughtful actions and decision making.
      1. Ethical speakers speak from responsible knowledge and cover all major relevant positions fairly and objectively.

III. Some basic learning principles can enhance the effectiveness of informative speaking. *(text pp. 381–385)*
   A. Speakers can motivate their listeners to learn by relating their topics to their needs and interests, directly or through examples and narratives.
   B. The following techniques can help speakers attract and sustain audience attention.
      1. Intensity of language and imagery can be very effective.
      2. The artful repetition of key words, sounds, or phrases can attract attention and help make a message memorable.
      3. Novelty can help gain audience attention.
      4. Physical or verbal activity can help attract and sustain attention.
      5. The use of contrast works because opposites attract attention.
         a. Vocal changes can be used for emphasis.
         b. Speakers can contrast situations or ideas.
      6. Stressing relevance gains attention by invoking needs and interests.
   C. Retention is important because information is useless if listeners do not remember it.
      1. Repetition can help listeners remember important points.
      2. Relevance is also important to retention.
      3. Well-organized messages are generally easier to remember.

IV. There are four major types of informative speeches. *(text pp. 385–390)*
   A. Speeches of description paint a clear picture of activities, objects, people, and/or places.

1. Speeches of description rely heavily on artful language use.
2. Speeches of description commonly use spatial, sequential, categorical, and comparative designs.
B. Speeches of demonstration aim at either understanding or application.
    1. Most speeches of demonstration follow a sequential design.
    2. Visual aids are usually appropriate for speeches of demonstration.
C. Speeches of explanation are appropriate for abstract or complex subjects.
    1. Speakers should define critical terms and offer examples and nonexamples.
D. A briefing is a short informative speech of explanation or description presented in an organizational setting.
    1. The following guidelines can help speakers prepare for briefings. Speakers should:
        a. be brief and to the point.
        b. organize their ideas and materials in advance when they anticipate giving briefings.
        c. rely on carefully verified facts and figures, expert testimony, and short examples.
        d. present their messages with confidence.
        e. be prepared to deal with tough questions forthrightly and honestly.

V. An appropriate design for arranging the main points of an informative speech is very important. *(text pp. 390–400)*
A. The following designs for informative speaking are also commonly used in persuasive and ceremonial speaking.
    1. Spatial designs are effective for describing places or locating subjects within a physical setting. Speakers should:
        a. determine a starting point and proceed in an orderly direction.
        b. complete patterns of description to satisfy audience needs for closure.
    2. Sequential designs move audiences through time, and are appropriate for speeches of demonstration that cover the steps of a process, or for historical explanations.
    3. Categorical designs are appropriate for subjects with natural or customary divisions. Speakers should:
        a. not have more than five categories in a short speech.
        b. begin and end with the most important or interesting categories.
    4. Comparative designs are helpful for new, abstract, or difficult subjects, for describing changes, and for contrasting different issues and proposals.
        a. Comparative designs work by relating topics to something the audience already understands.
        b. There are three basic types of comparative design.
            (1) A literal analogy draws subjects from the same field of experience.
            (2) A figurative analogy draws subjects from different fields of experience.
            (3) Comparison and contrast designs point out similarities and/or differences between subjects or ideas.
    5. A causation design explains a situation, condition, or event in terms of the causes that led up to it.
B. Many effective speeches use a combination of design strategies. Speakers should:
    1. plan a combined speech design carefully.
    2. use transitions to alert the audience when shifting from one design to the next.

USING END-OF-CHAPTER ITEMS

Discussion *(text p. 401–402)*

1. One testimonial to the power of information is the widespread practice of industrial and international espionage. Investigate a specific instance in which such a theft of information became widely known. In particular, seek for answers as to why this information was valuable

and secret. Ponder this issue: How much secrecy of government information can we tolerate in a society that depends on fully informed citizens as repositories of political power? Bring your thoughts and findings to class for discussion?

This can be used for homework or as a small-group activity followed by in-class discussion. You might coordinate this exercise by having your students investigate the same incident, or even looking up some secondary sources yourself and bringing them for class discussion. The past decade has seen multiple instances of political and corporate espionage. Recent tensions with China over American computer software copyrights illustrate the increasingly corporate nature of international espionage. Depending on the particular case being discussed, students may come to different conclusions. In cases of political espionage, the lives of agents abroad may be endangered, whereas in cases of corporate espionage, the right to capitalize on intellectual property is more often at stake. Regardless, focus class discussion on the relationship between information and power, and the tension that "free" societies must address between competing needs for security and freedom of expression and information flow.

2. **You probably recall one or several outstanding teachers in high school who helped you learn. How did they encourage learning in their classes? Share in class discussion your memories of their techniques for presenting information. What can you learn about communicating information, using them as models of excellence?**

This works best as homework followed by in-class discussion. You might preview this by briefing your students on the principles of motivating listeners to learn. You might expand it by having them contrast their observations with those (without names) of their "worst" high school teachers. For class discussion, push your students to ground their observations in concrete examples, and classify them with respect to the principles offered in the text. As high school classes are essentially captive audiences, your students will probably remember ineffective teachers who never stopped lecturing to solicit class input, read directly from the textbook, or always spoke in a monotone and avoided eye contact. They will probably have fond memories of teachers who, beyond being competent in their areas, went out of their way to involve their students, approached their subjects in an enthusiastic and (when appropriate) humorous fashion, and were always well organized, making effective use of presentation aids. Record your students' ideas on the chalkboard and try to move the class toward consensus criteria for effective and ineffective lecture styles.

3. **Over a typical week's viewing time, watch tabloid television programs that purport to be informative. Which informative functions do they fulfill? Are there qualitative differences among them, considered as media of information? Are they better characterized as entertainment programs? Do they sometimes serve persuasive purposes as well? Are they ethical providers of information? Discuss your observations and judgments in class.**

This works well for homework, or you might videotape some shows yourself and bring them for in-class viewing. Focus discussion on whether the shows represent news coverage or show business, and how or whether your students can tell the difference. Remember that all informative discourse is at least potentially persuasive in that it seeks to shape perceptions and set agendas. Tabloid news shows (and some say the corporate news media) have definitely torn down the barriers between informing and entertaining. Indeed, they usually sensationalize stories that have little more than celebrity interest. The recent overkill of O. J. Simpson coverage suggests that this influence has long since permeated mainstream sources.

Your students may raise concerns that the media are oblivious to the consequences of their discourse. At least since Aristotle and Aristophanes, critics have recognized that entertainment can be a powerful form of persuasion, and show business means giving the people what they want in order to maximize profits, but representatives for such shows typically continue to insist on the balanced objectivity of their coverage. In so doing, they abdicate the heightened sense of moral and social responsibility that accompanies persuasive speaking. On the other hand, media representatives might counter that we really cannot separate news and entertainment, and that their shows simply cater to a basic human need. For an alternative to this exercise, consider showing your students documentaries addressing controversial issues, such as "Silent Scream" or "The Guns of Autumn," that, while purporting to be informative, are obviously very persuasive.

For additional information on this topic, consult Bruce E. Gronbeck "Celluloid Rhetoric: On Genres of Documentary," in *Form and Genre: Shaping Rhetorical Action,* edited by Karlyn Kohrs Campbell and Kathleen Hall Jamieson (Annandale, Va.: SCA, undated [papers from 1976 conference held at the University of Kansas]), 139–161; Ibrahim M. Hefzallah, *Critical Viewing of Television: A Book for Parents and Teachers* (Lanham, Md.: University Press of America, 1987); or "Making the Media Work for You," *Media & Values,* Spring 1986 (entire issue devoted to developing media awareness).

Application *(text p. 402)*

1. **Analyze the speech by Stephen Lee in Appendix B in terms of its functions, type, and design. Consider how it gains and holds attention and motivates learning. Can you think of different designs for the speech? Would they be more or less effective?**

    This exercise works well as a written homework assignment. Stephen's speech fulfills two basic functions of informative speaking: sharing ideas and shaping perceptions. It is a speech of explanation. It follows a loose categorical design but could have been made easier to follow with better transitions. In addition, his second and third main points are inadequately developed. Because his topic might lack interest value for younger audiences, Stephen had to work hard to involve his audience. His introduction and conclusion are both very effective in this respect. Finally, he makes effective use of expert testimony, engaging examples, and light humor.

2. **Design the informative speech you prepare for class, being sure to include techniques to sustain attention. In the margin of the outline you turn in, specify what attention techniques you will use and why you believe they will be effective.**

    This is intended for homework in preparation for major speech assignments. Have your students include marginal notes or annotations on their outlines where they plan to use attention-getting strategies, and/or prepare a one-page analysis and justification of the techniques they intend to use. You might also use this as a small-group discussion activity. Divide your class into small groups to critique one another's ideas. They should focus on the relative appropriateness of their chosen attention-getting strategies and others that might prove more effective. This exercise should provide quality feedback for students to work into their actual presentations.

ADDITIONAL ACTIVITIES

Information and Power

Purpose: To illustrate for your students the relation between access to knowledge and power.

Directions: This works well as a small-group activity followed by class discussion. Briefly review the following five types of leadership power [see John R. P. French, Jr., and Bertram H. Raven, "The Basis of Social Power," in *Studies in Social Power,* edited by D. Cartwright (Ann Arbor: University of Michigan Press, 1959), 118–149]. Break your class into small groups, having each consider what power types are most appropriate in the following contexts: politics and law, work, school, family, lovers, close friends, and acquaintances. How do these power types shape relationships in these contexts? How does sharing and controlling access to information work into the process? What about the applicability of this dichotomy of power types to less formal or interpersonal relationships? Students should come up with real or hypothetical examples to illustrate their ideas and present them for class discussion. The following summary of power types may aid your discussion.

French and Raven's Power Types

Legitimate power over the behavior of others is vested in hierarchical position relationships, as with managers over subordinates in the workplace or state troopers over drivers on the highways. Position, not information, is the basis of legitimate power. Those with legitimate power often have more access to vital information, and unwillingness to share that information is usually perceived as an abuse of that power.

Coercive power is based on the ability to punish. It is often coupled with legitimate power and likewise may have little to do with information. However, those with coercive power often try to retain a sense of lost authority by deliberately withholding important information—which is generally perceived for what it is, making things even worse.

Reward power is based on the ability to grant payoffs for compliance. It may be, but is not necessarily, related to information. Sharing information can be a powerful form of reward that tends to increase feelings of inclusiveness. It is seldom perceived as abusive, unless it is coupled with an obvious "price" or threat of withholding information as punishment for noncompliance.

Expert power is related to competence. It is dependent on knowledge and information, and the perception of that special knowledge or expertise by others that matter. For that perception to exist, the information must be shared with others.

Referent power is based on identification and involves respect, likability, trustworthiness, and similarity of interests, values, or attitudes. The willingness to share information can lead to a greater perception of these factors, especially when they are consistent with the interests, values, or attitudes of the audience.

Informative Speech Construction

Purpose: To give your students practice planning and constructing mock informative speeches.

Directions: Use this either for homework or as a small-group activity followed by general class discussion. Have your students select informative topics, determine specific purposes, and develop two different outlines for the speech they might give, each illustrating a different choice among the various design options (spatial, categorical, comparative, sequential, causation, etc.). Have your students or groups submit rough key-word outlines of main ideas along with strategies to motivate learning. Encourage them to choose topics they are considering for their actual presentations. They should formulate specific-purpose and thesis statements, two different design schemes, two or three prospective main points for each and likely supporting information, and strategies for integrating learning principles into their presentations. Outline formats for these designs are available in the "Speech Designer" software program and on pp. 357–381 of this IRM. Have your students present their ideas for class discussion, focusing on the relationship between speech design and learning motivation as discussed in the text.

Informative Speech Analysis

Purpose: To give your students an opportunity to apply the concepts of informative speaking to actual student speeches.

Directions: This is intended for in-class viewing and discussion using the student speeches tapes provided as part of the *Public Speaking* package. You can easily convert it to a homework assignment by assigning your students an informative speech from Appendix B. For class discussion, have your students critique the speeches in terms of the informative functions fulfilled and the design(s) used to arrange main supporting ideas. Use this activity to underscore the fine line between informative and persuasive speaking, and emphasize what you will be looking for when you grade their informative presentations. To what extent do the speeches fulfill the informative functions of sharing ideas, shaping perceptions, setting agendas, and clarifying options? To what extent do they overstep the boundaries of informative speaking by advocating choices among options, addressing opposing views, or requesting the audience to assume great risks? What type of design strategy is utilized? Is it informative, persuasive, or a combination of both?

History as Rhetoric: A Primer

Purpose: To demonstrate for students how "objective" sources of historical information can reflect and reinforce the thinking and biases of their time.

Directions: Read or distribute the following passages from two different editions of *The World Book Encyclopedia* on the Kiowa Indians (this material is also presented in Chapter 6 of the text).* As an alternative, select different topics on which "information" may have changed with social changes and have your students bring copies of the encyclopedia entries to class for presentation and discussion or for use in a homework assignment. Focus on how these entries changed over thirty years, and how these changes might shape different perceptions of the Kiowas. Emphasize the importance of historical memory in shaping our perceptions of both ourselves and other peoples. Other forms of historical reckoning also tend to evolve and change with the times. Speculate on social, political, and cultural reasons for such changes and their probable consequences. How can language be used to tell different versions of the same story?

From the 1960 edition:

> **Kiowa,** *KI oh way*, **Indians** hunted buffalo on the southwestern plains of the United States. The Kiowa and their allies, the Comanche, raided many Texas ranches. They probably killed more whites than any other Indian tribe.
>
> For about 60 years, from 1832 to 1892, the Kiowa kept a record of their daring deeds on painted buffalo skins. The bright-colored pictures of horses and teepees showed their fights with the Cheyenne and Osage, and with United States troops. The paintings also showed the yearly celebration of the great sun dance; the coming of the deadly smallpox, cholera, and measles; and the making of a treaty with the whites. Their oldest tradition placed them in the area of the present Virginia City, Mont.
>
> Spanish records mention the Kiowa as early as 1732. In 1805 Lewis and Clark reported them as living on the North Platte River.
>
> By this treaty, signed in 1868, the Kiowa agreed to go with the Comanche to a reservation in Indian territory (now Oklahoma). But only the Kiowa chiefs had signed the treaty, and no chiefs could force their young men to make such a sacrifice. Many struggles and arrests occurred before the Kiowa finally went to live on the reservation. When trouble broke out in 1874, Satanta, one of the most daring Kiowa leaders, was arrested and sentenced to prison. There he committed suicide. The Kiowa then "put their hands to the plow." They now live peacefully as farmers. Several have become well-known artists.
>
> —*John C. Ewers*

From the 1990 edition:

> **Kiowa Indians,** *Ky oh wah* or *Ky oh way,* are a tribe that lives largely in Oklahoma and elsewhere in the Southwestern United States. The tribe has about 8,000 members, most of whom live in rural communities near Anadarko, Carnegie, and Mountain View, Okla. Other tribal members live in urban areas and work in law, medicine, teaching, and other professions.
>
> The Kiowa once hunted buffalo on the plains. They were fierce warriors and raided many white and Mexican settlements, especially from 1850 to 1870.
>
> According to tribal tradition, the Kiowa once lived as nomadic hunters in a region that was covered by snow much of the year. They later moved to the Rocky Mountains near

---

* Reprinted by permission of *World Book Encyclopedia*. This material was brought to our attention by Professor Gray Matthews of the University of Memphis.

what is now Yellowstone National Park. The Kiowa next migrated to the Black Hills of eastern Wyoming and southwestern South Dakota, and then to the Southwestern plains. In 1867, Kiowa chiefs agreed to settle on a reservation in the Indian Territory (now Oklahoma) with two other tribes, the Comanche and the Kiowa Apache. The three groups became known as the KCA tribes. They adopted a constitution in 1932.

In 1963, the KCA tribes abolished their constitution and, in 1970, the Kiowa adopted their own tribal constitution. The tribe is governed by the Kiowa Indian Council, which consists of members who are at least 18 years old. The Kiowa Business Committee, an elected group, manages tribal programs in such fields as business, education, and health.

—Everett R. Rhoades

Informative Speaking and Corporate Ethos

Purpose: To illustrate the often fine line between informative and persuasive speech in public relations rhetoric designed to defend the reputations or ethos of giant corporations.

Directions: Where there's controversy, you are likely to find a lot of pseudo-information—that is, persuasive speech advanced as informative. Look especially for statements by corporate spokespersons in response to crisis situations that threaten to destroy the company's (or even an industry's) good name. For instance, statements by Exxon, Valujet, or the tobacco industry in response to such crisis situations would be ideal for this activity. Such statements will usually purport to be informative, but they often contain persuasive and/or ceremonial appeals intended to defend the company's actions both prior and subsequent to "crisis" events or revelations. Often they seek to do this by boasting of full disclosure and asking for a dispassionate hearing of "the facts," which are then presented, of course, in a slanted fashion. Have your students consider why such spokespersons would purport to be purely informative, and emphasize the potential power of persuasion when it is successfully cloaked as objective discourse.

Katherine Rowan (Purdue University, West Lafayette, Indiana), "The Speech to Explain Difficult Ideas," *SCT* (Summer 1990), 2–3.

Goal: To provide students with research-based strategies for explaining difficult ideas and practice in explanatory speaking.

In this era, information may be easy to obtain but good explanations are rare. Everyone appreciates an excellent explanation of how microchips work or why the AIDS virus cannot be transmitted through swimming pools, but we also know that good explanations and good explainers are scarce.

An ideal way to teach strategies for effective explaining is to assign the "speech to explain difficult ideas." In this report, I summarize research on good explaining and describe the procedures I use to teach explanatory speaking. A unit on explaining works well in introductory, technical, or business speaking classes.

Definition. The speech to explain is a type of informative presentation. Informative speeches primarily create awareness or understanding, whereas explanatory speeches chiefly create understanding. For example, a speech on how to fax a document creates awareness, whereas a speech on how fax machines work deepens understanding.

Topics for explanatory speeches come from constantly asking "why" or "what does that mean?" Some of my favorites: Why do people yawn? What are modern artists trying to achieve? Why are water towers shaped like giant mushrooms? How does nuclear fusion work? Why is irradiated food healthful? What does "evolution" mean? What's a municipal bond?

According to my research, there are at least three ways in which answers to these and similar questions may be difficult for lay audiences to understand (for a review of this research, see Katherine E. Rowan, "A Contemporary Theory of Explanatory Writing," *Written Communication*, 5 (1988): 23–56). These include difficulties in (a) understanding the meaning and use of a term, (b) abstracting the main points from complex information, and (c) grasping an implausible or counter-intuitive proposition (such as Einstein's notion that we are accelerating toward the center of the Earth). The challenge for explanatory speakers is diagnosing the principal difficulty facing their audience and shaping their speech to overcome that difficulty.

Types of difficulties and explanations. If the audience's chief difficulty rests with understanding the meaning and use of a certain term, then speakers should develop speeches providing *elucidating explanations.* Elucidating explanations illuminate a concept's meaning and use. For example, speakers principally concerned with explaining concepts such as "evolution" and "municipal bond" should use elucidating explanations.

According to research (Merrill and Tennyson's *Teaching Concepts*, Englewood Cliffs, NJ: Educational Technology Publications, 1977) good elucidating explanations contain: (a) a definition that lists each of the concept's critical features, (b) an array of varied examples and nonexamples (nonexamples are instances that audiences often think are examples but are not), and (c) opportunities for audiences to distinguish examples from nonexamples by looking for the concept's critical features.

One particularly effective elucidating speech explained what "science" means. The student began:

> We all know what science is. It's what Carl Sagan and Mr. Wizard do, right? Since we know, we should agree on some basic ideas. How many people think biology is a science? (Nearly all hands rise.) How many think psychology is? (A few hands rise.) How about astrology? (A few hands rise.)

This speech was effective because, after establishing that "science" is hard to explain, the speaker offered a definition listing the concept's critical features, gave an array of examples and nonexamples of science (e.g., psychology vs. astrology), and offered the audience opportunities to distinguish examples from nonexamples with a short oral quiz.

If an idea is difficult chiefly because its complexity obscures its main points or the "big picture," then speakers should present a *quasi-scientific explanation*. Just as scientists try to develop models of the world, quasi-scientific explanations model or picture the key dimensions of some phenomenon for lay audiences. Speakers presenting complex topics to laypersons—topics such as how microchips work, the similarities and differences between Buddhism and Christianity, or how DNA molecules pass along genetic information—should use quasi-scientific explanations.

According to research, effective quasi-scientific explanations contain features that highlight the main points of the explanation, features such as titles, organizing analogies, visual aids, and signalling phrases (e.g., "The first key point is"). Good quasi-scientific explanations also contain features that *connect* key points, such as transitional phrases ("for example"), connectives ("because"), and diagrams depicting relationships among parts.

For example, a particularly good quasi-scientific speech explained how radar works. Using an organizing analogy, the speaker said that radar works essentially the way an echo does, except that radio waves, rather than sound waves, are sent and received. The presentation was effective because consistent references to this analogy highlighted its main points.

If the chief source of difficulty is not a particular term, nor a complex mass of information, but rather the counter-intuitivity of the idea itself, then speakers should design their talks as *transformative explanations*. For example, the idea that when people push on a concrete wall, that wall exerts an equal and opposite force on them (Newton's Third Law of Motion) contains no difficult terms and little detail, but, from a lay perspective, it just seems impossible. Transformative explanations are designed to present such counter-intuitive ideas by helping lay audiences transform their everyday "theories" of phenomena into more accepted notions. Questions best answered with transformative explanations might include: why we are accelerating toward the Earth's center, why irradiated food is healthful, or why perception is a subjective process.

According to research, transformative explanations are most effective when they: (a) state people's "implicit" or "lay" theory about the phenomenon; (b) acknowledge the apparent plausibility of this lay theory; (c) demonstrate its inadequacy; (d) state the more accepted account; and (e) demonstrate its greater adequacy.

Speech communication teachers often give good transformative explanations when they lecture on the notion that perception is a subjective, rather than an objective, process. As instructors, we know that simply asserting perception's subjectivity would not be effective. Consequently, we usually begin our lectures by acknowledging the apparent plausibility of the "objective-perceptions hypothesis." That is, we tell our students that it's natural to assume that what they perceive is exactly correspondent to reality. But then we demonstrate the inadequacy of the objective-perceptions hypothesis by using optical illusions or attribution exercises, showing that the mind partly creates the reality it perceives. Only after these exercises, do we explain the subjectivity of perception.

I have found that explanatory speech rounds are some of my favorites. Students try challenging topics and are impressed with how difficult it is to explain ideas well. Some have discovered that the strategies they learn for good explaining can also work as study tips. In this information era, it's good for us to slow down and thoroughly understand small but important bits of information. Explanatory speaking is a step in that direction.

SUPPLEMENTARY MATERIALS

Films and Videos

"Information Processing," CRM Productions, 29 minutes.

"Reporting and Briefing," Centron Films, 16 minutes.

"Informing People," Films for the Humanities, 20 minutes.

"Types of Information," Films for the Humanities, 15 minutes.

Student speeches videos to accompany *Public Speaking,* Houghton Mifflin.

Computer Software

"Speech Designer," Houghton Mifflin, 1991.

Transparency and Handouts *(see following pages)*

Steps in the Preparation of an Informative Speech (Transparency 12.1)

Spatial Design—Guidelines, Outline Work Sheet, and Check List

Sequential Design—Guidelines, Outline Work Sheet, and Check List

Categorical Design—Guidelines, Outline Work Sheet, and Check List

Comparative Design—Guidelines, Outline Work Sheet, and Check List

Causation Design—Guidelines, Outline Work Sheet, and Check List

STEPS IN THE PREPARATION OF AN INFORMATIVE SPEECH

1. **Select and analyze your topic.**

   A. Choose a worthwhile topic.
   B. Adapt your topic so that it is interesting and relevant.
   C. Limit your topic to something you can handle.
   D. Determine what you think will be your specific-purpose and thesis statements.

2. **Develop responsible knowledge on your topic.**

   A. Review what you already know.
   B. Use the library to expand your knowledge.
   C. Find facts and figures, testimony, examples, and narratives to add substance to your speech.

3. **Organize your material.**

   A. Determine the main points for your speech.
   B. Rethink your specific-purpose and thesis statements and revise if necessary.
   C. Arrange your main points so that your speech will be easy to follow, understand, and remember.
   D. Prepare your introduction and conclusion.

STEPS IN THE PREPARATION OF AN INFORMATIVE SPEECH (p. 2)

4. **Compose a working outline.**

   A. Share it with someone to see if it makes sense to them.
   B. Put it aside for a day, then review it.
   C. Revise as needed.

5. **Make a formal outline and practice presenting from it.**

   A. Make any further revisions that seem necessary.
   B. Practice from the formal outline at least three times.
   C. Tape your speech using your formal outline, let it sit overnight, then listen to it and revise as needed.
   D. Practice again, timing your presentation.

6. **Prepare a key-word outline and practice presenting from it.**

   A. Practice from it at least three times.
   B. Let it sit overnight, then practice again to be sure it still reminds you of what you want to say.

7. **Be ready when you are scheduled to speak.**

   A. Come to class well rested.
   B. Be sure you have everything you need, such as presentation aids, note cards, outline, etc.
   C. Review your key-word outline one final time before class.

GUIDELINES FOR USING A SPATIAL DESIGN

You should use a spatial design when your subject concerns places or objects that can be placed in a physical arrangement. This design takes your listeners on a systematic and orderly tour of your subject or systematically describes an arrangement so that your audience may visualize it accurately.

To develop the body of a speech using a spatial design, select a starting point and a direction of movement for the verbal journey on which you will take your listeners. Move in an orderly manner. Start a route and stay with it. Try not to backtrack or jump from place to place. Your speech should build in interest as you move along to the last place, which should be the most interesting.

OUTLINE WORK SHEET: SPATIAL DESIGN

TITLE (Optional): _____

Topic: _____

Specific purpose: _____

_____

Thesis statement: _____

_____

INTRODUCTION

Attention material: _____

_____

Credibility material: _____

_____

Preview: _____

_____

(Transition to body of speech)

_____

BODY

I. Main point 1 (location 1) _____

_____

    A. (subpoint) _____

_____

    B. (subpoint) _____

_____

(Transition to main point 2)

_____

OUTLINE WORK SHEET: SPATIAL DESIGN
(page 2)

II. Main point 2 (location 2) _____

_____

    A. (subpoint) _____

    _____

    B. (subpoint) _____

    _____

(Transition to main point 3)

_____

III. Main point 3 (location 3) _____

_____

    A. (subpoint) _____

    _____

    B. (subpoint) _____

    _____

(Transition to main point 4)

_____

IV. Main point 4 (location 4) _____

_____

    A. (subpoint) _____

    _____

    B. (subpoint) _____

    _____

OUTLINE WORK SHEET: SPATIAL DESIGN
(page 3)

(Transition to main point 5)

_____

V. Main point 5 (location 5) _____

_____

   A. (subpoint) _____

   _____

   B. (subpoint) _____

   _____

(Transition to conclusion)

_____

CONCLUSION

I. Summary: _____

_____

II. Concluding remarks: _____

_____

Works Consulted:

CHECK LIST FOR SPATIAL DESIGN OUTLINE

_____ I have selected a topic that involves places or things that can be located physically.

_____ I have clearly stated the purpose of my speech.

_____ My thesis statement is written as a complete declarative sentence.

_____ My introduction gains attention and interest, establishes my credibility, and previews the main points of my message.

_____ My first main point is the starting point for the verbal journey of my speech.

_____ My speech moves from place to place in an orderly fashion.

_____ My speech builds interest as it moves from location to location.

_____ I have adequate supporting material for each main point in my speech.

_____ I have positioned my subpoints under the main points to which they are related.

_____ My conclusion contains a summary that recaps my message and remarks that reflect on the meaning and significance of the speech.

_____ I have provided transitions where they are needed to make my speech flow smoothly.

_____ I have compiled a list of works consulted in the preparation of my speech.

GUIDELINES FOR USING A SEQUENTIAL DESIGN

A sequential design may be used to present the steps of a process or to provide a historical perspective on a subject.

When using a sequential design to present the steps in a process, you must first determine the necessary steps and the order in which they must take place. These steps become the main points of the speech. For an oral presentation, you should not try to discuss more than five steps. If you have more than this, see if you can cluster some of them into subpoints. Be sure to enumerate the steps as you present them so that the audience can follow your message.

When using a sequential design to present a historical perspective on a subject, be sure to follow a systematic chronological sequence. Do not jump around in time (e.g., start with 1990, jump back to 1942, then fast forward to 1971) or the speech will be hard for your listeners to follow. You can either begin with the beginnings of a subject and trace it to a later point in time or begin with the present and trace the subject back to its origins. When presenting a historical perspective, it is important to narrow your topic to manageable proportions by selecting the most important historical occurrences. Your speech should telescope time.

OUTLINE WORK SHEET: SEQUENTIAL DESIGN

TITLE (Optional): _____

Topic: _____

Specific purpose: _____

_____

Thesis statement: _____

_____

INTRODUCTION

Attention material: _____

_____

Credibility material: _____

_____

Preview: _____

_____

(Transition to body of speech)

_____

BODY

I. Main point 1 (step or occurrence 1) _____

_____

    A. (subpoint) _____

_____

    B. (subpoint) _____

_____

(Transition to main point 2)

_____

OUTLINE WORK SHEET: SEQUENTIAL DESIGN
(page 2)

II. Main point 2 (step or occurrence 2) _____

_____

    A. (subpoint) _____

_____

    B. (subpoint) _____

_____

(Transition to main point 3)

_____

III. Main point 3 (step or occurrence 3) _____

_____

    A. (subpoint) _____

_____

    B. (subpoint) _____

_____

(Transition to main point 4)

_____

IV. Main point 4 (step or occurrence 4) _____

_____

    A. (subpoint) _____

_____

    B. (subpoint) _____

_____

OUTLINE WORK SHEET: SEQUENTIAL DESIGN
(page 3)

(Transition to main point 5)

_____

V. Main point 5 (step or occurrence 5) _____

_____

    A. (subpoint) _____

_____

    B. (subpoint) _____

_____

(Transition to conclusion)

_____

CONCLUSION

I. Summary: _____

_____

II. Concluding remarks: _____

_____

Works Consulted:

CHECK LIST FOR A SEQUENTIAL DESIGN

_____ My topic involves a process that can be explained as a series of steps or a subject on which I wish to provide a historical perspective.

_____ I have clearly stated the purpose of my speech.

_____ My thesis statement is written as a complete declarative sentence.

_____ My introduction gains attention and interest, establishes my credibility, and previews the main points of my message.

_____ I have determined the main steps that must be taken (if applicable).

_____ I have arranged the steps in the order in which they must be taken (if applicable).

_____ I have selected the major occurrences or developments related to my topic (if applicable).

_____ I have presented the occurrences chronologically (if applicable).

_____ I have adequate supporting material for each main point in my speech.

_____ I have positioned my subpoints under the main points to which they are related.

_____ My conclusion contains a summary that recaps my message and remarks that reflect on the meaning and significance of the speech.

_____ I have provided transitions where they are needed to make my speech flow smoothly.

_____ I have compiled a list of works consulted in the preparation of my speech.

GUIDELINES FOR USING A CATEGORICAL DESIGN

You should use a categorical design for subjects that have natural or customary divisions. This design allows you to organize large amounts of material into a manageable format. Do not use a categorical design by default—because you are too lazy to think of any other way to arrange your information.

When using a categorical design, each category becomes a main point for the development of your speech. Limit yourself to five or fewer main points in a short speech. You should begin and end with the most important categories, since the first and last areas covered are the most easily remembered.

OUTLINE WORK SHEET: CATEGORICAL DESIGN

TITLE (Optional): _____

Topic: _____

Specific purpose: _____

_____

Thesis statement: _____

_____

INTRODUCTION

Attention material: _____

_____

Credibility material: _____

_____

Preview: _____

_____

(Transition to body of speech)

_____

BODY

I. Main point 1 (first category) _____

_____

   A. (subpoint) _____

_____

   B. (subpoint) _____

_____

(Transition to main point 2)

_____

OUTLINE WORK SHEET: CATEGORICAL DESIGN
(page 2)

II. Main point 2 (second category) _____

_____

    A. (subpoint) _____

    _____

    B. (subpoint) _____

    _____

(Transition to main point 3)

_____

III. Main point 3 (third category) _____

_____

    A. (subpoint) _____

    _____

    B. (subpoint) _____

    _____

(Transition to main point 4)

_____

IV. Main point 4 (fourth category) _____

_____

    A. (subpoint) _____

    _____

    B. (subpoint) _____

    _____

OUTLINE WORK SHEET: CATEGORICAL DESIGN
(page 3)

(Transition to main point 5)

_____

V. Main point 5 (fifth category) _____

_____

    A. (subpoint) _____

_____

    B. (subpoint) _____

_____

(Transition to conclusion)

_____

CONCLUSION

I. Summary: _____

_____

II. Concluding remarks: _____

_____

Works Consulted:

CHECK LIST FOR CATEGORICAL DESIGN OUTLINE

_____ I have selected a topic that has natural or customary divisions.

_____ I have clearly stated the purpose of my speech.

_____ My thesis statement is written as a complete declarative sentence.

_____ My introduction gains attention and interest, establishes my credibility, and previews the main points of my message.

_____ I have no more than five categories as main points in my speech.

_____ I have arranged my speech so that the most important categories are presented first and last.

_____ I have positioned my subpoints under the main points to which they are related.

_____ My conclusion contains a summary that recaps my message and remarks that reflect on the meaning and significance of the speech.

_____ I have provided transitions where they are needed to make my speech flow smoothly.

_____ I have compiled a list of works consulted in the preparation of my speech.

GUIDELINES FOR USING A COMPARATIVE DESIGN

You may wish to use a comparative design if your topic is new to your audience, abstract, highly technical, or simply difficult to understand. The comparative design aids understanding by relating your topic to something the audience already knows and comprehends. It may take the form of a literal analogy, a figurative analogy, or a comparison and contrast design, showing both similarities and differences.

The body of a speech using a comparative design may include up to five main similarities or differences. In a literal analogy, the topics are drawn from the same area—for example, word processing and typing are two forms of producing written information using a keyboard, so the comparison between them is literal. In a figurative analogy, the speaker draws together topics from different areas—for example, relating the body's struggle against infection to a military campaign by identifying who or what makes up the armies, how they fight, and the consequences of victory or defeat. In a comparison and contrast design, you show how two things are both similar and different.

OUTLINE WORK SHEET: COMPARATIVE DESIGN

TITLE (Optional): _____

Topic: _____

Specific purpose: _____

_____

Thesis statement: _____

_____

INTRODUCTION

Attention material: _____

_____

Credibility material: _____

_____

Preview: _____

_____

(Transition to body of speech)

_____

BODY

I. Main point 1 (first similarity or difference) _____

_____

    A. (subpoint) _____

    _____

    B. (subpoint) _____

    _____

(Transition to main point 2)

_____

OUTLINE WORK SHEET: COMPARATIVE DESIGN
(page 2)

II. Main point 2 (second similarity or difference) _____

_____

    A. (subpoint) _____

    _____

    B. (subpoint) _____

    _____

(Transition to main point 3)

_____

III. Main point 3 (third similarity or difference) _____

_____

    A. (subpoint) _____

    _____

    B. (subpoint) _____

    _____

(Transition to main point 4)

_____

IV. Main point 4 (fourth similarity or difference) _____

_____

    A. (subpoint) _____

    _____

    B. (subpoint) _____

    _____

OUTLINE WORK SHEET: COMPARATIVE DESIGN
(page 3)

(Transition to main point 5)

_____

V. Main point 5 (fifth similarity or difference) _____

_____

    A. (subpoint) _____

_____

    B. (subpoint) _____

_____

(Transition to conclusion)

_____

CONCLUSION

I. Summary: _____

_____

II. Concluding remarks: _____

_____

Works Consulted:

CHECK LIST FOR COMPARATIVE DESIGN OUTLINE

_____ I have selected a topic that is unfamiliar, abstract, or otherwise difficult to understand.

_____ The purpose of my speech is to compare and/or contrast two or more similar or dissimilar objects, ideas, situations, people, or events.

_____ I have clearly stated the purpose of my speech.

_____ My thesis statement is written as a complete declarative sentence.

_____ My introduction gains attention and interest, establishes my credibility, and previews the main points of my message.

_____ Each of my main points addresses one point of comparison or contrast.

_____ Each of my main points is supported with facts, statistics, testimony, examples, or narratives.

_____ The comparisons or contrasts I make are not strained.

_____ I have positioned subpoints under the main points to which they are related.

_____ I have included a summary statement that reviews the comparisons and contrasts.

_____ I have prepared concluding remarks that reflect on the meaning and significance of my message.

_____ I have provided transitions where they are needed to make my speech flow smoothly.

_____ I have compiled a list of works consulted in the preparation of my speech.

GUIDELINES FOR USING A CAUSATION DESIGN

You may wish to use a causation design for a speech of explanation that tries to make the world and the things in it more understandable. The causation design explains a situation, condition, or event in terms of the events or conditions that led up to it.

The body of a causation design typically begins with a description of existing conditions, then probes for their causes. The description of existing conditions becomes the first main point in the speech, with the causes being subsequent main points.

The causes may be separated into categories, which can then be arranged in order of their importance. The causes may also be presented in a historical design, which may begin with the distant past and work up to the present, begin with the present and work back to the origin of the situation, or begin with the present and make projections into the future.

OUTLINE WORK SHEET: CAUSATION DESIGN

TITLE (Optional): _____

Topic: _____

Specific purpose: _____

_____

Thesis statement: _____

_____

INTRODUCTION

Attention material: _____

_____

Credibility material: _____

_____

Preview: _____

_____

(Transition to body of speech)

_____

BODY

I. Main point 1 (description of existing conditions) _____

_____

    A. (subpoint) _____

    _____

    B. (subpoint) _____

    _____

(Transition to main point 2)

_____

OUTLINE WORK SHEET: CAUSATION DESIGN
(page 2)

II. Main point 2 (first cause) _____

_____

    A. (subpoint) _____

    _____

    B. (subpoint) _____

    _____

(Transition to main point 3)

_____

III. Main point 3 (second cause) _____

_____

    A. (subpoint) _____

    _____

    B. (subpoint) _____

    _____

(Transition to main point 4)

_____

IV. Main point 4 (third cause) _____

_____

    A. (subpoint) _____

    _____

    B. (subpoint) _____

    _____

OUTLINE WORK SHEET: CAUSATION DESIGN
(page 3)

(Transition to main point 5)

_____

V. Main point 5 (fourth cause) _____

_____

    A. (subpoint) _____

_____

    B. (subpoint) _____

_____

(Transition to conclusion)

_____

CONCLUSION

I. Summary: _____

_____

II. Concluding remarks: _____

_____

Works Consulted:

CHECK LIST FOR CAUSATION DESIGN OUTLINE

_____ I have selected a topic that involves a situation, condition, or event that can best be understood in terms of its causes.

_____ I have clearly stated the purpose of my speech.

_____ My thesis statement is written as a complete declarative sentence.

_____ My introduction gains attention and interest, establishes my credibility, and previews the main points of my message.

_____ The first main point of my speech describes the present condition, situation, or event.

_____ Subsequent main points of my speech explain the causes of the condition, situation, or event.

_____ The main points containing causes are arranged either categorically in terms of their importance or chronologically (see categorical and sequential designs).

_____ I have been careful not to oversimplify the cause-effect relationships.

_____ I have positioned my subpoints under the main points to which they are related.

_____ My conclusion contains a summary that recaps my message and remarks that reflect on the meaning and significance of the speech.

_____ I have provided transitions where they are needed to make my speech flow smoothly.

_____ I have compiled a list of works consulted in the preparation of my speech.

READINGS FOR ENRICHMENT

See guide to journal abbreviations on p. 37.

* Items marked with an asterisk are suitable for student enrichment.

Learning

Baird, John E., Jr. "The Effects of Speech Summaries upon Audience Comprehension of Expository Speeches of Varying Quality and Complexity." *CSSJ* (Summer 1974), 119–127.

Barr, Robert B., and John Tagg. "From Teaching to Learning—A New Paradigm for Undergraduate Education." *Change* (Nov.–Dec. 1995), 12–25.

* Bower, Gordon H., and Daniel G. Morrow. "Mental Modes in Narrative Comprehension." *Science*, 5 Jan. 1990, pp. 44–48.

Brissey, F. L. "The Factor of Relevance in the Serial Reproduction of Information." *JC* (Dec. 1961), 211–219.

"Cui Bono? Can Thinking Be Taught Separately from Knowledge?" *The Economist*, 12 Aug. 1989, pp. 75–76.

Dempster, Frank N. "Exposing Our Students to Less Should Help Them Learn More." *Phi Delta Kappan* (Feb. 1993), 432–437.

Ezzell, Carol. "Memories Might Be Made of This: Closing In on the Biochemistry of Learning." *Science News*, 25 May 1991, pp. 328–330.

* Gruner, Charles R. "The Effect of Humor in Dull and Interesting Informative Speeches." *CSSJ* (Fall 1970), 160–166.

Housel, Thomas J. "Conversational Themes and Attention Focusing Strategies: Predicting Comprehension and Recall." *CQ* (Fall 1985), 236–253.

Kandel, Eric R., and Thomas J. O'Dell. "Are Adult Learning Mechanisms Also Used for Development?" *Science*, 9 Oct. 1992, pp. 243–245.

* Knapp, Mark L., Cynthia Stohl, and Kathleen R. Reardon. "'Memorable' Messages." *JC* (Autumn 1981), 27–41.

Kotter, John P. "Lifetime Learning: The New Educational Imperative." *The Futurist* (Nov.–Dec. 1995), 27–29.

Lang, Annie. "Effects of Chronological Presentation of Information on Processing and Memory for Broadcast News." *Journal of Broadcasting and Electronic Media* (1989), 441–452.

Nadis, Steve. "The Energy Efficient Brain." *Omni* (Feb. 1992), 16.

Petrie, Charles M., Jr., and Susan D. Carrell. "The Relationship of Motivation, Listening Capability, Initial Information, and Verbal Organizational Ability to Lecture Comprehension and Retention." *CM* (Aug. 1976), 187–194.

Robinson, Sharon P. "Life, Literacy and the Pursuit of Challenges." *Daedalus* (Fall 1995), 135–142.

Shields, David. "Information Sickness." *Harper's* (June 1993), 28.

Siegel, Jannna, and Michael F. Shaughnessy. "Educating for Understanding." *Phi Delta Kappan* (Mar. 1994), 563–566.

Simon, Cheryl. "Memory, Chunk-Style," *Psychology Today* (Mar. 1988), 17.

* Spicer, Christopher, and Ronald E. Bassett. "The Effect of Organization on Learning from an Informative Message." *SSCJ* (Spring 1976), 290–299.

Thompson, Richard F. "The Neurobiology of Learning and Memory." *Science*, 29 Aug. 1986, pp. 941–947.

Tucker, Charles O. "An Application of Programmed Learning to Informative Speech." *CM* (June 1964), 142–152.

Wheeler, Lawrence R. "The Effects of Attitude, Credibility and Homophily on Selective Exposure to Information." *CM* (Nov. 1974), 329–338.

General

Baesler, E. James. "Construction and Test of an Empirical Measure for Narrative Coherence and Fidelity." *CR* (Summer 1995), 97–101.

Bernard, Robert M., and Gary O Coldevin. "Effects of Recap Strategies on Television News Recall and Retention." *Journal of Broadcasting and Electronic Media* (Fall 1985), 407–419.

Bower, Bruce. "Understanding Speech: I See What You Mean." *Science News,* 17 June 1995, p. 373.

Brinton, Alan. "On Viewing Knowledge as Rhetorical." *CSSJ* (Winter 1985), 270–281.

Broadwell, Martin M. "It's So Technical, I Have to Lecture." *Training* (Mar. 1989), 41–43.

Brown, William R. "The History of Public Address in an Age of Information." *CSSJ* (Winter 1981), 227–235.

Cangelosi, Vincent, D. M. Robinson, and L. L. Schkade. "Information and Rational Choice." *JC* (June 1968), 131–143.

Dahir, Mubarak. "Writing Science and Medical Nonfiction: It's Easier than You Think." *Writer's Digest* (Nov. 1995), 29–31.

* Davis, Jay. "Beyond the Myth of Objectivity." *Media and Values* (Summer 1990), 21.

Dervin, Brenda. "Strategies for Dealing with Human Information Needs: Information or Communication?" *Journal of Broadcasting and Electronic Media* (Summer 1976), 323–333.

Detz, Joan. *Can You Say a Few Words? How to Prepare and Deliver.* New York: St. Martin's Press, 1991.

* Drum, Dale D. "What Is Information?" *CE* (Sept. 1956), 174–178.

———. "Change, Meaning, and Information." *JC* (Winter 1957), 161–170.

Edwardskon, Mickie, Kurt Kent, and Maeve McConnell. "Television News Information Gain: Videotex versus a Talking Head." *Journal of Broadcasting and Electronic Media* (Fall 1985), 367–378.

Engstrom, Theresa. "Turning Computer Babble into Plain English." *Working Woman* (May 1987), 61–63.

Findahl, Olle, and Birgitta Hoijer. "Some Characteristics of News Memory and Comprehension." *Journal of Broadcasting and Electronic Media* (Fall 1985), 379–396.

Frandsen, Kenneth D., and Donald A. Clement. "The Functions of Human Communication in Informing: Communicating and Processing Information." In *Handbook of Rhetorical and Communication Theory,* edited by Carroll C. Arnold and John Waite Bowers, pp. 338–399. Boston, Mass.: Allyn and Bacon, 1984.

Frank, Milo O. *How to Get Your Point Across in 30 Seconds or Less.* New York: Simon & Schuster, 1986.

Funkhouser, G. Ray, and Nathan Maccoby. "Communicating Specialized Science Information to a Lay Audience." *JC* (Mar. 1971), 58–71.

Gordon, Charles. "Facts Can Just Ruin a Good Story." *Macleans,* 1 Aug. 1994, p. 9.

Gregg, Richard B. "Rhetoric and Knowing: The Search for Perspective." *CSSJ* (Fall 1981), 133–144.

* "Heroes Cited: Facts Slighted." *The New Republic,* 24 Feb. 1986.

Hickey, James R. "The Effects of Information Control on Perceptions of Centrality." *Journalism Quarterly* (Spring 1968), 49–54.

Hirschman, Elizabeth C. "Social and Cognitive Influences on Information Exposure: A Path Analysis." *JC* (Winter 1981), 76–87.

* "How to Analyze a News Story: Eight Guidelines for Reading Between the Lines." *Media and Values* (Summer 1990), 22.

* "Ignorance 101." *Discover* (Sept. 1988), 12.

Jansen, Sue Curry. "Power and Knowledge: Toward a New Critical Synthesis." *JC* (Summer 1983), 342–354.

Kernan, Jerome B., and Leslie B. Heiman. "Information Distortion and Personality." *Journalism Quarterly* (Winter 1972), 698–701.

Klapp, Orrin E. "Meaning Lag in the Information Society." *JC* (Spring 1982), 56–66.

Koshland, Daniel E., Jr. "Credibility in Science and the Press." *Science,* 1 Nov. 1991, p. 629.

Leeds, Dorothy. *PowerSpeak.* New York: Berkeley. 1991.

Lin, Nan. "Information Flow, Influence Flow and the Decision-Making Process." *Journalism Quarterly* (Spring 1971), 33–40.

Lyne, John Russell. "Rhetoric and Everyday Knowledge." *CSSJ* (Fall 1981), 145–152.

Marcus, Steven J. "No Failure to Communicate." *Technology Review* (July 1992), 5.

McAnany, Emile G. "Does Information Really Work?" *JC* (Winter 1978), 84–90.

McCombs, Maxwell E., and Donald Shaw. "The Agenda-Setting Function of the Mass Media." *Public Opinion Quarterly* (1972), 176–187.

Moffat, Susan. "To Be a Leader in Technology, You Must Share It." *Fortune*, 14 Jan. 1991, pp. 34–35.

Munn, William C., and Charles R. Gruner. "'Sick' Jokes, Speaker Sex, and Informative Speech." *SSCJ* (Summer 1981), 411–418.

Nicholson, Richard S. "Communicating Science." *Science*, 17 Aug. 1990, p. 721.

Parkhurst, William. *The Eloquent Executive: How to Sound Your Best: High-Impact Speaking in Meetings Large & Small*. New York: Avon, 1988.

Petrie, Charles. "Informative Speaking: A Summary and Bibliography of Related Research." *CM*, 79–91.

Ploman, Edward W. "Information as Environment." *JC* (Spring 1975), 93–97.

Porat, Marc Uri. "Global Implications of the Information Society." *JC* (Winter 1978), 70–80.

Read, William H. "Information as a National Resource." *JC* (Winter 1979), 172–178.

Robertson, Douglas S. "The Information Revolution." *CR* (Apr. 1990), 235–254.

Rogin, Gilbert. "How to Tackle Hard Subjects." *Discover* (Dec. 1986), 4.

Rowan, Katherine E. "Goals, Obstacles, and Strategies in Risk Communication: A Problem-Solving Approach to Improving Communication About Risks." *JACR* (Nov. 1991), 300–329.

Salmon, Charles T. "Message Discrimination and the Information Environment." *CR* (July 1986), 363–372.

Sawyer, Thomas M., Jr. "In Defense of Explanatory Speeches." *CE* (Sept. 1957), 196–199.

Schloff, Laurie, and Marcia Yudkin. *Smart Speaking: Sixty-Second Strategies*. New York: Holt, 1991.

Smith, Donald K. "Rhetoric of and in the Learning Society." *CE* (May 1979), 97–103.

Son, Jinok, Stephen D. Reese, and William R. Davie. "Effects of Visual-Verbal Redundancy and Recaps on Television News Learning." *Journal of Broadcasting and Electronic Media* (Spring 1987), 207–216.

Stamm, Keith. "Some Comments on Communication and Information." *Journal of Broadcasting and Electronic Media* (Summer 1976), 344–353.

Starck, Kenneth. "Values and Information Source Preferences." *JC* (Mar. 1973), 74–85.

* Thompkins, Phillip K. "Organizing the Speech to Inform." *CQ* (Sept. 1959), 21–22.

Walters, Lilly. *Secrets of Successful Speakers: How You Can Motivate, Captivate and Persuade*. New York: McGraw-Hill, 1993.

* Weimer, Walter B. "Why All Knowing Is Rhetorical." *JAFA* (Fall 1983), 63–71.

"Why Do We Fall for It? Journalistic Exploitation of Science." *U.S. News & World Report*, 21 Mar. 1988, p. 60.

* Wismer, Robert D. "Making an Effective Technical Presentation." *Research-Technology Management* (July–Aug. 1989), 9–10.

Wright, Ron. "That Never Really Happened!" *The Humanist* (July–Aug. 1994), 30–31.

Teaching Techniques and Materials

Adler, Barbara. "A Speech About a 'Great American Speech.'" *SCT* (Spring 1987), 7.

Berger, Charles R., and Patrick diBattista. "Communication Failure and Plan Adaptation: If At First You Don't Succeed, Say It Louder and Slower." *CM* (Sept. 1993), 220–238.

Clarke, John H. "Building a Lecture that Really Works." *Education Digest* (Oct. 1987), 52–55.

Frederick, Peter J. "The Lively Lecture—Eight Variations." *College Teaching* (1986), 43–50.

Frymier, Ann Bainbridge, and Gary M. Shullman. "'What's In It for Me?': Increasing Content Relevance to Enhance Students' Motivation." *CE* (Jan. 1995), 40–50.

Gorg, Robert. "The Use of Model Speeches on Videotapes (or See, Your Friends Can Do This Too!)." *SCT* (Fall 1993), 11–12.

Hawkinson, Ken. "Performing Personal Narratives." *SCT* (Spring 1995), 3–4.

Hollingsworth, J. E. "Oral Briefings." *Management Review* (Aug. 1968), 2–10.

Knox, Claire E. "Shared Short Talks Prepare Students for Oral Presentations." *Bulletin of the Association for Business Communication* (June 1989), 18–19.

Mino, Mary. "Application Speeches." *SCT* (Spring 1996), 6–7.

Powell, Kimberly A. "Increasing Appreciation for Diversity Through the Group Culture Speech." *SCT* (Winter 1996), 3–4.

Rowan, Katherine. "The Speech to Explain Difficult Ideas." *SCT* (Summer 1990), 2–3.

———. "A New Pedagogy for Explanatory Public Speaking: Why Arrangement Should Not Substitute for Invention." *CE* (July 1995), 236–250.

Schumer, Allison. "Custom Comparison Speeches." *SCT* (Fall 1989), 1.

Thompson, C. Lamar. "Suggestions for Making Lectures More Effective." *The Clearing House* (Dec. 1987), 186–187.

Tolar, Debra Olson. "My Favorite News Team: Comparative Analysis of the Nightly News." *SCT* (Fall 1992), 9.

Weaver, Richard L. "Effective Lecturing Techniques: Alternatives to Classroom Boredom." In *New Directions in Teaching,* edited by Wilbert J. McKeachie, pp. 25–35. San Francisco: Jossey Bass, 1980.

CHAPTER 13
Persuasive Speaking

OBJECTIVES

- To help your students recognize the characteristics of persuasive speaking.

- To help your students understand the steps in the persuasive process.

- To teach your students to adapt persuasive messages to different audiences.

- To help your students understand the major persuasive functions.

- To help your students select appropriate designs for their persuasive speeches.

SUGGESTIONS FOR TEACHING

Perhaps because of its obvious importance in our lives, persuasion can be an intimidating subject. It is easy to overwhelm freshmen-level students with the study of persuasion. At this level, the simplest ideas about persuasion are the most important. As a practical application, you may wish to stress the importance of persuasion in collective decision-making processes.

In this chapter, we cover the personal and social significance of persuasion, the differences between persuasive and informative speaking, the steps in the persuasive process, audience-centered challenges to successful persuasion, the functions of persuasive speaking, and design strategies for persuasive speaking. If, like many instructors, you like to emphasize argumentation skills with the persuasive assignment, coordinate the activities in this chapter with those covering evidence, proof, argumentation, and persuasive fallacies in Chapter 14. Emphasize two important and related factors of persuasive speaking. The first is that it is necessarily audience-centered. This is true of all public communication, but even more so when we seek to influence or persuade people. To be persuasive, a speech must be adapted to where a particular audience stands in relation to a topic and proposal. The second related point is that persuasion is rarely a complete success or failure, and so success should be considered in terms of degree. Just getting strongly polarized audiences to listen to other positions can sometimes be a tremendous victory. We tend to change our minds slowly and incrementally on issues that are of great importance to us, and almost never as the result of hearing a single message. Impress upon students the importance of knowing how to present messages incrementally in order to avoid committing the great expectation fallacy and creating a possible boomerang effect, and recognizing when it is time to take a more confrontational approach.

In this chapter we offer activities and exercises to help your students explore the differences between informative and persuasive speaking, make audience-centered adaptations of persuasive messages, use motivational appeals, and critique and construct persuasive messages. We also offer exercises and sample outlines to illustrate the process of structuring persuasive speeches.

CHAPTER OUTLINE

I. Persuasion is the art of convincing others to give favorable attention to our point of view. *(text pp. 415–417)*

    A. Persuasion is an integral part of our lives, and ranges from the ethical to the unethical.

        1. Becoming educated should involve learning how to resist bad persuasion while remaining open to constructive messages.

    B. Our political and social systems depend on free and open persuasion.

        1. Deliberation involves the open discussion of all sides of issues before reaching collective decisions.

        2. Persuasion is both more ethical and more practical than force or coercion.

        3. The freedom to voice unpopular views produces better decisions.

    C. Persuasion can be both ethical and beneficial.

        1. Ethical persuasion is based on sound reasoning, sensitivity to audiences, and appeals to people's better nature.

        2. Ethical persuasion helps us apply received wisdom to new situations, and improves the quality and humanity of our commitments.

II. Persuasive speaking differs from informative speaking in six important ways. *(text pp. 417–419)*

    A. Informative speakers reveal and clarify options, persuasive speakers advocate choices among options.

    B. Informative speakers provide information to enlighten, persuasive speakers provide evidence to justify recommendations.

    C. Persuasive speaking requires more audience commitment.

    D. Leadership is a more important issue in persuasive than in informative speaking.

    E. Appeals to feelings are more appropriate in persuasive than in informative speaking.

    F. Persuasive speakers must assume greater ethical obligations than informative speakers.

III. The persuasive process involves five major phases. *(text pp. 419–423)*

    A. The first step in the process is awareness of the issue.

        1. Speakers should make sure audiences know about, attend to, and understand how the issue affects their lives.

        2. Sometimes audiences must be convinced that a problem does or does not exist.

    B. The second stage is developing understanding.

        1. Beyond simply getting the point, audience members must be moved by our ideas and know how to carry out our proposals.

        2. Ethical persuasion expands our knowledge of arguments, demonstrates how some arguments are stronger than others, and provides evidence to support a position.

    C. The third stage of persuasion involves seeking agreement and helping audiences remember the reasons for their agreement.

        1. Total acceptance may not be possible, and success should be measured in terms of degree.

        2. Speakers may secure agreement by presenting indisputable facts with well-reasoned interpretations.

    D. The fourth stage is encouraging action.

        1. Getting listeners to raise hands, sign petitions, or voice agreement reinforces audience commitment.

    E. The final phase is the integration of new attitudes into belief and value systems.

        1. People often must modify existing attitudes and beliefs to integrate new ones.

            a. This is why listeners may agree momentarily, and then change their minds again.

        2. Because persuasion entails risk, speakers must demonstrate benefits, show that new attitudes are consistent with cherished values, and anticipate objections.

        3. It is unreasonable to expect listeners to change their value/belief systems as a result of hearing a single speech.

    F. Successful persuasion is rarely an all-or-nothing proposition.

1. It usually takes a series of persuasive attempts to change an audience's important values and beliefs.
2. Speakers should carefully consider their audiences and adapt to anticipated challenges.

IV. Persuasive speakers should prepare for the challenges of addressing specific audiences. *(text pp. 423–429)*
   A. Speakers should consider where their audiences stand, whether they are united, and how they might perceive them as speakers on the subject.
   B. Enticing reluctant audiences to listen can pose a major challenge.
      1. "Thoughtful attention" to opposing positions may be a reasonable goal.
      2. A co-active approach can help bridge differences. Speakers should:
         a. establish identification early by stressing common attitudes, beliefs, and values.
         b. emphasize common views before addressing points of opposition.
         c. emphasize explanation more than argument at the outset.
         d. cite authorities and evidence that the audience will be likely to respect and accept.
         e. set modest goals for change.
         f. make multisided presentations that help make those who agree resistant to later counterpersuasion.
      3. Strongly opposed audiences present a difficult challenge. Speakers should:
         a. enhance their ethos by being honest and and requesting a fair hearing.
         b. modify their purposes so that they don't try to accomplish too much.
            (1) An overly ambitious proposal may result in a boomerang effect.
            (2) The great expectation fallacy involves hoping for great change as a result of a single speech.
         c. realize that an immediate positive response is not the only mark of success.
            (1) A sleeper effect occurs when audiences change after a period of time.
   C. Removing barriers to commitment can be challenging. Speakers should:
      1. provide needed information.
      2. affirm and apply common values.
      3. strengthen their credibility by citing experts that the audience will trust and respect, using quality information, and making multisided presentations.
   D. It is often difficult to move listeners from attitude to action.
      1. Listeners may not see a personal connection, know what to do, or see any hope in acting.
      2. With reluctant listeners, speakers should:
         a. revitalize shared beliefs.
         b. demonstrate the need for audience involvement through examples and narratives.
         c. present a clear plan of action that shows their audiences how to proceed.

V. The three major forms of persuasive speeches correspond to their relative functions. *(text pp. 430–432)*
   A. Speeches addressing attitudes and values are aimed at forming, reforming, or reinforcing what people believe or the way they feel about something.
      1. They may pave the way for speeches urging action.
      2. They should begin on common ground.
   B. Speeches urging action go beyond attitude change by soliciting direct responses.
      1. Speakers may strive for individual or concerted group action.
      2. Speakers should provide good reasons to overcome caution.
   C. Speeches of contention refute opposing arguments to clear the way for proposed changes.
      1. Speeches of contention may be suitable when audiences are split on a topic.
         a. Speakers should target uncommitted listeners and reasonable opponents.
         b. Speakers should use tactful, carefully documented counterarguments.
      2. Speakers may sometimes want to "shock" strongly opposed audiences.

VI. Speakers must select an appropriate design for arranging their main ideas. *(text pp. 433–440)*
   A. Persuasive speeches may use some of the same designs as informative speeches.

1. The categorical design may be used to list reasons.
2. The sequential design may specify the steps in a plan of action.
3. The comparative design works well for speeches of contention.

B. The problem-solution design convinces listeners that they face a problem, then shows them how to deal with it.
    1. If the problem is not obvious, speakers should establish its existence and significance.
    2. Speakers should offer solutions that are concrete and easy to follow.

C. The stock issues approach is a variation of the problem-solution design based on general questions that listeners might ask.
    1. The stock issues design addresses the following questions.
        a. Is there a need for change because of some significant problem?
        b. What is the solution to this problem?
        c. Who will put this solution into effect?
    2. The stock issues design focuses on inherency.
        a. It considers whether a harmful effect is caused by the problem, and whether proposed solutions will solve it.
        b. It considers to what extent a harm is an inevitable part of a situation and therefore resistant to change.

D. The motivated sequence is also an elaboration of the problem-solution design.
    1. The motivated sequence design has five basic steps: (1) arousing attention, (2) demonstrating a need for change, (3) offering a plan of action, (4) visualizing results, and (5) calling for action.
    2. To use the motivated sequence effectively, speakers should consider where their audiences stand, then focus on the appropriate steps.

E. The refutative design raises doubt about competing positions by revealing their deficiencies.
    1. Speakers must understand the opposing positions before refuting them.
    2. Speakers may focus on faulty reasoning, poor evidence, or self-interest of opposing advocates.
    3. Speakers should address the weakest opposing viewpoints first.
    4. Speakers should follow five steps when refuting arguments: (1) state the point to be refuted, (2) tell how the point will be refuted, (3) present credible evidence, (4) interpret the evidence, and (5) explain the significance of the refutation.
    5. Speakers can strengthen their position by supporting a counterproposal.

USING END-OF-CHAPTER ITEMS

Discussion *(text p. 442)*

1. Examine magazine advertisements and newspaper articles for "infomercials"—persuasive messages cloaked as information. What alerts you to the persuasive intent? In what respects does such pseudo-information possess the characteristics of persuasion discussed in this chapter? In what respects does it possess the characteristics of informative speaking discussed in Chapter 12?

This exercise works well as a combined homework and in-class discussion activity. If you have your students find their own ads, remind them not to deface library periodicals. You might gather the items yourself for class discussion. Many ads for over-the-counter drugs, diet programs, and financial or legal services typically disguise themselves as objective news stories. Such advertisements typically contain more printed text than pictures, but little that reveals the actual purpose or bias. In newspaper supplements and tabloids, the word "Advertisement" is sometimes inserted at the top of the material to distinguish it from the text of the publication. As an alternative, videotape extended late-night infomercials and show them in class for discussion and analysis. Use the following questions to guide class discussion.

1. Does the ad present a variety of options, or does it urge one choice among options?

2. What does the advertisement ask of you? To change a belief or attitude? To take some action? To buy something? To make a donation?
3. Is the material in the advertisement directed at arousing a latent need?
4. Does the ad evoke strong positive or negative feelings? What are they?
5. Is the information in the ad credible? Why?
6. Is this an ethical advertising technique? Why?

2. **The letters to the editor section of the Sunday newspaper is often a rich source of persuasive material. Using a recent Sunday paper, analyze the persuasion attempted in these letters. Which do you think are most and least effective and why?**

This exercise works well as a written homework assignment. Again, remind students not to deface library materials. Instructors might collect an assortment of appropriate letters for in-class discussion and analysis. Divide your class into small groups, and have the members of each group critique one another's ideas before presenting them for general class discussion. Letters to the editor may range from reasonable, well-substantiated arguments to wild, irrational ravings. You might have your students concentrate on the organizational design of the letters, the specific claims and appeals, or the use, misuse, or lack of supporting information. You may wish to combine this exercise with Discussion item 3 from Chapter 14, addressing logical fallacies in editorial letters.

3. **The speech on slum housing that appears at the end of this chapter was prepared for a student audience at Kansas State University. What changes might you suggest in this speech if it were to be presented to a luncheon meeting of Realtors in Manhattan, Kansas? Why?**

This exercise works well as a combination homework and small-group activity to emphasize the importance of audience analysis in persuasive speaking—Realtors or landlords obviously have a vested interest against profit-threatening changes. Your students should carefully scan the text for references that might offend the new audience, and (where possible) reword without sacrificing ideas or the underlying purpose of the speech. Speakers might stress such factors as the costs of liability settlements for injuries, appeals to basic decency and business ethics, or reputation and prestige, as most of the audience would not appreciate being labeled "slumlords."

4. **When should a speaker give up trying to persuade a hostile audience and simply confront listeners directly with the position they oppose? Why would a speaker bother to do this? Is it possible that both speaker and audience might gain something from such a confrontation? Find an example of such a speech. Do you agree with the strategy used in it? Discuss in class.**

This exercise can be used for homework or in-class discussion. Persuasion is usually most effective when approached incrementally—small, reasonable steps toward a distant goal. A reasonable first step may be simply getting reluctant audiences to acknowledge a problem and listen to alternative positions. Later efforts might be directed toward changes in thinking or behavior. The process requires patience and persistence. Sometimes, however, incremental approaches are either practically, psychologically, or morally unacceptable. Some issues demand immediate attention, and when addressing highly volatile and controversial topics (gun control, abortion, etc.), it may be impossible to avoid confronting opposing positions. When audiences already know where you stand, they might appreciate the honesty of a direct but respectful confrontational approach. Before mixed audiences (including people who are strongly for, strongly against, or neutral toward the speaker's position), speakers might opt for a confrontational strategy, hoping to reach the neutral and reinforce the favorable segments of the audience. They should, however, take care to recognize the inherent risk of a boomerang effect when considering this approach. Many audience members may be offended by what they perceive to be an inappropriate assault on their values and beliefs. Furthermore, such speeches can increase polarization and alienation within groups. Audiences may end up rejecting both the proposal and the speaker, becoming even more firmly entrenched in their original positions.

Application *(text pp. 442–443)*

1. **Keep a diary of your day, identifying all the moments in which you confront and practice persuasion. Evaluate your adventure in persuasion. When were you most and least persuaded and most and least persuasive? Why? Did you encounter (or commit!) any ethical abuses?**

   Use this as an extended outside activity to impress upon students the prevalence of persuasion in all our lives. This activity can underscore the need to understand and appreciate the functions of persuasion. Have your students keep a running log for a week, recording at least three daily instances in which they attempt to persuade others or attempts are made to persuade them (preferably both). Many students may well be surprised by how constant a force persuasion is in their lives. They should consider a variety of contexts and media—advertising, work relations, intimate friends and family, strangers, etc. They should also consider the more subtle forms of persuasion implicit within communication, such as gender, race, and class stereotypes or underlying endorsements of predominant views, attitudes, and lifestyles. These more subtle messages can be difficult to recognize because we often do not think of them as persuasion. After a week or so, you might have your students highlight their observations in a short presentation. They should critique them in terms of their likely effectiveness and ethical considerations. As a shortened alternative, videotape several television ads for in-class viewing and discussion. Some critics believe that the implicit or subtle messages in advertising can be especially potent because the fast-paced montage format tends to break listeners out of a rational linear mode of consciousness and place them in one that is generally more emotive and reactionary.

2. **Read one of the persuasive speeches in Appendix B and identify the following:**

   a. **The challenge the speaker confronted**
   b. **The type of persuasive speech**
   c. **The design of the speech**

   Suggest an alternative design for the speech and discuss why you think that approach would work as well or better.

   This exercise works well for homework or small-group discussion. The following analysis of Bonnie Marshall, "Living Wills: Insuring Your Right to Choose," may help guide your discussion.

   Challenge: Bonnie faced several challenges in preparing and presenting her speech. First, she had to interest and involve her younger college classmates in her subject, living wills. Her use of narrative is especially effective in humanizing the topic and giving listeners a way to identify with it.

   Type: This speech address attitudes and urges individual action.

   Design: The speech follows a problem-solution design and also uses a sequential design to outline the plan of action.

   Optional Design: Monroe's motivated sequence might also have been an effective design strategy for this speech in that the five steps would have encompassed all of the dimensions of the problem that needed to be covered in an effective presentation.

3. **Select a controversial subject and outline the persuasive speeches you would present on the subject to:**

   a. **an uncommitted audience**
   b. **an audience in agreement**
   c. **a reluctant audience**

   Discuss the differences among your approaches.

This activity can be used for homework or as a small-group discussion activity. For in-class use, choose a controversial subject/thesis, divide your class into small groups, and assign each group an audience to work with. The group members should work together to generate a rough outline of a speech they might give to address this particular point and issue to this particular audience. Remember that for uncommitted audiences, speakers should emphasize the significance of their topics to their audiences, avoid emotional overkill, and cite high-quality information from well-respected sources. Speakers can move audiences who already agree to action by invoking shared beliefs and commitments, painting a clear picture of the need for change, and providing their audiences with a clear plan of action to solidify their involvement. With opposing audiences, speakers might use a direct confrontational approach, or a co-active approach that aims at a fair and dispassionate hearing. Have your students include specific-purpose and thematic statements, two or three main points, an appropriate design strategy, likely supporting materials, and strategies for introducing and concluding their speeches. Emphasize the importance of choosing a sound persuasive strategy, structure, and supporting materials with a particular audience in mind.

ADDITIONAL ACTIVITIES

Analyzing Persuasive Speeches

Purpose: To have your students apply the basic concepts of persuasion through critiques of actual student speeches.

Directions: This activity is intended for in-class viewing and discussion, although it can be used for homework by assigning speeches out of Appendix B. Show videotaped student speeches for in-class discussion and analysis. Use this to teach whatever you want to emphasize with respect to the text and your expectations from student speeches. You might have your students critique the viewed speeches in terms of their persuasive functions (to address attitudes and values, to promote action, to contend with opposing views), the design strategies used, and the stage of persuasion the speech appears to address. Your students might also consider the speaker's apparent purpose. What barriers to persuasion are presumed, and what strategies are employed to overcome them? As your students learn to distinguish among persuasive speeches in this fashion, they should eventually develop a heightened sensitivity to the importance of audience considerations in crafting strategically focused persuasive messages.

Why Should I Care?

Purpose: To provide your students an opportunity to investigate a variety of motivational appeals for specific topics and audiences.

Directions: This activity is intended for in-class use. Review the basic motivations covered in Chapter 4 of the text. For each pair of topics and audiences on the following list, have your students offer reasons why the stipulated audience should be concerned with the topic and state the need that is being appealed to. Give your students about ten minutes to gather their ideas before presenting them for class discussion. For example, if you wanted to convince a condominium homeowners' association to endorse adding insulation to all units, you might stress that they could live more comfortably and save money on heating bills. You would be appealing to the basic needs of comfort, the nurturance of family members, and economic security. Focus discussion on the often implicit nature of basic motive appeals in persuasive messages and discourse. You might collate the responses on the chalkboard under the headings "Why audience should care" and "Needs appealed to."

Topics and Audiences:

1. Painless backpacking for beginners
2. How to listen to get better grades: college freshmen in orientation
3. Spending a semester abroad: college students

4. Increasing peak experiences in your life: general mixed audience
5. Developing personal power: female college students
6. Making your home safer: off-campus student association
7. Winning the dating game: college students

Possible Responses:

Why the Audience Should Care	*Needs Appealed to*
1. Avoid injuries	Safety
Being with others	Friendship
Won't ache for a week	Comfort
2. Success in college	Achievement, accomplishment
Make Dean's list	Recognition
Help for future jobs	Independence, control
3. Be part of a close-knit group	Friendship
Do something different	Variety
Get away from home restrictions	Independence
4. Doing something rewarding	Success, recognition, enjoyment
Doing something different	Variety
5. Able to take care of yourself	Independence
Get a good job	Financial security, recognition
Become a leader	Dominance, recognition
Feel "in charge"	Control
6. Prevent robberies	Economic security, safety
Prevent accidents	Safety
7. Make friends	Friendship
Be popular	Recognition

Problem-Solution Impromptus

Purpose: To give your students experience enacting a basic persuasive message form.

Directions: Television commercials commonly make use of a basic problem-solution form of persuasive message to sell the advertised products. That is, they seek to create scenarios that pose a threat or "problem" for their targeted audiences, then promote their products as the most promising solution. This form of reasoning is clearly present in commercials ranging from those for personal hygiene products to those for automobile tires to those for life insurance. Follow the usual approach to impromptu speaking activity. Write the names of consumer products (deodorant, soda, bail bonds, condoms, etc.) on small slips of paper, fold them, and place them in a paper bag. Have each student draw three and choose one. You might quickly review the problem-solution design in preparation for this activity. Give your students five to ten minutes to make up a thirty-second commercial that uses a problem-solution format to sell the drawn product. Have your students give their products brand names.

Howard N. Schreier (Bloomsburg University, Bloomsburg, Pennsylvania), "Analyzing Persuasive Tactics," *SCT* (Summer 1989), 14.

Goal: To help students determine the appropriateness of employing specific tactics in persuasive messages.

Students enrolled in my junior level Persuasion class are required to write two editorial-type persuasive statements in which they take and maintain a position on a controversial and timely political, social, or moral issue. In addition to the written message—and of equal importance—students must write a comprehensive analysis of the persuasive tactics employed in the message.

Analysis of persuasive tactics meets two useful purposes. It suggests to students that multiple ways exist for approaching a persuasive message and this recognition compels them to consider both subject and audience as bases for choice. As a result of the required analysis, attempts to plagiarize are limited. No teacher can be familiar with all the editorials and position papers written by local newspapers or special interest groups. This approach discourages "borrowing" material written by others.

The first part of the analysis deals with the audience of persuasion. Since persuasive messages are created with the goal of influencing members of a target audience, the analysis should state who the specific audience is and why they were chosen. This analysis centers both on the demographics and "psychographics" of the audience. Information concerning the age, gender, educational, political, and ethnic and/or racial make-up of the target group is coupled with a determination of the group's values, beliefs, attitudes, and opinions on the subject of the message.

Second, since target audience members are, in part, influenced by emotional appeals, the analysis should focus on the motivators employed—those forces that stimulate or direct one's attitude or behavior—and why they were chosen, given the topic and the target audience. I introduce my students to a variety of motivators, such as fear, anger, sympathy, independence, ethnicity, devotion, and nostalgia, before giving the assignment. The analysis of motivators indicates how well the appeals fit the audience's needs, wants, and desires.

Third, since the manner in which a message is expressed has an effect on the audience, an analysis of language choices is required. Certain words or phrases may have been chosen, due to their ability to name things, connect thoughts, or spark an emotion. Other words or phrases are chosen for the meaning they carry. For example, in a message on hunting, the word *harvest* carries a very different meaning than *kill*, when used to describe what hunters do. Still other words or phrases may help to create mood, as when a beer manufacturer urges consumers to "Capture Canada's Bear of Beers," suggesting a mood of manly ruggedness and adventure.

Fourth, since some type of evidence usually is necessary to influence members of a target audience, the analysis centers on what approach has been taken. Persuaders may use evidence that appeals to the intellect of the audience. This *rational* approach to evidence employs facts, statistics, or other data that stand independent of the individual employing them. Persuaders may use evidence that appeals to the audience's emotions. This *dramatic* approach to evidence employs anecdotes and illustrations which provide characterization and setting, "forcing" audiences vicariously to experience the evidence. Yet another possibility is using a combination of both of these approaches to appeal to the "whole person."

Finally, since the manner in which arguments, evidence, and appeals to emotions are ordered has an effect on audiences, an analysis of the chosen organizational pattern is required. Students may employ a causal, topical, spatial, chronological, stock issues, or motivated sequence pattern, but it is important they understand that the choice is constrained by both the subject and the audience.

Student reaction to these analyses has been very positive for several reasons. They enable students to put into practice the theories of persuasion studied throughout the semester. They enhance students' ability to make meaningful choices among a variety of possible persuasive approaches. Moreover, since the persuasive message is presented in class, peers as well as the instructor have an opportunity to evaluate the message and the tactics employed. This allows for a thorough discussion of the strengths and weaknesses, the effectiveness and ineffectiveness of tactical persuasive choices.

SUPPLEMENTARY MATERIALS

Films and Videos

"How to Give a Persuasive Speech," Time-Life, color, 25 minutes.

"Persuasive Appeals," RMI Media Productions, 28 minutes.

"Endless Persuasion," RMI Media Productions, 28 minutes.

"Understanding Persuasion," Films for the Humanities, color, 15 minutes.

"Psycho-Sell: Advertising and Persuasion," Insight Media, 25 minutes.

"Speaking Persuasively," RMI Media Productions, 28 minutes.

"When You Buy: How Ads Persuade," Insight Media, 33 minutes.

Computer Software

"Speech Designer," Houghton Mifflin

Transparency and Handouts *(see following pages)*

The Process of Persuasion

Persuasive Speech Designs

Meeting the Challenges of Persuasion

Problem-Solution Design—Guidelines, Outline Work Sheet, and Check List

Stock Issues Design—Guidelines, Outline Work Sheet, and Check List

Motivated Sequence Design—Guidelines, Outline Work Sheet, and Check List

Refutative Design—Guidelines, Outline Work Sheet, and Check List

THE PROCESS OF PERSUASION

1. Listeners must be made aware of an issue or problem.

2. Listeners must understand arguments and proposals.

3. Listeners must agree with ideas and recommendations.

4. Listeners must be encouraged to act in accordance with their new beliefs.

5. Listeners must integrate their new commitments into their daily lives.

PERSUASIVE SPEECH DESIGNS

1. **Categorical designs: arrange reasons in familiar patterns.**

2. **Sequential designs: outline steps in plan of action.**

3. **Comparative designs: contrast weakness of opposition with strength of your position.**

4. **Problem-solution designs: show listeners how to deal with a problem.**

5. **Stock issues designs: focus on questions reasonable people might ask.**

6. **Motivated sequence designs: use five steps to lead people to action.**

7. **Refutative designs: directly address opposing positions.**

MEETING THE CHALLENGES OF PERSUASION

1. Enticing reluctant audiences to listen:
   - Establish identification and good will.
   - Begin with areas of agreement.
   - Emphasize explanation more than argument.
   - Cite authorities your listeners respect.
   - Set modest goals for change.
   - Offer a multisided presentation.

2. Removing barriers to commitment:
   - Provide needed information.
   - Affirm and apply values.
   - Strengthen your credibility.

3. Moving audiences to action:
   - Revitalize shared beliefs.
   - Demonstrate the need for involvement.
   - Present a clear plan of action.
   - Make it easy for listeners to comply.

GUIDELINES FOR USING THE PROBLEM-SOLUTION DESIGN

You may wish to use a problem-solution design when you must convince your audience that it should face up to a specific problem and that you have a solution that will deal with this problem. It is sometimes difficult to convince people that there really is a problem that deserves or even demands their attention. People often ignore problems until they reach a critical stage when drastic action is necessary. You can counteract this by depicting the crisis that will arise unless the audience makes the changes you suggest. The solution phase of a problem-solution design typically involves changing an attitude or taking action.

The body of a problem-solution design usually has only two main points: the presentation of the problem and the presentation of the solution. Subpoints under the problem main point describe the problem, highlight its importance, and suggest what might happen if the problem is ignored. Subpoints under the solution main point describe the solution, show how it solves the problem, present a plan of action, and picture the results of its implementation.

OUTLINE WORK SHEET: PROBLEM-SOLUTION DESIGN

TITLE (Optional): _____

Topic: _____

Specific purpose: _____

_____

Thesis statement: _____

_____

INTRODUCTION

Attention material: _____

_____

Credibility material: _____

_____

Preview: _____

_____

(Transition to body of speech)

_____

BODY

I. Main point 1 (statement of problem) _____

_____

    A. (Description of problem) _____

_____

        1. (Signs, symptoms, effects of problem) _____

_____

        2. (Example, narrative, or testimony) _____

_____

OUTLINE WORK SHEET: PROBLEM-SOLUTION DESIGN
(page 2)

B. (Importance of problem) _____

_____

    1. (Extent of problem) _____

    _____

        a. (Facts/statistics) _____

        _____

        b. (Expert testimony) _____

        _____

    2. (Who is affected) _____

    _____

        a. (Facts/statistics) _____

        _____

        b. (Example/narrative) _____

        _____

C. (Consequences of problem) _____

_____

    1. (Expert testimony) _____

    _____

    2. (Example/narrative) _____

_____

(Transition to main point 2)

_____

OUTLINE WORK SHEET: PROBLEM-SOLUTION DESIGN
(page 3)

II. Main point 2 (statement of solution) _____

_____

   A. (Description of solution) _____

   _____

      1. (How solution fits problem) _____

      _____

         a. (More than symptom relief) _____

         _____

         b. (Is workable) _____

         _____

      2. (How solution can be implemented) _____

      _____

         a. (Plan of action) _____

         _____

            (1) (Step 1 of plan) _____

            _____

            (2) (Step 2 of plan) _____

            _____

            (3) (Step 3 of plan) _____

            _____

            (4) (Step 4 of plan) _____

            _____

         b. (Costs and efforts) _____

         _____

OUTLINE WORK SHEET: PROBLEM-SOLUTION DESIGN
(page 4)

B. (Picture results) _____

_____

    1. (Describe expected results) _____

        _____

    2. (When results expected) _____

        _____

    3. (Additional benefits) _____

        _____

(Transition to conclusion)

_____

CONCLUSION

Summary: _____

_____

Concluding remarks: _____

_____

Works Consulted:

PROBLEM-SOLUTION DESIGN: CHECK LIST

_____   I have selected a topic that involves a problem that needs to be solved.

_____   I have clearly stated the purpose of my speech.

_____   My thesis statement is written as a complete declarative sentence.

_____   My introduction gains attention and interest, establishes my credibility, and previews the main points of my message.

_____   My first main point presents the problem.

_____   My subpoints for the first main point describe the problem, show its importance, and demonstrate the consequences of inaction.

_____   I have adequate supporting material for each of my subpoints relating to the problem.

_____   My second main point presents my solution to the problem.

_____   My subpoints for the second main point demonstrate how the solution addresses the problem, describe a plan of action, and picture the results of the solution.

_____   I have adequate supporting material for each of my subpoints relating to the solution.

_____   My conclusion contains a summary that recaps my message and remarks that reflect on the meaning and significance of my speech.

_____   I have provided transitions where they are needed to make my speech flow smoothly.

_____   I have compiled a list of works consulted in the preparation of my speech.

GUIDELINES FOR USING THE STOCK ISSUES DESIGN

You may wish to use the stock issues design when you anticipate that listeners will have questions in their mind about the existence or seriousness of a problem or the feasibility of your solution. The stock issues design is a variation of the problem-solution design. It attempts to answer the major general questions a reasonable person would ask before agreeing to a change in policies or procedures. The general questions related to the problem and its solution make up the framework of the body of the speech.

Like the problem-solution design, the stock issues design typically has two main points. The first main point in the body of a speech using the stock issues design addresses the problem: its background and significance and the harms or negative consequences that are associated with it. The second main point of the body of the speech addresses the solution to the problem. It includes consideration of the workability, practicality, and costs of the solution as well as the presentation of a plan of action.

OUTLINE WORK SHEET: STOCK ISSUES DESIGN

TITLE (Optional): _____

Topic: _____

Specific purpose: _____

_____

Thesis statement: _____

_____

INTRODUCTION

Attention material: _____

_____

Credibility material: _____

_____

Preview: _____

_____

(Transition to body of speech)

_____

BODY

I. Main point 1 (statement of problem/responses to questions of harm) _____

_____

    A. (Background of problem) _____

_____

        1. (When did problem begin?) _____

_____

        2. (How did problem originate?) _____

_____

OUTLINE WORK SHEET: STOCK ISSUES DESIGN
(page 2)

3. (What caused problem?) _____

_____

4. (How extensive is problem?) _____

_____

B. (Responses to questions of harms) _____

_____

    1. (What harms accrue from the problem?) _____

    _____

    2. (Are these harms inherent in the problem?) _____

    _____

    3. (Will harms continue or grow unless we change?) _____

    _____

(Transition to second main point)

_____

II. Main point 2 (statement of solution to problem and responses to questions of feasibility) _____

_____

A. (Will solution solve problem?) _____

_____

    1. (Is solution practical?) _____

    _____

    2. (Will costs be reasonable?) _____

    _____

    3. (Might there be additional benefits or problems?) _____

    _____

OUTLINE WORK SHEET: STOCK ISSUES DESIGN
(page 3)

B. (How can solution be enacted?) _____

_____

    1. (What is the plan of action?) _____

_____

        a. (Step 1 of plan) _____

_____

        b. (Step 2 of plan) _____

_____

        c. (Step 3 of plan) _____

_____

        d. (Step 4 of plan) _____

_____

    2. (Who will enact the plan?) _____

_____

        a. (Are they competent and responsible?) _____

_____

        b. (What role might listeners play?) _____

_____

C. (Picture results) _____

_____

    1. (What results can we expect?) _____

_____

    2. (When can we expect them?) _____

_____

OUTLINE WORK SHEET: STOCK ISSUES DESIGN
(page 4)

(Transition to conclusion)

_____

CONCLUSION

Summary: _____

_____

Concluding remarks: _____

_____

Works Consulted:

STOCK ISSUES DESIGN CHECK LIST

_____ I have selected a topic that involves a problem that needs to be solved but about which reasonable people might have questions.

_____ I have clearly stated the purpose of my speech.

_____ My thesis statement is written as a complete declarative sentence.

_____ My introduction gains attention and interest, establishes my credibility, and previews the main points of my message.

_____ My first main point addresses the problem and responds to questions people might have about it.

_____ My subpoints for the first main point describe the problem, discuss the harms associated with it, and demonstrate the consequences of inaction.

_____ I have adequate supporting material for each of my subpoints relating to the problem.

_____ My second main point presents my solution to the problem and answers questions reasonable people may have about its feasibility.

_____ My subpoints for the second main point demonstrate that my solution is workable, practical, and cost-effective, describe a plan of action; explain the roles of participants; and picture the results of the solution.

_____ I have adequate supporting material for each of my subpoints relating to the solution.

_____ My conclusion contains a summary that recaps my message and remarks that reflect on the meaning and significance of my speech.

_____ I have provided transitions where they are needed to make my speech flow smoothly.

_____ I have compiled a list of works consulted in the preparation of my speech.

GUIDELINES FOR USING THE MOTIVATED SEQUENCE DESIGN

You may wish to use a motivated sequence design for a persuasive speech intended to move people to action. The motivated sequence design is a highly structured variation of the problem-solution design. It concentrates on awakening an awareness of a need and then showing how that need can be satisfied, concluding with an explicit call to action. The motivated sequence contains five steps: (1) focusing attention on a problem, (2) demonstrating a need, (3) presenting a solution to satisfy that need, (4) visualizing the results of the implementation of the solution, and (5) issuing a call to action.

The first step in the motivated sequence design comes in the introduction of the speech. In the motivated sequence design, the introduction should arouse attention and directly focus this attention on the problem that will be addressed in the speech.

The second through fourth steps in the motivated sequence design are covered in the body of the speech, which will typically contain three main points. The first main point of the body of the speech covers step 2 of the motivated sequence design. It would be used to demonstrate a need related to the problem. The second main point covers step 3 of the motivated sequence design. It should present a detailed plan of action to satisfy the need. The third main point covers step 4 of the motivated sequence design. It should picture the positive results that will occur if the plan is adopted and/or the negative results that might be expected if the plan is ignored.

The fifth step in the motivated sequence design comes in the conclusion of the speech. It is a call to action.

When the motivated sequence design is used, audience analysis is extremely important. For example, if the audience already recognizes that there is a need for action, that step in the sequence can be covered briefly, and the major thrust of the speech would address the plan, visualization of results, and the call for action. Similarly, if the audience is convinced of the need and familiar with the plan, but needs its momentum renewed or needs to be prodded into action, the focus of the speech would be on visualizing the results and calling for action.

OUTLINE WORK SHEET: MOTIVATED SEQUENCE DESIGN

TITLE (Optional): _____

Topic: _____

Specific purpose: _____

_____

Thesis statement: _____

_____

INTRODUCTION

Attention material (focus attention on problem): _____

_____

Credibility material: _____

_____

Preview: _____

_____

(Transition to body of speech)

_____

BODY

I. Main point 1 (statement of need for action) _____

_____

   A. (Description of problem) _____

_____

      1. (Signs, symptoms, effects of problem) _____

_____

      2. (Example, narrative, or testimony) _____

_____

OUTLINE WORK SHEET: MOTIVATED SEQUENCE DESIGN
(page 2)

B. (Importance of problem) _____

_____

    1. (Extent of problem) _____

    _____

        a. (Facts/statistics) _____

        _____

        b. (Expert testimony) _____

        _____

    2. (Who is affected) _____

    _____

        a. (Facts/statistics) _____

        _____

        b. (Example/narrative) _____

        _____

(Transition to main point 2)

_____

II. Main point 2 (present solution that satisfies need) _____

_____

    A. (Description of solution) _____

    _____

        1. (How solution satisfies need) _____

        _____

        2. (How solution can be implemented) _____

        _____

OUTLINE WORK SHEET: MOTIVATED SEQUENCE DESIGN
(page 3)

a. (Plan of action) _____

_____

    (1) (Step 1 of plan) _____

    _____

    (2) (Step 2 of plan) _____

    _____

    (3) (Step 3 of plan) _____

    _____

    (4) (Step 4 of plan) _____

    _____

(Transition to main point 3)

_____

III. Main point 3 (visualize results) _____

_____

    A. (Describe expected results of action) _____

    _____

    B. (Describe consequences of inaction) _____

    _____

(Transition to conclusion)

_____

OUTLINE WORK SHEET: MOTIVATED SEQUENCE DESIGN
(page 4)

CONCLUSION

Summary: _____

_____

Call for action: _____

_____

Works Consulted:

CHECK LIST FOR MOTIVATED SEQUENCE DESIGN

_____ I have selected a topic that involves a problem that needs to be solved with action.

_____ I have clearly stated the purpose of my speech.

_____ My thesis statement is written as a complete declarative sentence.

_____ My introduction focuses attention on the problem, establishes my credibility, and previews my message.

_____ The first main point in my speech establishes the need for action.

_____ The second main point in my speech details a plan of action that satisfies the need.

_____ The third main point in my speech visualizes the results of action and the consequences of inaction.

_____ I have appropriate supporting material for each main point in my speech.

_____ The conclusion of my speech contains a summary statement and ends with a call to action.

_____ I have provided transitions where they are needed to make my speech flow smoothly.

_____ I have compiled a list of works consulted in the preparation of my speech.

GUIDELINES FOR USING THE REFUTATIVE DESIGN

You may wish to use a refutative design to raise doubts about, damage, or even destroy an opposing position by pointing out its weaknesses and inconsistencies. To make an effective refutation, you must be thoroughly familiar with the points the opposition would make in an argument. It is wise to attack the weakest points or arguments first. Don't try to refute more than three points or arguments in a short classroom presentation. Base your refutations on faulty reasoning or inadequate evidence. Avoid personal attacks on opponents unless credibility issues are inescapable. If time permits, support an alternative point or argument to replace the one(s) you have refuted.

In the body of your speech, your main points will be the points or arguments you are refuting or supporting. Refutation follows a five-step sequence: (1) state the point you will refute and explain its importance to the opposing position, (2) tell how you will refute the point, (3) present evidence to refute the point, (4) show how the evidence refutes the point, and (5) explain the significance of the refutation. A refutative speech is strengthened if you can support an alternative point or argument for each one that you refute. Use the same five steps to demonstrate the superiority of your position. The inclusion of a supported point helps to counteract the negativity associated with straight refutation and provides the audience with a sense of completeness and closure.

OUTLINE WORK SHEET: REFUTATIVE DESIGN

TITLE (Optional): _____

Topic: _____

Specific purpose: _____

_____

Thesis statement: _____

_____

INTRODUCTION

Attention material: _____

_____

Credibility material: _____

_____

Preview: _____

_____

(Transition to body of speech)

_____

BODY

I. Main point 1 (first point you will refute/weakest point of opposition) _____

_____

    A. (Explain importance of point) _____

    _____

    B. (Explain how you will refute point) _____

    _____

    C. (Present evidence to refute point) _____

    _____

OUTLINE WORK SHEET: REFUTATIVE DESIGN
(page 2)

    1. (Facts/figures) _____

_____

    2. (Expert testimony) _____

_____

D. (Explain how evidence refutes point) _____

_____

E. (Explain significance of refutation) _____

_____

    1. (Facts/figures/expert testimony) _____

_____

    2. (Example/narrative) _____

_____

(Transition to main point 2)

_____

II. Main point 2 (second point you will refute or counterpoint you will support) _____

_____

A. (Explain importance of point) _____

_____

B. (Explain how you will refute/support point) _____

_____

C. (Present evidence to refute/support point) _____

_____

    1. (Facts/figures) _____

_____

    2. (Expert testimony) _____

_____

OUTLINE WORK SHEET: REFUTATIVE DESIGN
(page 3)

D. (Explain how evidence refutes/supports point) _____

_____

E. (Explain significance of refutation) _____

_____

    1. (Facts/figures/expert testimony) _____

    _____

    2. (Example/narrative) _____

    _____

(Transition to main point 3)

_____

III. Main point 3 (third/second point you will refute) _____

_____

A. (Explain importance of point) _____

_____

B. (Explain how you refute point) _____

_____

C. (Present evidence to refute point) _____

_____

    1. (Facts/figures) _____

    _____

    2. (Expert testimony) _____

    _____

D. (Explain how evidence refutes point) _____

_____

E. (Explain significance of refutation) _____

_____

OUTLINE WORK SHEET: REFUTATIVE DESIGN
(page 4)

1. (Facts/figures/expert testimony) _____

_____

2. (Example/narrative) _____

_____

(Transition to main point 4)

_____

IV. Main point 4 (next point you will refute or counterpoint you will support) _____

_____

   A. (Explain importance of point) _____

_____

   B. (Explain how you refute/support point) _____

_____

   C. (Present evidence to refute/support point) _____

_____

    1. (Facts/figures) _____

_____

    2. (Expert testimony) _____

_____

   D. (Explain how evidence refutes/supports point) _____

_____

   E. (Explain significance of refutation/support) _____

_____

    1. (Facts/figures/expert testimony) _____

_____

    2. (Example/narrative) _____

_____

OUTLINE WORK SHEET: REFUTATIVE DESIGN
(page 5)

(Transition to conclusion)

_____

CONCLUSION

Summary: _____

_____

Concluding remarks: _____

_____

Works Consulted:

REFUTATIVE DESIGN: OUTLINE CHECK LIST

_____ I have selected a topic that involves an issue that has strong opposition.

_____ I have clearly stated the purpose of my speech.

_____ My thesis statement is written as a complete declarative sentence.

_____ My introduction gains attention and interest, establishes my credibility, and previews the main points of my message.

_____ My first main point refutes the opposition's weakest point.

_____ Each main point for refutation is clearly stated and its importance explained.

_____ I describe how I will attack each point and present credible evidence to support my refutation.

_____ I clearly explain what each refutation means.

_____ I have supported a counterpoint for each point I have refuted, following the same format used for each refutation.

_____ I have avoided personal attacks in my refutations.

_____ My conclusion contains a summary that recaps my message and concluding remarks that reflect on the meaning and significance of my speech.

_____ I have provided transitions where they are needed to make my speech flow smoothly.

_____ I have compiled a list of works consulted in preparation for my speech.

READINGS FOR ENRICHMENT

See guide to journal abbreviations on p. 37.

* Items marked with an asterisk are suitable for student enrichment.

Ethics

* Bier, Jesse. "A Nation of Hookers: The Morality of Celebrity Endorsements and Advertising." *The Humanist* (Nov.–Dec. 1995), 41.

Cunningham, Stanley B. "Sorting Out the Ethics of Persuasion." *CS* (Winter 1992), 233–245.

Herrick, James A. "Rhetoric, Ethics, and Virtue." *CS* (Fall 1992), 133–149.

Johannesen, Richard J. *Ethics in Human Communication*, 4th ed. Prospect Heights, Ill.: Waveland, 1996.

* Minnick, Wayne C. "A New Look at the Ethics of Persuasion." *SSCJ* (Summer 1980), 352–362.

Attitudes

Anderson, N. H. "Integration Theory and Attitude Change." *Psychological Review*, 78 (1971), 171–206.

Berger, Ida E., and Andrew A. Mitchell. "The Effect of Advertising on Attitude Accessibility, Attitude Confidence, and the Attitude-Behavior Relationship." *Journal of Consumer Research* (Dec. 1989), 269–279.

* Dillard, James Price. "Persuasion Past and Present: Attitudes Aren't What They Used to Be." *CM* (Mar. 1993), 90–97.

Eagly, Alice H., and Shelly Chaiken. *The Psychology of Attitudes*. Fort Worth, Tex.: Harcourt Brace Jovanovich, 1993.

McGuire, William J. "Attitudes and Attitude Change." In *The Handbook of Social Psychology*, vol. 1, edited by Gardner Lindzey and Elliot Aronson, pp. 233–346. New York: Random House, 1985.

Miller, Gerald R., Michael Burgoon, and Judee K. Burgoon. "The Functions of Human Communication in Changing Attitudes and Gaining Compliance." In *Handbook of Rhetorical and Communication Theory*, edited by Carroll C. Arnold and John Waite Bowers, pp. 400–474. Boston: Allyn & Bacon, 1984.

Morley, Donald Dean, and Kim B. Walker. "The Role of Importance, Novelty, and Plausibility in Producing Belief Change." *CM* (Dec. 1987), 436–442.

Petty, Richard E., and John T. Cacioppo. *Communication and Persuasion: Central and Peripheral Routes to Attitude Change*. New York: Springer-Verlag, 1986.

Wicklund, R. A., and J. W. Brehm. *Perspectives on Cognitive Dissonance*. Hillsdale, N.J.: Erlbaum, 1976.

Propaganda

* Combs, James E., and Dan Nimmo. *The New Propaganda: The Dictatorship of Palaver in Contemporary Politics*. New York: Longman, 1993.

* Pratkanis, Anthony R., and Elliot Aronson. *The Age of Propaganda: The Everyday Use and Abuse of Persuasion*. New York: Freeman, 1992.

* Rohatyn, Dennis. "Propaganda Talk." In *Selected Issues in Logic and Communication*, edited by Trudy Govier, pp. 73–92. Belmont, California: Wadsworth, 1988.

Sproule, J. Michael. "Propaganda Studies in American Social Science: The Rise and Fall of the Critical Paradigm." *QJS* (Feb. 1987), 60–78.

Social Movements

Bowers, John W., Donovan J. Ochs, and Richard J. Jensen. *The Rhetoric of Agitation and Control.* Prospect Heights, Ill.: Waveland, 1993.

Condit, Celeste Michelle. "Democracy and Civil Rights: The Universalizing Influence of Public Argumentation." *CM* (Mar. 1987), 1–18.

Procter, David E. "Bridging Social Change Through Mythic Regeneration." *CS* (Fall 1992), 171–181.

Vanderford, Marsha L. "Vilification and Social Movements: A Case Study of Pro-Life and Pro-Choice Rhetoric." *QJS* (May 1989), 166–182.

General

* Alexander, Ernest R. "After Rationality: Planning, Politics, and Power." *Society* (Nov.–Dec. 1988), 15–19.

* Bandow, Doug. "The Power to Persuade: How to Be Effective in Government, the Public Sector, or Any Unruly Organization." *Fortune,* 27 June 1994, p. 133.

Bettinghaus, Erwin P., and Michael J. Cody. *Persuasive Communication,* 4th ed. New York: Holt, Rinehart & Winston, 1987.

Booth-Butterfield, Steve, Peggy Cooke, Annette Andrighetti, Beth Casteel, Tracy Lang, Doug Pearson, and Brendaly Rodriquez. "Simultaneous versus Exclusive Processing of Persuasive Arguments and Cues." *CQ* (Winter 1994), 21–35.

Bostrom, Robert N. *Persuasion.* Englewood Cliffs, N.J.: Prentice-Hall, 1983.

* Bower, Bruce. "Roots of Reason: Our Daily Deliberations Provoke Scientific Debate." *Science News,* 29 Jan. 1994, pp. 72–75.

Bretl, Daniel J., and James Price Dillard. "Persuasion and the Internality Dimension of Cognitive Responses." *CS* (Summer 1991), 103–113.

Carlson, Richard A., David H. Lundy, and Robin G. Yaure. "Syllogistic Inference Chains in Meaningful Text." *American Journal of Psychology* (Spring 1992), 75–99.

Cialdini, Robert B. *Influence: The Psychology of Persuasion,* rev. ed. New York: Quill, 1993.

Clark, Ruth Ann. *Persuasive Messages.* New York: Harper and Row, 1984.

* "A Critique of Pure Reason." *The Economist,* 4 July 1992, pp. 73–74.

* Demo, Mary Penasack. "The Persuaders." *CE* (July 1979), 244–249.

Dillard, James Price. "Self-Inference and Foot-in-the-Door Technique." *HCR* (Spring 1990), 422–447.

Dillard, James Price, and Kim Witte. "Possessions Theory of Persuasion." *CS* (Fall 1993), 188–199.

* Foss, Sonja K., and Cindy L. Griffin. "Beyond Persuasion: A Proposal for an Invitational Rhetoric." *Communication Monographs,* 62 (1995), 2–18.

* Goldfaden, Gloria. "Winning Hearts and Minds." *The Humanist* (Nov.–Dec. 1988), 13.

Greene, Chris. "Higher Education: Elevated Thinking?" *Psychology Today* (Apr. 1986), 14.

* Haass, Richard. *The Power to Persuade.* Boston: Houghton Mifflin, 1994.

Jensen, Keith, and David A. Carter. "Self-Persuasion: The Effects of Public Speaking on Speakers." *SSCJ* (Winter 1981), 163–174.

Johnson, Darrin, and Timothy Sellnow. "Deliberative Rhetoric as a Step in Organizational Crisis Management: Exxon as a Case Study." *CR* (Winter 1995), 54–60.

Johnston, Deirdre D. *The Art and Science of Persuasion.* Dubuque, Iowa: W.C. Brown, 1994.

Kahane, Howard. *Logic and Contemporary Rhetoric: The Use of Reason in Everyday Life,* 5th ed. Belmont, Calif.: Wadsworth, 1988.

* Kenton, Sherron B. "Speaker Credibility in Persuasive Business Communication: A Model Which Explains Gender Differences." *The Journal of Business Communication* (Spring 1989), 143–157.

King, Florence. "QED: The Politics and Ethics of Logic in Liberal Thought." *National Review,* 7 (Oct. 1991), 56.

* ———. "Ex Pede Herculem: The Decline of the Respect for and Use of Logic in American Society." *National Review,* 15 Nov. 1993, p. 72.

Larson, Charles. *Persuasion: Reception and Responsibility,* 6th ed. Belmont, Calif.: Wadsworth, 1992.

Levine, Timothy R., and Eugenia E. Badger. "Argumentativeness and Resistance to Persuasion." *CR* (Summer 1993), 71–78.

Littlejohn, Stephen W., and David M Jabusch. *Persuasive Transactions*. Glenview, Ill.: Scott, Foresman, 1987.

* McVey, Stephanie. "Giving Presentations that Persuade." *Management World* (Jan.–Feb. 1989), 6–8.

Nemeth, Charlan Jeanne. "Differential Contributions of Majority and Minority Influence." *Psychological Review* (1986), 23–32.

O'Keefe, Daniel J. *Persuasion: Theory and Research*. Newbury Park, Calif.: Sage, 1990.

Perloff, Richard M. *The Dynamics of Persuasion*. Hillsdale, N.J.: Erlbaum, 1993.

Reardon, Kathleen Kelley. *Persuasion in Practice*. Newbury Park, Calif.: Sage, 1991.

* Rosenbaum, Bernard. "Making Presentations: How to Persuade Others to Accept Your Ideas." *American Salesman* (Feb. 1992), 16–18.

Sanders, Judith, Robert Gass, Richard Wiseman, and Jon Bruschke. "Ethnic Comparison and Measurement of Argumentativeness, Verbal Aggressiveness, and Need for Cognition." *CR* (Winter 1992), 50–56.

Sanders, Judith A., Richard L. Wiseman, and Robert H. Gass. "Does Teaching Argumentation Facilitate Students' Critical Thinking?" *CR* (Winter 1994), 27–35.

Simons, Herbert. *Persuasion: Understanding, Practice, and Analysis*, 2nd ed. New York: Random House, 1986.

Smith, Mary John. *Persuasion and Human Action: A Review and Critique of Social Influence Theories*. Belmont, Calif.: Wadsworth, 1982.

* Sonnenberg, Frank K. "Presentations that Persuade." *Journal of Business Strategy* (Sept.–Oct. 1988), 55–58.

Sproule, J. Michael. "Progressive Propaganda Critics and the Magic Bullet Myth." *CSMC* (Sept. 1989), 225–246.

Suzuki, Shinobu, and Andrew S. Rancer. "Argumentativeness and Verbal Aggressiveness: Testing for Conceptual and Measurement Equivalence Across Cultures." *CM* (Sept. 1994), 256–279.

vos Savant, Marilyn. *The Power of Logical Thinking*. New York: St. Martin's, 1996.

* Waldrop, M. Mitchell. "Causality, Structure, and Common Sense." *Science*, 11 Sept. 1987, 1297–1299.

Woodward, Gary C., and Robert E. Denton, Jr. *Persuasion and Influence in American Life*, 2nd. ed. Prospect Heights, Ill.: Waveland, 1992.

Teaching Options

Bahti, Cynthia L. "And Now, a Commercial Word From . . . ." *SCT* (Fall 1989), 9.

Bozik, Mary. "An Exercise in Inference Making." *CE* (Oct. 1984), 401–403.

Cammilleri, Sandra. "Creating Persuasive Commercials." *SCT* (Winter 1995), 10–11.

Dittus, James K. "Grade Begging as an Exercise in Argumentation." *SCT* (Summer 1991), 5.

Drewis, Rob. "PSAs: Persuasive Speaking in a Minute." *SCT* (Fall 1992), 10–11.

Fregoe, David H. "Informative vs. Persuasive Speaking: The Objects Game." *SCT* (Winter 1989), 13–14.

Garrett, Roger L. "The Premises of Persuasion." *SCT* (Spring 1991), 13.

Glick, I. David. "Tossing LAP'S into Their Laps." *SCT* (Winter 1990), 15.

MacDonald, Madlyne A. "The Key to Persuasion." *SCT* (Fall 1986), 14–15.

Nelson, Lee Ann. "Sell Us Monroe's Motivated Sequence." *SCT* (Spring 1995), 13.

Phillips, Terilyn Goins. "Name That Analogy: The Communication Game." *SCT* (Winter 1996), 10–11.

Powell, Kimberly A. "Debate as the Key to Teaching Persuasion Skills." *SCT* (Fall 1994), 10–11.

Ross, Charlynn. "The Challenging Audience Exercise." *SCT* (Spring 1987), 15–16.

———. "Vaccinating Against Inoculations: McGuire's Theory as an Experiential Learning Activity." *SCT* (Summer 1995), 6–7.

Schneider, Valerie L. "Four Steps Produce a Print Promotional Piece." *SCT* (Fall 1988), 4–5.

Schnell, Jim. "The Developmental Speech Sequence Model (DSSM)." *SCT* (Winter 1987), 15–16.

Schreier, Howard N. "Analyzing Persuasive Tactics." *SCT* (Summer 1989), 14.

Webb, Lynn. "The Analogy Speech." *SCT* (Fall 1986), 2.

Challenges and Strategies

Allen, Mike. "Meta-Analysis Comparing the Persuasiveness of One-sided and Two-sided Messages." *WJSC* (Fall 1991), 390–404.

———. "Determining the Persuasiveness of Message Sidedness: A Prudent Note About Utilizing Research Summaries." *WJC* (Winter 1993), 98–103.

Allen, M., et al. "Testing a Model of Message Sidedness: Three Replications." *CM* (Dec. 1990), 275–291.

Allen, Mike, and James B. Stiff. "Testing Three Models for the Sleeper Effect." *WSCJ* (Fall 1939), 411–426.

Beatty, Michael J., and Michael W. Kruger. "The Effects of Heckling on Speaker Credibility and Attitude Change." *CQ* (Spring 1978), 46–50.

Bell, Robert Alan, Matthew Cholerton, Kevin E. Fraczek, Guy S. Rohlfs, and Brian A. Smith. "Encouraging Donations to Charity: A Field Study of Competing and Complementary Factors in Tactic Sequencing." *WSJC* (Spring 1994), 98–115.

Boster, F. J., and P. Mongeau. "Fear-Arousing Persuasive Messages." In *Communication Yearbook 8*, edited by Robert N. Bostrom, pp. 330–375. Beverly Hills, Calif.: Sage, 1984.

Brown, William J. "Culture and AIDS Education: Reaching High-risk Heterosexuals in Asian-American Communities." *ACR* (Aug. 1992), 275–291.

Burgoon, M. J., P. Dilard, and N. E. Doran. "Friendly and Unfriendly Persuasion: The Effects of Violations of Expectations by Males and Females." *HCR* (Winter 1983), 283–294.

Burke, Julie A. "A Comparison of Methods for Eliciting Persuasive Strategies: Strategy Selection Versus Message Construction." *CR* (Summer 1989), 72–82.

* Crump, Kathy, and Casey Davidson. "Celebrities Speak Easy: Celebrity TV Commercials." *Entertainment Weekly*, 4 Aug. 1995, p. 17.

Dillard, James Price, and Jerold L. Hale. "Prosocialness and Sequential Request Compliance Techniques: Limits to Foot-in-the-Door and the Door-in-the Face?" *CS* (Winter 1992), 220–232.

Glynn, Carroll J., and Jack M. McLeod. "Public Opinion, Communication Processes, and Voting Decisions." In *Communication Yearbook 6*, edited by Michael Burgoon, pp. 759–774. Beverly Hills, Calif.: Sage, 1982.

* Golden, Linda L., and Mark I. Alpert. "Comparative Analysis of the Relative Effectiveness of One- and Two-sided Communication for Contrasting Productions." *Journal of Advertising* (Winter 1987), 18–25.

* Govier, Trudy. "Are There Two Sides to Every Question?" In *Selected Issues in Logic and Communication*, edited by Trudy Govier, pp. 43–54. Belmont, Calif.: Wadsworth, 1988.

Grant, Jo Anna, Paul E. King, and Ralph Behnke. "Compliance-Gaining Strategies, Communication Satisfaction, and Willingness to Comply." *CR* (Summer 1994), 99–108.

Hale, Jerold L., Paul A. Mongeau, and Randi M. Thomas. "Cognitive Processing of One- and Two-sided Persuasive Messages." *Western Journal of Speech Communication* (Fall 1991), 380–389.

Hamilton, Mark A., and John E. Hunter. "The Effect of Language Intensity on Receiver Attitudes Toward Message, Source, and Topic." In *Persuasion: Advances Through Meta-Analysis*, edited by M. Allen and R. W. Preiss. Beverley Hills, Calif.: Sage [in press].

Hovland, Carl I., Arthur A. Lumsdaine, and Fred D. Sheffield. "The Effects of Presenting 'One Side' versus 'Both Sides' in Changing Opinions on a Controversial Subject." In *Experiments on Mass Communication*, Princeton, N.J.: Princeton University Press, 1949, pp. 201–227.

Infante, Dominic A., and Andrew S. Rancer. "Relations Between Argumentative Motivation, and Advocacy, and Refutation on Controversial Issues." *CQ* (Fall 1993), 415–426.

* Karetz, Jack D. "Rational Arguments and Irrational Audiences: Psychology, Planning, and Public Judgement." *Journal of the American Planning Association* (Autumn 1989), 445–456.

Kendall, Kathleen E., and June Ock Yum. "Persuading the Blue-Collar Voter: Issues, Images, and Homophily." In *Communication Yearbook 8*, edited by Robert N. Bostrom, pp. 707–722. Beverly Hills, Calif.: Sage, 1984.

McCombs, M. E. "The Agenda-setting Approach." In *Handbook of Political Communication*, edited by D. D. Nimmo and K. R. Sanders, pp. 121–140. Beverly Hills, Calif.: Sage, 1981.

McGuire, William J. "Inducing Resistance to Persuasion." In *Advances in Experimental Social Psychology*, edited by L. Berkowitz, pp. 191–229. New York: Academic Press, 1964,

* Lau, Barbara. "Communicating Under Fire." *Management Quarterly* (Spring 1987), 17–20.

Milburn, T. W., and K. H. Watman. *On the Nature of Threat: A Social Psychological Analysis.* New York: Praeger, 1981.

O'Keefe, Daniel J. "The Persuasive Effects of Message Sidedness Variations: A Cautionary Note Concerning Allen's (1991) Meta-Analysis." *WJC* (Winter 1993), 87–97.

Pfau, Michael, and Michael Burgoon. "The Efficacy of Issue and Character Attack Message Strategies in Political Campaign Communication." *CR* (Summer 1989), 53–61.

Pfau, Michael, Roxanne Parrott, and Bridget Lindquist. "An Expectancy Theory of Explanation of the Effectiveness of Political Attack Television Spots." *ACR* (Aug. 1992), 235–253.

Reel, Bradley W., and Teresa L. Thompson. "A Test of the Effectiveness of Strategies for Talking About AIDS and Condom Use." *ACR* (May 1994), 127–140.

Snyder, Leslie B., and Deborah J. Blood. "Caution: Alcohol Advertising and the Surgeon General's Alcohol Warnings May Have Adverse Effects on Young Adults." *ACR* (Feb. 1992), 37–53.

* Tracy, Lawrence L. "Taming the Hostile Audience." *Training and Development Journal* (Feb. 1990), 32–36.

Whaley, Bryan B., and Austin S. Babrow. "Analogy in Persuasion: Translator's Dictionary or Art?" *CS* (Fall 1993), 239–253.

Wheeless, Lawrence B., Robert Barraclough, and Robert Stewart. "Compliance-Gaining and Power in Persuasion." In *Communication Yearbook 7,* edited by Robert N. Bostrom, pp. 105–145. Beverly Hills, Calif.: Sage, 1983.

Witte, Kim, and Kelly Morrison. "Using Scare Tactics to Promote Safer Sex Among Juvenile Detention and High School Youth." *ACR* (May 1995), 128–142.

CHAPTER 14
Evidence, Proof, and Argument

OBJECTIVES

- To help your students use supporting materials as powerful evidence.

- To help your students develop their evidence into persuasive proof.

- To help your students arrange proof into compelling arguments.

- To help your students recognize and avoid defects of evidence, proofs, and arguments.

SUGGESTIONS FOR TEACHING

Most of the materials in this chapter coordinate logically with those of Chapter 13. To argue reasonably for our assertions is our promising birthright as a species. All of us persuade and are persuaded on a regular basis. But while we frequently make claims reflecting beliefs and convictions that others will not necessary share, we do not always argue constructively for our positions, or even recognize the need to do so; we too often assume that our positions are self-evident and need no support. However, everyone can learn to reason, and teaching basic argumentative skills from an audience-centered perspective is a crucial part of developing persuasive communication and critical listening skills. It is also important to participative democracy and enlightened public deliberation.

Perhaps the most basic steps in learning to argue are: (1) learning to recognize our own persuasive claims as well as the claims implicit within those claims, (2) learning to offer appropriate reasoning and evidence in support of disputed claims, and (3) learning to constructively engage opposing positions rather than simply reacting against them. As with most communication skills, students will learn and appreciate these concepts more effectively through practice and critique.

In this chapter, we offer numerous activities and exercises to teach the basic concepts of argumentation, proofs, and evidence. We have exercises that help illustrate the varicus types of persuasive fallacies, and have your students construct and critique their own arguments. Other activities have your students consider alternative approaches to reasoning using myth and metaphor.

CHAPTER OUTLINE

    I. Evidence, proof, and argument form the tapestry of reasoning that drives the persuasive process and explains its power. *(text pp. 450–471)*

        A. Responsible evidence use adds the strength, authority, and objectivity needed to substantiate persuasion.

1. Facts and figures help to establish the reality of a situation.
2. Examples can help move audiences and arouse emotions.
3. Narratives help illustrate the meaning of major points, create a sense of dramatic reality, and build identification between speakers, messages, and audiences.
4. Testimony calls forth witnesses to strengthen persuasive positions. Speakers should:
   a. specify the qualifications of their sources of testimony.
   b. use expert testimony to establish the validity of claims.
   c. use prestige and lay testimony to stress values and build identification.
   d. cite reluctant witnesses whenever possible.
B. Proofs weave together evidence to provide reasons for changing attitudes or behaviors.
   1. Proof by logos includes facts, figures, and expert testimony.
      a. The basic pattern of proof by logos is to interpret information, and reason from it to a conclusion. There is:
         (1) an assertion that must be proved.
         (2) evidence to support the statement.
         (3) a conclusion that ties the statement and the evidence together.
      b. Proof by logos demonstrates faith in the audience's intelligence.
   2. Proof by pathos is based on the fact that people are moved by emotions.
      a. Emotional appeals may be necessary to involve and move audiences to action.
      b. Examples and narratives can be very effective for arousing emotions.
      c. Speakers should invoke emotional appeals cautiously.
         (1) Obvious emotional appeals can come across as manipulative.
         (2) Strong fear and guilt appeals can offend audiences and result in a boomerang effect against both speakers and their messages.
      d. Proof by pathos is generally more sound and effective when it is used in conjunction with proof by logos.
   3. Proof by ethos is based on the fact that people may be persuaded by the credibility of sources.
      a. Appeals based on ethos usually involve the use of testimony.
      b. Listeners will evaluate sources of important information in terms of their perceived competence, character, likability, and forcefulness.
   4. Proof by mythos helps listeners understand how the speaker's recommendations fit into the total belief and value patterns of their group.
      a. It is often expressed through traditional narratives, sayings, and symbols.
      b. Speakers often need not tell stories in their entirety to invoke mythos.
   5. The art of persuasion involves weaving the right combination of proofs.
      a. Logos reassures listeners who are unaware or uncertain of the facts of a situation.
      b. Pathos helps to promote human involvement and understanding.
      c. Ethos is important in confusing or uncertain situations.
      d. Mythos can associate messages with cultural traditions and values.
C. Arguments weave proofs into persuasion using basic patterns of human reasoning.
   1. Arguments should answer the following basic questions:
      a. Is the message based on principles that I accept?
      b. Are the conclusions based on careful observations?
      c. Can we learn something by considering closely related situations?
   2. The three major forms of argument relate to the questions above.
      a. Deductive arguments work from generally accepted principles to specific observations.
         (1) Deductive arguments follow a pattern that moves from major premise (generally accepted truth or principle) to minor premise (specific observation) to a conclusion.
         (2) In real life, arguments are never certain, and so speakers should use qualifiers.
         (3) The following suggestions can help develop deductive reasoning.
            (a) Be certain your audience will accept your major premise.

        (b)   Once major premises are established, concentrate on supporting minor premises.

        (c)   Demonstrate the relationship between major and minor premises.

        (d)   Be certain your reasoning is free from logical errors and fallacies.

        (e)   Be sure your conclusion offers a clear direction for your listeners.

  b. Inductive arguments work from specific observations to general assertions.

     (1) Inductive reasoning is often used to demonstrate the reality of a situation.

     (2) As we develop our critical thinking skills, we want arguments based on observations.

     (3) Inductive and deductive reasoning should complement each other.

        (a)   Inductive reasoning can verify major premises for deductive arguments.

        (b)   Inductive and deductive reasoning usually converge at the minor premise.

     (4) The following questions can help speakers develop inductive arguments.

        (a)   Do your observations adequately justify your conclusions?

        (b)   Have you read and observed enough?

        (c)   Are your observations recent and reliable?

        (d)   Are you objective enough to see the situation clearly?

        (e)   Are your observations representative or the exception?

        (f)   If your observations are based on people's views, have you sampled enough people?

  c. Argument by analogy provides strategic perspectives on issues and situations by relating them to something similar.

     (1) Analogical arguments combine deductive and inductive elements.

        (a)   The deductive part is based upon the presumed value of comparisons.

        (b)   The inductive part attends to the particulars of compared problems.

     (2) Because analogies are based upon concentrated observations, they are generally less reliable than inductive reasoning.

 D. All arguments depend on clear definitions of terms.

II. Persuasive fallacies may involve the use of evidence, proofs, arguments, and designs. *(text pp. 471–477)*

 A. Defective evidence is a common source of persuasive fallacy.

  1. Facts are often misused in persuasive messages.

    a. The slippery slope fallacy assumes that events and proposals represent irreversible trends.

    b. Persuasive speakers may confuse facts and opinions.

    c. The red herring fallacy involves the introduction of extraneous materials to divert attention from the issue at hand.

  2. Statistical evidence can be used deceptively.

    a. The myth of the mean creates an illusion of averages that can distort reality.

    b. Speakers may make predictions from statistical comparisons that start from unequal bases.

  3. The use of testimony is defective when speakers:

    a. use obsolete or outdated testimony without revealing its date.

    b. misrepresent the qualifications of sources.

    c. cite experts out of context.

    d. cite celebrities and laypersons to establish factual validity.

  4. Some fallacies are based upon the willful misuse of evidence.

    a. Speakers may use the wrong forms of evidence.

     (1) Facts and figures may be used to dehumanize problems.

     (2) Examples may be used to arouse emotions and overwhelm reason.

     (3) Examples, narratives, and testimony may be substituted for factual data.

 B. Any form of persuasive proof can be used in error.

  1. Speakers may over-rely on pathos.

  2. Mythos can be misused to support cultural elitism and intolerance.

  3. Speakers abuse proof by ethos when:

      a.   they resort to argument *ad hominem* by attacking the character of their opponents.

      b.   they over-rely on testimony and lack facts to support claims.

   4. Begging the question involves making claims the audience will not necessarily accept without offering proof.

C. All forms of arguments are susceptible to various fallacies.

   1. It is unethical to knowingly commit argumentative fallacies, and irresponsible to commit them inadvertently.

   2. Most deductive errors relate to unsound major premises.

      a.   Speakers should watch out for the confusion of probability and certainty.

      c.   The *post hoc* fallacy assumes that association implies causality.

      d.   The *non sequitur* fallacy occurs when major and minor premises do not relate or when minor premises are irrelevant.

   3. Hasty generalizations may be based on insufficient evidence.

   4. Defective analogies occur when speakers compare things that are essentially dissimilar.

D. Some persuasive fallacies are design-related.

   1. Problem-solution designs implying that they are only two alternatives are characteristic of either-or thinking.

   2. The straw man fallacy, in which opposing positions are misrepresented to make them easier to refute, is common in speeches of contention.

USING END-OF-CHAPTER ITEMS

Discussion *(text p. 479)*

1. **Bring to class examples of advertisements that demonstrate the four basic types of persuasive proof: logos, pathos, ethos, and mythos. What factors in the product, medium of advertising, or intended audience might explain the emphasis in each example? Do the ads make use of other types of proof as well? How effective is each ad?**

This works either for written homework or as a small-group activity followed by general class discussion. Remind students to photocopy ads and submit them with their analyses, and not to deface library magazines. For in-class use, bring an assortment of old magazines (or have each student bring one), divide your class into small groups, and have each find ads with effective and ineffective examples of the four types of proof. Each group should then share their observations with the class.

    Ads for drugs, vitamins, and cosmetics often use proof by logos—a form more frequently found in print than in TV ads. Such ads typically contain more text than pictures. Proof based on pathos is common in ads for charitable appeals. Ads sporting celebrity endorsements or expert testimony use proof by ethos. Proof by mythos is reflected in ads with regional or patriotic themes. In class discussion, push your students to explore the differences between proofs in advertising and in persuasive speaking, especially the manner in which visuals are used in concert with text to advance persuasive claims or sell a product.

2. **Analyze the tapestry of evidence, proof, and argument that develops in the speech by Bonnie Marshall, reprinted in Appendix B. How powerful is this design of persuasive materials? Might it have been even stronger? How?**

Bonnie begins her speech with a narrative to involve her student audience with her topic (living wills) and arouse compassionate emotions. She continues to provide factual examples that demonstrate the extent of the problem. She carefully provides evidence in the form of facts and figures from reputable sources citing government statistics and Supreme Court decisions. She relies most strongly on proof by logos and proof by pathos. Throughout the speech, Bonnie provides clear definitions for unfamiliar or technical terms. She argues from induction, citing sufficient evidence to make not accepting her claims highly unlikely.

3. **Look for examples of defective persuasion in the letters to the editor section of your local newspaper. Bring them to class for discussion.**

You might combine this activity with Discussion item 2 from Chapter 13. It can be used for homework or in-class discussion. In preparation for this activity, briefly review the text on argumentative fallacies. Project the transparency "Abuses of Argument" to help guide class discussion. Have your students record their observations and share them for general class discussion. Emphasize that common fallacies in persuasive speaking, such as hasty generalization or begging the question, are usually a matter of audience perception, and that reluctant or opposed audiences will be more likely to scrutinize our reasoning for potential weak spots. Speakers should also assume that well-educated audiences will not be impressed by argumentative fallacies even when they already agree with the speaker's proposals. As always, remind your students not to deface library materials.

Application *(text p. 479)*

1. **Find a news story that interests you. Taking the information provided, (1) show how you might use this information as evidence in a persuasive speech, (2) structure a proof that would make use of this evidence, and (3) design an argument in which this proof might be functional.**

This is intended for homework to help illustrate how arguments can be structured from supporting materials. Require students to submit photocopies of their articles with their analyses. For in-class use, simply photocopy the stories yourself and have your students construct arguments from them, working in small groups before presenting their ideas for class discussion. What argumentative claims does the information in the article seem to suggest? Remind students that the strength of inductive argument lies in the quality and variety of evidence used to support it, which is determined ultimately by their primary audiences. Have them make short presentations of their ideas for class discussion.

2. **In *The Ethics of Rhetoric*, Richard Weaver observed that frequent arguments over the definitions of basic terms in the major premises of syllogisms are a sign of division within a social group. Look for examples of public argument over the definition of one of the following terms:**

   a. **Community-based schooling**
   b. **Welfare**
   c. **Tax fairness**
   d. **Abortion**
   e. **Gun control**
   f. **Alternative lifestyles**
   g. **Political correctness**

   Do the arguments reflect the kind of social division Weaver suggested?

This assignment can be used for homework or for small-group discussion. A quick look at the editorial pages of a major newspaper should suggest numerous terms of dispute. Bitter social disputes and debates over public moral issues commonly get stuck on the inability to find common definitions to work from. The definition (or lack thereof) of abortion stands as a classic and obvious example. If this exercise is used for homework, make sure your students understand the meaning of major premises and Weaver's basic terms. You might collect an assortment of such materials and duplicate them for in-class use. Divide your class into small groups, providing each with artifacts related to issues or key terms of dispute. Students should search for conflicting definitions and report their findings for class discussion.

3. Will your next persuasive speech develop both deductive and inductive patterns of argument? Which will it emphasize and why? Will you make any use of analogical argument? Why or why not?

This exercise can be used for homework or for small-group discussion. It is especially useful for illustrating the applications and relative strengths and weaknesses of deductive and inductive argument forms. It is also a good way to get students started on their own persuasive speeches by considering which argument forms might be most appropriate to establish their claims. Break the students into groups and have them critique and brainstorm ideas for one another's topics and claims. In presenting their ideas to the class, students should explain why the forms they chose would be most appropriate for their particular claims.

ADDITIONAL ACTIVITIES

Advertising and Evidence Abuse

Purpose: To illustrate for your students fallacious misuses of evidence in commercial advertising.

Directions: Use this for homework, or as a small-group activity followed by class discussion. Have your students look for what they perceive to be misuses of evidence in newspaper or magazine advertisements. You might review some common persuasive fallacies related to misuse of evidence in preparation for this activity, such as willful misrepresentation of facts and testimony, using nonrepresentative examples, and making hasty generalizations. Have your students photocopy their ads and bring them for class discussion, and remind them not to deface library materials. *Consumer Reports* exposes abusive ads in a monthly section entitled "Selling It," and your local Better Business Bureau may make complaints filed on local ads available for public scrutiny. For in-class use, collect the ads yourself and bring them in for small-group discussion and analysis. Focus on types of misuse identified, probable motives, and your students' reactions to them. What do these advertisements say about the credibility of the products represented? Emphasize that the fact that such ads "work" suggests that there are a lot of people in our society who have not sufficiently developed their critical listening and argumentative skills, which are crucial to protecting ourselves and our communities from the designs of unscrupulous persuasive communicators.

Critiquing Testimony as Evidence

Purpose: To have your students critique effective and ineffective uses of testimony as evidence in student persuasive speeches.

Directions: Use this for homework or as a small-group activity followed by class discussion. Have your students find examples of effective and ineffective uses of testimony in the persuasive student speeches in Appendix B of the text. As an alternative, you may wish to show one of the persuasive student speeches from the Houghton Mifflin videotapes. For class discussion, students should identify the examples of testimony in the speeches and justify their evaluations. Do the speakers adequately document their sources? Are expert, lay, and prestige forms of testimony used appropriately and effectively? How might the speaker's use of testimony be made more effective?

Find the Fallacy

Purpose: To give your students practice identifying major argumentative fallacies.

Directions: Distribute copies of the "Find the Fallacy" exercise on p. 446. Have your students identify the fallacies in each of the items. Refer them to the appropriate section of the text (pp. 471–477) on persuasive fallacies. Break your students into small groups, allowing them approximately fifteen minutes to consider the items, and then have them present their ideas for class discussion.

Answers:

1. Incomparable percentages. (In 1931 far fewer workers were employed than in 1945.) 2. Slippery slope. 3. *Post hoc.* 4. Argument *ad hominem.* 5. Hasty generalization. 6. *Non sequitur.* 7. Faulty analogy. 8. Myth of the mean. (Top executives might make around $450,000 a year while tellers make around $13,000.) 9. Red herring. 10. Confusing fact and opinion.

See Major Premises Play

Purpose: To demonstrate for students how major premises or warrants function implicitly as well as explicitly in persuasive discourse.

Directions: A basic first step in learning how to argue effectively is learning to recognize our own arguments and the major premises implicit within or presumed by them. You cannot really consider opposing views until you know where you are coming from yourself. Considering the major claims implicit within an argumentative position can help speakers discover what needs to be argued for in order to convince their audiences.

Use this exercise for a small-group activity or general class discussion. It can help to emphasize how some premises assumed by the things we say and advocate are so basic that we tend not to recognize them even as we invoke them. If they run with this, your students may well come up with observations you do not recognize yourself. Read or distribute the following list of unsupported persuasive claims and have your students consider (a) major premises implied by the claims, and (b) which ones would need to be argued for in order to convince their audience and which would probably be accepted without support. What types of evidence would be most effective for supporting the claims that need support? What opposing views would probably need to be addressed? If necessary, how might the thesis be modified to give it a better chance for success? If you wish, invert any of the following questions and argue the opposite conclusion.

1. We should increase taxes to raise the quality of education.
2. We should oppose attempts at gun control at all cost.
3. We should teach sex education in our high schools.
4. Ronald Reagan was a good president because he dramatically cut domestic spending.
5. Laboratory testing using animals for whatever reason should be abolished.
6. People who cannot speak English should not be allowed to apply for U.S. citizenship.

Suggestions for discussion:

1. This statement assumes that education is good, that the state of education needs improvement, that higher tax revenues would improve the quality of education, and that higher taxes would be worth paying. The latter two assumptions would need support for most audiences (especially taxpayers). Taxes have never been very popular, and over the last few decades the idea that spending money on problems does not necessarily solve them has become a common theme in American political rhetoric.

2. This is a strong stand that many people would take issue with, especially people from urban areas with high crime rates. It assumes either that there is not a problem sufficient to warrant gun control, or that gun control efforts simply would not work and would have negative consequences such as leaving law-abiding citizens without protection. To be effective, speakers would probably have to argue for at least one if not both of these implicit major premises. To give themselves a better chance for success, speakers might moderate and qualify this to something like "We should oppose X proposal for Y reasons."

3. This is another controversial stand. It assumes that information on sex is not being sufficiently taught elsewhere. Furthermore, it assumes that the state has a right to interfere with issues traditionally considered to be in the family domain. With undecided audiences, you would

probably want to express respect for family rights while arguing that the problems caused by lack of sex education outweigh these rights, and offer plenty of supporting information in support of that assertion. You might qualify this claim by clarifying your position on related issues such as distributing contraceptives and discussing premarital sex.

4. Cutting spending is an increasingly popular issue with middle- and upper-class taxpayers, and many of these same people remember Reagan as a hero for abolishing as much domestic spending as he could. Others (mostly liberals and the poor) despise his memory for the same reasons. This statement assumes that domestic spending needed to be cut. Either it had not worked or (as Reagan himself said many times) it had somehow destroyed the spirit of individual thrift that had once made this country great. With mildly opposed or undecided audiences, speakers should probably argue that the perceived rise in social problems since the Reagan years is not a result of his policies, and offer supporting information to support this point as well as the negative effects of pre-Reagan era domestic spending levels.

5. This is a radical thesis that many people would obviously take issue with. It assumes that animal testing is either unnecessary, obsolete, or so inhumane that the medical and technological gains are simply not worth it. Without moderating or qualifying this thesis to something like, "We should abolish X type testing for Y reasons," speakers would need to argue one of these points. Many animal rights activists argue that computer technology is making animal testing unnecessary. Others push religious and spiritual values to support the second claim.

6. With the growing emphasis on multiculturalism, many people are likely to be offended by this thesis. They would argue that it implies a racist cultural elitism, or at least that English is superior to other languages. The basic implication is that people should eschew their language and heritage to blend into an "Anglo" mold of Americana. Of course not all people who believe English should be our exclusive language believe all this, but speakers would have to address suspicions of this type in the minds of opposing audiences. You would probably want to distance yourself from any claims of cultural supremacy and base your argument primarily on pragmatic reasons, such as difficulties and tensions that bilingualism causes in the workplace, school, or society in general.

Appreciating Opposing Views and Arguments

Purpose: To impress upon students the primary importance of knowing and appreciating prevalent opposing views and arguments when preparing an argumentative thesis.

Directions: This works well for homework or as a small-group activity followed by in-class discussion in preparation for speeches of contention. A major step in learning to argue effectively is to engage and appreciate opposing viewpoints and convictions instead of simply being disgusted by and reacting against them. This exercise is intended to have your students systematically and dispassionately evaluate opposing positions so that they may later argue more effectively against them.

For homework, your students should identify the two or three predominant views opposed to their persuasive claims. Note that if there really are no opposing views, then the student does not have much of an argument, and if there are more than three salient opposing views with the particular audience, the student may be attempting too much and setting himself or herself up for a boomerang effect.

Your students should try to express opposing positions in their most effective or eloquent form. They might imagine themselves preparing for a debate on the issue against the greatest of all possible advocates. What will be his or her strongest points? What kinds of supporting information will he or she be likely to use? What looks to be the weakest point of your argument, where your opponent will probably attack first? For in-class or small-group discussion, have students critique one another's ideas in terms of opposing views they might be missing and possible straw man fallacies or mischaracterizations of opposing views to make them easier to refute.

You might also have your students follow up by brainstorming different strategies for effectively refuting these positions. Remind students that the point is to be constructive and help one another argue more effectively. Learning to argue against yourself and for positions you do not necessarily agree with can be an effective way to sharpen your deliberative skills. You might have your students prepare a written statement of opposing views and arguments to be turned in with their formal outlines.

The Metaphors of Argument

Purpose: To have your students consider alternative ways of envisioning the process of argumentation.

Directions: This exercise takes some thought and may work best as an outside writing assignment, although you might adapt it for in-class discussion. Review some basic concepts of metaphor (Chapter 10), emphasizing its potential function of shaping and giving meaningful form to abstract or complex ideas and phenomena. Metaphors of conflict and battle are a time-honored (some say sexist and inhumane) approach to teaching argumentation [see Sonja K. Foss and Cindy L. Griffin, "Beyond Persuasion: A Proposal for an Invitational Rhetoric," *CM* (March 1995), 2–17]. Quintilian used images of combat formations to visualize the structure of an effective argument. We commonly speak of "attacking" or "shooting down" opposing positions, and it is easy to liken the strategy of addressing an interlocutor's weakest views first to that of outflanking an opposing army. Lately, this foundation metaphor has been seriously challenged. It has been called overly masculine, conquest-oriented, amoral, and destructive of any ideal model for communication. We fight wars from a competitive and one-sided perspective. The goal is to win and to defeat (kill) an enemy rather than to transcend differences, discover common ground, maintain harmonious relationships, and deal with greater problems facing both participants and their communities. Some have gone so far as to reject the concept of argument and dialectic altogether, and scholars have offered alternative metaphors such as dance to emphasize a more constructive process of deliberative interaction.

For this assignment, have your students come up with their own metaphors to symbolize a more constructive and mutually beneficial process of argument. They should look for images that, while allowing for the engaging of differing positions, emphasize a greater sense of interdependence and mutual regard among participants, developing more enlightened positions on all sides of important issues, growing together and discovering mutual interests and ideals, and, in general, the greater transcendent quality to the process as a whole. Students should come up with their own images, but the following ideas may help to stimulate class discussion:

- A chorus
- A painting
- A traffic intersection
- A dance (any kind)
- A meandering river
- An invitation
- A business contract or partnership
- An exploration team
- A chess match
- A sports event
- Making children
- A rainbow
- Two rivers flowing together
- A task force
- A "truth" scale
- An ecosystem

Have your students explore their selected images in terms of their relative strengths and weaknesses as compared with those of dialectical conflict. Encourage them to stretch their imaginations to incorporate the various aspects and principles of enlightened argumentation, and have them present their ideas for class discussion.

Mythos and Argument

Purpose: To impress upon students the persuasive and argumentative functions of rhetorical myth.

Directions: This activity may be used for homework or as a small-group discussion activity. You might start things off by soliciting various definitions of myth and its significance from your students. Many will define myth as a primitive way of thinking expressed in popular narrative. Others may well hold out the idea that myth serves a higher function of upholding basic values and collective identity. Write their ideas on the board. Then ask them to consider themes that are common in American political discourse, such as the American Dream and individual self-sufficiency. Are these true? In what way? What core beliefs and values do we conjure up and reaffirm when speakers praise the deeds of heroes such as Susan B. Anthony, George Washington, and Martin Luther King? What does it mean when speakers imply (as presidents are literally expected to) that we are one nation under God, with a special providential status and mission to enlighten and save a beckoning world with our visions and values?

You might approach this subject by having your students choose a "great speech" for mythic analysis, or choose one yourself and bring it for class discussion. Ceremonial speeches are generally rich with myth and would work perfectly. You might combine this with the activity on presidential inaugural addresses in Chapter 15. Have your students respond to the following questions and share their responses for class discussion. If the exercise is used for homework, have them write a short essay or prepare a short presentation of their ideas for class discussion.

1. What themes in their artifacts strike them as mythic, and why?
2. What are the core visions and values associated with these themes as invoked in this artifact?
3. How is the past construed in relation to these core visions and values?
4. How is the present depicted in relation to these core visions and values?
5. What motives might account for the advocate's associating his or her topic with these themes?
6. What are some likely positive and negative consequences of this use of myth, both in general and with respect to the specific subject it is being associated with?

You might present the following mini-lecture to orient your students to the subject of rhetorical myth and preview this activity. For more readings on rhetorical myth, see the bibliography at this end of this chapter.

Mini-lecture on Myths

Myths are potent forms of collective meaning that can be extremely effective when successfully invoked. However, this can be a difficult subject to approach, as there are so many popular and academic views on the subject, many of which are fiercely opposed to one another. Consulting a dictionary seems to point us in several directions at once. *The American Heritage College Dictionary,* Third Edition (Boston: Houghton Mifflin, 1993, p. 903) defines myth as:

> **1. a.** A traditional story dealing with supernatural beings, ancestors, or heroes that informs or shapes the world view of a people, as by explaining aspects of the natural world or delineating the customs or ideals of society. **b.** Such stories considered as a group. **2.** A story, a theme, an object, or a character regarded as embodying an aspect of a culture: *the pioneer myth.* **3.** A fiction or half-truth, esp. one that forms part of an ideology. **4.** A fictitious story, person, or thing.

Their are two predominant views reflected in the above definitions. The first and most popular view regards myth as a set of popular beliefs in narrative form that are essentially false and that serve to naturalize and perpetuate ignorance and injustice. We commonly hear "scientists" decry the "primitive" use of myth to explain natural phenomena. Your text notes that myths at their worst tend to advocate cultural elitism and intolerance of outsiders. Marxist critics attack popular American myths and themes for rationalizing the injustces of capitalism, and feminists speak of myths of femininity that serve to keep women in their place. More generally, we often hear champions of "repressed" peoples critiquing various myths of cultural supremacy and their inhumanity. The point of this predominant approach is to expose myths for the fallacies they are and the ignorance and injustice they perpetuate.

More recently, critics have sought to balance this with a more sympathetic approach. Many have come to see myth as an inherent part of political culture and rhetorical expression. No matter how much they have been exposed as false by academics and intellectuals, myths continue to exert tremendous influence on American politics. In this view, mythic themes embody the basic truths, values, and themes of a people and culture, and it makes little sense to critique them as right or wrong in and of themselves. Rather, we should focus on the human functions served by myth (not all of which may be negative) in discourse, as well as the appropriateness and likely consequences of specific applications. When popular critics speak disparagingly of myths, it is usually because they are being invoked by people or associated with propositions the critics do not like. The same liberals who were disgusted by Reagan's use of American mythos would probably be more open to the same themes if they were associated with calls for social reform or more money for education. The text notes that at their best, myths promote a healthy sense of collective identity, pride, and purpose, and critics in our field have suggested that rhetorical myth may serve therapeutic if not spiritual functions for the maintenance of a healthy cultural psyche.

Whatever their positive or negative functions, critics generally agree that myths remain a potent force in political rhetoric. They are often used in conjunction with universal imagery, especially in ceremonial speaking when speakers seek to regenerate the core visions and values that define a sense of collective identity and purpose (see text Chapter 15). Many scholars believe that the themes implicit within myth reflect archaic and universal forms of collective consciousness. It is interesting to consider how a culture's core political myths transcend the issues and ideologies they inform and embody. Presidential hopefuls, for instance, have sough to cast themselves in the image of the populist outsider at least since the time of Andrew Jackson, and most big league politicians and movement leaders in our country find it incumbent upon themselves to associate their propositions and "vision" with the American Dream. Other common themes in American political mythos are the Horatio Alger stories of the self-made man risen from common origins, the cowboy and the Western frontier, and biblical and religious themes and values. The predominant values or "truths" endorsed by American political mythology focus on freedoms—political, individual, economic, and religious. Presidents and other politicians commonly imply in their speeches that America has a providential status on Earth along with a special obligation to spread our (His) ideals to a benighted world.

Popular interpretations of history (which are of course commonly decried by professional historians as mythic) play a very important function in rhetorical and political myth. The overwhelming tendency is for politicians to weave past deeds, heroes/heroines, and struggles into a meaningful narrative that gave rise to a special sense of identity and purpose as a people. Past events and struggles are commonly interpreted as testing our resolve to live in accordance with that higher vision. Certainly Martin Luther King, Abraham Lincoln, and George Washington and our other founding fathers have all been mythologized. Events such as the Revolutionary War, the Civil War, and, more recently, Vietnam have been reconstructed as having greatly redefined or challenged our vision of our nation and our sense of its direction. Speakers such as Pat Robertson commonly imply that the Revolution was a sacred beginning when a providential covenant and mission was established between our "fathers" and God.

Another interesting focus for criticism concerns the interplay of mythic themes and their evolution within a historical context. The text notes that differing mythic themes coexist as a sort of delicate and not always harmonious ecology. They are often brought to bear against each other in the course of public deliberation. Indeed, the same themes are commonly invoked against each other. Walter Fisher has argued that contradictory versions of the American Dream are actually interrelated parts of the same overall mythology, continuously subverting and reaffirming each other's preeminence in American culture. While at any given time one form will tend to predominate as it illuminates perceived situations, the other form is always lying in wait for the prevailing form to lose its probability. Other critics have argued a similar interplay between New and Old South mythic themes in Southern rhetoric.

Scholars are not in agreement concerning how to isolate myths in speeches and other messages for study and analysis. At a recent Speech Communication Association Convention in Chicago, Robin Rowland argued that critics were reckless about labeling myths and advocated rigid formal criteria for identifying the presence of myth in discourse. Jan Rushing contended that advocates can invoke powerful forms of ethos-enhancing myth simply through their choice of background music at rallies. Michael Osborn (co-author of your text) suggested that mythic themes can even function implicitly within persuasive claims in a fashion similar to major premises. Your text notes that these themes are commonly invoked in the form of truncated narratives or through ideographs and culturetypes such as "freedom," "equality," and (more recently) "diversity." This is often most effective when speakers characterize situations or problems as threats to or proofs of our sense of mythic purpose and identity.

Myth is obviously an extremely potent source of persuasion, and coming to better understand its role and importance in our lives promises to teach us more about ourselves and who we are. It is important to remember that any one use of a transcendent cultural form is but a fragmentary reflection of a larger and ongoing process that continuously defines and redefines our very identity as a people and as a culture. When people invoke myths successfully in their speeches (especially powerful people like presidents), they at least temporarily redefine who we are, have been, and aspire to be— a feat of considerable social and cultural significance. The effectiveness of the use of myths roughly corresponds to the extent to which listeners accept the association of the speaker's topic and propositions with their most salient values, beliefs, and "stories." This remains an important focus for rhetorical inquiry.

Joan A. Yamasaki (California State University, Hayward), "Teaching the Recognition and Development of Appeals," *SCT* (Spring 1994).

Goal: To demonstrate the differences among persuasive appeals and to develop skill in applying appeals to meet the requirements of varying situations.

Many factors comprise audience adaptation. I introduce students to one of these factors, use of appeals, by defining the differences among appeals to reason, source credibility, and the emotions and discussing how speakers may make choices among appeals in order to clarify meaning for their listeners.

I begin by asking students to write down their last logical decision—the most recent example of a choice made from reasoned review of alternatives. Students contribute examples such as shopping insurance rates or airline fares and then choosing the lowest rate for the same service. Next, I ask if students have examples of relying on the recommendation of another person to make a decision. Far more examples are offered, including choice of colleges, entertainment, and jobs.

Finally, I ask if there are other factors that can affect decisions. Students note that they have been bullied or frightened into making choices, that they have responded to another's grief, or that some choices just "feel right." Since students both give and receive appeals, I ask them to identify those emotional influences they find are most often used by others to convince them and those they most often use to convince others.

Given students' ease at recognizing and developing emotional appeals, I present situations and ask that they rank order the appeals in terms of accomplishing the intended goal. For example:

Purpose: Convince child to shut refrigerator door.

Appeal to Reason: When the door is open, the refrigerator has to work harder because it is keeping the kitchen cold too. When the refrigerator works harder, it costs us more money so we have less for other things.

Appeal to Source Credibility: I'm your mother and I'm telling you to shut that door.

Appeal to Emotions: Shut the door or no dessert.

Students agree that although the first appeal offers reasons for the action, the second appeal is more likely to succeed while the last appeal is most likely to accomplish the speaker's purpose. We discuss why the threat of no dessert, an emotional appeal which will frighten this particular audience, rather than an explanation is used. I also ask students when such an appeal might fail. They generally cite a difference in the relationship between speaker and listener as the single most important factor. Should the conversation take place between roommates, with one reminding the other of the cost of electricity, the logical appeal might be far superior; by using ethos one roommate would be condescending to the other, while the threat of the emotional appeal would be insulting.

We analyze additional emotional appeals in another case:

Purpose: Borrow brother's car.

Appeal to Reason: As a married woman, over 30, living in the suburbs, the actuarial tables show that your car is in safer hands with me than it is with you driving.

Appeal to Source Credibility: I'm your sister and I've always taken good care of your things.

Appeal to Emotions: Unless I get there, my life will be ruined (said while crying).

Again, students rank the likely effectiveness of the appeals. What seems to doom the appeal to reason is a failure to acknowledge the relationship between the speaker and listener. Students acknowledge that in making the same request to a different audience, such as a supervisor, a reminder of being loyal and trustworthy or an appeal to logos in which the speaker might describe how the car will be used would prove more effective. The choice between these two appeals would be determined by the speaker's reputation and relationship with the supervisor. An emotional appeal, students agree, would damage the credibility of the speaker, who might be seen as behaving unprofessionally or even acting too unstable to be regarded as a good worker. So, while it might succeed in the short run, use of an emotional appeal would harm the relationship between the speaker and supervisor and diminish the speaker's reputation.

Finally, I ask students to solve a problem by developing appeals. I remind them to write the emotional appeal first, since they are most practiced at that strategy, then develop appeals to source credibility and logic:

Problem: As the public relations director for the local Humane Society, you want to convince people to adopt an animal.

Most students contribute emotional appeal examples that demonstrate their awareness of the persuasiveness of the power of language. They urge the adoption of "cute," "cuddly," "loving" pets who will be "put to sleep" if they can't be "part of your family." We discuss situations in which such appeals would not be effective—for example, if you wanted to adopt a pet but your roommate did not. Students agree that another approach might be more effective in approaching someone resistant to the idea.

We discuss the added power of appeals to ethos in appealing to the reputation of the agency. The speaker could remind the roommate that the Humane Society has been placing animals in homes in the community for over 50 years and is a reputable source for healthy pets. Further, as one student suggested, one could argue that the Humane Society specializes in "used pets," a group ignored by pet stores. As a true specialist, they would be a reliable place from which to adopt an animal.

Finally, we develop logical appeals for adopting a pet. Usually examples appeal to pragmatic values such as an exchange of services: dogs provide protection, companionship, and exercise, and help keep one on a regular schedule. Further, students argue that adopting a pet is a social responsibility, reducing the number cared for at public expense and allowing funds to be used for other needed services. As students generate additional examples, they refine logical appeals and develop practice in this strategy. Like the hypothetical roommate, they acknowledge that potential animal owners might be more effectively moved by reason rather than emotions, and that even situations that seem first to lend themselves primarily to emotional appeals may be argued by logic.

The purpose of this exercise is to increase student awareness of the relationship among speaker, audience, and type of appeal. By defining the three appeals and practicing use of all three strategies in application to familiar situations, students become more conscious of their own reliance on and susceptibility to emotional appeals while learning to develop and use logical appeals which meet the needs of their listeners.

SUPPLEMENTARY MATERIALS

Films and Videos

"Credibility Factor: What Followers Expect from Leaders," CRM Films, 22 minutes.

"PsychoSell: Advertising and Persuasion," Insight Media, 25 minutes.

"When You Buy: How Ads Persuade," Insight Media, 33 minutes.

"Reason and Emotion," Films for the Humanities, 15 minutes.

"Credibility," CRM Films, 42 minutes.

"Presenting an Argument," Films for the Humanities, 20 minutes.

"Persuasion Gone Awry," RMI Media Productions, 28 minutes.

"Understanding Persuasion," Films for the Humanities, 15 minutes.

"Critical Thinking: How to Evaluate Information and Draw Conclusions," Insight Media, 47 minutes.

"Persuasive Appeals," RMI Media Productions, 28 minutes.

"Truth and the Dragon," McGraw-Hill, 10 minutes.

Transparencies and Handouts

Persuasive Proofs (Transparency 14.1)

Argument and Persuasion (Transparency 14.2)

Abuses of Argument (Transparency 14.3)

Find the Fallacy

PERSUASIVE PROOFS

Proof by logos

- Uses appeals based on rationality
- Relies on facts, figures, and expert testimony
- Is basic to all ethical persuasion

Proof by pathos

- Uses appeals based on emotions
- Relies on examples and narratives
- May be necessary to moving people to action
- May boomerang if overused or misused
- Should be used in conjunction with logos

Proof by ethos

- Uses appeals based on credibility
- Includes expert, prestige, and lay testimony

Proof by mythos

- Uses appeals based on cultural heritage
- Relies on examples and narratives
- Involves appeals to patriotism, cultural pride, historic deeds, heroes/heroines
- Can help bring audiences together

ARGUMENT AND PERSUASION

Deductive argument

- Works from generally accepted principles to specific observations.
- Follows a syllogistic form having major and minor premises and a conclusion.
- Uses basic values and beliefs as major premises.

Inductive argument

- Works from specific observations to general claims and assertions.
- Must be based on sufficient, reliable, recent, and representative observations.
- Is useful for establishing the existence of problems or introducing new ideas.
- Is often used to establish major premises.

Argument by analogy

- Provides strategic perspectives on issues.
- Associates the issue with something familiar.
- Can create positive or negative associations.
- Depends for its effectiveness on acceptance of the comparison.

ABUSES OF ARGUMENT

Abuses of evidence

- Confusing facts and opinion
- Slippery slope fallacy
- Red herring fallacy
- Myth of the mean
- Incomparable percentages
- Using obsolete/outdated testimony
- Misrepresenting the qualifications of sources
- Citing out of context
- Misusing types of testimony

Abuses of proof

- Using pathos to hide the lack of a substantive argument
- Using mythos to promote cultural elitism or intolerance
- Argument *ad hominen*
- Over-relying on testimony to hide the absence of substantial information
- Begging the question

Abuses of arguments, per se

- Unsound major premises
- Categorical imprecision
- Confusion of probability and certainty
- *Post hoc* reasoning
- *Non sequiturs*
- Hasty generalizations
- Contamination of conclusions
- Either-or thinking
- Setting up a straw man

FIND THE FALLACY

1. In 1931 approximately 6,000 workers were killed in industrial accidents in the United States. In 1945 over 9,000 workers were killed in industrial accidents. The rate of workers killed in industrial accidents rose dramatically between 1931 and 1945.

2. If we allow the Communists a toehold in San Salvador, Mexico will be next.

3. Because the Great Depression began during Hoover's presidency, it is safe to assume that his economic policies were its primary cause.

4. Don't listen to environmentalists complaining about acid rain. They're just a bunch of pot-smoking hippies.

5. My brother got a bad grade in algebra. My roommate got a bad grade in algebra. The girl sitting next to me in history class got a bad grade in algebra. Nobody makes a good grade in that class!

6. You know she can't be a good Republican. Her father was a liberal.

7. What's good for General Motors is good for America.

8. Salaries are really good at Gulf State Bank. They average over $62,000 per year.

9. Don't tell me about recycling and the environment. By not being a vegetarian, you're ultimately contributing to environmental destruction yourself.

10. Everyone knows that taxes are bad for the economy.

READINGS FOR ENRICHMENT

See guide to journal abbreviations on p. 37.

* Items marked with an asterisk are suitable for student enrichment.

Problems in Reasoning and Argumentation

Aldrich, Alan. "Locating Fallacies and Reconstructing Arguments." In *Argumentation and Values: Proceedings of the Ninth SCA/AFA Conference on Argumentation*, pp. 519–524. Annandale, Va.: Speech Communication Association, 1995.

Bakke, John, and Michael Osborn. "Debate as Victim: The Impact of Journalism upon Public Argument in the Memphis Sanitation Strike of 1968." In *Argumentation and Values: Proceedings of the Ninth SCA/AFA Conference on Argumentation*, pp. 213–218. Annandale, Va.: Speech Communication Association, 1995.

Hample, Dale. "Dual Coding, Reasoning, and Fallacies." *JAFA* (Fall 1982), 59–78.

* Ivins, Molly. "What about Apple Pie?" *The Progressive* (Nov. 1988), p. 37.

* Jason, Gary. "Are Fallacies Common? Look at Two Debates." In *Selected Issues in Logic and Communication*, edited by Trudy Govier, pp. 20–34. Belmont, Calif.: Wadsworth, 1988.

Langsdorf, Leonore. "No One Has Ever Died from Contradictions: Argumentation in a Rhetorical Lifeworld." *Argumentation and Values: Proceedings of the Ninth SCA/AFA Conference on Argumentation*, pp. 274–280. Annandale, Va.: Speech Communication Association, 1995.

* Osborn, Michael. "The Abuses of Argument." *SSCJ* (Fall 1983), 1–11.

Postrel, Virginia. "Fatal Fallacies." *Reason* (Feb. 1995), 4–5.

Remland, Martin. "The Implicit *Ad Hominem* Fallacy: Nonverbal Displays of Status in Argumentative Discourse." *JAFA* (Fall 1982), 79–86.

Snyder, Leslie B., and Deborah J. Blood. "Caution: Alcohol Advertising and the Surgeon General's Alcohol Warnings May Have Adverse Effects on Young Adults." *ACR* (Feb. 1992), 37–53.

Spiker, Barry K., Tom D. Daniels, and Lawrence M. Bernabo. "The Quantitative Quandary in Forensics: The Use and Abuse of Statistical Evidence." *JAFA* (Fall 1982), 87–96.

Yoos, George E. "Licit and Illicit in Rhetorical Appeals." *WJSC* (Fall 1978), 222–230.

Ethos

Benoit, William L. "Argument and Credibility Appeals in Persuasion." *SSCJ* (Winter 1987), 181–197.

* Bier, Jesse. "A Nation of Hookers: The Morality of Celebrity Endorsements and Advertising." *The Humanist* (Nov.–Dec. 1995), 41.

* Burgoon, Judee K. "The Ideal Source: A Reexamination of Source Credibility Measurement." *CSSJ* (Fall 1976), 200–206.

Decker, Bert. *You've Got to Be Believed to Be Heard*. New York: St. Martins, 1992.

Delia, Jesse G. A Construct Analysis of the Concept of Credibility." *QJS* (Dec. 1976), 361–375.

Elston, Catherine F. "Following the Nez Perce Trail: A Guide to the Ne-Me-Poo National Historic Trail with Eyewitness Account." *The American Indian Quarterly* (Winter 1993), 128–129.

* Friedman, Hershey H., and Isaac C. Friedman. "Whom Do Students Trust?" *JC* (Spring 1976), 48–49.

Gill, Mary M. "Accents and Stereotypes: Their Effect on Perceptions of Teachers and Lecture Comprehension." *ACR* (Nov. 1944), 348–360.

Gill, Mary M., and Diane M. Badzinski. "The Impact of Accent and Status on Information Recall and Perception Formation." *CR* (Summer 1992), 99–106.

Infante, Dominic A., Kenneth R. Parker, Christopher H. Clarke, Laverne Wilson, and Indrani A. Nathu. "A Comparison of Factor and Functional Approaches to Source Credibility." *CQ* (Winter 1983), 43–48.

* Kenton, Sherron B. "Speaker Credibility in Persuasive Business Communication: A Model Which Explains Gender Differences." *Journal of Business Communication* (1989), 143–157.

Lashbrook, William R., William B. Snavely, and Daniel L. Sullivan. "The Effects of Source Credibility and Message Information Quality on the Attitude Change of Apathetics." *CM* (Aug. 1977), 252–262.

Lawrence, Samuel G., and Mike Watson. "Getting Others to Help: The Effectiveness of Professional Uniforms in Charitable Fund Raising." *ACR* (Aug. 1991), 170–185.

MacIntrye, Peter D., and Kimly A. Thivierge. "The Effects of Speaker Personality on Anticipated Reactions to Public Speaking." *CCR* (Fall 1995), 125–133.

McCroskey, James C., and Thomas J. Young. "Ethos and Credibility: The Construct and Its Measurement After Three Decades." *CSSJ* (Spring 1981), 24–34.

* Overstreet, R. Larry. "Understanding Charisma Through Its History." *CSSJ* (Winter 1978), 275–282.

Pfau, Michael, and Michael Burgoon. "The Efficacy of Issue and Character Attack Message Strategies in Political Campaign Communication." *CR* (Summer 1989), 53–61.

Pfau, Michael, Roxanne Parrott, and Bridget Lindquist. "An Expectancy Theory of Explanation of the Effectiveness of Political Attack Television Spots." *ACR* (Aug. 1992), 235–253.

Portnoy, Enid J. "The Impact of Body Type on Perceptions of Attractiveness by Older Individuals." *CR* (Summer 1993), 101–108.

* Richmond, Virginia P., and James C. McCroskey. "Whose Opinion Do You Trust?" *JC* (Spring 1975), 42–50.

Rosenfeld, Lawrence B., and Timothy G. Plax. "The Relationship of Listener Personality to Perceptions of Three Dimensions of Credibility." *CSSJ* (Winter 1975), 274–278.

White, Sylvia E. "A Content Analytic Technique for Measuring the Sexiness of Women's Business Attire in Media Presentations." *CRR* (Fall 1995), 178–185.

Mythos

Andrews, James R. "If God Prosper Us: Daniel Webster and the Historical Foundations of American Nationalism." In *Argumentation and Values: Proceedings of the Ninth SCA/AFA Conference on Argumentation*, pp. 21–27. Annandale, Va.: Speech Communication Association, 1995.

Baesler, E. James. "Construction and Test of an Empirical Measure for Narrative Coherence and Fidelity." *CR* (Summer 1995), 97–101.

Balthrop, V. William. "Culture, Myth and Ideology as Public Argument: An Interpretation of the Ascent and Demise of 'Southern Culture.'" *CM* (Dec. 1984), 339–352.

* Barthes, Roland. *Mythologies*. Translated by Annette Lavers. New York: Hill & Wang, 1972.

Bormann. Ernest G. "Fantasy and Rhetorical Vision: The Rhetorical Criticism of Social Reality." *Quarterly Journal of Speech*, 58 (1972), 396–407;

* Campbell, Joseph. *The Hero with a Thousand Faces*. Princeton: Princeton University Press, 1949.

* ———. *Myths to Live By*. New York: Bantam, 1973.

Carpenter, Ronald H. "Frederick Jackson Turner and the Rhetorical Impact of the Frontier Thesis." *QJS* (Apr. 1977), 117–129.

———. "America's Tragic Metaphor: Our Twentieth Century Combatants as Frontiersmen." *QJS* (Feb. 1990), 1–22.

Cloud, Dana. "The Rhetoric of <Family Values> and the Public Sphere." In *Argumentation and Values: Proceedings of the Ninth SCA/AFA Conference on Argumentation*, pp. 281–289. Annandale, Va.: Speech Communication Association, 1995.

Communication Studies: Special Section: "On Mythic Criticism." *CS* (Summer 1990), 101–160.

Crable, Richard E., ed. "On Mythic Criticism: The Conversation Continues." *CS* (Winter 1990), 278–298.

* Crump, Kathy, and Casey Davidson. "Celebrities Speak Easy: Celebrity TV Commercials." *Entertainment Weekly*, 4 Aug. 1995, p. 17.

Dorsey, Leroy G. "The Frontier Myth in Presidential Rhetoric: Theodore Roosevelt's Campaign for Conservation." *WJC* (Winter 1995), 1–19.

* Edelman, Murray. "Language, Myths, and Rhetoric." *Transaction: Social Science and Modern Society* (July–Aug. 1975), 14–21.

Fisher, Walter F. "Narration as a Human Communication Paradigm: The Case of Public Moral Argument." *Communication Monographs*, 51 (1984), 1–22.

Fuller, Edmund, ed. *Bullfinch's Mythology.* New York: Dell, 1959.

Jung, Carl J., ed. *Man and His Symbols.* New York: Dell, 1968.

Lee, Ronald, and Loren Murfield. "Christian Tradition, Jeffersonian Democracy, and the Myth of the Sentimental Family: An Exploration of the Premises of Social Conservative Argumentation." In *Argumentation and Values: Proceedings of the Ninth SCA/AFA Conference on Argumentation,* pp. 36–42. Annandale, Va.: Speech Communication Association, 1995.

McGee, Michael Calvin. "The Origins of 'Liberty': A Feminization of Power." *CM* (Mar. 1980), 23–45.

——. "Power to the People." *CSMC* (Dec. 1987), 432–437.

McGee, Michael Calvin, and John S. Nelson. "Narrative Reason in Public Argument." *JC* (Autumn 1985), 139–155.

Miller, Greg, and Brad Lotterman. "Disassociating Myth and Practice: Pete Wilson's Campaign against Immigration." In *Argumentation and Values: Proceedings of the Ninth SCA/AFA Conference on Argumentation,* pp. 196–203. Annandale, Va.: Speech Communication Association, 1995.

Nelson, John S. "Virtual Politics: Mythic Persuasion Through Experience in Campaign Advertising on Television." In *Argumentation and Values: Proceedings of the Ninth SCA/AFA Conference on Argumentation,* pp. 557–563. Annandale, Va.: Speech Communication Association, 1995.

O'Leary, Stephen, and Michael McFarland. "The Political Use of Mythic Discourse: Prophetic Interpretation in Pat Robertson's Presidential Campaign." *QJS* (Nov. 1989), 433–452.

* Ortner, Sherry. "On Key Symbols." *American Anthropologist* (1973), 1338–1346.

Osborn, Michael. "Rhetorical Depiction." In *Form, Genre and the Study of Political Discourse,* edited by Herbert W. Simons and Aram A. Aghazarian, pp. 79–107. Columbia: University of South Carolina Press, 1986.

* Osborn, Suzanne. "Reagan's Rhetorical Montage." In *Argument and Critical Practices: Proceedings of the Fifth SCA/AFA Conference on Argumentation,* edited by Joseph Wenzel, pp. 223–228. Annandale Va.: Speech Communication Association, 1987.

Procter, David E. "Bridging Social Change Through Mythic Regeneration." *CS* (Fall 1992), 171–181.

Rodden, John. "Uses of the Past: Versions of Buchenwald." *The Christian Century,* 26 Apr. 1995, pp. 457–459.

* Rushing, Janice Hocker. "The Rhetoric of the American Western Myth." *CM* (Mar. 1983), 14–32.

* ——. "Mythic Evolution of 'The New Frontier' in Mass Mediated Rhetoric." *CSMC* (Sept. 1986), 265–298.

——. "Evolution of 'The New Frontier' in *Alien* and *Aliens:* Patriarchal Co-optation of the Feminine Archetype." *QJS* (Feb. 1989), 1–24.

* Sagan, Carl. *The Dragons of Eden.* New York: Ballantine, 1977.

Solomon, Martha. "The 'Positive Woman's' Journey: A Mythic Analysis of the Rhetoric of STOP ERA." *Quarterly Journal of Speech,* 65 (1979), 262–274.

Weal, Bruce W. "The Force of Narrative in the Public Sphere of Argument." *JAFA* (Fall 1985), 104–114.

Wilson, Kirt H. "And Equality for All: The Foundations of African American Civil Rights Argument." In *Argumentation and Values: Proceedings of the Ninth SCA/AFA Conference on Argumentation,* pp. 204–212. Annandale, Va.: Speech Communication Association, 1995.

Logos

Check, Terence. "The Evaluation of Scientific Evidence on the Exxon Valdez Oil Spill." In *Argumentation and Values: Proceedings of the Ninth SCA/AFA Conference on Argumentation,* pp. 397–402. Annandale, Va.: Speech Communication Association. 1995.

* Engel, S. Morris. *With Good Reason: An Introduction to Informal Fallacies.* New York: St. Martin's, 1990.

* Fisher, Walter R. "Toward a Logic of Good Reasons." *QJS* (Dec. 1978), 376–384.

* Govier, Trudy, ed. *Selected Issues in Logic and Communication.* Belmont, Calif.: Wadsworth, 1988.

* Harrison, Tyler R. "Are Public Opinion Polls Used Illegitimately? 47% Say Yes." In *Argumentation and Values: Proceedings of the Ninth SCA/AFA Conference on Argumentation,* pp. 383–388. Annandale, Va.: Speech Communication Association, 1995.

* Harte, Thomas B. "The Effects of Evidence in Persuasive Communication." *CSSJ* (Spring 1976), 42–46.

Hartney, Ann M. "Argument Through Example: An Exploration and Case Study." In *Argumentation and Values: Proceedings of the Ninth SCA/AFA Conference on Argumentation*, pp. 408–412. Annandale, Va.: Speech Communication Association, 1995.

Hollihan, Thomas A. "Evidencing Moral Claims: The Activist Rhetorical Critic's First Task." *WJC* (Summer 1994), 229–234.

Kazoleas, Dean C. "A Comparison of the Persuasive Effectiveness of Qualitative Versus Quantitative Evidence: A Text of Explanatory Hypotheses." *CQ* (Winter 1993), 40–50.

* Kellerman, Kathy. "The Concept of Evidence: A Critical Review." *JAFA* (Winter 1980), 159–172.

* King, Florence. "QED: The Politics and Ethics of Logic in Liberal Thought." *National Review*, 7 Oct. 1991, p. 56.

* ———. "Ex Pede Herculem: The Decline of the Respect for and Use of Logic in American Society." *National Review*, 15 Nov. 1993, p. 72.

Luchok, Joseph A., and James C. McCroskey. "The Effect of Quality of Evidence on Attitude Change and Source Credibility." *SSCJ* (Summer 1978), 371–383.

Nakayama, Thomas. "Disciplining Evidence." *WJC* (Spring 1995), 171–175.

Reinard, John C. "The Empirical Study of the Persuasive Effects of Evidence: The Status After Fifty Years of Research." *HCR* (Fall 1988), 3–59.

Reynolds, Rodney A., and Michael Burgoon. "Belief Processing, Reasoning, and Evidence." In *Communication Yearbook 7*, edited by Robert N. Bostrom, pp. 83–104. Beverly Hills, Calif.: Sage, 1983.

Smith, Craig. "Criticism as Rational: An Argument from Disciplinary Integrity." In *Argumentation and Values: Proceedings of the Ninth SCA/AFA Conference on Argumentation*, pp. 456–460. Annandale, Va.: Speech Communication Association, 1995.

Stiff, James B. "Cognitive Processing of Persuasive Message Cues: A Meta-Analytic Review of the Effects of Supporting Information on Attitudes." *CM* (Mar. 1986), 75–89.

Wallace, Karl R. "The Substance of Rhetoric: Good Reasons." *Quarterly Journal of Speech*, 49 (1963), 239–249.

Western Journal of Communication, Special Issue, "The Dialogue of Evidence: A Topic Revisited" (Winter 1994).

Pathos

Boster, Franklin J., and Paul Mongeua. "Fear-Arousing Persuasive Messages." In *Communication Yearbook 8*, edited by Robert N. Bostrom, pp. 330–375. Beverly Hills, Calif.: Sage, 1984.

* Damasio, Antonio R. *Descartes' Error: Emotion, Reason, and the Human Brain.* New York: Putnam 1994.

Garrett, Mary M. "*Pathos* Reconsidered from the Perspective of Classical Chinese Rhetorical Theories." *QJS* (Feb. 1993), 19–39.

Hamilton, Mark A., and Becky L. Stewart. "Extending an Information Processing Model of Language Intensity Effects." *CQ* (Spring 1993), 231–246.

* Hyde, Michael J. "Emotion and Human Communication: A Rhetorical, Scientific, and Philosophical Picture." *CQ* (Spring 1984), 120–132.

* Karetz, Jack D. "Rational Arguments and Irrational Audiences: Psychology, Planning, and Public Judgment." *Journal of the American Planning Association* (1989), 445–456.

Rogan, Randall G. "Language Intensity: Testing a Content-based Metric." *CR* (Summer 1995), 128–135.

Smith, Craig R., and Michael J. Hyde. "Rethinking the 'Public': The Role of Emotion in Being-with-Others." *QJS* (Nov. 1991), 446–466.

Waddell, Craig. "The Role of Pathos in the Decision-Making Process: A Study in the Rhetoric of Science Policy." *QJS* (Nov. 1990), 381–400.

Witte, Kim. "Putting the Fear Back into Fear Appeals." *CM* (Dec. 1992), 329–349.

Witte, Kim, and Kelly Morrison. "Using Scare Tactics to Promote Safer Sex Among Juvenile Detention and High School Youth." *ACR* (May 1995), 128–142.

General

Berger, Charles R., and Patrick di Battista. "Communication Failure and Plan Adaptation: If At First You Don't Succeed, Say It Louder and Slower." *CM* (Sept. 1993), 220–238.

Blair, J. Anthony. "Everyday Argumentation from an Informal Logic Perspective." In *Argument and Critical Practices: Proceedings of the Fifth SCA/AFA Conference on Argumentation*, edited by Joseph Wenzel, pp. 177–184. Annandale Va.: Speech Communication Association, 1987.

* Bower, Bruce. "Roots of Reason: Our Daily Deliberations Provoke Scientific Debate." *Science News*, 29 Jan. 1994, pp. 72–75.

* Brockriede, Wayne. "Characteristics of Arguments and Arguing." *JAFA* (Winter 1977), 129–132.

Canary, Daniel J., Jeanette E. Brossmann, Brent G. Brossman, and Harry Weger, Jr. "Toward a Theory of Minimally Rational Argument: Analyses of Episode-Specific Effects of Argument Structures." *CM* (Sept. 1995), 183–212.

Carlson, Richard A., David H. Lundy, and Robin G. Yaure. "Syllogistic Inference Chains in Meaningful Text." *American Journal of Psychology* (Spring 1992), 75–99.

* "A Critique of Pure Reason." *The Economist*, 4 July 1992, pp. 73–74.

* Eagly, Alice H., and Shelly Chaiken. *The Psychology of Attitudes.* Fort Worth, Tex.: Harcourt Brace Jovanovich, 1993.

Eilers, Perthenia. "Depiction as Argumentative Strategy in Rachel Carson's *Silent Spring.*" In *Argumentation and Values: Proceedings of the Ninth SCA/AFA Conference on Argumentation*, pp. 371–377. Annandale, Va.: Speech Communication Association, 1995.

* Greene, Chris. "Higher Education: Elevated Thinking?" *Psychology Today* (Apr. 1986), 14.

* Haass, Richard. *The Power to Persuade.* Boston: Houghton Mifflin, 1994.

Hample, Dale. "A Cognitive View of Argument." *JAFA* (Winter 1980), 151–158.

———. "The Cognitive Context of Argument." *WJSC* (Spring 1981), 148–158.

Jenson, J. Vernon. *Argumentation: Reasoning in Communication.* New York: D. Van Nostrand, 1981.

Kahane, Howard. *Logic and Contemporary Rhetoric: The Use of Reason in Everyday Life*, 5th ed. Belmont, Calif.: Wadsworth, 1988, p. 38.

Kaplowitz, Stan A., and Edward L. Fink. "Attitude Change and Attitudinal Trajectories: A Dynamic Multidimensional Theory." In *Communication Yearbook 6*, edited by Michael Burgoon, pp. 364–394. Beverly Hills, Calif.: Sage, 1982.

Kauffeld, Fred. "On the Difference Between Assumptions and Presumptions." In *Argumentation and Values: Proceedings of the Ninth SCA/AFA Conference on Argumentation*, pp. 509–514. Annandale, Va.: Speech Communication Association, 1995.

* Kipnis, David, and Stuart Schmidt. "The Language of Persuasion." *Psychology Today* (Apr. 1985), 40–46.

* Nelson, John S., and G. R. Boynton. "How Music and Image Deliver Argument in Political Advertisements on Television." In *Argumentation and Values: Proceedings of the Ninth SCA/AFA Conference on Argumentation*, pp. 543–549. Annandale, Va.: Speech Communication Association, 1995.

O'Keefe, Daniel J. *Persuasion: Theory and Research.* Newbury Park, Calif.: Sage, 1990.

O'Keefe, Daniel J., and Sally Jackson. "Argument Quality and Persuasive Effects: A Review of Current Approaches." In *Argumentation and Values: Proceedings of the Ninth SCA/AFA Conference on Argumentation*, pp. 88–92. Annandale, Va.: Speech Communication Association, 1995.

Palmerton, Patricia R. "Teaching Skills or Teaching Thinking?" *ACR* (Aug. 1992), 335–341.

* Pellegrino, James W. "Anatomy of Analogy." *Psychology Today* (Oct. 1985), 49–54.

Perloff, Richard M. *The Dynamics of Persuasion.* Hillsdale, N.J.: Erlbaum, 1993.

Reardon, Kathleen Kelley. *Persuasion in Practice.* Newbury Park, Calif.: Sage, 1991.

Rieke, Richard D., and Malcolm O. Sillars. *Argumentation and the Decision Making Process*, 2nd ed. Glenview, Ill.: Scott Foresman, 1984.

* Roberts, Donald F., Peter Christenson, Wendy A. Gibson, Linda Mooser, and Marvin E. Goldberg. "Developing Discriminating Consumers." *JC* (Summer 1980), 94–105.

* Rokeach, Milton. "Persuasion that Persists." *Psychology Today* (Sept. 1971), 69–71, 92.

* Rosenbaum, Bernard. "Making Presentations: How to Persuade Others to Accept Your Ideas." *American Salesman* (Feb. 1992), 16–18.

Sanders, Judith, Robert Gass, Richard Wiseman, and Jon Bruschke. "Ethnic Comparison and Measurement of Argumentativeness, Verbal Aggressiveness, and Need for Cognition." *CR* (Winter 1992), 50–56.

Sanders, Judith A., Richard L. Wiseman, and Robert H. Gass. "Does Teaching Argumentation Facilitate Students' Critical Thinking?" *CR* (Winter 1994), 27–35.

* Sillars, Malcolm O. "Values: Providing Standards for Audience-Centered Argumentation." In *Argumentation and Values: Proceedings of the Ninth SCA/AFA Conference on Argumentation*, pp. 1–6. Annandale, Va.: Speech Communication Association, 1995.

* Sproule, J. Michael. "The Institute for Propaganda Analysis: Public Education in Argumentation, 1937–1942." In *Argument in Transition: Proceedings of the Third Summer Conference on Argumentation*, edited by David Zarefsky, Malcolm O. Sillars, and Jack Rhodes, pp. 486–499. Annandale, Va.: Speech Communication Association, 1983.

Suzuki, Shinobu, and Andrew S. Rancer. "Argumentativeness and Verbal Aggressiveness: Testing for Conceptual and Measurement Equivalence Across Cultures." *CM* (Sept. 1994), 256–279.

Toulmin, Stephen, Richard Rieke, and Allan Janik. *An Introduction to Reasoning*, 2nd ed. New York: Macmillan, 1984.

* Waldrop, M. Mitchell. "Causality, Structure, and Common Sense." *Science*, 11 Sept. 1987, pp. 1297–1299.

* Weiler, Michael. "Arguments from Ignorance in Multicultural Discourse." In *Argumentation and Values: Proceedings of the Ninth SCA/AFA Conference on Argumentation*, pp. 187–190. Annandale, Va.: Speech Communication Association, 1995.

* Wenzel, Joseph W. "Toward a Rationale for Value-Centered Argument." *JAFA* (Winter 1977), 150–158.

Wiethoff, William E. "A Classical Rhetoric for 'Powerful' Argumentation." *JAFA* (Summer 1980), 1–10.

Wilson, Barrie A. The Anatomy of Argument. Landham, Md.: University Press of America, 1980.

Alternative Teaching Activities

Beal, Carol. "Challenging Your Convictions: Critical Thinking Speech Activities for Secondary Students." *SCT* (Spring 1994), 6–7.

Cammilleri, Sandra. "Creating Persuasive Commercials." *SCT* (Winter 1995), 10–11.

Dittus, James K. "Grade Begging as an Exercise in Argumentation." *SCT* (Summer 1991), 5.

Downey, Sharon, and Karen Rasmussen. "A Claim-Making Exercise for Critical Writing in Rhetoric." *SCT* (Spring 1990), 10–11.

Drewis, Rob. "PSAs: Persuasive Speaking in a Minute." *SCT* (Fall 1992), 10–11.

Garrett, Roger L. "The Premises of Persuasion." *SCT* (Spring 1991), 13.

Gill, Mary. "Non-Debaters Realize the Value of Debate." *SCT* (Spring 1990), 14–15.

Glick, I. David. "Tossing LAP'S into Their Laps." *SCT* (Winter 1990), 15.

Grainer, Diane. "What's Evidence?" *SCT* (Winter 1993), 10–11.

Hamlet, Janice D. "Editorial Sessions: A Different Approach to Teaching Argumentation." *SCT* (Fall 1994), 8.

Hankins, Gail Armstead. "Don't Judge a Book By Its Cover." *SCT* (Summer 1991), 8.

Johnson, Craig. "Nothing to Fear but Fear . . . Or Is There?" *SCT* (Winter 1990), 1.

Kauffman, James. "Collecting and Evaluating Evidence." *SCT* (Winter 1992), 12.

MacDonald, Madlyne A. "The Key to Persuasion." *SCT* (Fall 1986), 14–15.

Nelson, Lee Ann. "Sell Us Monroe's Motivated Sequence." *SCT* (Spring 1995), 13.

Newburger, Craig. "Testing Students' Ability to Distinguish Facts from Inferences." *SCT* (Winter 1994), 13–14.

Powell, Kimberly A. "Debate as the Key to Teaching Persuasion Skills." *SCT* (Fall 1994), 10–11.

Proctor, Russell E., II. "Using Feature Films to Teach Critical Thinking." *SCT* (Spring 1993), 11–12.

Ross, Charlynn. "Vaccinating Against Inoculations: McGuire's Theory as an Experiential Learning Activity." *SCT* (Summer 1995), 6–7.

Schreier, Howard N. "Analyzing Persuasive Tactics." *SCT* (Summer 1989), 14.

Spicer, Karin-Leigh. "Stereotypes and Appearances." *SCT* (Winter 1995), 10.

Spicer, Karin-Leigh, and William E. Hanks. "Critical Thinking Activities for Communication Textbooks." *SCT* (Summer 1993), 6–7.

Yamasaki, Joan M. "Teaching the Recognition and Development of Appeals." *SCT* (Spring 1994), 12–13.

Argumentation in Particular Settings

Allen, Mike, and William Donohue. "The Mediator as Arguer." In *Argument and Critical Practices: Proceedings of the Fifth SCA/AFA Conference on Argumentation,* edited by Joseph Wenzel, pp. 279–282. Annandale Va.: Speech Communication Association, 1987.

* Bandow, Doug. "The Power to Persuade: How to Be Effective in Government, the Public Sector, or Any Unruly Organization." *Fortune,* 27 June 1994, p. 133.

Birdsell, David. "Argumentation in Urban Public and Not-for-Profit Management." In *Argumentation and Values: Proceedings of the Ninth SCA/AFA Conference on Argumentation,* pp. 71–74. Annandale, Va.: Speech Communication Association, 1995.

Boynton, George R. "Telling a Good Story: Models of Argument; Models of Understanding in the Senate Agriculture Committee." In *Argument and Critical Practices: Proceedings of the Fifth SCA/AFA Conference on Argumentation,* edited by Joseph Wenzel, pp. 429–438. Annandale Va.: Speech Communication Association, 1987.

Crawford, John E. "Toward a Model of Effective Public Argumentation: A Case Study of Executive Presentations to City Councils." In *Argument in Transition: Proceedings of the Third Summer Conference on Argumentation,* edited by David Zarefsky, Malcolm O. Sillars, and Jack Rhodes, pp. 500–515. Annandale, Va.: Speech Communication Association, 1983.

* Gouran, Dennis S. "The Failure of Argument in Decisions Leading to the 'Challenger Disaster': A Two-Level Analysis." In *Argument and Critical Practices: Proceedings of the Fifth SCA/AFA Conference on Argumentation,* edited by Joseph Wenzel, pp. 439–448. Annandale Va.: Speech Communication Association, 1987.

* Hart, Roderick P. *The Political Pulpit.* West Lafayette, Ind.: Purdue University Press, 1977.

* Schuetz, Janice. "Legal and Research Evidence and the O. J. Simpson Trial." *WJC* (Fall 1995), 347–354.

Sheppard, Sally Asbell, and Richard D. Rieke. "Categories of Reasoning in Legal Argument." In *Argument in Transition: Proceedings of the Third Summer Conference on Argumentation,* edited by David Zarefsky, Malcolm O. Sillars, and Jack Rhodes, pp. 235–250. Annandale, Va.: Speech Communication Association, 1983.

CHAPTER 15
Ceremonial Speaking

OBJECTIVES

- To help your students appreciate the importance of ceremonial speaking.

- To help your students understand and use the techniques of identification and magnification.

- To help your students prepare and present speeches of tribute, acceptance, introduction, and inspiration.

- To teach your students how to prepare a toast or an after-dinner speech.

- To teach your students how to act as a master of ceremonies.

SUGGESTIONS FOR TEACHING

We strongly recommend the ceremonial speaking assignment. It provides a nice sense of closure for the course, giving your students one last chance to fine-tune and show off their presentation skills. It also gives them a chance to reflect on and voice their broader ideals and moral commitments—a vitally significant "community-building" function of public speaking. The benefits are real, and many will recognize the practical applications of making toasts, paying tribute to others at work or in social organizations, and other formal ceremonial speaking skills. Effectively enacted, ceremonial speaking can greatly enhance a speaker's perceived ethos and leadership potential within a given organization or community. Finally, the ceremonial assignment gives instructors a chance to introduce some basic ideas about rhetoric and culture.

Like all public communication, ceremonial speaking is concerned with the timely. But ceremonial speakers celebrate specific people, events, ideas, and accomplishments by reaffirming them and associating them with the core values, forms, and beliefs that help define and are perceived to be essentially timeless within that particular community. As such, ceremonial speaking is fertile ground for explorations of mythic narrative, metaphor, archetypes, and culturetypes. The materials in this unit are geared primarily toward teaching the practical benefits of ceremonial speaking, along with an awareness of its significance in our lives.

Most of the exercises and activities have your students present or critique ceremonial artifacts using the principles of identification and magnification covered in this chapter. No new design strategies are added, and so students may find it helpful to consult the "Speech Designer" computer software program in structuring their presentations. We suggest that you use final speaking assignments or activities to review the progress that students have made over the course of the semester and offer last suggestions for improvement. Many instructors like to combine last-day activities with a party, to which they bring munchies and soft drinks to celebrate the completion of the course and the coming vacation.

454

CHAPTER OUTLINE

I. Ceremonial speaking celebrates the sharing of identities, values, and aspirations that unites people into communities. *(text pp. 487–488)*
   A. Ceremonial speaking answers four basic questions:
      1. Who are we?
      2. Why are we?
      3. What have we accomplished?
      4. What can we become together?
   B. Ceremonial speaking spotlights the speaker and puts his or her leadership skills on display.
   C. Ceremonial speaking affirms values.

II. Ceremonial speaking relies heavily on identification and magnification. *(text pp. 488–491)*
   A. Identification is promoted by:
      1. invoking narratives related to group activities and traditions.
      2. recognizing group heroes.
      3. renewing group identity.
   B. Magnification amplifies certain features of people or events, such as
      1. overcoming obstacles.
      2. superior or unusual accomplishment.
      3. pure, unselfish motives.
      4. benefit to society.

III. The major types of ceremonial speeches are speeches of tribute, acceptance, introduction, and inspiration and the after-dinner speech. *(text pp. 491–505)*
   A. Speeches of tribute celebrate accomplishment in its own right or for its symbolic significance.
      1. A speech of tribute should:
         a. not embarrass honorees by exaggerating their accomplishments beyond believability.
         b. focus on the honoree, not the speaker.
         c. create vivid images of accomplishments through narratives and examples.
         d. reflect sincerity, warmth, pride, and appreciation.
      2. Award presentations should explain the nature of the award and how the recipient earned it.
      3. Eulogies are tributes delivered upon the death of a person.
      4. A toast is a minispeech of tribute. It should be:
         a. eloquent.
         b. planned in advance.
         c. memorized and practiced.
         d. brief.
   B. Speeches of acceptance are presented by recipients of awards or honors. Speakers should:
      1. be modest as they express gratitude and acknowledge those who make it possible.
      2. recognize the values the award represents.
      3. present speeches that match the dignity and formality of the occasion.
   C. Speeches of introduction introduce featured speakers. They should:
      1. welcome the speaker.
      2. strengthen the speaker's ethos.
      3. orient the audience and create anticipation without previewing the speech.
      4. be short.
   D. Speeches of inspiration help audiences appreciate, commit to, and pursue a goal, purpose, or set of values and beliefs.
   E. After-dinner speeches should be noncontroversial and positive in tone.
      1. Humor is an essential ingredient of most after-dinner speeches.
      2. An after-dinner speech should be carefully planned, developed, and practiced.

IV. Masters of ceremonies introduce participants, may present awards, and keep a program moving. *(text pp. 505–507)*
   A. They should:
      1. plan a good opener for the program.
      2. be prepared to introduce the participants.
      3. know the timetable so that they can keep the program moving.
      4. plan their comments ahead of time.
      5. practice their presentations.
      6. be ready for the inevitable glitches.
      7. end the program strongly.

USING END-OF-CHAPTER ITEMS

Discussion *(text p. 508)*

1. **The speeches in Appendix B by Hillary Rodham Clinton and Elizabeth Dole are ceremonial addresses. How do they relate to the basic questions of "Who are we?" "Why are we?" "What have we accomplished?" and "What can we become together?" What values do they celebrate?**

This exercise works well as a written homework assignment. You may wish to review the material on values from Chapter 4 at this time and distribute the "Value Survey" instruments from this IRM to serve as a guide for the analysis. Since these speeches were presented under drastically different circumstances (one as a keynote address at the Beijing Conference on Women and one as a commencement address), you may wish to ask students to note differences in tone and tenor that are attributable to the occasion.

2. **Is there a speech of inspiration you heard some time ago that you still remember? Why do you feel it made such an impression on you?**

This works best as a written homework assignment. Speeches of inspiration are often memorable because they touch upon our basic values, the inner core of our attitude and belief systems. Students may remember speeches from high school banquets, commencement addresses, or sermons they found especially meaningful. Such presentations may actually help people to visualize who they are and what they want to be—at least for the moment. Students should consider what it was that made such an impression on them. Was it the speaker's presentation or the occasion? What values, beliefs, and commitments were reaffirmed on that occasion, and how?

3. **List five heroes that you think are often mentioned in ceremonial speeches. Why do speakers refer to them so frequently? What does this tell us about the nature of these admired persons, about contemporary audiences, and about the ceremonial speech situation? Be prepared to discuss this in class.**

This activity, which helps illustrate the relationship between cultural heroes and the reaffirmation of identity, can be used as a homework assignment and/or as an in-class discussion piece. Some obvious political heroes might include George Washington, Thomas Jefferson, Abraham Lincoln, Emmeline Pankhurst, Franklin Delano Roosevelt, Rosa Parks, John F. Kennedy, Martin Luther King, Malcolm X, Mahatma Gandhi, and Ronald Reagan. Focus discussion on what types of accomplishments characterize these heroes, what realms of life are most frequently represented (e.g., political, religious, civil rights, athletics, entertainment) and why, what values these heroes embody, and whether females or minorities are included in the list and why or why not. What types of audiences would these heroes appeal to, and what might this tell us about our culture?

Application *(text p. 508)*

1. **Select a public figure you admire and prepare a speech of tribute honoring that person. Discuss the aspects of that person's life you chose to magnify and why.**

   This works well as homework followed by a short in-class speaking activity. It can easily be expanded into a graded activity, and makes an interesting alternative to speeches of self-introduction (see Chapter 2). You might review the functions and techniques of effective speeches of tribute with your students in preparation for this exercise. Have your students research their admired public figures in terms of impressive accomplishments, obstacles overcome, benefits to society, and the values and ideals embodied in their words and/or deeds. Remember that speeches of tribute magnify impressive feats in terms of ideals reaffirmed for the audience. Push your students to reflect on what their admired heroes embody with regard to who "we" are as a community.

2. **Prepare a toast for a classmate who you feel either (a) has made the most progress as a speaker this semester or (b) has given a speech you are likely to remember long after the class is over. Strive for brevity and eloquence in your toast. Be ready to present your toast in class.**

   This activity works well as a final presentation in the last regular class meeting. As an alternative, break your students into dyads so that everyone has someone to toast. Allow about ten minutes for them to interview each other regarding the progress they've made thus far in the course, their strongest and weakest skills as speakers, and what communication skills they would like to further develop in the future.

   For alternatives to this application, have your students toast favorite heroes or heroines, causes, events, the "meaning of life," or anything that holds special significance and meaning for them. You might review the text on making effective toasts. Your students should memorize their presentations and strive to be brief and eloquent. They should focus on what qualities or characteristics the objects of their toasts represent for them, and offer examples to illustrate their points. Limit the toasts to one minute. Have a glass available for your students to use while making them. Evaluate the toasts in terms of appropriateness of the speaker's message and demeanor, brevity, eloquence, appropriateness, worthiness of the toasted, and the speaker's general presentation skills.

ADDITIONAL ACTIVITIES

The "Vision" Thing: Presidential Inaugurals and American Reaffirmation

Purpose: To illustrate the primary functions of ceremonial discourse by considering a classic American exemplar of the genre.

Directions: This works well for homework or as a small-group activity followed by in-class discussion. In the right context, ceremonial speaking can be extremely important. It gives us an opportunity to observe the historic and cultural significance of discourse. Indeed, the most celebrated speakers in Western history, from Pericles to Reagan, are most remembered for their ceremonial addresses.

Ceremonial rhetoric centers on images reaffirming the "visions" and values that define a given community and are perceived by its members to be timeless. It commonly couches its vision of renewal in rich mythic and universal images, and lavishly expressive language use. This is nowhere better illustrated than in presidential inaugural addresses, which, as Kathleen Hall Jamieson and Karlyn Khors Campbell argue, function to renew our sense of ourselves as special people with a transcendent sense of identity and purpose [see Karlyn Khors Campbell and Kathleen Hall Jamieson, "Inaugurating the Presidency," in *Methods of Rhetorical Criticism: A Twentieth-Century Perspective*, edited by Bernard L. Brock, Robert L. Scott, and James W. Chesbro (Detroit: Wayne State University Press, 1989), pp. 343–360].

Choose a presidential inaugural address, and have your students analyze it in terms of the ceremonial functions discussed in the text. How does the chosen speech couch the new president's political agenda in terms of answering the four basic questions that ceremonial oratory addresses: "Who are we?" "Why are we?" "What have we been in the past?" and "What can we become together?" What culturetypes and universal symbols are invoked to embody the president's vision of an America renewed? What heroes and historic events are cited, and what do they signify for the president's message? Many students will appreciate reading the inaugurals of sitting presidents, which also tends toward lively discussion. Emphasize the importance of ceremonial discourse for both redefining political identity and establishing shared convictions and "deep" premises upon which later more explicitly persuasive messages can be based.

The Celebration of Values Speech

Purpose: To offer a valuing approach to the ceremonial speaking assignment.

Directions: To be human is to value, and to reaffirm our more important values from time to time. A principal function of ceremonial speaking is to reaffirm the visions and values that sustain a sense of group identity and purpose. Have your students choose a value, belief, or cause that they feel is of great importance to their communities, and prepare a speech of inspiration to affirm or reaffirm a sense of commitment to it. Students should find supporting materials to magnify and enhance audience identification with their value or cause. They might accomplish this by stressing its direct significance or associating it with basic values and beliefs shared with the audience, by citing heroic deeds and examples that embody the cause, or by citing sources of testimony the audience knows and respects. After defining and exalting their "visions," your students should focus on where and how they apply today, what threats to them need to be overcome, and what their audiences can do to reaffirm them and make them a reality. Their speeches should build toward a call for renewed commitment.

Students should avoid controversial or divisive stands that may alienate and offend some audience members and are not really appropriate on formal ceremonial occasions. Rather, they should focus on values and imperatives that are generally accepted in our culture, such as participative democracy, the American Dream, progress and economic prosperity, law and order, freedom of expression and other constitutional liberties, political or education reform, free trade, the individual work ethic, racial and sexual equality, the value of multicultural diversity, and tolerance for alternative lifestyles. Encourage your students to be enthusiastic and energetic when making their presentations, and remind them to spotlight their ideas as they express them.

Introducing Your Dream President 2000

Purpose: To provide your students an interesting alternative for the ceremonial speaking assignment.

Directions: Have your students select a favorite presidential hopeful, and imagine that they have been entrusted with the task of introducing him or her at their national party convention to accept the nomination for the presidency of the United States in the year 2000. Typical choices might include Al Gore, Ross Perot, John Kerry, Jesse Jackson, Robert Dole, Newt Gingrich, Dianne Feinstein, Carol Moseley-Braun, or even Rush Limbaugh. Your students should focus their speeches on establishing their nominee's ethos and qualifications for the highest job in the land by magnifying his or her past deeds and accomplishments attesting to his or her competence, integrity, and trustworthiness. They should seek to enhance their candidate's identification with the American people by emphasizing the core values and visions that inspire their candidacy and their hopes for our country. Speakers should begin with opening remarks reflecting humility regarding their task on this momentous occasion, and previewing their message. They should build their conclusions to a climactic, "My fellow Americans, I give you the next President of the United States, _____ _____!" In preparation for their presentations, students will need to do some background reading to find out what their "dream" candidates stand for, and what they have accomplished toward these ends in the past. Instructors may want to obtain a videotape or text of a real-life sample so that students can become familiar with this interesting subgenre of introductory speech in preparation for this assignment.

Ceremonial Speaking and Intercultural Communion

Purpose: To illustrate for your students the intercultural significance of ceremonial rhetoric.

Directions: Use this for homework, or as a small-group activity followed by general class discussion. Have your students analyze a prominent speech that addresses the issue of race or cultural diversity in contemporary American society. President Clinton presented a speech entitled "Racism in the United States: The Responsibility of Fatherhood" at the University of Texas in the fall of 1995 (see *Vital Speeches*) that would be perfect for this exercise. Speakers seeking to transcend cultural boundaries and address multiple audiences commonly use a ceremonial form of discourse. This is especially true when speakers are addressing topics such as racial injustice and bigotry, since ceremonial rhetoric is a community-building discourse that unites people by invoking shared ideals and values. Crusaders for social justice, such as Martin Luther King, Jr., invoked the power of ceremonial speech in order to convince a majority of Americans that the status quo on race was a betrayal of the values and aspirations that define us as a people. Yet this method comes at a price, as ceremonial is inherently a discourse of moderate conciliation, one that tends to preclude any sense of separate community and obliges minority subcultures to celebrate community ideals and culturetypes that in the past have been used to justify and even ennoble their own oppression. Student reactions to the Clinton speech may vary. Most "moderates" will probably read it as a reasonable and equitable statement of the concerns of "white" and "black" people in this country, whereas members of minority groups might read it as a condescending speech that blames problems in the African American community on young black males. Focus class discussion on what is gained versus what is lost as minority communities are read into the text of the dominant culture. Ceremonial rhetoric, like proof by mythos, can be wonderfully constructive when used to unite human communities, but is sometimes used to suppress our appreciation for the differences that enrich our lives.

Eulogies as Ceremonial Speaking

Purpose: To give your students a chance to apply the concepts of ceremonial speaking to a classic and highly significant form of the genre.

Directions: Use this for homework or as a small-group activity followed by general class discussion. When prominent figures die, eulogies celebrating the ideals and values embodied by the person's life are typically presented. When prominent figures die during decisive periods of history, the more important eulogies delivered are often history-making themselves, as leaders stand to cast their visions for reaffirming what the fallen hero had stood for. Many of the most celebrated speeches in history, from Pericles' "Funeral Oration" to Lincoln's "Gettysburg Address," were eulogies. Choose a prominent contemporary eulogy and have your students analyze it in terms of the basic functions of ceremonial speaking as discussed in the text. What ideals is the lost hero celebrated in terms of, and what is asked of the audience to see them to fruition? The eulogies presented after the assassination of Yitzhak Rabin in the fall of 1995 (most of which were published in the *New York Times*, 7 Nov. 1995) would be perfect for this exercise. Most speakers present at his funeral used the occasion to call for unity and a recommitted sense of devotion to a peace process for which Rabin had been killed by a right-wing fanatic. Again, use this as an opportunity to emphasize the social and cultural significance of ceremonial rhetoric.

Writing Your Own Tribute

Purpose: To give your students another interesting alternative for the ceremonial speaking assignment.

Directions: Try this for homework followed by a last-day speaking activity. If you were to die tomorrow, how would you like to be remembered? What did you accomplish, and what did you stand for? How would you have your fellow citizens act in terms of reaffirming what you stood for? Refer your students to the text on the basic functions of speeches of tribute and the themes of magnification, and have them craft their own eulogies; these should be a minute and one-half to two minutes in length. As an alternative, you might have your students eulogize one another, or a friend or family member of special importance to them. Their speeches should center around one meaningful accomplishment and the ideals or values that are of significance to their community that are embodied.

Using Humor

Purpose: To provide students with an opportunity to assess their comfort with using humor in a speech.

Directions: Administer the Humor Orientation Scale from p. 463 of this IRM. Students may score this themselves, or you may score it for them and return it during the next class period. As the scale is scored, the scores for the following items should be reversed: 3, 6, 7, 9, 10, 13, and 14. The higher the score on the scale, the more comfortable students will be with using humor in their speeches.

SUPPLEMENTARY MATERIALS

Films and Videos

"Special Speech Occasions," Films for the Humanities, color, 15 minutes.

Computer Software

"Speech Designer," Houghton Mifflin, 1991.

Transparencies and Handouts *(see following pages)*

Preparing a Speech of Tribute

Making a Toast

Humor Orientation Scale

PREPARING A SPEECH OF TRIBUTE

1. Do not exaggerate your tribute so much that it embarrasses the person being honored.

2. Keep the focus on the person, group, or event being honored. Don't talk about yourself.

3. Create vivid images of accomplishments through narratives and examples.

4. Explain the significance of the accomplishments in terms of the values they represent.

5. Present your tribute with true sincerity, warmth, and pride.

MAKING A TOAST

1. Prepare in advance if you think you might be asked to make a toast.

2. Keep your remarks short and to the point.

3. Select one important characteristic of the person or occasion and illustrate it with an example or narrative.

4. Accentuate the positive: a toast is a time of celebration.

5. Use language that befits the occasion.

6. Memorize your toast so that you can present it with graceful aplomb.

7. Rise from your seat to present your toast.

HUMOR ORIENTATION SCALE*

Please respond to the following statements in terms of how well they describe your typical behavior. Use the following scale of agreement.

5 = Strongly agree
4 = Agree
3 = Neutral
2 = Disagree
1 = Strongly disagree

_____ 1. I regularly tell jokes or funny stories when I am with a group.

_____ 2. People usually laugh when I tell a joke or story.

_____ 3. I have no memory for jokes or funny stories.

_____ 4. I can be funny without having to rehearse a joke.

_____ 5. Being funny is a natural communication style with me.

_____ 6. I cannot tell a joke well.

_____ 7. People seldom ask me to tell stories.

_____ 8. My friends would say that I am a funny person.

_____ 9. People don't seem to pay close attention when I tell a joke.

_____ 10. Even funny jokes seem flat when I tell them.

_____ 11. I can easily remember jokes and stories.

_____ 12. People often ask me to tell jokes and stories.

_____ 13. My friends would not say that I am a funny person.

_____ 14. I don't tell jokes or stories even when asked to.

_____ 15. I tell stories and jokes very well.

_____ 16. Of all the people I know, I'm one of the funniest.

_____ 17. use humor to communicate in a variety of situations.

* Adapted from Steve Booth-Butterfield and Melanie Booth-Butterfield, "Individual Differences in the Communication of Humorous Messages," *SSCJ* (Spring 1991), 32–40. Reprinted by permission of the Speech Communication Association.

READINGS FOR ENRICHMENT

See guide to journal abbreviations on p. 37.

* Items marked with an asterisk are suitable for student enrichment.

General

Beale, Walter H. "Rhetorical Performance Discourse: A New Theory of Epideictic." *Philosophy and Rhetoric* (Fall 1978), 221–246.

Carpenter, Ronald H., and Robert V. Seltzer. "Situational Style and the Rotunda Eulogies." *CSSJ* (Spring 1971), 11–15.

Chase, J. Richard. "The Classical Conception of Epideictic." *QJS* (Oct. 1961), 293–300.

Condit, Celeste M. "The Function of Epideictic: The Boston Massacre Orations as Exemplar." *CQ* (Fall 1985), 284–298.

Duffy, Bernard K. "The Platonic Functions of Epideictic Discourse." *Philosophy and Rhetoric*, no. 2 (1983), 79–93.

Dundes, Alan. "What's So Funny? Political Humor." *Mother Jones* (Jan.–Feb. 1996), 18–19.

Foss, Karen A. "John Lennon and the Advisory Function of Eulogies." *CSSJ* (Fall 1983),187–194.

Johnson, Samuel R. "The Non-Aristotelian Nature of Samoan Ceremonial Oratory." *WJSC* (Fall 1970), 262–273.

Majors, Randall E. "Practical Ceremonial Speaking: Three Speech Activities." *SCT* (Winter 1989), 2–3.

Matthews, Gray. "Epideictic Rhetoric and Baseball: Nurturing Community Through Controversy." *SSCJ* (Summer 1995), 275–291.

Oravec, Christine. "'Observation' in Aristotle's Theory of Epideictic." *Philosophy and Rhetoric* (Summer 1976), 162–174.

Osborn, Randall Parrish. "Jimmy Carter's Rhetorical Campaign for the Presidency: An Epideictic of American Renewal." Southern States Communication Association Convention, Memphis, March 1996.

Samosky, Jack A., and John E. Baird. "The Epideictic Speech as a Contest Event." *JAFA* (Spring 1983), 274–278.

Humor

* Amiel, Barbara. "A Tasteless Joke and a Moral Dilemma." *Macleans*, 29 May 1995, p. 13.

* Barnes, Don. "The Seriousness of Being Funny." *National Underwriter Life & Health—Financial Services Edition*, 16 Oct. 1987, p. 17.

* Berger, Arthur Asa. "Anatomy of the Joke." *JC* (Summer 1976), 113–115.

* Berger, Arthur Asa, and Aaron Wildavsky. "Who Laughs at What?" *Society* (Sept.–Oct. 1994), 82–86.

Booth-Butterfield, Steve, and Melanie Booth-Butterfield. "Individual Differences in the Communication of Humorous Messages." *SSCJ* (Spring 1991), 32–40.

* Brandt, John. "In Praise of Fools: Importance of Humor in Business Careers." *Industry Week*, 1 Apr. 1996, p. 6.

* Cantor, Joanne R. "What Is Funny to Whom? The Role of Gender." *JC* (Summer 1976), 164–172.

Chang, Mei-Jung, and Charles R. Gruner. "Audience Reaction to Self-disparaging Humor." *SSCJ* (Summer 1981), 419–426.

Chapman, Antony J., and Nicholas J. Gadfield. " Is Sexual Humor Sexist?" *JC* (Summer 1976), 141–153.

Foot, H. "Humour and Laughter." In *A Handbook of Communication Skills*, edited by O. Hargie, pp. 355–381. London: Croom Helm, 1986.

Goldstein, Jeffrey H. "Theoretical Notes on Humor." *JC* (Summer 1976), 104–112.

Goodchilds, J. "On Being Witty: Causes, Correlates, and Consequences." In *The Psychology of Humor*, edited by J. Goldstein and P. McGhee, pp. 173–193. New York: Academic, 1972.

* Gruner, Charles R. "Advice to the Beginning Speaker on Using Humor—What the Research Tells Us." *CE* (Apr. 1985), 142–147.
* "The Humor Advantage." *D & B Reports* (Sept.–Oct. 1988), 62–63.
Kane, T., J. Suls, and J. Tedeschi. "Humour as a Tool of Social Interaction." In *It's a Funny Thing, Humour,* edited by A. Chapman and H. Foot, pp. 13–16. Oxford: Pergamon, 1977.
Kaplan, Robert M., and Gregory C. Pascoe. "Humorous Lectures and Humorous Examples: Some Effects upon Comprehension and Retention." *Journal of Educational Psychology,* 69 (1977), 61–65.
La Fave, Lawrence, and Roger Mannell. "Does Ethnic Humor Serve Prejudice?" *JC* (Summer 1976), 116–123.
Leventhal, Howard, and Gerald Cupchik. "A Process Model of Humor Judgment." *JC* (Summer 1976), 190–205.
* Machan, Dyan. "Do You Sincerely Want to Be Funny? Humor in Business Situations." *Forbes,* 15 Oct. 1990, pp. 212–213.
* Marklein, Mary Beth. "Leave Them Laughing: Businesswomen Using Humor in Speeches." *Nation's Business* (October 1989), 49.
* Martin, Hosea L. "What's So Funny? Sense of Humor in Men." *Essence* (Apr. 1992), 46.
* Martin, James. "Contemplation in Action: Humor—Religion in TV Advertising." *America,* 8 Apr. 1995, p. 21.
* "No Laughing Matter: Legal Aspects of Ethnic Jokes." *Time,* 16 Mar. 1987, p. 37.
O'Connell, W. "The Social Aspects of Wit and Humor." *Journal of Social Psychology* (1969), 183–187.
* Provine, Robert R. "Laughter." *American Scientist* (Jan.–Feb. 1996), 38–49.
* Queenan, Joe. "Americans Have Always Been of Two Minds About Jokes in Poor Taste." *People Weekly,* 13 May 1996, p. 15.
Sherman, L. "Humor and Social Distance." *Perceptual and Motor Skills* (1985), 1274.
Smith, Christie McGuffie, and Larry Powell. "The Use of Disparaging Humor by Group Leaders." *SSCJ* (Spring 1988), 279–292.
Stat, Joanie. "John Cleese Teaches Through Laughter: How to Use a Punchline to Get Your Points Across." *Communication World* (Apr. 1988), 34–35.
* Udall, Morris K. *Too Funny to Be President.* New York: Holt, 1988.
Wanzer, Melissa Bekelja, Melanie Booth-Butterfield, and Steve Booth-Butterfield. "The Funny People: A Source-orientation to the Communication of Humor." *CQ* (Spring 1995), 142–154.
———. "Are Funny People Popular? An Examination of Humor Orientation, Loneliness, and Social Attraction." *CQ* (Winter 1996), 42–52.
* Winick, Charles. "The Social Contexts of Humor." *JC* (Summer 1976), 124–128.
* Zolf, Larry. "On Navigating Treacherous Waters: Political Correctness and Political Jokes." *Macleans,* 29 May 1995, p. 64.

Introductions

* Flanagan, William G. "Unaccustomed as I Am. . . " *Forbes,* 16 Jan. 1995, p. 100.
* Sabath, Anne Marie. "How to Say Thanks (or No Thanks)." *Sales and Marketing Management* (Dec. 1990), 113–114.
* Tarver, Jerry L., and Sara Means Geigel. "It Is with Great Pleasure that I Introduce. . . ." *Communication World* (June 1988), 30–32.

Roasts

* "The Gentle Art of the Resounding Put-Down." *American Scholar* (Summer 1987), 311–318.
* Migdall, Dave. "Roasting to Perfection: The Careful Selection of Speakers Makes the Difference Between Staging a Successful Roast and Simply Skewering the Honoree." *Meetings and Conventions* (Jan. 1990), 45–47.

Toasts

Braude, Jacob M. *Complete Speaker's and Toastmaster's Library: Definitions and Toasts.* Englewood Cliffs, N.J.: Prentice-Hall, 1965, pp. 88–123.
* Collins, Larry. "A Host of Toasts." *Reader's Digest* (Canadian) (Dec. 1984), 7–9.
* Edwards, Owen. "What Every Man Should Know: How to Make a Toast." *Esquire* (Jan. 1984), 37.
* Hetherington, Joan K. "The Art of Toasting." *TWA Ambassador* (Mar. 1988), 26–32.
Lin, Wendy. "Let's Lift a Glass, Say a Few Words, and Toast 1996." *Memphis Commercial Appeal,* 28 Dec. 1995, p. C3
* Maxa, Rudy. "Here's to the Toast: It Shouldn't Mention Sex or Money." *Washingtonian* (Sept. 1986), 158–159.

After-Dinner Speeches

Mahaffey, R. D. "After Dinner Speaking." *WJSC* (Nov. 1940), 10–13.
* Morris, Sylvia Jukes. "Five of Clare Boothe Luce's After-Dinner Stories." *Forbes,* 23 Oct. 1995, pp. 100–101.

Teaching Activities and Exercises

Cates, Carl. "Eulogies as a Special Occasion Speech." *SCT* (Winter 1996), 6–7.
Lamansky, Martin. "Getting to Know My Hero: The Speech of Tribute." *SCT* (Winter 1993), 10.
Poyner, Barry Cole. "Adding a Ceremonial Touch." *SCT* (Fall 1992), 12.
Siddens, Paul L., III. "Figures of Speech in Poetic and Everyday Discourse." *SCT* (Spring 1994), 13–14.
Sikes, Shirley. "Introducing the Speaker." *SCT* (Fall 1991), 14.
Walter, Suzanne. "Introduction of a Speaker: Multipurpose and Multicultural." *SCT* (Spring 1993), 3.

APPENDIX A
Group Communication

OBJECTIVES

- To introduce students to the basic principles of group discussion.

- To teach students some basic group problem-solving skills.

- To help students understand the roles and responsibilities of participants.

- To help students understand the roles and responsibilities of leaders.

- To provide students with guidelines for planning and conducting meetings.

- To introduce the fundamentals of parliamentary procedure for formal meetings.

SUGGESTIONS FOR TEACHING

Many of the activities in the text and in this IRM require students to work in small groups and to apply problem-solving skills. The material in this section is designed to provide them with the basics they need to participate more effectively in such situations. If you want to incorporate such activities in your teaching of the course, you could assign this material early in the semester, picking and choosing what you believe will be most helpful to your students.

LECTURE/DISCUSSION OUTLINE

I. Organizations often use small groups as a means of solving problems and making decisions. *(text p. A2–A4)*
    A. Group problem solving and decision making has many advantages.
        1. It allows a variety of perspectives on problems.
        2. It stimulates creativity.
    B. There are also problems associated with group problem solving.
        1. Cultural gridlock may occur when people do not share the same basic assumptions and expectations.
        2. Groupthink can lead to development of a one-track, uncritical frame of mind.

II. Reflective thinking is a common technique used in problem-solving groups. It involves: *(text pp. A4–A7)*

     A. defining the problem.
     B. generating solution options.
     C. evaluating solution options.
     D. developing a plan of action.
     E. evaluating results.

III. Other methods of group problem solving may be used to reach decisions. *(text pp. A7–A10)*
     A. The Successive Integration of Problem Elements (SIE) method focuses on integrating elements from different proposals into a final solution.
     B. Collaborative problem solving is helpful when participants have diverse backgrounds.
     C. Dialogue groups focus on understanding problems as a precursor to problem solving.

IV. Group participants have specific responsibilities. *text p. A10)*
     A. They should come to meetings prepared to contribute.
     B. They should be open-minded, willing to listen and to learn from others.
     C. They should be constructive listeners.

V. Leaders help a group get the job done. *(text pp. A10–A12)*
     A. There are a variety of leader types.
       1. Task leaders are goal-directed.
       2. Social leaders initiate positive communication behaviors.
       3. Transactional leadership is based on power relationships.
       4. Transformational leadership may help bring about collaboration in diverse groups.
     B. Ideal leaders:
       1. have experience, knowledge, and insight into the problems confronting the group.
       2. help define problems, set goals, initiate action, and keep the group going.
       3. are considerate and sensitive.
       4. mediate conflicts.
       5. recap and articulate group consensus.
       6. adapt to changing circumstances.
       7. represent the group to others.

VI. Group communication skills are used in meetings. *(text pp. A12–A13)*
     A. Meetings should be called to:
       1. share information.
       2. determine what needs to be done.
       3. lay out a plan of action.
       4. report on progress.
     B. Meetings should be planned so that they run smoothly.
       1. Meetings should have a specific objective and purpose.
       2. The leader should prepare an agenda.
       3. Meetings should be short.
       4. Meetings should have a small number of participants from near the same level in the organization.

VII. To conduct an effective meeting, you should: *(text pp. A13–A14)*
     A. begin and end on time.
     B. prepare and present information concisely.
     C. lead the meeting, don't run it.
     D. be enthusiastic.
     E. be tolerant of differences of opinion.
     F. urge all members to participate.
     G. keep discussion centered on the issue.
     H. recap what has happened.

VII. Formal meetings often follow parliamentary procedure. *(text pp. A14–A16)*

CLASSROOM ACTIVITIES

Evaluating Group Communication Activities

Purpose: To provide a structured format for the evaluation of group discussions.

Directions: Assign a small-group activity from one of the chapters in this IRM. Distribute the "Group Discussion Participant Evaluation" form from p. 471 of this IRM. Inform the class that each student will be required to evaluate another member of his or her small group at the end of the discussion activity. You should assign the students to be evaluated.

What Is Your Leadership Potential?

Purpose: To allow students to self-assess their leadership potential.

Directions: Distribute the "Leadership Potential Questionnaire" on p. 472 of this IRM. Allow students approximately ten minutes to complete the questionnaire. Use the following guide for scoring the leadership questionnaire. Remind students that this measures their propensities toward leadership behavior. If they score low, it means that they are not very interested in becoming leaders, but it does not mean that they cannot learn leadership skills that would help them be effective leaders in the future. Also advise them that their propensities may change as they grow and have more experience in leadership positions.

Scoring for leadership potential questionnaire

1. A=2, B=1, C=3; **2.** A=1, B=3, C=2; **3.** A=3, B=2, C=1; **4.** A=1, B=3, C=2; **5.** A=3, B=1, C=2; **6.** A=1, B=2, C=3.

A score of 15–18 indicates strong tendencies to *want* to lead and to be successful in leadership situations (whether business, civic, or political).

A score of 10–15 indicates a mixture of some leadership tendencies and hesitation about taking on too many leadership tasks.

A score below 10 suggests that you are not very *interested* in being a leader.

Leader and Follower Styles

Purpose: To provide students with an opportunity to assess the style of leadership they are most prone to use and the type of leader they prefer to follow.

Directions:

1. Distribute the "What Kind of Leader Are You?" questionnaire from pp. 473–474 of this IRM. Allow five to ten minutes for students to complete the questionnaire.

2. Distribute the "What Kind of Follower Are You?" questionnaire from pp. 475–476 of this IRM. Allow five to ten minutes for students to complete the questionnaire.

3. Have students score their questionnaires.

4. Explain the three types of leadership styles:

   The autocratic leader makes decisions without consulting others and expects compliance. He or she works mainly from a base of legitimate or coercive power (see pp. 348–349 of this IRM). Follower behaviors include obedience, submission, fear, and mistrust. The focus is on control.

The participative leader consults with others when making decisions and welcomes input and advice. He or she typically functions from an expert or referent power base but may rely on reward power to sustain motivation (see pp. 348–349 this IRM). Follower behaviors include participation and cooperation. The focus is on involvement.

The free-rein leader may leave decisions up to followers. He or she may function from referent or expert power base but rarely exercises any type of power to direct or control the behavior of others. This leadership style is most effective with highly competent, self-motivated employees. The focus is on autonomy.

5. Discuss the differences between students' preferences for leading and following.

SUPPLEMENTAL MATERIALS

Films and Videos

"The Dynamics of Groups," Films for the Humanities, 15 minutes.

"Group Productivity," CRM, 21 minutes.

"Meeting the Meeting Challenge," CRM, 35 minutes.

"Groupthink," CRM, 22 minutes.

"Guidelines for Groups," Films for the Humanities, 15 minutes.

"The Leadership Challenge," CRM, 26 minutes.

"Interpersonal and Small-Group Communication," Insight Media, 27 minutes.

"How to Conduct a Meeting," Coronet/MTI Films and video, 18 minutes.

Handouts

Group Discussion Participant Evaluation Form

Leadership Potential Questionnaire

What Kind of Leader Are You?

What Kind of Follower Are You?

GROUP DISCUSSION PARTICIPANT EVALUATION FORM

Person being evaluated _____

Your name _____ Date _____

Use the following scale to describe the person assigned to you. Indicate your evaluation by circling one of the numbers to the left of each statement. You must describe and evaluate this student's performance.

1 = Poor, 2 = Below average, 3 = Average, 4 = Above average, 5 = Superior

1 2 3 4 5   Appeared committed to the goals of the group.

1 2 3 4 5   Participated frequently in group deliberations.

1 2 3 4 5   Made contributions that were clear, relevant, and helpful.

1 2 3 4 5   Performed task leadership functions.

1 2 3 4 5   Performed social leadership functions.

1 2 3 4 5   Helped resolve conflict within the group.

1 2 3 4 5   Encouraged participation of other group members.

1 2 3 4 5   Helped keep the discussion focused on the problem.

1 2 3 4 5   Performed in comparison with other group members.

1 2 3 4 5   Emerged as the leader of this group.

Leadership Potential Questionnaire*

Leadership is composed of many facets. The ability to establish confidence, respect, and good rapport is required. Many people are afraid of assuming a leadership role. Others grow into it, although they feel at first that they are not qualified. What about you?

This quiz is designed to help you measure your leadership potential by thinking back on real situations in your life and projecting yourself into possible future circumstances where leadership might be required. Its purpose is to start you *thinking about* your leadership potential. It is not a scientifically developed measuring instrument. Respond as honestly as you can to the following items and see what you can learn about your leadership potential.

1. Your instructions were not followed and everything got messed up. Why?
   A. You did not foresee all the blunders your subordinates could make.
   B. It seems impossible to get halfway intelligent people to work these days.
   C. You did not explain the assignment in sufficient detail.

2. You are asked to organize a group to improve your neighborhood. How would you react?
   A. Use an excuse, such as being too busy, to get out of it.
   B. Ask someone who had organized such a group before to help you.
   C. Feel flattered and accept the assignment, even though it's a first for you.

3. Someone higher up in your group gives you an order. What are you most likely to do?
   A. Question the order and possibly suggest an alternative.
   B. Discuss the pros and cons and finally agree.
   C. An order is an order, and I carry it through as best I can.

4. You read about the chaotic state of affairs in another country. Finally a strong person takes over and puts everything in better working order. How do you react to this news?
   A. Is he or she a dictator? I don't know, and if so, so what?
   B. It was necessary to introduce strong measures. The people always have to be led; later on they can participate again in decisions.
   C. Had the people been properly informed, they would have taken the right measures themselves.

5. You read the following statement: "He was relentless. He drove himself and others. He did not rest until he had reached a goal." What is your reaction?
   A. I am just like him.
   B. He is an unhappy person. I prefer to enjoy myself.
   C. If he could relax in between it's okay, otherwise I pity him.

6. You read in a person's obituary that he never complimented anyone in his organization. He watched every little detail. Managers were fired at the slightest pretext. He was feared by everybody, but he created a successful company.
   A. That is a very heavy price to pay. Probably nobody really liked him.
   B. Sometimes that is the only way to lead. The end result is really the important thing.
   C. He might have been more successful had he been more human and caring.

---

* Adapted from Ernest Dichter, *Total Self-Knowledge* (New York: Stein & Day, 1976), pp. 211–214. Copyright © 1976 by Ernest Dichter. Originally published by Stein & Day, Inc. Reprinted with permission of Scarborough House/Publishers and the author.

WHAT KIND OF LEADER ARE YOU?*

For each of the following questions, circle the answer that best applies to you.

Yes No 1. Do you enjoy "running the show"?

Yes No 2. Generally, do you think it's worth the time and effort to explain the reasons for a decision or policy before putting it into effect?

Yes No 3. Do you prefer the administrative end of your leadership job—planning, paperwork, and so on—to supervising or working directly with your subordinates?

Yes No 4. A stranger comes into your department, and you know he's the new employee hired by one of your assistants. On approaching him, would you first ask *his* name rather than introducing yourself?

Yes No 5. Do you keep your people up to date as a matter of course on developments affecting the group?

Yes No 6. Do you find that in giving out assignments you tend to state the goals and leave the methods to your subordinates?

Yes No 7. Do you think that it's good common sense for a leader to keep aloof from his or her people because in the long run familiarity breeds lessened respect?

Yes No 8. Comes time to decide about a group outing. You've heard that the majority prefer to have it on Wednesday, but you're pretty sure Thursday would be better for all concerned. Would you put the question to a vote rather than make the decision yourself?

Yes No 9. If you had your way, would you make running your group a push-button affair, with personal contacts and communications held to a minimum?

Yes No 10. Do you find it fairly easy to fire someone?

Yes No 11. Do you feel that the friendlier you are with your people, the better you'll be able to lead them?

Yes No 12. After considerable time, you figure out the answer to a work problem. You pass along the solution to an assistant, who pokes it full of holes. Will you be annoyed that the problem is still unresolved rather than become angry with the assistant?

Yes No 13. Do you agree that one of the best ways to avoid problems of discipline is to provide adequate punishments for violations of rules?

Yes No 14. Your way of handling a situation is being criticized. Would you try to sell your viewpoint to your group rather than make it clear that, as boss, your decisions are final?

Yes No 15. Do you generally leave it up to your subordinates to contact you as far as informal, day-to-day communications are concerned?

---

* Adapted from *Mastery of Management* by Auren Uris (1968) by permission of the Berkeley Publishing Company.

Yes No 16. Do you feel that everyone in your group should have a certain amount of personal loyalty to you?

Yes No 17. Do you favor the practice of appointing committees to settle a problem rather than stepping in to decide on it yourself?

Yes No 18. Some experts say differences of opinion within a work group are healthy. Others feel that such differences indicate basic flaws in group unity. Do you agree with the first view?

Scoring and Interpretation

To get your score, circle the question numbers 1 through 18 to which you answered yes. Then compare your answers with the groupings below.

A. 1, 4, 7, 10, 13, 16
B. 2, 5, 8, 11, 14, 17
C. 3, 6, 9, 12, 15, 18

If most of your yes answers correspond with Group A, chances are that you tend to be an autocratic leader. If your total of yes answers was highest in Group B, you probably have a predisposition toward being a participative leader. If Group C is the one in which you had the greatest number of yes answers, you are probably inclined toward being a free-rein leader.

WHAT KIND OF FOLLOWER ARE YOU?*

For each of the following questions, circle the answer that best applies to you.

Yes No   1. When given an assignment, do you like to have all the details spelled out?

Yes No   2. Do you think that by and large most bosses are bossier than they need to be?

Yes No   3. Is initiative one of your stronger points?

Yes No   4. Do you feel a boss lowers him or herself by "palling around" with subordinates?

Yes No   5. In general, do you prefer working with others to working alone?

Yes No   6. Do you prefer the pleasures of solitude (reading, listening to music) to the social pleasures of being with others (parties, get-togethers, and so on)?

Yes No   7. Do you tend to become strongly attached to the boss you work for?

Yes No   8. Do you tend to offer a helping hand to the newcomers among your colleagues and coworkers?

Yes No   9. Do you enjoy using your own ideas and ingenuity to solve a work problem?

Yes No 10. Do you prefer the kind of boss who knows all the answers to one who comes to you for help?

Yes No 11. Do you feel it's okay for you boss to be friendlier with some members of the group than with others?

Yes No 12. Do you like to assume full responsibility for assignments rather than just do the work and leave the responsibility to your boss?

Yes No 13. Do you feel that "mixed" groups—men working with women, for example—naturally tend to have more friction than unmixed ones?

Yes No 14. If you learned your boss was having an affair with his or her secretary, would your respect for your boss remain undiminished?

Yes No 15. Have you always felt that "he travels fastest who travels alone"?

Yes No 16. Do you agree that a boss who couldn't win loyalty shouldn't be a boss?

Yes No 17. Would you be upset by a colleague whose inability or ineptitude obstructs the work of your department or company as a whole?

Yes No 18. Do you think *boss* is a dirty word?

---

* Adapted from *Mastery of Management* by Auren Uris (1968) by permission of the Berkeley Publishing Company.

Scoring and Interpretation

To get your score, circle the question numbers 1 through 18 to which you answered yes. Then compare your answers with the groupings below.

A.   1, 4, 7, 10, 13, 16
B.   2, 5, 8, 11, 14, 17
C.   3, 6, 9, 12, 15, 18

If most of your yes answers correspond with Group A, chances are that you prefer autocratic leadership. If your total of yes answers was highest in Group B, you probably prefer participative leadership. If Group C is the one in which you show the most yes answers, you probably prefer free-rein leadership

READINGS FOR ENRICHMENT

See guide to journal abbreviations on p. 37.

* Items marked with an asterisk are suitable for student enrichment.

General

Aiken, Milam, Mahesh Vanjami, and James Krosp. "Group Decision Support Systems." *Review of Business* (Spring 1995), 38–42.

Andrews, Patricia Hayes, and Richard T. Herschel. *Organizational Communication: Empowerment in a Technological Society.* Boston: Houghton Mifflin, 1996.

Bernthal, Paul R., and Chester A. Insko. "Cohesiveness Without Groupthink: The Interactive Effects of Social and Task Cohesion." *Group and Organization Management* (Mar. 1993), 66–87.

Cline, Rebecca J. Welch. "Detecting Groupthink: Methods for Observing the Allusion of Unanimity." *CQ* (Spring 1990), 112–126.

Communication Studies, Special Issue: "Revitalizing the Study of Small Group Communication" (Spring 1994).

Cragan, John F., and David W. Wright. "Small Group Communication Research of the 1980s: A Synthesis and Critique." *CS* (Fall 1990), 212–236.

Gouran, Dennis S., and B. Aubrey Fisher. "The Functions of Human Communication in the Formation, Maintenance, and Performance of Small Groups." In *Handbook of Rhetorical and Communication Theory*, edited by Carroll C. Arnold and John Waite Bowers, pp. 622–658. Boston: Allyn and Bacon, 1984.

Guetzow, Harold, and John Gyr. "An Analysis of Conflict in Decision-Making Groups." *Human Behavior* (1954), 367–382.

* Hurt, Floyd. "Better Brainstorming." *Training and Development* (Nov. 1944), 57–59.

Issacs, William N. "Taking Flight: Dialogue, Collective Thinking, and Organizational Learning." *Organizational Dynamics* (Autumn 1993), 24–39.

* Jablin, Frederic M. "Cultivating Imagination: Factors That Enhance and Inhibit Creativity in Brainstorming Groups." *HCR* (Spring 1981), 245–258.

Janis, I. L. *Groupthink: Psychological Studies of Policy Decisions and Fiascoes.* Boston: Houghton Mifflin, 1982, pp. 245–246.

* Kay, Gail. "Effective Meetings Through Electronic Brainstorming." *Management Quarterly* (Winter 1994), 15–26.

* Kettelhut, Michael C. "How to Avoid Misusing Electronic Meeting Support." *Planning Review* (July–Aug. 1994), 34–38.

Maier, Norman R. F., and Richard A. Maier. "An Experimental Test of the Effects of 'Developmental' vs. 'Free' Discussion on the Quality of Group Decisions." *Journal of Applied Psychology* (1957), 320–323.

* Neck, Christopher P., and Charles C. Manz. "From Groupthink to Teamthink: Toward the Creation of Constructive Thought Patterns in Self-Managed Work Teams." *Human Relations* (Aug. 1994), 929–952.

Pavitt, Charles. "Describing Know-How About Group Discussion Procedure: Must the Reaction Be Recursive?" *CS* (Fall 1992), 150–170.

———. "Does Communication Matter in Social Influence During Small Group Discussions? Five Positions." *CS* (Fall 1993), 216–227.

Pavitt, Charles, Gail G. Witchurch, Heather McClurg, and Nancy Petersen. "Melding the Objective and Subjective Sides of Leadership: Communication and Social Judgments in Decision-Making Groups." *CM* (Sept. 1995), 243–264.

Poole, Marshall Scott. "Do We Have Any Theories of Group Communication?" *CS* (Fall 1990), 237–247.

Putnam, Linda L., and Cynthia Stohl. "Bona Fide Groups: A Reconceptualization of Groups in Context." *CS* (Fall 1990), 248–265.

* Rao, Srikumar S. "Meetings Go Better Electronically: Do Hard-Nosed Bosses Stifle Discussion? Try Conferencing Software." *Financial World*, 14 Mar. 1995, pp. 72–73.

Smagorinsky, Peter, and Pamela K. Fly. "The Social Environment of the Classroom: A Vygotskian Perspective on Small Group Process." *CE* (Apr. 1993), 159–171.

Sykes, Richard E. "Imagining What We Might Study if We Really Studied Small Groups from a Speech Perspective." *CS* (Fall 1990), 200–211.

* Thiagarajan, Sivasailam. "Take Five for Better Brainstorming." *Training and Development Journal* (Feb. 1992), 37–42.

* Zemke, Ron. "In Search of Good Ideas." *Training* (Jan. 1993), 46–51.

Leadership

Baker, Deborah C. "A Qualitative and Quantitative Analysis of Verbal Style and the Elimination of Potential Leaders in Small Groups." *CQ* (Winter 1990), 13–26.

Barge, Kevin J. "Leadership as Medium: A Leaderless Group Discussion Model." *CQ* (Fall 1989), 237–247.

* Schuster, John P. "Transforming Your Leadership Style." *Association Management* (Jan. 1994), 39–43.

Zorn, Theodore E., and Gregory B. Leichty. "Leadership and Identity: A Reinterpretation of Situational Leadership Theory." *SCJ* (Fall 1991), 11–24.

Zorn, Theodore E., and Michelle T. Violanti. "Measuring Leadership Style: A Review of Leadership Style Instruments for Classroom Use." *CE* (Jan. 1993), 70–78.

Problem-Solving and Decision-Making Groups

Beatty, Michael J. "Group Members' Decision Rule Orientations and Consensus." *HCR* (Winter 1989), 279–296.

Berger, Charles R., and Patrick di Battista. "Information Seeking and Plan Elaboration: What Do You Need to Know to Know What to Do?" *CM* (Dec. 1992), 368–387.

Gouran, Dennis, Randy Y. Hirokawa, Kelly M. Julian, and Geoff B. Leatham. "The Evolution and Current Status of the Functional Perspective in Decision–Making and Problem-Solving Groups." In *Communication Yearbook 16*, edited by Stanley A. Deetz, pp. 573–600. Newbury Park, Calif.: Sage, 1993.

Hirokawa, Randy Y., and Marshall Scott Poole, eds. *Communication and Group Decision-Making*. Newbury Park, Calif.: Sage, 1986.

* Hood, Jacqueline N., Jeanne M. Logsdon, and Judith Kenner Thompson. "Collaboration for Social Problem Solving: A Process Model." *Business and Society* (Spring 1993), 1–17.

* Isaacs, William M. "Taking Flight: Dialogue, Collective Thinking, and Organizational Learning." *Organizational Dynamics* (Autumn 1993), 24(16).

* Schein, Edgar H. "On Dialogue, Culture, and Organizational Learning." *Organizational Dynamics* (Autumn 1993), 40(12).

Teaching Techniques

Blom, Patricia. "Using Group Activities in Basic Public Speaking." *SCT* (Fall 1989), 10–11.

Bourhis, John. "Video Groups." *SCT* (Summer 1992), 12.

Bozik, Mary. "Playing Games with the Small Group Project." *SCT* (Spring 1995), 13–14.

Brunson, Deborah A. "A Perceptual Awareness Exercise in Interracial Communication." *SCT* (Fall 1994), 2–4.

Bytwerk, Randall L. "Teaching Parliamentary Procedure in Group Communication." *SCT* (Winter 1988), 4–5.

Dittus, James K. "Giving Students What They Want: A Role-Playing Exercise with True-to-Life Groups." *SCT* (Summer 1993), 2–3.

Eldred, Jean Parker. "A Procedure for Teaching Criteria Generation." *SCT* (Winter 1996), 9–10.

Fagella, Kathy. "Solid Gold Problem Solving." *Instructor* (Jan. 1992), 35–37.

Faries, Liz. "The Upside Down Exercise." *SCT* (Summer 1992), 10.

Haleta, Laurie. "Activities to Facilitate the Application of Parliamentary Procedure." *SCT* (Summer 1991), 10–11.

Hochel, Sandra. "An Exercise in Understanding Ethnocentrism." *SCT* (Summer 1994), 10–11.

Hofer, Katy. "Final Exam Exercise." *SCT* (Winter 1992), 5.

Hyde, Richard Bruce. "Council: Using a Talking Stick to Teach Listening." *SCT* (Winter 1993), 1–2.

Johnson, Scott D. "Exploring the Influences of Culture on Small Groups." *SCT* (Winter 1995), 6–7.

Kaye, Tom. "Respecting Others' Point of View." *SCT* (Spring 1990), 12.

Neumann, David. "Building and Destroying Groups." *SCT* (Spring 1992), 13–14.

Scherer, Robert F., and Crystal L. Owen. "Demonstrating Group Dynamics in the Classroom: The Real Gorilla." *SCT* (Fall 1992), 3.

Smith, Lindsley F., and Peter M. Kellett. "Self-Directed Teams in the Classroom." *SCT* (Fall 1995), 14–15.

Smith, Robert E., Jr., and Sandi S. Smith. "Focus Group Interviews for Course Evaluations: Projects for the Small Group Class." *SCT* (Winter 1991), 13.

Stearns, Susan. "Small Group Activities and Student Empowerment." *SCT* (Summer 1995), 3–4.

Thompson, Carol, and Christina Standerfer. "Interactive Public-Speaking Activities." *SCT* (Summer 1992), 2–3.

Walter, Suzanne. "Experiences in Intercultural Communication." *SCT* (Summer 1995), 1–3.

Yook, Eunkyong Lee. "Students Creating Intercultural Sensitizers: Storytelling and Attribution." *SCT* (Spring 1996), 11–12.

Zalewski, James W., and Larry J. Walters. "Playing Games with Small Groups." *SCT* (Summer 1993), 1–2.

Meetings

* Jones, Becky, Midge Wilker, and Judy Stoner. "A Meeting Primer." *Management Review* (Jan. 1995), 30–32.

* Patnode, Darwin. *Robert's Rules of Order: Modern Edition.* Nashville: Thomas Nelson, 1989.

* Ramsey, Robert D. "Making Meetings Work For You." *Supervision* (Feb. 1994), 14–16.

Groups and Diversity

Bantz, Charles R. "Cultural Diversity and Group Cross-Cultural Team Research." *ACR* (Feb. 1993), 1–20.

Hammer, Mitchell R., and Judith N. Martin. "The Effects of Cross-Cultural Training on American Managers in a Japanese-American Joint Venture." *ACR* (May 1992), 162–183.

* Hequet, Marc. "The Fine Art of Multicultural Meetings." *Training* (July 1993), 29–33.

Klopf, Donald W., and Catherine A. Thompson. *Communication in the Multicultural Classroom.* Edina, Minn., Burgess, 1992.

Lee, Wen Shu. "On Not Missing the Boat: A Processual Method for Intercultural Understanding of Idioms and Lifeworld." *ACR* (May 1994), 141–161.

Sanders, Judith, Robert Gass, Richard Wiseman, and Jon Bruschke. "Ethnic Comparison and Measurement of Argumentativeness, Verbal Aggressiveness, and Need for Cognition." *CR* (Winter 1992), 50–56.